The BEST PLACES TOKISS
in the NORTHWEST

KATE CHYNOWETH

EDITION 9

SASQUATCH BOOKS
SEATTLE

Printed in the United States of America
Published by Sasquatch Books
Distributed by Publishers Group West
10 09 08 07 06 05   8 7 6 5 4 3 2 1

Cover and interior design: Stewart A. Williams
Cover photograph: S. Plant/Masterfile
Interior maps: GreenEye Design
Project editor: Kurt Stephan
Copy editor: Karen Parkin
Proofreader: Laura Gronewold
Indexer: Michael Ferreira

ISBN 1-57061-458-X
ISSN 1546-525X

Sasquatch Books
119 South Main Street, Suite 400
Seattle, WA 98104
(206) 467-4300
www.sasquatchbooks.com
custserv@sasquatchbooks.com

CONTENTS

OREGON

WASHINGTON

Contributors

Three time's a charm for Seattle-based writer and editor **Kate Chynoweth**, who counts this new edition as her third book in the *Best Places to Kiss* series; she edited the previous Northwest edition, authored *The Best Places to Kiss in Northern California*, and still found energy to kiss and tell about Seattle's most romantic hideaways for this volume. She is the author of *The Bridesmaid Guide: Etiquette, Parties, and Being Fabulous*, published by Chronicle Books. Her writing on travel, food, and lifestyle appears in *Real Simple*, *Sunset*, *Seattle*, and other magazines and books.

Seattle native **Karen Bullard** has traveled extensively throughout the Pacific Northwest as both a bicycle tour guide and lifetime resident, so it wasn't a stretch for her to write about Oregon's Willamette Valley as well as Washington's North and Central Cascades. She has written for the *Best Places* series and helped establish the defunct Web site Seattle Sidewalk (now known as Citysearch.com). She spends the winters in Seattle and summers in Hood River, Oregon, with her husband and two young sons.

Bend-based writer **Kim Cooper Findling** grew up on the Oregon coast and has spent the last 10 years coming to love the dry side of the state. Her essays and articles appear regularly in *Alaska* and *Horizon Air*, *Bend Living*, *Oregon Business*, and *Oregon Quarterly*. She contributed to the chapters on the Central, Southern, and Crater Lake regions of her native state for this edition.

Originally a Vancouverite, freelance writer **Sue Kernaghan** fell hopelessly in love with Salt Spring Island while on a research trip for Fodor's Guides. She moved to the island in 1999 and has since written about BC for a variety of publications, including *Best Places Northwest* and *Fodor's Escape to Nature Without Roughing It*. She used her insider knowledge to great advantage in updating the Vancouver Island and Southern Gulf Islands chapters.

Mid-Columbia–based **Anna King** loves nothing more than an adventure in Washington wine country or her girlhood backyard, the South Sound, the two regions she covered for this edition of *Best Places to Kiss*. She writes for the *Tri-City Herald* about wine, agriculture, and the environment. She also contributes to *Wine Press Northwest*.

Okanagan contributor **Sandra Kochan** is a hardy Saskatchewan original, but two decades in Kelowna have transformed her into a consummate local. After years working as a lawyer, winery owner, chef, and contributor to *BC Wine Trails* and Vancouver's *CityFood* magazine, she is now an independent consultant, and continues to be a passionate advocate for the region's culinary and cultural offerings.

Portland-based writer **Nancy Levenson** arrived from the East Coast in 1995, and has called the City of Roses home ever since. Her love affair with Oregon inspired the chapters on Portland, Mount Hood, and the Columbia River Gorge. She also writes for Citysearch.com about Portland nightlife, shopping, and spas.

Freelance writer **Anna Joe Savage** was raised on Bainbridge Island and lives in Indianola, making her a confirmed "other side of the water" dweller. Updating the Kitsap and Olympic Peninsula chapters for *The Best Places to Kiss* offered her a chance to re-explore the inspired beauty of her regional stomping grounds and discover new "just for two" romantic destinations. Other publications she has written for include *Northwest Home + Garden* and *Best Places Seattle*.

Seattle-based freelance writer **Calin Taylor** is a fourth-generation North-westerner, and spent most summers in her childhood boating around north Puget Sound—a perfect preparation for writing about the San Juan Islands, as she did for this edition. Inspired, she and her husband purchased their own best place to kiss, a piece of property on Orcas Island. Taylor's work appears in *Seattle* and *Seattle Bride* magazines.

After she had spent 15 years exploring the country, the Oregon Coast finally lured writer **Lori Tobias** into settling down, and she relays the region's many charms in her chapters. Her work appears in numerous magazines and newspapers, including Alaska Airlines' in-flight magazine, *The Oregonian*, the *Seattle Times*, and *Ladies' Home Journal*.

Vancouver-based food and travel writer **Kasey Wilson** is also a radio personality: she co-hosts *The Best of Food and Wine* (a weekly live radio show on CFUN). She is the editor of *Best Places Vancouver*, the author of several cookbooks, and a regular contributor to national magazines. She contributed chapters on Vancouver, Whistler, and the Sunshine Coast.

Acknowledgments

Thanks to this edition's fabulous team of writers whose ability to kiss and tell (and travel) is a true talent. Appreciation also goes to David Griffith for putting up with yet another *Best Places to Kiss* book, and the subsequent bad jokes about whether or not he's my best person to kiss. He is. A big thank you also goes to Judi Lees, Jane Mundy, and Mark Laba for their roadwork and contributions to the Sunshine Coast and Whistler chapters. Great appreciation goes to the team at Sasquatch Books, including series editor Terence Maikels, project editor Kurt Stephan, and designer Stewart A. Williams. Finally, gratitude for invaluable services rendered goes to copy editor Karen Parkin and proofreader Laura Gronewold.

About Best Places® Guidebooks

PEOPLE TRUST US. *Best Places®* guidebooks, which have been published continuously since 1975, represent one of the most respected regional travel series in the country. In 2004, we incorporated the *Best Places to Kiss* guidebooks into our publishing series, beginning with the previous (eighth) edition of *The Best Places to Kiss in the Northwest,* bringing our reputable stamp of high quality and research to this much-loved series. Our reviewers know their territory. They have your romantic interests at heart, and they strive to function as reliable guides for your amorous outings. The *Best Places to Kiss* guides describe the true strengths, foibles, and unique characteristics of each establishment listed. *The Best Places to Kiss in the Northwest* specifically seeks out and highlights the special parts of this region that harbor romance and splendor, from restaurants, inns, lodges, wineries, and bed-and-breakfasts to spectacular parks, pristine beaches, and romantic drives. In this edition, couples will find all the information they need: when to visit a place to find the most privacy, where to find the most intimate restaurants, which rooms to request (and which to avoid), and how to find each destination's most romantic activities.

NOTE: *The reviews in this edition are based on information available at press time and are subject to change. Romantic travelers are advised that places listed may have closed or changed management, and thus may no longer be recommended by this series. Your romantic feedback assists greatly in increasing our accuracy and our resources, and we welcome information conveyed by readers of this book. Feel free to write us at the following address: Sasquatch Books, 119 S Main St, Suite 400, Seattle, Washington, 98104. We can also be contacted via e-mail: bestplaces@sasquatchbooks. com.*

Lip Ratings

The following is a brief explanation of the lip ratings awarded each location.

◖◗◖◗   *Simply sublime*

◖◗◖◗   *Very desirable; many outstanding qualities*

◖◗◖◗   *Can provide a satisfying experience; some wonderful features*

◖◗   *Romantic possibilities with potential drawbacks*

UNRATED   *New or undergoing major changes*

Price Range

Prices for lodgings are based on peak season rates for one night's lodging for double occupancy (otherwise there wouldn't be anyone to kiss!). Prices for restaurants are based primarily on dinner for two, including dessert, tax, and tip, but not alcohol. Peak season is typically Memorial Day to Labor Day; off-season rates vary, but can sometimes be significantly lower. Because prices and business hours change, it is always a good idea to call ahead to each place you plan to visit.

$$$$ *Very expensive (more than $100 for dinner for two; more than $250 for one night's lodging for two)*

$$$ *Expensive (between $65 and $100 for dinner for two; between $150 and $250 for one night's lodging for two)*

$$ *Moderate (between $35 and $65 for dinner for two; between $85 and $150 for one night's lodging for two)*

$ *Inexpensive (less than $35 for dinner for two; less than $85 for one night's lodging for two)*

Romantic Highlights

The Romantic Highlights section of each chapter provides a guide to the most romantic activities in the region. These pursuits are designed to be intimate and relaxing for couples, and might include strolling to a lighthouse, taking an easy guided kayaking tour, or enjoying an alfresco lunch. In Romantic Highlights, the establishments or attractions that appear in boldface are recommended, and addresses and phone numbers are supplied. Every attempt has been made to provide accurate information on an establishment's location and phone number, but it's always a good idea to call ahead and confirm.

Lodgings

Many romance-oriented lodgings require two-night minimum stays throughout the year (especially on weekends); during some holiday weekends or high-season periods, this requirement might be extended to three nights. It is a good idea to call in advance to check the policy at your lodging of choice. In the spirit of romance, popular family lodgings are mostly not included; however, some accommodations included do allow children, particularly over age 12. Many have safeguards for your privacy, such as separate breakfast times (one seats children, the other is adults-only) or providing detached suites removed from other guests for those traveling with children. If having a kid-free environment is critical to your intimate weekend away, call ahead to find out an establishment's policy. For more information about where to find pet-friendly rooms, see the pet sidebar (page 340) or refer to the pet index (page 457) at the back of this book.

Indexes

In addition to the index of pet-friendly accommodations mentioned above, this book also features a wedding index. Organized by region, this index lists romantic lodgings with facilities to accommodate wedding parties of at least 50 people. (Since one of the most auspicious times to kiss is the moment after you exchange wedding vows, we felt this was appropriate!)

Credit Cards

Many establishments that accept checks also require a major credit card for identification. Some places accept only local checks; this is noted in the reviews. Credit cards are abbreviated as follows: American Express (AE); Bravo (B); Carte Blanche (CB); Diners Club (DC); Discover (DIS); Enroute (E); Japanese credit card (JCB); MasterCard (MC); Visa (V).

"As usual with most lovers in the city, they were troubled by the lack of that essential need of love—a meeting place."

—THOMAS WOLFE

♡ The Fine Art of Kissing

THIS IS THE NINTH EDITION OF *The Best Places to Kiss in the Northwest*, and we are proud to be providing better-than-ever coverage of the most romantic destinations in Washington, Oregon, and British Columbia with features such as the "Romantic Highlights" section, which appears in every chapter and details each region's most romantic activities. As ever, our research is enthusiastic, our investigations thorough, and our criteria increasingly more restrictive. We gather numerous reports from local and traveling inspectors before recommending a place for romance. We highly value our mission as one of the few travel books to review romantic properties with a candid and critical eye, and we treasure the feedback from readers who report that our reviews offer a breath of amorous fresh air.

We admit a strong bias in our feelings about the Northwest. Without question, this area provides the best kissing territory anywhere in the continental United States and Canada, and we strive to recommend the most romantic times of year to visit particular regions. Ultimately, however, each season brings its own rewards, from the pink cherry blossoms of spring and warm, clear days of summer to the brilliant colors of crisp autumn or the dramatic storms of winter. Oh, and about the rain—it does. Enough said. Don't be one of those couples who wait until summer to travel and then decide not to go because it might be too crowded! The style and approach of the people in the Northwest are highly conducive to intimacy and affection. We are confident that, no matter when or where you travel, you will relish this glorious part of the world as much as we do.

Any travel guide that rates establishments is inherently subjective—and *Best Places to Kiss* is no exception. We rely on our professional experience, yes; we also rely on our reporters' instincts to evaluate the heartfelt, magnetic pull of each establishment or region. Whether or not we include places is determined by three main factors: setting, privacy, and ambience. Setting is quite straightforward, referring simply to location and view, but we feel the latter two categories deserve some clarification. In regard to privacy, our preference is for cottages and suites set away from main buildings: such locations allow amorous couples to say or do what they please without fear of being overheard or disturbing others. However, many truly wonderful bed-and-breakfasts and hotels require sharing space; in these cases, we look for modern soundproofing techniques, as well as expert innkeepers who know how to provide guests with a sense of intimate seclusion. We also applaud the notion of private breakfasts, whether delivered straight to your suite or served at an intimate table for two in the dining room. (Here, as with all dining experiences, a warm and friendly greeting, knowledgeable and helpful service, and the ability of the staff to be nearly invisible when you lock eyes across the table is our ideal.)

Ambience is the final major criteron, and it includes a multitude of factors. Intimate environments require more than four-poster beds and lace pillows, or linen-covered tables set with silver and crystal. Ambience requires features that encourage intimacy and allow for uninterrupted affectionate discourse, and relates more to the degree of comfort and number of gracious appointments than to image and frills. We also keep an eye out for details such as music, fresh flowers, and candles. Ambience is also created in part by innkeepers, and if you are traveling for a special romantic occasion, we highly recommend informing them in advance. With notice, the best innkeepers take extra care to ensure that an especially intimate ambience welcomes you and your loved one. They can also inform you of any "special occasion packages," which might include chilled champagne, breakfast in bed, and special touches during turndown service, such as dimmed lights and your beloved's favorite music playing in the background to set the right romantic mood.

If a place has all three factors going for it, inclusion is automatic. But if one or two of the criteria are weak or nonexistent, the other feature(s) have to be superior before the location will be included. For example, a place that offers a breathtakingly beautiful panoramic vista but is also inundated with tourists and children on field trips would not be featured. A fabulous bed-and-breakfast set in a less than desirable location might be included, however, if it boasts a wonderfully inviting and cozy interior that outweighs the drawback of the location. It goes without saying that we consider myriad other factors, including uniqueness, excellence of cooking, cleanliness, value, and professionalism of service. Luxuries such as complimentary champagne and handmade truffles, or extraordinary service, are noteworthy extras, and frequently determine the difference between lip ratings of three-and-a-half and four. In the final evaluation, keep in mind that every place listed in this book is recommended. When you visit any of the places we include here, you should look forward to some degree of privacy, a beautiful setting, heart-stirring ambience, and access to highly romantic pursuits.

PORTLAND & ENVIRONS

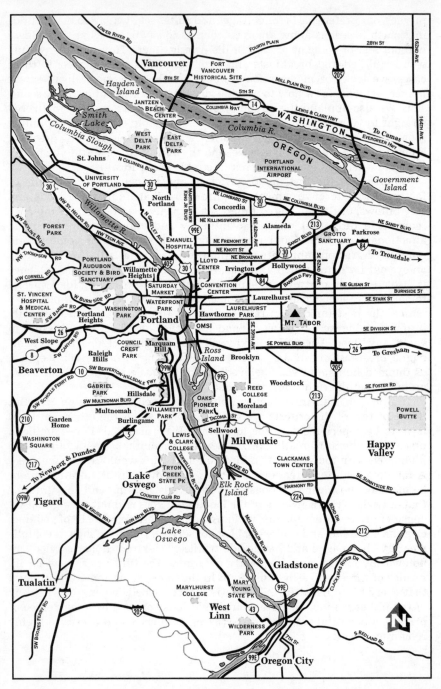

*"You may conquer with the sword, but you are
conquered by a kiss."*

—DANIEL HEINSIUS

♡ PORTLAND & ENVIRONS

Portland is one of the Northwest's true jewels, a friendly city that boasts sophisticated urban pleasures, lush parks and gardens, and a stunning natural setting on the Willamette River. Most getaways here will involve both outdoor and indoor excursions. The Pearl District, a wonderful place to soak up sophisticated street life, is home to hundreds of artists' lofts, galleries galore, and excellent shopping. Meanwhile, the city's green space adds up to more than 37,000 stunning acres. Whether you explore the tiny, two-foot-long Mill Ends Park or the mammoth 5,000-acre Forest Park, the largest urban wilderness in the nation, you'll find lots of secluded spots here for stealing a kiss.

For romantic travelers, there are plenty of great day-trips from Portland even if you're visiting for just a weekend. A short drive west puts you on the decidedly irresistible, rough-and-tumble Oregon Coast. Two volcanic mountains, Mount St. Helens and Mount Hood, are equally accessible day-trip destinations. The city itself is divided in two by the Willamette River (local pronunciation stresses the second syllable), which can be traversed via one of ten bridges that provide plentiful opportunities for gorgeous views and riverside walks.

Portland's manageable size, along with its expertly executed urban plan, makes it easy to navigate. And, unless it's rush hour, crossing the city—diagonally from southeast to northwest, for instance—takes no longer than 15 minutes by car. Parking is rarely difficult. Couples who prefer two-wheel transport will find Portland refreshingly bike friendly. When it rains (a frequent occurrence from November through May), the two of you can take refuge from the wet weather in one of the cozy coffee shops that seem to be on every corner, or in one of Portland's many brew pubs. When the sunny summer months do arrive, the city blossoms—literally. Flowering trees line the streets, and the roses for which the city is famous bloom in brilliant hues. Interstate 5 offers easy access to Portland from the north or south, and travelers approaching from the east can use Interstate 84.

PORTLAND

ROMANTIC HIGHLIGHTS

As home to three highly acclaimed rose gardens, Portland has earned the affectionate nickname of the "City of Roses," which sounds tailor-made for a romantic getaway. Shakespeare might have said that a city by any other name would be just as sweet, and we'd have to agree. With endless options for beautiful walks, cultural outings, and culinary adventures, everything to make your romantic sojourn complete is at your fingertips.

Portland offers countless paths for hiking and biking within city limits. With so many trails to choose from, couples often find themselves in the company of no one but each other—and what better opportunity to sneak a kiss? No trip to Portland is complete without a wander through the **International Rose Test Gardens** (400 SW Kingston; 503/823-3636), located within Washington Park. If you visit during a summer weekend, chances are good there'll be at least one couple saying "I do" in this idyllic setting. For a more secluded garden stroll, head to the nearby **Japanese Gardens** (611 SW Kingston; 503/223-1321) and enjoy the serene surroundings.

If it's a beautiful day and nothing sounds better than a picnic, gather gourmet provisions at **City Market NW** (735 NW 21st Ave; 503/221-3007) and drive west (away from the river) on West Burnside, following signs to the **Pittock Mansion** (3229 NW Pittock Dr; 503/823-3624); here you can spread out your picnic and enjoy the views through the trees on the mansion's well-manicured grounds. Walking tours of the 16,000-square-foot landmark home are held in the afternoons. Another kiss-worthy destination in the West Hills is **Council Crest Park** (SW Council Crest Dr; 503/823-2223). One of Portland's highest points, it's a prime spot for gazing at the stars, the mountains, and each other.

Outdoor space may be the city's hallmark, but Portland's got a lot of indoor romance going for it too—especially if you spend an evening at the theater and share an intimate supper afterward. The **Portland Center for the Performing Arts** (1111 SW Broadway; 503/248-4335) is host to four venues, which feature theater, opera, ballet, and symphony performances throughout the year. You can also wander hand in hand through the **Portland Art Museum** (1219 SW Park Ave; 503/226-2811; www.portlandart museum.org), or tour downtown's public artwork on SW Fifth and Sixth Avenues—here you'll find Norman Rockwell's notorious **Kvinneakt**, the nude that Portlanders know as former mayor Bud Clark's accomplice in the "Expose Yourself to Art" poster. Or explore contemporary artwork at fine galleries in the **Pearl District**. This formerly industrial neighborhood is now home to artsy retail shops, high-priced loft spaces for living and working, and an array of tempting eateries. Strolling around amid the "beautiful people" in the Pearl is a quintessential Portland experience.

Spending a day near the river is always a treat. For most of the year, you can shop to your heart's content underneath the Burnside Bridge among the artisans at the **Saturday Market** (108 W Burnside St; 503/222-6072; Sat–Sun weekly, Mar–Christmas). Homespun crafts range from pottery and stained glass to hand-dipped candles and decadent chocolates. If the crowds are too much, duck away for a delicious breakfast at the nearby **Bijou Café** (132 SW 3rd Ave; 503/222-3187). From there, walk toward the river and find the paved path at **Tom McCall Waterfront Park**, a beautiful strip of green that's popular with runners, walkers, and bikers alike. Turn north and head to **Riverplace Marina**, a boardwalk that begins at the **Riverplace Hotel**. This line of shops and cafes was made for arm-in-arm strolling. In the evening, set sail on the **Portland Spirit** (503/224-3900) for a dinner cruise with breathtaking city views and tasty fare—just the recipe for romance.

Don't let wet weather put a damper on your visit to Portland. Think of the rain as a perfect excuse to explore the city's bookstores, shops, and wonderful restaurants. For lovers of all things literary, an entire rainy day could be spent inside **Powell's City of Books** (1005 W Burnside St; 503/228-4651), which happens to be the largest bookstore in the whole country. Get lost together in the stacks of this mazelike mecca for readers, and recite poetry into each other's ears. The unpretentious shops along Hawthorne Boulevard reflect the street's laid-back reputation as a hippie haven and make for great browsing. Give your noses something to do at **Escential Lotions & Oils** (3638 SE Hawthorne Blvd; 503/236-7976), where you can stir your senses with more than 100 scents (try Portland Rain), then purchase your own custom-blended massage lotion, shampoo, or bubble bath to savor back at your room. If lingering over an afternoon meal sounds tempting, join locals for lunch along Hawthorne. The **Bridgeport Ale House** (3632 SE Hawthorne Blvd; 503/233-6540) serves soups, sandwiches, and salads that far surpass what you'd expect from a brew pub. **Bread and Ink Café** (3610 SE Hawthorne Blvd; 503/239-4756) offers a great brunch, with favorites like blintzes or the egg, lox, and onion scramble, or pick up your own gourmet picnic fixings at **Pastaworks** (3735 SE Hawthorne Blvd; 503/232-1010).

When the sun goes down, the two of you should go up—and treat yourself to a bird's-eye view of the city. Take an elevator to the 30th floor of the U.S. Bank Tower to **Portland City Grill** (111 SW 5th Ave; 503/450-0030) and get a window seat for drinks or dinner while you gaze over the sparkling city. The **Heathman Hotel** (1001 SW Broadway; 503/241-4100) is a haven for late-night romance; its three bars are among Portland's most chic and offer delicious light meals, live music, and sumptuous decor.

Access and Information

Portland International Airport (PDX) (7000 NE Airport Wy; 503/460-4234; www.portlandairportpdx.com) is served by most major airlines, with excellent connections from points around the Pacific Northwest and beyond. Allow at least 30 minutes—more during rush hour—between the airport and town. All major car-rental companies operate from the airport. Taxis and shuttles are readily available; expect to pay at least $25 for the trip downtown. The most economical ride ($1.65) is via the Metropolitan Area Express (MAX) train. Catch MAX just outside baggage claim; the ride to Pioneer Courthouse Square takes about 40 minutes.

Most drivers reach Portland via either Interstate 5, which runs north-south, or Interstate 84, which runs east-west and connects visitors to the beautiful Columbia River Gorge. Rush hours in Portland can mean gridlock, but if you arrive midday (after 9am, but before 3pm) or after 7pm, you should have smooth sailing into town. If you're traveling from Seattle, the drive takes approximately three hours. **Amtrak** (503/273-4866 locally or 800/USA-RAIL; www.amtrak.com) operates out of lovely Union Station (800 NW 6th Ave), just north of downtown. This elegant structure memorializes the romance of train travel in a bygone era. Trains come and go from points north, east, and south daily.

From May until August, the city celebrates the Portland Rose Festival with parades, concerts, and various other events. For information on area happenings, contact the **Portland Oregon Visitors Association** in Pioneer Square (701 SW 6th Ave; 503/275-8355 or 877/678-5263; info@pova.com; www.pova.org).

Romantic Lodgings

AVALON HOTEL AND SPA
◐◐◐◖

0455 SW Hamilton Ct, Portland / 503/802-5800 or 888/556-4402
If you're seeking a luxurious retreat in the middle of the city, look no further than this river-side address. The elegant Avalon Hotel prides itself on catering to its guests' every whim. Located south of downtown, the property sits on the Willamette River in the upscale Johns Landing neighborhood. Pampering is taken seriously here, and the indulgent atmosphere will set you both at ease from the moment you enter the lobby. Each of the 99 stylish rooms is designed with your ultimate comfort in mind and combines Northwest casual with Asian-influenced decor, including Chinese wedding cabinets hiding the televisions. The softest cotton sheets, vintage velvet couches, marble baths, and warm tones throughout combine to create an inviting, sumptuous atmosphere. Most rooms offer direct balcony access

(some are more private than others), so you and your sweetie can take advantage of the superb panoramic views of Mount Hood or the Willamette River. Enjoy room service from Rivers (503/802-5850), the hotel's restaurant, or opt for alfresco dining on the water when the weather permits. All guests have access to the full-service spa and fitness club, just off the hotel lobby. The fitness club offers classes like yoga and Pilates, plus a full spectrum of free weights and cardiovascular machines. Arrange to enjoy nurturing spa services—such as a chamomile body scrub, a massage, or a mud wrap—in one of the soothing treatment rooms, or, for the ultimate splurge, order an in-room spa experience, such as a soothing Coastal Evergreen bath or Aromatherapy Bath for two.
$$$–$$$$ *AE, DC, DIS, MC, V; checks OK; www.avalonhotelandspa.com.* &

THE BENSON HOTEL
✿✿❅

309 SW Broadway, Portland / 503/228-2000 or 888/523-6766
It's easy to get swept away by the grandeur of the Benson's massive lobby, where Austrian crystal chandeliers, Italian marble floors, a stamped-tin ceiling, and rare walnut wood paneling imported from Russia are just a few of the details that make it a sight to behold. By choosing to stay in one of the 286 rooms, you'll be following in a long line of famous footsteps: presidents, movie stars, and big-time musicians often stay here when they're passing through Portland. The rooms are tastefully and traditionally decorated in beige and black, each with a comfy chair and ottoman, and many offer city views. Bright, spotless baths and plush his-and-her robes are standard. Truly special occasions call for a Grand Suite, which includes a baby grand piano, fireplace, and jetted tub. There are two notable restaurants attached to the Benson. El Gaucho (503/227-8794) is known for serving some of the city's finest steaks, with many dishes prepared tableside. The more romantic option is the London Grill (call the main hotel number), where classic meals like chateaubriand for two are served in an elegant, formal setting.
$$$–$$$$ *AE, DC, DIS, MC, V; checks OK; www.bensonhotel.com.*

BLUE PLUM INN
✿✿❅

2026 NE 15th Ave, Portland / 503/288-3848 or 877/288-3844
Within walking distance of this sweet Victorian inn are B&Bs that beg passersby to turn their heads. With thousands of twinkling lights, circular drives, and opulent fountains outside, visitors can only hope that what's inside is half as enchanting. And then there's the Blue Plum Inn. Like the City of Roses itself, it's a beautifully cared for home that's so unpretentious and comfortable, you'll want to take up residence here. Hostess Suzanne Hansche and her husband, Jonathan, take great care with details that matter, such as an abundance of fresh flowers, in-room chocolates, and

delectable, hearty breakfasts. Each of three rooms has its own bath and is furnished with precious heirlooms, but the two that can be reserved as suites are our picks for romance seekers. The Hydrangea Suite on the lower level is the most spacious, with two bedrooms, a bathroom with a tub and shower, and a sitting room with a TV and VCR. Having an extra bedroom is indeed a luxury, but the resulting privacy is worth the splurge. Upstairs, the Tulip Room doubles in size with its adjoining living room. Shut the French doors and curl up with your other half to watch a movie or read, and then retire to the queen bed with its intricate pink and green quilt. Special occasions call for special requests, and your hosts will cheerfully arrange for local wines, chilled champagne, or just about anything else you desire upon your arrival. $$–$$$ *MC, V; checks OK; www.bluepluminn.com.*

HOTEL VINTAGE PLAZA
❤❤❤
422 SW Broadway, Portland / 503/228-1212 or 800/243-0555
Even with a location smack in the middle of downtown, there's no place quite like this in Portland for getting away from it all. Everything about the Vintage Plaza is cozy, beginning with the lobby, which is highlighted by rich jewel tones and offers sumptuous sofas warmed by a marble fireplace. Each evening, guests are invited into the lobby to taste some of the notable Northwest wines after which many of the guest rooms upstairs are named. Any one of the 107 room choices would be a good one; the standouts, however, are spectacular. On a cloudless night, snuggle under a twinkling sky in one of the Starlight Rooms, featuring solarium-style windows with electric blinds for nighttime stargazing. (Kiss all you'd like; the windows are tinted for privacy.) Secluded outdoor Jacuzzis enhance the otherwise standard Garden Spa Rooms and are well worth the splurge. And for true romance (with enough space for a game of hide-and-seek!), choose a luxurious bilevel Townhouse Suite and top it off with a romance package: chilled champagne, rose petals scattered on the king-size bed at turndown, and breakfast delivered to your room when you rise. For a taste of fine Northern Italian cuisine, try Pazzo Ristorante (503/228-1515); it's adjacent to the hotel's ground floor and serves breakfast, lunch, and dinner daily. And since you're right in the heart of the city, your options abound for fine dining, theater, shopping, and exploring Portland's best romantic offerings. $$$–$$$$ *AE, DC, DIS, MC, V; no checks; www.vintageplaza.com.* ঙ

THE LION AND THE ROSE
❤❤❤
1810 NE 15th Ave, Portland / 503/287-9245 or 800/955-1647
Now a City of Portland–designated landmark, this 1906 Victorian bed-and-breakfast is also on the National Register of Historic Places. The location,

one block away from busy NE Broadway, makes for a less than peaceful setting, but it does offer excellent access to shopping, dining, and soaking up the feel of Portland's Irvington neighborhood. Each of the six guest rooms meets a high standard of Victorian elegance, and the hosts let few details go untended, from candles in the baths to in-room beverages to luxurious, fluffy robes. The most spacious room is the Lavonna, which wins our hearts despite the fact that its private bath is across the hall. Nonetheless, the light and airy lavender and white decor immediately draws you in, making it worthy of romantic consideration. Also, the room's reading nook with bay windows is perfect for two (with or without a book of Shakespeare's sonnets). Joseph's Room is distinctive in its own right. The rich burgundy and gold tones, private bath, fainting couch, and lavish four-poster bed set the stage for romance. Not to be forgotten is the Rose Room. Although it's located off the main living room, it offers a beautiful garden view and is ideal for those who want to soak in the B&B's only Jacuzzi tub. Arriving guests are greeted with afternoon tea, and the hearty morning meal is served around a large formal table in the stately dining room.
$$ AE, DIS, MC, V; checks OK; www.lionrose.com.

MACMASTER HOUSE
✪✪✪
1041 SW Vista Ave, Portland / 503/223-7362 or 800/774-9523
If we absolutely *had* to stay inside all weekend long, we'd be sure to lock ourselves into this palatial residence (and throw away the key!). Built in the 1880s, this elegant mansion boasts a rich history and was at one time host to some of Portland's swankiest soirees. MacMaster isn't just another house on the hill—it's a house on King's Hill, an elite neighborhood close to downtown, trendy shops on NW 23rd Avenue, and the must-see gardens in Washington Park. No matter which of the seven deluxe guest rooms you choose, your stay here will be a special one—although romantic travelers should note that only two rooms have private baths. Each room is furnished with European antiques, and dreamy murals by local artist Myrna Anderson grace the walls throughout. We recommend the two options with in-room baths. The McCord Suite's safari theme, canopied wicker bed, and carved-wood furnishings are beautiful; add to that a working fireplace and a private deck, and it makes for a near-perfect place for an amorous adventure. A close second is the less extravagant Artist's Suite. This garretlike room with sloped ceilings, located on the top floor, made us feel as if we were in Paris. Relax in the king-size bed for hours, or have a soak in the claw-foot tub. The other five rooms have shared baths, but are nicely decorated and less expensive than the luxury suites. Whatever you do, don't miss breakfast. The fruit-laden first course—perhaps poached pears or sweet baked

apples—is divine. If you feel too full after the savory second course, not to worry: you can always head back upstairs for a late-morning nap. $$ *AE, DIS, MC, V; checks OK; www.macmaster.com.*

PORTLAND'S WHITE HOUSE
❂❂❂

1914 NE 22nd Ave, Portland / 503/287-7131
The "oohs" and "ahhs" begin as soon as you turn into the circular drive of this historic Greek Revival home in the northeast quadrant of the city. With its bubbling fountain set in lovingly manicured grounds, and a remarkable resemblance to the First Couple's abode, be assured that a stay here is suitable for heads of state. The location is prime for exploring the myriad shops and boutiques along nearby NE Broadway—the short walk will take you past more of the city's finest residences. Inside, the lavish surroundings will make your heart jump. The grand entrance hall dazzles with a cascading staircase and hand-painted murals. An inviting parlor features French doors and a grand piano; the exquisite formal dining room is set with European table linens and fine china for up to 18 guests. Breakfast here is a serious affair. Innkeeper Lanning Blanks is the house chef (as well as the house decorator), and the tempting aroma of his breakfast creations will gently stir you from your slumber. No expense was spared when the home and its adjacent Carriage House were restored, and the fact that each room has its own bath (many with claw-foot tubs) is a testament to that. For the most romantic getaway, we recommend the Chaffeur's Quarters. With its four-poster king-size bed, double-headed shower, and Jacuzzi tub, you may find little reason to venture out. Our next favorite is the Canopy Room. It's decorated in rich, romantic reds and boasts an oversize jetted tub. With any room you choose, Moonstruck chocolates waiting in the rooms assure a sweet arrival. Thinking of tying the knot in Portland? The White House hosts some of the city's most exquisite affairs, from beautiful rehearsal dinners and receptions to the ultimate romantic wedding night for the newlyweds.
$$-$$$ *AE, DIS, MC, V; checks OK; www.portlandswhitehouse.com.*

Romantic Restaurants

ASSAGGIO
❂❂❂

7742 SE 13th Ave, Portland / 503/232-6151
Head east across the Sellwood Bridge to get to the historic neighborhood of Sellwood. In addition to working up a healthy dinner appetite, an afternoon of exploring here will bring delights, like a chance to shop in Portland's antiques alley (SE 13th Street) and an up-close view of some of the city's most lovingly restored Victorian homes. Italian cuisine is the sustenance of

choice in these parts, and our favorite source is Assaggio. This neighborhood trattoria's popularity is the result of its appealing combination of consistently delicious Italian food and a beautiful yet relaxed setting. The amber walls reflect the flickering votives in the main dining room, casting a warm glow. Couples who like to share everything will swoon for the house specialty: a trio of pastas chosen by the chef each evening. It could be penne sautéed with leeks, garlic, and pistachios; farfalle cooked al dente with seasonal vegetables and pecorino cheese; and spaghetti *alla puttanesca*. Enhance these mouthwatering dishes with some Italian wine from the adjoining wine bar, Enoteca, and it's the perfect dinner à deux. End the evening on a sweet note with handmade chocolates or the fruity house-made sorbet and cookies.

$$ AE, DIS, MC, V; checks OK; dinner Mon–Sat; beer and wine; reservations recommended; www.assaggiorestaurant.com. &

CARLYLE
✪✪✪✪
1632 NW Thurman St, Portland / 503/595-1782
We admire the fact that Portlanders frequently head out to upscale restaurants without dressing up for dinner. Relaxed couples wearing jeans and T-shirts—even hiking boots—are par for the course. But if you relish the idea of getting dolled up for a special evening, put your best foot forward and step into Carlyle, a splendidly sophisticated locale hidden in a hushed northwest neighborhood surrounded by industry and overpasses. As you enter, take a few moments to bask in the magical glow of the bar, which is illuminated so that the entire room feels like a work of fine art. Only a handful of tables fit into the intimate dining room, accented with dark woods with elegant lamps lighting each table. Share a variety of small tastes such as crepes filled with duck and wild mushrooms or radicchio-wrapped goat cheese. Then indulge in equally decadent entrées, ranging from grilled rib-eye steak to duck breast served with confit and polenta. Saving room to share a dessert takes some restraint, but it's worth it to enjoy the sweet rewards of the hazelnut-chocolate mousse with caramel–peanut butter *semifreddo* or the creamy espresso-infused crème brûlée.

$$$–$$$$ AE, MC, V; no checks; lunch Tues–Fri, dinner Tues–Sat; full bar; reservations recommended; www.carlylerestaurant.com.

HIGGINS
✪✪
1239 SW Broadway, Portland / 503/222-9070
This restaurant on a corner near the theater district may not look exactly like an intimate haven, but its delicious food casts a romantic spell—and it's widely considered one of the city's finest dining establishments. Chef-owner Greg Higgins's dedication to Northwest cuisine has earned him many

kudos, including an award from the James Beard Foundation in 2002. Soft lighting and a multitiered design turn a sizable space into a cozy one. None of the tables are secluded, but the lowest level is the quietest, as it escapes the clamor of the open kitchen. As for the food: if it's on the menu, it's local and in season. Seafood dishes shine, including the warming red-wine cioppino with crab, prawns, mussels, and clams. Vegetarians will be thrilled with choices like risotto of Oregon truffles, leeks, and chèvre. Spectacular presentation accompanies everything, especially the desserts, which might include a chocolate soufflé cake or an apple-rhubarb crisp with buttermilk ice cream. *$$$ AE, DC, DIS, MC, V; checks OK; lunch Mon–Fri, dinner every day; full bar; reservations recommended; www.higgins.citysearch.com.* &

HOLDEN'S BISTRO
◖◗◖

524 NW 14th Ave, Portland / 503/916-0099
If spontaneity floats your romantic boat, it's still good to have options. Even on a weekend, it's unlikely that you'll need a reservation to eat at this hip, underappreciated Pearl District restaurant. Clean lines and industrial-chic decor set Holden's apart from the lavish (and spendy) dining destinations that dot this artsy neighborhood. The minimalist space is warmed by romantic lighting, with votives at each table, and brightly colored fresh flowers are everywhere you look. Opt for a booth over the less comfy tables. The menu focuses on lighter fare, leaving enough room for a gooey brownie sundae and two spoons. But we're getting ahead of ourselves: for your meal, enjoy a bowl of the daily soup, a fresh salad with seared flank steak, or an entrée of grilled tombo (Hawaiian for albacore) tuna tacos. Afterward, cozy up to the bar for a freshly mixed cocktail, some prime people watching, and an after-dinner kiss. *$ AE, MC, V; no checks; dinner Tues–Sat; full bar; reservations recommended.* &

IL PIATTO
◖◗◖

2348 SE Ankeny St, Portland / 503/236-4997
Chef-owner Eugene Bingham has created one of southeast Portland's most charming restaurants. This lovable neighborhood place is surrounded by houses, so only those who know its exact location will find it. Inside, lucky diners privy to the secret will find a color scheme of soothing gold and wine, along with rustic decor, hand-painted pottery, and antique furniture. Couples don't mind waiting for a table on the comfy sofa in back, wineglasses in hand. The menu is Italian through and through, with pastas for every taste, risottos bursting with flavor, and signature dishes such as pork saltimbocca with sage and prosciutto. For an extra dose of romance, request booth

C-8, also known as "the proposal table." Cozy up next to each other on the velvet-padded bench and whisper sweet nothings all evening.
$$ DIS, MC, V; checks OK; lunch Tues–Fri, dinner every day; beer and wine; reservations recommended; www.ilpiatto.citysearch.com.

LUCY'S TABLE
❍❍❍❶

704 NW 21st Ave, Portland / 503/226-6126
If one word could sum up the delicious dining experience you'll enjoy at this unassuming 21st Avenue gem, we'd select indulgent. If you arrive by car, eschew the stress of finding a rare, open parking spot nearby. Simply pull up to the corner of NW 21st Avenue and Irving Street and hand your keys to the valet. It feels like an indulgence but only costs a few dollars. Once inside the intimate dining room, we suspect the ambience will encourage hand-holding across the table. The gold walls are accented by dark velvet curtains for a luxe look. Tables are well spaced and invite intimate conversations, but you'll find the most private seats in the nook farthest from the door, with a painting of two embracing lovers watching overhead. The deeply flavorful fare will do wonders for your senses, whether you order several small plates to share—standouts include goat cheese ravioli and grilled romaine hearts—or opt for more traditional entrées such as lavender-blackened ahi tuna or lamb rubbed with cocoa and espresso. Cap off your meal with a final indulgence: not-to-be missed desserts such as flourless chocolate cake and apple tart with cheddar cheese.
$$ AE, DC, MC, V; checks OK; dinner Mon–Sat; full bar; reservations recommended; www.lucystable.com. ♿

MINT
❍❍❶

816 N Russell St, Portland / 503/284-5518
The city's long-reigning queen of cocktails, Lucy Brennan, isn't only the master mixologist at one of the hippest restaurants around—she's the owner. With names like Love on the Rocks and Mandarin Kiss, her masterfully concocted drinks are at least as, if not more, tempting as the dinner offerings. Food-wise, the menu consists of intensely flavorful dishes drawn from Latin cuisine. Seafood items such as tuna ceviche and smoky sautéed mussels shine, and main dishes like the Brazilian mixed grill or wild mushroom risotto won't leave your palates disappointed. Don't let the dining room's chic see-and-be-seen atmosphere intimidate you; request a table for two so you can focus on each other. Or, ask to be seated at the tiny bar in back and steal kisses when no one is looking.
$$–$$$ AE, MC, V; no checks; dinner Mon–Sat; full bar; reservations recommended; www.mintrestaurant.com. ♿

NOBLE ROT
✿✿✿

2724 SE Ankeny St, Portland / 503/233-1999

Wine is always romantic, but it soars to new heights at this popular Eastside wine bar/dinner destination. Inside, make your way through the narrow space between the bar and cozy booths and into the back room, where exposed brick calls to mind a wine cellar. Let us count the ways we adore this little place. First, it's set up like a wine shop in that each selection is priced at retail, so enjoying a bottle here is easy on the wallet. On-site drinkers will pay a corkage fee. Note: bringing your own is discouraged. Second, it's the kind of establishment where if you're waffling between the cabernet and the pinot noir, the patient servers will give you a taste of each to help you along (by-the-glass selections only). Last but certainly not least, the menu of small plates lends itself to sharing. Don't be fooled—just because you're in a wine bar doesn't mean you can't leave feeling satisfied. Choices change with the seasons but usually include a cheese plate, a savory terrine, a salad or two, and a creamy macaroni and cheese.

$$ AE, MC, V; local checks only; dinner Mon–Sat; beer and wine; no reservations. ♿

PALEY'S PLACE
✿✿✿

1204 NW 21st Ave, Portland / 503/243-2403

Set in a lovingly renovated house in Nob Hill's restaurant row, Paley's Place has been a popular destination for fine dining since chef Vitaly and his wife, Kimberly, first opened their doors in 1995. Cream-colored walls, white linen–covered tables, and hardwood floors make for a simple, intimate setting. The main dining area is not as cozy, so opt for one of a handful of tables in the back room or, in warm weather, on the lovely porch. Begin your meal with something made to share: Paley's signature mussels steamed with garlic, parsley, and white wine, served with perfectly browned hand-cut fries and mustard aioli. Entrées change with the seasons and range from grilled Alaskan prawns to roasted rabbit and crispy veal sweetbreads. The award-winning dessert menu offers one of the city's best crème brûlées and a chocolate soufflé cake to sweep you both off your feet.

$$$ AE, MC, V; local checks only; dinner every day; full bar; reservations recommended; www.paleysplace.citysearch.com.

VERITABLE QUANDARY
✿✿✿

1220 SW 1st Ave, Portland / 503/227-7342

In the evenings, Portland's bridges light up the sky, providing an irresistible backdrop for kissing by the Willamette River. Sadly, most of the city's riverside restaurants leave much to be desired in the romance department. But

don't fret: the former tavern now affectionately known as "The VQ" rises to the occasion. Dining alfresco in the Northwest is an experience to be savored in summer, and no patio is better suited for an amorous evening meal than this one. Hanging baskets bursting with blooms and well-kept gardens of lush greenery provide the ideal ambience. In inclement weather, get cozy in the gently lit dining room, which provides respite from the noisy bar. The restaurant's extensive wine list offers plenty of modestly priced bottles and over 50 selections by the glass to sip while you sup. Chef Annie Cuggino's menu changes with the seasons, but always includes her signature osso bucco—a mouthwatering rendition. You'll find hints of Italy in other entrées such as grilled sausage and white beans or salmon served with risotto. As you're deciding on your main course, consider this: the chocolate soufflé (which must be ordered when your order your meal to give ample preparation time) is lighter than air and a heavenly way to end your dinner.
$$-$$$ *AE, DIS, MC, V; no checks; lunch Mon–Fri, dinner every day, brunch Sat–Sun; full bar; reservations recommended; www.veritable quandary.com.* &

WILD ABANDON
❂❂❂
2411 SE Belmont St, Portland / 503/232-4458
To say that Wild Abandon has character is an understatement. The velvety interior, friendly wait staff, and varied menu offerings are anything but ordinary. Inside an unassuming terra-cotta–tinted building, the long, narrow dining area feels loungelike and inviting. A bevy of festive light fixtures hangs from above, illuminating the place just enough for you to make out the dreamy painted fresco of lounging Dionysian figures on the back wall. Choosing from the tempting dinner menu can be a bit of a challenge, but never fear, any choice you make will be delicious. Keep it simple with one of the pastas or a Red Velvet Burger, or splurge on the Wild Cioppino, a hearty, satisfying stew of scallops, prawns, clams, and other delights from the sea. Linger after your meal with a glass of port or dessert wine from the bar.
$$-$$$ *AE, DIS, MC, V; local checks only; dinner every day, brunch Sat–Sun; full bar; reservations recommended.* &

COLUMBIA RIVER GORGE & MOUNT HOOD

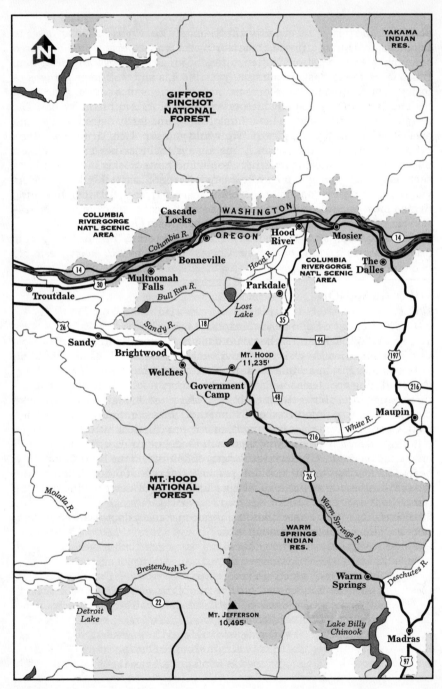

"Let him kiss me with the kisses of his mouth: for thy love is better than wine."
—SONG OF SOLOMON

♡ COLUMBIA RIVER GORGE & MOUNT HOOD

Some of the Northwest's greatest natural treasures can be found in and around the Columbia River Gorge, the beautiful chasm that separates part of Washington from Oregon. An obvious choice for adventures of all kinds—including amorous ones—the region stretches from The Dalles in the east to Troutdale in the west. Blessed with panoramic vistas, fields full of wildflowers, an abundance of magnificent waterfalls, quaint towns dotted with charming country inns, and boundless opportunities for invigorating outdoor activities, the Columbia River Gorge offers an excellent setting for romance. Located less than an hour east of Portland, it can make a romantic day-trip or inspire a weekend-long escape.

The sights in this historically rich area are best savored with a meandering drive along the Historic Columbia River Highway, a road that was built specifically to display the Gorge and that has been in operation since 1915. Keep your eye out for the intricate stonework, arched bridges, viaducts, tunnels, and lookout points tailor-made for romantic discovery. For a memorable excursion, drive a stretch of the old highway from Troutdale to Multnomah Falls, Oregon's most popular (and most photographed) tourist attraction.

Another popular destination here is the town of Hood River, the main hub of activity on the Oregon side of the Gorge. Known for its thousands of fruit trees—mostly apples and pears—that blossom into beauty each year, Hood River is also the windsurfing capital of the Northwest. The town serves as an ideal base for starry-eyed couples exploring the area, with its plentiful eating establishments, wide array of good lodging options, and easy access to Mount Hood, Oregon's highest peak. On clear days, snowy Mount Hood seems just a few steps away from almost anywhere in central Oregon—and, in fact, it is easily accessible by car. As the seasons shift, so do the opportunities for romantic activities around the mountain (which is also an active volcano). Summer offers the chance to backpack, golf, hike, climb, and share quiet days of fishing or dipping bare feet in the Salmon River. Winter provides ample opportunity for skiing or snuggling by a cozy fire. The mountain's crown jewel is Timberline Lodge, one of the only year-round ski resorts in the United States. The Timberline Lodge is worth a visit in any season. Other options for snow-kissed fun are Mount Hood Meadows—the largest ski area on the mountain—and Mount Hood SkiBowl, the largest night-skiing area in the United States. (See Mount Hood section for ski area contact information.)

COLUMBIA RIVER GORGE

ROMANTIC HIGHLIGHTS

Because there is so much to see and do on any given weekend in the Columbia River Gorge, one visit alone will not be enough. Spend a few days (or more) exploring in the summertime, when the wildflowers are in bloom, and then treat yourselves to another getaway in the fall, to enjoy the leaves and the abundance of the harvest in the fruit-producing Hood River Valley.

If you're heading east on Interstate 84 from Portland, Troutdale is your first stop, and the town serves as an ideal entry point for any visit to the Columbia River Gorge. The main attraction in Troutdale, and one not to be missed by any pair of lovers, is **McMenamins Edgefield** (2126 SW Halsey, Troutdale; 503/669-8610 or 800/669-8610), a 38-acre estate run by local microbrew barons Mike and Brian McMenamin. Built in 1911 as a working farm, Edgefield is now a haven for cozy dining and drinking, quirky artwork, gardens made for wandering, golf, and cinema. It's also a sought-after wedding site. For daytime visitors, highlights include meals at the **Black Rabbit Restaurant** (see Romantic Restaurants), libations at the **Little Red Shed**, daily tastings at the **Edgefield Winery**, and luxurious on-site massages.

Continuing east, the next stretch of the Historic Columbia River Highway is one of the most romantic drives in the state. The **Vista House** (40700 E Historic Columbia River Hwy; 503/695-2230; mid-Apr–mid-Oct) at Crown Point should be your first stop. On a clear day, this octagonal stone structure, built atop a 733-foot cliff, is an exhilarating place to experience the beauty of the Columbia River Gorge. In summer, you can explore the historical displays and gift shop. For a tour of waterfalls, continue heading east; you'll see **Latourell Falls** as you cross a lovely bridge that arches over the water rushing to the Columbia. Next is **Bridal Veil Falls**—like the blushing bride it's named after, it hides from passing motorists. A steep two-thirds-of-a-mile round-trip hike from the parking lot is worth the effort, especially with a kiss as your reward at the top. Next, you'll pass **Wahkeena Falls**, whose name means "most beautiful." While it is indeed lovely, it's just a warm-up for what's to come: 620-foot **Multnomah Falls**, the nation's second-largest year-round waterfall. After you've taken a few photos of each other before the falls and felt the mist refresh your faces, sit down to a rustic, romantic lunch of homemade soup and sandwiches inside the **Multnomah Falls Lodge** (50000 Historic Columbia River Hwy 30 E, Bridal Veil; 503/695-2376).

The second-largest city in the Gorge is the very romantic Hood River, located off Highway 84. Top-notch restaurants; plenty of lodgings tastefully tailored to lovers; and an adorable, very walkable downtown make it an irresistible place to spend time with your special someone. (The largest town, The Dalles, is an industrial area ill-suited to a romantic getaway.)

On Saturdays in summer, visit the **Hood River Saturday Market** (on Cascade St between 5th and 7th Aves; mid-May–mid-Oct) for fresh local produce, baked goods, and handcrafted gifts such as delicate jewelry and wonderfully scented soaps. And if you time it right, you can soak up more local culture at **Hood River's First Friday Art Walk**, held on the first Friday night of the month between March and December. From 5pm to 8pm, local restaurants and shops transform themselves into art galleries and welcome you in to browse the work of local artists, hear live music, and sample delicious fare.

For a unique and romantic tour of the fruit orchards of the Hood River Valley, take the train. The **Mount Hood Railroad** (110 Railroad Ave; 541/386-3556 or 800/872-4661; www.mthoodrr.com) leaves from downtown Hood River and offers four-hour excursions that stop in the tiny town of Parkdale, where you'll enjoy stunning views of Mount Hood. The brunch or dinner trains are even more romantic, and offer four-course meals served in nicely restored 1940s dining cars.

Or take a leisurely drive on what's affectionately known as the "Fruit Loop," a 35-mile route that leads you through the valley's orchards, forests, farmlands, and towns. Take in the spectacular scenery and make a few stops along the way to sample the local fruit. Pick your own flowers, berries, or vegetables at **Rasmussen Farms** (3020 Thomsen Rd; 541/386-4622) or purchase from the bounty of ready-picked varieties. Free wine tastings are held at both **Cathedral Ridge Winery** (4200 Post Canyon Dr; 541/386-2882 or 800/516-8710) and **Hood River Vineyards** (4693 Westwood Dr; 541/386-3772). Both are also perfect spots for picnics. For a breathtaking view of the valley leading to Mount Hood, stop at Panorama Point, a half mile south of Hood River on Highway 35.

Access and Information

The Columbia River Gorge is most commonly approached from Portland via Interstate 84 east. Follow the freeway through the Gorge to Hood River and The Dalles. Another, more scenic option is to exit at Troutdale and take the Historic Columbia River Highway. From Mount Hood, take Highway 35 north to Hood River. Travelers from Seattle should drive south on Interstate 5 to Portland, then east on Interstate 84. Visit in mid-April to experience the charming small-town atmosphere of the Blossom Festival, which celebrates the natural beauty of the area's orchards in spring. For tourist information, contact the **Columbia River Gorge Visitors Association** (2149 W Cascade Ave, #106A, Hood River; 800/984-6743; www.crgva.org).

Romantic Lodgings

COLUMBIA GORGE HOTEL
♥♥♥
4000 Westcliff Dr, Hood River / 541/386-5566 or 800/345-1921
As soon as you catch your first glimpse of this beautiful Spanish-style villa, you'll know you've come to the right place. Located on a forested bank above the Columbia River, the hotel's grounds are expertly groomed and include lush lawns, stone bridges that make for excellent kissing spots, and a glorious 208-foot waterfall named Wah Gwin Gwin Falls. The excitement builds as you enter the lavish lobby and turn the corner to the hotel's elegant restaurant, the Columbia Court Dining Room (see Romantic Restaurants), where in the morning you'll enjoy the wonderful World Famous Farm Breakfast. The 40 individually decorated guest rooms are attractive but a bit of a letdown after you've seen the pristine grounds, fancy lobby, and restaurant. For the price, we'd expect the rooms to be larger, with all of the furnishings in tiptop shape. Many rooms are a tad too small, but if you don't mind paying extra, request one with a canopied bed and gas fireplace. Still, as one of the area's premier destinations for romantic couples, there are plenty of reasons to stay here. The nightly turndown service includes roses and chocolates. And for a small charge, the two of you can indulge in some squeaky-clean fun with an extra basket of bath goodies set out in the bathroom. In the morning, any disappointments about your room will disappear when you sit down to the seemingly never-ending breakfast that's included with your room rate (nonguests pay $57 for two). The meal starts with fresh fruit with hot apple fritters, and moves on to oatmeal, three eggs, breakfast meats or grilled Idaho trout, golden hash browns, biscuits with honey, and,

finally, a stack of buttermilk pancakes. A hand-in-hand stroll around the beautiful grounds is the perfect conclusion to your morning feast. $$$–$$$$ *AE, DC, DIS, MC, V; checks OK; www.columbiagorgehotel.com.* &

HOOD RIVER HOTEL
◑◖

102 Oak Ave, Hood River / 541/386-1900 or 800/386-1859
If finding yourselves steps away from all the shops and restaurants in Hood River is a top priority, the Hood River Hotel might be just the ticket. Built in 1912, the charming red-brick building has a European flair, with French doors opening up to the inviting, high-ceilinged lobby. Each of the 41 guest rooms is tastefully decorated with antique reproductions, and for the most part they're quite small, so you'll never be far from your special someone. The suites are best suited for romance and are appointed with canopied beds, Oriental rugs, and kitchenettes. We recommend asking to see rooms before you agree to book one, as some are infiltrated by the red light of the hotel sign, some are too dark, and some overlook the unsightly parking lot. Just off the lobby, Pasquale's serves Mediterranean-influenced Pacific Northwest cuisine in a casual setting. Despite its drawbacks, the Hood River Hotel is a good, and less expensive, alternative to the pricey Columbia Gorge Hotel—even when you add in the price of champagne and roses. $–$$ *AE, DC, DIS, MC, V; checks OK; www.hoodriverhotel.com.* &

INN AT THE GORGE
◑◑◑◑

1113 Eugene St, Hood River / 541/386-4429
Located within walking distance of downtown, this sunny yellow Victorian, one of Hood River's historic jewels, lives up to our high standards for romantic hideaways—and then some. In summertime, nasturtiums pour off the oversize wraparound porch. Each of the five rooms has distinctive decor and a private bath, so you can't go wrong—but that doesn't mean we don't have our favorites. Even though it's just off the kitchen, the Terrace Bedroom on the main floor is a paradise for lovers. Its spacious marble bathroom boasts a jetted tub for two, along with French doors leading to the porch swing on the back patio—undeniably the inn's best place to kiss. The Cascade Suite stands out for its view of Mount Adams. Hosts Marilyn Fox and Jon Johnson aren't your typical innkeepers. Both are avid windsurfers, skiers, and mountain bikers, making them experts on the activities that draw adventure-loving travelers to the area. They'll also gladly point you to a lovely picnic spot or winery tour, instead. $$ *MC, V; checks OK; www.innatthegorge.com.*

LAKECLIFF
✿✿✿❁

3820 Westcliff Dr, Hood River / 541/386-7000
Jim and Allyson Pate have turned this historic 1908 summer home into a peaceful, woodsy retreat tucked away on 3 acres of prime Columbia River property. Nearly every room in the house offers a spectacular river view. A huge stone fireplace serves as the living room's centerpiece, and the back deck is just the place for enjoying the sublime surroundings and watching the visiting geese and eagles. Cheery colors and fresh flowers grace the four guest rooms, all of which have private baths. All but one, the Forget-Me-Not, have fireplaces. Lilac is the largest room and also offers the best views; its only shortcoming is that the room's private bath is across the hall. The river views from Daffodil make it another top choice. Your hosts go to great lengths to ensure a truly pampering experience, with luxurious touches like fluffy robes, hot coffee outside your bedroom door before breakfast, and a delicious morning meal. After breakfast, take a leisurely stroll around the grounds or snuggle up by the aforementioned fireplace and savor every moment of this intimate river-side escape. Celebrating a special occasion? Arrange for a bottle of wine or chilled champagne to greet you upon arrival. Raise your glasses and toast your weekend together in the privacy of Lakecliff.
$$–$$$ *MC, V; checks OK; www.lakecliffbnb.com.*

MOSIER HOUSE BED AND BREAKFAST
✿✿

704 3rd Ave, Mosier / 541/478-3640
Perched atop a knoll overlooking the Columbia River, this bed-and-breakfast in a restored Queen Anne home is the only place to stay in Mosier. The charms of the beautiful 1904 home begin with its location and easily outweigh its romantic drawback, which is that four of the five rooms have shared baths. Mosier, with fewer than 400 residents, serves as an ideal base for couples who wish to enjoy the splendors of the Gorge without the tourism of Hood River. With so few distractions, a weekend for two here offers a peaceful respite with endless romantic possibilities. The careful restoration and impeccable attention to detail of the house have paid off: it's a sight to behold, especially from the outside. Inside, antique furniture and colorful quilts complement the architectural style. Up the wooden staircase are the five guest rooms. If you can, book the Master Bedroom and have a luxurious soak in the delightful claw-foot tub beneath a well-placed skylight. The Master Bedroom also has its own entrance and a porch overlooking the creek—an irresistible place to kiss. The sweeping views from the river-facing Columbia Room make it our second favorite, and an in-room washbasin makes sharing a bath less of an issue. You're going to want to enjoy as much of breakfast as possible, so consider eating dinner early the

night before. Two delicious courses offer more-than-generous portions of made-from-scratch pastries, locally grown fruits, and specialties like eggs Florentine. *$$ MC, V; checks OK; www.mosierhouse.com.*

PHEASANT VALLEY ORCHARDS
◑◑◑◖

3890 Acree Dr, Hood River / 541/386-2803
You and your loved one can experience the essence of romantic Hood River by choosing a stay at Pheasant Valley. Multitalented hosts Scott and Gail Hagee grow eight varieties of organic pears and apples and produce nearly 10 types of wine while maintaining one of the most comfortable B&Bs in the Columbia River Gorge. Pleasantly off the beaten path, this delightful farmhouse welcomes travelers with two large living rooms, working fireplaces, and a wide porch with a view. All rooms offer pretty views of the orchards as well as of Mount Hood. Our favorite place to snuggle is upstairs in the Comice Suite. The huge room features an inviting king-size bed, private deck, and oversize bathroom. Be sure to make time for a leisurely soak in the raised Jacuzzi tub as well as for a steamy shower in the double-headed stall. Another very private option is the cottage affectionately known as "the coop." Located just a few yards from the house, the two-bedroom coop gives no hint of its former use as an authentic chicken coop and is perfect for longer stays or for those wishing to prepare their own meals (there's even a grill). Wherever you choose to sleep, you'll wake to rich, fresh-brewed coffee and a sumptuous breakfast that always includes fruits and juices from the orchard. As longtime residents of the area, Gail and Scott are happy to suggest ways to spend quiet, fun-filled days in the Hood River Valley, ending with a romantic visit to the Pheasant Valley Winery tasting room, just a short stroll from the house. *$$ MC, V; checks OK; www.pheasantvalleyorchards.com.*

Romantic Restaurants

BLACK RABBIT RESTAURANT
◑◑◖

2126 SW Halsey St, Troutdale / 503/492-3086
Located on McMenamins Edgefield's 25-acre grounds, the Black Rabbit is the most elegant of the estate's many dining options. Arrive early and visit the colorful gardens and on-site tasting room, a romantic hideaway lit with twinkling lights where you can sample the McMenamins label pinot noir. The dining room's large space is softened with wall sconces and white tablecloths, and there are high-backed booths along the perimeter. On a summer evening, reserve a spot outside in the gorgeous New Orleans–style

courtyard. Try the crispy calamari with Romescu sauce and a hearty main course such as grilled New York steak with roasted potatoes and herb butter or Moroccan-style lamb ribs with saffron-cinnamon couscous. No meal here is complete without a serving of the house-made apple pie, served with vanilla-bean ice cream and topped with caramel sauce. Note that staying overnight is also possible at Edgefield, but we don't recommend the hostel-style lodgings for romantic getaways; the 12 new suites added in 2004 offer more privacy but we nonetheless prefer other area lodgings for true romance. Luckily, you don't have to be an overnight guest to enjoy an intimate meal at the Black Rabbit.

$$–$$$ *AE, DIS, MC, V; no checks; breakfast, lunch, dinner every day; full bar; reservations recommended; www.mcmenamins.com.*

BRIAN'S POURHOUSE
◑◑◖

606 Oak St, Hood River / 541/387-4344
In a town the size of Hood River, it's not surprising that the most popular local hangouts multitask. It's true that the front of this establishment feels more like a neighborhood bar than a romantic spot for fine dining. Fortunately, there's more than meets the eye, and the tables away from the door offer a more couple-friendly setting. Here you can enjoy the welcoming, attentive service and the relaxing surroundings of the dining room: neutral walls, white linen on the tables, abundant fresh flowers, and plenty of window-side seating. On warm summer nights, opt for the patio. The Pourhouse happens to serve some of the most delicious, creative fare in the area. With options like smoked chicken linguine and coconut green curry, the food here goes miles beyond what you'd find at a typical bar. The menu also offers ample servings of tasty steaks, fresh seafood, and a fish taco plate that will add just the right amount of spice to your lives. Desserts are made in house and are worth a visit on their own. Or take some delicious brownies and a slice of cheesecake to go and enjoy them in the blissful privacy of your own room.

$$–$$$ *MC, V; checks OK; dinner every day; full bar; reservations recommended for parties of 6 or more; www.brianspourhouse.com.* ⅙

COLUMBIA RIVER COURT DINING ROOM
◑◑◑◖

4000 Westcliff Dr (Columbia Gorge Hotel), Hood River / 541/386-5566 or 800/345-1921
If a meal at the award-winning dining room inside the Columbia Gorge Hotel (see Romantic Lodgings) doesn't sweep you off your feet, the breathtaking views of the river below and the 208-foot cascading waterfall on the hotel grounds surely will. The World Famous Farm Breakfast, where five delicious courses add up to a morning extravaganza, attracts visitors from

all over the Northwest. (While the meal is included with a stay at the hotel, it's a bit pricey if you're not a hotel guest.) Request a table by the windows; sample a little bit of everything (the berry-blossom honey will send you into rapture); and plan to spend a couple of hours enjoying the views, the food, and—most of all—your dining companion. In the evening, the ambience is more sophisticated, and the entrées are well-loved classics: filet mignon and lobster tail, rack of lamb, and grilled Northwest salmon, to name a few. Start things off with a wilted-spinach salad prepared tableside and end your meal with the wonderfully rich, apple-laden tarte Tatin.

$$$ *AE, DC, DIS, MC, V; checks OK; breakfast, lunch, dinner every day; full bar; reservations recommended; www.columbiagorgehotel.com.* ♿

STONEHEDGE GARDENS
❂❂❂

3405 Cascade Dr, Hood River / 541/386-3940
Tucked away at the top of a winding gravel road is one of Hood River's most popular dinner destinations—and once you arrive, you'll immediately know why. When Mike and Shawna Caldwell bought the place in 2000, they put their energy into beautifying the grounds—sending the romance quotient sky-high. The resulting five-level garden is a stellar setting, making this the best spot for alfresco dining in the Gorge. In cooler months, head indoors with your sweetie and request a table for two near the crackling fire. Choose from well-prepared entrées like tender filet mignon, scrumptious portobello-mushroom ravioli, or pork scaloppini. All servings are generously portioned and are accompanied by fresh bread, steamed veggies, and a special house salad with pecan vinaigrette. It's tempting to go overboard here, but do your best to save room for Stonehedge Gardens' bread pudding for two, topped with a layer of crème brûlée and finished with bourbon caramel sauce. Another restaurant in town, North Oak Brasserie (113 3rd St, Hood River; 541/387-2310), run by the same owners, is also an inviting spot for great Italian food.

$$–$$$ *AE, DIS, MC, V; checks OK; dinner every day; full bar; reservations recommended; www.stonehedgegardens.com.*

MOUNT HOOD

ROMANTIC HIGHLIGHTS

The snowy peak of Mount Hood beckons visitors year-round for beautiful scenery and recreation; as Oregon's highest peak (11,235 feet), this fabled mountain takes romance to new heights. The surrounding area offers a bounty for active nature lovers as well as for those simply seeking a quiet mountain retreat. With beautiful lakes, hiking and biking trails, and pristine ski slopes, there's never a shortage of ways to take in the fresh air and stunning surroundings. The popularity of this destination with climbers, backpackers, and snowboarders means that many of the accommodations are geared to adventurers seeking a place to rest in between activity-filled days; happily, more lodging options catering to romance seekers have popped up in the last few years.

Timberline is the main attraction at Mount Hood. This singular resort offers year-round skiing, fine dining, and accommodations in the impressive Timberline Lodge. Other towns that offer lodging close to the glacial peak include Welches, Brightwood, Parkdale, and Government Camp. Trust your instincts and avoid staying in Government Camp; this is the most commercial and least romantic of the towns. Just a few miles down the road, Welches offers several good restaurant options, an espresso shop, an information center, and the charming **Wy'east Book Shoppe and Gallery** (67195 E Hwy 26; 503/622-1623). Note that many amorous couples choose to stay about an hour away in the charming town of Hood River, with its wonderful lodgings, hiking, and restaurants.

It won't come as a surprise that winter is the busiest time on the mountain. Skiers often book their rooms months in advance and take advantage of the bargain-priced lift tickets offered by many of the lodgings. Whatever your level of expertise (or lack thereof), the five ski resorts in the area offer something for everyone—along with plenty of romantic opportunities to warm up with hot cocoa in front of the fireplace. While Cooper Spur and Summit are geared more to families (and thus register lower on the romance meter), they do offer easier terrain for beginners. **Cooper Spur** (Hwy 35, 11000 Cloud Cap Rd; 541/352-6692; www.cooperspur.com), on the north side of Mount Hood, offers inexpensive day and night skiing. At an elevation of 7,300 feet, **Mount Hood Meadows** (2 miles north of Hwy 35 on Forest Rd 3555; 503/337-2222; www.skihood.com) is the largest and most popular area on the mountain, boasting eighty-seven runs; four high-speed quads; six double chairlifts; and a Nordic center with groomed tracks, instructors, and rentals.

In the town of Government Camp, **Mount Hood SkiBowl** (87000 E Hwy 26; 503/272-3206 or 503/222-2695, recorded information; www.skibowl.com) offers the best place to ski under the stars, with 34 lighted runs. At 4,306 feet, **Summit** (Hwy 26, near rest area at east end of Government Camp; 503/272-0256) is good for beginners. At 6,000 feet, **Timberline** (4 miles north of Hwy 26, just east of Government Camp; 503/622-7979; www.timber linelodge.com) has six lifts and offers year-round skiing.

For an easy—and romantic—way up the mountain any time of year, take Timberline's **Magic Mile Sky Ride**, a six-minute ride on an express chairlift to the 7,000-foot mark. Once you reach the top, hold each other tight and take in the magnificent view. Once the snow melts in spring, hiking opportunities spring up like mushrooms after rain. The **Magic Mile Interpretive Trail** leads back to Timberline Lodge. Another excellent hiking option is the **Timberline Trail**, which leads 4½ miles west from Timberline Lodge to flower-studded Paradise Park. Energetic twosomes can continue another 5½ miles to the sublimely beautiful mist of Ramona Falls. In June and July, lower parts of the Timberline Trail burst with rhododendrons and wildflowers. Each of these kiss-worthy trails is accessible from the lodge.

Two of the area's lakes are prime destinations for romantic summer picnics. East of Government Camp on Highway 26 you'll find **Trillium Lake**. An easy walking trail circles the lake; wintertime explorers can tour it on cross-country skis or snowshoes.

Farther toward Hood River is **Lost Lake** (541/386-6366 for driving directions), another paradise for couples. Trails are open for hikers, bikers, and horseback riders alike. On a clear summer day, take advantage of the lake by renting a rowboat or canoe to soak up the sunshine, cast a line for trout and salmon, or serenade your sweetie. Campsites and cabins are available for rustic overnight stays.

Access and Information

From Portland, take Highway 26 to Mount Hood. From the north, Highway 35 from Hood River connects with Highway 26. In winter, traction devices are often required on Mount Hood. Call the **Oregon Department of Transportation** (503/588-2941 outside Oregon or 800/977-6368 inside Oregon) to find out if roads are snowy or icy. The online Travel Advisor (www.tripcheck. com) has excellent, up-to-date information on road conditions. Also, an Oregon Department of Transportation Winter Sno-Park Permit is required if you plan to stop. Permits are sold at Timberline Lodge (see Romantic Lodgings), as well as at service stations, Department of Motor Vehicles offices, and sporting-goods stores in the Gorge and on the mountain. In summer, you'll need a Northwest Forest Pass ($5 per day), which you can purchase at ranger stations and sports stores. The **Mount Hood Information Center** (65000 E Hwy 26, Welches; 503/622-4822 or 888/622-4822; www. mthood.info) provides tourist information, including hiking maps.

Romantic Lodgings

BRIGHTWOOD GUEST HOUSE
✿✿✿✿
64725 E Barlow Trail, Brightwood / 503/622-5783 or 888/503-5783
To have anything but a stellar experience at this Japanese-style guest house

would be highly out of the ordinary. Innkeeper Jan Estep wouldn't think of providing you and your love with anything less than a perfect weekend full of pampering. Between the peaceful, secluded surroundings, Estep's scrumptious gourmet cooking, and an entire house to yourselves, the two of you are practically guaranteed to fall in love all over again. And speaking of love, the setting will inspire rapture. The guest house, with its private deck beside a koi pond, is separate from the main house; both the cottage and house are set on 2 secluded acres surrounded by meadows and flourishing daylilies, foxglove, roses, irises, and ferns. (The flowers can also be admired in the bouquets that adorn the rooms.) The Asian-style decor is tasteful and bright. Wall hangings, pottery, tea sets, fans, and lanterns create a relaxed, refined setting. None of the guest house's rooms are particularly large, but your hostess has put great care into making the house self-contained, with a fully equipped kitchen, plenty of reading material, and sweet-smelling bath products. The residential town of Brightwood is easily missed on a drive to the mountain, so finding this place is like finding a hidden treasure. Drink tea from the well-stocked cupboards, snuggle up to watch a movie, or ride the bicycles provided for your use. Winter options include nearby cross-country skiing and snowshoeing. In the morning, fresh baked goods and an expertly prepared (and presented) full breakfast are delivered at your requested time. With a little notice, Jan will also prepare special-occasion gift baskets; provide champagne; or arrange picnics, massages, and other luxurious and romantic options.

$$ *No credit cards; checks OK; www.mounthoodbnb.com.*

MT. HOOD HAMLET BED AND BREAKFAST
◊◊◊◊

6741 Hwy 35, Mount Hood / 541/352-3547 or 800/407-0570

A better setting for this New England–style Colonial would have been hard to find. Not only does it overlook the 9-acre farm where owner Paul Romans was raised, but magnificent Mount Hood appears close enough to touch. Paul and his wife, Diane, make it their mission to ensure that the two of you are spoiled every step of the way. Bask in the outdoor Jacuzzi tub for extraordinary views of Mounts Hood and Adams by day, or for stargazing at night. With the heated deck, you'll stay cozy even when you emerge from the hot, bubbly water. Two of the largest rooms, Vista Ridge and Orchard, both boast Jacuzzi tubs, making them prime kissing quarters. You can see Mount Hood from the soothing water of the tub in Vista Ridge's bathroom; Orchard's fireplace and pair of rocking chairs make it a comfy love nest to behold. The charm and the Colonial theme of the inn are further enhanced by original artwork on the walls and period furnishings. All rooms are equipped with TV/VCRs, and there is a good selection of movies. Plush robes are provided, too. To top all this off, the morning meal here is reason enough to book a stay. Delicious offerings include veggie omelets, smoky sausage,

a bottomless basket of freshly baked scones, and *very* local jams and jellies—they're homemade by your hosts.
$$ *AE, DIS, MC, V; checks OK; www.mthoodhamlet.com.*

OLD PARKDALE INN
◐◐◐

4932 Baseline Rd, Parkdale / 541/352-5551 or 877/687-4669
One of the things that set this retreat apart is that it offers the quaintness of a B&B while also allowing for plenty of self-sufficiency and privacy. It's a honeymooner's dream-come-true—but who says lovers should wait for a special occasion to spoil themselves? Convenient self–check-in, full in-room kitchens, and the option to have the award-winning breakfasts delivered to your door (apple crepes and sausage, perhaps) remove any real need to venture out. Even the colorful gardens—complete with a pond and waterfall—that surround the house provide an idyllic setting for a late-morning stroll. Each of the three themed rooms reflects owners Mary and Steve Pellegrini's passion for art. Named Monet, Gauguin, and Georgia O'Keeffe, each has a private bath, distinctive decor, artwork, and quotes from the artist written on the door. You don't have to be art lovers—lovers pure and simple will do—to enjoy this playful place. Furthermore, Parkdale makes a good base for a weekend away. The town itself is tiny and charming, and the breathtaking scenery and activities in Hood River and around Mount Hood are all within easy reach.
$$ *MC, V; checks OK; www.hoodriverlodging.com.*

THE RESORT AT THE MOUNTAIN
◐◖

68010 E Fairway Ave, Welches / 503/622-3101 or 800/669-7666
Although this 160-room, Scottish-themed resort looks more like an apartment complex than a charming inn, the sublime setting helps to make up for the building's aesthetic shortcomings: it's nestled in 300 acres of evergreen woodland in the foothills of the Huckleberry Wilderness Area in the Mount Hood National Forest. The scenery is breathtaking in any season, but spending a weekend here when the grounds are covered in snow is nothing short of spectacular. The rooms may not be deluxe, but they're large and comfortable, and even the standard rooms come with a deck or patio (ask for one with a forest view). Each Fireside Studio offers a full kitchen and the added warmth of a wood-burning fireplace glowing on a platform near the king-size bed. Before you arrive, pick up provisions—bottled water, logs for the fireplace, coffee, and popcorn are provided—so that once you settle in, your room can become a self-contained unit. When you're ready to venture out, the resort offers two restaurants, tennis and volleyball courts, a golf course, an outdoor heated pool, a Jacuzzi tub, a fitness center, hiking trails, and

more. For couples seeking a true mountain retreat, the fresh air, walks in the woods, and stunning scenery all offer an appealing respite from busy lives. $$–$$$ *AE, DIS, MC, V; checks OK; www.theresort.com.* &

TIMBERLINE LODGE
○○

Timberline Ski Area, Timberline / 503/231-5400 or 800/547-1406
On a winter's day, driving up the road to Timberline, with its snow-covered trees and increasingly angelic views, is like climbing up to heaven. The lodge sits at a 6,000-foot elevation, about halfway up Mount Hood. The history of this massive timber-and-stone lodge is rich: it was built in just 15 months in the 1930s, as part of President Roosevelt's Works Progress Administration program to create jobs. Evidence of masterful craftsmanship comes through in well-preserved details such as glass mosaics, stone chimneys, and hand-made tapestries and fabrics in the main lodge. Because the 70 guest rooms are designed to reflect the era in which they were built, a stay here is more rustic than luxurious. But a recent upgrade added premium mattresses and new carpeting, making the steep prices a bit easier to justify. The outdoor pool and spa have also been renovated and are open year-round. Your best bet for a private soak under the stars is to come midweek (or just keep your fingers crossed). The spacious Fireplace Rooms, equipped with cozy hearths, offer the most romantic potential and are also the most expensive. Ask for one with a view of Mount Hood's snowy peak. With the ski area here open 12 months of the year, these accommodations are booked far in advance, so plan ahead to avoid getting left out in the cold. The Northwest cuisine at the Cascade Dining Room (see Romantic Restaurants) is worth a splurge after a day of hiking or skiing—and kissing. $$$ *AE, DIS, MC, V; checks OK; www.timberlinelodge.com.*

Romantic Restaurants

CASCADE DINING ROOM
○○○

Timberline Lodge, Timberline / 503/622-0700
With its grand beauty, magical surroundings, and rich history, Timberline Lodge (see Romantic Lodgings) can be a thrill, and for those seeking to celebrate a special occasion or simply to enjoy a refined meal on Oregon's highest peak, the thrills can keep coming right through dessert. In the evening, the rustic, casual dining room takes on a soft glow. Tables in the center of the room are a bit cramped, so ask to sit by the windows for more privacy. For the past 20 years, chef Leif Eric Benson has been preparing sophisticated, creative cuisine worth lingering over. His method is to start with a bounty of local ingredients and then weave in flavors from around the world. Make

your taste buds tingle with Brazilian barbecue pork loin glazed with orange and ginger, grilled Alaskan wild king salmon, or wild chanterelle–crusted rack of lamb with goat cheese. Complement your meal with a bottle from the 13-page wine list, or, better yet, have one of the competent waitpersons make a recommendation. Not-to-be-missed desserts include vanilla-kissed crème brûlée and the Chocolate Dream, a decadent flourless cake. **$$$–$$$$** *AE, DC, DIS, MC, V; checks OK; breakfast, lunch, dinner every day; full bar; reservations recommended; www.timberlinelodge.com.*

DON GUIDO'S ITALIAN CUISINE
✪✪✪

73330 E Hwy 26, Rhododendron / 503/622-5141
Don't be fooled by the sign outside, with its bright neon and "espresso" in big letters underneath the restaurant's name. The inviting atmosphere here is undeniably romantic, with very low lighting, candles in wax-covered Chianti bottles, and a huge stone fireplace, all of which set the stage for a meal you won't soon forget. In the dining room, housed in the historic "Log Lodge," the interior has been transformed from its formerly rustic state. Large booths shaped like half-moons mean getting close enough to kiss is a cinch. Whatever your heart desires, it's likely to be on the menu here. Choose from classic Italian favorites like minestrone soup, fettuccine primavera, lasagne bolognese, and chicken marsala. Portions are plentiful, but if you can save room, share a serving of some of the best tiramisù around. **$$$** *AE, DIS, MC, V; checks OK; dinner Thurs–Sun (every day in summer); full bar; reservations recommended; www.donguidos.com.*

THE RENDEZVOUS GRILL AND TAP ROOM
✪✪

67149 E Hwy 26, Welches / 503/622-6837
In the Mount Hood area, finding restaurants that overflow with romantic potential can be a bit of a challenge. And though the Rendezvous may not be filled with doe-eyed couples, this unassuming spot in a shopping center along Highway 26 serves some of Mount Hood's best meals. Chef/co-owner Kathryn Bliss's emphasis is on seasonal, local produce, including chanterelle mushrooms and huckleberries. The comfortable main room features high ceilings, hunter-green hues, and an assortment of tables and booths. Pasta lovers will swoon for the house specialty: rigatoni with alder-smoked chicken in a champagne cream sauce with toasted hazelnuts, dried cranberries, and fresh spinach. In the mood to splurge? Order the mouthwatering char-grilled New York Steak with Oregon white truffle butter. And don't even think about skipping dessert—sharing the chocolate pecan tart with chocolate mousse makes for nothing short of a heavenly finish. **$$–$$$** *AE, DIS, MC, V; checks OK; lunch, dinner Wed–Sun (every day in summer); full bar; reservations recommended; www.rendezvousgrill.net.* ♿

WILLAMETTE VALLEY

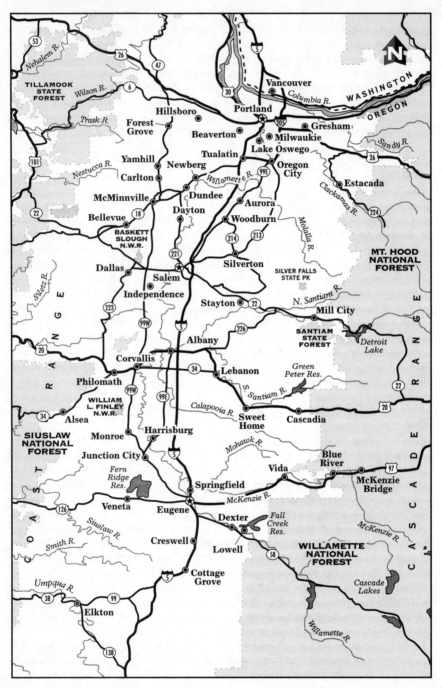

"To be thy lips is a sweet thing and small."
—E. E. CUMMINGS

♡ WILLAMETTE VALLEY

Geographically speaking, Portland lies at the north end of the Willamette Valley, the broad and fertile river basin bounded on the west by the gentle countenance of the Coast Range and on the east by the glacial peaks of the Cascades, on the north by the Willamette River's confluence with the Columbia and on the south by the hills of southern Oregon. Romantically speaking, however, the valley starts once you leave Portland's urban core and suburban fringe and find yourselves among the wineries, farms, small towns, and groves of oak and Douglas fir that characterize this picturesque and history-rich area.

The wine country in and around Yamhill County, southwest of Portland, is simply made for romance. Excellent restaurants are tucked into historic homes and eye-catching new buildings, and among the myriad small B&Bs dotting the region are several of honeymoon caliber. And then there's the wine: from the fruity elegance of a fine pinot noir to the sprightly festivity of a sparkling wine, you'll find something for every taste. You can't get much more romantic than a day built around wine-tasting: a little driving, a little tasting, a little picnicking and kissing under the oaks. The touring needn't stop at the Yamhill County line; the Willamette Valley appellation continues south as far as Lorane, southwest of Eugene, with vineyards and dozens more wineries scattered on the hills mostly west of the river.

Among the region's small cities and towns, several have plentiful lodging and dining choices, and these make excellent bases for romantic explorations. Eugene offers rose gardens, opera and symphony, and miles of riverside walking paths; Albany is known for antiquing; and Salem has a lively downtown shopping core and historic homes and parks. Lovers will no doubt be pulled back out of town to the rural tranquility for exploring—to the Willamette and its mellow tributaries crossed by ferries and covered bridges; to the dashing McKenzie River; to the solitude of the Finley National Wildlife Refuge in fall or winter; or to the warmth of Heirloom Old Garden Roses in summer (for details, see Romantic Highlights). Because of its mild climate, generous amounts of rain in winter, and long, sunny summers, everything grows well in the Willamette Valley—and romance is in bloom year-round.

Interstate 5 runs the length of the Willamette Valley and provides quick access to the major cities. For a more romantic drive, take Highway 99W from the wine country at the valley's north end down to Eugene in the south—you'll pass through the wine-country hubs of Newberg, Dundee, and McMinnville; unobtrusive blue signs point the way to wineries.

WINE COUNTRY

ROMANTIC HIGHLIGHTS

A 30-minute drive southwest from Portland brings you into the Willamette Valley, home of the famous Oregon wineries. Embraced by the gentle rise of the Coast Range in the west and the glacial peaks of the Cascades in the east, and featuring rolling, oak-covered hills and lush vineyards, this is romance country. Pinot noir grapes thrive in the mild climate, influenced by the nearby Pacific; what's good for the grapes is good for the visitor. The number of wineries has more than doubled in the past decade, and many of Oregon's pinot noirs have achieved international renown (and have the prices to prove it). There are more than 50 wineries to visit, and, as with wine, some have more character than others. Go on your own romantic expedition, or try our recommendations (see Romantic Wineries). Our favored kissing destinations are in the North Willamette Valley appellation, but intrepid explorers should know that wineries and vineyards stretch all the way south past Salem and Eugene. A word to the wise: if you are considering a long day of wine tasting, be sure to choose a designated driver or book with a wine tour company that provides transportation.

The Willamette Valley wine country is a lovely destination any time of year, and most wineries are open at least on weekends year-round. In spring, beautiful clouds of blossoms arrive on the fruit trees; summer's hot days are ideal for picnics; fall brings crisp air, golden leaves, and the wine crush. With winter comes rain, but from the cozy interior of a tasting room, it needn't dampen your spirits. In the Romantic Wineries section, we highlight places that hold special interest for couples seeking idyllic wine-country moments. (The list is not meant to indicate which wines are best in the region—a highly subjective matter, in any case.) For help in planning your trip, be sure to get a copy of *Vintage Oregon Winery Guide*, the excellent publication from the Oregon Wine Advisory Board (1200 NW Naito Pkwy, Ste 400, Portland, OR 97209; 800/242-2363; www.oregonwine.org). Since the back roads can be hard to navigate, we also suggest bringing a map. Tasting is free at most places; some charge a small fee (which can be applied toward any wine you purchase). Some wineries feature cozy tasting rooms and exquisite flower gardens; others are plain roadside buildings that make up for their lack of atmosphere with the excellence of their wines. Whether you choose to visit one or all, and whether you consume or not, your entire winery-hopping tour will be an intoxicating joy. And if you're pleased by what you taste, purchase a bottle or two to enjoy at home with a toast to happy memories of your romantic adventure.

If you tour the region by car via the "wine road"—Highway 99W—you will find wonderful stops at nearly every turn. Many of the wineries are concentrated near the picturesque small towns of Newberg, Dundee, Dayton, and McMinnville. Each town has its own appeal, and each can make a good headquarters for wine touring. Dundee, considered the culinary capital of northern Oregon's wine country, makes an excellent midday stop. Indulge in an elegant repast at the **Dundee Bistro** (see Romantic Restaurants), then cross the street to try the sparkling wines at **Argyle Winery** (691 Hwy 99W; 503/538-8520 or 888/427-4953; www.argylewinery.com), open for tastings 11am to 5pm daily. Farther along on the wine road is McMinnville. Don't be scared off by the strip malls as you drive into town. Once you turn off the highway onto Third Street, you'll be charmed by the gracious, tree-shaded streets of the old town, where you can explore cafes, restaurants, and boutiques. Check out the local wine bar, **Noah's** (525 NE 3rd St; 503/434-2787), which also offers dinner; or visit the **McMenamins' Hotel Oregon** (310 NE Evans St; 503/472-8427 or 888/472-8427; www.hoteloregon.com), where you have three bars to choose from, including a rooftop bar, the casual ground-floor family pub, and a romantic wine cellar hidden away in the basement.

To explore off the beaten path, take Highway 47 to wineries farther north, near the towns of Gaston or Forest Grove. You can visit these wineries on your way to or from Portland, since several highways link back to the city (and Interstate 5) from these northern areas. For the most luxurious afternoon, pack a picnic before you depart; the wineries in this area are somewhat remote, and stores have meager supplies. Along Highway 47, the tiny town of Carlton offers a sweet respite for lovers who like to leave the modern world behind. Snap a few pictures in front of the charming 19th-century brick and stone storefronts or the old-fashioned feed store, or taste (for a small fee) at **The Tasting Room** (105 W Main St; 503/852-6733; www.pinot noir.com), which offers wines from exclusive wineries generally closed to the public. The tiny, shady outdoor patio has picnic tables if you decide to buy a bottle and pop it open on the spot.

Organized wine tours are not exactly private affairs, since you generally travel with others. However, they have one great advantage—you can soak up scenery, and sip wine, to your heart's content while someone else does the driving. Several tours leave from Portland. **Grape Escape Winery Tours** (503/283-3380; www.grapeescapetours.com) offers a variety of options, including full-day trips with a gourmet lunch. **Wine Tours Northwest** (503/439-8687 or 800/359-1034; www.winetoursnorthwest.com) specializes in smaller groups and will even take twosomes on their own, for a slightly higher fee. A more exciting means of exploration is a romantic hot-air balloon flight with **Vista Balloon Adventures** (503/625-7385 or 800/622-2309; www.vistaballoon.com) out of Newberg. Flights depart close to dawn, last for about one exquisite hour, and conclude with a delicious champagne breakfast.

Access and Information

Travelers from Seattle or Portland usually arrive in the wine country by car via Interstate 5. Or you can fly into **Portland International Airport**, also known as PDX (7000 NE Airport Wy; 503/460-4234 or 877/739-4636; www. portlandairportpdx.com), rent a car, and then proceed on to wine country. A popular, and scenic, alternate route from Portland to the northern Willamette Valley is via the old US Highway 99W, parallel to Interstate 5 west of the Willamette. At the north end, where it's known as the "wine road," it passes through Newberg, Dundee, and McMinnville; blue signs point the way to wineries. All three towns make good headquarters for wine touring. McMinnville even has a helpful **Chamber of Commerce** (417 N Adams St; 503/472-6196; www.mcminnville.org). For an overview of the Willamette Valley or for general information, try the **Albany Visitors Center** (250 Broadalbin SW, #110; 541/928-0911 or 800/526-2256; www.albanyvisitors. com).

Be prepared for more traffic on summer and holiday weekends; on the other hand, one benefit of visiting during busy periods is that even the smaller wineries open their doors. Generally, driving conditions are fine, even in winter.

Romantic Wineries

ANNE AMIE
♥♥

6580 NE Mineral Springs Rd, Carlton / 503/864-2991 or 800/248-4835
Formerly known as Chateau Benoit, this winery changed ownership in 1999 and was re-christened in May 2004 as Anne Amie (pronounced on-ah-me), after the new owner's two daughters. At this hilltop winery, serene pastoral views and exquisite sunsets over the Coast Range provide a wonderful backdrop for the excellent wine. There are plenty of lovely tables with shade umbrellas in front of the French-style chateau, which doubles as a tasting room and facade for the wine warehouse. Over the past several years, winemaker Scott Huffman and new owner Dr. Robert Pamplin have been hard at work upgrading the winemaking facilities and quality of fruit to create

world-class pinot noirs. Find romance over a glass of one of the many pinot noir blends or, for a lighter touch, opt for a sip of pinot gris or Riesling. *10am–5pm every day; www.anneamie.com.*

DAVID HILL VINEYARDS AND WINERY
❂❂❂❂

46350 David Hill Rd, Forest Grove / 503/992-8545 or 877/992-8545
After you've descended a dirt driveway, this pristine, beautifully restored 1883 home, surrounded by lush green lawns and brilliant flower gardens, is a refreshing sight. The bright, airy tasting room, located inside the historic home, is abundantly pleasant and charming. There are plenty of tempting wine choices, including a delicious pinot noir and heavenly port, as well as a wonderful selection of books and gourmet treats for sale. For a truly sublime romantic moment, step outside and share a kiss beneath the shady trees. It's a lovely spot for a private picnic, and it's no wonder that some couples choose to tie the knot here.
Noon–5pm Tues–Sun; www.davidhillwinery.com.

ELK COVE VINEYARDS
❂❂❂❂

27751 NW Olson Rd, Gaston / 503/985-7760 or 877/ELKCOVE
Drive up the long, winding road to get here and you will discover one of Oregon's most wildly romantic wineries. Kissing in this scenic spot is almost unavoidable, whether you visit in summer, when the vineyards are lush and green, or in fall, when the landscape turns red and golden. In the tasting room, sip a single-vineyard pinot noir, a pinot gris, or a sweet dessert wine. A small, charming English garden courtyard adjoins the tasting room; from the patio, enjoy lovely views of vineyards enclosed by stately Douglas firs. This is a popular spot for weddings, but if you can get the lovely gazebo to yourselves, it's also a perfect place to steal a kiss.
10am–5pm every day; www.elkcove.com.

ERATH VINEYARDS
❂❂❂

9409 NE Worden Hill Rd, Dundee / 503/538-3318 or 800/539-9463
You will want to drink in the sights, as well as the wines, on offer at this scenic winery. The cozy tasting room, nestled among vineyards high in the beautiful Dundee Hills, has stunning views in every direction. Sample the pinot noir, pinot blanc, Riesling, or Dolcetto. When we visited, we spotted not one but two couples kissing on the vine-covered terrace outside. Tables here provide an ideal spot for a picnic to go with your newly purchased wine; a small selection of gourmet treats can be found inside if you forget to bring your own.
11am–5pm every day; www.erath.com.

MONTINORE ESTATE
🗢🗢

3663 SW Dilley Rd, Forest Grove / 503/359-5012
A driveway lined with 100-year-old oak trees leads to a grand Victorian mansion surrounded by expansive manicured lawns—a kiss-worthy setting indeed. Unfortunately, the winery's tasting room is housed in a separate building offering considerably less aesthetic pleasure (although the estate house is available for special events). Here, the ceilings are low, windows are few, ambience is lacking, and, if your entrance is not perfectly timed, you may find yourselves elbowed out of the way by hordes of visitors just off the tour bus. Nonetheless, the grounds here are truly lovely, and the pinot noir, pinot gris, and Gewürztraminer will not disappoint. The best thing to do is to purchase your favorite and, with a bottle in one hand and your sweetheart in the other, find a secluded spot outside to enjoy yourselves in private.
11am–5pm every day; www.montinore.com.

REX HILL VINEYARDS
🗢🗢🗢

30835 N Hwy 99W, Newberg / 503/538-0666 or 800/739-4455
Lush, terraced lawns, divided by railroad ties and anchored by a forest of fir trees, provide a beautiful setting for the prestigious Rex Hill winery, which is nestled among acres of vineyards. However, while the grounds are ideal for picnics and relaxation, there are few secluded spots for kissing; this is also a tour-bus destination, so crowds may detract from your experience. Once you taste the outstanding pinot noir, however, you'll forget all about these slight drawbacks. This is truly world-class wine. The tasting room welcomes visitors with a massive stone fireplace, antiques, tapestry rugs, and wine barrels displayed in the brick-lined cellar. Rex Hill also offers champagne breakfast/hot-air balloon rides from late spring to early fall. After getting up with the birds, you'll find yourselves soaring with them. Now that's romantic.
11am–5pm every day (10am–5pm summer weekends); www.rexhill.com.

TORII MOR WINERY
🗢🗢🗢

18325 NE Fairview Dr, Dundee / 503/538-2279 or 800/839-5004
Sometimes it's the most difficult path that yields the greatest reward. Such is the case with this small winery hidden high in the hills. Once you've dusted off from the long, gravel-road drive, go into the delightful Japanese garden—complete with a small rock garden, grassy alcoves, and moss-covered pathways. Most rewarding of all, you'll likely have the place to yourselves. Samples of Torii Mor's high-end wines, including a remarkable pinot noir, can be sipped in a Japanese-style tasting room adjacent to the

garden. Be sure and walk over to the vineyard, where spectacular views will take your breath away.
11am–5pm Weds–Mon; www.toriimorwinery.com.

Romantic Lodgings

GAHR FARM B&B COTTAGE
❂❂

18605 SW Masonville Rd, McMinnville / 503/472-6960
Nature lovers will go wild over this comfortable three-room cottage, located on a 350-acre farm surrounded by wetlands and forests. Just 15 minutes from downtown McMinnville and 30 minutes from Newberg, this spot will be most romantic for couples who love the great outdoors—in one afternoon here, you might see herds of elk, red-winged blackbirds, pheasants, and hawks. The modest cottage's interior isn't fancy, but features include a full kitchen, a wood-burning stove, a queen-size bed, and a covered front porch overlooking the wetlands and nearby hills. The main house is 600 feet away, and breakfasts are generally served here (although, if you prefer, the hostess can prepare the meal in your kitchen at a prearranged time). The tempting repast might include home-baked biscuits, a savory egg dish, and fresh fruit. Afterward, explore the wetlands, which are home to several species of endangered plants and animals (tread gently), or take a romantic stroll (or vigorous hike) along the grassy trails that weave through 150 acres of woodland. At night, enjoy a true country experience as you sit outside on the porch listening to the chorus of hundreds of frogs in the nearby wetlands.
$ *AE, DIS, MC, V; checks OK; www.gahrfarm.com.*

MATTEY HOUSE
❂❂❂

10221 NE Mattey Ln, McMinnville / 503/434-5058
Coming upon this stately 1892 Queen Anne Victorian house, nestled between a vineyard and an orchard, feels like a delightful discovery. The charcoal-gray two-story home, with colorful stained-glass windows and inviting wraparound porch amid towering trees, wows at the end of a dirt road. All four upstairs bedrooms are appointed with period antiques, patchwork quilts, antique light fixtures, and color schemes of pink, rose, and burgundy. We like the small Riesling Room—more specifically, its claw-foot tub with views overlooking the orchards; be forewarned, however, that the charming antique bed is not exactly roomy. The Chardonnay and Pinot Noir Rooms offer regular queen-size beds but are decorated less gracefully. The bright, sunny Blanc de Blanc Room has a bath in the hall but is popular nonetheless (it, too, has an antique bed, also on the smaller side). This being wine country, you might order a bottle of champagne to enjoy in your room, or sip

a glass of local wine on the tiny patio set above the home's front entrance. The light-filled sitting room has white wicker furniture and lace curtains, while piles of slightly shabby games and books lend a lived-in look. Come morning, enjoy a family-style meal in the country-style dining room, where the English proprietors dispel the poor reputation of British cooking with dishes like Dutch apple pancakes, herb-baked eggs, and plenty of fresh scones. Lovely refreshments are offered in the late afternoon. Last, but not least in terms of romance, are the grounds. A newly planted vegetable garden, surrounded by a white picket fence, includes a cutting garden, which guests are welcome to indulge in. Or, explore the secluded cedar grove marked by a white arched entryway, curl up on the porch swing, or kiss beneath the magnificent copper beech.
$$ *MC, V; checks OK; www.matteyhouse.com.*

SPRINGBROOK HAZELNUT FARM
◐◐◐◐

30295 N Hwy 99W, Newberg / 503/538-4606 or 800/793-8528
A Craftsman-style farmhouse, surrounded by lawns, gardens, and orchards, is the centerpiece of this working hazelnut farm. While the interior of the home is extraordinary, with a striking yellow foyer that opens to a terrace overlooking the grounds, and the four rooms and upstairs suite are pleasant, they are most appropriate for groups or for serious wine connoisseurs who are more interested in sips than lips. You'll want to book the Carriage House or the Cottage (which inspired the sky-high lip rating). Similar in design, each elegant abode has Craftsman-style furnishings, lovely fir floors, large windows, and charming tiled kitchens with glass-front cabinets and big butcher-block tables. They also feature gas fireplaces, queen-size beds, and cream-colored walls with forest-green trim. Popular with honeymooners, the delightful Carriage House offers the most space, but our favorite is the cozy Cottage, with its rose garden, terra cotta–tiled bathroom, and postage-stamp dining room overlooking a pond surrounded by irises and daffodils. You'll likely hear the mating call of red-winged blackbirds; what you won't hear are noisy jetted tubs, telephones, or televisions. And although Highway 99W runs nearby, the traffic diminishes considerably as night progresses and shouldn't disturb your sleep. Breakfast is supplied in the fridge so you can serve yourselves in the morning, which is especially helpful for those who get up early for hot-air ballooning. Delicious treats include hard-boiled eggs, croissants, scones, and satisfying ham-and-cheese crepes. For an incredibly romantic stroll, walk through the hazelnut orchard to the adjacent Rex Hill Vineyards. Or, visit the historic barn on site, which houses a one-man operated winery, J. K. Carriere Wines (503/554-0721; www.jk carriere.com), as well as another amazing surprise (you have to visit to find

out what it is). In warm weather, lounge by the beautifully tiled outdoor pool or play a game of tennis on the newly refurbished courts.
$$–$$$ *DIS, MC, V; checks OK; www.nutfarm.com.*

WESTFIR LODGE
✿✿❦

47365 1st St, Westfir / 541/782-3103
This welcoming bright-pink B&B run by owners Gerry Chamberlain and Ken Symons is a hidden treasure and holds a lifetime of antiques from their travels around the world (ask about their gramophone collection). Located across the street from Office Bridge, the longest covered bridge in Oregon, and at one end of the Aufdereide National Scenic Drive, it is a favorite of cyclists, hikers, and travelers alike. Beautiful historical photos line the walls of this exquisite inn, built in 1925 to house lumber company offices, but converted to a B&B in 1990 by the current owners. Five guest rooms ring the main floor, which also contains the living area, with three more private spaces up a wide flight of stairs. All are filled with antiques, flowery wallpaper, and luxurious linens, and all have modern, private baths. A full English breakfast is served in the formal dining room, and the table is set with exquisite china and crystal. You might start with fresh fruit and yogurt, followed by an elegant egg dish served with English bangers (Ken's mother's recipe) and freshly baked scones or muffins. Don't forget to take a romantic stroll, wandering among the cottage gardens and over to the scenic covered bridge, lit up spectacularly at night.
$ *No credit cards; checks OK; www.westfirlodge.com.*

WINE COUNTRY FARM
✿✿❦

6855 Breyman Orchards Rd, Dayton / 503/864-3446 or 800/261-3446
Relax on the porch of this renovated 1910 French stucco farmhouse and take in the magnificent views of the valley, mountains, and Wine Country Farm's vineyards. With such outstanding scenery, it's not surprising that the interior of this bed-and-breakfast, which includes some outdated decor, pales in comparison. The real pleasures here involve strolling through the 13-acre estate, unwinding in the shared hot tub or sauna, and scheduling a relaxing treatment in the on-site massage room. All nine rooms feature private baths, down comforters, and lovely views. In the main house, we prefer the two rooms downstairs over the four standard rooms upstairs, despite their proximity to the potentially noisy living room and front door. The Courtyard Room has a king-size canopy bed, fireplace, and private entrance, while the Willamette Room offers a queen-size bed, bay windows, and a wonderful view. However, come nightfall, the most private options are the three rooms set above the recently expanded wine-tasting area. There's the simply appointed Vineyard Room, with standard bath,

or—our preference—the Sunset and Oregon Rooms, both added in 2003, with king-size canopy beds, separate sitting areas, cozy fireplaces, and outside decks. Note that come daytime, visitors will be sampling wines in the tasting room below these rooms between 11am and 5pm (weekends only Memorial Day to Labor Day). A hearty farm breakfast is served in the sunny dining room. Couples can take advantage of the nearby horse stables by arranging a highly romantic private picnic: with advance notice, the proprietor will pack a gourmet lunch—complete with wine, silverware, and a big blanket—and take the two of you via horse-drawn buggy into nearby orchards, where you will be alone for as long as your hearts desire. $$–$$$ *MC, V; checks OK; www.winecountryfarm.com.*

YOUNGBERG HILL VINEYARDS & INN
◓◓◓◔

10660 Youngberg Hill Rd, McMinnville / 503/472-2727 or 888/657-8668
Climb a little closer to heaven at this magnificent bed-and-breakfast built in 1989 but with a turn-of-the-century feel. A steep, mile-long driveway winds past rolling fields, oak forests, and vineyards to this stunning inn, prominently perched on a hill. At night, the lights of McMinnville twinkle in the distance. Choosing from among the three luxurious two-room suites and four delightful guest rooms (two with fireplaces) isn't easy; all feature elegant decor, private baths, inviting beds with down comforters, and outstanding views. Gleaming wooden antique-replica furnishings and carved headboards are set against walls of pleasing plum, sage, and buttercup-yellow hues. For the most space, try the Jackson Suite or the Martini Suite, both with king-size beds, French doors opening onto private decks, and luxurious baths; the Jackson has a double-headed shower, the Martini a jetted tub. The front-facing Jura Suite has amazing views through the bay windows, plus wingback chairs in the sitting area. The first-floor Gamay Room, despite its location near the front door, charms with its wood-burning fireplace and private deck. Since this spacious and popular inn can accommodate quite a few guests at once, on busy weekends you may spend some time visiting with (or possibly overhearing) others. In the morning, watch fog roll into the valley from the bright, airy dining room as you indulge in pears poached in wine sauce, freshly baked muffins, and puffed pancakes with stuffed sausages. In the afternoon, stroll the surrounding vineyards—or visit with owners Wayne and Nicolette Bailey and hear their exciting plans to expand the current offerings, including a new outdoor event site, which opened in July 2004, a spectacular spot for a romantic wedding. $$$ *MC, V; checks OK; www.youngberghill.com.*

Romantic Restaurants

BISTRO MAISON
❂❂

729 E 3rd St, McMinnville / 503/474-1888
Enjoy a romantic meal over candlelight in this cheery French cafe based on the ground floor of a historic bungalow in downtown McMinnville. If the weather is clear, opt for a private table for two on the charming outdoor patio. Opened in 2003 by chef Jean-Jacques and his wife, Deborah, who live upstairs, it is a welcome addition with its yellow French-country wallpaper and red leather–backed booths. There is a wine-tasting bar up front as well as a comfortable waiting area at the top of the stairs. Start with an aperitif and sample the *moules*—cooked in three different styles—served with *frites* and saffron aioli. Classics such as escargots *en croûte de bourguignonne*, coq au vin, and steak tartare, as well as daily specials, such as poached leeks, are mouthwatering fare. Don't forget to save room and prep time (10–15 minutes) for the *moelleux au chocolat*—molten chocolate cake served warm. End the meal by sampling sublime local hazelnuts.
$$ *DIS, MC, V; local checks only; lunch Wed–Fri, dinner Wed–Sun, brunch Sun; full bar; reservations recommended; www.bistromaison.com.*

DUNDEE BISTRO
❂❂❂

100-A SW 7th St, Dundee / 503/554-1650
For the most privacy at this sleek, bustling bistro set along Highway 99 within a small upscale development, be sure to request a booth. The outdoor patio overlooks a courtyard of emerald green lawn (and the parking lot beyond); the light-filled interior has large windows and a color scheme that evokes Tuscany, with warm sage and pumpkin tones. A cozy fireplace warms things up in winter. On busy evenings, noise can be a factor, but the inventive seasonal Northwest menu outweighs this minor drawback. Daily menu changes focus on ingredients available at nearby farms and ranches, and a local farmers market can be found in front of the restaurant on Sundays. An autumn dinner might start with chanterelle-mushroom crostini with grilled sweet onion, or paprika and fennel–cured salmon on grilled flatbread. Tempting entrée choices include prosciutto-wrapped sea scallops and locally caught sturgeon with a charred-pepper mascarpone risotto. Pizza, a specialty, appears as an appetizer at dinner or an entrée at lunch, topped with unusual combinations that are not always successful: the version we tried, with bland chunks of butternut squash, made a good argument for more traditional ingredients. Nonetheless, most of the dishes here are successful. Enhance your meal with one of the handful of desserts

and something from the eclectic wine list, not long but well chosen—a dozen are available by the glass.

$$ *AE, MC, V; local checks only; lunch, dinner every day; full bar; reservations recommended; www.dundeebistro.com.*

JOEL PALMER HOUSE
◆◆◆◆

600 Ferry St, Dayton / 503/864-2995

A romantic getaway in Oregon's wine country is simply not complete without an evening at the Joel Palmer House. Chef Jack Czarnecki is both world famous and a renowned authority on cooking with wild mushrooms; rare is the dish that emerges from his kitchen without some variety of fungus to tempt you. The backdrop for his culinary creations is one of Oregon's most famous historic homes, the Joel Palmer House, which is found on both state and national historic registers. Inside the 1849 Southern Revival–style house, the cozy dining rooms evoke that bygone era, with lace or green velvet curtains, tables adorned with linen and fresh flowers, and period antiques and artwork. Ingredients are mostly Northwest, including fresh local produce and herbs from a charming onsite garden, but the cooking is freestyle. Appetizers might include a three-mushroom tart, escargot with black chanterelles, or a silky corn chowder with dried cèpes. The rack of lamb comes with a rich pinot noir–hazelnut sauce, while wild-mushroom duxelles and a Creole–pinot gris sauce accompany tender sautéed scallops. Service is friendly if not lighting-quick, but the unrushed pace suits the charming surroundings. The wine cellar, which boasts more than 5,000 bottles and leans heavily toward Oregon pinot, is sure to have just the right something special to accompany this romantic meal. On warm twilight evenings, enjoy dining on the lovely outdoor patio.

$$-$$$ *AE, DIS, MC, V; local checks only; dinner Tues–Sat; full bar; reservations recommended; www.joelpalmerhouse.com.*

NICK'S ITALIAN CAFE
◆◆◗

521 E 3rd St, McMinnville / 503/434-4471

As the name suggests, Nick's offers a casual ambience—the lavish, multi-course Italian meals, however, often keep diners in their seats for upward of two hours. With its funky charm, mismatched plates, and location in a former luncheonette, Nick's is not nearly as slick as the newer places along Dundee's "restaurant row." However, it has a long history as the region's first culinary headquarters, and its luscious pastas keep Italian-food lovers—and lovers in general—coming back. While the menu changes nightly, it is always a five-course extravaganza that features the best that local markets have to offer. New head chef Jeremy Buck, just back from a year of culinary study in Italy, specializes in duck and salmon dishes and uses many

family recipes including ravioli and minestrone. Among the seasonal specialties are handmade pastas; rabbit braised in Oregon pinot gris; a pesto, chanterelle, and hazelnut lasagne; salt-grilled Chinook salmon; and grilled fresh asparagus. Ordering à la carte is also an option. Nick's has two dining rooms, but we recommend the front room, with its charming private booths. A single candle tops every table and low lighting makes the wood interior glow, while the extensive wine list offers over eighty different Oregon pinot noirs. Dessert choices of crème brûlée, truffles, or tiramisù make your evening all the sweeter.
$$$ AE, MC, V; checks OK; dinner Tues–Sun; beer and wine; reservations recommended; www.nicksitaliancafe.com.

RED HILLS PROVINCIAL DINING
⬡⬡⬡

276 Hwy 99W, Dundee / 503/538-8224
This restaurant, located in a lovely 1912 Craftsman-style home, offers a testament to the wonders restoration can do. Two dining rooms, both appointed with linen-covered tables and fresh flowers, highlight the beauty and functionality of the home's original design features, including a built-in buffet and drawers (in the front room) and leaded crystal windows throughout. Chocolate- and cream-colored walls add to the warm and inviting ambience. The location, above Highway 99, is not entirely scenic—but everything in Dundee is found along this so-called wine road, and the drawback is slight given the surroundings. The simple European-country dinner menu changes monthly, and the choices are all intriguing: veal osso buco with creamy polenta, fricassee of game hen with chanterelle and black trumpet mushrooms, or a classic coquilles St.-Jacques—scallops in a creamy wine sauce with a browned bread-crumb-and-cheese topping. The kitchen gets all the culinary details just right and pulls much of the ingredients, including herbs and berries, from twelve raised-bed gardens as well as numerous fruit trees located on the property. Whether it's bread dusted with fresh rosemary, a crisp mesclun salad, or luscious desserts such as poached pears with caramel sauce and chocolate ganache, the result is exquisite. Add to this an award-winning wine list with a huge selection from all over the world, and you have a recipe for romance indeed.
$$ AE, MC, V; checks OK; dinner Tues–Sun; full bar; reservations recommended.

TINA'S
⬡⬡⬢

760 Hwy 99W, Dundee / 503/538-8880
Raving about the food here has become a wine-country tradition, and this small, unassuming restaurant along the highway is a favorite gathering spot for the local wine crowd. But while this insider quality gives Tina's an

authentic feel, the restaurant is not exactly designed for romance. Inside, the pleasant dining room has white walls and framed prints, but the lighting is too bright and the acoustics are poor. A cozy double-sided fireplace is not always lit on chilly evenings; when it is, the ambience is considerably warmer. The bias toward local ingredients is welcome, and nearly every item on the seasonal, French-influenced menu looks tempting. Start with a creamy soup or a tasty crisp salad, and a glass of the famous Oregon pinot noir. Sample an appetizer highlighting wild mushrooms, and don't miss the Oregon rack of lamb from Sudan Farms in nearby Canby. Main courses are slightly less reliable—we encountered overcooked halibut and a duck dish with sauce that was nearly viscous. A bright spot is the plate of tasty, tender sea scallops. Despite the occasionally uneven food, couples should find plenty to enjoy at this wine-country haven. You can count on fresh, high-quality ingredients, an ever-changing menu, an impressive wine list, and house-made desserts to provide a sweet finish.
$$–$$$ *AE, DIS, MC, V; checks OK; dinner every day; full bar; reservations recommended.*

SALEM & HISTORIC OREGON

ROMANTIC HIGHLIGHTS

Is it a coincidence that Oregon's statehood anniversary falls on Valentine's Day? Oh, probably, but there's plenty to love about this state, particularly among the small, historically intriguing towns that dot the countryside around Salem. Wineries are within easy reach, but the mid-Willamette Valley offers its own kind of peaceful escape. True, there aren't a lot of choices for exceptionally romantic accommodations, but neither are there overwhelming numbers of tourists late fall through spring. Summer is busier, but is still an appealing season for visiting romance seekers: the abundant rose gardens are in bloom, and strawberries and marionberries are ripe for the picking at roadside stands. Outdoor activities—from concerts to whitewater rafting—beckon. Winter has its own rewards, with its solitude, uncrowded restaurants, and plentiful opportunities for snuggling by the fireside at a B&B. In any season, you can duck under a covered bridge for an atmospheric kiss; with nearly 50 covered bridges, Oregon is the roofed-span capital of the country.

Attractive as it is, capped with a golden pioneer statue and decorated inside with Depression-era murals, the State Capitol Building in Salem is probably truly appealing only to lobbyists in love. Instead, stroll the campus of neighboring **Willamette University** (900 State St; 503/370-6300; www.

willamette.edu), the oldest university in the West (established in 1842); be sure to pop into the second-largest art museum in Oregon, **Hallie Ford Museum of Art** (700 State St; 503/370-6855; www.willamette.edu/museum_ of_art; open 10am–5pm Tues–Sat). Historic buildings abound in Salem, and you'll find several of them in **Historic Mission Mill Village** (1313 Mill St SE; 503/585-7012; www.missionmill.org; tours 10am–5pm Mon–Sat). This impressive 42-acre cluster of restored buildings from the 1800s includes a woolen mill, a parsonage, a Presbyterian church, and several houses. On a warm day, plan a leisurely exploration of **Bush's Pasture Park** and the **Bush House Museum** (600 Mission St SE; 503/363-4714; www.salemart.org/bush; tours Tues–Sun; call for tour hours), with its conservatory, rose gardens, hiking paths, barn-turned-gallery, and—for one weekend in mid-July— outdoor Salem Art Festival (www.salemart.org/fair). Bring a picnic, or head downtown to the **Arbor Café** (380 High St NE; 503/588-2353) for homemade soup or a savory muffaletta panini. The *Queen Mary* it's not, but the rail of the stern-wheeler **Willamette Queen** (503/371-1103; www.willamettequeen. com) has its own vintage charm as a kissing venue; both short excursions and brunch, lunch, and dinner cruises are available year-round. South of town, the views are just as romantic as the wine at **Willamette Valley Vineyards** (8800 Enchanted Way SE, Turner; 503/588-9463 or 800/344-9463; www.wvv.com).

Follow State Highway 221 or back roads south to the Eola Hills, which are home to several acclaimed wineries, including **Stangeland** (8500 Hopewell Road NW; 800/301-9482; www.stangelandwinery.com), **Witness Tree** (7111 Spring Valley Rd NW; 888/478-8766; www.witnesstreevineyard. com), **Cristom** (6905 Spring Valley Rd NW; 503/375-3068; www.cristom wines.com), and **Bethel Heights** (6060 Bethel Heights NW; 503/581-2262; www.bethelheights.com), all generally open weekends (plus some weekdays in summer) noon to 5pm. Watch for blue signs pointing the way. Cross the river on the charming, four-car **Wheatland Ferry** (503/588-7979; www. wheatlandferry.com)—river crossings for passengers are free (cars cost a dollar and change)—and disembark on the other side to explore the scenic, flat walking paths of **Willamette Mission State Park** (www.oregonstate parks.org/park_139.php).

Head west on State Highway 22 for a few miles and watch for signs south to Independence, where you and your sweetheart can sip sodas at historic **Taylor's Fountain and Gift** (296 S Main St; 503/838-1124) or browse the work of local artists at **The River Gallery** (184 S Main St; 503/838-6171; www. oregonlink.com/rivergallery; open 11am–5pm Tues–Sun). Follow Buena Vista Road south to remote **Buena Vista House Café** (11265 Riverview St; 503/838-6364) to enjoy a scone and an espresso, or a pizza from the wood-fired oven, served in the 110-year-old farmhouse or under the apple trees out back. The cafe is just two blocks from the tiny **Buena Vista Ferry** (503/588-7979; 7am–5pm Wed–Fri, 9am–7pm Sat–Sun). If you're not in a hurry, be sure to take this charming ride—it's the only way to cross the Willamette between Albany and Independence. (If you're driving from Interstate 5, take exit 242 and follow signs west about 5 miles to the ferry.) If you're used to riding the huge car ferries on Puget Sound, you'll love this altogether more leisurely ferry experience; Oregon has only a handful of boats—small crafts that are nostalgic remnants of an earlier era. This particular ride gets you into the farm-and-wine country west of the river.

Time and the interstate have passed by Albany, the next big town to the south. Stroll the 50-block Monteith Historic District to see everything from colorful Queen Anne houses to Craftsman bungalows, or experience the romance of covered bridges (there are six within an 8-mile radius of Scio, northeast of Albany). For either excursion, contact the Albany Visitors Center for maps (see Access and Information). Then head to First Avenue and the side streets to browse antique shops; stop for something hot at **Boccherini's Coffee and Tea House** (208 1st Ave SW; 541/926-6703). Bring a blanket and a picnic to one of the many outdoor summer concerts at **Monteith Riverpark** (Water Ave and Washington St; 541/917-7772; www.riverrhythms.org).

For a beautiful drive south, follow the river road to Corvallis and then take a romantic stroll along the recently revitalized **Riverfront Park** near the handsome Oregon State University campus. This beautifully paved pedestrian esplanade runs for several blocks along the Willamette River and includes a lovely fountain, stone benches, picnic tables, and interesting sculptures by Northwest artists—the perfect spot for a romantic picnic or quick smooch. This is also the home of the local Saturday farmers market, which runs May through October. Afterward, stop for a well-earned espresso at **The Beanery** (500 SW 2nd St; 541/753-7442). You're likely to be all alone but for the dusky Canada geese when you stroll the trails at **Finley National Wildlife Refuge** (541/757-7236), 10 miles south of town on Highway 99W.

Tiny Silverton, east of Salem, is not to be missed by the romantically inclined. Stroll its historic downtown, festooned with hanging baskets overflowing with flowers in summer, and browse the shops; then refresh yourselves with lunch or high tea at **Oregon Tea Garden** (305 Oak St; 503/873-1230; www.oregonteagarden.com), which is named after the **Oregon Garden** (503/874-8100 or 877/674-2733; www.oregongarden.org), about 2 miles southwest of town off Highway 213. At the garden, skip the narrated group shuttle-bus tour and walk the paths hand in hand at your own pace— much more romantic. Southeast of town is lush **Silver Falls State Park** (off Hwy 214, 26 miles east of Salem; 503/873-8681; www.oregonstateparks. org/park_211.php); there's not a more dramatic place to kiss than behind 177-foot South Falls or 136-foot North Falls. Iris farmers cultivate acres of fields around Silverton, creating a brilliant palette in late May; that's also the time to wander **Cooley's Iris Display Gardens** (11553 Silverton Rd NE; 503/873-5463; www.cooleysgardens.com). North of Silverton, browse the many antique shops in well-preserved Aurora, which was founded in 1856 as a communal settlement by a group of Pennsylvania Dutch. You can learn their intriguing story at the **Old Aurora Colony Museum** (15018 2nd St NE; 503/678-5754; www.auroracolonymuseum.com).

Access and Information

The town of Salem makes a good base for exploring the historic (and romantic) charms of the mid-Willamette Valley. Most travelers arrive by car via Interstate 5; its four lanes (at Eugene) widen to six around Salem. A more leisurely route is the scenic old US Highway 99W, parallel to Interstate 5 west of the Willamette. Travelers from farther afield can fly into Portland or Eugene before starting the drive. Another romantic option is to take the train (800/USA-RAIL; www.amtrak.com) from Seattle or Portland; **Amtrak's Coast Starlight** route stops at Salem, Albany, and Eugene on its way south to Los Angeles.

Vintage Oregon Winery Guide is an invaluable guide for winery touring; get a copy from the Oregon Wine Advisory Board (503/228-8336 or 800/242-2363; www.oregonwine.org) or at most wineries. You can also get travel tips from the **Salem Convention and Visitors Association** (503/581-4325 or 800/874-7012; www.scva.com). **The Albany Visitors Center** (250 Broadalbin SW, #110; 541/928-0911 or 800/526-2256; www.albanyvisitors.com) is another excellent resource—request their map of covered bridges in the area. Those traveling to Corvallis can check in with its **Convention and Visitors Bureau** (553 NW Harrison Blvd; 541/757-1544 or 800/334-8118; www.visitcorvallis.com).

Romantic Lodgings

HANSON COUNTRY INN
♥♥◖

795 SW Hanson St, Corvallis / 541/752-2919
It's just a few minutes' drive from Corvallis, but you'll feel you've gone deep into the rural Willamette Valley countryside when you arrive at Hanson Country Inn. It's no wonder the inn, with its surrounding formal lawn and garden, is a favorite among local brides. This wood-and-brick 1928 farmhouse was once the centerpiece of a prosperous poultry ranch; it's now on the Benton County Historical Register, thanks to extensive renovation by former San Franciscan Patricia Covey. Downstairs, you can enjoy a book or a kiss (or both!) by the fireplace in the gleaming wood-paneled living room, in the light-washed sun-room, or in the library. Three large guest suites upstairs (two with their own sitting rooms and decks, and all with private

baths) feature beautiful wallpaper and fine bed linens. After breakfasting on crepes with blackberries or a fresh frittata, explore the grounds and the original egg house. For the utmost privacy, take the charmingly decorated, quiet two-bedroom cottage tucked in the trees up behind the main house. Guests here enjoy the complimentary breakfast as well, but may also want to bring fresh groceries and stay in for dinner; with a living area, a fully equipped kitchen, a private bath, and two bedrooms (one with a queen-size bed, one with a double), you'll have everything you need for a cozy weekend à deux.
$$ AE, DIS, MC, V; checks OK; www.hcinn.com.

WATER STREET INN
🟢🟢
421 N Water St, Silverton / 503/873-3344 or 866/873-3344
After a day of waterfall-watching at Silver Falls State Park or strolling in the Oregon Garden, collapse into luxury at the Water Street Inn, the most luxurious accommodations for miles around. Originally built as the Wolford Hotel in 1890, it was gutted and rebuilt by the new owners, who in 2001 reopened it as a handsome bed-and-breakfast. Sheila, Laurie, and Rob Rosborough come from a family of innkeepers in England, and they know how to treat guests right. Each of the five guest rooms is elegantly and individually appointed with period-style furniture, heavy cut-velvet drapes, and thick comforters; some rooms also have feather beds. Each has a TV/VCR and private bath with shower, and all but Room 2 have queen-size beds. Room 2's twin mattresses, however, can be combined into a spacious king; here you can also luxuriate together in the oversize, heated whirlpool tub. We also recommend spacious Room 4's double shower and feather bed, or Room 5's fireplace and jetted tub for two. Original dark-stained Douglas-fir floors gleam in the guest rooms as well as in the large, high-ceilinged living room and formal dining room, where guests gather in the morning to enjoy a full and tasty homemade breakfast—served family-style at the polished mahogany table. Be sure and linger over the savory Grand Marnier French toast served with yogurt and fresh fruit or sweet cheese blintzes with seasonal berries—assuredly, a romantic way to start the day.
$$ AE, DIS, MC, V; checks OK; www.thewaterstreetinn.com.

WILLAMETTE GABLES RIVERSIDE ESTATE
🟢🟢🟢
10323 Schuler Rd, Aurora / 503/678-2195
Rhett Butler and Scarlett O'Hara have nothing on you as you ascend the polished hardwood steps of the spiral staircase, passing under the crystal chandelier, to your lavish guest room at the top of the stairs. It could be an old mansion, well restored, but in fact the Willamette Gables Riverside Estate is a *new* mansion, built as a B&B in Southern Plantation style and

perched on a bluff overlooking the Willamette River. Open since March 2001, this inn, with its 5 acres of beautifully landscaped grounds and its elegantly appointed interior, is already a favorite for weddings. Downstairs, the lower parlor invites you to lounge by the fireplace with a book, to dabble at the baby grand piano, or to just relax and enjoy the view of the river through the trees. The spiral staircase leads upstairs to all five guest rooms, each with private bath and individually decorated with antiques (and convincing reproductions). Stretch out in the Captain's Room, with its king-size sleigh bed, fireplace, and claw-foot tub; a day bed tucked under the eaves makes an inviting reading retreat. The Music Room is smaller, but the decor has romantic appeal; the queen-size four-poster bed is spread with a wedding-ring quilt. The Monet Room offers a wood-burning fireplace and a view of the river. Varina's Room, with its antique Eastlake double bed, is charming, but small. Breakfast—from blueberry pancakes with homemade blueberry syrup to Dungeness crab quiche—is prepared from scratch; dine with other guests at the large table overlooking the river, or have a private table set upstairs, outside your room. For a small extra fee, the two of you can breakfast alone in your room.
$$$ *MC, V; checks OK; www.willamettegables.com.* &

Romantic Restaurants

IOVINO'S
●●
126 SW 1st St, Corvallis / 541/738-9015
Work up an appetite for your romantic dinner with a leisurely stroll through Corvallis's recently rehabbed riverfront, then pop across First Avenue to Iovino's for a taste of big-city atmosphere and flavor. With its concrete floors and high ceiling, this former garage has a stylish sophistication you don't expect in small-town Oregon. Start with a drink from the bar's innovative martini menu, accompanied perhaps by bruschetta swathed in piquant caramelized onions, tomatoes, capers, and Gorgonzola (you'll need a fork for this finger food), or *insalata de noce*—chopped greens with delicious minced hazelnuts. The nouvelle-Italian menu is full of surprises—all of them pleasant. The sweet marsala sauce on the turkey scallops melds brilliantly with mashed ricotta potatoes, and a basil dressing happily marries the plate of tiger prawns to the herb-breaded eggplant underneath. Many entrées are offered in either smaller or full-size portions. The tiramisù is terrific, as is the chocolate mousse, served in a lemonade glass.
$$ *AE, MC, V; checks OK; lunch Mon–Fri, dinner every day; full bar; reservations recommended.* &

J. JAMES RESTAURANT
◆◆

325 High St, Salem / 503/362-0888
Couples who find good food more important than an intimate dining atmosphere on a romantic evening out will appreciate chef-owner Jeff James's restaurant, on the fringe of downtown Salem. An Oregon native, James uses the region's seasonal ingredients in simple yet creative dishes, including starters such as Oregon shrimp, whole kernel corn, and fresh dill risotto, and an Oregon white cheddar and goat cheese tart with spicy onion jam and citrus reduction. The entrée selections include a good mix of meat and seafood dishes, such as grilled pork loin marinated in molasses and salmon poached in a lightly spiced broth. The large dining room is softened by white linens, floor-to-ceiling windows, and warmly hued walls, and the service is crisp and professional. The wine list is moderately priced. Bring healthy appetites and enjoy what this restaurant does best—delicious meals and desserts that are worth the indulgence.
$$ *AE, MC, V; local checks only; lunch Mon–Fri, dinner Mon–Sat; full bar; reservations recommended; www.jjamesrestaurant.com.* &

LE BISTRO
◆◆

150 SW Madison Ave, Corvallis / 541/754-6680
The atmosphere at this quietly elegant French restaurant is almost stark in its simplicity; here, the focus is on the food. French chef Robert Merlet came to Corvallis via Paris, Bordeaux, and the Bay Area, and couples seeking an intimate dinner à deux are glad he did. Dishes don't necessarily dazzle, but ingredients are fresh, and everything is expertly prepared. Roast duckling might come with fresh rhubarb and a French sweet-and-sour demi-glace; grilled fish choices have light sauces; and cheese tortellini comes with diced vegetables and roasted-garlic pesto. Furthermore, not all restaurants get risotto right—but Le Bistro does. The menu includes not only escargots and sweetbreads but also a simple plate of sliced tomatoes with a bit of anchovy and feta. Dessert choices include profiteroles, a fresh fruit tartlet, and a melt-in-your-mouth chocolate mousse.
$$ *MC, V; local checks only; dinner Tues–Sat; full bar; reservations recommended; www.lebistro.com.*

MORTON'S BISTRO NORTHWEST
◆◆◆

1128 Edgewater St, Salem / 503/585-1113
If the two of you are looking for exquisite food in an intimate setting, make your way to Morton's. Tucked below the road off a busy highway in West Salem, the dining room's low ceiling, dark wood beams, and soft lighting add up to romantic ambience. It can be noisy, but not in a way that detracts

from the experience: this is one of those rare and pleasant places that create intimacy with noise, as no one will overhear your sweet nothings above the lively hubbub of conversation surrounding you. The restaurant's food, staunchly Northwestern with hints of international influences, has been singled out by national magazines as among the best in Oregon. A salmon fillet might be accompanied by a savory potato-pumpkin mash with basil and balsamic–braised tomatoes; vegetarian lasagne combines roasted red peppers, mushrooms, goat cheese, and spinach. Give serious consideration to the mixed grill and the cioppino. Service is expert and pleasant, and there's a good selection of reasonably priced Northwest wines.
$$ MC, V; checks OK; dinner Tues–Sat; full bar; reservations recommended; www.mortonsbistronw.com. &

SILVER GRILLE CAFÉ & WINES
🌣🌣🌣
206 E Main St, Silverton / 503/873-4035
The Silver Grille, with its tiny, softly lit dining room, dark wood wainscoting, and deep red grass-paper walls, embraces you warmly from the moment you walk in the door. Once you taste the food, you'll be hooked. The menu changes seasonally, with specials written on a chalkboard, and features the bounty of Willamette Valley farms and fields. Winning seasonal dishes include locally foraged wild mushrooms merged with white Oregon truffles in a faultless risotto, and a perfectly seared ahi fillet on a bed of black rice, bathed in a truffle wine sauce. Start with a salad of local organic greens or a terrine of smoked salmon and bay shrimp, and end your meal with a dense chocolate cake laced with essence of marionberries. The wine selection is displayed just inside the front door as a convenience for retail customers; diners choose their wine here, too, and then add a modest corkage fee.
$$ AE, DIS, MC, V; checks OK; lunch Tues–Sat, dinner Tues–Sun; full bar; reservations recommended; www.silvergrille.com. &

SYBARIS
🌣🌣🌣
442 SW 1st, Albany / 541/928-8157
In ancient Greece, the city of Sybaris was synonymous with luxury and pleasure. So it is with this elegant restaurant, which opened in 2001 in the former Capriccio Ristorante space on Albany's historic First Street. The former owners kept the exposed brick and large windows when they renovated, adding an English-style wood-burning fireplace and scattering tables throughout the high-ceilinged room. Enter current chef-owner Matt Bennett along with his wife, Janel, whose rotating menus reflect a fearless and playful approach to food. On any given day, "spaghetti and meatballs" might mean balls of ahi tuna in a ginger-tomato sauce with black squid-

ink pasta; "roast" could be venison loin with mashed root vegetables and a huckleberry-port sauce. Bennett relies on a couple of local farms for many of his ingredients and plans his monthly menus according to what's in season there. The generous entrée portions may lead you to pass on dessert—which would be a shame, for you'd miss the Sybaris chocolate hazelnut cake, a dense, flourless, decadent work of art filled with a cache of crème brûlée. The wine list is short but well matched to the menu. Monteith Riverpark is just across the street; extend the evening's pleasure with a starlit stroll by the river. $$ AE, MC, V; local checks only; dinner Tues–Sat; full bar; reservations recommended; www.sybarisbistro.com. &

EUGENE AREA

ROMANTIC HIGHLIGHTS

Portland's laid-back sister lies at the south end of the Willamette Valley, where the Cascade and Coast Range foothills both draw close to enclose the town in a green embrace. Eugene may be the state's second-largest urban area, but it's still something of an overgrown small town, with enough secluded romantic spots and local color to keep your getaway interesting. The high point within Eugene's city limits is Skinner Butte, which provides breathtaking sunset views. A road leads to the top of the butte; from here, look west to the pink and gold clouds, east to the snow-covered Three Sisters mountains, and south to the city lights stretching out toward forested Spencer's Butte. Such views offer a perfect glimpse of the natural beauty that abounds in this region, and that makes it so suitable for romance.

At the base of Skinner Butte is the **Owen Rose Garden** (end of N Jefferson St, at the Willamette River), home to Charisma, French Perfume, Golden Slippers, and dozens of other rose varieties, including climbing roses trained to heart-shaped trellises. In summer, there's not a sweeter-smelling spot to wander hand in hand (or, if the time is right, pose a query on bended knee!). Trails here connect to an extensive network of riverside paths and river-spanning bicycle/pedestrian bridges. In spring, **Hendricks Park** (Summit Ave and Skyline Dr) is Romance Central. Ten acres of dazzling rhododendrons and azaleas burst into bloom from late April to early June; between plantings lie swaths of green lawn practically begging for a blanket and picnic basket. Even after the bloom, the park and its tall stands of Douglas fir provide a welcome retreat from a hurried world. For more information, contact the parks department for the city of Eugene (541/682-4800; www.ci.eugene.or.us/parks).

The broad lawns and walkways and historic buildings of the University of Oregon campus (13th Ave and University St) are made for leisurely strolling, whether your brain is full of test questions or romantic purring. Sneak a kiss at the waterfall fountain behind the science complex, or linger in the **Jordan Schnitzer Museum of Art** (1430 Johnson Ln; 541/346-3027; uoma.uoregon.edu), which reopened in January 2005 after a $12 million extension and renovation, or the **Museum of Natural and Cultural History** (1680 E 15th Ave; 541/346-3024; natural-history.uoregon.edu) which reopened in February 2005. There's no shortage of great coffeehouses, fabulous bakeries, intriguing art galleries, and trendy brew pubs in Eugene. For the latter, try **Steelhead Brewery** (199 E 5th Ave; 541/686-2739), in the Fifth Avenue historic district. Enjoy a drink and live music at **Jo Federigo's Jazz Club** (259 E 5th Ave; 541/343-8488) or **Luna** (30 E Broadway; 541/434-5862; www.lunajazz.com), a stylish bar located next to the restaurant Adam's Place that schedules live music every night (see Romantic Restaurants). Eugene has not one but two serious chocolatiers: **Euphoria** (6 W 17th Ave; 541/343-9223; www.euphoriachocolate.com) and **Fenton & Lee** (35 E 8th Ave; 541/343-7629; www.fentonandlee.com), and there's an elegant French tea shop—**Savoure** (201 W Broadway; 541/242-1010; www.savoure. com)—in the Broadway Place development. April through the second week in November, spend a morning at **Saturday Market** (8th Ave and Oak St; 541/686-8885; www.eugenesaturdaymarket.org), the state's oldest outdoor crafts fair.

Ready to get out of town? Head west on Highway 126 to Veneta for a bite at **Our Daily Bread** (88170 Territorial Rd; 541/935-4921; www.our dailybreadbakery.net), a bakery and cafe housed in a former church (hence the name). Take Territorial Highway west a short distance to visit **Secret House Vineyards** (88324 Vineyard Ln; 541/935-3774 or 800/497-1574); once you're finished here, head south and watch for blue signs leading to three more excellent wineries: Italian-inspired **Silvan Ridge/Hinman Vineyards** (27012 Briggs Hill Rd; 541/345-1945; www.silvanridge.com); **King Estate** (80854 Territorial Rd; 541/942-9874 or 800/884-4441; www.kingestate.com), with a palatial hilltop home; and woodsy and intimate **Chateau Lorane** (27415 Siuslaw River Rd; 541/942-8028; www.chateaulorane.com). All are open weekends, noon to 5pm; some are open weekdays, as well. Return north on Territorial Road and turn east on Hamm Road to savor the heady scents and sights at **Sawmill Ballroom Lavender Farm** (29251 Hamm Rd; 541/686-9999; www.sawmillballroom.com).

The wild McKenzie River lies to the east of Eugene; follow it along State Highway 126 past small mountain towns, boat launches, and riverside parks and picnic sites to **Belknap Resort and Hot Springs** (541/822-3512), where an outdoor swimming pool full of hot mineral water awaits. (There's no privacy, but there's no rule against kissing in the pool, either!) The pool is relaxing in any season, but pure magic when snow is falling. Cross the river on a footbridge to stroll the adjacent extensive formal gardens in the woods. A detour up State Highway 242 (open summer and fall only) is especially appealing in autumn, when the vine maples turn gold and crimson and the hiking trails and picnic sites are yours alone.

Couples who enjoy music festivals and fairs will find much to consider when planning a trip to Eugene. (If you prefer to avoid crowds, steer well clear during the most popular summer events.) What, for example, could be more romantic than a full orchestra and chorus engaged in the perfect harmony of a Bach oratorio? The second weekend in July, the world-class **Oregon Bach Festival** (541/682-5000 or 800/457-1486; www.oregonbach festival.com) concludes its two-week run at the Hult Center for the Performing Arts and smaller concert venues around town. A truly alternative experience awaits at the **Oregon Country Fair** (541/343-4298; www.oregon countryfair.org), a wild and wacky three-day celebration held on a wooded retreat west of town that draws more than 40,000 visitors. There's food, art, music, men dressed like flamingos parading on stilts, women wearing a smile and little else—call it a throwback, but we prefer to think of it as love, counterculture style.

Access and Information

Commuter airlines America West, Horizon Air, and United Express serve the **Eugene airport** (north of town, off Hwy 99; 541/682-5544; www.euge-neairport.com). Car rentals are available at the airport and in town. Most travelers arrive by car via Interstate 5; it's less than two hours from Portland to Eugene. More leisurely north-south travelers prefer the scenic, older US Highway 99W, parallel to Interstate 5 west of the Willamette River. Winter driving is generally easy, but if you're worried about road conditions contact the **Oregon Department of Transportation** (503/588-2941 or 800/977-6368 outside Oregon; www.tripcheck.com) For old-fashioned travel, **Amtrak's Coast Starlight** route (800/USA-RAIL; www.amtrak.com) from Seattle and Portland stops at Salem, Albany, and Eugene on its way south to Los Angeles.

Romantic Lodgings

CAMPBELL HOUSE
ⓞⓞⓞⓒ
252 Pearl St, Eugene / 541/343-1119 or 800/264-2519
From the gorgeous guest rooms to the lavish landscaping to the tables for two in the breakfast room, the Campbell House is designed for romance. Built in 1892 and lovingly restored as a grand bed-and-breakfast, the house

is set on an acre of beautiful grounds with a quiet yet convenient location two blocks from Fifth Street Public Market. Elegant, light-filled rooms have both Old World charm (four-poster beds, high ceilings, dormer windows) and modern amenities (TV/VCRs tastefully hidden, wireless Internet access, stocked mini-fridges), not to mention smart, attentive service. Complimentary tea, coffee, and wine are served in the Victorian parlor each evening. Lovely mauve and green couches, hardwood floors covered with area rugs, and large picture windows make this an inviting place to unwind. Adjoining the parlor is the library, filled with books, games, and an extensive video collection available for guests' use. Throughout the house, a few quirks lend an aura of authenticity; unusually shaped rooms and dormer ceilings create some extremely cozy quarters. Each of the 13 rooms in the main house has a private bath stocked with plush robes. Some have claw-foot tubs, and some offer romantic amenities such as gas fireplaces and jetted tubs. One—the Dr. Eva Johnson Room—has a luxurious bathroom alcove with jetted tub. The inn is designated nonsmoking, but the Cogswell Room offers a private entrance that opens onto a pretty patio for those who must. We were particularly won over by the five suites in the Carriage House, with their spacious sitting areas, jetted tubs, and wet bars; for further privacy, check out the Celeste Cottage, a separate guest house located next door and available as a one- or two-bedroom option, complete with gas fireplace and wet bar. A full breakfast is served in the main house overlooking the grounds; feast on mini Belgian waffles, homemade granola, and such specialties as pear pancakes or chile-cheese eggs. As of September 2004, guests can now have dinner on site at the newly added restaurant known as The Dining Room at the Campbell House. The menu focuses on appetizers and à la carte items and turns out dishes like roast albacore Louis with ratatouille and tapanade or lasagne of summer vegetables. If you like the personalized service of a B&B but don't like to feel hovered over, if you love country-cottage decor but know your limits, this is your kind of place.
$$–$$$$ *AE, DC, DIS, MC, V; no checks; www.campbellhouse.com.* &

MCKENZIE VIEW BED & BREAKFAST
🏵🏵🏵

34922 McKenzie View Dr, Springfield / 541/726-3887 or 888/625-8439
This large, contemporary country home, run by proprietors Scott and Roberta Bolling, is 15 minutes—and seemingly a world—away from downtown Eugene. The only things between your room and the wide, placid lower McKenzie River are the broad back porch, immaculate gardens, lawns dotted with hammocks big enough for two, and a maple-shaded deck overhanging the river's edge. The four rooms, all with private baths, range from modestly priced but comfortable to spacious and expensive; three overlook the river through large picture windows, two have gas fireplaces, and all are well appointed with antiques and quality reproductions, luxurious

comforters, and fluffy pillows. The spacious, ground-floor Woodland Suite is especially appealing: a cherry-wood headboard crowns the queen-size bed; French doors open to a private porch with views of the forest; and the bathroom has both a sunken tub with a view of the garden and a separate tiled shower. It's pricey but an excellent bet for a splurge. Feel free to grab the clippers and a vase and cut your own bouquet in the inn's own cutting garden. Join other guests in the formal dining room and enjoy a generous breakfast featuring sour cream pancakes with blueberry syrup; between meals, you have recourse to the well-stocked mini-fridge and cookie jar. With no TVs or phones in the guest rooms, it's easy to forget the cares of the outside world and create a world of your own; crack the window to enjoy the river's musical riffle all night long.
$–$$$$ *AE, DC, MC, V; checks OK; www.mckenzie-view.com.* &

SECRET GARDEN
❀❀❀
1910 University St, Eugene / 541/484-6755 or 888/484-6755
One of Eugene's most romantic B&Bs, the Secret Garden is tucked into a residential neighborhood just a few steps from the University of Oregon campus and a few minutes' drive from the voluptuous blooms of the Hendricks Park rhododendron gardens. Originally built in 1910 as a farmhouse, this hilltop haven at the corner of 19th and University is now an airy, enchanting 10-room inn. An exquisite bouquet of flowers—and Angus, the house dog—greet you in the great room, featuring the home's original hardwood floors covered with area rugs, plush draperies framing the generous windows, and a baby grand piano. Thoughtfully chosen art and antiques give the inn a refined feeling reminiscent of the Edwardian era, from which the house's namesake novel sprung. Decor in each room varies, from the rusticity of the Barn Owl to the refinement of the Scented Garden. We especially like the Apiary Room, with its French-country style, gas fireplace, and European soaking tub. All rooms have private baths as well as TV/VCRs, mini-fridges, phones, plush robes, and electric bed warmers. At the heart of the inn's own secret garden is an outdoor shower and hot tub, disguised with wattling and shielded from the street by abundant foliage (but—beware—visible to guests upstairs). The inventive, generous breakfasts—always featuring fresh fruit, freshly baked bread, homemade granola, and an entrée—are served in the downstairs dining room. Depending upon the season, noise from boisterous university students may penetrate your romantic cocoon, but aside from this rare occurrence, you'll find the quiet and seclusion you crave here.
$$–$$$$ *AE, DIS, MC, V; checks OK; www.secretgardenbbinn.com.* &

Romantic Restaurants

ADAM'S PLACE
✪✪✪

30 E Broadway, Eugene / 541/344-6948
Whether you're here to pop the question or to celebrate the anniversary of your first kiss, Adam's Place is *the* place for special occasions. From the elegant interior to the highly professional service to the inventive entrées perfectly arranged on the plate, Adam's manages to be both sophisticated and warmly unpretentious. Chef-owner Adam Bernstein, a third-generation restaurateur who trained at the Culinary Institute of America, changes the menu with the seasons. Try the appetizer of salmon and dill potato pancake with dill crème fraîche and salsa, or the grilled eggplant, tomato, and warm duck salad. For your entrée, consider porcini-dusted summer-run Pacific halibut; Misty Isles farm-raised filet mignon; or candied maple leaf duck à l'orange. Vegetarian options are always interesting, desserts are stunning, and the wine list would please the most discriminating oenophile. End the evening with brandy and live jazz in Luna, attached to the restaurant.
$$–$$$ *AE, MC, V; checks OK; dinner Tues–Sat; full bar; reservations recommended; www.adamsplacerestaurant.com.* ⅃

CAFE SORIAH
✪✪

384 W 13th Ave, Eugene / 541/342-4410
Wedged between a dress shop and an auto-repair business west of downtown, Cafe Soriah is a diamond in the rough. Squeeze past the tiny, busy bar to reach the pretty, well-appointed dining room in back, airy and smart with original art and fine woodworking. In good weather, proceed outside to the leafy walled terrace. Chef-owner Ibrahim Hamide focuses the menu on Mediterranean and Middle Eastern cuisines, though he's not afraid to take liberties with tradition. The two of you could make a meal of the signature appetizer plate of hummus, *baba gannoujh*, and stuffed grape leaves, but you'll not want to miss the entrées, which might range from lamb tagine and moussaka to roasted salmon with a coconut-curry sauce, or a spicy Lebanese-style marlin. Among the memorable desserts is a subtly exotic cardamom-scented flan.
$$ *AE, MC, V; checks OK; lunch Mon–Fri, dinner every day; full bar; reservations recommended; www.soriah.com.* ⅃

CHANTERELLE
✪✪✪

207 E 5th St, Eugene / 541/484-4065
Walk in to Chanterelle, and you might think you've been transported to an intimate French *auberge*: a warm welcome from the dining-room captain,

white table linens, and the heady fragrance of Gruyère-topped French onion soup and escargots bubbling in red wine all greet you at once. The muted lighting and uncluttered interior keeps diners' attention focused on one another—and on the food. The small menu reflects chef Ralf Schmidt's classical French culinary sensibilities and hints at his Austrian roots. A dozen entrée choices, from delicate coquilles St.-Jacques to richly sauced tournedos of beef and a classic *zwiebelsteak*, are supplemented by a wide selection of specials, such as spring lamb and Chinook salmon. All come with salad and choice of potatoes or spaetzle. You'll also find a respectable wine list and extraordinary desserts made by the chef's wife, Gisele. Or consider a nightcap and tête-à-tête in Chanterelle's intimate, stylish lounge; there's live music—usually small ensembles—on Friday and Saturday nights. **$$$** *AE, DC, MC, V; checks OK; dinner Tues–Sat; full bar; reservations recommended.* &

EXCELSIOR INN RISTORANTE ITALIANO
◐◐◖

754 E 13th Ave, Eugene / 541/342-6963 or 800/321-6963
Pick your pleasure: a glass of wine and hand-holding across an intimate table at an airy, European-style bar, or snuggling by the fire in the embrace of a formal dining room. The Excelsior offers both—and a sky-lit indoor terrace and walled outdoor courtyard, too. Owner/executive chef Maurizio Paparo has brought his Italian background to both the menu and the interior of this elegant establishment. Try the medallions of elk sauced with a fig-molasses demi-glace, fresh fettucine with chicken in a garlic-rosemary-sherry sauce, or filet mignon topped with a brandy-mushroom demi-glace. Celebrations call for one of pastry chef Milka Babich's outstanding desserts, from a simple crème caramel to the Grand Marnier–infused Maurizio's cake, topped with white and dark chocolate curls. The wine list is extensive. **$$–$$$** *AE, DC, DIS, MC, V; no checks; breakfast, dinner every day, lunch Mon–Fri, brunch Sun; full bar; reservations recommended; www.excelsior inn.com.* &

MARCHÉ
◐◐◖

296 E 5th Ave, Eugene / 541/342-3612
Lovers with refined palates will appreciate the well-crafted combinations of fresh and often organically grown local foodstuffs at the heart of Marché's meals. This sophisticated restaurant on the ground floor of the Fifth Street Public Market celebrates the seasonal Northwest bounty with menus that change daily and entrées prepared with a French sensibility. In fall, pork chops from local farms may come with an autumn fruit-and-onion confit, and the sage-infused roasted leg of venison is accompanied by sweet potato purée, baked apple, and huckleberry sauce. Lunch is lighter, with the addi-

tion of a few *pizzettas* (picture pancetta, delicata squash, sage, and Romano cheese) and sandwiches such as portobello mushroom with sun-dried tomato relish and smoked mozzarella on homemade flatbread. The wine list and dessert menu reflect the same regional leanings and attention to detail. The interior—elegantly hip with dark, gleaming wood and wry artwork—sets the stage for an enjoyable and tasty evening with your sweetheart.
$$–$$$ *AE, DC, DIS, MC, V; checks OK; lunch, dinner every day, brunch Sun; full bar; reservations recommended; www.marcherestaurant.com.* &

RED AGAVE
◗◗

454 Willamette St, Eugene / 541/683-2206
Voted one of the best new restaurants by the *Eugene Weekly* in 2003, Red Agave is a distinctive blend of Nuevo-Latino cuisine. Although it has a quasi high-energy atmosphere, its Latin roots recommend it for romance. (For a quieter experience, arrive later in the evening.) The high ceilings and warm yellow walls make the open floor plan feel lively, vibrant, and a bit sexy. Ask to be seated in a tucked-away corner for more intimacy. Start with a whole-leaf Tijuana Caesar salad for two and move on to local pattypan squash vegetarian tamales or rum-marinated pork loin, pan seared and served with a jalapeño-Jamaica drizzle. Mixmaster Jeff Morgenthaler adds his own special twist to the full bar, and desserts range from spiced Mexican chocolate cheesecake with warm caramel–arbol chile sauce to an aged manchego cheese plate served with quince paste, cayenne, toasted almonds, and Palace Bakery baguette. Quite a mouthful, whatever you choose.
$$–$$$ *MC, V; local checks only; dinner Mon–Sat; full bar; reservations recommended.* &

RING OF FIRE
◗◗

1099 Chambers St, Eugene / 541/344-6475
In the mood for Asian cuisine? Your sweetie will be impressed by Ring of Fire's elegant, tranquil atmosphere; the tasty, festive tropical drinks from the stylish Lava Lounge; and the flavorful, well-prepared dishes, none of which will set you back much more than dinner at the humbler Chinese-American place down the street. The menu claims inspiration from many Pacific Rim cuisines, but mainly Thai and Indonesian. Start with a Korean-style vegetable tempura served with Japanese *tagaragi* spice, or a taste of beef satay with black bean–ginger sauce. Thai-style curries are coconut-based, and noodle dishes include the reliable phad Thai as well as *phad se yu*, with sweet wheat noodles and broccoli. Eat in, or rent a romantic video and get it to go; takeout is available until midnight.
$$ *MC, V; no checks; lunch, dinner every day; full bar; reservations recommended; www.ringoffirerestaurant.com.* &

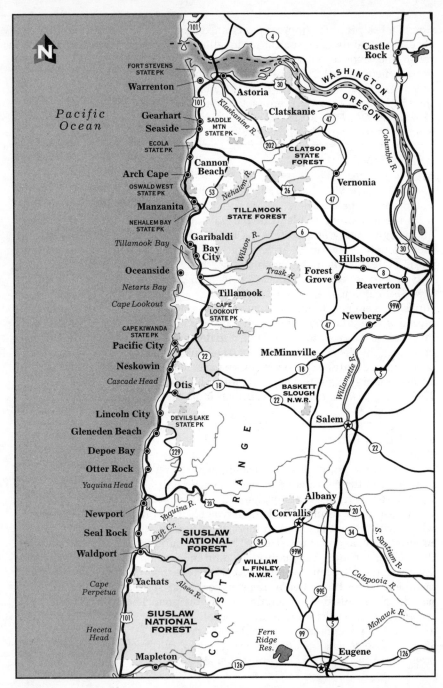

"The sound of a kiss is not so loud as that of a cannon, but its echo lasts a great deal longer."
—OLIVER WENDELL HOLMES

♡ OREGON COAST

You could travel far and wide and never come upon a stretch of highway quite like Oregon's Highway 101. This winding coastal road runs the length of the state, and almost every mile of it showcases awe-inspiring scenery. Thank goodness for the many turnoffs, parks, trails, coves, and inlets, where you can stop and drink in the view at your own leisurely pace—or satisfy the urge for a scenery-inspired kiss. Thank goodness, too, for the gorgeous coastal towns where the beauty of this area can be experienced for days at a time.

Constant changes in the weather enhance the boundless drama of the Oregon Coast. At times the mixture of fog and sea mist settles like a gauzy veil over the region. At other times, dramatic tempests brew on the horizon. Yet even on the calmest summer days, the siren song of the waves breaking over beaches, headlands, and rocks is simply spellbinding. Time shared on the Oregon Coast can rekindle your relationship with the world—not to mention with each other. Not only is the scenery stupendous, but also the two of you can amuse yourselves with a multitude of activities here, hiking through coastal rain forest, beachcombing for agates, clamming, exploring tide pools, kite flying, whale watching, or building a toasty bonfire.

On the northern coast, romance is easy to find in quaint, cultured little towns like Cannon Beach, while the central coast offers both the sophisticated pleasures of boutiques and fine dining and the charm of working harbors where fresh seafood abounds. Farther south, the remote terrain feels wild and unsettled—the perfect setting for romance-infused exploration. Driving the entire coast would take the better part of a day, even without stops. So you're better off choosing a region and really getting acquainted with it. If, however, you have the time, a few days spent meandering from one port to the next would certainly make for a memorable journey.

NORTHERN COAST

ROMANTIC HIGHLIGHTS

First-time visitors to the northern Oregon Coast will find that each town, from Astoria to Seaside to Cannon Beach, offers a distinctly different flavor, and each has charms of its own. Wherever you decide to stay, be sure and find a front-row seat in the evening—your hotel deck, the beach, a park bench—to watch the spectacular sunsets that have earned the Oregon Coast its nickname, "Sunset Empire." On a clear evening, as the sun descends to the sea, you'll watch its rays infuse the lavender-blue dusk with brilliant shades of golden amber and blaze red before they disappear completely and the sky changes to cobalt and then, finally, inky black.

The northernmost romantic destination here is Astoria, a picturesque town on the mouth of the Columbia River characterized by its working waterfront. The ships, sailboats, fishing vessels, and tugs create a lively panorama of color and commerce as they ferry their goods in and out of port. Although parts of Astoria can seem industrial and run-down, its stunning views, hillside neighborhoods of brightly hued Craftsman and Victorian homes, and rich history more than make up for this drawback. For an excellent introduction to the waterfront, cuddle up with your favorite travel companion on the **Riverfront Trolley**, which runs daily during the summer and Friday through Sunday the rest of the year (catch it at marked stops all along the riverfront). The 4-mile journey along the river over old railway lines takes in the recently expanded Columbia River Maritime Museum, many historic buildings, working boat crews, and, of course, beautiful views. Once you've enjoyed the scenery up close, get a bird's-eye view by climbing the spiraling staircase of the **Astoria Column** (1 Coxcomb Hill; 503/325-2963; open 8am–dusk). Built as a tribute to the Lewis and Clark Expedition, the 125-foot-tall structure has been inspiring lofty kisses since 1926. Daylight brings sweeping views of surrounding rivers, mountains, the bay, and the ocean, along with the 4-mile-long Astoria-Megler Bridge, which connects Oregon and Washington. At night, be sure to catch the newly lighted column twinkling in all its luminous glory high about the town. With a long list of movies filmed here to its credit, Astoria fascinates film fans, and romantic visitors won't feel left out. It was at a restaurant at West Mooring Basin that Arnold Schwarzenegger traded passionate kisses with co-star Penelope Ann Miller in *Kindergarten Cop.* As local lore has it, boat owners helped set the mood by leaving their lights on during the nighttime filming. The stone and marble building that houses the **Columbia River Day Spa** (1215 Duane St; 503/325-7721) is the sort of grand old building that keeps Hollywood coming. You'll want to indulge in the spa's Couple's Package, which includes a warm-up in the sauna, side-by-side Swedish massages, and a hot soak in the Japanese geisha tub.

At first glance, there's almost nothing romantic about **Seaside**, a town 20 miles south of Astoria, where the ocean has been obscured by hyperactive motel developers with little sensitivity for the landscape. In the summer, families flock here by the thousands to frequent the arcades, mini-malls, and popular beachfront. Fortunately, you can still find plenty of places to kiss on the vast beaches at the north and south ends of town. In the off-season, you might even find yourselves alone on Seaside's famous Prom, the mile-and-a-half-long cement trail that meanders along the beachfront near the thundering surf. Stay away from the video arcades and the kid-lined streets of the town center and you may find Seaside more romantic than you had hoped—this is especially true, of course, when school is in session and there is nary a child in sight.

Cannon Beach, just a few miles south of Seaside, is a decidedly quieter and more sophisticated destination. With more than 7 miles of firm sand and rolling waves, this town beckons dreamers and lovers alike to roll up their jeans, hold hands, and stroll at the edge of the churning surf. Start your day with a fresh-baked Danish at the **Cannon Beach Bakery** (240 N Hemlock St; 503/436-0399), then walk down the beach to the base of the free-standing monolith called **Haystack Rock**, the third largest of its kind in the world and a true natural wonder. At low tide, you'll find tidal pools alive with sea stars, hermit crabs, sea anemones, and other marine life, while seabirds—cormorants, harlequin ducks, pigeon guillemots, and black oystercatchers, to name a few—soar overhead. Back in town, wander Hemlock Street's art galleries and boutiques, and drop in on a glass-blowing demonstration at **Icefire Glassworks** (corner of Hemlock and Gower Sts; 503/436-2359), where visitors can watch artists from a special viewing area. After lunch, get an ice cream cone from **Osburn's Ice Creamery** (240 N Hemlock St; 503/436-2578), then sit side by side on the sprawling front porch and watch the world go by.

Another romantic highlight nearby is **Hug Point** (8 miles south of Cannon Beach; 800/551-6949). Even when the parking lot is full, there is still plenty of room at this windswept beach in Tolovana Park to make you feel as if you have the place to yourselves. If you're here during low tide, explore the soaring cliffs along the beach, gouged with caves and crevasses of varying shapes and proportions, and dotted with tide pools where you can observe the abundant and varied marine life.

If you're looking for the peace and quiet of a relatively undiscovered shore, spend some time in lovely **Manzanita**, set between the Pacific Ocean and the base of Neahkahnie Mountain. Although this little town has been steadily growing in recent years, it still qualifies as tranquil and uncrowded. What to do here? Treat yourselves to a cup of organic coffee and a homemade pastry at **Manzanita News & Espresso** (500 Laneda Ave; 503/368-7450), or try flying a kite, beachcombing, or—that favorite of sweethearts everywhere—nothing at all.

Couples who love being on the water in addition to admiring it from afar flock to the town of **Wheeler**, just 18 miles south of Cannon Beach, for excellent kayaking. When the summer sun shines and the gentle waters of the Nehalem River gleam invitingly, this sport can be incredibly romantic. What could be more relaxing than cutting through the water with a soft breeze on your face and your loved one in tow? Follow the curve of the river south past country meadows and groves of trees to Nehalem Bay, or simply spend the afternoon exploring the river's edge. Calm waters make this a relaxing trip even for beginners, and the folks at the **Wheeler Marina** (278 Marine Dr; 503/368-6055) will make sure you paddle away with all the information you need.

Access & Information

Driving is your best bet to and from the northern Oregon Coast. From Seattle, take Interstate 5 to Longview, Washington, cross the interstate bridge, and follow Highway 30 west to Astoria. From downtown Portland, take Highway 26 west (the road traverses the Coast Range mountains and can be dangerous in winter) to its intersection with Highway 101 at the Cannon Beach Junction. Highway 6 from Portland isn't quite as direct a route to the north coast, but it's also popular. Highway 101 (also known as the Coast Highway) is the only road along Oregon's coast. The **State Welcome Center** (111 W Marine Dr, Astoria; 503/325-6311 or 800/875-6807) and the **Seaside Visitors Bureau** (7 N Roosevelt Dr, Seaside; 503/738-3097 or 888/306-2326) are good starting points. The **Oregon Coast Visitors Association** (888/628-2101;visittheoregoncoast.com) also offers helpful information.

Romantic Lodgings

ASTORIA INN BED AND BREAKFAST
🌣🌣🌣

3391 Irving Ave, Astoria / 503/325-8153 or 800/718-8153
Although the Astoria Inn is just minutes from downtown, its location above the city provides expansive views of the Columbia River and good old-fashioned peace and quiet—making it a good place to kiss. Set high on a grassy knoll in a residential neighborhood, this gray-and-white home is fronted by a small veranda. All four guest rooms are cozy retreats with private baths, inviting comforters, and lovely window treatments crowned with dried flowers. Three rooms are located on the second floor and share a small common area. The rooms named for Cape Lookout and Cape Meares face

the river and afford the best views. Our favorite, however, is Cape Virginia, with its dark green walls and a whimsical canopy above the bed; stained-glass windows, a claw-foot tub, and a pedestal sink embellish the modest bathroom. The fourth room is situated off the dining room, which could make sleeping through breakfast difficult if other guests prove talkative in the morning. However, you won't want to miss breakfast, which may include warm Dutch pastries, French toast, or homemade quiche.
$ *DIS, MC, V; checks OK; www.astoriainnbb.com.*

CLEMENTINE'S BED AND BREAKFAST
♥♥《

847 Exchange St, Astoria / 503/325-2005 or 800/521-6801
This stylish Italianate Victorian, built in 1888, is conveniently located on the edge of downtown. Innkeepers Judith and Cliff Taylor possess a wealth of knowledge about Astoria and the surrounding region, and their B&B has a pleasantly lived-in look, with a baby grand piano and a crystal chandelier in the living room and a bevy of antiques throughout, including a collection of vintage glassware and bowls. Five rooms feature private baths, antique wrought-iron beds, and warm, welcoming floral decor. For romance, book an upstairs room with a private balcony and captivating river vista; the spacious Clementine's Suite, done in shades of apricot and green with separate sitting area and gas fireplace, is our favorite. Judith serves one of Astoria's finest breakfasts: you might feast on hand-crafted wild-mushroom omelets and baked French toast stuffed with cream, cottage cheese, and peaches, plus a stunning array of sweet treats.
$$ *AE, DIS, MC, V; checks OK; www.clementines-bb.com.* &

EAGLE'S VIEW BED AND BREAKFAST
♥♥《

37975 Brooten Rd, Pacific City / 503/965-7600 or 888/846-3292
Set inland about 70 miles south of Cannon Beach, and surrounded by gently rolling countryside, Eagle's View is hands-down the best kissing bargain along the Oregon Coast. The house, constructed in 1995, commands sweeping views of Nestucca Bay from its perch atop a quiet hill. Four acres of nature and all its glories can be yours for a weekend at unexpectedly reasonable prices. All five guest rooms are comfortably appointed with goose-down comforters, European armoires, and plenty of sunshine. The Garden Room downstairs offers a private entrance and a whirlpool tub; however, we prefer the four rooms upstairs, with their high knotty-pine ceilings and serene vistas. Love Spoken Here and Whimsy boast whirlpool tubs and incredible views of Nestucca Bay, while the remaining two rooms overlook the forest. Dine in the privacy of your own room or join other guests downstairs in the Great Room for fresh fruit, homemade pastries, and innkeepers Steve and Toni Westmoreland's famous German pancakes or Nestucca Eggs:

scrambled eggs mixed with smoked salmon, cream cheese, and green onions, served over a warm croissant.
$$ DC, DIS, MC, V; checks OK; www.eaglesviewbb.com. &

GILBERT INN
♥♥♥
341 Beach Dr, Seaside / 503/738-9770 or 800/410-9770
A white picket fence surrounds this picturesque yellow Victorian, located just a block from Seaside's popular beachfront. In the height of summer, when throngs of tourists are a force to be reckoned with, the inn's location can feel like a disadvantage—until you step inside, that is. Once you've checked in, you'll find that Seaside's crowds simply fade into oblivion. Even the smallest of the inn's 10 guest rooms offers all kinds of comfort and charm. Fir paneling gives homespun appeal to rooms in the older wing, where we discovered the best getaway of all: the Turret Room. A circular wall of windows allows loads of sunlight into this cozy room, which is furnished with an inviting four-poster cherry-wood bed. The newer wing contains a series of brightly accented suites featuring wicker furniture, handsome wood armoires, country fabrics, and private bathrooms. Fluffy down comforters and armfuls of pillows embellish the antique beds in every room. Raspberry French toast or blueberry pancakes might be featured in the generous morning meal, which is served at individual white wrought-iron tables tucked into a lovely pink breakfast nook on the main floor.
$$ AE, DIS, MC, V; checks OK; www.gilbertinn.com.

HOTEL ELLIOTT
♥♥♥♥
357 12th St, Astoria / 503/325-2222 or 877/EST-1924
The Hotel Elliott, Astoria's newest boutique hotel—and arguably its most luxurious—is an old city treasure originally built in 1924 and made new in 2003 with a $4 million renovation. In the lobby, Honduran mahogany, period carpet, and original oversize cove moldings set a distinguished tone. The 32 rooms come with 440-count Egyptian cotton sheets, goose down pillows, featherbeds, and sumptuous terry robes. Spa tubs, heated stone bathroom floors, marble vanities, and spun glass sinks add to the undeniably lush setting. For the ultimate indulgence, the top floor, five-room Presidential Suite with petite baby grand piano (complete with cassette and player piano mode for those less adept at tinkling the ivories), handcrafted mahogany finishes, and private circular staircase to the rooftop garden wins our most enthusiastic nod. Whatever room you cozy up in, on clear nights you'll want to check out the rooftop for stargazing by the outdoor fire pit. If Astoria's moody weather prevails, in-room fireplaces, wet bars, and designer furniture make staying in a treat. You'll also find a CD/DVD player in your room and an up-to-date library of DVD selections—some of the classics, too—at

the front desk. The entire menu from the neighboring Schooner 12th Street Bistro (see Romantic Restaurants) is available by room service morning 'til night, and if you can't find it on the menu you may be able to persuade the very amenable staff to fetch it for you. Do slip downstairs to the Vintner's Room wine cellar/bar to soak up the Casablanca atmosphere and raise a toast to you two. A wine reception is held every evening from 5pm to 6pm, and summer weekends will find the rooftop deck swinging with live music, locally brewed beers, and barbecue. With views of the mighty Columbia River for a backdrop, it's a definite scene setter for romance. In the morning, choose between a complimentary fresh-fruit-and-muffin continental breakfast or discounted gourmet fare at the Schooner. Better yet, stay in bed and have it brought to you.
$$$–$$$$ *AE, DC, DIS, MC, V; checks OK; www.hotelelliott.com.* ⅄

INN AT CANNON BEACH
❂❂❂

3215 S Hemlock St, Cannon Beach / 503/436-9085 or 800/321-6304
While the Inn at Cannon Beach, one of the town's newer lodgings, does not have ocean views, it offers amenities you don't often find in a coastal setting: lush green lawns, a koi pond, and gardens—all meant to be enjoyed by romance seekers from the Adirondack chairs dotting the property. Four rustic natural-wood bungalows, with private decks and porches, house the rooms and are tucked among old trees—lending the property a surprisingly secluded feel. An art gallery on site gives the place an air of culture, while inside the bungalows, casual but chic furnishings in natural tones and nature themes suggest simple sophistication. All rooms come with fireplaces and kitchenettes; eleven rooms offer corner Jacuzzis for two. In the morning, hot and cold cereals, waffles, bagels, muffins, fresh fruit, and juices are served in the art gallery.
$$$ *AE, DC, DIS, MC, V; checks OK; www.atcannonbeach.com.* ⅄

THE INN AT MANZANITA
❂❂❂

67 Laneda Ave, Manzanita / 503/368-6754
Set amid coastal pines and spruce trees, this contemporary Northwest inn sits a mere 200 feet from Manzanita's 7-mile stretch of beach. Guest rooms in the main building suggest a hybrid of sunny log cabin and comfortable hotel room, with pine and cedar walls that rise dramatically to form vaulted ceilings, and private decks that afford partial views of the ocean through the treetops. The rooms are further enhanced by all the romantic frills a couple could want: two-person Jacuzzi tubs; gas fireplaces; wet bars; and firm, cozy beds with down comforters. Adjacent to the main building is a stunning two-level cottage called the North Building. The four units here are decorated in soothing neutral tones and wood paneling, and include Jacuzzi

tubs and small decks. Captain's beds with down comforters are tucked into snug, sunlit nooks separated from the living area by curtains. The downstairs units are comfortable and intimate; the upstairs units feature vaulted ceilings, treetop views, and, in the northern units, a skylight over the bed for the ultimate in cozy stargazing. Considering the reasonable prices and the luxurious Northwest-style comfort, the Inn at Manzanita could easily become one of your favorite getaways along the coast. *$$–$$$ MC, V; checks OK; www.innatmanzanita.com.*

OCEAN LODGE
◖◖◖◖

2864 S Pacific St, Cannon Beach / 503/436-2241 or 888/777-4047
The newest oceanfront lodging in Cannon Beach, Ocean Lodge combines rustic elegance—think open-beamed ceilings and massive stone hearths—with the nostalgic style of an old-time beach resort. The result is truly delightful. Reclaimed-hardwood floors from an old warehouse and thick beam stairs that were once local gymnasium bleachers add a timeless warmth. The decor, in neutral and dark tones, is tasteful and understated. In-room amenities include corner Jacuzzi tubs and fireplaces, and 33 of the main lodge's 37 rooms have oceanfront views. While most of the rooms are similar, units 207 and 309 feature vaulted ceilings and bigger oceanfront decks. Bungalows across the street lack the views, but they make up for it in cozy privacy and also come with Jacuzzis and king-size beds. Service is first-rate, as are the locally baked breakfast goodies. *$$$–$$$$ AE, DC, DIS, MC, V; checks OK; www.theoceanlodge.com.* ♿

ROSEBRIAR HOTEL
◖◖◖

636 14th St, Astoria / 503/325-7427 or 800/487-0224
Recognized as a historic landmark, this magnificent 1902 Neoclassical home has been beautifully restored. Even better, it retains much of its original charm, while offering modern-day comforts. Inside, you'll find a fir-paneled front desk and a cozy parlor with overstuffed floral couches, elegant window treatments, and a fireplace with a wooden mantel. Ten guest rooms are handsomely decorated with sage walls, mahogany furnishings, and elegant moldings. Our top vote for romance goes to the new Captain's Suite on the third floor, with its queen-size sleigh bed, large soaking tub with river views, breakfast nook, and sitting room with fireplace. Adjacent to the hotel and its courtyard, the 1885 carriage house offers the most privacy, as well as a kitchenette, a fireplace, a jetted tub, and stained-glass windows. In the morning, the seductive aromas of the homemade full breakfast—think French toast, eggs Benedict, or sweet potato pancakes—will lure you to the

dining area, where you can either take your place at one of the tightly spaced tables or get your breakfast to take back to your room.
$$–$$$ *AE, DC, DIS, MC, V; checks OK; www.rosebriar.net.* &

ROSE RIVER INN BED & BREAKFAST
❍❍❬

1510 Franklin Ave, Astoria / 503/325-7175 or 888/876-0028
With a blush-pink exterior and lush gardens teeming with flowering shrubs, evergreens, and climbing rosebushes, the Rose River Inn is a favorite for weddings, anniversaries, and getaways of all kinds. Finnish proprietor Kati Tuominen-Maki lends European flair to this circa-1912 lodging, which exemplifies American four-square architecture. Our pick for the most romantic room is the Rose Room, complete with fireplace and canopied queen-size bed. For something a little different, reserve the River Suite and sweat away your worries in a Finnish sauna paneled in Alaskan yellow cedar. Follow this with a soak in the claw-foot tub, then gaze in utter relaxation at the Columbia River from your private sun porch. If it's a chilly evening, curl up with a warm beverage in the glow of the parlor fireplace. If you're in the mood for some pampering, ask Kati, a licensed masseuse, for an in-house massage.
$$ *DIS, MC, V; checks OK; www.roseriverinn.com.* &

SANDLAKE COUNTRY INN
❍❍❍❍

8505 Galloway Rd, Cloverdale / 503/965-6745
When planning a romantic getaway to the Oregon Coast, most couples look for oceanfront accommodations, or at least an ocean view. While this attitude is perfectly understandable, it has the unfortunate drawback of depriving amorous travelers of the wonderful Sandlake Country Inn. Bountiful flower gardens fill the front yard of this 111-year-old farmhouse hidden on a quiet country road off the Three Capes Scenic Loop, about 10 miles north of Pacific City. The inn's countrified, farmlike surroundings give little hint of the elegance and luxury that await you in the four very private suites. The spacious Starlight Suite is situated behind a curtain at the top of the stairs in the original farmhouse; the four connecting rooms in this suite have doors that can be closed for privacy. A double-sided fireplace warms the suite's master bedroom and extra sitting room; you'll also find a TV/VCR, French doors that open onto a private deck, and a wood-paneled bathroom with a whirlpool tub for two. Downstairs in the Timber Room, sumptuous linens cover a four-poster king-size bed; French doors open onto a private deck and gardens; Oriental rugs cover the hardwood floors; and a large bathroom boasts a sunken whirlpool tub set behind lace curtains. The gracious innkeepers tend to all the details, including freshly baked cookies and sweet apple cider, to ensure that your stay is comfortable. In the morning,

an overwhelmingly generous three-course breakfast is delivered for you to enjoy undisturbed in your room.
$$ *DIS, MC, V; checks OK; www.sandlakecountryinn.com.* &

ST. BERNARDS
⬡⬡⬡

3 E Ocean Rd, Arch Cape / 503/436-2800 or 800/436-2848
Reminiscent of an Old World castle and located just a few miles south of Cannon Beach, the expansive wood-shingled chateau that is St. Bernards is like a treasure chest waiting to be explored. New owner Barbara Dau adds warmth and hospitality, and has already built a reputation as a fabulous cook. Plush white carpets extend throughout the house, which is accented with French doors, beautiful tile work, and pieces from the owner's private art collection. The inn's seven guest rooms are bona fide masterpieces, and all of them enjoy views of the ocean, across Highway 101. White lace and pale peach walls decorate the Tower Room, which hosts a Louis XIV carved bed and a raised sitting area with a handsome settee beneath a pointed turret. Everything about the Tapestry Room is spacious, including its king-size bed and large bathroom with two-person soaking tub. When the gas fireplace is lit, this room becomes especially cozy. If it's the French countryside you're hankering for, request the Provence Room, with its cathedral ceiling, authentic French linens, terra-cotta floors, and French doors that lead to a private patio. A wood-accented tiled Jacuzzi is an added luxury here. Breakfast at St. Bernards is an all-out affair, with gourmet goodies like broiled grapefruit, butter-almond shortbread cake with crème anglaise, and salmon soufflé on a bed of wilted spinach with cucumber sour cream sauce.
$$$ *AE, DIS, MC, V; checks OK; minimum-stay requirement on weekends; www.st-bernards.com.* &

STEPHANIE INN
⬡⬡⬡⬡

2740 S Pacific, Cannon Beach / 503/436-2221 or 800/633-3466
When it comes to luxurious beachfront accommodations, look no further than the Stephanie Inn. The surf practically laps at the foundations of this New England–style inn and its adjacent Carriage House, and a fire is always glowing in the river-rock hearth in the front parlor, where overstuffed sofas, impressive wood detailing, and hardwood floors create an inviting and elegant ambience. Aperitifs, wine, and hors d'oeuvres are served here in the early evening, accompanied by delicious sunsets. The inn's 46 sophisticated rooms are all equipped with plush terry-cloth robes and four-poster beds made up with beautiful floral linens, and nearly every room has a private deck, a gas fireplace, and a corner Jacuzzi or whirlpool tub in its spacious bathroom. The Mountain View rooms are the least expensive—but also the

least romantic, since they face the parking lot. If you can, splurge on an Ocean Front room; the views of the vast sandy beach, crashing surf, and jagged sea stacks are indescribably beautiful. A complimentary breakfast buffet is served in the inn's mountain-view dining room.
$$$$ *AE, DC, DIS, MC, V; checks OK; www.stephanie-inn.com.*

TURK'S LODGINGS
◐◐◐

50 Hwy 101, Cannon Beach / 503/436-1809
Good news: a renovation has restored the Turk's reputation as one of the Oregon Coast's most extraordinary places to kiss. This unusual house, crafted from rough-cut spruce and fir and supported by stilts on one side, juts out over the western slope of a steep, forested hillside, where a wrap-around deck offers compelling views of the Oregon coastline. Designed to accommodate one party, the interior is equally stunning, with cathedral-style pine ceilings, a sunken kitchen, expansive floor-to-ceiling windows, and a wood-burning stove that glows hot enough to warm the entire house. In the spacious two-level master bedroom, you'll find an open rock-lined shower and an oversize spa tub overlooking the trees. You can also get cozy under a patchwork quilt on the king-size bed and watch the fire crackling in the stone hearth. If you're looking for something more affordable, ask about the unassuming cottage and studio next door, with quiet views of the trees and distant ocean. The studio offers a kitchenette, a queen-size bed with floral accents, and an electric fireplace; the cottage has a full kitchen, skylights, a wood-burning stove, a sectional sofa with ocean view, a Jacuzzi tub, and a separate bedroom with king-size bed. Both choices are more homey than romantic (worthy of only a two-lip rating), but are charming in their own right.
$$$–$$$$ *MC, V; checks OK; www.clatsop.com/turkslodging.*

Romantic Restaurants

BAKED ALASKA
◐◐

1 12th St, Ste 1, Astoria / 503/325-7414
It's hard to believe that this charming little waterfront restaurant grew out of a mobile soup wagon in Alaska. Back in the '80s, owners Chris and Jennifer Holen coined the phrase "Have soup, will travel," and took their wagon on the road all over the 49th state. Today, the pair has finally retired the wagon and created a romantic little spot in Astoria. Their signature dishes include Salad Niçoise—seared albacore tuna atop mixed greens with fresh veggies, hard-boiled eggs, and served with whole grain mustard vinai-grette—and Campfire Salmon, marinated with the restaurant's own Alaska

Amber–barbecue sauce. There are also duck à l'orange, Dungeness crab fettucine, and sourdough pizza with toppings such as grilled chicken and barbecue sauce, or shrimp and garlic. To make dining that much sweeter, every seat in the place comes with its own view of the Columbia River.
$$ *AE, DC, DIS, MC, V; no checks; lunch, dinner every day; full bar; reservations not necessary.* &

BISTRO
◐◐◖

263 N Hemlock St, Cannon Beach / 503/436-2661
This Tudor-style cottage is nestled within a cluster of small shops a comfortable distance off the main thoroughfare in Cannon Beach. Past the bustling bar area, you'll find a snug dining room handsomely appointed with dark wood trim, blue tablecloths, and glowing candles. You might begin your feast with mouthwatering Manila clams dipped in herbed broth and drawn butter, then move on to roasted chicken breast stuffed with goat cheese and herbs over shallot and wild mushroom sauce, or sockeye salmon served with leeks, shiitake mushrooms, and soy-garlic sauce. All entrées may be ordered à la carte or as part of a full dinner that includes soup or salad and fresh bread. Bistro is slightly noisier than most places we recommend for amorous encounters, but tables are sufficiently spaced to ensure the privacy for a kiss or two.
$$$ *MC, V; local checks only; dinner every day (Wed–Mon Nov–Mar); full bar; reservations recommended.* &

GUNDERSON'S CANNERY CAFÉ
◐◐

1 6th St, Astoria / 503/325-8642
If you and your sweetie are pining for a view, you'd have a hard time finding a better one than this. Located in a 100-year-old former cannery building, this restaurant features excellent views of marine activity on the Columbia River from every one of its tables. Decor, much of it salvaged from the original structure, includes old fir floors, nautical charts, and vintage glass windows. Everything on the menu is made daily from scratch; fish is fresh and caught locally. The clam chowder is authentic and the panini du jour is made with thick slices of focaccia. Meat eaters can indulge in a blackened rib-eye or teriyaki-glazed flank steak. Just added: a new full-service bar showcasing the best regional wines. Once you're sated, wander down to the end of the 6th Street Pier or out to the riverfront viewing tower for even better panoramas.
$$ *DC, DIS, MC, V; checks OK; lunch and dinner every day (no dinner Mon Nov–Mar); full bar; reservations recommended; www.cannerycafe. com.*

JP'S
◖◖◖

240 N Hemlock, Cannon Beach / 503/436-0908
The European-style JP's has moved but still offers the same simple and sophisticated dining experience. Now located in the Coaster Village, the new JP's is larger and loftier, with sky-high ceilings, fine art, mahogany tables, and white linen. Even the bathrooms—works of art in purple and orange—win raves. Chef Bill Pappas calls his award-winning fare of seafood, poultry, pasta, or beef "à la minute," which means as fresh as possible. While that may mean waiting just a bit longer for your food, it's worth the wait. The crab cakes are moist and surprisingly creamy, yet still crisp on the outside. The clam chowder, flavored with a touch of salmon and topped with hazelnuts, is utterly delicious. The award-winning wine list offers a nicely balanced selection of Oregon wines, an outstanding array of Washington vintages, and some unusual bottles that might spice up a romantic dinner, such as a Girardet baco noir or a Hood River zinfandel.
$$ *DIS, MC, V; local checks only; lunch, dinner Mon–Sat; beer and wine; reservations recommended.* ♿

PACIFIC WAY BAKERY AND CAFÉ
◖◖

601 Pacific Wy, Gearhart / 503/738-0245
If you want to taste absolutely sensational baked goods, this rustic, unassuming cafe is the place to go. For a scrumptious afternoon snack, order hot espresso and fresh cinnamon rolls for two. The cafe's cheerful yellow exterior is set off by a green-striped awning; inside, natural wood tables with rush-seated Italian maple chairs surround a wood-burning fireplace. An eclectic array of old-fashioned knickknacks and photographs decorates the walls, and a small brick courtyard offers outdoor seating in nice weather next to an Italian fountain. Though the staff is laid-back, the room is immaculate and all the food nicely presented. Lunch is superior, with generous sandwiches, delicious soups, fresh breads, and exact seasonings. Dinners—casual and relaxed—feature world fusion dishes accented by fresh herbs.
$$ *MC, V; checks OK; lunch, dinner Thurs–Mon; beer and wine; reservations recommended for dinner.*

ROSEANNA'S RESTAURANT
◖◖

1490 Pacific St, Oceanside / 503/842-7351
Roseanna's is Oceanside's only oceanfront restaurant. In fact, except for the little coffee shop down the road, it's the only restaurant in town, period. But even if there were a number of dining establishments to choose from, we would still recommend eating here. While the atmosphere is easygoing, the kitchen takes its job seriously, producing delicious and healthy breakfasts,

lunches, and dinners. Views of the ocean and Three Arch Rocks offshore help make meals memorable, and the food is simply a delight. The menu highlights regional cuisine and fresh seafood; expect salads chock-full of crisp, fresh vegetables, and a variety of satisfying, creative pasta dishes. In the evening, nature prepares another treat to enhance your meal: an ambrosial sunset for two.

$$ *MC, V; local checks only; breakfast Sun, lunch, dinner every day; full bar; no reservations.* &

SCHOONER 12TH STREET BISTRO

360 12th St, Astoria / 503/325-7882
One of the city's newest restaurants, the Schooner is located in the up-and-coming downtown neighborhood some have dubbed "the side street of dreams." The character here is decidedly contemporary, with local art, custom African mahogany furniture, and wide open windows for people watching. The downstairs level is not the most intimate, but for those first-date nights, it's the place to see and be seen. Move upstairs for a little more privacy, but beware the decor is a work in progress. Food here is fresh, with an international flair. Appetizers and light fare are the bistro forte, but dinner specials every night merit a taste, too. Some of our favorites: Dungeness crab fritters (rich local seafood with just the right seasoned crunch); spicy Cajun shrimp; Northwest cioppino, so juicy and dripping with seafood you'll wish you had a bib; and who can resist a down-home plate of spaghetti and meatballs once in awhile? All wine is available by the glass and martinis are a house specialty, which is how the Schooner's Lemon Drop came to be known as the best in town.

$$ *AE, DC, DIS, MC, V; no checks; breakfast, lunch, dinner every day; full bar; reservations recommended for dinner.* &

CENTRAL COAST

ROMANTIC HIGHLIGHTS

At the heart of the central Oregon Coast is Newport, a little town blessed with both a bay and an ocean. On one side of town you'll find the calm waters of Yaquina Bay; on the other, the mighty Pacific. Joining the two, the Yaquina Bay Bridge is a picturesque arc of graceful steel and the perfect backdrop for romantic photos. Newport is also home to one of the largest fishing fleets on the coast—fishermen sell their catch fresh from the docks—and to two lighthouses and the aquarium that once held the now world-famous orca Keiko.

Other destinations on this part of the coast include Depoe Bay, a colorful little town with a stretch of shops set right on the water's edge; it's Oregon's prime spot for whale watching. Yachats is an artsy community harbored in the Siuslaw National Forest, and one of the few places where the coastal mountain range actually merges with the shoreline. The hiking terrain here ranks with the best on the coast, and the beaches are relatively remote and empty. Better yet, Yachats has some of the most impressive and romantic bed-and-breakfasts in the area. Lincoln City is a bit too commercial to be truly romantic, but it's an excellent place to take advantage of Oregon's tax-free outlet stores.

Start your day with a cup of something hot and fresh goodies from **Panini Bakery** (232 NW Coast, Newport; 541/265-5033) in Newport, then make your way to the **Yaquina Head Lighthouse** (follow the signs off Hwy 101 in Newport; 541/574-3100), which is considered by some to be one of the most beautiful lighthouses in the country. The stately structure stands at the tip of a coastal headland jutting far out into the Pacific. Beyond the lighthouse there's a grassy hillside of wildflowers and sea grass (did someone say picnic?). Hike the nature trails that lead to magical views or wander down to Cobble Beach, made of basalt rock, where you'll find tidal pools, harbor seals, and maybe, if you visit during migration times (Mar to May; Dec to early Feb), a gray whale. For more marine life, visit the **Oregon Coast Aquarium** (2820 SE Ferry Slip Rd, Newport; 541/867-3474). Tucked into the woods on Yaquina Bay, this surprisingly romantic aquarium houses the largest walk-through seabird aviary in North America. Passages of the Deep is an undersea exhibit viewed from a 200-foot underwater tunnel, with nearly 360-degree views of sharks, wolf eels, and 5,000 other sea creatures.

Easily the most romantic neighborhood in Newport is **Nye Beach**, comprising several blocks of oceanfront property lined with quaint boutiques and shops. Sample wine at the **Nye Beach Gallery** (715 NW 3rd; 541/265-3292), enjoy the local artwork at **Tsunami Ceramics** (310 NW Coast; 541/574-7958), or treat yourself to high tea at **Tea & Tomes** (716 NW Beach; 541/265-2867). With the beach right at your feet, it's always the right time for a sandy stroll. Or cross Highway 101 to the **Bay Front**, where you'll find a colorful mix of fine art and funky souvenirs. Grab a light lunch at **The Coffee House** (156 SW Bay Blvd; 541/265-6263) and watch the boats going out to sea. If you're staying in a place with a kitchen, buy fresh ingredients at any of the local grocery stores or seafood shops and cook up a tasty dinner; or purchase fresh cooked crab from the fishermen on the dock, grab a blanket, and nestle someplace private on the beach for a seafood feast for two.

If you happen to be in town when the **Nye Beach Writers Series** (www. writersontheedge.org) is hosting its monthly Saturday-night reading series, stop by for an evening of words, wit, and good cheer. Visiting writers read from their work; then the stage is turned over to aspiring authors for an open mike. Perhaps there's a love poem in your pocket you've been meaning to share? The series is under new direction and the location will change, but you'll find all the information you need at their Web site.

There are also lots of romantic outdoor activities available on the coast. Rent a kayak for two at the **Embarcadero Resort** (1000 SE Bay Blvd, Newport; 541/265-8521) and paddle about Yaquina Bay, where you'll pass sea lions, seabirds, and sailboats; fly a kite; beach comb for agates; or simply stroll the miles upon miles of sand. You'll discover plenty of vantage points from which to observe the astounding mixture of rock, sand, and surf so common to this stretch of coast. **Fogarty Creek State Park** (on Hwy 101, 1 mile north of Depoe Bay; $6 day-use parking fee) may not look like much at first—signs from the highway lead to a rather unattractive parking area with a few picnic tables scattered about. But once you take the pedestrian underpass to the other side of the highway, you're in for a treat. This small stretch of beach is an ideal setting for picnics and for whale watching. Snuggle together while you take in the dramatic display of waves and mist as the turbulent surf breaks against the rugged rock formations, or, if the sea is in a more tranquil mood, explore marine life in the peaceful tide pools.

Located in Yachats in the 2,700-acre Cape Perpetua Scenic Area, the **Devil's Churn** is accessible via an exciting descent down a steep flight of wooden stairs that leads to a rocky, narrow channel. At the exchange of tides, the movement of water through this natural cut into the land is simply electrifying. Make a stop at the **Cape Perpetua Interpretive Center** (2400 Hwy 101, Yachats; 541/547-3289; open May–Sept) and stock up on hiking maps for a diverse range of trails. A tour map is also available for those who want to see the area by car; the drive is fantastic. There's a $3 day-use fee per vehicle for each location.

Access & Information

US Highway 101 follows the Pacific coastline from Washington to Southern California and links most of the towns along the central Oregon Coast. Highway 101 parallels Interstate 5 and can be accessed via any number of secondary roads throughout the state. From Interstate 5, travelers heading toward the central coast can take 99W to Highway 18 or, from the Corvallis area, Highway 20 or 34. For more information, call the **Newport Chamber of Commerce** (555 SW Coast Hwy, Newport; 541/265-8801 or 800/262-7844; www.newportchamber.org) or the **Lincoln City Visitor & Convention Bureau** (801 SW Hwy 101, Lincoln City; 541/994-8378; www.oregoncoast.org). The **Oregon Coast Visitors Association** (888/628-2101; www.visittheoregoncoast.com) is also a good place to start for general information.

Romantic Lodgings

CHANNEL HOUSE INN
✿✿✿

35 Ellingson St, Depoe Bay / 541/765-2140 or 800/447-2140
This appropriately named, towering blue building sits high upon the rocky cliffs of Depoe Bay and overlooks one of the world's smallest channels (it's only 50 feet wide). The interior of this cozy getaway features a nautical theme, from the whales etched into the glass doors at the entrance to guest rooms with names like Channel Watch, The Bridge, and Crow's Nest. Maritime antiques, such as brass ship fittings, a polished captain's wheel, and part of an ancient diving suit, are scattered throughout the hallways. Almost all of the 12 contemporary units feature views of waves crashing against the coastline. The larger, more desirable oceanfront rooms and suites have their own private decks, where you can lie back in a steaming hot tub for two and watch the evening sun disappear into the sea. In rooms like Whale Watch, the bedroom seems to jut out over the water like the cliffs themselves; here you can lie in bed, surrounded by two walls of windows, and bask in the sights, sounds, and smells of the ocean in total privacy. (Boat traffic during the day is a pleasing distraction.) Each room is decorated in shades of blue and includes pine furnishings, plush comforters, and a pair of binoculars for whale watching. Several units offer the additional convenience of small kitchenettes. In the morning, head downstairs to the cheery breakfast nook for a buffet of fresh fruit and pastries.
$$$–$$$$ *AE, DIS, MC, V; checks OK; www.channelhouse.com.*

CLIFF HOUSE
✿✿✿

1450 Adahi Rd, Waldport / 541/563-2506
Perched on a cliff overlooking the clamorous surf, this bed-and-breakfast is full of personality, from its bright blue exterior to the eclectic decor of intriguing antiques, heirlooms, and knickknacks. All four guest rooms are plush, with chandeliers and exquisite American antiques. Some guest rooms, as well as the common area, feel a bit too cluttered for comfort, but guests with a taste for this style will undoubtedly find them charming. In the Morning Star Room, inhale the fresh ocean air on the private balcony or stargaze through skylights above the king-size bed. A panoramic view and a private entrance make the Alsea Room a good choice, as well. The best room in the house, though, is The Suite, featuring supreme privacy in addition to ocean views, a wood-burning stove, and a private balcony. Furnishings in this room include a four-poster mahogany king-size bed, an English settee, and matching antique English chairs. Soak your cares away in the large Jacuzzi tub in the fully mirrored bathroom, or try out the two-headed shower for some good, clean fun. After your rich and satisfying

morning meal, be sure to take advantage of the large shared deck, which has a panoramic view of the ocean to the north, west, and east. In the center of the glassed-in deck you'll find a massive hot tub with massaging jets that move up and down your spine—a terrific way to begin your day on the Oregon Coast.

$$$-$$$$ *MC, V; checks OK; www.cliffhouseoregon.com.*

FAIRHAVEN VACATION RENTALS
✪✪✪✪

1109 SW Fall St, Newport / 541/574-0951 or 888/523-4179
After spending a few nights in any one of these new houses—three Victorian, one Cape Cod—it's a safe bet that kissing couples won't want to go home. Set in the charming Nye Beach neighborhood, these elegantly appointed houses are two blocks from the beach, shops, and cafes, and just across the street from the Newport Performing Arts Center. Inside, the homes feature slate accents, designer decor, fireplaces, window seats, full kitchens, washer/dryers, and views of the town and the ocean. Out back, there's a private garden, hot tub, and barbecue. A couple looking for the perfect place to make memories could hardly ask for more. There's a two-night minimum year-round, and a three-night minimum during holidays and special events. If you must bring along friends or family, the houses offer sleeping accommodations for six to nine, and each has two full bathrooms. While the houses are a bit large for two, if you're looking for privacy and upscale living, this is as classy as it gets.

$$$ *MC, V; checks OK; www.newportnet.com/fairhaven.*

HECETA HEAD LIGHTHOUSE BED & BREAKFAST
✪✪✪

92072 Hwy 101 S, Yachats / 541/547-3696
Once the lighthouse keeper's home, this Queen Anne–style house at the foot of the lighthouse now welcomes travelers to what may be one of the most ruggedly romantic settings you'll ever encounter. Set on the cliff, with dramatic views of the ocean and beach, the B&B features five rooms decorated in turn-of-the-century style. The new oceanfront Mariner's Room has spectacular, up-close views of the ocean and comes with a private bathroom with marble shower. "I've had couples say they got in bed and never left," says innkeeper Michelle Korgan, who notes, "You can see the ocean and coastline right from the bed." The Lightkeeper's Room has an exclusive view of the lighthouse and an elegant claw-foot soaking tub; the country-style Victoria's Room is the largest and offers a four-poster queen-size bed with touches of wicker and lace throughout, as well as a marble shower. We think amorous travelers will find the Queen Anne Room the most inspiring. There's an elegant four-poster queen-size bed with Austrian sheers, as well as chaise longues. The innkeepers describe it as "a fantasy room fit for a

queen and a king." One drawback: the bathroom is across the hall and shared with another room (though it does have a lovely claw-foot tub). **$$–$$$** *MC, V; checks OK; www.hecetalighthouse.com.*

KITTIWAKE
🗝🗝🗝

95368 Hwy 101, Yachats / 541/547-4470
The ocean views from this contemporary gray home are so sensational, you'll wonder if the innkeepers ever experience high tide in their living room—the careening ocean surf seems that close. The three light and airy oceanfront guest rooms are appointed with brightly colored linens, lovely wood furnishings, and French doors that open out to the crashing surf. Guests in rooms 2 and 3—the obvious romantic choices—can appreciate the inn's gorgeous location from the vantage point of a large, private whirlpool tub. Breakfast is served in your room and may begin with fresh juices, home-baked coffee cake, and lox and bagels, followed by a European entrée such as stuffed crepes or Austrian pancakes. You can take a walk along the beach at any time of day or night and in any season, thanks to the innkeepers' thoughtful supply of beach amenities, including boots, hats, scarves, rain ponchos, warm jackets, and flashlights. We recommend a pre-breakfast stroll to whet your appetite for the extravaganza to come. There's a two-night minimum stay year-round, so you can't rush the experience—nor will you want to.
$$$ *MC, V; checks OK; www.kittiwakebandb.com.*

NEWPORT BELLE BED & BREAKFAST
🗝🗝🗝

2301 SE Marine Science Dr, Newport / 541/867-6290
Those in search of a unique bed-and-breakfast experience need only step aboard the Newport Belle. This three-story stern-wheeler riverboat, firmly docked at the Newport Marina, has a white and cherry-red exterior that gleams invitingly on Yaquina Bay's quiet waters. The massive paddle wheel at its stern lies dormant except when the owner starts up the boat to give the paddles their weekly workout. Even though you won't be braving the high seas during your stay, a night here is guaranteed to rock the boat when it comes to romance. Built in 1991, the 97-foot-long riverboat offers a surprising amount of space, with five guest rooms, three decks, and a main salon. All five staterooms are on the snug side (which encourages snuggling, after all), but each has a private full bath; each room is also distinguished by its own subtle motif, from cowboy hats and a rocking horse in the Montana-inspired room to the sheepskin and stuffed koala bear in the Australian-themed room. Most feature either a king- or queen-size bed, although one room is equipped with a double and a twin day bed. Room 4, a.k.a. The Honeymoon Suite, is the most romantic; its top-floor corner

location affords views of the Yaquina Bay Bridge clear out to the ocean. Room 5 is the Captain's Suite and offers picturesque views of the marina with all its bobbing boats. Awaken early to catch the sunrise from the Belle's bow; in the evening, steal away to the stern for a brilliant sunset. In between, you can set crab pots near the dock or simply cozy up to read or dream in the main salon. Sherry, the Belle's skipper, serves a buffet-style gourmet breakfast, which may include omelets, waffles, French toast, or quiche, along with fresh fruit and homemade granola.
$$ *AE, DIS, MC, V; checks OK; www.newportbelle.com.*

NYE BEACH HOTEL
◑◑◖

219 NW Cliff St, Newport / 541/265-3334
Set on the ocean bluff in an old but recently revitalized neighborhood, this cosmopolitan hotel sparkles. Outside, the shingle-sheathed facade has been painted a striking chile-pepper red, while inside, a hunter green lobby and banisters accented with splashes of taupe and cranberry are equally eye-catching. (The lobby is also home to a lovebird named Killer, who likes to greet guests with a friendly chirp.) All 18 guest rooms are identical, with fireplaces, bent-willow love seats, black-lacquered bed frames imported from Holland, thick down comforters, and small private baths. We recommend the six rooms with Jacuzzi soaking tubs and unobstructed ocean views. Open the sliding glass door to your tiny balcony and you can kiss to the continuous melody of the nearby ocean surf. Theater posters, a lobby piano, an ocean-view deck, hanging plants, and eclectic accents add up to give the inn a decidedly cultured flair.
$–$$ *AE, DIS, MC, V; checks OK with check-guarantee card; www.nye beach.com.*

OCEAN HOUSE BED AND BREAKFAST
◑◑◑◑

4920 NW Woody Wy, Newport / 541/265-6158 or 800/562-2632
Ever since it opened in 1984, this blue and wood-shingled, two-story Cape Cod with stellar ocean views has been garnering rave reviews from customers, many of whom come first to honeymoon and then return to celebrate anniversaries. Now guests have even more reason to rave. Innkeepers Bob and Marie Garrard have meticulously remodeled every inch of the Ocean House, making it even more charming and sophisticated. Its eight rooms are furnished in antiques and wicker, with slate accents, gas fireplaces, and designer details. With the exception of the Rainbow Room, which features a private deck with view, each has a lovely sitting area with breathtaking views of the ocean and lovely gardens below. Couples will find any of the rooms a worthy retreat for a romantic interlude, but we have some favorites. The Cottage, a small house in itself with private entrance, has country charm

with hardwood floors, a king-size wrought-iron bed with patchwork quilt, and wood ceilings. In the main house, the intimate Overlook Room offers a white king-size wrought-iron bed, wicker chairs facing an expanded bay window, a double Jacuzzi, and a wood-beam ceiling. The gardens, Asian in design, feature pebbled paths, birdhouses, and benches for quiet musings à deux. A private staircase winds down to Agate Beach, where 4 miles of firm sand summon those who like to shed their shoes and comb the beach for seashells and agates. Come back to enjoy the satisfying breakfast of Belgian waffles, pancakes, omelets, or quiche served downstairs in the dining room each morning.
$$–$$$ AE, DIS, MC, V; checks OK; www.oceanhouse.com. &

SEA QUEST BED AND BREAKFAST
✿✿✿✿
95354 Hwy 101, Yachats / 541/547-3782 or 800/341-4878
Everything you could possibly want in a romantic getaway is here—and much, much more. A mere 50 feet from the ocean, this contemporary 7,000-square-foot wood home exemplifies Oregon Coast architecture at its best. And in 2003, it got even bigger and better with the addition of the 1,000-square-foot "Tis Suite." The suite occupies its own wing of the house and comes with a king-size bed, a private entrance, a fireplace, a large jetted tub, oversize furniture, and spectacular ocean views from 40 feet of glass spanning ceiling to floor. The five other beautifully designed guest rooms feature bright linens and wallpaper, thick down comforters on queen-size beds, private entrances, and tantalizing views. Shutters open from the bedrooms onto spacious Jacuzzi soaking tubs in the tiled bathrooms. Eclectic framed artwork covers just about every inch of wall space, while corners and sitting areas overflow with knickknacks and trinkets. A room off the common area called "General Mess" is generously filled with beach toys, boots, and jackets for guests to use. Upstairs, a crackling fire warms the shared dining/living room, where three walls of windows showcase the fantastic ocean view. The enormous brick fireplace boasts a different imaginative mantelpiece each season; when we visited, large sunflowers adorned an old-fashioned bicycle hung from the ceiling. This comfortable room is where you'll enjoy the buffet-style breakfast of homemade granola and jams, fresh fruit, a variety of baked breads, coffee cake, and delicious croissants stuffed with eggs, cheese, and mushrooms. The enthusiastic innkeepers are a delight, but if you want privacy, say so—or, during breakfast, you may find yourselves included in the cheery socializing.
$$$–$$$$ MC, V; checks OK; www.seaq.com.

SERENITY BED AND BREAKFAST
❍❍❍❛

5985 Yachats River Rd, Yachats / 541/547-3813
Don't make the mistake of bypassing this outstanding romantic destination simply because it's not on the ocean—you'd be missing out on a haven
of unexpected luxury and opulence if you do. A 6-mile drive inland from
Highway 101 brings you to this large white home and accompanying guest
house, sprawled on a 10-acre sweep of lawn lined with red alders and kissed
by breezes from the distant ocean. We had difficulty choosing between the
four ornate guest rooms, because each one has been lavished with sensuous details and given a unique theme. Alt Heidelberg, the smallest room,
features a double bed and antiques from Heidelberg, Germany, while the
Bavaria Suite is brimming with Bavarian knickknacks and accented with
beautiful blond wood. The Europa Suite holds an enticing assortment of fine
European antiques, including an iron bed draped in blue-and-white linens.
The most opulent room is La Italia, also called the Honeymoon Suite; it has
a white-veiled wrought-iron canopy bed, tall ceilings, and a large, tiled
Jacuzzi tub. Skylights and a wall of windows enhance its sunny disposition.
Each suite boasts a two-person Jacuzzi tub and French doors that open to
private decks or patios overlooking the nearby gardens and distant mountains. If you can tear yourselves away from your romantic oasis for breakfast, you won't be disappointed. The innkeeper is known for her authentic
German-style breakfasts, which include a layered dish of German bread,
shaved ham and eggs, a potato dish or German pancakes, and her famous
secret-recipe hot cocoa, all served at one shared table in the main house,
amid European antiques and lace.
$$ *MC, V; checks OK; www.pioneer.net/~serenitybnb/serenity.htm.* ♿

TYEE LODGE OCEANFRONT BED AND BREAKFAST
❍❍❛

4925 NW Woody Wy, Newport / 541/265-8953 or 888/553-8933
Named for the Chinook word for salmon, this contemporary home embraces
the Native American heritage of the Pacific Northwest. Situated on a cliff
overlooking the ocean, the lodge offers breathtaking views of Agate Beach
and Yaquina Head from almost every part of the house. Each guest room
honors a different local tribe, with names like Tillamook, Siletz, and Alsea.
All five feature fireplaces; down comforters on queen-size beds, each facing
a large picture window with wide open views to the beach; private baths
with skylights; pine furnishings; and wrought-iron mirrors. Distinctive art-
work adorns the cream walls in each room. In the Yaquina Room, an inviting
bay window is a perfect spot to sit close and watch the waves roll in on the
beach below. The Chinook Room, however, outshines all the others, with its
gas fireplace and extraordinary view to the southwest. Follow the switch-
back trail down to the sandy beach, where you can explore tide pools to your

hearts' content. Or watch a brilliant sunset from the outdoor fire pit. Indoor types will find contentment in the sunlit grand room, tastefully decorated in subtle greens and beiges, with large windows facing the sparkling ocean. Get comfy in the overstuffed plaid chairs near the slate fireplace as you sip complimentary coffee or tea. Mornings here begin with a full breakfast of such gourmet delights as stuffed French toast, poppy-seed pancakes, frittatas, and smoked-salmon quiche.
$$ *AE, DIS, MC, V; checks OK; www.tyeelodge.com.*

Romantic Restaurants

APRIL'S AT NYE BEACH
❍❍❍

749 NW 3rd St, Newport / 541/265-6855
Imaginative Mediterranean-inspired cuisine shines at this little cafe in Nye Beach. There are just 12 tables in the warm and charming space, which means intimacy is never a problem, though privacy could be. The seafood is particularly noteworthy: grilled wild salmon is topped with saffron aioli and surrounded by Manila clam broth, tomatoes, and fresh herbs; halibut comes coated with romescu sauce; and a half-dozen fish and shellfish are rolled into cannelloni tubes redolent of lemon, dill, and tarragon. Other good choices are the house-made Italian turkey sausage layered with polenta with arrabbiata sauce and three cheeses; and the Portuguese-style clams served with grilled *linguiça* sausage, zesty tomato herb broth, and crispy polenta. The wine list includes 70 bottles, with 10 wines sold by the glass at reasonable prices.
$$ *DIS, MC, V; checks OK; dinner Wed–Sun; closed Jan; beer and wine; reservations recommended.*

BAY HOUSE
❍❍❍❍

5911 SW Hwy 101, Lincoln City / 541/996-3222
This weathered building, all by itself off the main highway, would be easy to pass by, but then you'd miss the flawless view of tidal Siletz Bay, the driftwood-strewn shoreline, and the flow of the clear blue water—not to mention the consistently outstanding meals. Just about every table is blessed with its share of the lovely scenery, and the newly renovated interior is elegant and modern, with large picture windows, upholstered chairs, and private booths edged in cherry wood. The menu lists an enterprising assortment of Northwest creations made from local fish and meats. Oregon wild-mushroom *queso fundido* or Dungeness crab and potato-chive cakes with lemon mayonnaise and shaved fennel are excellent appetizer choices. When choosing an entrée, consider the splendid seared fresh scallops and

clams in a chardonnay sauce with butternut squash and avocado risotto, or the roasted Cattail Farms rack of lamb and *merguez* sausage with pinot noir–fig sauce and sweet potato–fontina gratin. Equally wonderful are the desserts—the signature special is black bottom cheesecake with amaretti and chocolate crumb topping. If you forget to save room, order one to share.

$$$ AE, DIS, MC, V; checks OK; dinner every day (Wed–Sun in winter); full bar; reservations recommended. ⅖

FATHOMS RESTAURANT & BAR
🔷🔷

4009 SW Hwy 101 (Inn at Spanish Head), Lincoln City / 541/994-1601
Fathoms sits atop the Inn at Spanish Head Resort Hotel and possesses utterly spectacular views of the coastline, the ocean, and the beach below. The main dining room tends to draw families and large parties, so we recommend, instead, that you sup on light fare and drinks in the stylishly appointed lounge, or order your meal to be enjoyed from the plump chairs by the fireplace. Standard dining-room fare includes live Maine lobster, fresh salmon, Dungeness crab, and thick, juicy steak; the Sunday brunch is wonderfully expansive.

$$ AE, DC, DIS, MC, V; checks OK; breakfast, lunch, dinner every day (lounge opens at 4pm every day); full bar; reservations recommended; www.spanishhead.com.

LA SERRE RESTAURANT
🔷🔷🔷

160 W 2nd St, Yachats / 541/547-3420
Although the ambience isn't exactly wildly romantic, La Serre is your best bet for a pleasant evening out in Yachats. Set just off Highway 101, the casual restaurant is filled with large, leafy potted plants and greenery that hangs from the atrium-like ceiling. The oak tables are topped with oil lamps, and frilly white curtains partly shield diners from the outside world. An open kitchen and the restaurant's popularity mean the atmosphere in the two dining rooms can get noisy. Service is friendly, but may be a bit slow on busy nights. Fresh, local seafood is the kitchen's specialty. We recommend starting your meal with steamed clams with drawn butter and lemon, then moving on to either Dungeness crab cakes with Cajun tartar sauce and mild red peppercorns, or filet mignon wrapped with bacon and topped with sautéed mushrooms in a light cream sauce. After your meal, step outside and cap it all off with a deep breath of the fresh ocean air.

$$ AE, MC, V; local checks only; dinner Wed–Mon; closed Jan; full bar; reservations recommended.

QUIMBY'S
🔶🔶

740 W Olive St, Newport / 541/265-9919
Quimby's offers a casual beach neighborhood setting and consistently good Pacific Northwest fare. The ambience, enhanced by stained glass and nautical accents, is comfortable and relaxed. For lunch, the Table Top Mountain sandwiches of roast beef, smoked turkey, and tuna are piled high with avocado, wild greens, and other treats. At dinner, the food is a bit more elegant. The Seafood Stew—fresh salmon, halibut, and prawns in an herb-infused broth of tomatoes, onions, saffron, shrimp stock, and Oregon Riesling—is absolutely delicious and comes in huge portions. Equally good are the chef's famous crab cakes and crispy oyster sauté, both served with rémoulade and rice pilaf.
$$ *AE, DC, DIS, MC, V; local checks only; lunch, dinner every day (Tues–Sat in winter); full bar; reservations recommended.* &

SAFFRON SALMONS
🔶🔶🔶

859 SW Bay Blvd, Newport / 541/265-8921
In the 1½ years it's been in town, Saffron Salmons, the Bay Front's newest addition in gourmet fare, has established a stellar reputation for fine regional dining. With excellent food, a waterfront setting, and contemporary art decor, this cozy place fills every one of the 13 tables most nights. The signature Saffron Salmon is pan-seared local Chinook salmon served with saffron crème sauce, risotto cake, basil chiffonade, and roasted tomato confit. Also big with regulars are the clam chowder, crab cakes, and rack of lamb; the crème brûlée has been called the best in town. Owners Michael and Stacy Waliser, who created Saffron Salmons with an eye toward catering to couples, strive to offer a menu of fresh foods, locally obtained and prepared in the Northwest tradition. Wines come from Northwest vineyards; beer is from the Rogue Ale Brewery. Even the art coloring the saffron walls comes from nearby Bay Street Gallery.
$$–$$$ *MC, V; local checks only; lunch, dinner Thurs–Tues; beer and wine; reservations recommended.* &

VILLAGE MARKET & DELI
🔶🔶

741 NW 3rd St, Newport / 541/574-9393
What this new little eatery lacks in intimacy it more than makes up for in scene. Set in the lovely nook of Newport that is Nye Beach, the Village Market & Deli has that European sidewalk-cafe feel—indoors and out. Most of the handful of tables are positioned for a view of the quaint neighborhood and are set amid the shelves of gourmet market fare and wine. The deli opened as a place for a light lunch, but after only one year has nurtured

a big enough fan base to warrant a dinner menu. We love the salmon BLT for lunch fare, and the custom-crafted meat and cheese platter is great for finger food à deux. For dinner, the pork tenderloin with butternut squash and candied walnuts served with orange-glazed carrot au gratin and a French brown sauce is scrumptious, as is the hoisin-glazed grilled salmon on a bed of sautéed spinach and Yukon gold potatoes with paprika crème fraîche. *$$ AE, DIS, MC, V; local checks only; lunch, dinner Fri–Tues; beer and wine; reservations recommended.*

SOUTHERN COAST

ROMANTIC HIGHLIGHTS

The farther south you travel on Highway 101, the more rural and sparsely populated the coast becomes. On the plus side, that means fewer crowds, little traffic, and rarely a line for anything. On the downside, of course, it means fewer choices in restaurants and lodging and fewer amenities when you do find a place to stay. The fact is there is nothing very romantic about many of the communities straddling the southern portion of 101—but if you venture a few miles east or west, you might easily find yourselves someplace unexpectedly charming.

Florence is just such a hidden gem; on the outskirts it offers little beyond an overabundance of gas stations and mini-marts, but the historic old town, situated along the Siuslaw River, is an absolute delight. Here, in the quaint surroundings of old, wooden two-story buildings, you can park the car and wander about the gift, candy, and coffee shops to your hearts' content. Treat yourselves to a homemade ice cream at **BJ's Ice Cream Parlor** (1441 Bay St; 541/902-7828), then savor it at the riverfront gazebo. Florence is also home to the **Oregon Dunes National Recreational Area**, stretching 38,000 acres and 42 miles from Florence to Coos Bay. Unless you consider noise and grit romantic, pass on the dune buggies for rent and hike the nature trails, which take you to Sahara-sized dunes, coastal rain forests, ocean overlooks, beaches, and wetlands. Because of the diversity of the landscape, what you will find in some parts of the dunes you will not find in others, but tundra swans, great blue herons, bald eagles, snowy plovers, osprey, hummingbirds, and great egrets, among other birds, have all been spotted here. Keep your eyes out also for the berries—strawberries, huckleberries, salmonberries, and blackberries, to name a few—that grow in wild abundance here. Northwest Forest Passes ($5) are required and may be purchased at any Forest Service office or at the **Oregon Dunes Visitor Center** (855 Hwy, Reedsport; 541/271-3611).

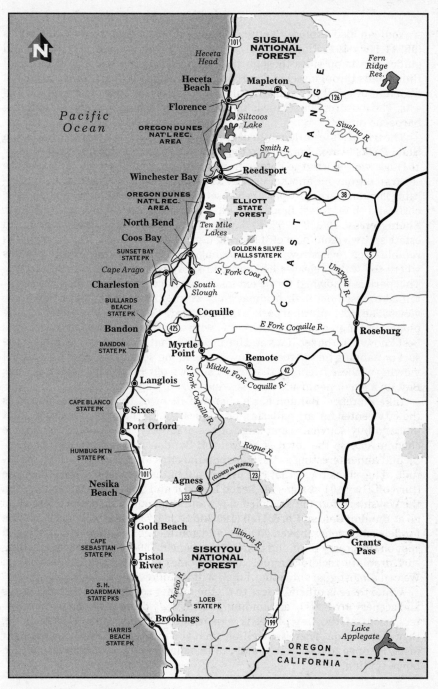

SIUSLAW NATIONAL FOREST

COAST RANGE

Pacific Ocean

101

Heceta Head

Heceta Beach

Mapleton

Florence

Fern Ridge Res.

126

Siltcoos Lake

Siuslaw R.

OREGON DUNES NAT'L REC. AREA

Smith R.

Winchester Bay

Reedsport

38

ELLIOTT STATE FOREST

OREGON DUNES NAT'L REC. AREA

Ten Mile Lakes

North Bend

Coos Bay

GOLDEN & SILVER FALLS STATE PK

S. Fork Coos R.

Umpqua R.

5

SUNSET BAY STATE PK

Cape Arago

Charleston

South Slough

BULLARDS BEACH STATE PK

Coquille

E Fork Coquille R.

Roseburg

Bandon

425

BANDON STATE PK

Myrtle Point

Remote

42

Langlois

Middle Fork Coquille R.

S Fork Coquille R.

CAPE BLANCO STATE PK

Sixes

Port Orford

Rogue R.

HUMBUG MTN STATE PK

101

Nesika Beach

Agness

(CLOSED IN WINTER)

23

33

Gold Beach

Illinois R.

Grants Pass

CAPE SEBASTIAN STATE PK

Pistol River

SISKIYOU NATIONAL FOREST

5

S. H. BOARDMAN STATE PKS

Chetco R.

LOEB STATE PK

Lake Applegate

Brookings

199

HARRIS BEACH STATE PK

OREGON

CALIFORNIA

You can also explore the dunes mounted on a horse from **C&M Stables** (90241 Hwy 101, Florence; 541/997-7540), which is open year-round and guides guests on rides through the forest and by the sea. The Dune Trail Ride winds through scenic dunes and beach, while a Coast Range Ride will fill a half or a full day and will take you from ocean vistas to evergreen forests. The most romantic ride is the Sunset Ride, which includes an optional barbecue dinner.

The trio of state parks south of Coos Bay known collectively as **Charleston State Parks** (watch for signs to the parks; they're 12 miles due west of Hwy 101) are well worth the detour from the main road. Though the parks are separated from one another by only a few miles, each one has distinctive terrain. The northernmost park is **Sunset Bay** (541/888-3778), where majestic cliffs and thick forest flank a small, calm ocean inlet. A bit farther south, **Shore Acres** (541/888-3732; $3 day-use fee) is home to the remains of an old estate sprawled out on a cliff soaring high above the coast. Intriguing paths ramble over rock-strewn beaches gouged with caves and granite fissures where the water releases its energy in spraying foam and crashing waves. This park is renowned for its extensive botanical gardens, which are maintained to resemble their original glory. Numerous lookouts offer bird's-eye views. The most informal park is **Cape Arago** (541/888-3778), an outstanding picnic spot high above the shoreline, with a northern view of the coast. It is best known for the sea lions and harbor seals that can be seen romping in the surf or napping on the rocks below. Bring along your binoculars for optimal viewing of these friendly creatures. The town of Charleston is south of Coos Bay, on a small peninsula 30 miles due west of Highway 101.

Like Florence, **Bandon** has a charm of its own. The old-town district is the city center for art galleries, boutiques, and gift shops. It's also a great place to buy souvenir samplings of the cranberry delights and handmade cheddar cheese the town is known for. Bandon beaches are just as spectacular and interesting as the more popular sites farther north, with a multitude of haystack rocks that rise in tiers out of the ocean. **Face Rock Wayside** (turn off Hwy 101 at signs for Beach Loop Dr and follow this until you reach the Wayside) offers unparalleled views and stupendous scenery. Get lunch to go at **Bandon Baking Co. & Deli** (160 2nd St; 541/347-9440), a local favorite for deli sandwiches, baked goodies, and gourmet coffee, then find a secluded spot on the grassy bluff and take in the magical 180-degree view of crashing surf, dramatic rock formations, and awesome expanse of sandy beach below. We can almost guarantee that lunch will be followed by a kiss.

While there is officially less to do the farther south you travel, the views and scenery are utterly astounding. If a leisurely drive with chance encounters at out-of-the-way places is your idea of a lovely, romantic afternoon, then continue on. There's no telling what you might see, or whom you might meet. Be open to the sheer wonder of this place, and you're bound to return home smiling.

Access & Information

US Highway 101 follows the Pacific coastline from Washington to Southern California and links most of the towns along the southern Oregon Coast. From Interstate 5, two-lane paved roads follow rivers west to the south coast; from Eugene, Highway 126 follows the Siuslaw River to Florence; from Drain, Highway 38 follows the Umpqua River to Reedsport; from Roseburg, Highway 42 follows the Coquille River to Bandon and Coos Bay; and from Grants Pass, Highway 199 follows the Smith River, then cuts through the redwoods and dips into Northern California near the Oregon border and Brookings. All of these routes are scenic. For information, call the **Bay Area Chamber of Commerce** (50 Central Ave, Coos Bay; 541/269-0215 or 800/824-8486) or the **Brookings-Harbor Chamber of Commerce** (16330 Lower Harbor Rd, Brookings; 800/535-9469). The **Oregon Coast Visitors Association** (888/628-2101; visittheoregoncoast.com) is also a good place to start for general information.

Romantic Lodgings

COAST HOUSE
○○○○
Off Coastal Hwy 101, Florence / 541/997-7888
If it's privacy you're after, you'll find it in abundant supply at this tranquil retreat located 10 miles north of Florence. A short lantern-lit pathway meanders through a grove of evergreens to this round, cedar-shake rental home set high on a towering cliff overlooking the blue waters of the Pacific. An expansive deck, complete with outdoor shower and wooden chairs, offers a stunning view of the mesmerizing terrain. (Please note that the deck sits very high and is not fenced.) Inside the house, throw rugs cover hardwood floors and an antique woodstove supplies cozy warmth. Floor-to-ceiling windows in the comfortable living room allow a view of the ocean through lofty pines. Ladders lead to two sleeping lofts, where you can stargaze through windows and skylights. In the bathroom, a claw-foot tub sits next to windows looking out on the ocean. Stock up on provisions in Florence before you arrive, because the only staples you'll find here are coffee, tea, and a complimentary bottle of wine (a nice romantic touch). The house is equipped with a full kitchen, a microwave oven, and a stereo with a collection of tapes and CDs; there is no TV or telephone.
$$$ No credit cards; checks OK; www.coasthouseflorence.com.

THE EDWIN K BED AND BREAKFAST
✿✿❤

1155 Bay St, Florence / 541/997-8360 or 800/8-EDWIN-K
Beautifully tended flower gardens surround this white Craftsman-style home located at the edge of old-town Florence and across the street from the Siuslaw River. (Unfortunately, the inn's river views are obstructed by a building and a large parking lot.) Built in 1914, the home has been lovingly refurbished to provide thoroughly comfortable accommodations. The six guest rooms are named after seasons and times of the year. We prefer the four very spacious upstairs rooms, all of which are appointed with stained and leaded glass windows, period antiques, contemporary pastel fabrics and linens, and tiled bathrooms with large tubs or showers. Some have patios that overlook a rock waterfall at the back of the house. The Winter Room, with its blue and silver color scheme and queen-size four-poster bed, is crowned by a lovely wall canopy; however, the step-up tiled bathroom is part of an open floor plan, with no actual door separating the bathroom (which means the toilet situation is not exactly private). Fortunately, the inviting claw-foot tub should help you look past this awkward layout. The other rooms do have bathrooms with doors you can close, so if you prefer more privacy, book one of them. Two additional, traditionally furnished guest rooms are located on the main floor, just off the antique-filled common area, but they are not as lavish as the upstairs rooms. When you awaken, follow your nose to the wood-paneled Victorian dining room for a formal breakfast served on fine china at one large table. Quiches, soufflés, freshly baked breads, fruit compote, and white chocolate–apricot scones are just a few of the culinary creations offered each morning. Complimentary sherry, tea, and cookies can be enjoyed each afternoon.
$$–$$$ *DIS, MC, V; checks OK; www.edwink.com.*

FLORAS LAKE HOUSE BED AND BREAKFAST
✿✿❤

92870 Boice Cope Rd, Langlois / 541/348-2573
If you windsurf or kite sail (or want to learn), Floras Lake's steady Northwest winds and proximity to the ocean make it an ideal spot for you. The owners of this lovely B&B rent sailboards and wet suits, and even give lessons for all skill levels. But you don't have to windsurf to enjoy staying at this wood-and-brick contemporary home. The four attractive guest rooms are very spacious, with cathedral ceilings and abundant windows, and come with antique beds, patchwork quilts, wicker furnishings, and pastel accents. We like the South Room, with its king-size four-poster bed and country-Victorian touches, and the Nautical Room, which is done in navy and red. Two rooms have fireplaces, and all have private entrances that open onto a weathered wraparound deck facing the beautiful gardens, Floras Lake, and, in the distance, the Pacific. This same view can be enjoyed from the airy

common room, which is crowned by a 20-foot-high, open-beamed ceiling and furnished with several comfy couches and a woodstove. A continental breakfast buffet is served here each morning. Before or after breakfast, take a long walk on the beach or follow one of the hiking trails that wind along the bluffs to secluded coves and a waterfall. These areas remain empty most of the year, so you'll have the privacy to kiss to your hearts' content.
$$ *MC, V; checks OK; closed mid-Nov–mid-Feb; www.floraslake.com.*

LIGHTHOUSE BED & BREAKFAST
✿✿
650 Jetty Rd, Bandon / 541/347-9316
If you do nothing else here but cuddle up and take in the stunning views, your stay will be memorable. This spacious, warm contemporary house is oriented toward the mouth of the Coquille River, which means guests get front-row seats for the lighthouse, the river, *and* the ocean. At any given moment you might spy windsurfers, seals, or seabirds—or maybe even a migrating whale. All of the five rooms are spacious, with private baths and homey decor. Our favorite is the Gray Whale Room, with king-size bed, fireplace, wood-burning stove, and whirlpool tub for two. Breakfast specialties include three-cheese quiche, fruit platters, croissants, homemade muffins, and French toast.
$$ *MC, V; checks OK; www.lighthouselodging.com.*

MOONSET
✿✿✿✿
90675 Hwy 101, Florence / 503/223-1425 or 800/768-9488
Designed specifically as a romantic oceanfront getaway, the phenomenal octagonal Moonset is a one-of-a-kind contemporary home set on an acre of meadows and trees 8 miles north of Florence. The interior of this architectural masterpiece features wood-paneled walls and wraparound floor-to-ceiling windows that showcase views of the nearby woods, the sprawling ocean dunes, and the blue Pacific in the distance. A loft bedroom holds a king-size bed covered with colorful goose-down pillows and a down comforter. The full sunken kitchen (breakfast is up to you) and tiled bath are modern and luxurious. Romantic amenities include a sauna, an outdoor Jacuzzi tub and shower, a video library, and a wood-stocked fireplace. On a sunny morning, retreat to the circular decks outside and get closer to nature—and each other.
$$$ *AE, DIS, MC, V; checks OK; www.touroregon.com/moonset.*

TU TU' TUN LODGE
◐◐◐◐

96550 N Bank Rogue, Gold Beach / 541/247-6664 or 800/864-6357
Be prepared for enchantment at this renowned Northwest retreat located 7 miles from Gold Beach. Tu Tu' Tun (meaning "people by the river") is nestled in the heart of a quiet forested valley, next to the winding Rogue River. Ivy cloaks the wood pillars of the cedar lodge, colorful flower boxes line the stairs, and the manicured grounds include a heated outdoor lap pool and stone terrace. The lodge's sixteen attractive rooms, two suites, and two private homes are all decorated with a distinctive Northwest flavor. Unique art pieces and sumptuous linens and fabrics, along with open-beamed ceilings, set the stage for romance. Tile entryways, wool carpeting, and small refrigerators are additional features. Some units offer slate fireplaces; others have sliding doors that open onto private balconies or patios where guests can relish river views from a "moon soaker" tub. (Be sure to specify the amenities you desire when booking, since only seven rooms have hot tubs and only eight have fireplaces.) Bouquets of fresh flowers adorn each room, and turndown service and fresh cookies are provided nightly. There's also a "Look Good–Feel Good Basket" full of complimentary toiletries in each room in case you've forgotten anything. The only accommodation here that does not have a river view is a private three-bedroom home sheltered in a nearby apple orchard (it's too large for a couple anyway). For an extra charge, breakfast, hors d'oeuvres, and dinner are served in a comfortable common lodge (May–Oct only), warmed on cool evenings by a crackling fire in an immense river-rock fireplace. All meals are served family-style at several round eight-person tables, which puts the kibosh on romantic intimacy. However, you can request a candlelit dinner for two served in your very own room.
$$$ MC, V; checks OK; www.tututun.com.

Romantic Restaurants

CHIVES
◐◐◖

21292 Hwy 101, Gold Beach / 541/247-4121
Every table at this oceanfront restaurant enjoys an ocean view, and the food is excellent. Romantic detractions, however, include the fact that the restaurant is set smack in the middle of a parking lot, and the interior decor is extremely minimal. Nevertheless, the menu, created by owner and former San Francisco Four Seasons Hotel chef Rick Jackson (along with his wife, Carla) is impressive. On any given night, openers might include asparagus soup, shrimp bisque, crispy salmon cakes, or rock shrimp risotto. Jackson's dazzling entrées include a classic osso buco and chicken stuffed

with Brie and hazelnuts. A variety of fresh fish is served on a daily basis and may include seared ahi sided with hot pepper noodles; spicy cioppino; and halibut and prawns tossed with garlic fettucine, bacon, Romano, and chives. The dessert and pastry menu changes at the chef's whim but may include chocolate pot-au-crème, zabaglione, or warm bread pudding spiked with Jack Daniels.

$$ *MC, V; checks OK; dinner Wed–Sun; open by reservations only Nov–May; full bar; reservations recommended.*

SPINNER'S SEAFOOD, STEAK & CHOP HOUSE
✿✿
29430 Ellensburg Ave, Gold Beach / 541/247-5160
As the restaurant's name suggests, the menu here offers something for everyone, but the sweeping views of the water should especially delight romancing couples. Every table overlooks the ocean, and the sunset panoramas are impressive. You might begin with a wild-mushroom napoleon bathed in an herb-cognac sauce, then move on to a charbroiled whiskey steak, cedar-planked salmon garnished with a pinot noir reduction, or one of a slew of chicken preparations (for example, grilled lime-ginger breast) or pasta plates (maybe seafood fettuccine tossed in an Asiago cheese sauce). Mandarin salad with candied walnuts and grilled prawns, lamb chops marinated in garlic and herbs, and pan-roasted halibut smeared with citrus sauce are other good choices. Burgers—massive half-pounders served with shoestring fries—are the south coast's finest.

$$ *AE, MC, V; checks OK; dinner every day; full bar; reservations recommended.*

WILD ROSE BISTRO
✿✿
130 Chicago St, Bandon / 541/347-4428
This cozy little place in Bandon's old town specializes in fresh seasonal food, with an emphasis on all things organic. Vegetables often come straight from the bistro garden, and seafood specials are made fresh from the catch at the local docks. There's an impressive selection of vegetarian dishes, and locals rave about the chocolate torte. The restaurant is small and simple, though it's not without a certain friendly charm; linens cover the tables at night, but there's no stuffy formality. Special requests are happily accommodated whenever possible. This is the kind of place that's custom-made for couples looking for a quiet place to enjoy tasty food with a healthy twist.

$$ *AE, DIS, MC, V; checks OK; dinner Thurs–Mon; full bar; reservations recommended.*

SOUTHERN OREGON

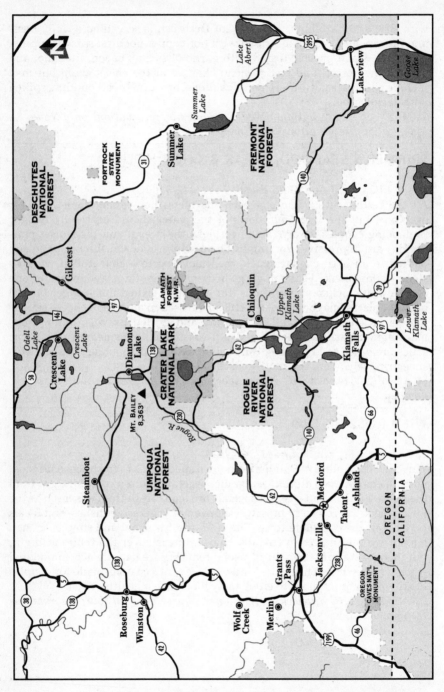

"A kiss can be a comma, a question mark, or an exclamation point. That's basic spelling that every woman ought to know."

—MISTINGUETT

♡ SOUTHERN OREGON

Majestic mountains, vast stretches of wilderness, roaring rivers, and forested valleys make southern Oregon a paradise for lovers of outdoor adventure. People come from all over for the white-water rafting, back-country hikes, and scenic bike tours, but, in this setting of rugged outdoor beauty, visitors will also find a flourishing cultural scene and plenty of opportunities for quiet romance.

Numerous small cities and towns, each with their own distinctive character, dot this region. Ashland, home to Southern Oregon University, is noted for its Shakespeare festival and progressive lifestyle, while Medford, the largest city in southern Oregon, is the retail heart of the area, home to shopping, golf courses, antiques shops, and the Harry and David's flagship store. A third and smaller town, Jacksonville, is all about history and makes a lovely place for a leisurely hand-in-hand stroll. Beyond the cities and suburbs, a short drive in almost any direction will take visitors deep into the countryside, where wineries, fruit orchards, and small farms thrive.

Summers here are hot, with temperatures often peaking in the triple digits, while winters bring snow to the high country, but milder temperatures and rain to the valley. Avoid the extremes by visiting in late spring or early fall, when tourist attractions are still going strong and the landscape is brilliantly colored with early blossoms or turning leaves.

ASHLAND & ROGUE VALLEY

ROMANTIC HIGHLIGHTS

Tranquil neighborhoods, a dynamic downtown teeming with shops and restaurants, and a world-class cultural center make Ashland a wonderful place to visit. Outside town, pristine countryside and mountainous terrain bordering fertile river valleys offer easy escapes. Ashland's famous Oregon Shakespeare Festival, which begins in February and runs through October, draws theater fans from literally all over the world. Romance in a place like this is rarely more than a heartbeat away, but while it may be tempting to schedule something for every hour of the day, remember to leave time for leisurely wandering. Do bear in mind that during the summer—when a cast of thousands descends for the Shakespeare Festival—quiet, romantic dining spots can be difficult to find. Everyone wants to eat before the show, so restaurants are packed and rushed between 5pm and 7:30pm. If you don't have evening tickets, and if your appetites can be put off, book a reservation for later in the evening. Alternately, bypass dinner altogether and have a big lunch: **Pilaf** (18 Calle Guanajuato; 541/488-7898) serves amazingly flavorful vegetarian cuisine of the Mediterranean, Middle East, and India, indoors and on a delightful patio overlooking Ashland Creek. Another great option is **Market of Choice** (1475 Siskiyou Blvd; 541/488-2773), where a plethora of delicious take-out food (the sushi is wonderful) will allow you to dine in whatever romantic location you choose. Visit Ashland knowing that this little town is a place full of possibilities, and you never know where the next step might take you.

What could be more romantic than snuggling together at dusk in an outdoor Elizabethan theater, listening to romantic love poetry written by England's leading authority on the subject? Thanks to the **Oregon Shakespeare Festival** (541/482-4331; www.osfashland.org), you can see a variety of the Bard's works in several different theaters (both indoor and out) in downtown Ashland. And since not all performances are Shakespearean, you can find other kinds of shows to enjoy as well. Season after season, the costumes are spectacular, the sets are imaginative, and the acting is superb. Be sure to arrive early to catch "The Green Show," a music-and-dance presentation that precedes every outdoor performance. This 30- to 45-minute production can be as engaging and enjoyable as the main feature.

Ashland's **Lithia Park**, a national historic landmark, begins in the heart of Ashland's theater district and extends southward for roughly a mile. With more than 100 acres of forest, lawns, ponds, and flower gardens, this lovely playground encompasses plenty of space for intimate moments. Stroll arm-in-arm beneath the ponderosa pines—just one of 100 different kinds of trees and shrubs here—or share a kiss on one of the small bridges spanning a burbling creek. Rhododendrons, dogwood trees, azaleas, and forget-me-nots fill the park with brilliant displays of color each spring. Picnic tables are liberally sprinkled throughout the park, so on a sunny day, you have an appointment here. Immaculate paved walkways eventually turn into trails as you wind your way upward to a panoramic view of Ashland and the valley beyond.

The town of Ashland is crowned by the 7,500-foot summit of **Mount Ashland** (541/482-2897; www.mtashland). In winter, Nordic buffs hit the more than 100 miles of cross-country ski trails that snake their way through forests, open fields, and crystal-clear mountain lakes, while alpine skiers schuss their way down terrain ranging from easy cruisers to steep chutes. In spring and summer, the steep trails are equal parts challenging and beautiful, and reward your toil with spectacular views.

For sheer indulgence, consider the Double Delight massage or body treatment at the **Blue Giraffe Day Spa** (51 Water St; 541/488-3335). This stylish spa, set on the banks of Ashland Creek, offers massages, facials, body polishes, wraps, and hydrotherapy treatments, as well as a full complement of hair and nail services. Couples can start with soothing neck wraps followed by an aromatherapy session, and then move to the double room for dual massages. Finish up with a soak in a tub made of a stone called "tumbled marble," big enough for two.

Southern Oregon is famous for its white-water adventures, and trips are offered by any number of licensed guides. For a particularly romantic river tour, **Kokopelli Kayak** (1655 Parker St; 541/201-7694; www.kokopelli kayak.com) offers a custom trip for two. Your guide will lead you down the Klamath River, where you'll paddle through the scenic quiet of forest and meadow, home to blue herons, deer, otters, and all sorts of creatures great and small. You'll be served a light lunch accompanied by wine off river, then delivered back to your hotel doorstep.

Plan to spend at least one day in the charmingly historic small town of Jacksonville, where old-fashioned brick buildings house antiques shops, art galleries, wine-tasting rooms, and boutiques. Nestled in the foothills of the Siskiyous, Jacksonville's scenic setting is naturally romantic. Take a self-guided walking tour with a map available from the **Visitor Information Center** (185 N Oregon St; 541/899-8118); it features 101 historical buildings and landmarks. The center can also provide maps of the Applegate Valley vineyards, where five wineries, including the much-acclaimed **Valley View Winery** (800/781-9463), are ideal places to while away an afternoon. Cap off your visit to Jacksonville with an evening at the **Peter Britt Music Festival** (800/882-7488; www.brittfest.org; June–Sept), held at an outdoor concert venue set amid pine and madrona trees on the hillside estate of 19th-century photographer Peter Britt. The festival lineup always includes world-class artists in jazz, folk, classical, country, and pop music, as well as comedians, dancers, and other international performers. For the full Britt Fest experience, board the vintage trolley to the festival grounds with gourmet fare at the ready; picnic baskets, wine, and beer (no "hard" alcohol) are permitted (as are blankets and chairs with legs of 4 inches or less in height). Food, wine, beer, ice cream, espresso, and popcorn are also available from the concessionaires at the festival. With the stars overhead and great music on the stage, love is definitely in the air.

Access & Information

The primary access to Ashland is via Interstate 5. Visitors traveling from the east can connect with Highways 62, 66, or 140, all of which meet up with Interstate 5; from the west, take Highway 199, which also connects with the interstate. For more information about the area, contact the **Ashland Chamber of Commerce** (110 E Main St; 541/482-3486).

Romantic Lodgings

A MIDSUMMER'S DREAM
✿✿✿
496 Beach St, Ashland / 541/552-0605 or 877/376-8800
This blue Victorian house set on a quiet Ashland street takes the Shakespeare theme to a tastefully elegant place. Opened in 2002, the bed-and-breakfast features five suites, each designed with modern-day romance in mind. This means king-size beds, fireplaces, two-person tubs, sumptuous robes—and no TVs. For the utmost in privacy, choose the Romeo Suite, in the cottage out back, where furnishings include a plush chaise longue, a canopied bed, and a corner spa tub. A three-course gourmet breakfast, complimentary in-room snack baskets, and port served in the game room are all part of the dreamy package.
$$$ AE, DIS, MC, V; checks OK; www.amidsummer.com. ♿

ASHLAND CREEK INN
✿✿✿✿
70 Water St, Ashland / 541/482-3315
Innkeeper Carolyn Sheldon has created what is without a doubt one of the finest bed-and-breakfast experiences in town. The seven suites, all with private decks on Ashland Creek, have been designed in international themes from exotic to elegant, furnished with antiques and fine art, and given private entrances and kitchens. The Matsu suite is a Japanese-theme space with raised platform king bed, antique tansu, Asian artwork, and views of the koi pond. If you're looking for cozy and sweet, consider the Caribe suite, a Caribbean vision in white and pastel. It's the smallest room, but also the

sunniest. Or, for something truly exotic, we like the Marrakech, with its vaulted-ceiling king bedroom, Moroccan antiques, and oversize deck. Wine-tasting weekends are a guest-only treat, and breakfasts are a three-course gourmet affair with fresh smoothies, seasonal fruit dishes, and main courses of frittatas or French toast with praline syrup. $$$–$$$$ *MC, V; checks OK; www.ashlandcreekinn.com.*

ASHLAND SPRINGS HOTEL
🖤🖤

212 E Main St, Ashland / 541/488-1700 or 888/795-4545
One of the most recognizable landmarks in town, this historic hotel has stood on the corner of East Main and First since 1925, when it was considered the most luxurious hotel between San Francisco and Portland. The boutique hotel's most recent remodel gave it a pretty naturalist theme, with shells, birds, and pressed herbs on display in the quiet and comfortable lobby, where weary travelers can settle into cozy sofas and chairs to peruse local publications or take in Ashland's bustling Main Street through the hotel's oversize windows. Rooms feature crisp white linens, French down comforters, and the original 1920s oversize windows overlooking downtown. Daily from May to October, the hotel offers afternoon tea on the mezzanine, complete with petite sandwiches, chocolate-dipped strawberries and grapes, fresh scones, and Oregon cheeses. (As it's both a lovely and a popular way to pass an Ashland afternoon, reservations are strongly recommended.) $$–$$$ *AE, DC, DIS, MC, V; checks OK; www.ashlandspringshotel.com.* ♿

BYBEE'S HISTORIC INN
🖤🖤🖤

883 Old Stage Rd, Jacksonville / 541/899-0106 or 877/292-3374
Built in 1857 by one of Jackson County's most influential and wealthy residents, William Bybee, this classic revival Victorian home on 3½ idyllic acres outside of Jacksonville was completely remodeled from its former existence as a private residence and opened as Bybee's Historic Inn in June 2003. Owners Mike and Tricia Sullivan achieved a perfect blend of history and romance by tailoring renovations to both the luxury and comfort of travelers and the criteria of the National Historic Register, on which the building is listed. Start your day with coffee in the exquisite library, which boasts the home's original ornate plaster ceiling and Italian marble fireplace. Furnishings are accurate to the period but not so elegant that you don't feel comfortable curling up contentedly with a book—or your sweetie. The six guest rooms achieve this same balance of glamour and ease. Our favorites are the Elizabethan Room on the ground floor, which has plush, felt-lined walls, a jetted tub, and a candlelit fireplace, and the Renaissance Room upstairs, which has a lighted canopy over the bed and is decorated

with gentle pastel shades. The Americana Room, located in the old carriage house, is roomy, private, wheelchair accessible, and pet-friendly. Details in each room are designed for optimum romance—beds are triple sheeted, towels are thick and luxurious, and organic soaps are on hand. Breakfasts of homemade crepes, chicken-apple sausage, broiled grapefruit, or Mike's signature homemade granola keep you well nourished for a day spent lounging by Bybee's three-tier cascading koi pond or strolling Jacksonville's historic streets.

$$–$$$ MC, V; checks OK in gift shop only; www.bybeeshistoricinn.com. &

COOLIDGE HOUSE
❍❍❨

137 N Main St, Ashland / 541/482-4721 or 800/655-5522
Coolidge House, a finely restored Victorian, makes a good first impression with manicured shrubs and gardens adorning the front yard and flower baskets lining the porch. The interior confirms it. Of the six guest rooms, four are in the main house and two are in the Carriage House behind. Rooms in the main house vary in size, but all have private baths and are furnished with gorgeous antiques. Romantics will especially love the regal Parlor Room, with its hardwood floors, fabulous window seat, luxurious furnishings, and spacious bathroom with Jacuzzi tub for two. The Carriage House rooms have the advantage of being larger, but are short on the lovely antiques found in the main house. Those sensitive to noise, however, should choose one of these rooms, since they are shielded from Main Street. Full gourmet breakfasts are offered each morning. Depending on the season, you can enjoy your morning meal in the dining room, on the flower-trimmed brick patio behind the house, or on the second-story balcony at charming white iron tables for two.

$$$ MC, V; checks OK; www.coolidgehouse.com.

COUNTRY WILLOWS BED AND BREAKFAST
❍❍❍❍

1313 Clay St, Ashland / 541/488-1590 or 800/WILLOWS
This ranch estate, located 2½ miles from downtown Ashland, continues to be a marvelous kissing destination under the attentive custody of new owners Chuck and Debbie Young. A bright yellow sign reminding you to drive slowly because of the "Geese and Quackers" greets you as you drive up the gravel road. Huge willows, a groomed lawn bordered by lovely gardens, and a duck pond beautify the property, which lies at the foot of wooded hills and also boasts a huge heated pool and a hot tub. Four rooms are located on the second floor of the farmhouse, where an expansive deck with willow furniture provides a place to sit and appreciate the country landscape. Lodged in an adjacent barn, the aptly named Barn Suites offer the ultimate privacy and comfort, and are the absolute best places to kiss on the property.

Our favorite is the luxurious Pine Ridge Suite, a stunning, spacious room with a fireplace, high open-beam ceilings, skylights, a small kitchen, and a dazzling slate bathroom with two-person open shower and Jacuzzi tub for two. The fresh Northwest-style decor—a peeled-log king-size bed frame, pine furnishings, and coordinating pine-tree wallpaper and linens—creates an overall effect that is simply glorious, and entirely tasteful. Sunrise is accompanied by fresh coffee and culinary delights like roasted banana with lime yogurt, chocolate chip pancakes, or omelets filled with vegetables from the property's huge gardens. Details like compote made from banana and fresh orange juice and tiny, heart-shaped scones exemplify Country Willow's quest for romantic excellence.
$$–$$$ *AE, DIS, MC, V; checks OK; www.countrywillowsinn.com.* &

COWSLIP'S BELLE
✿✿✿
159 N Main St, Ashland / 541/488-2901 or 800/888-6819
Each of the five rooms at this retreat (two in the 1913 bungalow and three in the adjacent carriage house) is named for a flower mentioned in a Shakespeare play. Our favorite rooms are the carriage house accommodations, each with a private entrance, a down comforter, and the softest linens you've ever snuggled in. The upstairs Daffy Down Dilly suite is the most spacious of the three and features a handmade twisted-juniper bed with attached burl-wood nightstand, a triple-sided fireplace, a Jacuzzi tub, and a view of the mountains. Cuckoo-Bud has a magnificent four-poster bent-willow canopied bed entwined with carved roses, an antique stained-glass window, a beamed ceiling, upholstered floral chintz walls, and a star-quilt wall hanging. Love-in-Idleness has a beautiful antique brass bed and a damask love seat. Air-conditioning in all rooms provides comfort during the sweltering heat of Ashland's summers. The morning meal at Cowslip's Belle is an event in itself. (The innkeepers also operate a popular cookie company, so you know the treats have got to be good!) Served on the main floor of the bungalow, breakfast may include fresh fruit, homemade coffee cake, and sour cream Belgian waffles with pecan maple syrup or cornmeal crepes with shrimp-vegetable stuffing. Indulge.
$–$$$ *MC, V; checks OK; closed Nov–Feb; www.cowslip.com.*

FLERY MANOR BED & BREAKFAST
✿✿◖
2000 Jumpoff Joe Creek Rd, Grants Pass / 541/476-3591
Those seeking opulence in a quiet country setting will adore this large blue house a few miles north of Grants Pass. Nestled on 7 mountain-view acres, the inn features an ornate two-story common living room with arched windows, antiques, lavish window treatments, and plush carpeting. On the grounds, you'll be delighted by ponds, waterfalls, walking paths, streams—

and spectacular views. Each of the five guest rooms is richly appointed with lace and satin accents, fluffy pillows, framed art prints, faux-textured walls, and lots of antiques. A private garden entrance leads to the Vintage Suite, which features a king-size canopied feather bed, an antique wood-burning fireplace, a two-person Jacuzzi—complete with one-way window over-looking the garden—and a spacious glass-enclosed shower. Consider also the Moonlight Suite, where red satin sheets top the king-size bed and a love-note pillow by the bed lets you write sweet nothings in addition to whis-pering them. The oversize room has a private balcony ideal for watching the sunset, along with a marble fireplace for cooler nights. But most spectacular is the suite's spa room, where the two of you can soak in the pink double Jacuzzi tub surrounded by flickering candles. In the morning, as you savor a three-course breakfast in the formal dining room, a bubbling little waterfall fountain provides soothing background music. The signature breakfast dish is "eggs on a cloud"—eggs baked on mounds of bread, served with hollan-daise sauce and salmon. Breakfast dishes also often include organic produce from the garden. Note: this B&B is about a 45-minute drive from Ashland, so it's not a good choice for serious theater attendees. **$$–$$$** *MC, V; checks OK; www.flerymanor.com.*

JACKSONVILLE INN
✿✿✿

175 E California St, Jacksonville / 541/899-1900 or 800/321-9344
This landmark brick hotel is located in the heart of downtown Jacksonville. Built in 1861 and lovingly restored over the years, the inn mixes old and new to create comfortably elegant lodgings. All of the eight second-floor rooms have exposed-brick walls, private baths, handsome antique armoires, oak furnishings, comfortable beds, and a great deal of elaborate Victorian style. The inn also rents out four charming, private guest cottages approxi-mately a block away, which provide the optimum option for romance. A white picket fence surrounds these side-by-side cottages, and gardens line the walkways. Three are newly built and have a more modern style, with vaulted ceilings, large Jacuzzi tubs with steam showers, and double-sided gas-log fireplaces. The oldest cottage is also a wonderful little hideaway, with country-Victorian furnishings, a lace-canopied bed, a gas fireplace, a kitchenette, and a steam shower with Jacuzzi tub. Cottage guests can have a fruit-and-champagne breakfast delivered to them or venture to the inn's famous Victorian dining room for a full breakfast. We love the fresh fruit with raspberry sauce, salmon Benedict, and hash browns. During Sunday brunch, champagne from local wineries is served with the meal. **$$$–$$$$** *AE, DC, DIS, V; checks OK; www.jacksonvilleinn.com.* ♿

MORICAL HOUSE GARDEN INN
❀❀❀

668 N Main St, Ashland / 541/482-2254 or 800/208-0960
A major renovation in 2002 transformed this Eastlake-style Victorian farm-house into a study in Eastern elegance. The six guest rooms on the upper floors of the main house feature finely crafted Asian furniture, natural-fiber window and floor coverings, luxurious linens, and down comforters. Guests will also find orchids, plush bathrobes and slippers, and custom organic soaps awaiting them. Out back, a garden carriage house offers three luxury suites, any one of which will set the tone for a romantic interlude. Suites 6 and 7 include king-size beds, vaulted ceilings, cozy window seats, fireplaces, kitchenettes, double showers, and Jacuzzi tubs. Suite 8, at the top of a private staircase, has a wet bar, king-size bed, and double shower. Guests awaken to a three-course gourmet organic breakfast served on custom-fired porcelain plates and including such delectables as mandarin orange spritzers, mocha-pear coffee cake, marionberry crepes, and eggs Florentine with orange scones and orange hollandaise sauce.
$$–$$$ *AE, MC, V; checks OK; www.garden-inn.com.* ♿

MT. ASHLAND INN
❀❀❀❀

550 Mt Ashland Rd, Ashland / 541/482-8707 or 800/830-8707
Sheltered by pine trees near the summit of Mount Ashland and placed practically on top of the Pacific Crest Trail, this handcrafted cedar inn provides an extraordinarily romantic Northwest alpine lodge experience. Arrive early enough to take a stroll through the woods, then take a dip in the outdoor hot tub with views of Mounts Shasta and McLoughlin before settling in for a gloriously private night in one of five serene, Early American–decorated guest rooms. In the second-story McLoughlin Suite, you'll feel like you're in your very own cabin, with exposed-log walls and a rose-marble gas fireplace near the foot of the king-size bed. A lovely rectangular window above the bed perfectly frames Mount McLoughlin, while Mount Shasta rises off to the south. However, even the delightful McLoughlin can be topped—journey upward to the third-floor Sky Lakes Suite, where the bathroom centerpiece is a small river-rock waterfall that sends water cas-cading into a two-person Jacuzzi tub. A skylight, walk-in double-headed shower, king-size bed, river-rock fireplace, microwave, refrigerator, and wet bar all leave nothing to be desired. In the morning, witness from bed as a salmon-colored sunrise illuminates Siskiyou forests and the slopes of Mount Shasta. The inn's main living room is cozy, with peeled-log columns; a 17th-century fireplace in a massive stone wall; furniture handmade by both the prior and current innkeepers; and plenty of books, photos, and games. Days at the Mount Ashland Inn start with a full breakfast that may include chilled mango and kiwi soup or spiced cran-apple pears, followed by an

entrée such as toasted almond–cheese French toast. Amenities also include complimentary snowshoes, skis, and mountain bikes, as well as a Finnish cedar sauna. Consider bringing a take-out supper from town, as there are no dinner dining options near the inn—plus, once you check in to the Mt. Ashland Inn, it's likely you'll never want to leave.
$$$ DIS, MC, V; checks OK; closed in Nov; www.mtashlandinn.com.

PEERLESS HOTEL
ɔɔɔɕ
243 4th St, Ashland / 541/488-1082 or 800/460-8758
A bold name like "Peerless" sets up lofty expectations in a traveler's mind. Happily, this inn lives up to its name by offering a memorable and unique-to-Ashland experience. With colorful flower boxes adorning the windows and an old Coca-Cola sign painted on one outer wall, the exterior of this turn-of-the-20th-century brick building gives no indication of the polished magnificence inside. All six of the grand guest rooms are decorated with large murals or intricate stencil work, and feature towering 12-foot ceilings, original woodwork, rich colors and fabrics, and glistening hardwood floors warmed with Oriental rugs. Although each room is different, a flamboyant and stylish Victorian theme prevails throughout, accomplished with antiques, queen-size beds, and sumptuous furnishings and linens. Suite 3 has side-by-side claw-foot tubs and a spacious sitting area adjacent to the bedroom; the French-influenced Room 5 has a two-person Jacuzzi tub positioned beneath a skylight; and Suite 7 (our favorite) features a four-poster mahogany bed, two-person shower, and a jetted tub for two framed by lace curtains. This elegant suite is painted a calming green, complemented by hardwood floors and white shutters. Ceiling fans help cool the sunlight-filled room, and a private patio adds an extra-special touch. Turndown service is provided in the evening, but otherwise, once you check in, you are left alone—perfect for those with romance on their minds. The hotel's romantic restaurant is simply outstanding (265 Fourth St, Ashland; 541/488-6067).
$$$ AE, DIS, MC, V; checks OK; closed in Jan; www.peerlesshotel.com. &

TOUVELLE HOUSE
ɔɔɔ
455 N Oregon St, Jacksonville / 541/899-8938 or 800/846-8422
Built in 1916, this lovely, well-preserved house sits just outside the charming town of Jacksonville. You'll find many of the home's original features intact, including built-in hutches, push-button light switches, and, outside, the wonderful wraparound porch. In 2004, new owners redecorated the great room to match the home's fundamental Mission styling, and the effect is more distinguished than the previous Victorian decor. Some guest rooms still boast the delicate floral motifs of the Victorian era, however; of the six rooms, we like the Garden Suite for its abundance of natural light and the

third-floor Granny's Attic for its coziness and view of Mount McLoughlin. Thanks to two gigantic oak trees that shade the entire home, some of the rooms are a bit on the dark side (which can prove a bonus in the summertime), and the lovely grounds are highlighted by a partially shaded in-ground pool surrounded by trees and a wooden fence—it's a welcome refreshment at the end of a hot summer day. Changes were underway when we visited, but chef Gary Balfour promises to add a whole new batch of breakfast selections, including items made from fresh Rogue Valley pears. $$ *AE, MC, V; checks OK; www.touvellehouse.com.*

WEISINGER'S VINEYARD COTTAGE
◔◔◖

3150 Siskiyou Blvd, Ashland / 541/488-5989 or 800/551-9463
If a private cottage set on 10 acres of luscious vineyards and quaint farm-land fits your idea of romance, then you and your love will have a time to remember here. This petite modern home has everything you could desire for an intimate getaway: a comfy floral love seat positioned directly across from a gas fireplace; a private hot tub on the outside deck; a TV/VCR and stereo hidden away in an attractive armoire; air-conditioning; and a basket of wine, cheese, crackers, and light breakfast items awaiting your arrival. The kitchen is stocked with utensils, a toaster oven, and a microwave. In the spacious bedroom, where green-and-white decor sets the mood for rest and relaxation, you'll find a queen-size bed, ivy-patterned linens and wallpaper, and a skylight ideal for midnight stargazing. Yet there's trouble in paradise: the cottage is within earshot of a nearby home, and, when we visited, two huge antennas and an unsightly shack cluttered the landscape. Luckily, from the bubbling hot tub, all you see is the vineyard. $$$ *MC, V; checks OK; www.weisingers.com.*

Romantic Restaurants

AMUSE
◔◔◔◖

15 N 1st St, Ashland / 541/488-9000
With its polished concrete floor, velvet drapes, and hand-blown lamps, this sophisticated little place is at once intimate and elegant. The heavenly menu is best described as French with a Northwest twist. The dining experience begins with the traditional French *amuse-bouche* (hence the restaurant's name), a savory treat designed to be a prelude to the meal, and finishes with a small sweet; on our visit a lovely lemon meringue tart was served in a square of golden blown glass. Entrée offerings change almost daily but might include a dish like wood-grilled rib-eye steak with *pommes frites*, baby spinach, and shallot butter. The service is excellent, the food a delight.

In the summer, dine alfresco on the restaurant's new, airy patio. Chances are good you'll leave here ready for a kiss.

$$$ *AE, DC, DIS, MC, V; local checks only; dinner Tues–Sun (Wed–Sun in winter); beer and wine; reservations recommended; www.amuserestaurant. com.* &

CHATEAULIN RESTAURANT
✿✿✿❨

50 E Main St, Ashland / 541/482-2264
Conveniently located in the heart of Ashland's theater district, this ivy-covered French-country restaurant is one of the best places in town to enjoy a romantic meal, whether you're headed for the theater or not. Inside, the subtle lighting is augmented by flickering candlelight. Exposed-brick walls are decorated with champagne bottles and copper kettles, and rosy stained-glass windows frame the restaurant's bar area. Lace window treatments, scarlet carpeting, and dark woodwork create a romantic ambience. The seating perhaps too intimate, particularly when diners are crammed too tightly together just before show time. Try booking one of the window tables for more space. Creatively prepared pâtés and free-range veal dishes with subtle sauces are the specialties here, and the seafood is always fresh and delicious. Desserts at Chateaulin border on euphoric, so save room for one of our favorites: the Chambord pot de crème with raspberry coulis.

$$$ *AE, DIS, MC, V; local checks only; dinner every day (Wed–Sun in winter); closed first 3 weeks of Jan; full bar; reservations recommended; www.chateaulin.com.*

GOGI'S
✿✿❨

235 W Main St, Jacksonville / 541/899-8699
This cozy restaurant tucked off Jacksonville's busy Main Street entices many a lover of both romance and first-class cuisine. The stylish interior, which includes warm colors, rich wood, and cheerful works of art, exudes quiet elegance. The well-stocked bar, formed from beautiful mahogany and dominating one corner of the room, is the source of tasty mixed drinks and a thorough wine list, which includes selections from local wineries Valley View and Griffin Creek, as well as more worldly varietals. White linen–set tables are spaced generously enough to promise privacy, and the overall feeling is quiet and relaxing. But it's chef William Prahl's excellent and eclectic fine dining fare—crafted with French techniques, yet Northwest influenced—that most delights. The grilled romaine salad—a unique take on the classic starter made from half a head of romaine dipped in marinade, then grilled briefly and stuffed with parmesan and croutons—is highly recommended. Entrées such as mushroom-crusted ahi tuna with saimin noodles and wasabi aioli are as creative as they are delicious. Desserts, such

as a warm individual chocolate cake with chocolate and raspberry sauces, are equally decadent. Lighter but equally tasty fare is available in Gogi's Britt Boxes; order by 2pm to ensure that you'll dine on an especially gourmet picnic dinner at your Britt Festival show.

$$$ *DIS, MC, V; local checks only; dinner Wed–Sun; full bar; reservations recommended; www.gogis.net.* &

IL GIARDINO CUCINA ITALIANA
◑◑◖

5 Granite St, Ashland / 541/488-0816
You and your beloved are in for a cozy Italian treat at Il Giardino. This family-run restaurant is both casual and personable, with family photographs and colorful Art Deco advertisements covering the bright blue walls. Linen-covered tables are close to their neighbors, but the ambience has charm nonetheless. Just off the dining room, a garden patio allows alfresco dining beneath wisteria vines and hanging baskets of flowers. No matter where you sit, be aware that the restaurant is usually too noisy and bustling for intimate conversation; instead, you might just want to gaze into each other's eyes and let the food speak for itself. The authentic Italian cuisine is prepared with the utmost care and expertise. Try the savory homemade soup, which changes with the seasons; every single pasta dish is delicious. We highly recommend the linguine with clams in a light tomato sauce, or the capellini with tomato and basil. Even the classic spaghetti bolognese is a masterpiece. Before we walked in, we had been tempted to leap on the antique scooter parked in front of the restaurant and drive off into the sunset. But you'd have to be crazy to miss food like this.

$$ *AE, DIS, MC, V; local checks only; dinner every day; full bar; reservations recommended; www.ilgiardinoashland.com.*

MCCULLY HOUSE INN
◑◑◑

240 E California St, Jacksonville / 541/899-1942 or 800/367-1942
This historic Gothic Revival mansion sits with dignity at the edge of Jacksonville's little downtown. The remarkable gourmet cuisine is served in one of two separate indoor dining rooms, in the garden, or out on the rose-bordered front lawn. The internationally inspired cuisine, such as pan-seared scallops with andouille sausage served on baby greens, boldly combines flavors with wonderful results. The menu changes several times a year, with specials featuring seasonal seafood and local organic produce. For the budget-conscious, the American Classics menu, featuring lighter fare such as macaroni and cheese or liver and onions for a bargain price, is an excellent choice. Be sure to give the dessert menu a once-over. What lover

of sweets could resist blueberry crème brûlée or New York–style cheesecake with blueberry amaretto?

$–$$ *AE, DIS, MC, V; checks OK; breakfast, lunch for big parties and by reservation only, dinner every day; full bar; reservations recommended; www.mccullyhouseinn.com.* &

MONET RESTAURANT
❀❀❀

36 S 2nd St, Ashland / 541/482-1339
Named after the famous French Impressionist, this restaurant is as pretty as a picture. The culinary masterpieces on offer include smoked salmon wrapped around a heavenly avocado mousse; creamy broccoli soup drizzled with sour cream; and the robust *poulet alsacienne*, paprika-spiced chicken on a bed of linguine. Most meals come with fresh whole-grain French bread. A delightful garden outside, filled with plants resembling those in Monet's garden, is a perfect spot for dining in the summer. The interior has been decorated in the pale pinks and greens of the artist's palette, with peach curtains framing the front windows; the walls are adorned with replicas of Monet's paintings. Fresh flowers, floral tablecloths, and comfortable, elegant chairs complement each table. Our only complaint is that the tables are a little too close together—but all is forgiven once the meal begins.

$$ *MC, V; local checks only; dinner every day (Tues–Sat off-season); closed Jan–mid-Feb; full bar; reservations recommended; www.mind.net/monet.*

NEW SAMMY'S COWBOY BISTRO
❀❀

2210 S Pacific Hwy, Talent / 541/535-2779
From the outside, this bistro looks like nothing so much as a rundown roadside shack. The exterior is painted in vivid colors, and a flashing arrow (with lots of bulbs missing) is the only sign indicating the restaurant. As you enter the first set of doors, you might wonder if you are in the right place. But continue on—you won't want to miss what awaits inside. Attractive country wallpaper, pastel accents, Fiestaware, and candles on the tables make for a dining room that is reminiscent of a quaint little dollhouse. The kitchen emphasizes fresh, organic, regional ingredients, and the food ranks among the best in the Northwest. The French-inspired menu usually lists a handful of entrées, such as duck breast with spinach, chicken with spicy couscous, and salmon with dill sauce and vegetables (perfectly cooked). The wines include more than 2,000 choices from Oregon, California, and France. The extremely tiny dining room holds only six tables, so you'll have to make reservations up to three months in advance to get a taste of this place.

Looking for a unique experience? Consider yourselves adventurous? Don't mind planning far in advance? This place is worth seeking out.
$$$$ MC, V; checks OK; dinner Thurs–Sun; closed in Jan; beer and wine; reservations required. ♿

WINCHESTER COUNTRY INN
⬢⬢⬢

35 S 2nd St, Ashland / 541/488-1115 or 800/972-4991
The main floor of a renovated Queen Anne Victorian house is the setting for this winningly romantic restaurant. Tables are placed casually throughout the two front rooms, with plenty of space in between for privacy. Windows look out onto tiered gardens where you can also dine; the mood is always cordial and relaxed. The kitchen specializes in international cuisine prepared with finesse and skill. The Teng Dah beef (filet mignon marinated in soy, garlic, nutmeg, and lemon zest) delivers a delicious harmony of flavors; the crab avocado croissant with orange hollandaise served at brunch is divine. Bread and soup or salad accompany the entrées, and a prix-fixe meal—different each night—is also offered. Service is prompt—the servers are eager to help you make opening curtain. Just make sure you leave time for dessert; the apricot bread pudding and chocolate-hazelnut tureen are both outstanding. The inn also includes 19 guest rooms and a wine bar.
$$–$$$ AE, DIS, MC, V; checks OK; dinner every day (call for seasonal hours in winter), brunch Sun (summer only); full bar; reservations recommended; www.winchesterinn.com.

CRATER LAKE

ROMANTIC HIGHLIGHTS

This region is famous worldwide for its extraordinarily beautiful lake. It's hard to wrap your mind around the dimensions of this volcanic formation, cut into the earth thousands of years ago by natural forces so grand they make the Mount St. Helens eruption seem about as big as a firecracker on the Fourth of July. At 1,932 feet deep, Crater Lake is the deepest lake in the United States, and the seventh deepest in the world. A towering border of golden, rocky earth encompasses this inconceivably blue body of water. It is an astounding spectacle to behold. You can revel in the views as the two of you drive around the entire perimeter (except in the winter and early spring), take a two-hour boat ride from Cleetwood Cove to Wizard Island, or hike down to the lake and embrace amid scenery that will take your breath away. Alas, the caravans of summer tourists can also take your breath away and mar some otherwise prime kissing opportunities. Snow lasts nine months of the year here, and cross-country trails ranging in length from 1 to 10 miles will delight skiers of all abilities.

Access & Information

Crater Lake is off Highway 62, 80 miles northeast of Medford and 60 miles northwest of Klamath Falls. It is about a two-hour drive from either Ashland or Bend. The lake is accessible from Bend via Highway 97 or Roseburg via Highway 138 (Diamond Lake). For information on activities at Crater Lake, including ranger-led walks and boat tours, call the **Steel Visitor's Center** (541/594-3100), or, during the summer months, the **Sinnott Memorial Center** at Rim Visitor's Center (541/594-3090).

Romantic Lodgings

CRATER LAKE LODGE
❀❀❀

Rim Dr, Crater Lake National Park / 541/830-8700
This 1915 lodge, renovated in the mid-1990s, sits on the southern rim of the Crater Lake caldera near Rim Village. A handsome stone-and-wood exterior is accented with chalet-style shutters. Inside, an extensive collection of black-and-white photographs and a detailed display area recount the history of the original building and its recent (and extraordinary) transformation. One of the original stone fireplaces still stands in the main lobby, where Douglas fir floors, columns made from tree trunks, and walls of stone and wood create a rustic Northwest ambience you won't soon forget. Next to the lobby is the Great Hall, which was part of the original 1915 lodge. Here you'll find a gigantic stone fireplace and an assortment of Craftsman-style chairs and sofas. After a day of outdoor adventures, take in the breathtaking views of Crater Lake from the lodge's large patio. You won't find any phones or TVs in the lodge's 71 guest rooms, but neither will you miss them: half the rooms offer incredible views of Crater Lake, and the other half face the Klamath Lake basin. The nicely decorated rooms are a small step up from standard hotel rooms, with contemporary oak furnishings, rather ordinary linens, and small private bathrooms; some also have cushioned window seats. Rooms on the third and fourth floors have sloped ceilings. Four spacious loft rooms are also available, but these are better suited for families than for couples looking for a romantic getaway. Few activities or recreational amenities are available inside the lodge, aside from a selection of board games and cards. Bring a good book just in case the weather proves uncooperative. The lodge's dining room, though spectacular in appearance,

is what happens when no other culinary competition exists for miles: unpredictable dishes and crowded tables put a damper on dining here.
$$$ *AE, DC, DIS, MC, V; checks OK; closed mid-Oct–mid-May; www. crater-lake.com.*

STEAMBOAT INN
❂❂

42705 N Umpqua Hwy (Hwy 138), Steamboat / 800/840-8825
It may feel like you're in the middle of nowhere, but the Steamboat Inn is approximately halfway between Interstate 5 and Crater Lake, in the heart of the Umpqua National Forest. Its remote location along the rushing North Umpqua River is the best reason to stay at this rustic lodge. Hiking to a dozen different waterfalls, wading in the river, and fly-fishing top the list of potential activities. Accommodations come in a variety of shapes and sizes. The five Hideaway Cottages, set in forested surroundings, are spacious and very private. Each one features comfortable furnishings, knotty-pine walls, a white-tiled soaking tub, a wood-burning fireplace, a small kitchenette, and a spacious bedroom and living room. The only thing they lack is a river view. That feature is available in the two higher-priced River Suites, freestanding cottage-style private structures that feature king-size beds, soaking tubs, fireplaces, and private decks overlooking the river. At the least-expensive end of the price spectrum are eight small cedar-paneled Streamside Cabins, which share a pleasant veranda that overlooks the river. These spartan but clean cabins serve as a reminder that many guests come here more to fish than to kiss. The rusticity is part of the fun, and the secluded setting really does allow you to get away from it all.
$$$ *MC, V; checks OK; closed Jan–Feb, open Sat–Sun only Mar–Apr, Nov–Dec (call for seasonal closures); www.thesteamboatinn.com.* &

UNION CREEK RESORT
❂❸

56484 Hwy 62, Union Creek / 541/560-3565 or 866/560-3565
If you're looking for something off the beaten path, the affordable Union Creek Resort might be for you. Located 23 miles west of Crater Lake, the resort offers 14 cabins on 12 acres surrounded by the Rogue River National Forest and is just minutes from horseback riding, snowmobile trails, pristine hiking, cross-country skiing, salmon and steelhead fishing, and absolute solitude. Cabins are simple and somewhat dated, but this is in keeping with the rustic setting—a favorite of Zane Grey, Jack London, and Herbert Hoover. "Sleeping" cabins are equipped with microwaves, coffee makers, and bedding; "housekeeping" cabins come with fully equipped kitchens. There's a country store, ice cream shop, and cafe just a romantic stroll away.
$ *AE, DC, DIS, MC, V; no checks; www.unioncreekoregon.com.* &

CENTRAL OREGON

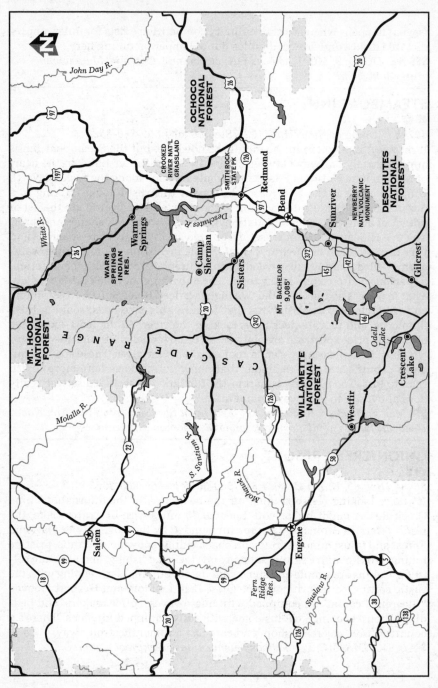

"Where kisses are repeated and the arms hold there is no telling where time is."

—TED HUGHES

♡ CENTRAL OREGON

Distinguished by the rugged peaks of Mounts Jefferson, Washington, and Bachelor, this land of high mountain lakes, dense pine forests, and tumbling streams beckons lovers of the outdoors—and just plain lovers—to play year-round. Set just west of the true center of the state, the Central Cascade region of Oregon remains one of the rare places in the United States that is still more wild than tamed, with just enough towns—mostly small and rugged—to make creature comforts easily accessible.

The terrain is varied and dramatic, with the mountain landscape changing abruptly from lush alpine to high desert just east of the Cascade Range. Here, at 4,000 feet, canyons and rivers carve paths through dry expanses brightened by the red bark of the ponderosa pine, berried junipers, manzanita, and sage. With at least two quite romantic destinations—the city of Bend and the neighboring small town of Sisters—this region merits more than just one visit. Even the journey, along quiet country roads through mountains and valleys, is a destination in itself.

Central Oregon draws visitors during all four seasons; it has an ideal climate year-round. Humidity is low, nights are cool, and temperatures are reasonably mild, with the average July high peaking at 83 degrees F and January lows at 20 degrees F. Winters bring abundant snow and cold temperatures, perfect for downhill or cross-country skiing, snowmobiling, skating, snowshoeing, or simply cuddling up by a warm fire. Summers are pleasantly mild in the higher regions, warmer in the lower elevations, and ideal for fishing, hiking, biking, boating, or enjoying a romantic picnic by a hidden lake. For those who like their outdoor adventure on the quiet side, there are shops to browse, county fairs to visit, outdoor concerts and summer fests to attend—each with its own possibilities for romance. The highways in and around the Cascades, many of them closed from late fall through early spring, showcase stunning views of volcanic cones, lava flows, basalt cliffs, waterfalls, and twisting gorges.

BEND & MOUNT BACHELOR

ROMANTIC HIGHLIGHTS

Blessed with scenic beauty and a mild climate, and cultivating a personality that can be both sophisticated and simple, Bend offers the sort of setting that can make even routine things seem romantic. Forty-odd years ago, this small city in the heart of Oregon was barely known beyond its borders. That all changed in 1957, when Mount Bachelor, then called Bachelor Butte, opened as a ski resort. (For more on winter skiing, see Access and Information, below.) Today, the little town is not quite so little anymore. With a population of 62,000, innumerable parks (including the 11-acre Drake Park, with its picturesque Mirror Pond), as well as hiking trails, golf courses, and the state's largest ski resort, opportunities for leisure and play abound. Add incredible natural beauty to the mix, and romance is a natural.

Downtown Bend offers just enough urban variety and bustle to keep life interesting, but without the hectic pace of larger cities. Ponder the possibilities of the day with coffee and quiche or a bagel at **Tuffy's** (961 NW Brooks St; 541/389-6464), where cafe seats take in views of both Mirror Pond and the Deschutes River.

If you visit Bend during the summer, check the calendar for a full moon, then sign on with **Wanderlust Tours** (541/389-8359; www.wanderlusttours. com) for a very romantic moonlight canoe trip on the Cascade Lakes. Tours are led by a naturalist, who will point out all the geographic wonders of the area as you paddle your canoe across still waters beneath a nighttime summer sky. After a break on the shore for hot apple cider and desserts from local bakery **Nancy P's** (1054 NW Milwaukee Ave; 541/322-8778), you'll paddle back to the dock for the drive home. You won't have the lake to yourselves; there will be others—also romantics at heart, no doubt—along on the tour, but the memories you can share all alone.

Gazing at the sunset in Bend is essential to any romantic rendezvous. Watch twilight fall from the sloping lawns of **Drake Park**, in the heart of downtown Bend on the Deschutes River, or snuggle as you view the changing sky from atop **Pilot Butte**, on the east side of town on Highway 20 (the turn is well signed). There are many possibilities for summer day-trips from Bend, but our favorite is the meandering drive along the **Cascade Lakes National Scenic Byway**. Before you set out, pick up a delectable picnic for two at **Appetite Deli** (335 SW Century Dr; 541/617-8885). The peaceful drive along blacktop winds past pristine lakes, forests of ponderosa pine, the Deschutes River, basalt lava flows, and awe-inspiring views of some of the area's biggest mountains. There are plenty of lake beaches to lounge on, or if you prefer a more active search for romance, take one of the fabulous hikes that begin right from the road. Except for on the busiest of summer weekends, after a mile or two of walking you are likely to have the forest to yourself; you might even feel as if you're the only two people left in a world of wild beauty. When you return to town, you just might be in need of refreshment, which you'll find at the **Maragas Winery Tasting Room** (643 NW Colorado Ave; 541/330-0919). You and your love can sit at a patio table and sample one of the winery's delicious signature varietals, Legal Zin or Pinot Riche.

You don't have to be a skier to appreciate the stunning beauty of **Mount Bachelor**. The warmer months bring unsurpassed views, fields of bright wildflowers, and sightings of all sorts of wildlife, both feathered and furry. If you and your sweetie are especially athletic, you can hike to the top, but between Independence Day and Labor Day romantics can hop on the Pine Marten Lift for a relaxing ride to the mid-mountain lodge, where **Scapolos Italian Bistro** (541/382-2442), over a mile in the air, offers sunset dinners with front-row seats to the breathtaking mountain scenery. Sit outside, order something cold to drink, then share hearthmade wood-oven pizza or homemade pasta while reveling in the scenery.

Traveling 8 miles over a washboard dirt road is hardly our idea of a romantic thing to do, but just wait till you receive your reward: stars like you've never seen them before (except, perhaps, in each other's eyes), courtesy of the **Pine Mountain Observatory** (from Bend, take Hwy 20 east toward Burns, turn right (south) on a dirt road just beyond the abandoned Millican gas station, and continue about 8 miles to the top; 541/382-8331; Fri–Sat evenings, late May–late Sept). The observatory offers three telescopes—15, 24, and 32 inches in diameter, respectively—providing views of sunspots and sunflares, the discs and rings of planets, distant galaxies, and the star clouds of the Milky Way. Focus on your favorite constellation, then let your sweetheart make a wish. With stargazing this good, neither of you will mind if it doesn't come true. Come to the observatory prepared; once you leave Bend, there are no stores or gas stations. Be sure you have enough fuel for the return trip, and bring along bottled water and some warm clothing; you may want to linger up here among the heavens.

If you and yours are charmed by towns small and decidedly Western, plan to spend a few hours wandering the streets of **Sisters**. Located 20 miles west of Bend on Highway 20, Sisters is named for the three mountain peaks—Faith, Hope, and Charity—that dominate the horizon. Surrounded by mountains, trout streams, and pine and cedar forests, Sisters is perfect for both lovers of nature and those whose idea of a good afternoon outing is browsing small shops filled with antiques, art, and souvenirs while enjoying a good old-fashioned ice cream cone. One word of warning: Sisters in the summer is not the place for solitude, especially during the second weekend in June or the second weekend in July, when the rodeo and outdoor quilt show, respectively, draw crowds.

But privacy is only a short drive away. We would be the first to admit that a fish hatchery is hardly anyone's idea of a place made for *amour*, but so singular is the setting of the **Wizard Falls Fish Hatchery** (take Hwy 20, 10 miles west of Sisters, and look for Rd 14), that it would be a crime to omit it here. In fact, the drive alone will no doubt inspire a few kisses: the road leads deep within the Deschutes National Forest, surrounding you in lush woods of pine and cedar and all manner of wildlife. Before you leave Sisters, grab a picnic lunch to go from **Angeline's Bakery and Café** (121 W Main Ave; 541/549-9122) or **Seasons Café & Wine Shop** (411 E Hood Ave; 541/549-8911). You'll know you've arrived when you spot the stretch of rushing river so incredibly blue you'll look twice to be sure you haven't imagined it. Trails run both upstream and downstream of the river, leading to all sorts of beautiful spots where you can indulge in a passionate picnic in the woods. Finding such delightful seclusion often requires a more arduous journey than this one, all the more reason to seize this chance for a private interlude surrounded by nature.

Access & Information

Access to Bend or Sisters from the Salem region is via Interstate 5 to Highway 20, which runs over the Santiam Pass. From Eugene, take Highway 126 to access Highway 20. From southern Oregon, you can reach the region from Highway 97 (via Highway 62 if you're coming from Interstate 5). From Portland and the north take Highway 26 from Interstate 5. During the winter months, traction devices and good snow tires are musts. For snow and road conditions, call the **Oregon Department of Transportation** (800/977-ODOT). For more information about Bend, call the **Central Oregon Visitors Association** (800/800-8334). For information on Sisters, call the **Sisters Area Chamber of Commerce** (541/549-0251).

Mount Bachelor Ski Area (on Century Dr, 22 miles southwest of Bend; 541/382-7888 for ski report or 800/829-2442; www.mtbachelor.com) is one of the biggest in the Northwest, with seven high-speed lifts (ten lifts in all) feeding skiers onto 3,100 vertical feet of groomed and dry-powder runs. The tubing park has a surface lift and five groomed runs. When you and your ski bunny have worked up your appetites, the **Skier's Palate** (located at mid-mountain in the Pine Marten Lodge) serves excellent lunches; **Scapolo's** (on the lodge's lower level) features hearty Italian cuisine. Skiing closes on Memorial Day, but the slopes re-open July 1 for summer sightseeing. During the high season, Mount Bachelor offers a ski school, racing, a day care, rentals, and an entire Nordic program and trails.

Romantic Lodgings

BLUE SPRUCE BED & BREAKFAST
○○€

444 S Spruce, Sisters / 541/549-9644 or 888/328-9644
Built in 1999, this farmhouse-style inn nestled in a grove of evergreens offers rustic comforts with a dash of luxury. If you sit out on the expansive front porch, you'll be entertained by deer, squirrels, and all manner of wildlife prowling the woods. Inside, the great room features a stone fireplace, leather sofas, oversize chairs, a player piano, and a game table. The four guest rooms are generous, and each is decorated according to a theme: choose from among Hunting, Logging, Fishing, and Western. Each comes with a king-size bed, a private bath with two-person spa, a shower with waterfall head, and, says innkeeper Vaunelle Temple, "the only towel warmers in central Oregon." (But what you're guaranteed to remember here are the mouse-hole nightlights: cut into the wall, each nightlight is a miniature copy of the guest room it's in, and absolutely adorable.) The family-style breakfast, served at an enormous round table with a large lazy Susan in the middle, may not be the most intimate affair, but the fresh-squeezed orange juice, fresh blueberry syrup, orange-pecan stuffed French toast, and bacon, ham, or sausage will provide hearty fuel for your day of romantic fun.
$$ AE, DIS, MC, V; checks OK; www.blue-spruce.biz.

CONKLIN'S GUEST HOUSE
○○€

69013 Camp Polk Rd, Sisters / 541/549-0123
Set in 5 acres of fields dotted with two ponds, and featuring a large grassy yard with a swimming pool, this turn-of-the-20th-century farmhouse on the outskirts of Sisters sparkles. The picturesque grounds make a perfect backdrop for weddings, and in summer the inn is popular with couples tying the knot. Twosomes with romance on their minds naturally gravitate to the gazebo that juts charmingly out over the pond closest to the house; inviting benches that line this pond's banks also beckon. New ownership promises yet more romance on the grounds; plans for 2005–06 include adding new cottages, among other changes. But the accommodations this inn already offers are delightful. In the Forget-Me-Not Room on the main floor, a black iron-canopied queen-size bed stands as the room's centerpiece, complemented by white wicker furniture, a gas fireplace, and a day bed. This room also has its own private entrance. Upstairs, the charming Morning Glory Suite has gorgeous views of the ponds and gardens, pastures and mountains—sure to inspire romance. Pleasant framed prints, terra-cotta–hued walls, and a black-iron canopied queen-size bed furnish the room. In the morning, a lovely terra-cotta–tiled solarium next to the pool is the perfect setting for a breakfast that may include corned-beef hash with baked eggs,

eggs Benedict with grated kielbasa, or an assortment of muffins. Fresh flowers and herbs from the garden adorn each dish.

$$ *No credit cards; checks OK; www.conklinsguesthouse.com.* ⅋

CRICKETWOOD COUNTRY BED & BREAKFAST
🖤🖤

63520 Cricketwood Rd, Bend / 877/330-0747

As its name suggests, the Cricketwood Country B&B is all about country living. Set on 10 acres of parklike lawn and grassy fields, the inn is just 5 miles from Bend—but you and your love will feel as though you're in another world. Three guest rooms—two are suites—have garden themes; the Secret Garden Room doubles as a honeymoon suite, and features a double Jacuzzi, portable massage table, candles, scented oil, and even some romantic (naughty but nice!) games. But it's the hospitality here that makes this B&B stand out. Innkeepers Jim and Tracy Duncan have mastered the fine art of providing superb service—they do just enough to make you feel entirely welcome, without annoying you with their constant presence. Breakfasts are made to order from a large menu that may include such delights as crème brûlée–baked French toast or New Orleans bread pudding with rum sauce. Guest refrigerators are fully stocked, and bedtime cookies and morning beverages are on the house. After you've fed the local ducks or taken the perfect 2-mile walk around the countryside, continue to enjoy the bucolic scenery—from the hot tub.

$$ *AE, DIS, MC, V; checks OK; www.cricketwood.com.*

LARA HOUSE BED AND BREAKFAST
🖤🖤

640 NW Congress St, Bend / 541/388-4064 or 800/766-4064

Guests never fail to comment on Lara House's picturesque location, and for good reason: built in 1910, this bed-and-breakfast on a quiet residential corner features bay windows and a large front porch that frame pretty views of tranquil Drake Park and Mirror Pond. The one guest room on the first floor and four on the second floor of the house come with queen-size beds and private baths, but for the utmost in intimacy, we favor the Summit Suite, tucked up under the eaves of the third floor and offering a king-size bed and cozy living room. In winter, a cup of steaming, delicious spiced cider greets your arrival; genuine smiles from the innkeepers come with every season. In the morning, an ample breakfast of stuffed French toast, fresh fruit, and locally roasted organic coffee is served at your private table in the glass-enclosed sunroom. Although Lara House is not exceedingly elegant, it's a wonderful place to relax, unwind, and spend cozy time together.

$$ *AE, DIS, MC, V; checks OK; www.larahouse.com.*

METOLIUS RIVER RESORT
❍❍❍❍

25551 SW Forest Service Rd 1419, Camp Sherman / 541/595-6281 or 800/81-TROUT

Not to be confused with the lower-priced, well-worn, and well-loved Metolius River Lodges across the bridge, these 11 gracious cabins on the west bank of the river offer the height of rustic romance. Trimmed in wood-shake and featuring river-rock fireplaces, most of the cabins have river views, master bedrooms and lofts, furnished kitchens, and French doors leading to large, river-facing decks. In this setting tucked snugly within the Deschutes National Forest, you'll awaken to the sweet sounds of birdsong and the rushing river, then wind down in the evening to the evocative chirping of crickets and frogs. Whether you choose to snuggle inside by the fire or sit out on the deck, take a peaceful stroll through the woods or cast your fishing line on the river, time spent here can't help but be romantic. Because the cabins are privately owned, the interiors, though consistently luxurious, are all different; most include a CD player and TV/VCR with satellite dish. *$$$ MC, V; checks OK; closed first 2 weeks of Dec; www.metoliusriver resort.com.*

PINE RIDGE INN
❍❍❍❍

1200 SW Century Dr, Bend / 541/389-6137 or 800/600-4095

Set on a bluff above the Deschutes River, this charming luxury inn, one of Bend's finest, caters to romantics by offering the ultimate in personal attention and privacy. Amenities in most of the 20 guest rooms include large, well-stocked baths; TV/VCRs; kitchenettes; Jacuzzi tubs; and evening turn-down service. Suites have step-down living rooms with both antique and reproduction-antique furniture, gas-log fireplaces, and private porches. For the ultimate in indulgence, the 900-square-foot Hyde Suite, on the second floor, takes the cake. With a luxurious king bedroom, a living/dining room, a two-person Jacuzzi, an adjoining powder room, a pair of decks, and expansive windows framing glorious views of the river, this is hands-down the best place to kiss in the inn. In the evenings, wine and cheese are served in the communal fireside parlor. The delicious complimentary breakfast is also served in the parlor and includes a hot entrée, fruit, breads, and cereals. Inn guests are invited to take advantage of the nearby athletic club, which features exercise facilities and a huge outdoor pool. *$$$ AE, DC, DIS, MC, V; no checks; www.pineridgeinn.com.* ♿

RIVER RIDGE AT MOUNT BACHELOR VILLAGE RESORT
◐◐◐

19717 Mount Bachelor Dr, Bend / 541/389-5900 or 800/452-9846
Tucked in the heart of Mount Bachelor Village Resort, River Ridge offers tastefully finished, contemporary suites with one to three bedrooms, and "executive" suites. The executive suites, similar to a room in a nice hotel, are the smallest and least expensive, but don't have views. The one-bedroom suites offer plentiful space, full kitchens, and relaxing views of the forest or river. The two- and three-bedroom suites, however, are the crème de la crème, each featuring a full kitchen, a hot tub on the deck, a Jacuzzi tub in the master suite, and a gas fireplace. The price is steep, but well worth it for your romantic getaway. River Ridge is set within a larger resort (meaning you'll have little privacy in common areas), but once you are enclosed in your suite you'll notice nothing but idyllic isolation. The luxurious decor and spectacular view—not to mention melodious sounds of the river—will make you feel as if you're the only two in the whole wide world. The resort also offers access to many more amenities, including the 2.2-mile nature trail—perfect for a romantic meander—and athletic club and swimming pool, both open year-round.
$$–$$$ *AE, DC, DIS, MC, V; checks OK; www.mtbachelorvillage.com.* &

SUNRIVER RESORT
◐◐

1 Center Dr, Bend / 541/593-1000 or 800/547-3922
Encompassing a stunning 3,200 riverside acres, this self-sufficient community comes complete with its own post office, grocery store, and paved runway for private planes. Much of the resort's reputation is built around its three 18-hole championship golf courses, but the surrounding mountains, the Deschutes River, and the resort itself offer all kinds of recreational opportunities. Twenty-eight tennis courts, 35 miles of paved bike paths, swimming pools, horseback riding, cross-country skiing, and white-water rafting are all available for you and your athletic honey at this all-around vacation destination. Unlike many resorts, Sunriver is well spread out, so you aren't forced to have a family experience even when you're traveling without children. Various companies manage the many vacation rentals, so your best bet for finding the romantic retreat of your dreams is to let the reservation staff know your hearts' desire and let them guide you to the appropriate accommodations. Lodge dining includes the Meadows, an acclaimed showplace for lunch, dinner, and Sunday brunch. Elsewhere in the town of Sunriver, you can find everything from Chinese to pizza, but for a really romantic meal, travel up the road to the Grille at Crosswater (541/593-3400), a golf-course restaurant that's above par and open to Sunriver guests only.
$$–$$$$ *AE, DIS, MC, V; checks OK; www.sunriverresort.com.* &

Romantic Restaurants

CAFE ROSEMARY
◒◒◒

1110 NW Newport Ave, Bend / 541/317-0276
Cafe Rosemary moved in 2004 from its popular downtown location to a small bungalow on Bend's west side, and though the new space is more casual, the restaurant's charm and style are intact. In fact, the new location seems friendlier to a wider range of romance seekers. Café au lait–colored walls displaying antique botanical prints and portraits provide a formal mood, tempered by cheerful white wainscoting and lace curtain–draped stained glass windows. Lunch is pleasant, offering a wide variety of reasonably priced salads, including the restaurant's trademark rosemary salad with field greens, Gorgonzola, fresh fruit, honey-roasted nuts, and a poppy seed dressing. Dinner is a more elaborate (and expensive) affair, though there's no doubt that the foie gras with pomegranate drizzle or jumbo Maryland soft-shell crab appetizers will make you and your sweetie melt with happiness. The entrée menu includes rack of lamb, beef tenderloin, and the inimitable chef game sampler (rattlesnake sausage, boneless quail, and rocky mountain elk). Desserts such as the chocolate truffle cake with freshly made ice cream or the chocolate croissant bread pudding with crème anglaise will round out your romantic evening properly.
$$$ AE, DIS, MC, V; checks OK; lunch Tues–Fri, dinner Tues–Sun; full bar; reservations recommended.

CORK
◒◒◒

150 NW Oregon, Bend / 541/382-6881
Named "Best New Restaurant in Oregon 2002" by *Northwest Palate* magazine, this intimate and elegant downtown restaurant offers "American eclectic" cuisine—that is to say, they cook up a little bit of everything. There's filet mignon, seared ahi tuna, chicken breast, and risotto. The signature dish is the scallops, tender bits pan-seared in their own milk and so rich and tasty they could almost pass for lobster. Both the restaurant and its separate wine bar (open Tues–Sat at 5pm) offer an extensive wine list, with a good number served by the glass (in Riedel glassware, no less). You and your sweetheart will relish the French-press coffees, specialty domestic and imported beers, and homemade desserts. Works by local artists adorn the walls, and the abundant flickering candles and fresh flowers enhance the romantic air. Because the space is small and the tables close together, come here for the charming atmosphere and fine food rather than for privacy.
$$$ AE, MC, V; no checks; dinner Tues–Sat; beer and wine; reservations recommended. &

HANS
●●

915 NW Wall St, Bend / 541/389-9700
This warm and welcoming downtown cafe offers a fine selection of salads and intriguing daily specials. While service can be a bit brisk, the bustle is hospitable and the room itself—hardwood floors, Tuscany-hued plaster walls adorned with frescoes—is inviting. Lunch menus feature mix-and-match sandwiches with all kinds of breads, cheeses, and other ingredients. Dinner ratchets up the cuisine several notches, as choices include grilled portobello appetizers, unique pizzas, seafood pasta, salmon, and tenderloin—all with creative yet simple sauces and flavors. For a cozy treat for two to finish things off, look no farther than the case of pastries and decadent sweets.
$$ MC, V; checks OK; lunch, dinner Tues–Sat; beer and wine; reservations recommended. &

KOKANEE CAFÉ
●●●

25545 SW Forest Service Rd 1419, Camp Sherman / 541/595-6420
This hidden-away cafe earns regular raves from folks both near and far. Though it's small, making privacy elusive, this shingle-sided cottage's setting, tucked among the ponderosa pines of the Deschutes National Forest and just off the Metolius River, is romantic indeed. The river-rock fireplace and covered heated porch make it even more so. Here the food is eclectic, upscale Pacific Northwest cuisine and includes signature dishes such as Oregon duck with maple-ginger butter sauce and wild Pacific salmon, served with a reduced pinot noir sauce and crispy potatoes. Food this delicious in a setting this wonderfully wild can't help but inspire a kiss.
$$$ MC, V; no checks; dinner every day (June–Aug), Tues–Sun (May, Sept–Oct); closed Nov–Apr; beer and wine; reservations recommended. &

MERENDA
●●

900 NW Wall St, Bend / 541/330-2304
Occupying a corner building downtown with exposed brick walls and high ceilings and accented with rich gold and red tones throughout, Merenda is where urban trendy meets Old World charm. Launched in 2002 by San Francisco chef Jody Denton, Merenda has developed a reputation as the place to see and be seen in Bend. This popularity means that, especially during happy hour or on weekend nights, it can be packed and noisy. But romance isn't out of the question, and Merenda is definitely a great date destination. Secure yourselves a booth or window table (or better yet, a spot upstairs in the quieter fireplace room, usually open for dining on weekends) and you'll soon be so enchanted by the extensive wine list and excellent French- and

Mediterranean-inspired cuisine (and each other, of course) that you'll forget about the bustle. Start with a wine flight—four 2-ounce pours grouped by varietal or origin that the two of you can trade sips from—before choosing a glass or bottle from Merenda's large wine cellar. If you're still in the sharing mood, the hors d'oeuvres are all superb—absolutely don't miss the risotto fritters. Entrées include nightly specials from the wood-fired oven; choose leg of lamb or duck, as well as steaks, seafood, and impeccably prepared vegetable side dishes. Save room for dessert: the beignets—served hot with chocolate, caramel, and whipped cream for dipping—will leave a sweet taste lingering on your lips and tide you over until your next kiss.

$$ *AE, DC, DIS, MC, V; checks OK; lunch, dinner every day; full bar; reservations recommended; www.merendarestaurant.com.* &

SCANLON'S
❂❂❂

61615 Mount Bachelor Dr, Bend / 541/382-8769

It's true that Scanlon's shares a building with an athletic club—but don't let that scare you away. Offering consistently exceptional Northwest and Mediterranean cuisine and attentive yet unobtrusive service, Scanlon's is wonderful for either a lovely, casual lunch or a leisurely, extravagant dinner. High-backed booths of rich, dark oak, with comfy, cushioned seats offer plenty of privacy for kissing twosomes. Each table is beautifully set with white linens and decanters of olive oil and balsamic vinegar to accompany the fresh baked breads from Scanlon's wood-fired oven. Both the house salad, with dried cranberries and hazelnuts, and the Caesar salad, sprinkled with pine nuts and sun-dried tomatoes, are delightful. The entrée menu, inspired by flavors Asian to European, changes twice yearly and might include hazelnut-crusted salmon or tataki ahi drizzled with wasabi crème fraîche and accompanied by Asian greens with sake vinaigrette. Your server will no doubt tempt you with a tray of house-made desserts; the Key lime pie is a sublime combination of tart and sweet, and the peanut butter pie is nothing less than original decadence. Seasonal outdoor patio seating is available but will put you closer to the athletic club's swimming pool and lawn—areas that might be noisier and less attractive than you might prefer; if your goal is privacy and quiet, also avoid nights when the club hosts outdoor concerts.

$$ *AE, DIS, MC, V; checks OK; lunch, dinner every day; full bar; reservations recommended; www.athleticclubofbend.com.* &

SEATTLE & ENVIRONS

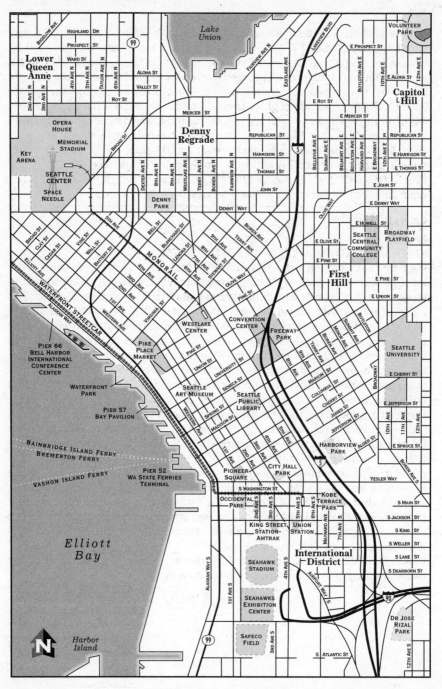

"What of soul was left, I wonder, when the kissing had to stop?"

—ROBERT BROWNING

♡ SEATTLE & ENVIRONS

Seattle's awe-inspiring natural beauty attracts droves of visitors, all of whom fall in love with its eccentric, charming, and rugged personality. The views never fail to astound, and few cities in the world offer such a spectacular setting. Not only are there numerous glistening waterways, anchored by Puget Sound, but also everywhere you look there are mountains, mountains, mountains: the snowcapped peaks of the Olympic Mountains in the west; the jagged Cascade Mountains in the east; and Mount Rainier, one of the world's most beautiful mountains, playing hide-and-seek in mist to the south.

Fantastically successful companies like Microsoft, Amazon.com, Nordstrom, and Starbucks have given Seattle a reputation for innovation, while the city's espresso obsession (drive-thru latte, anyone?) has also attracted national notice. There are big-city drawbacks here, ranging from congested freeways to crowded restaurants, but a lively downtown, lush and abundant parks, and ever-increasing numbers of acclaimed dining destinations make for tempting benefits. Yet for all its urbanity, Seattle holds fast to its small-town roots. Its many neighborhoods are fiercely individualistic, and each prides itself on the history, shops, restaurants, and people that define it. Across the floating bridge to the east, the booming region known as the Eastside is creating a life of its own, and destinations such as Woodinville, with its acclaimed wineries, and the waterfront town of Kirkland draw tourists year-round. A short ferry ride across Puget Sound leads to woodsy Bainbridge Island, which features a quaint downtown and provides the link from Seattle to the magnificent Olympic Peninsula.

What tends to bring the people of this city together is a shared passion for the outdoors. From bicycling, hiking, and inline skating to boating, windsurfing, and skiing, outdoor recreation is a serious year-round pursuit in Seattle. Any season is an excellent time to visit, from the verdant, blossom-filled spring or brilliant, sunny summer to the crisp autumn or the famously rainy winter (perfect for cozying up with your sweetheart). The ski slopes are only an hour's drive east of the city; excellent theater, music, opera, and late-night entertainment can be found almost any night downtown; island getaways are just an hour away by ferry; and opportunities for beautiful hikes and walks abound. In short, Seattle boasts enough kissing destinations to keep two people occupied with romance for a lifetime.

SEATTLE

ROMANTIC HIGHLIGHTS

For an authentic Seattle experience, there is no better place to visit than the beloved **Pike Place Market** (on busy summer weekends, be prepared to kiss amid the crowds). Fresh seafood (some of the best crab and mussels you'll ever taste), colorful regional produce, gorgeous flowers made into bouquets ready for your table, and locally made arts and crafts are among the market's bountiful offerings. As you stroll down the cobblestone alleys, pass the famous flying-fish stand (watch your head!), or do as the Seattleites do and order a latte at the original Starbucks—the unique spell of this waterfront city will take hold. Go off the beaten path and explore charming Post Alley all the way to its northern end, where you'll find gems like **Rose's Chocolate Treasures** (1906 Post Alley; 206/441-2936), the **Perennial Tea Room** (1910 Post Alley; 206/448-4054), and **The Tasting Room** (1924 Post Alley; 206/770-9463), where you can sample delicious Washington wines at an elegant tasting bar and learn more about the state's famous vintages. For more market information, pick up a map and self-guided-tour pamphlet at the information booth (corner of 1st Ave and Pike St; 206/682-7453).

If you're up for a romantic meal in the market, duck into our favorite French-inspired hideaway, **Place Pigalle** (81 Pike St; 206/624-1756), for picture-postcard views of Elliott Bay; warm, professional service; and delicious lunch or dinner fare. Summertime terrace seating at the bustling **Pink Door** (1919 Post Alley; 206/443-3241) is less intimate, but in warm weather it's an alfresco treat. If you're up for exploring beyond the market, shop in the sleek downtown stores near Pine Street and Fifth Avenue. Or stroll north along First Avenue to the Belltown neighborhood, Seattle's restaurant central. Here, the acclaimed **Macrina Bakery & Café** (2408 1st Ave; 206/448-4032) provides an inviting spot for lunch, weekend brunch, or just strong, hot coffee and heavenly cookies.

South of downtown, on First and Second Avenues, you'll find the quaint cobblestone streets, historic brick buildings, and leafy streets of Pioneer Square. It's fun to poke around in the many little shops here, and you could spend hours browsing at Seattle's best-known bookstore, the **Elliott Bay Book Company** (101 S Main St; 206/624-6600). With its terraced layout, exposed-brick walls, cozy downstairs cafe, and more than 150,000 titles to choose from, this legendary independent store will inspire *amour* among book lovers. Afterwards, repair to the well-hidden but charmingly formal terraced dining room for an elegant Italian repast at **Il Terrazzo Carmine** (411 1st Ave S; 206/467-7797; lunch Mon–Fri, dinner every day; reservations recommended).

Museums are not always romantic, but the delightful **Seattle Art Museum** (100 University St; 206/654-3100; www.seattleartmuseum.org) certainly is. The airy lobby invites you in, and as you ascend the grand marble staircase guarded by massive stone rams and camels that leads to the exhibits, you'll have fun deciding what sort of art fits your mood. Seattle's got many other kinds of cultural offerings, and the staff of any area lodging can help you seek out tickets to the opera, theater, ballet, or concerts. For a more "moving" form of entertainment, ride the city's famous **Monorail** from downtown's Westlake Center to the **Space Needle** (206/905-2100; www.spaceneedle.com). Brave the line: The view that awaits at the top is highly romantic on a clear day. All the region's glories are readily visible, from the mountains and islands to the city's many neighborhoods, encircled by green. And, while it may sound cheesy, we are nevertheless unafraid to recommend the **Sky City at the Needle restaurant** (Seattle Center; 206/905-2100; reservations recommended). The restaurant makes a full revolution each hour (don't worry, it's so gradual you'll hardly notice you're moving), and its ever-changing view, combined with a summer sunset, candlelight, and fresh king salmon, makes for an excellent—if touristy—date.

If you'd like to explore beyond downtown, head for the city's quiet parks and intriguing neighborhoods. In lively **Capitol Hill**, if you're in the mood for street life, check out the cool bars and hot boutiques along Pine Street; or, if it's more of a pastoral excursion you're after, wander around pretty **Volunteer Park** (1400 E Prospect St), with its magnificent trees and splendid Victorian conservatory filled with flowers. Even better for nature-inspired kissing is the beautiful **Washington Park Arboretum** (2300 Arboretum Dr E; 206/543-8800; open daily until dusk). Wander hand in hand through this sylvan realm just south of the University of Washington, where 5,500 different kinds of plants transform the land into a verdant oasis. Special highlights include the Rhododendron Glen, the Woodland Garden, and, for a small admission fee, the lovely Japanese Garden (closed Dec–Feb). In spring, the clouds of white and pink cherry blossoms are astonishing, and autumn turns the foliage to ardent shades of red and gold. If you work up an appetite looking at leaves, consider brunch at the nearby, 100 percent vegetarian yet delightfully gourmet **Café Flora** (2901 E Madison St; 206/325-9100).

Among Seattle's many quirky and charming neighborhoods, **Fremont** prides itself on its eccentricity: to get the vibe, note the signs that say "Welcome to Fremont: Center of the Universe," or visit the European-style flea market held on Sundays (N 34th St between Evanston and Phinney Aves;

206/282-5706). The angled streets here are filled with highly browsable antique, secondhand, and retro-kitsch stores and inviting neighborhood hideaways like the **35th Street Bistro** (709 N 35th St; 206/547-9850; lunch, dinner Tues–Sun). We are also partial to **Ballard**—both old Ballard, with its Scandinavian heritage, and new Ballard, with its chic shops along cobblestone Ballard Avenue; after an afternoon browsing the boutiques (which sell everything from home adornments and hand-crafted Italian shoes to seductive French underclothing), step into the cozy **Portalis Wine Bar** (5310 Ballard Ave; 206/783-2007), an elegant bar space with exposed-brick walls that's also half-retail so you can shop for a special vintage to bring home with you. Farther west, along the water, are the **Hiram M. Chittenden Locks** (3015 NW 54th St; 206/783-7059), where every year as many as 100,000 pleasure and commercial boats transition from Lakes Washington and Union to Puget Sound. Gaze at gleaming wooden sailboats from the plush, sloping lawns above the water, or explore the nearby 7-acre English gardens. You'll find lots of idyllic places to picnic, and the gardens are worth a visit even in winter.

Yet another of Seattle's assets is its proximity to the jewel-like islands in Puget Sound. While locals may use the **Washington State Ferries** (206/464-6400 or 800/843-3779; www.wsdot.wa.gov/ferries/) as a means of transportation, we think they're ideal for romance—and you'll hardly find a better vantage point for a sweeping view of the majestic mountains. If you're feeling adventurous, make a day of it: put on your walking shoes and take the ferries to explore some nearby ports of call. Granted, they're not the Love Boat—the interiors are industrial and there's no privacy—but for very little money, you and yours can bundle up and head out onto the open deck to enjoy a glowing sunset. The crisp, salty air is bound to inspire some snuggling, and who could resist a few kisses with sublime views of the Seattle skyline for a backdrop?

Access & Information

Interstate 5 is the main north-south arterial in Seattle. If you choose to drive while you're here, be forewarned: surveys rank Seattle as among the top ten least drivable cities in the country (along with Los Angeles and San Francisco) and traffic jams are as common as cloudy skies and drizzle. Two east-west arterials connect to Eastside cities such as Bellevue via floating bridges—Interstate 90 (south of downtown) and Highway 520 (north of downtown); the major Eastside north-south highway is Interstate 405. Downtown Seattle is divided into avenues (starting with First near the waterfront) running north-south, and streets running west-east. A further warning to prospective drivers: many streets are one-way.

Getting to downtown from **Seattle-Tacoma International Airport** (17801

Pacific Hwy S, SeaTac; 206/431-4444) is a 35-minute straight shot north on Interstate 5 (make sure to avoid peak rush hours: 7–9:30am and 4:30–7pm). **Gray Line Airport Express** (206/626-6088) runs airport passengers to and from major downtown hotels for about $8.50 one-way. Taxis from the airport to downtown cost $30–$35. By law, taxis to the airport from downtown Seattle must charge a flat fee of $25 (some cabbies might need reminding). Large car-rental agencies have locations near the airport, in downtown Seattle, and in the suburbs.

Amtrak (303 S Jackson St; 206/382-4126 or 800/USA-RAIL; www. amtrak.com) trains arrive at and depart from King Street Station. Seattle is a stop on Amtrak's Coast Starlight route; the Portland-to-Seattle section, much of which runs along the shores of Puget Sound, is especially scenic—and rather romantic.

The city's **Metro Transit** (206/553-3000; transit.metrokc.gov) serves Seattle and the Eastside and connects with buses from greater Puget Sound to the north and south. Metro buses are free until 7pm in the downtown core (between the waterfront and Interstate 5, and Jackson and Bell Sts). The charming old-time streetcar (part of Metro) serves the waterfront, Pioneer Square, and the city's Chinatown/International District. For off-road transport, ride the space-age Monorail (see Romantic Highlights), which in 90 seconds glides between downtown's Westlake Center (Pine St and 4th Ave, 3rd floor) and the Seattle Center.

The **Seattle–King County Convention and Visitors Bureau** (800 Convention Pl, Galleria level; 206/461-5840; www.seeseattle.org) is a good source for information and maps. In summer, visit their outdoor kiosks at Seattle Center and Pioneer Square.

Romantic Lodgings

ALEXIS HOTEL
♥♥♥
1007 1st Ave, Downtown / 206/624-4844 or 800/426-7033
When the Sultan of Brunei stayed at this historic, 109-room downtown hotel, he did more than relax at the Aveda Spa or enjoy the wine tastings and restaurant. He redecorated his room in dark purples and grays and brought in a collection of world-class antiques. He came, he saw, he stayed—and then left almost everything to the hotel. For just over $400 a night, you, too, can live like a sultan. Also consider the Fireplace Suites, which feature king-size beds hidden behind Japanese screens, large formal living rooms, TV/VCRs, tall windows, antiques, and wood-burning fireplaces. The spacious Spa Suites, with jetted tubs for two, are almost guaranteed to spark some romance. Rooms with creative themes (such as the Author's Room, filled with autographed books) and bold, European-style decor—maize-yellow

hues and opulent fabrics—are hallmarks of the hotel's artistic bent. Of the smaller rooms, try those on the quiet inner courtyard (209 or 211); we prefer them to the larger one- and two-bedroom suites with their long hallways and dull kitchens. Book an "Art of Romance" package if you'd like extras such as chilled champagne and chocolates in your room, plus an Aveda gift box and late (3pm) checkout. The hotel's small lobby features a massive octopus-like sculpture by a Northwest icon, glass artist Dale Chihuly. The hotel restaurant, the Library Bistro (206/624-3646), offers breakfast, lunch, and weekend brunch—the high-backed booths are terrific for exchanging *sotto voce* sweet nothings. The Bookstore Bar (206/382-1506) offers lunch, dinner, and late-night dining, and shares a kitchen with the Bistro; the menu of upscale comfort food includes options such as halibut fish-and-chips and roast chicken. For dessert, the warm and chocolaty s'mores should inspire a sweet kiss.
$$$–$$$$ *AE, DC, DIS, E, JCB, MC, V; checks OK; www.alexishotel.com.* ♿

CHELSEA STATION ON THE PARK
🐾🐾
4915 Linden Ave N, Fremont / 206/547-6077 or 800/400-6077
Wake up and smell the roses—literally!—at this charming bed-and-breakfast across from the Woodland Park Rose Gardens. Located a 10-minute drive (via Highway 99) north of downtown Seattle, this pair of 1920s Federalist and Tudor homes offer a rosy, cozy retreat from the city as well as easy access to Fremont, one of Seattle's most-loved neighborhoods. All nine guest rooms offer Craftsman-style decor and come with private, albeit standard, baths; the one exception is the three-room Margaret Suite, which boasts a soaking tub. Of all the rooms, however, we prefer the coral-and-cream Morning Glory Room on the ground floor, across from the parlor. The room's hardwood floors, lace curtains, and sunny sitting room add up to elegance, while an antique working pump organ provides some fun. Directly upstairs, the Sunlight Suite, a wonderful place for catching Seattle's elusive rays, offers a four-poster queen-size bed and outstanding views of the Cascades. If it's privacy you and your sweetheart are after, request the Woodland Park Suite, which has its own private entrance and small deck. Throughout both homes, you'll find comfy Arts and Crafts furniture (made, in fact, by the talented proprietor), along with period antiques and watercolors of Northwest scenes. Perks include off-street parking and wireless access in all the rooms. In the morning, enjoy ginger pancakes with lemon sauce, a baked grapefruit drizzled with honey, or eggs Florentine. Guests sit family-style at the dining-room table or at a table in the parlor. After breakfast, walk down to Green Lake, one of Seattle's most popular parks, or hold each other tight amid the grizzly bears and lions at the excellent Woodland Park Zoo, right across the street.
$$ *AE, DC, DIS, MC, V; checks OK; www.bandbseattle.com.*

THE EDGEWATER
❂❂❰
2411 Alaskan Wy/Pier 67, Downtown / 206/728-7000 or 800/624-0670
If you like the rustic look, this hotel is made for you—but even if tree-bark pillars and antler furniture don't make your heart go pitter-pat, the views from the Edgewater Inn may just sway you into staying. This 241-room hotel prides itself on being Seattle's only waterfront hotel, and the unobstructed views of Puget Sound and the Olympic Mountains are truly outstanding. Behind the flashy new exterior of aluminum shingles designed to evoke silvery fish scales, you'll find a sunny, inviting lobby; this is an excellent, if not very private, place to watch the sunset. Or, if the day is gray (and oh! in Seattle, it just might be), cuddle up on the couch beside the statuesque river-rock fireplace. When making your reservation, be sure to request a waterfront room; otherwise, you'll be staring up at skyscrapers or down into a parking lot. The small, standard-looking rooms have log frames for the king-size beds and comfortable armchairs; some have fireplaces. An armoire hides the TV, and it *should* stay hidden because all the entertainment you'll require is the view from your patio of seabirds swooping over the whitecaps. The Six Seven Restaurant & Lounge (206/269-4575) features Northwest cuisine and uninterrupted views of Elliott Bay, Puget Sound, and the Olympics. The waterfront, downtown Seattle, and Pike Place Market are a short walk (or complimentary shuttle ride) away; you can also hop on the waterfront trolley, which stops right across the street and passes through Pioneer Square before terminating near the International District and the ballparks.
$$$ *AE, DC, DIS, MC, V; checks OK; www.edgewaterhotel.com.*

FAIRMONT OLYMPIC HOTEL
❂❂❂❰
411 University St, Downtown / 206/621-1700 or 800/441-1414
Just holding hands in the opulent lobby of this 1920s landmark is a romantic experience, but the mood is slightly less amorous in the spacious accommodations (some of which have separate parlors and living rooms): office amenities and rather standard decor seem aimed more at business travelers than at starry-eyed couples. What will sweep you away are the exquisite tea room, elegant restaurant, gracious service, and sensational on-site amenities. After a morning workout at the complimentary health club—which has a lap pool, a 20-person spa tub, and a modest exercise room—you can arrange for fresh coffee, eggs Florentine, and the paper to be delivered to you poolside or out on the sunny garden patio. For afternoon tea or for evening cocktails and dancing, head to the Garden Court Lounge, with its lush greenery, marble floors, 40-foot-tall windows, and well-spaced settees. If you and your sweetie like extras, ask about the Romance package, which offers champagne upon arrival and breakfast goodies delivered to your

door, or the Honeymoon package, which goes for the gold with chocolate-covered strawberries, personalized robes, and continental breakfast in bed. The hotel's fine dining restaurant, the Georgian Room (206/621-7889)—with soaring ceilings, elegant appointments, a pianist, and uncompromisingly high service standards—is ideal for an intimate evening (thankfully, the stuffy dress code was discarded). The menu features a Northwest seasonal twist. All in all, when you talk about grand accommodations in the heart of downtown Seattle, you're talking about the Fairmont Olympic.
$$$$ *AE, DC, DIS, JCB, MC, V; checks OK; www.fairmont.com.*

GASLIGHT INN
❂❂

1727 15th Ave, Capitol Hill / 206/325-3654
The Gaslight Inn offers eight rooms in an appealing turn-of-the-20th-century home on Capitol Hill's busy 15th Avenue, with a spacious annex next door that contains seven additional suites. Guests are sure to find a room that suits their fancy with fifteen unique accommodations. Rooms in the main house are homey and slightly worn, each decorated with rich Northwest colors, Mission- and Arts and Crafts–style furnishings, Native American art, and handsome antiques. Unfortunately, only five rooms have private baths—but one room features a gas fireplace, and two have decks that overlook the backyard pool and downtown Seattle. For more romantic accommodations, try to reserve one of the attractive, self-contained suites in the adjacent annex (rooms 201–207), which are remarkably airy and comfortable. All feature richly colored walls, carpeting, full kitchens, private bathrooms, living areas with comfy couches, and large windows overlooking the courtyard and surrounding neighborhood. We strongly recommend room 206, an exceptionally spacious option with a gas fireplace; the top-floor location showcases spectacular views of the Seattle skyline. The innkeepers invite guests to unwind in the inn's wood-paneled common rooms. Cozy sofas are set in front of a crackling fireplace in one room, while the other features deep green walls and a mounted deer head over the couch. In the morning, follow the scent of freshly brewed coffee and locally made teas to the main-floor dining room for the complimentary continental breakfast.
$$–$$$ *AE, MC, V; checks OK; www.gaslight-inn.com.*

HILL HOUSE BED AND BREAKFAST
✿✿✿

1113 E John St, Capitol Hill / 206/720-7161 or 800/720-7161

AMARANTH INN
✿✿

1451 S Main St, Central District / 206/720-7161 or 800/720-7161
Of these two lovely inns, our hands-down favorite is the Hill House Bed and Breakfast, which is housed in two tastefully renovated Victorian homes on a pretty residential street within strolling distance of Volunteer Park. The Amaranth Inn is equally elegant, but its location, south of Capitol Hill, is less convenient. Fortunately, the hospitality and expertise of the gracious innkeepers, Herman and Alea Foster, appear in every fine detail at both lodgings—from the perfectly made beds (nary a crease in sight) to the fresh flowers in all the rooms. The three upstairs rooms at Hill House are a bit too small for romance (and two share a small standard bath), but the two garden-level suites are much more spacious. Both feature striking decor, enticing down comforters, separate seating areas with sofas, brightly tiled standard bathrooms, and heavenly private entrances guarded by a magnificent willow tree. Additional lodgings at Hill House are located in a second home directly next door, which offers two quite private upstairs guest rooms with lace-covered canopy beds, antique furnishings, and large private baths. In the morning, an exquisitely prepared breakfast is served on china and crystal; treats include baked cinnamon apples and walnut French toast. The other house operated by the Fosters, the eight-room Amaranth Inn, is located in a 1906 Craftsman near Chinatown and Pioneer Square. Hardwood floors, rich Oriental rugs, queen-size antique beds, and original art grace the rooms; all but one come with gas fireplaces, and a few have Jacuzzi tubs. Two cozy attic-level rooms share a bath but are remarkably affordable for lovebirds on a budget; for the most space and charm, try the inviting Freesia Room, which has a view of Mount Rainier and a large private bath. At press time, these bed-and-breakfasts had been put up for sale, so you may want to call to find out the latest before booking.
$$$ AE, DC, DIS, MC, V; no checks; www.seattlebnb.com or www. amaranthinn.com.

HOTEL ANDRA
✿✿✿◖

2000 4th Ave, Belltown / 206/448-8600 or 800/448-8601
Quite a buzz surrounded the spring 2004 opening of this ultrasleek downtown destination, and not *just* because Lola (206/441-1430), the newest restaurant from famed Seattle restaurateur Tom Douglas, adjoins the hotel (and provides room service). It's easy to say good things about the Andra: To our eye, it not only outdoes the W Hotel in terms of chic decor and modern

amenities, but it also provides a refreshingly down-to-earth Seattle-style welcome. The lobby's vaulted ceilings, distressed plank floors, massive fire-place made of local split-grain granite, and floating steel-wrapped plasma screen projecting an ever-changing collection of art is pure Northwest-meets-millennium. Even the hallways, illuminated by light that mimics underwater bubbles, provide a pleasant backdrop (luckily, kissing is allowed here). The hotel's 119 rooms and suites—with khaki walls, charcoal-colored fuzzy alpaca headboards, warm dark-wood furniture, and brushed stain-less–steel accents—are stylishly minimal without feeling spare or chilly. The Andra Suites offer cozy seating areas as well as large polished-wood desks. The hotel, originally built in 1926, shows off its historic charm in unexpected places, such as in the bathrooms, where the original white tile is intact and contrasts beautifully with the well-chosen blue of the walls. Every room detail is both practical and luxurious, from the double-paned windows that open, private bars, and flat-screen televisions to the 315-thread-count Egyptian-cotton linens, Frette towels, spa robes, and sleek bedside Tivoli radios. If money is no object, the Monarch Suite is where you'll want to celebrate a special occasion; the elegant bathroom with sand-hued walls, fluffy white throw rugs, a Jacuzzi tub overlooking the cityscape, and glassed-in double showers is especially memorable. Plans to add a 2,000-square-foot spa by the end of 2005 will only add to the luxury. Check into the romance package if you'd like a little bubbly and a box of gourmet chocolates awaiting your arrival.

$$$–$$$$ *AE, DIS, MC, V; checks OK; www.hotelandra.com.*

HOTEL MONACO
❂❂❂

1101 4th Ave, Downtown / 206/621-1770 or 800/945-2240
Walk in to the spectacular, Mediterranean-style lobby of the Hotel Monaco, and the busy streets of downtown Seattle will seem worlds away. Let your senses come back to life as you take in the brightly hued furniture, giant potted palms, gold-framed mirrors, and dolphin mural adorning the vaulted ceiling. Tied-back velvet curtains divide the main sitting area from a window alcove that holds a "kissing couch"! (Unfortunately, this isn't really one of the best places to kiss, unless you're undaunted by passersby watching you through the windows.) Tiered bronze-and-glass chandeliers, tasseled throw pillows in bright paisleys and stripes, several chaise longues, and round portal mirrors complete this magnificent entry. You'll be sorry to leave it—but you can come back in the evening for the nightly wine recep-tion. The hotel's 189 guest rooms, filled with vivid splashes of pink, yellow, and cream, or bold displays of red, green, and charcoal, along with ornate layered patterns and striped wallpaper, are definitely not for the faint of heart. Cherry-wood and whitewashed furniture and TVs hidden in armoires are standard. Of the 45 suites, we find the Monte Carlo the most romantic,

with pinstriped curtains that separate the sitting room from the bedroom. We're also partial to the Mediterranean Suite, which features a large jetted tub in its spacious bathroom. Of the amenities offered, perhaps the most interesting is the delivery to your room of a pet goldfish (in a fishbowl) to keep you company—not exactly romantic, but definitely unique. To finish your Seattle day on an intimate note, we highly recommend the warmly inviting New Orleans–style hotel restaurant, Sazerac (206/624-7755; www. sazeracrestaurant.com). Its flamboyant decor, delicious food—try the signature flash-fried catfish with lemon whipped potatoes and jalapeño-lime meunière—and lively ambience make it a favorite with locals.

$$$$ *AE, DC, DIS, JCB, MC, V; checks OK; www.monaco-seattle.com.*

HOTEL VINTAGE PARK
♥♥♥
1100 5th Ave, Downtown / 206/624-8000 or 800/624-4433
The romance quotient of the Hotel Vintage Park is enhanced by its ideal location downtown, just a few blocks away from fine boutiques, upscale department stores, the delightful Pike Place Market, and the 5th Avenue Theatre. The hotel's intimate elegance and supreme comfort standards also make it a winner. A tastefully done winery theme plays throughout the 126 guest rooms, with suites named after Washington vineyards and a truly convivial, complimentary evening wine hour in the hotel lobby, where you can sip on plush velvet settees or leather armchairs before a blazing fireplace. Inside the rooms, you'll find stately cherry-wood furnishings, TVs in wooden armoires, tall ceilings and windows, sofas and chairs upholstered in rich tapestries, sumptuous linens in shades of deep plum and hunter green, and attractively appointed bathrooms. Although the exterior rooms have no views, we prefer them because they provide a bit more space. Noise from the nearby Interstate 5 on-ramp might be noticeable from the lower floors, but the soundproofing helps—and it's a small price to pay for the convenient downtown location. If you happen to have money to burn, you'll find an especially kiss-worthy ambience in the Chateau Ste. Michelle Suite, with its gold and bright blue color scheme, wood-burning fireplace, canopied bed, and Jacuzzi tub for two. A competent staff provides attentive service to all guests, and 24-hour room service (as well as three meals daily) is available from the adjacent Tulio Ristorante (206/624-5500), which is lively and well-regarded. Sit down to a plate of tasty pasta and order your favorite Italian or Northwest vintage to celebrate your escape.

$$$ *AE, DC, DIS, JCB, MC, V; checks OK; www.vintagepark.com.*

INN AT THE MARKET
✿✿✿

86 Pine St, Pike Place Market / 206/443-3600 or 800/446-4484
Set right in the heart of the colorful Pike Place Market, this stylish inn perched on a steep slope above Puget Sound offers terrific views of either the bustling city streets or Elliott Bay and the snowcapped Olympics. As you enter through the airy, ivied courtyard you'll notice a gentle blurring of indoor and outdoor, which seems appropriate for this quintessentially Seattle hotel. Indulge in some of the city's best assets right outside your door, from the excellent dining downstairs at Campagne (see Romantic Restaurants) to the myriad shops and stalls of the market. When it's warm, lounge on the rooftop patio and relish one of the best overlooks in the city. On rainy days, the overstuffed sofa arranged beside a blazing fire in the common room makes for a cozy refuge. Decor in the 70 guest rooms is utterly fresh and tasteful, with French-country pine furnishings and color schemes of soft taupe, copper, and green. Plump down duvets and thick terry-cloth robes up the comfort quotient. TVs are tucked discreetly into large wooden armoires, and the private baths are roomy enough for two. All rooms above the fifth floor afford views, and those on the west have floor-to-ceiling windows that open to catch the breeze off the Sound. Breakfast is not included in your stay, but Campagne has a cafe downstairs offering a hearty, delicious French-inspired morning repast. And if that doesn't tempt you, not to worry: you're in the middle of an outdoor market, after all, and fruit stands and delicious bakeries abound.
$$$–$$$$ *AE, DC, DIS, JCB, MC, V; checks OK; www.innatthemarket.com.*
&

SALISBURY HOUSE
✿✿✶

750 16th Ave E, Capitol Hill / 206/328-8682
Situated on a quiet, tree-lined residential street in a long-established and beautiful part of Capitol Hill, this inviting 1904 Prairie-style house offers a peaceful oasis from the neighborhood's vivid street life. The handsome common rooms on the main floor are appointed with comfortable couches and chairs, polished maple floors, Oriental rugs, fireplaces, and leaded-glass windows. On the second floor, a glass-enclosed sun-room filled with wicker furniture and plants overlooks the lush backyard, with views of the lawn, trees, flower gardens, and brick courtyard below. All five simple yet elegant guest rooms have queen-size beds made up with crisp linens and down comforters, attractively renovated baths (one has a six-foot-long claw-foot soaking tub), and a mixture of antiques and contemporary furnishings; two have cozy window seats. For complete privacy, request the Suite, a spacious room on the lower level offering such romantic amenities as a private entrance, fireplace, whirlpool tub, and shower for two. Don't be fooled by

the rooms' country quaintness—all feature high-speed wireless Internet access. In keeping with the dignified air of this getaway, however, only one room (the Suite) has a television, which keeps things quiet and enables you to enjoy each other to the fullest. A full vegetarian breakfast of eggs, pancakes, fresh fruit, juice, and coffee is served each morning in the pretty, formal dining room.

$$ *AE, MC, V; checks OK; www.salisburyhouse.com.*

SORRENTO HOTEL
✿✿✿

900 Madison St, First Hill / 206/622-6400 or 800/426-1265
Step into the lobby of this architecturally stunning 1909 Italianate Renaissance hotel, and its old-world elegance will immediately envelop the two of you. The rich interior woodwork, ornate details, and soft lighting offer a romantic change of pace from the modern entrances to many urban hotels. The hotel is located on the western slope of First Hill, five blocks uphill from the heart of the city; for energetic couples it's easily walkable, and the removed location brings considerable quiet. But you might not be going anywhere, since you could easily spend days shuttling between your room and the inviting bar and restaurant downstairs. Of the hotel's 76 accommodations, the regal suites are the most romantic, with their plush furnishings, yellow and green hues, large windows, stereos, goose-down pillows, and elegant fabrics. The standard rooms are not remarkable and feature uninspired bathrooms that are not exactly roomy. But everything else is simply exemplary: on chilly nights, for example, turndown service includes a hot water bottle placed under the sheets for a warm evening snuggle. Rooms include concessions to the technological age: direct TV, CD players, and high-speed Internet access; there's also a small exercise room. You'll be drawn irresistibly downstairs to the utterly cozy Fireside Room, where you can order a traditional afternoon tea for two; enjoy live music in the evening; or curl up before the hand-painted fireplace in one of the many elegant settees, sofas, and armchairs to sip an after-dinner cognac. The award-winning Hunt Club restaurant (see Romantic Restaurants) serves consistently fine meals in a series of seductive mahogany-paneled rooms.

$$$$ *AE, DC, DIS, JCB, MC, V; checks OK; www.hotelsorrento.com.*

W SEATTLE HOTEL
✿✿✿

1112 4th Ave, Downtown / 206/264-6000 or 877/W-HOTELS
This hotel is made for modern love. With five branches in Manhattan alone, not to mention locations from San Francisco to Sydney, the W Hotel has perfected a hip, urban persona that seems to please young and old alike (if not those whose eyes light up at the sight of flowers and lace). The W Seattle has an ideal location in the heart of downtown, a terraced lobby with vaulted

ceilings, postmodern art, chocolate-colored velvet drapes on soaring windows, and plush contemporary furniture. While the see-and-be-seen mood, which almost makes the lobby feel like a nightclub (especially at night when they turn up the techno dance music), isn't necessarily conducive to intimate conversation, there are places to find respite in the hotel, from the cozy cocktail bar, often busy with an after-work crowd, to the excellent hotel restaurant, Earth & Ocean (206/264-6060). Check the Internet for specials when booking your room. The rooms are on the smaller side, with low ceilings, and the decor is both spare and neutral. Expect muted taupe and black fixtures and small Zen-inspired water sculptures. The nod to peaceful meditation ends there, as rooms are totally wired and include 27-inch TVs with Internet access, CD and video players, and high-speed Internet connections. Bathrooms are not large, but the stainless-steel and glass fixtures are delightfully sleek. Request one of the many rooms offering an impressive downtown vista; otherwise, you may find yourselves gazing onto dreary rooftops or a parking lot. Rooms feature either one king-size or two double "W Signature Beds," sheathed in goose-down duvets and pillows and 250-thread-count sheets. You might not want to leave this paradise of linens, except that lively downtown Seattle awaits, just outside the hotel's huge glassed-in front doors.
$$$$ *AE, DC, DIS, JCB, MC, V; checks OK; www.whotels.com.*

Romantic Restaurants

ANDALUCA
❂❂❂
407 Olive Wy (Mayflower Park Hotel), Downtown / 206/382-6999
This lively yet intimate spot, located downtown in the Mayflower Park Hotel, is an excellent choice for a first date; if you hit a conversation lull, the surrounding buzz will easily fill in the silence. However, if it's quiet cooing you're after, go early to beat the crowds, or come for post-theater dessert. The inviting, old-fashioned rosewood booths and tables brightened with fresh flowers make an excellent setting for the seasonal Mediterranean cuisine. Among the entrées, good choices include the cumin-scented shellfish stew and the Cabrales-crusted beef with grilled pears, blue cheese, and marsala glaze. The menu of small plates is perfect for sharing. Try the delicious roasted mussels with chile pepper, lemon, and rosemary; crispy duck cakes served with apricot chutney; or warm lentil ragout served with crispy pancetta, along with a bottle of wine. This approach will leave plenty of room for dessert, which includes a decadent warm liquid chocolate cake served with caramel and espresso-chip ice cream. While the mahogany and stained glass–filled lobby and sitting room of the hotel itself has charm,

the rooms are rather impersonal; Andaluca's delightful food and jewel-box dining room have the lion's share of romance at this property.
$$$ *AE, DC, DIS, MC, V; checks OK; breakfast, dinner every day, lunch Mon–Sat; full bar; reservations recommended; www.andaluca.com.*

CAMPAGNE
✿✿✿
86 Pine St (Inn at the Market), Pike Place Market / 206/728-2800

CAFÉ CAMPAGNE
✿✿✿
1600 Post Alley, Pike Place Market / 206/728-2233
Situated in Seattle's famous Pike Place Market, Campagne serves up superior French food in a stately setting. During the summer, sit outdoors in the brick courtyard, where flickering candles give off a dreamy light; in other seasons, choose the chic but simple dining room, which overlooks Elliott Bay and features hardwood floors, large fresh-flower arrangements, and white linens. We also like the lounge, with its floral-upholstered chairs, muted gold tablecloths, and dark wood accents. (Lovers who like to stay up until the wee hours will enjoy the late-night menu, available Friday and Saturday until midnight.) The creative fare would please a Gallic purist. Try the *entrecôte rôti*, naturally raised boneless rib-eye with braised shallots and garlic in red-wine foie gras sauce, or enjoy the Northwest's famous seafood with dishes such as *poisson du jour*, pan-roasted fish served on celeriac and Puy lentil ragout with pistachio oil. Café Campagne, set underneath its stylish sibling, is a more casual but charming French bistro open for lunch and dinner (it also serves a charming weekend brunch). The classic bistro fare is reliably delicious; for dinner, try the *steak frites*, Roquefort butter–topped pan-roasted beef and some of Seattle's best *frites*; at lunch, you can't miss with the classic croque madame, a ham and Gruyère sandwich served with a fried egg and a green side salad. For the most formal date, book a table for two at the elegant restaurant; when a festive lunch is your quarry, try the cafe.
$$$** *(Campagne);* **$$ *(Café Campagne) AE, DC, MC, V; no checks; dinner every day (Campagne), lunch, dinner Mon–Fri, brunch, dinner Sat–Sun (Café Campagne); full bar; reservations recommended; www.campagne restaurant.com.*

CANLIS
✿✿✿✿
2576 Aurora Ave N, Queen Anne / 206/283-3313
Perched high above Lake Union right next to the Aurora Bridge, the legendary Canlis restaurant has been a Seattle landmark since 1950. The dress code has eased over the years, but men are still asked to wear jackets. The

steep (borderline extravagant) prices tend to draw in a wealthy clientele, but the fine service and superb cuisine make it worthy of a special-occasion romantic splurge. The lodgelike entry welcomes you with a floor-to-ceiling fireplace, dark wood beams, rugged rock walls, and warmly hued decor. Asian accents infuse the dining room, which offers white linen–cloaked tables and candlelight, panoramic views, cushioned banquettes, and classical melodies from a pianist. Start with decadent appetizers like the signature prawns with dry vermouth, garlic, red chiles and lime, or simply elegant white sturgeon caviar on warm buckwheat blini with crème fraîche. The famous copper broiler yields dishes such as troll-caught salmon with a cherry and beet emulsion, or New York cuts of beautifully marbled Kobe-style beef. When ordering your entrée, put in an advance request for the dark chocolate lava cake with molten interior; the kitchen needs extra time to prepare this luscious, and not-to-be-missed, treat. When you're in the mood to spoil yourselves, Canlis will do very nicely. For the ultimate in romance, book Caché, the legendary, intimate dining space for two upstairs, which comes with its own private server. Furnished with an intimate table and a fainting couch (should the romance of it all overwhelm you), the corner setting offers panoramic views of Lake Union and the Cascades that are especially splendid on summer evenings when the light doesn't wane until late.
$$$$ *AE, DC, DIS, MC, V; checks OK; dinner Mon–Sat; full bar; reservations required; www.canlis.com.*

CHEZ SHEA
◖◖◖◖

94 Pike St, 3rd Floor, Downtown / 206/467-9990
In the evening, after you've walked through a deserted Pike Place Market watching the vendors close up shop, climb the steps to Chez Shea for dinner at a memorably charming hideaway. If you haven't made an advance reservation for the dining room, you can try for a table at Shea's Lounge, the restaurant's bar area: All tables share the view of Puget Sound across the rooftops of the market. Come at dusk to see the evening sky turn from blue to crimson. In the small, intimate dining room, tall arched windows, cinnamon-colored walls, dark-wood floors, and linen-clad tables set the stage. Fresh seasonal fare characterizes the four-course menu ($44 per person) or eight-course chef tasting menu ($65, with an additional $30 for wine pairings). A recent winter four-course offering included an *amuse-bouche* of gougère with truffle cream; roasted apple–parsnip bisque with cinnamon oil; salad of blood oranges, candied walnuts, and shaved fennel; and sea scallops with Meyer lemon cream and French lentils or beef tenderloin with foie gras butter, demi-glace, and horseradish mashed potatoes. At Shea's Lounge, you'll find a menu of small plates (think fresh oysters, crab cakes, ahi tartare) and the chance to order some of the tempting entrées on

the dining room's menus à la carte. Whether you choose restaurant or bar, Chez Shea is the perfect place to take your special someone.

$$$ *AE, MC, V; no checks; dinner Tues–Sun; full bar; reservations recommended; www.chezshea.com.*

DAHLIA LOUNGE
✿✿✿

1904 4th Ave, Downtown / 206/682-4142
With its interior of crimson, gold brocade, and whimsical papier-mâché fish lanterns, and with nationally known chef-owner Tom Douglas at the helm, the Dahlia Lounge is an Emerald City tradition. Relax into your cushioned booth (we prefer these to the tables and chairs) and soak up the casual sophistication of the dining room. The menu fuses Northwest and Asian cuisine with creative flair, and changes seasonally; entrées range from Copper River salmon with Yakima asparagus and fingerling potatoes to lobster hot pot soup with rice noodles. The portions are just right, and the presentation is flawless. For dessert, try the bag of tiny, delicious doughnuts or the pillowy coconut cream pie, which should inspire some almost tropical kisses. To enable intimate conversation, request a table toward the back of the restaurant, well away from the often-crowded bar.

$$ *AE, DC, DIS, MC, V; local checks only; lunch Mon–Fri, dinner every day; full bar; reservations recommended; www.tomdouglas.com.*

GENEVA
✿✿✿

1106 8th Ave, First Hill / 206/624-2222
This restaurant's location, crammed between two city buildings and around the block from a hospital on First Hill, is not exactly romantic, but that ceases to matter the instant you enter the lovely, tree-shaded courtyard. Inside the small dining room, hung with plush tapestries, the tables are draped in white linen and set beneath an arched dome ceiling. Venerable antiques, crystal chandeliers, and lace-curtained windows convey a sense of refinement. Although the tables are arranged somewhat snugly, the intimate ambience and strains of Mozart promote privacy, as does the outstanding, award-winning service. Dine on signature entrées such as Jägerschnitzel, lightly crusted pork medallions with a bacon–wild-mushroom sauce and buttered spaetzle; or Veal Bernoise, a ragout of veal in a wine and cream sauce loaded with mushrooms. Lovers with sweet tooths won't want to skip dessert, which includes delights such as warm apple strudel and bittersweet chocolate mousse with raspberry sauce in a Florentine cookie basket.

$$$ *AE, MC, V; no checks; dinner Tues–Sat; full bar; reservations recommended.*

THE HUNT CLUB
✦✦✦✦
900 Madison St (Sorrento Hotel), First Hill / 206/343-6156
A hallowed Seattle dining spot for years, this seductively lit room oozes gentility. Honduran mahogany paneling and exposed brick walls provide an inviting backdrop for cozy booths and white linen–covered tables, while wall sconces glow invitingly throughout the handsome interior. The wait staff performs with panache, and the food lives up to the atmosphere, with exceptionally creative and carefully prepared meals. Your every need, including privacy, will be obligingly met. Succulent Sonoma duckling, incredibly moist and delicious Alaskan king salmon, and remarkable sauces—not to mention the impressive wine list—are some of the highlights of this superlative dining experience. Enjoy dessert, coffee, and cognac in the wood-paneled Fireside Room, off the lobby, to the tinkling of live piano music. In summer, have your meal at the alfresco cafe that is set up in the hotel's circular drive amid fountains and palm trees.
$$$ AE, DIS, MC, V; checks OK; breakfast, lunch, tea, dinner every day, brunch Sat–Sun; full bar; reservations recommended; www.hotelsorrento. com.

LARK
✦✦✦
926 12th Ave, Capitol Hill / 206/323-5275
The surprises come fast and furious at Lark, from the ever-changing menu of creative small plates to the location itself; its nondescript exterior on an out-of-the-way Capitol Hill block belies the bustling charm of this chic new restaurant. Tables for two line one side of the dining room, characterized by crisp white linen, candlelight, and polished wood accents, while the room's central tables and opposite booths seat four. Panels of gauzy fabric suspended from the high ceiling soften the industrial feel of the space. A tempting selection of cheeses from around the world starts off the menu, which also lists categories of alluring small plates: from "vegetables," choose a savory dish of farro with black kale, red kuri squash, and mascarpone or roasted potatoes with clabber cream; or, from the list of "charcuterie," sample jamon serrano with pickled red currants or chicken liver parfait with walnuts. Experimentation brings rewards here, such as the dish of roasted eel with saba and new potatoes or roast quail with chestnut honey, brussels sprouts, and house-made pancetta. Chef Jonathan Sundstrom, who earned his reputation cooking at a series of impressive Seattle restaurants, delivers on even the most daringly creative or unlikely sounding specials. The service, quite simply, is excellent. We rarely recommend restaurants that don't take reservations (Lark takes them only for parties of six or more) but feel it's merited here; the tiny but pleasant bar space in the back isn't a terrible place to wait. If the light, creamy, and

delicious butterscotch pudding is on the dessert menu, don't hesitate for a moment; besides, the more you can do to draw out a meal this pleasant, the better.

$$$ MC, V; no checks; dinner Tues–Sun; full bar; reservations for 6 or more only.

LE GOURMAND
❂❂❂❅

425 NW Market St, Ballard / 206/784-3463
Ballard is a neighborhood best known for its Scandinavian heritage, yet Le Gourmand is 100 percent French. This elegant little dining room is situated in a modest brick building in a residential area; the windows are covered to deflect the sights and sounds of traffic. Once you're inside, the dining room is completely charming, with a whimsical pastel mural of a pastoral scene and pink crushed-silk pillows on the bench lining the room, and the appealing ambience is complemented by gracious service. Prix-fixe meals are expensive but memorable, and are prepared from local, organically grown ingredients. Delectable starters include sole and shrimp mousseline and blintzes of sheep's milk cheese with chive butter. For the main course, try roast pork with rich rhubarb sauce and toasted hazelnuts; half-rack of Washington lamb with a sauce of plum and lavender; or a poached king salmon fillet topped with creamy fresh sorrel sauce that's a delicate masterpiece. A mixed green salad with edible flowers is a refreshing end to the meal—that is, unless you have saved room for dessert. The homemade ice creams and profiteroles are nothing short of magnifique. Sambar (206/781-4883; closed Sun), the hip, intimate lounge that adjoins the restaurant, is worthy of a visit on its own for the excellent martinis and classic bistro food; the French *frites* make the perfect cocktail snack. After a luxurious meal at Le Gourmand, it's also a fabulous place for a nightcap.

$$$ AE, MC, V; checks OK; dinner Wed–Sat; beer and wine; reservations recommended.

PONTEVECCHIO
❂❂❅

710 N 34th St, Fremont / 206/633-3989
At first glance, Pontevecchio's location, on a busy street in the artsy Fremont neighborhood, seems unlikely to provide much in the way of romance, but a closer look reveals that this Italian restaurant caters almost exclusively to couples. A sign posted in the intimate, softly lit dining room says it all: "We reserve the right to refuse service to anyone not in love." Small and somewhat stark, the dining room features a sleek tiled floor, marbled brown walls, and artistic black-and-white photographs; on some weekend evenings, a tenor singing Puccini fills the space with song. The room holds a mere seven candlelit tables, arranged on opposite sides of the room to

enhance privacy. You can't help but get close to one another at the tiny round tables (the tables are so small, in fact, that we scarcely had room for our plates!). The gracious wait staff encourages long, leisurely meals. Fortunately, the classic Italian cuisine is excellent, so you'll enjoy lingering over every bite of savory grilled antipasti, pasta entrées done to perfection, fresh seafood and chicken dishes, and homemade hazelnut gelato for dessert. *$$ MC, V; local checks only; lunch Mon–Fri, dinner Mon–Sat; beer and wine; reservations recommended; www.pontevecchiobistro.com.*

ROVER'S
❍❍❍❍

2808 E Madison St, Madison Valley / 206/325-7442
An unassuming neighborhood location, a discreet interior subtly lit, white walls hung with pastel art, and some of the most sumptuous cuisine you will ever taste await you at Rover's. The decor is a bit too stark for our tastes, but that only serves to sharpen the focus on the flawless and elegant cuisine. Summer months allow for more intimate dining in the restaurant's fragrant garden courtyard. The incredibly skilled chef-owner has a worldwide reputation, and this fact is proven night after night in delicious, jewel-like dishes. An example is one of our favorite appetizers: eggs scrambled with garlic and chives, then layered with crème fraîche and lime juice in an eggshell cut into a tiny cup and topped with white sturgeon caviar. Main courses—such as roasted monkfish with smoked apple bacon and rich red wine sauce, roasted squab with onion confit and a warm pecan vinaigrette, and venison medallions with chanterelle mushrooms in a remarkable Armagnac sauce—are simply outstanding. *$$$$ AE, DC, MC, V; checks OK; lunch Fri, dinner Tues–Sat; beer and wine; reservations required; www.rovers-seattle.com.*

SERAFINA
❍❍❍

2043 Eastlake Ave E, Eastlake / 206/323-0807
Low lighting, soft live jazz, and an Italian-influenced menu make any night at Serafina undeniably romantic. While the room does get busy and the small tables are set close together, the cozy ambience makes it a favored Seattle destination for intimate dates. On weekends, the atmosphere can be clamorous and the service rushed, but the ever-changing lineup of music, from Afro-Cuban to Latin, keeps the mood upbeat and festive. Spanish anchovies with Belgian endive and green olive tapenade, delicious goat cheese and pickled pepper bruschetta, or other antipasto options make a savory start. Pasta dishes such as roasted pumpkin ravioli with brown butter–sage sauce and entrées such as slowly braised lamb shank served with mashed cannellini beans showcase the restaurant's Italian roots. Food can sometimes be uneven, but if it's a romantic mood you're after, Serafina

won't disappoint—and warm weather dining on the outdoor patio is sublime. The dessert menu also changes, but if it lists the profiteroles, definitely order them; these ice cream–filled, chocolate sauce–drizzled pastries are outstanding, and nearly as sweet as a kiss.

$$ *MC, V; checks OK; lunch Mon–Fri, dinner every day; full bar; reservations recommended; www.serafinaseattle.com.*

SOSTANZA TRATTORIA
❍❍❍
1927 43rd Ave E, Madison Park / 206/324-9701

Madison Park is a charming and totally gentrified neighborhood, but you still don't need to dress up here; this is Seattle, after all, and despite the multimillion-dollar homes lining the area, casual rules. Just around the corner from the upscale shops and boutiques, Sostanza captures a mood of rustic Tuscan elegance. Amber stucco walls, a wood-beamed ceiling, soft lighting, a large gas fireplace, and nicely spaced tables fill this Italian trattoria with warmth and comfort. Upstairs, a second dining room features Caravaggio prints and an outdoor deck overlooking Lake Washington. The menu concentrates on dishes that hail from centuries-old Northern Italian traditions. Start with a classic caprese, or sautéed spinach with garlic, pine nuts, and lemon. Pastas are richly flavorful: try the pappardelle with veal sauce or penne *alla grappe* with green onions, green peppercorns, and a creamy sauce flavored with grappa. The quail wrapped and grilled in pancetta, served on a bed of risotto with sage and shallots and drizzled with a Chianti demi-glace, is as fabulous as it sounds. Kiss inspiration abounds here for couples who want to enjoy excellent cuisine near the lake. On a chilly evening, the table for two in front of the fireplace is a most romantic spot.

$$–$$$ *AE, DC, MC, V; local checks only; dinner Mon–Sat; full bar; reservations recommended.*

STUMBLING GOAT
❍❍❍
6722 Greenwood Ave N, Phinney Ridge / 206/784-3535

Tucked into a row of storefronts in Phinney Ridge, a quiet neighborhood north of downtown, is this stand-out neighborhood bistro. Decor in the scarlet dining rooms includes red velvet draperies and green carpet—but it works; and best of all, noise is absorbed rather than echoed around the room. Combine this hushed setting with the homey, friendly ambience, and you'll understand why this restaurant is one of our favorite spots for intimate dinner conversation in Seattle. We applaud the new addition, in early 2005, of an intimate cocktail bar at the back of the restaurant. Complete with crimson walls, dark wood, and ornate wrought-iron accents, this candlelit setting charms, offering just a handful of seats at the bar and a couple of tables (note that a glass of wine is safer than one of the oversweet, carelessly made cocktails). The eclectic menu features seasonal local ingredients: winter might bring a beet salad with chunks of Stilton or a rich mushroom risotto. The crispy-tender pan-roasted chicken with pillowy mashed potatoes and pan juices, a signature dish, is absolutely first-rate, and daily seafood specials are always an excellent choice. A well-thought-out wine list offers a number of good wines by the glass. The service can be laid-back, even lapsing at times into lackadaisical or worse, uninformed—but with each other and such reliably delicious food to enjoy, our bet is that you'll happily settle in for a long, romantic evening nonetheless. Desserts change seasonally but are worth saving room for; the luscious lemon cake is particularly memorable.

$$ *MC, V; local checks only; dinner Tues–Sat; beer and wine; no reservations.*

EASTSIDE

ROMANTIC HIGHLIGHTS

When it comes to romance in the Seattle area, it used to be that east was east and west was west—and west was definitely best. People living east of Lake Washington, in suburbs like Bellevue, Woodinville, Kirkland, and Redmond, shuttled to Seattle for cultural events, fine restaurants, and downtown shopping, while Emerald City dwellers passed through the Eastside only on their way to the Cascades. Well, times have changed. Today, the Eastside is booming, thanks in large measure to Microsoft and other large companies whose office parks sprawl across these once-quiet rolling hillsides. For romance seekers, the benefit of all this growth is the ever-increasing number of acclaimed restaurants, adorable shops, and luxurious lodgings dotting the area.

The traffic here is practically famous, and the two floating bridges that connect Seattle and Bellevue, Interstate 90 and Highway 520, are crammed with cars going both ways at all hours. Farther east, toward the mountains, visitors are drawn to the thundering spectacle of the 268-foot Snoqualmie Falls (just up Hwy 202 from I-90), and the luxurious **Salish Lodge & Spa** (see Romantic Lodgings).

The famous wineries in the quiet hamlet of **Woodinville** rank among the Eastside's biggest draws. Built in the style of a French country estate, **Chateau Ste. Michelle** (14111 NE 145th St; 425/488-3300; www.chateauste-michelle.com; free tours and tastings daily) offers the chance to stroll 87 acres of well-tended grounds after a complimentary wine tasting and a cellar tour. The winery's shop offers all the essentials for a gourmet picnic;

simply choose a sunny spot on the lawn and gaze at the lush grapevines as you nibble portable treats. A summer-long series of outdoor concerts attracts fun-loving crowds to the outdoor amphitheater. Across the street, **Columbia Winery** (14030 NE 145th St; 425/488-2776; www.columbiawinery. com; open daily, tours Sat–Sun) is the oldest premium winery in the state (although, truth be told, it's not quite as pretty as its neighbor). If you tire of the mighty grape, visit the palatial **Red Hook Brewery** (14300 NE 145th St; 425/483-3232) nearby to sample the beers or to enjoy food and live music at its pub, Forecasters, open daily. If it's a casual sandwich you're more in the mood for (or a tasty balsamic chicken salad), visit the nearby **Purple Café** (14459 Woodinville-Redmond Rd; 425/483-7129; www.thepurplecafe.com).

The vibrant waterfront town of **Kirkland** evokes a seaside village in California with a welcome dash of the Northwest in its vistas of the Seattle skyline. The quaint downtown, lined with boutiques and restaurants and set directly on the scenic shores of Lake Washington, is practically designed for romantic excursions. Art lovers, and lovers in general, will enjoy the gallery at the historic brick **Kirkland Arts Center** (620 Market St; 425/822-7161; www.kirklandartscenter.org), or the **Kirkland Art Walk**, held the second Thursday of every month.

In summer, you can sneak a kiss on the open water with the excellent lake tour offered by **Argosy Cruises** (206/623-4252; www.argosycruises. com), which departs from the Kirkland waterfront. Revel in fabulous views of Mount Rainier and the water, and relax on deck chairs in the sunshine as you take in the 1½-hour live narrated tour, which points out the grand Lake Washington homes of Seattle's rich and famous. The ride even carries you past the **mansion of Bill Gates**, located in the Medina area of Bellevue. His $54 million, 20,000-square-foot waterfront home isn't particularly romantic (unless you live there, we guess), but it is unique. Afterward, stroll into town for an early-evening margarita on the outdoor patio at **Cactus** (121 Park Ln; 425/893-9799; lunch Mon–Sat, dinner every day) or sophisticated martinis and small plates at **Jäger** (148 Lake St; 425/803-3310; dinner Mon–Sat).

There's less charm immediately visible in the traffic-clogged streets of downtown **Bellevue**, but with a little bit of effort, you will be rewarded. The lion's share of the romance resides in the beautiful **Bellevue Botanical Garden** (12001 Main St; 425/452-2750), a serene haven with walking trails and a 19-acre nature preserve. Quiet paths lead past an alpine rock garden, filled with mountain hemlock and tiny wildflowers, to the exquisite Yao Garden. Pass beneath its traditional Japanese gate and you'll find delicate maples and vibrant azaleas and rhododendrons. Elsewhere in Bellevue, you can also find romance in a little well-deserved self-indulgence. Anyone whose heart jumps at the thought of good chocolate will delight in the exquisite trays of truffles at **Fran's Chocolates** (10305 NE 10th St; 425/453-1698). A number of excellent spas also fit the romantic-indulgence bill: choose from among the stunning **Spa at Pro Sports Club** (4455 148th Ave NE; 425/885-

5566; www.proclub.com), near the Microsoft campus; the **Bellevue Club** (see Romantic Lodgings); or **La Serenity Spa** (10301 NE 10th St; 425/990-0043; www.laserenityspa.com), where every treatment begins with a foot soak amid aromatherapy scents and the falling-water glass sculpture in the moss-green lounge.

Access & Information

From Interstate 5, there are two east-west arterials connecting to the East-side communities via floating bridges: Interstate 90 (south of downtown Seattle) and Highway 520 (north of downtown). The major Eastside north-south highway is Interstate 405.

Located northeast of Seattle, Woodinville is easily accessed by either Interstate 405 or State Route 522. For more information, contact the **Woodinville Chamber of Commerce** (425/481-8300; www.woodinvillechamber. org). Set right on Lake Washington, Kirkland encompasses the waterfront downtown and the upscale development of Carillon Point. For more information, contact the **Kirkland Chamber of Commerce** (425/822-7066; www.kirklandchamber.org). Bellevue is located between Interstate 90 and Highway 520; for more about the city, contact the **Bellevue Chamber of Commerce** (425/454-2464; www.bellevuechamber.org).

Romantic Lodgings

BELLEVUE CLUB HOTEL
◗◗◗◗
11200 SE 6th St, Bellevue / 425/454-4424 or 800/579-1110
Attached to the Eastside's most exclusive health club, this 67-room boutique hotel will remind you that exercise isn't the only thing that can get your heart pumping. If the elegant, Asian-influenced lobby, with its ceramic and glass artwork, subdued lighting, and infusion of warm earth tones, doesn't raise your pulse rate, the rooms almost certainly will: with handcrafted cherry-wood furniture, original art on the walls, and 12-foot ceilings, they are both spacious and lovely. The handsome Club Rooms on the ground floor are the most inviting, with private terra-cotta tile patios and attractive outdoor furniture. If you're in the mood for a splurge, request either the Wilburton Suite or the Fountain Suite; both feature a slate entry, sitting room with fireplace, and jetted tub. But for a truly special night, reserve the Rainier Suite, which features hardwood floors, a double shower, and a Roman bath. All the rooms include luxurious beds with plump duvets and feather pillows, and TVs hidden within lovely armoires. The opulent bathrooms, which feature soaking tubs, glass-enclosed showers, marble and granite surfaces, and a

hedonistic array of toiletries, will keep the TV in its armoire and the two of you covered in bubbles. Unlimited use of the state-of-the-art health club, with its gorgeous adjoining full-service spa, is an added benefit. As sublime as all this sounds—and it is sublime—the ambience is slightly marred by a nearby freeway. Chances are you won't notice, wrapped up in each other as you'll be. The hotel's dining room, Polaris, open to hotel guests and club members only, is an exceptional place for breakfast, lunch, or dinner, and the wine list features a number of premium Northwest bottles.
$$$–$$$$ *AE, DC, MC, V; checks OK; www.bellevueclub.com.*

HOLLY HEDGE HOUSE
✿✿✿✿

908 Grant Ave S, Renton / 425/226-2555 or 888/226-2555
Set high up a hillside in Renton—a suburb decidedly less flashy than its northern neighbors—this English country cottage is a delightful and very private retreat for two. From the moment you open the gate and step onto the perfectly manicured grounds, bordered by a beautiful, century-old holly hedge, you will be swept up into the quiet charm of this singular accommodation. Inside the immaculate cottage, a pretty, floral decor—which has won prestigious awards—sets the stage for your country getaway. The sitting room provides entertainment with a gas fireplace and movie and CD library; the dining room and gourmet kitchen are bright and cheerful. The tidy, rather standard bathroom has one indulgent touch in the whirlpool tub. Decorated in pine and pink floral, the cozy bedroom will almost guarantee you a good night's sleep; the only sounds you'll hear will be the morning birds. Upon waking, indulge in the delicious complimentary breakfast stocked by the thoughtful hosts, then spend hours in the luxurious Jacuzzi tub nestled outside in the charming gazebo. During warm weather, read a book and sip lemonade by the small kidney-shaped pool, or cool off with a dip. Spread out on the lawn with a picnic, or swing yourselves to a nice afternoon nap in the hammock. Later, watch the sun sink over the Olympic mountain range as you snuggle on the cozy love seat in the glassed-in veranda and plan your activities with the tempting brochures on offer. But don't be in a hurry to leave; privacy and comfort this perfect are meant to be savored. The summer months fill up quickly at this popular honeymoon hideaway, so be sure to call in advance.
$$–$$$ *MC, V; checks OK; www.hollyhedgehouse.com.*

THE SALISH LODGE & SPA
✿✿✿

6501 Railroad Ave SE, Snoqualmie / 425/888-2556 or 800/826-6124
The Salish Lodge and Spa has everything going for it: a respected name, a celebrated location at the top of beautiful Snoqualmie Falls, a full-service luxury spa (including 4 new treatment rooms in 2004) and thoroughly

romantic guest rooms. All 91 of the plush suites feature ample spa tubs, well-stocked wood-burning fireplaces, and comfortable furnishings that invite tenderness; as you might expect, the outstanding accommodations go hand in hand with outstanding prices, which grow more outstanding as the view of the falls improves. But there is one major drawback: the throngs of tourists that invade the place day in and day out, particularly on weekends. Thankfully, the guest wings are accessible only with guest room keys, so some privacy is afforded. Only a handful of these exquisite rooms have views of the falls; the rest look out on the road or the power plant upstream. That said, the inviting amenities include an afternoon tea served to lodging guests daily from 4pm to 6pm in the main-floor library, and the chance to haunt the wine bar after the day-trippers have all gone home. If you choose not to spend the night, you can still enjoy the extremely intimate Salish Lodge Dining Room, headed up by a chef who previously hailed from the renowned Meadowood Resort in Napa Valley; his French training can be seen on the upscale menu, emphasizing seafood, game, and Northwest produce. Four prix-fixe options at dinner, and a wine list offering more than 1,000 labels, make this an opulent (and expensive) place to dine. Lunch is also served daily, and Sundays bring a popular multicourse brunch. The restaurant is elegantly appointed, with handsome cherry-wood paneling, a wood-burning fireplace, and romantic lighting. Almost every seat in the house affords some kind of view through the floor-to-ceiling windows, but the very best tables are those directly beside the windows facing the falls. Reservations are recommended, so you might as well ask if any of those seats are available. To find out more about packages of many varieties, including romance or eagle watching, check out the lodge's Web site. If you're in the mood for the ultimate indulgence, splurge on tandem massages in one of the spa's two couple's treatment rooms; the one with the fireplace is especially romantic.

$$$ AE, DC, DIS, MC, V; checks OK; *www.salishlodge.com.*

SHUMWAY MANSION
◖◖

11410 99th Pl NE, Kirkland / 425/823-2303
Built in 1909, this four-story, post-Victorian estate now houses a curious blend of bed-and-breakfast rooms and banquet facilities. Surrounded by ample parking (enough for 60 cars) and fronted by a busy street, the 10,000-square-foot mansion also features a nicely tended lawn, pretty flower gardens, and an adjacent duck pond. Doors open from the downstairs ballroom onto a covered patio and the backyard, where you'll find an arched trellis covered with climbing roses and a gazebo embraced by wisteria. The mansion is best known for the more than 150 weddings a year that take place here. When the wedding party stays elsewhere, the guest rooms can be rented out; however, the cozy, handsomely decorated common areas may be inundated with celebrants around the time of the ceremony. Fortunately, you can

always escape for a hand-in-hand walk amid the nature trails at Juanita Bay Park, just blocks away. The eight simple guest rooms are appointed with homey Victorian-style furnishings, patterned wallpaper, lace curtains, and dried floral arrangements; but they are too dimly lit, even for romantics. Each room has a queen-size bed, and all include private tiled bathrooms (one is detached). Antique furnishings such as the four-poster cherry-wood bed in the Redmond Room add romantic appeal to the otherwise standard accommodations. In the morning, a full buffet-style breakfast is served downstairs at one long table in the handsome dining room.
$$ AE, MC, V; checks OK; www.shumwaymansion.com.

WILLOWS LODGE
⬣⬣⬣⬣
14580 NE 145th St, Woodinville / 425/424-3900 or 877/424-3930
Ever since this beautiful 88-room luxury hotel opened in 2000, it's had no trouble maintaining its status as one of the most romantic jewels in the Northwest. While the cedar-shingled exterior, surrounding parking lot, and quiet, rural location may not inspire immediate rapture, just wait. After you've stepped into the lodge-style lobby, with its massive stone-surround fireplace, slate floors, and exposed beams; caught a glimpse of the exquisitely landscaped garden through glass doors at the hotel's center; and let yourselves in to your inviting, sleek, tasteful room, the spell of the Willows will be upon you. As with all truly outstanding hotels, it's the spirit of the place, and not just the upscale amenities, that creates the lovely ambience. The lodge excels at offering an utterly romantic experience. The pinnacle of intimacy is the Do Not Disturb package, which includes an unforgettable in-tub finale following dinner: when you return to your room, you'll find oysters on the half shell, strawberries with hot chocolate fondue and whipped cream, and delicious chilled sparkling wine, all to be enjoyed in the privacy of your soaking tub, scattered with rose petals. But even an ordinary stay here can't help but be romantic. All of the rooms have fireplaces, king- or queen-size beds, stereo-DVD-CD systems, high-speed Internet connections (Microsoft's just down the road, after all), and lush bathrooms. Some rooms also feature jetted tubs and heated towel racks, and balconies or patios with views that might take in the hotel gardens, the Chateau Ste. Michelle winery, the Sammamish River and its popular bike trail, or Mount Rainier, on a clear day. The luxury suites are especially posh, with the price tag to go with it. Relax in the outdoor Jacuzzi tub, pamper yourselves at the spa, and have dinner at the casually elegant Barking Frog restaurant or the famous Herbfarm restaurant (see Romantic Restaurants), which are on the grounds.
$$$–$$$$ AE, DC, DIS, JCB, MC, V; checks OK; www.willowslodge.com.

THE WOODMARK HOTEL & SPA
♦♦♦
1200 Carillon Point, Kirkland / 425/822-3700 or 800/822-3700
Situated on the eastern shores of Lake Washington, this hotel is truly an intimate and romantic Northwest retreat, despite its rather standard exterior. The elegant lobby, with its overstuffed couches, glowing fireplace, sumptuous color schemes, and tall windows framing views of sparkling Lake Washington, will invite you to idle the day away in style. And the Library Room, with its armchairs, crackling fire, artworks, and inviting bar, is an appealing spot for a romantic nightcap before turning in. Unfortunately, the guest rooms are not as impressive as the common rooms. While decor in the 100 rooms is tasteful, with cream and beige linens, pretty watercolors, pine furnishings, and king-size beds, the rooms feel somewhat generic; you'll never forget you're in a large hotel. Be sure to request a room with a full lake view, or you may end up with an excellent vantage of the specialty shops across the street. The Petite Suites and the Parlor Suites offer extra space. We recommend ferreting out weddings when you book, since celebratory crowds flock to this premier Northwest wedding site in summer. (Luckily, the receptions take place on the bottom level of the hotel.) Waters Lakeside Bistro (425/803-5595) downstairs is an ideal waterfront spot to enjoy a fresh seafood entrée—and each other's company. Midnight snackers will be overjoyed to learn that the restaurant opens its kitchen at 11:30pm for guests to "raid the pantry," which essentially means helping yourselves to sandwiches, drinks, and desserts arranged appetizingly on a linen-covered table in the half-darkened dining room. It makes for a surprisingly sweet and romantic moment. You can also avail yourselves of the luxurious services at the spa. **$$$–$$$$** *AE, DC, JCB, MC, V; checks OK; www.thewoodmark.com.*

Romantic Restaurants

CAFE JUANITA
♦♦♦♦
9702 NE 120th Pl, Kirkland / 425/823-1505
This sublime Eastside destination soars higher on the romance scale than many of Seattle's most acclaimed restaurants. Even without a special event to celebrate, an evening here will make romantically-minded couples feel all the more amorous. Owner Holly Smith, the chef you may spy in the open kitchen, creates Italian-inspired dishes so good we have almost wept with joy. Her glowing national reputation leads to high expectations, and the simple, delicious fare absolutely delivers. The single-page menu launches into gourmet orbit with appetizers such as a savory house-smoked trout *crespelle* (Italian crepe) with English peas, and a *frisée* salad with house-made

bacon, soft-cooked egg, pecorino cheese, and oil-poached potato. For the pasta course try the delicate ravioli stuffed with crisp cauliflower, pine nuts, and currants. The main course brings even more bounty: a delicious whole roasted fish (the type of fish on offer changes daily), or a saddle of lamb adorned with artichokes and pine nuts. Finish with the Valrhona chocolate truffle cake or the caramelized lemon tart. The carefully selected wine list takes into consideration varied budgets and tastes. The modest, L-shaped interior is simply but beautifully decorated, with linen-covered tables, hardwood floors, and fresh flowers; in daylight, enjoy pretty views of the creek out back. For an open kitchen, it's surprisingly quiet, and a fireplace lends coziness; the congenial service is excellent. Our favorite tables are the corner banquettes for two, but if you don't mind sacrificing a little privacy, choose the table set before the fireplace.

$$$ *AE, MC, V; local checks only; dinner Tues–Sun; full bar; reservations recommended.*

THE HERBFARM
✪✪✪✪
14590 NE 145th St, Woodinville / 425/784-2222

One of the most acclaimed fine-dining destinations in the Northwest, the Herbfarm, located on the grounds of the posh Willows Lodge (see Romantic Lodgings), is a must for couples who love serious food and formal service almost as much as they love each other. The nine-course, five-hour, prix-fixe dinner with wine, which costs about $175 per person, certainly qualifies as a gourmet indulgence. Nationally renowned chef Jerry Traunfeld presides over menus that reflect seasonal local produce and herbs—much of which is grown in the Herbfarm's own substantial gardens. The food is immaculately presented—and carefully explained—in a cozy, tasteful interior filled with art and memorabilia. An evening's repast could include a starter of rosemary mussel skewer with marjoram aioli, flat oyster with nettles, and caviar on chive flan; Alaskan shrimp consommé with lemon verbena and fava beans; a trio of asparagus preparations including one with white-truffle hollandaise; lovingly hand-filled carrot ravioli with currants and fried sage; and chamomile-honey ice to cleanse the palate before the main event of Copper River king salmon, slow-roasted on the skin and served with lentil cake, morel mushrooms, and a pinot noir–fennel sauce. Finish with a refreshing spring salad with artisan sheep's milk cheese and a tart cherry turnover, followed by a trio of light strawberry desserts including strawberry-angelica shortcake and a strawberry, lavender, and chocolate sorbet sundae. A final selection of small sweet treats, such as chocolate truffles, arrives to go with your coffee. You will be looked after with great care by the hovering army of staff, who will anticipate your every need, pouring your wines and deftly clearing away the Christofle flatware and crystal just as soon as you're finished using it. Arrive a half-hour before dinner for a tour around the beautifully landscaped gardens. This coveted, one-of-a-kind destination must be booked months in advance, especially for holidays.

$$$$ AE, MC, V; checks OK; dinner Thurs–Sun; full bar; reservations required; www.theherbfarm.com.

SEA STAR RESTAURANT AND RAW BAR
◐◐◖

205 108th Ave NE, Bellevue / 425/456-0010
Offering a seemingly endless parade of the freshest Northwest oysters, along with a creative menu by James Beard award–winning chef-owner John Howie, this restaurant has become an Eastside fixture since its 2002 opening. Vaulted ceilings inside soar above the linen-clad tables in a bright, airy interior warmed by striking orange glass chandeliers in evocative sea-weed shapes. While the tables for two here are comfortable, the dining room is a bit too large to feel intimate and the views to the street aren't inspiring. Fortunately, the raw bar's vast selection of aphrodisiacs—fresh oysters—will help you overlook these minor romantic drawbacks. The seafood dishes are spectacular, particularly the signature dish of sesame-peppercorn seared ahi served on jasmine rice cakes with creamed wasabi and ginger-soy reduction. Hearty New York steaks and a selection of pastas round out the options. For dessert, try the fabulous banana spring-roll sundae—a crispy, cinnamon-rolled fried banana served with vanilla ice cream and rich caramel sauce. The fun-to-read wine list has garnered prestigious awards and will be demystified in a moment by the refreshingly down-to-earth sommelier. The $30-and-under price range includes more than 20 bottles.

$$$ AE, DC, MC, V; checks OK; lunch Mon–Fri, dinner every day; full bar; reservations recommended; www.seastarrestaurant.com.

THIRD FLOOR FISH CAFE
◐◐◐

205 Lake St S, Kirkland / 425/822-3553
As the sun dips below the horizon, the lights in this Kirkland restaurant dim for optimal viewing of the marina in the foreground and Seattle's skyline in the distance. The best time to come here for a romantic dinner is later in the evening, when the after-work crowds have dispersed. Although the window seats provide the best views, they are in a high-traffic area, so snuggle up instead in one of the high-backed booths on the less frantic upper level; you'll still have a nice view to look at when you can tear yourselves away from each other. As the restaurant's name suggests, your best bet here is fish, such as the pan-seared salmon with fennel and red onion salad. Also con-sider the sea scallops with stewed organic-vegetable ragout in a tarragon broth. The five- and seven-course tasting menus, with accompanying wines, are quite good—and show that the chef has skills well beyond fish. Service

is unwaveringly polished and professional. The wine list of mostly domestic bottles is carefully selected, but skimpy at the low end, with just a bottle or two priced below $30. Desserts range from an oven-roasted plum cake with plum caramel and whipped cream to a triple-chocolate *semifreddo*.
$$$ *AE, DC, DIS, MC, V; local checks only; dinner every day; full bar; reservations recommended.*

YARROW BAY GRILL
✪✪✪
1270 Carillon Pt, Kirkland / 425/889-9052
Dotted with sailboats and yachts, Lake Washington's blue waters take center stage at this waterfront restaurant, located in the upscale Carillon Point development next to the Woodmark Hotel & Spa (see Romantic Lodgings). All of the restaurant's windows face west, while booths near the restaurant's center (far from the back room, where large groups tend to congregate) are ideal for enjoying the sunset with a little privacy. Chocolate-colored walls and metal sculptures lend character to the interior. The creative, seasonally influenced menu changes frequently. Appetizers such as Louisiana-style barbecue prawns bathed in a spicy Cajun broth will heat up your lips—you might need a kiss or two to cool them off. Fresh seafood dishes are a good choice, with seductive options such as lobster risotto with wild mushrooms, braised greens, and goat cheese; other main courses range from pork tenderloin sauced with apricot–ancho chile mole to grilled rib-eye steak with porcini rub, portobello mushrooms, and roasted-garlic mashed potatoes. Cap off the evening with a honey-roasted pear with marcona almond streusel, sweet mascarpone cream, and port syrup, or a rich, decadent chocolate-hazelnut cake. For more casual fare, head downstairs to the Beach Café (425/889-0303; lunch, dinner every day), which serves up an array of less expensive dishes. If the sun is shining, snag a table on the outdoor deck overlooking the marina.
$$$** *(Yarrow Bay Grill);* **$$ *(Beach Café) AE, DC, DIS, JCB, MC, V; no checks; lunch Mon–Fri, dinner every day, brunch Sun; full bar; reservations recommended; www.ybgrill.com.*

BAINBRIDGE ISLAND & KITSAP PENINSULA

ROMANTIC HIGHLIGHTS

Bainbridge Island's charming downtown and beautiful parks and gardens, and the scenic 35-minute ferry ride from Seattle, make it appealing as a romantic getaway. At the north end of the island, cross over Agate Passage on the Highway 305 bridge to reach the Kitsap Peninsula. Here you'll find Poulsbo, with its quaint Scandinavian motif and shop-lined streets, along with tiny, scenic communities such as Port Gamble and Seabeck, which are set along Hood Canal and offer exquisite views of the snowcapped Olympic peaks. Some of the larger cities on the Kitsap Peninsula, such as the naval port of Bremerton, have reputations that are decidedly less than romantic; but those willing to venture down roads less traveled will be rewarded with surprising finds, such as **Cafe Destino** (1223 McKenzie Ave; 360/782-0711), a waterside restaurant that serves a delightful Sunday brunch and shows movies screened against the building's outer wall on summer nights. With its small towns and unfailingly spectacular views of rugged nature, this region is worthy of romantic exploration.

The start of your romantic travels can begin on the ferry ride to Bainbridge. On blue sky days, you and your loved one can bask in the light on the top deck and enjoy the beautiful waterscape that surrounds. If it's overcast or rainy, step onto the back deck of the main level and hold each other for warmth while fog-embanked Seattle slips into the distance.

Once on Bainbridge, you can spend an incredibly romantic afternoon visiting the gorgeous **Bloedel Reserve** (7571 NE Dolphin Dr; 206/842-7631; open Wed–Sun by reservation only). An afternoon excursion here leads through 150 acres of splendid Northwest gardens, from landscaped meadows to forested dells. Wander through the bird sanctuary and exquisite Japanese gardens, pause at the quiet reflecting pool, and admire the dense moss garden. All is divine.

For an afternoon of small-town pleasures, stroll the streets of downtown Bainbridge, indulging in shopping and refreshments. Start with a strong coffee and luscious lemon tart from the **Blackbird Bakery** (210 Winslow Wy E; 206/780-1322), and then continue on to the handsome independent bookstore **Eagle Harbor Book Company** (157 Winslow Wy E; 206/842-5332) or **Bainbridge Arts & Crafts** (151 Winslow Wy E; 206/842-3132). If an afternoon drink sounds divine on a sunny day, you'll find a cozy spot for two on the postage-stamp deck of **The Harbour Public House** (231 Parfitt Wy SW; 206/842-0969). Watch the boat masts bobbing gently in the marina as you enjoy the quiet together (or rub elbows with locals during the busy noon hour). If you find you've worked up an appetite, order the tasty fish-and-chips—classic pub fare that is fried to perfection here. Another pleasing option is to sit down at **Cafe Nola** (see Romantic Restaurants) for an excellent lunch.

Bainbridge Island is the perfect place for a romantic waterside picnic. You can pick up goodies in town at **Town & Country Market** (343 Winslow Wy E; 206/842-3848) or get a few heavenly fresh pasta dishes at the hole-in-the-wall **Mon Elisa's** (450 Winslow Wy E; 206/780-3233) and then tote them to one of the island's parks. Our favorite destination is **Fort Ward State Park** (2241 Pleasant Beach Dr NE; 206/842-4041), on the island's south end. It's a scenic drive along some of the island's back roads to get here; bring a map and good directions. An easier-to-find option is the small beachfront **Fay Bainbridge State Park** (15446 Sunrise Dr NE; 206/842-3931; from downtown Bainbridge, take SR 305 north to the turnoff at Day Rd E and follow signs). While a playground, picnic shelters, and a campground mean this park might be slightly more crowded than you would like, the expanse of pebbled beach is nicely suited to a long, hand-in-hand walk. On your way here, stop off at **Bainbridge Island Vineyards and Winery** (8989 Day Rd E; 206/842-WINE; www.bainbridgevineyards.com; open Fri–Sun) for wine tastings and a self-guided tour of the vineyard.

The tiny waterfront town of **Poulsbo**, just north of Bainbridge across Agate Pass, is best known for the charming (OK, touristy) Scandinavian motif of its coffee shops, restaurants, and storefronts. You'll certainly be drawn in by the tantalizing aroma of fresh apple-cinnamon bread wafting out of the popular **Sluy's Poulsbo Bakery** (18924 Front St NE; 360/779-2798). Once you've selected your pastries (easier said than done), head for the boardwalk along Liberty Bay, where you can rent a kayak from **Olympic Outdoor Center** (18971 Front St NE; 360/697-6095). After you've worked up an appetite, try **MorMor Bistro & Bar** (see Romantic Restaurants) for a tasty lunch in pleasant surroundings. **Boehm's Chocolates** (18864 Front St NE; 360/697-3318) has an outpost here, if you find yourselves in the mood to share sweets with your sweetheart. No matter how you amuse yourselves, you'll find that Poulsbo has more charm than its ersatz facade promises. Venture out of town and you'll discover distinctly romantic destinations in the countryside that are not to be missed. North of town, enjoy a quiet walk at **Kitsap Memorial State Park** (from Poulsbo, head north on Hwy 3; look for signs to the park 4 miles south of the Hood Canal Bridge), where a 1,797-foot stretch of saltwater shoreline awaits exploration. In the scenic farmland of Poulsbo, the **Farm Kitchen** (24309 Port Gamble Rd; 360/297-6615; www.farmkitchen.com; open Sat only) is a welcoming breakfast oasis—complete with red barn and two pastured horses—that offers a rotating baked goods and early morning menu.

Near the fishing town of **Hansville** to the east are a couple of the prettiest, most accessible, and least-explored beaches on the peninsula. The first, Point No Point, boasts a beautiful lighthouse. But even better is **Foul-weather Bluff** (follow the road from Hansville to the west). Don't be put off by its name; you'll find a secluded paradise of a beach where you can picnic amid the sand and driftwood. You may even spot a soaring eagle. The short trail through the woods is a little hard to find, so look for the Nature Conservancy sign on the south side of the road.

Near the Hood Canal Bridge, you'll discover the intriguing town of **Port Gamble**. Built in the mid-19th century by the Pope & Talbot timber company, whose founders traveled here by clipper ship from Maine, this is the quintessential company town. In fact, everything is still company owned and maintained—though the company these days is Olympic Resource Management. The town was modeled on a New England village and features beautiful Victorian houses, a lovely church, a vital and well-stocked company store, and **LaLa Land Chocolates** (32279 Rainier Ave NE; 360/297-4291), a combination chocolatier and tearoom that makes sinfully decadent chocolate truffles. The historic **Port Gamble Museum** (32400 Rainier Ave; 360/297-8074) is a gem, with a fascinating presentation of the community's societal and industrial heritage. From Port Gamble, roads lead south past Bremerton to the waterfront town of **Port Orchard**, which hugs Sinclair Inlet; here you'll find a boardwalk, beach access, and a waterfront **Saturday farmers market** (Marina Park, 1 block from Bay St; late Apr–Oct).

Access & Information

Washington State Ferries (206/464-6400 or 800/843-3779; www.wsdot.wa.gov/ferries/) run regularly between downtown Seattle and Bainbridge Island. This ferry route is one of the more popular ways to begin a trip to the Olympic Peninsula (via the Hood Canal Bridge), where the Northwest's largest national park and some of the state's most spectacular scenery await.

You could drive around Puget Sound to reach the Kitsap Peninsula, but the Washington State Ferries provide more scenery and more romance. There is a ferry departing regularly from Seattle to Bremerton. Boats also dock on the Kitsap Peninsula in Kingston (catch the ferry from Edmonds, north of Seattle), and in Southworth, near Port Orchard (ferry from Fauntleroy in West Seattle). For more information on destinations on the Kitsap Peninsula, contact the **Kitsap Peninsula Visitor and Convention Bureau** (360/297-8200; www.visitkitsap.com).

For more information about Bainbridge Island, contact the **Bainbridge Chamber of Commerce** (590 Winslow Wy E; 206/842-3700; www.bainbridge-chamber.com). Locals and tourists alike crowd the Bainbridge Island ferry; summertime, and most weekends during the rest of the year, can bring horrendous lines and frustrating delays. If you just want to explore Winslow, you can avoid hassles by leaving your car behind; downtown is within easy walking distance of the ferry terminal, and you can reach the terminal on the Seattle side by bus or waterfront trolley.

Romantic Lodgings

ALDERBROOK RESORT & SPA
🌑🌑🌑

7101 E State Route 106, Union / 800/622-9370
From the window seat of one of Alderbrook's Marine View Rooms, the view is spectacular: in winter, a light blanket of fog envelops the tree-lined Hood Canal horizon, and, in summer, the cool blue water sparkles in the sunlight. Set on the very southern shores of Hood Canal—where the Kitsap Peninsula meets the mainland—the resort is reached from Seattle via the Bremerton ferry (a 60-minute ride plus 30-minute drive) or by driving from Seattle to Tacoma, turning west onto Highway 16, connecting to southwest Highway 3, and then taking Scenic Route 106 (this drive takes about 90 minutes). No matter where you're coming from, the idea is to stay put once you've arrived, since this destination resort provides activities, restaurants, spa service, and transfixing views. Reopened in June 2004 after a complete make-over, the resort's lodge boasts 77 guest rooms, most with views of Hood Canal and the Olympic Mountains, 15 two-bedroom cottages, and 1 one-bedroom cottage complete with full kitchen and fireplace. All are decorated in warm, soothing earth tones, such as sage green and autumn red, and have creature comforts like down comforters, room service, and cable and DVD players. The cottages are more suited for families, and most look out onto a common lawn area. If you're interested in romance, the main lodge's Marine and Olympic View rooms offer what you're looking for: interiors featuring dark-wood accents, soft lighting, and plush king- and queen-size beds make the guest rooms feel like secluded cocoons. Other features include standard-size elegant bathrooms with deep soaking tubs. Request a room with a private deck, then you can order room service, stay in your bathrobe, and enjoy morning pancakes outside at the deck's table. If only the Alderbrook Restaurant (360/898-5500) could live up to the promise of the rooms and the spectacular setting; the uneven food (also overpriced) could use improvement. Fortunately, there are plenty of romantic distractions: Walk the 1,500-foot-long dock over the glistening water, take a dip in the pool housed in a greenhouse alongside the canal, order an afternoon martini in the resort's restaurant bar, unwind in the luxury spa's sauna, and enjoy a basalt hot stone massage. More athletic pursuits include canoe and kayak rentals at the resort, tennis and golf nearby, and many accessible hiking trails. **$$$–$$$$** *AE, CB, DC, MC, V; checks OK; www.alderbrookresort.com.* ♿

THE BUCHANAN INN

♥♥

8494 NE Odd Fellows Rd, Bainbridge Island / 206/780-9258 or 800/598-3926

Hidden away on a scenic country road, this beautifully renovated 1912 B&B is surrounded by lush grounds full of colorful flowers, blossoming cherry trees, and a beautiful old madrone tree. For your romantic retreat, choose from four spacious suites with large private baths. The Bilberry, in a building adjacent to the main house, is the honeymoon suite and boasts a Jacuzzi tub, as well as mint-hued walls with white trim, and an adorable red love seat next to the gas fireplace. Our favorite room, however, is the Loch Lomond, directly above the Bilberry; it doesn't have a private Jacuzzi, but if you feel like a soak, you can enjoy the cedar cottage–housed hot tub in the beautiful gardens, which is available to all guests. This bright accommodation has a private entrance, high ceilings, playful artwork, lush green plants, Oriental carpets warming the polished hardwoods, and comfortable mahogany furnishings. The suites in the main house offer slightly less privacy, but are very pretty, nonetheless. Amenities in all rooms include silky robes, Egyptian cotton linens and towels, CD players, coffee makers, and mini-fridges stocked with complimentary beverages. In keeping with the spirit of a romantic getaway, the sole TV is located in the main house's guest living room. At 5:30 each evening, enjoy a cocktail hour with wine and cheese served on the deck and take in views of the garden. Breakfast is served family-style in the spare white dining room in the main house; the oft-changing artwork here comes from a local gallery. Fort Ward State Park and the beach are nearby, so after breakfast, head out for a romantic stroll along the water.

$$ *AE, DC, DIS, JCB, MC, V; checks OK; www.buchananinn.com.* &

THE EAGLE HARBOR INN

♥♥♥

291 Madison Ave S, Bainbridge Island / 206/842-1446

Located by the marina in Bainbridge's downtown area of Winslow, The Eagle Harbor Inn, which opened in September 2004, blends convenience with tasteful design. The inn is part of a building constructed in three sections, all of which cluster around a quaint garden courtyard. One part of the building includes condominiums for permanent residents, the rest is the inn. Parts of the courtyard are residents' private spaces, as are a few of the parking spaces, but there are no signs saying so—everything looks communal—leaving guests wondering where to relax outside, where to park their cars, or where to address questions (there is no reception desk). Instead, when guests reserve space via phone or e-mail, owners Cihan and Bonnie Anisoglu provide them with a private code for keyless entry. While those who like the warm welcome of a B&B might find this a tad lonely, some kissing couples might just enjoy the extra privacy. The inn's main section has a comfortable entryway with four of the six available suites branching from it. One suite, the Rockaway Beach Room, is a romantic second-story room with lofty, vaulted ceilings; a king-size bed; and views in three directions, including a vantage of peaceful Eagle Harbor. Perfectly styled to follow a driftwood-and-blue beach theme, the room looks like it was decorated for the pages of a Pottery Barn catalog. The second section of the inn—with a separate entry—houses the remaining suites, with the top-floor Vineyard Suite being the most grand of all six. Besides having a gas fireplace, private deck, king-size bed, pullout sofa, and full commercial kitchen, the apartment's French Provençal look includes large-beam raised ceilings, crafted forest-green cabinetry and granite counters in the kitchen, and a light-filled living room. Fresh coffee is offered in the entryway of the main building each morning, but otherwise there is no food or drink included in the stay. This isn't a big concern, however, since it creates the excuse to explore the nearby charming restaurants and cafes (see Romantic Highlights). **$$$** *AE, DIS, MC, V; no checks; www.theeagleharborinn.com.* ♿

ILLAHEE MANOR
◗◗◗◗
6680 Illahee Rd NE, Bremerton / 360/698-7555 or 800/693-6680
The urban sprawl of Bremerton does little to prepare you for this luxurious getaway, where attention to detail and luxurious amenities result in one of the finest bed-and-breakfasts in the region. The main house, which resembles a small castle, sits on a landscaped bluff above the sparkling waters of Puget Sound. (A hot tub on the large deck shares the splendid view.) Majestic trees, an apple orchard, a calming babbling brook, and three separate vacation homes are spread out on the 6 acres surrounding the main house, whose five suites all feature gas fireplaces or woodstoves, beautifully restored antiques, and private bathrooms. The second-story Penthouse Suite is spacious and dramatic, with a vaulted ceiling, safari-style decor including a leopard-print rug and vast leather sofa, a stereo, a woodstove, an enormous Jacuzzi tub, and a palatial king-size bed. A full kitchen and separate bath are also included. While the Penthouse is extraordinary, the other four rooms will do very nicely for a romantic weekend. Even the Library, a tiny guest room on the main floor, has a highlight; although it's located across the hall, the enormous private bathroom features skylights in the two-person shower, and a huge spa tub and sauna. The spacious Beach House, Cottage, and Hill House, all separate from the main house, are best for families or multiple couples traveling together. Nothing at this romantic getaway will disappoint—certainly not the gourmet breakfasts served at intimate tables in the grand, airy conservatory. Fresh blueberry scones, creamy scrambled eggs, apple-stuffed croissant French toast, and delicious fresh fruit will entice

you out of your room. In the afternoon, relax on white wicker furnishings on the elegant veranda and enjoy the views of the water.
$$–$$$ *AE, DC, DIS, MC, V; checks OK; www.illaheemanor.com.* &

SELAH INN
◐◐◐

130 NE Dulalip Landing, Belfair / 360/275-0916 or 877/232-7941
There aren't many deluxe accommodations on the north shore of Hood Canal, but in the small town of Belfair, Selah Inn's prime beachfront property, beautiful guest rooms, gourmet breakfasts, and dinners featuring fresh Northwest seafood make it a premier romantic destination. Furthermore, golfers-in-love will appreciate the proximity to several excellent courses. Two buildings house seven guest suites, all with private baths and extra soundproofing to ensure privacy. In the main house, the King Room features a green marble fireplace, a double Jacuzzi tub, and a large deck with a view of the canal. The best views, however, are from the three rooms in the adjacent Canal House, set right on the water. Whether you stay in the main house or the Canal House, you'll enjoy a first-class bed with luxurious linens. All guests are free to unwind in the inn's common areas, which include a library, a tiled sunroom, and a comfortable modern living room with a massive stone fireplace. Breakfast, which is served in the main house, is included, and other meals are available for an additional cost. If you aim to make the Friday lunch, you'll get your weekend off to an excellent early start—and avoid the traffic from Seattle. Dinners, available by reservation, include five courses made with local seafood and produce; enjoy hors d'oeuvres on the deck, and then adjourn to your private table for options like roast salmon with roasted-garlic herb butter. Finish the evening with tiramisù or lemon mousse with berries. For a delicious afternoon snack, you're welcome to dig for clams on the beach (shovels are provided); grill them over the outdoor fire pit until they pop open.
$$–$$$ *MC, V; checks OK; www.selahinn.com.* &

WILLCOX HOUSE
◐◐◐◑

2390 Tekiu Rd NW, Seabeck / 360/830-4492 or 800/725-2600
The grandeur of the Willcox House belongs to a bygone era. The drive to get here winds past 14 miles of towering evergreens and rolling countryside to the turnoff for the house, where the road plunges to the water before winding up to the copper-roofed, terra-cotta–tiled mansion. The location, on a forested bluff with superb views of Hood Canal and the Olympic Mountains, is nothing short of sublime. Wisteria climbs a trellis in the backyard, where walking paths wind through palatial gardens, past a swinging hammock, a swimming pool, and a goldfish pond. The aura of the place is romantic 1930s Hollywood: with good reason, as the home's original owners

ran in the same circle as Clark Gable, who often stayed here as a guest (one of the rooms is now named after him). The impressive 10,000-square-foot interior includes many common areas, marked by extravagant, if slightly eclectic, decor. Relax by the grand piano in the wood-paneled guest parlor, amuse yourselves with darts in the game room, or socialize with other guests over wine and cheese in the upstairs library overlooking the water. All five guest rooms feature copper-framed fireplaces, walnut paneling, and wood parquet floors. But despite recent renovations, still more are in order. The windows need new treatments, and, overall, the rooms could use more spit and polish; nevertheless, the advantages of this noble lodging cannot be denied. Some rooms offer sweeping views, two have Jacuzzi tubs, and one has a private balcony. Breakfast is a remarkable presentation of fresh fruits, granola, and crepes topped with strawberry-blueberry syrup, all served in a glass-enclosed dining room with great views. Lunch is also an option for guests staying multiple nights, as is the prix-fixe dinner (also open to nonguests on weekends by reservation). Diners rave about the roasted pork tenderloin served Saturdays, and, if you're lucky, you'll come on a night when the decadent chocolate truffle cake is offered for dessert. Count on a half-hour drive from the Bremerton ferry, though guests also arrive by boat or floatplane.
$$$ DIS, MC, V; checks OK; www.willcoxhouse.com. &

Romantic Restaurants

CAFE NOLA
◕◕◕
101 Winslow Wy E, Bainbridge Island / 206/842-3822
Located on a corner in charming downtown Bainbridge, this cheerful, elegant restaurant offers an inviting haven for locals and island visitors alike. While the restaurant has recently been expanded, it has retained its warm, cozy atmosphere, complete with sunny yellow walls adorned with tasteful artwork, linen-covered tables—including a few private booths—and an attentive, youthful staff. Windows overlook the street and an inviting outdoor patio—a popular lunch spot in summer. The restaurant is run by Kevin and Whitney Warren; Kevin was formerly a sous chef at Marco's Supperclub in Seattle, and his menu offers an intriguing and eclectic selection of dishes. Popular with lunch crowds are the hearty soup—from clam chowder to butternut squash—and the grilled salmon sandwich dressed with seasonal greens and sturdy Essential Bakery bread. Dinner brings forth herb-wrapped filet mignon with a red wine demi-glaze, served with mashed potatoes; also consider the pan-seared scallops served over yellow corn–grit cakes with roasted pepper–garlic sauce. Don't miss the desserts,

which range from delicious confections of white chocolate–caramel bread pudding to crème brûlée and a decadent cappuccino-chocolate roulade. $$ *AE, MC, V; checks OK; lunch Mon–Fri, dinner every day, brunch Sat–Sun; full bar; reservations recommended.* &

THE FOUR SWALLOWS
❁❁❁❁

481 Madison Ave N, Bainbridge Island / 206/842-3397
This picturesque yellow 1889 farmhouse, within walking distance of the ferry landing, is wonderfully romantic. Turn-of-the-20th-century antiques, a polished black-and-ivory bar, and leaded-glass windows enhance the interior's charm. Cozy dark-wood booths fill the intimate bar area in the back, while the several elegantly simple dining rooms at the front are ideal for romance; tables set into the bright and airy rooms' nooks and crannies create the illusion that you've been given your very own dining room. The menu has Mediterranean overtones and features delicious starters such as delicate mussels with Spanish sherry, leeks, tomatoes, smoked paprika, and cream; beef carpaccio; and a generous antipasto plate. Entrées are exceptional, too. Try the savory hand-roasted beef tenderloin with brandy and green peppercorn sauce and accompanied by mashed potatoes, or pillowy crab cakes served with a tangy lemon aioli and shoestring fries. The clam linguine offers a blast of flavor, with pancetta and lots of garlic. Top off the dinner with a rich vanilla crème brûlée. With its sophisticated yet easygoing ambience, and food that borders on the magical, this popular island restaurant provides an intimate harbor for island-going couples. $$ *MC, V; local checks only; dinner Tues–Sat; beer and wine; reservations recommended.* &

ISLAY MANOR
❁❁❁

4738 Lynnwood Ct Rd NE, Bainbridge Island / 206/780-9303
Formerly known as Ruby's on Bainbridge and originally located in Lynnwood Center alongside the retro movie theater, Islay Manor now sits across the road, atop a hill overlooking Lynnwood and the water—same owners, still serving impressive food, just under a new name and in a new location. Truly a manor, the sprawling building has dramatic peaked rooflines and an attractive wood-paneled interior. Unfortunately, the large main dining room can get noisy due to bad acoustics on busy nights, and the food can be uneven when there's a crowd. But the casual, French-country mood, appetizing menu options, intimate tables warmed by candles, and extensive wine list make it worth a stop. For a more romantic, private experience make reservations for an early weeknight or ask to sit in the Library Bar; it is a more intimate space with only a few tables—ideal for a kiss-perfect, quiet dinner. And during the summer, there's the light-strewn patio to enjoy. To

begin the evening, try the mixed green–curry salad with jicama, fried ginger, and a curry-peanut sauce. Make sure to check out the specials of the night. Offered one night was an impressive mixed grill of halibut, scallops, salmon, and prawns in a red wine–tomato cream sauce. For a smooth, rich dessert, the sweet cream with a light raspberry sauce is ideal. Follow it all up with a movie showing at the nearby historic Lynnwood Theatre (sit in the back to sneak a few unobtrusive kisses). **$$$** *AE, MC, V; checks OK; dinner every day; full bar; reservations recommended; www.islaymanor.com.* &

MORMOR RESTAURANT
♥♥€

18820 Front St NE, Poulsbo / 360/697-3449
This spare, sophisticated restaurant is a welcome addition to the offerings in quaint, Scandinavian-styled Poulsbo. The clean interior, filled with white linen–clad tables and black-and-white, color-tinted family photographs, feels like a sleek urban haven in this kitschy waterfront village. While on busy nights it can be noisy, and the open, airy room lacks secluded nooks and corners to harbor romantic couples, the delicious food and relaxed atmosphere make up for these slight drawbacks. Owners John and Laura Nesby are both accomplished chefs with a passion for fresh ingredients and creative food. Each inspired by their grandmothers' cooking, the couple bought the restaurant, formerly Benson's, and renamed it MorMor, a Scandinavian word that translates to "mother's mother." The menu changes on a nightly basis—all dependent on what is being sold at the local farmers markets and what the catch-of-the-day is. For example, served one night was the flat-iron steak with a truffle-wine demi-glaze accompanied by butter-whipped potatoes and butter-braised wild chanterelles; while the following night the steak was complemented by oven-roasted celery root, grilled fennel, and roasted new potatoes. The dessert menu changes every four weeks or so. But what is always offered is some deliciously rich chocolate cake, perhaps a deconstructed German chocolate cake with chocolate ganache and toasted coconut, served with a cold shot of Ovaltine—John's family tradition. **$$** *AE, MC, V; checks OK; lunch, dinner Wed–Mon; full bar; reservations recommended.*

PUGET SOUND

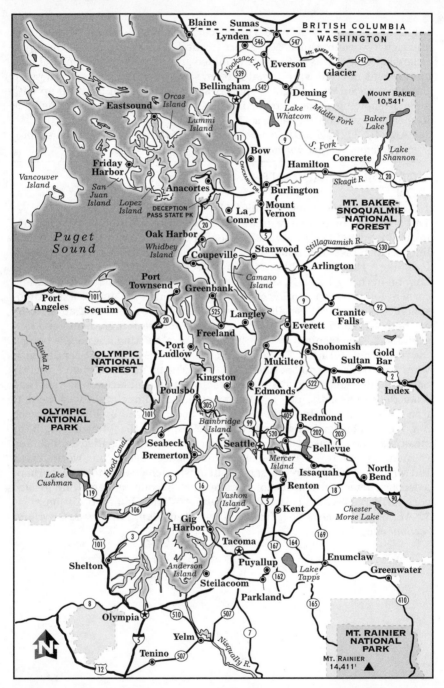

Blaine   Sumas   BRITISH COLUMBIA
Lynden   546   WASHINGTON
        547   MT. BAKER HWY.   542
Nooksack R.   Everson   Glacier
539
Bellingham   542   Deming   ▲ MOUNT BAKER
                              10,541'
Orcas
Island   Lake   Middle Fork
Eastsound   Whatcom   Baker
        Lummi   9   Lake
        Island   S. Fork
11   Bow   Concrete   Lake
                              Shannon
Friday   Hamilton
Harbor   Burlington   Skagit R.   20
Vancouver   Anacortes   Mount   MT. BAKER-
Island   San   Vernon   SNOQUALMIE
        Juan   DECEPTION   La   NATIONAL
        Island   Lopez   PASS STATE PK   Conner   FOREST
        Island   20   5
Puget   Oak Harbor   Stanwood   Stillaguamish R.   530
Sound   Whidbey   Coupeville
        Island   Arlington
Port   Camano
Townsend   Greenbank   Island
Port   101   9   Granite
Angeles   Sequim   525   Langley   Falls   92
        20   Everett   Snohomish   Gold
        Freeland   Bar
Elwha R.   Port   Mukilteo   Sultan   2
        Ludlow   522   Monroe   Index
OLYMPIC   Kingston   Edmonds
NATIONAL   Poulsbo   99   405   Redmond
FOREST   305   520   202   203
OLYMPIC   Bainbridge   Seattle   Bellevue
NATIONAL   Island   North
PARK   Seabeck   Mercer   Issaquah   Bend
Lake   Bremerton   Island   90
Cushman   3   16   Renton   18
119   106   5   Kent   Chester
        Vashon   Morse Lake
        Island
        Gig   169   Enumclaw
        Harbor   Tacoma   164   Greenwater
101   3   Anderson   Puyallup   167   Lake
Shelton   Island   Steilacoom   162   Tapps   410
        Parkland   165
8   510   507   MT. RAINIER
Olympia   7   NATIONAL
5   Yelm   Nisqually R.   PARK
Tenino   507   MT. RAINIER
12   14,411'   ▲

N

"Soul meets soul on lovers' lips."
—PERCY BYSSHE SHELLEY

♡ PUGET SOUND

The landscape of the greater Puget Sound region, with its pastoral farm-land, sparkling waterways, and jewel-like islands, is naturally blessed with scenic splendor. Hemmed in by the vast Cascade Range to the east and the magnificent Olympic Mountains in the west, the region offers views of jagged snow-capped peaks against the horizon (OK, only on clear days) from nearly every vantage point. The long days of Puget Sound summers are easily celebrated at the many romantic destinations within short traveling distance of Seattle. Winter brings the infamous rain, and chilly evenings that call for fireside suppers. Fortunately, with not infrequent clear after-noons and moderate temperatures year-round, lovers of the outdoors can indulge in scenic walks in any season. And the inclement weather pays off in spring, when the farmlands are a lush green and the meadows explode with blossoms.

Interstate 5 is the main route through this populous, verdant stretch of Washington state, from Olympia at the southern end of Puget Sound to Bellingham near the border with Canada. This part of the state not only is the headquarters of the state's port, shipping, fishing, and naval indus-tries, but it also offers some of the region's most idyllic getaways. If you're driving north from Seattle, the interstate takes you to the region's famous tulip capital, the Skagit Valley, which, in addition to tulip field after tulip field, offers waterfront towns and villages such as Anacortes and La Conner; farther north is the pretty city of Bellingham, with its parks, sparkling lakes, university, and restored historic districts. However, Puget Sound is best explored by leaving the freeway and traveling on the back roads, some of which lead to the state's most-visited islands, including Whidbey and the San Juans—known for their picturesque island villages and stretches of unspoiled beach, inviting travelers with romance on their minds to linger and explore.

WHIDBEY ISLAND

ROMANTIC HIGHLIGHTS

A side from being one of the most easily accessible islands in the Seattle area—and one of the most sophisticated—Whidbey Island is also the longest island in the continental United States, with miles of lovely, scenic coastline and pastoral green meadows. If you're looking for a quick escape from city life, Whidbey is an exemplary destination and offers an unusually large selection of good restaurants, wonderful bed-and-breakfasts, and beautiful parks.

Nestled on a bluff above the water's edge, the small town of Langley, with its mesmerizing views of Mount Baker, the Cascades, and Saratoga Passage, is one of the island's most romantic spots. In the downtown area, the shops and galleries on First Street are designed for hand-in-hand strolling and browsing. Shop for diamonds *and* chocolates in the antique-and-candy-filled shop **Wayward Son** (202 1st St; 360/221-3911), or browse for that perfect summer read at the friendly, inviting **Moonraker Books** (209 1st St; 360/221-6962). The **Artists' Gallery Cooperative** (314 1st St; 360/221-7675) showcases work from more than 40 island artists and craftspeople. After a day of exploring, catch a movie (and sneak a kiss) at downtown's tiny, charming **Clyde Theatre** (213 1st St; 360/221-5525).

For refreshments, duck into the **Langley Village Bakery** (221 2nd St; 360/221-3525) and indulge in luscious fresh pastries and piping-hot espresso. Hidden away on a charming side street, **Langley Tea & Sushi** (112½ Anthes Ave; 360/221-6292; open Thurs–Mon) offers an unusual combination of fare: in the airy, terra-cotta–tiled room, you can enjoy either an English tea with traditional scones and Devon cream, or Japanese green tea and delicious sushi rolls. Another pleasant interlude is to be found via a 10-minute drive on a scenic, forested road to Bayview Corner, near the junction of Highway 25. Here you can stroll through the beautiful gardens and vast outdoor nursery at **Bayview Farm & Garden** (2780 Marshview Ave; 360/321-6789); afterward, join the locals for a tasty lunch at the whimsical **Smilin' Dog Coffee House and Café** (5603 S Bayview Rd; 360/321-7686).

In Langley itself, our favorite spot for a casual alfresco meal is the lively **Star Bistro** (201½ 1st St; 360/221-2627), located upstairs from a genuine mercantile outpost. Its charming, heated deck offers a bird's-eye view of the street and the water, which goes well with tasty Northwest cuisine. On more formal occasions, consider the local favorite **Cafe Langley** (see Romantic Restaurants), or the **Edgecliff** (510 Cascade Ave; 360/221-8899), an upscale steak and seafood restaurant perched above the water with sweeping views of sparkling Saratoga Passage. For afternoon eats, perhaps the most romantic option is a wine-lovers' picnic: stock up on gourmet lunch provisions at **Langley's Star Store** (201 1st St; 360/221-5222) and head about a mile south of town to **Whidbey Island Vineyards and Winery** (5237 S Langley Rd; 360/221-2040; www.whidbeyislandwinery.com). Inside the quaint, shingled tasting room, sip Madeleine Angevine, a delicate white wine made with grapes grown on Whidbey Island, or try merlot or syrah made with Eastern Washington–grown grapes. Afterward, enjoy a wine-infused kiss—and your lunch—at one of the picnic tables on the groomed lawn in full view of the lush vineyards.

If you head north on Whidbey Island, past the town of Langley, the small community of **Greenbank** will pass by in a flash; but *do* consider stopping here. Particularly if you find yourselves blessed with a glorious spring day, we highly recommend a stroll through **Meerkerk Rhododendron Gardens** (3531 Meerkerk Ln; 360/678-1912; www.meerkerkgardens.org; open 9am–4pm every day; small admission fee). This 43-acre wooded preserve is home to many varieties of rhododendron, and gardening buffs can gain valuable knowledge—and even buy the rhododendrons in bloom. Those with planting kisses rather than rhodies on their minds can simply enjoy the blooms while walking hand in hand; their glorious peak occurs April through May.

As with all of Puget Sound's beautiful islands, Whidbey is full of beaches and parks that beckon with the promise of romantic solitude. Pack a picnic and drive to **Double Bluff Beach**, northwest of Langley, to discover an unspoiled beach and watch the sunset while snuggling with your sweetie. Northwest of Coupeville, you can explore the bluff and beach at 17,000-acre **Ebey's Landing** and **Fort Ebey State Park**. As for the town of **Coupeville** itself, it may not look particularly romantic as you drive down the commercial Main Street, but patience has its rewards: continue on and you'll find a tiny, one-street stretch of picturesque and old-fashioned waterfront. Browse the small selection of turn-of-the-20th-century, harbor-style storefronts for antiques and trinkets, or stop for homemade ice cream in one of several sweets shops. These quiet streets can and do get crowded during annual community events such as the **Penn Cove Mussel Festival**, the first weekend in March; and the **Coupeville Arts & Crafts Festival**, the second weekend in August (360/678-5116; www.coupevilleartsandcraftsfestival.org).

Be sure to visit the north end of Whidbey Island for the exhilarating views of the beautiful, treacherous gorge of **Deception Pass**. Words can't describe the heart-stopping sensation of driving across the narrow bridge that spans this chasm; all the more reason to cling to your companion. This is also the site of **Deception Pass State Park**, which comprises 2,300 acres of prime camping land, forests, and beach (although the area's highly hazardous currents mean you should avoid the water). You can cross the bridge over Deception Pass that links Whidbey to Fidalgo Island and the mainland via State Route 20 to Interstate 5; or take the Whitney–La Conner Road south to **La Conner** (see the Skagit Valley section of this chapter).

Access & Information

From Seattle, take Interstate 5 north about 25 miles, past Lynnwood, then take State Routes 526 east and 525 north about 5 miles to Mukilteo; driving time is about 45 minutes. Take the **Washington State Ferry** (206/464-6400 or 800/843-3779; www.wsdot.wa.gov/ferries/) from Mukilteo to Clinton; crossing time is approximately 20 minutes. From Clinton, drive north on State Route 525 and Langley Road to Langley, about 10 minutes north.

From farther afield, fly into **Seattle-Tacoma International Airport** (17801 Pacific Hwy S, SeaTac; 206/433-5388)—13 miles south of Seattle and 16 miles north of Tacoma—from where you'll have easy access to Interstate 5. You'll need a car to best explore the region; most car-rental agencies have outlets at Sea-Tac Airport.

Romantic Lodgings

CHAUNTECLEER HOUSE, DOVE HOUSE, AND POTTING SHED COTTAGES
◆◆◆◆

5081 Saratoga Rd, Langley / 360/221-5494 or 800/637-4436
You'll be feeling romantic the moment you set foot on this enchanting property, where three gorgeous cottages sit on a beautiful bluff overlooking scenic Saratoga Passage. In the early spring, you're even likely to spot a pod of gray whales spouting and breaching on the horizon—a breathtaking sight! Sheltered among 6 acres of lush gardens and lawns, each of these three accommodations is unique, with luxurious touches that include jetted tubs and full kitchens. The two-story Chauntecleer House is perhaps the most sublimely romantic, with its large hot tub ensconced in the garden, spacious deck with panoramic water views, and sunset views from the bed. The double-headed shower in the beautifully tiled bathroom is an added bonus. The living room features English pine antiques and inviting plaid couches flanking the brick hearth. Blond hardwood floors, wooden roosters arranged here and there, and tasteful artwork add charming detail. The warmly inviting Dove House doesn't have the Chauntecleer's view, but its cedar walls, bright skylights, woodstove, terra-cotta floors, colorful fabrics and artwork, and cozy breakfast nook with hand-painted fish tiles in the sunny kitchen make it delightful nonetheless. The Potting Shed, set next to the English garden, is smaller yet, but still enchanting. The interior has a whimsical garden motif, handmade twig bed, two-person jetted tub, and glass-front wood stove. Provisions for a delicious breakfast are stocked in each kitchen. We simply can't think of a better place to seclude yourselves and enjoy the beauty of Whidbey Island than one of these three retreats. $$$–$$$$ *AE, MC, V; checks OK; www.dovehouse.com.*

CLIFF HOUSE AND SEACLIFF COTTAGE
❂❂❂❂

727 Windmill Dr, Freeland / 360/331-1566

This utterly lavish luxury retreat for two with views over sparkling Admiralty Inlet is unparalleled in both its setting and its design. After one glimpse of this architecturally splendid, unique timber home, recipient of numerous architecture awards, you'll know your romantic excursion is off to a wonderful start. The house's centerpiece 30-foot glass-enclosed atrium and high, open wood-beamed ceilings impart a sense of spacious ease that envelops you as soon as you walk in the door. Impressive floor-to-ceiling windows frame the view, which can also be enjoyed outside from the hot tub or hammock. The stone floors, wood-paneled walls, and earth-toned color scheme flatter the tasteful antique furnishings. Two upstairs bedrooms, a sunken living room with fireplace, and a full gourmet kitchen complete this private retreat. The larger bedroom loft is our favorite. Its king-size feather bed, down comforter, and boutique pillows will make you feel delightfully pampered; a small Jacuzzi tub awaits in the bathroom. Such luxury, of course, comes at a price; a fee in the $400 range definitely makes this a splurge. For considerably less money, check in to the smaller, utterly charming Seacliff Cottage, which features cozy wood-paneled walls, plush furnishings, a wood-burning stove, and a full kitchen. Relax on the private deck, with its views of boats navigating Puget Sound, or while away the afternoon swinging peacefully in the hammock. At night, you'll be happy to retreat to the bedroom, with its inviting queen-size bed and cushioned window seat overlooking the water. Just before dusk, be sure to pay a visit to the tree house on the grounds—it's a perfect vantage point for the sunset—and toast each other beneath the starlit sky. Both lodgings offer TV/VCRs, stereos, and extensive video and music collections for your enjoyment, as well as a continental breakfast. Simply put, you have found your island utopia built for two.

$$$$ *(Cliff House);* $$$ *(Seacliff Cottage) No credit cards; checks OK; www. cliffhouse.net.*

COUNTRY COTTAGE OF LANGLEY
❂❂❂

215 6th St, Langley / 360/221-8709 or 800/713-3860

Located just a few blocks from downtown Langley and surrounded by lush, colorful gardens, this getaway offers five charming cottage-style retreats. All feature private entrances, luxurious feather beds, down comforters, TV/VCRs, stereos, refrigerators, and coffee makers. New owners Tom Felvey and his wife, Jackie, have added welcome new touches to the interiors, including the tasteful original artwork now adorning the walls. Two cottages, Lynn's Sunrise and Sand N See, share a single gazebo-style structure with a deck overlooking the water (across a semi-busy street).

Lynn's Sunrise has cheerful yellow walls, a garden motif, and beautiful antiques, while the seaside-styled Sand N See features a crisp white-and-blue color scheme. Located slightly closer to the main house, the nautical Captain's Cove, decorated in blue, holds a beautifully appointed bed facing the water. A large Jacuzzi tub tucked beneath a picture window overlooks a private deck, and a wood-burning stove will warm you on chilly nights. Next door, the pretty Whidbey Rose has an inviting four-poster canopy bed, a love seat beside the gas fireplace, and a large rose-tiled Jacuzzi tub that takes center stage. But the most romantic option is the spacious Cabernet Cottage. Enjoy a beautiful water view from the private wraparound porch, cuddle in the elevated king-size bed, or gaze at a crackling fire from the enormous two-person Jacuzzi tub. In the morning, fresh fruit, pastries, and main dishes such as savory strata or quiche wait outside your door in a nicely packed basket.

$$–$$$ *AE, MC, V; checks OK; www.acountrycottage.com.*

FRENCH ROAD FARM COTTAGE AND HOME BY THE SEA
🟢🟢🟢

2388 E Sunlight Beach Rd, Clinton / 360/321-2964
These two tasteful retreats share the same gracious owners and charming amenities. French Road Farm, built in 1918, is a secluded and utterly romantic cottage set deep in the quiet countryside. Home by the Sea, the owners' private residence on the water, harbors the Sandpiper Suite, a beachfront getaway surrounded by a bird sanctuary. Both are within 10 minutes' driving distance of the village of Langley. At the French Road Farm Cottage, situated in the middle of 10 acres of verdant woods, you can explore the rambling flower gardens or swing gently on the hammock amid stately evergreens. Inside, French doors in nearly every room open onto the deck for lovely garden views, and a charming, eclectic mix of antiques fills the living room (which also has a wood-burning stove), an open kitchen, and a small, bright bedroom. One of the most romantic features of this sublimely private retreat is the large, airy bathroom, with its stone-tiled floor and seven-foot-long Jacuzzi tub set next to a window overlooking the gardens and vineyard. (Contact the owner for driving directions to French Road Farm Cottage.) Miles away, located right on the shoreline, the Sandpiper Suite, completely redesigned and renovated in 2002, showcases views of Admiralty Inlet and the jagged Olympic Mountains. It's attached to the main house via an entryway and shares the yard, but feels utterly private and self-sufficient. There is a fully equipped kitchen, living room with wood-burning stove, sparkling white-tiled bathroom with Jacuzzi tub, and small bedroom with TV hidden away in an armoire. Outside, sand walkways wind through sea grasses and wild roses, and two kayaks and a canoe allow you to explore the serene waterways. Birders will be interested to know that the waterside setting was recently designated one of the state's richest bird habitats; you will

find yourselves in a birdwatchers' paradise. With both accommodations, a breakfast basket with fresh fruit and baked goods is provided.
$$$ *MC, V; checks OK; www.frenchroadfarm.com or www.homebythe seacottages.com.*

GALITTOIRE, A CONTEMPORARY GUEST HOUSE
🔶🔶🔶🔶
5444 S Coles Rd, Langley / 360/221-0548
Expect the unexpected at this sleek wood-and-glass guest house enveloped by a sloping lawn and 10 acres of tranquil woods. The meticulous owner, an architect turned innkeeper and photographer, has overlooked no detail in the design of this exquisite home. This story is true: a couple concluding their honeymoon at Galittoire decided to take one last morning ramble in the woods. After walking several yards, they stumbled across a luxurious feather bed nestled in an enchanted forest grove, prepared especially for them. While we can't promise an exact duplicate of this experience, you get the idea. Only two guest suites are available, located at opposite ends of the innkeeper's house. The smaller, ground-level Garden Suite has elegant modern appointments, Japanese flower arrangements, and a bed covered with white linens and draped with white fabric. The Sky Suite boasts similarly streamlined decor, but it is far more grand and luxurious: guests of this room enjoy exclusive use of a cozy wood sauna, a triple-headed tiled shower, an exercise room, a two-person Jacuzzi tub, and an immense hot tub—and did we mention the private living room with massive entertainment center? An upstairs bedroom features lovely pomegranate-colored walls and spectacular floor-to-ceiling windows that survey the sky and surrounding property. In the home's common room, you can cuddle on sumptuous white sofas set before the black glass-and-rock fireplace and look out upon the elegant grounds. The talented innkeeper, who is also a master chef, serves full gourmet breakfasts in the dining room or outside on a large patio. Set a mile and a half from the town of Langley, this location is filled with country serenity. Kiss quietly out on the patio: you're likely to see deer.
$$$–$$$$ *No credit cards; checks OK.*

GARDEN PATH INN
🔶🔶◗
111 1st St, Langley / 360/221-5121
Located just a few steps from Langley's bustling First Street, the Garden Path Inn isn't exactly secluded—but it feels as if it is. Cloaked in wisteria and heavenly with nature's scents in springtime, a brick garden path leads away from the busy shopping street to the front door of this inn. Once inside, you'll find skylights brightening the stately living room, which is filled with impressive antiques, colorful artwork, and artistic touches such as the hand-carved chessboard displayed next to the love seat. There are two

tasteful suites to choose from; a spring 2002 remodel brought new furnishings, new white tile in the bathrooms, and new tailored window treatments. Both suites include all the amenities required for a romantic getaway: fireplace, TV/VCR, private kitchen, and inviting bedrooms. The front suite is more spacious and luxurious, with windows looking out upon Saratoga Passage and downtown Langley, a Jacuzzi tub, and a bed with Asian-style linen headboard. On the opposite side of the building, the second, smaller suite faces the back parking lot; nevertheless, this unit is lovely and immaculate, with a gracious, daylight-filled sitting room and French-country antiques. A wrought-iron chandelier casts a soft glow on the high-backed plaid chairs flanking the beautifully set table for two, and sunshine floods in through skylights in the fully equipped kitchen and small but cheery bedroom. A skylight also brightens the private bathroom, equipped with a hand-thrown ceramic sink and glass-enclosed shower. Both suites include a continental breakfast delivered to your door. You won't regret having chosen this inn, which offers the perfect combination of garden hideaway and village convenience.

$$–$$$ *MC, V; checks OK; www.islandsgetaways.com/gardenpath.*

GUEST HOUSE LOG COTTAGES
🏵🏵🏵
24371 Hwy 525, Greenbank / 360/678-3115
Straight out of a fairy tale, these five authentic log cabins and luxurious log home enfolded in 25 acres of gorgeous meadow and forest are a study in privacy. The cabins, each surrounded by shady trees, are decorated with old-fashioned country touches, including patchwork quilts adorning sumptuous feather beds, knotty-pine walls, and rustic oak furniture. Tidy little kitchens, Franklin stoves, TV/VCRs, and private spa tubs (in some of the cabins) supply plenty of romantic potential. Each is stocked with a generous supply of fresh breakfast items, including eggs from the owners' chickens, tempting pastries, and savory ham-and-cheese croissants. If you ever do feel like leaving your cozy cabin, we encourage you to explore the property's forested acreage and to make use of the outdoor hot tub, heated swimming pool, and exercise room, which are available to all guests. Serious romantics with a $300-plus nightly budget should by all means sequester themselves in the spacious log mansion, which has been custom designed for lovers and set at the edge of a duck pond. Cathedral ceilings soar above the rustic but elegant interior, where a fire crackles in an immense rock fireplace and floor-to-ceiling windows overlook the pond. There's a full kitchen, TV/VCR, and stereo. A fascinating collection of antiques and relics fills the house; the mounted deer head imparts lodgelike authenticity. The serene loft bedroom upstairs includes an enormous king-size bed covered in luscious

white linens, a giant in-room Jacuzzi tub, a private bath and sitting area, and views of the pond.

$$$–$$$$ DIS, MC, V; checks OK; www.guesthouselogcottages.com.

HONEYMOON COTTAGE
◍◍◍

EAGLES NEST INN
◍◍◖

4680 Saratoga Rd, Langley / 360/221-5331 or 800/243-5536

Two one-bedroom private cottages set on separate premises (but under the same ownership as the Eagles Nest Inn) are highlights of this Whidbey Island hideaway. Both cottages offer comforts such as fireplaces, DVD players, jetted tubs in the bathrooms, full kitchens (stocked with a deluxe continental breakfast), and CD players (don't forget your favorite romantic soundtracks). The Honeymoon Cottage is set on a steep bluff with incredible views of sparkling Saratoga Passage and has a private outdoor Jacuzzi tub; yes, the tub is bright red and heart-shaped. Inside, the slightly eclectic floral-and-lace decor is offset by soothing white walls; the living room's central wood-burning stove is charming. Outside, a staircase to the shoreline leads to romantic beach walks. On the hill below the Honeymoon Cottage is the comfortable Hunter House, which also overlooks the water. Soft sofas and chairs in the living room, fly fisherman–themed artwork, a bedroom loft, a jetted tub in the bathroom, and a private brick patio out back offer creature comforts. For a more traditional B&B experience, opt for one of the four spacious suites in the Eagles Nest Inn, the comfortable, elegant main home. Three of the four suites have stunning views of Saratoga Passage and Mount Baker, and all have access to a shared outdoor spa tub. Best is the Eagles Nest Room at the top of the house, with its sweeping, 360-degree view, a plush queen-size bed, impressive wooden eagle sculptures, and a petite Vermont Castings stove. The Saratoga Room, located just beneath it, has similar views and a deck facing Saratoga Passage; the Forest Room features a beautiful bed fashioned of driftwood. The Garden Suite, on the ground floor, is a haven for bird-watchers. Breakfast brings fresh, healthful Northwest gourmet fare with delicious treats such as seasonal fruit plates, autumn-pear pancakes with caramel sauce, and the innkeepers' famous wild blackberry coffee cake.

$$–$$$ DIS, MC, V; local checks only; www.eaglesnestinn.com.

THE INN AT LANGLEY
◍◍◍◖

400 1st St, Langley / 360/221-3033

For as long as we can remember, the Inn at Langley has been one of Whidbey Island's sleekest, most desirable, and best-known places to kiss. Set high on a bluff, the wood-shingled inn overlooks Saratoga Passage, and each of the 24 rooms boasts glorious views of the mountains and water. Asian artwork and elegant furnishings fill the guest rooms (we prefer those on the upper level), which also feature wood-burning fireplaces, quarry-tiled bathrooms with alder-twig hooks, and private decks. Deep, two-person spa tubs, fronted by shower areas the size of small rooms, are precisely placed to take in both the view and the fireplace. Thick comforters and crisp white linens render the cushy beds quite inviting. Two spacious townhouse suites adjacent to the main building offer more of the same polished decor and impressive amenities. Guests can access the nearby beach via an inviting, grassy walking path above the shoreline—watch for magnificent soaring eagles. But the heart of the inn is its acclaimed formal country kitchen, which provides the delicious complimentary continental breakfast. Enjoy the meal à deux at a table by the river-rock fireplace, or carry a piled-high tray back to the privacy of your room. Weekends bring six-course prix-fixe dinners—epicurean productions that offer tantalizing Northwest meals to guests and visitors alike (by reservation). The on-site locally owned and operated Spa Essencia (360/221-0991) offers even more options for pampering. With so much to recommend it, we understand why tour groups and business retreats flock to this inn, with its grand waterfront conference room; the crowds can impose some distraction from romance, but the minor drawbacks of popularity are far outweighed by the luxurious amenities and majestic views.

$$$$ *AE, MC, V; no checks; www.innatlangley.com.*

ISLAND TYME
◐◐◖

4940 Bayview Rd, Langley / 360/221-5078 or 800/898-8963
Slow down and relax; you're now operating on island "tyme." Tucked far away from the road on 10 serene acres of woods and pastureland, this multicolored new Victorian offers guests an abundance of space and privacy. In 2004, new owners gave the living and dining rooms an inspired face-lift, replacing the cluttered country-style decor with a clean and sophisticated look. In the dining room, new Tuscan-inspired terra-cotta hues brighten the walls, and four smaller tables have replaced the family-style dining table. The living room now shines in eggplant hues with gold and white accents, and is adorned with dark wood and leather upholstered furnishings. The owners are now progressively renovating each guest room to an equal the sophistication of the living and dining rooms. For now, bath amenities have been upgraded, and comfy new robes are supplied to wrap up in after a soak in the outdoor Jacuzzi tub. The inn also offers wireless access. All five guest rooms, located on the main and second floors, feature private baths, queen- or king-size beds, and an eclectic mix of antiques and country furnishings. Glowing fireplaces and shared or private decks are found in three rooms,

and every room has a TV/VCR. The Heirloom Room, done in mauve florals, is a popular choice of honeymooners—it features an antique fireplace; a private deck overlooking the property's quiet, wooded setting; and a Jacuzzi tub off the bedroom. A windowed tower inspired the name for the Turret Room, where you'll find a two-person Jacuzzi tub, American pine antiques, and a shared deck. The Masterpiece Room also has a spacious Jacuzzi tub and king-size bed, as well as a semiprivate deck. On weekdays, morning brings an expanded continental buffet with seasonal fruit, cereals, yogurt, freshly baked goods, and local Mukilteo coffee; on the weekends, breakfast is a sit-down affair with fare such as homemade cinnamon rolls, fresh fruit, and homemade quiche. After you've eaten your fill, you'll want to explore the property and say hello to the pet pygmy goats. Honeymooners should consider arranging in advance for one of the owner's unique gift baskets, which will add a charming romantic touch to your arrival. $$ *AE, DIS, MC, V; no checks; www.islandtymebb.com.*

SARATOGA INN
✿✿✿

201 Cascade Ave, Langley / 360/221-5801 or 800/698-2910
Everything about this sprawling country inn would be absolutely perfect—if only it were on the other side of the street. The inn's spectacular views of Saratoga Passage are interrupted by the main thoroughfare leading into Langley, which can see heavy traffic in the summer months. The two-story inn itself, professionally managed by the Four Sisters Inn group (which also owns hotels in California), is lovely, with its classic wood-shingle exterior and wraparound veranda. The inviting and homey downstairs, with cozy fireplace, elegant furnishings, and views of the water, is a great spot to relax with complimentary tea and cookies. You can choose from among fifteen upscale guest rooms and one honeymoon suite, the Carriage House. In the rooms, green-and-taupe color schemes, tasteful plaid or floral linens, down comforters, enticing cushioned armchairs, framed botanical prints, and gas fireplaces create cozy, attractive interiors. The bathrooms offer beautifully tiled, spacious walk-in showers and plush robes. Rooms on the top floor are especially appealing, with high cathedral ceilings and supreme water views, but the traffic noise may bother light sleepers. Away from the water, room 15 is the quietest. The most private and most expensive—and most romantic!—option is the adjacent Carriage House, a beautifully designed suite in which Oriental rugs cover gleaming hardwood floors, a seductive claw-foot tub awaits in the spacious marble bathroom, an enormous deck offers water views, and a gorgeous king-size sleigh bed stands ready to enfold you. A TV/VCR, CD player, and large open kitchen are additional romantic features. No matter which room you stay in, a full buffet-style

breakfast is included; dine at one of several tables downstairs, or carry the goodies back to enjoy in the privacy of your room.

$$$–$$$$ *AE, DC, DIS, MC, V; no checks; www.saratogainnwhidbeyisland. com.*

VILLA ISOLA
✦✦✦

5489 S Coles Rd, Langley / 360/221-5052 or 800/246-7323
More than 3½ acres of towering pines and fastidiously maintained gardens envelop this Italian-style Northwest retreat. On a beautiful day, relax in one of the Adirondack chairs or the inviting hammock among the lush lawns and enjoy the scenery. Indoors, guests can spend time in the elegant, comfortable common areas or retire to the luxury of their own private accommodation. Five large, sumptuous suites feature oversize baths, jetted tubs, queen-size beds, down comforters, and CD players; two suites share a deck. Each is named after a different Italian destination, and all offer plenty of space and attractive decor. A Jacuzzi tub in the black-and-white-tiled bathroom and a wrought-iron bed are the highlights of the sleek Venice Suite. The largest option, the Tuscany Suite, is also the most romantic and features skylights, a fireplace, and a wall of windows surveying the lush grounds. In the evening, guests can enjoy chocolate and homemade cranberry-pecan biscotti in the downstairs common areas before slipping into the plush robes provided in the rooms to stargaze from the outdoor hot tub. In the morning, poached pears with raspberry syrup, hazelnut French toast, Italian frittata with sausage, and double-chocolate cranberry bread are served in a dining room that overlooks the flower-laden yard, or, in summer, on the deck.

$$–$$$ *MC, V; checks OK; www.villaisola.com.*

Romantic Restaurants

CAFE LANGLEY
✦✦✦

113 1st St, Langley / 360/221-3090
Cafe Langley has been serving up reliably delicious Greek cuisine—and lots of romantic ambience—for years. A handful of oak tables and chairs are scattered around the small dining room, which features white textured walls, wood-beamed ceilings, and terra-cotta floors. Though the mood is casual, the tables are spaced far enough apart that you can turn the evening into an intimate experience for two under the softly glowing candle lantern that illuminates your table. The menu showcases Mediterranean cuisine and includes delicious renditions of classics like hummus with warm pita bread. Starters include Penn Cove mussels in saffron broth and a tangy, refreshing Greek salad. For your main dish, try a feast of seafood stew, a lamb shish

kebab, or a creative preparation of Northwest salmon or halibut, in season. Every dish is cooked to perfection, and the service is friendly and attentive. You will be thoroughly satisfied by the time you've finished dessert (we recommend the Russian cream—it's outstanding). This cafe is one of Langley's best bets, so be sure to make a reservation (especially on weekends). **$$** *AE, MC, V; checks OK; lunch, dinner every day (closed Tues in winter); beer and wine, limited bar; reservations recommended (dinner only); www. langley-wa.com/cl.*

TRATTORIA GIUSEPPE
◔◔◖

4141 E Hwy 525, Clinton / 360/341-3454
Harbored in a shopping plaza just off Whidbey Island's main highway— admittedly an unlikely spot for romance—Giuseppe's is well known throughout the island for its authentic Italian cuisine and heartwarming ambience. Cathedral ceilings with large skylights lend an open, cheerful feel to the restaurant's three dining rooms, which are filled with dried flowers, candles, and pottery. Chandeliers cast a soft light on the yellow-and-peach-colored stucco walls, and the snugly arranged tables are covered in yellow linens. Note that noise from the open kitchen can be a distraction, and the tables are a little on the packed-in side, but the chef's tasty Italian cuisine will make up for all that. Whether you order the superbly fresh grilled-vegetable antipasto or the homemade minestrone, *pennette* tossed with chicken and mushrooms in Gorgonzola cream or fusilli primavera with prawns and scallops, rest assured that you won't be disappointed. The menu also has an enticingly wide range, offering everything from light seafood and pasta to hearty entrées such as roasted pork loin and grilled New York steak. For dessert, the tiramisù is a must—but wait, so are the cannoli: pastry shells filled with ricotta, chocolate shavings, and almonds. You may just have to order one of each, and feed each other bites. On weekend evenings, live classical piano music accompanies your meal. **$$–$$$** *AE, DIS, MC, V; local checks only; dinner every day; full bar; reservations recommended; www.trattoriagiuseppe.com.*

SKAGIT VALLEY

ROMANTIC HIGHLIGHTS

Guarded by the colossal, snowcapped peak of Mount Baker, beautiful Skagit Valley lights up with a succession of brilliant flowers in spring. Given the flood of daffodils in late March, patchwork tulip fields in April, and dazzling irises that last through June, it's no wonder this pastoral destination is popular in the warm months—but in fact, each season offers a romantic aura all its own. Any time of year, the 1,500 acres of prime farmland in the valley create a serene panorama, making it a wonderful choice for a quiet getaway in any season. (Crowds do arrive during the famous Skagit Valley Tulip Festival in spring; see Access and Information for details.) While the soul of the region is farmland, its heart lies in the charming town of La Conner, a picturesque spot on the Swinomish Channel. The larger towns of Mount Vernon and Anacortes are nearby, and both offer some promising places to kiss, as well.

Because La Conner is famous for the antiques stores and distinctive boutiques that line its lively main street, no visit here would be complete without a morning spent browsing in the shops. If you're lucky enough to have sunny weather, celebrate with a leisurely outdoor lunch at one of several waterfront restaurants; if it's cool, enjoy a meal at cozy **Calico Cupboard** (720 S 1st St; 360/466-4451). The sleek, modern interior and congenial atmosphere at the **La Conner Brewing Company** (117 S 1st St; 360/466-1415) make it a good spot for enjoying great salads, crispy wood-fired pizzas, and a refreshing beverage.

For a pleasant stroll just a few miles from town, walk the 2-mile shore-line trail just south of the **Breazeale Interpretive Center** at the Padilla Bay Reserve (10441 Bayview-Edison Rd; 360/428-1558; open 10am–5pm Wed–Sun). The center can be packed with kids on the weekends, but if you're bird lovers, brave the small fry to see the fun exhibits. Energetic hikers will want to visit **Larrabee State Park** (off Chuckanut Dr; 360/902-8844; www.parks.wa.gov); while it's traditionally considered a playground for inhabitants of the northern city of Bellingham, the park is easily reached by car from La Conner (see the Bellingham section of this chapter). For a trip to the "big city"—Skagit Valley style—visit the neighboring town of **Mount Vernon**, and browse the shelves at **Scott's Bookstore** (121 Freeway Dr; 360/336-6181) or explore the shops in the historic **Granary Building** at the north end of town.

Not far from La Conner, and with considerable charms of its own, the city of **Anacortes** boasts several nice kissing locales (see Romantic Lodgings). Known primarily as the gateway to the San Juan Islands, Anacortes is actually on an island itself: Fidalgo Island. Although most visitors rush through this town on their way to the ferry, romantic travelers will find its fine qualities worth a stop. The scenery of spectacular **Washington Park** (less than a mile west of the ferry terminal) merits a little detour; it's got excellent picnic spots, a scenic loop road, and marked footpaths that wind through old-growth timber. Also in Anacortes, you can hike or drive up to lookout points at the top of **Mount Erie** for panoramic views of the islands and the Olympic Mountains. No matter where your romantic wanderings take you, visit **Geppetto's** (3320 Commercial Ave; 360/293-5033) first for picnic provisions. This tiny shop specializes in packaging delicious Italian food to go, so snap up some panini sandwiches and homemade tiramisù. You might end up toting your picnic to small, nearby Guemes Island for a day of exploring.

But if the two of you really like to get off the beaten path, consider staying on quiet **Camano Island** (getting here does not require taking a ferry). Although it's not technically part of Skagit Valley, the island offers the same quiet, pastoral pleasures. There isn't much here besides miles of flat farmland surrounding rural, tree-lined country roads—but then again, that's the appeal. Spend a peaceful day exploring the island's relatively secluded waterfront and forested areas, then satisfy the appetites you've worked up with a casual dinner.

While it's true that the Skagit Valley provides the perfect jumping-off point for romantic day-trips to the San Juans, Whidbey Island, or the Cascades, the relaxed pace here will inspire you to loosen your tightly scheduled itinerary. You'll find yourselves wondering where the days go, as you spend them treasuring quiet time together.

Access & Information

Driving north from Seattle, Interstate 5 carries you to exits for Camano Island and La Conner, and then on to the tulip town of Mount Vernon, located just off the interstate. Camano Island can be reached directly by car: take exit 212 from Interstate 5 and follow the main thoroughfare through Stanwood. There are several ways to get to La Conner, but taking backcountry roads is by far the most romantic: take exit 221, drive east on Fir Island Road, and follow the signs. The countryside is ideal for bicyclists, so do bring your bikes if you're so inclined; however, it's best to leave them at home during the annual **Tulip Festival** (360/428-5959; www.tulipfestival. org), when crowds descend. For more information about the area, contact the **La Conner Chamber of Commerce** (PO Box 1610; 360/466-4778 or 888/642-9284; www.laconner.net).

Romantic Lodgings

ALICE BAY BED & BREAKFAST
✿✿✿

11794 Scott Rd, Samish Island, Bow / 360/766-6396 or 800/652-0223

Alice Bay is a nesting spot for great blue herons, and in this immaculate guesthouse overlooking the water, romantic couples may feel inspired to do a little nesting themselves. Located about 15 miles outside La Conner on quiet Samish Island, this retreat provides the rural calm and serenity you expect from Skagit Valley. Floor-to-ceiling glass doors on the ground level showcase the view and can be either opened to welcome a breeze in summer or kept closed to frame the fury of a winter storm. A vintage 1920s woodstove and small, fully equipped kitchen are equal parts beauty and function; cold drinks and fresh flowers await your arrival. The simple queen-bed room upstairs has large windows overlooking the bay, and in the bathroom, you'll find cozy robes to keep you warm on the journey to the outdoor hot tub—a beautiful spot for relaxing under the stars. The owner published a cookbook of her recipes because so many people asked her to do so, and the breakfasts are indeed sublime; your feast might include grand Dutch babies with triple-crown blackberries, savory frittata, or pancakes with homemade strawberry sauce. Best of all, the meal is delivered to your door at the time you specify. The owners live directly adjacent to the guesthouse (separated only by a breezeway) and their well-behaved children are on the premises, but we found this doesn't detract from the pleasures offered by this quiet retreat. You may even want to spend some time with the pleasant hosts and charter their boat for an exploration of local islands or beaches, with a picnic lunch in tow. If you visit during crab season, you might be lucky enough to share in a late-afternoon feast of the local catch. There are no houses east of this cozy spot, so you can explore with abandon; a 10-minute walk along the rocky beach leads to a beautiful secluded point—if you don't do some kissing here, you're missing out.

$$ *AE, DIS, MC, V; checks OK; www.alicebay.com.*

AUTUMN LEAVES
✿✿◖

2301 21st St, Anacortes / 360/293-4920 or 866/293-4929

Anacortes is the departure point for ferries to the San Juan Islands, and for most travelers, the town goes by in a blur as they rush to catch the boat. The arrival of this romantic new bed-and-breakfast could turn the tide; why not be pioneers and spend a few days in this luxurious lodging? At the very least, you'll avoid the ferry lines. Nestled into a cul-de-sac in a hilltop neighborhood, the building's setting is newly developed and residential, but step inside and you will be enveloped by an authentic and historic Victorian ambience featuring exquisite antiques, lovely lamps and chandeliers, and

even a phonograph in the sitting room. The house, built specifically to be a bed-and-breakfast, combines the best of both worlds: a traditional Victorian floor plan has been enhanced with modern features such as spacious rooms, high ceilings, soundproofing, gas fireplaces, and a sound system that plays romantic music throughout the house. All the rooms feature fireplaces, TVs, robes and slippers, CD players, and gorgeous antique beds and nightstands along with other Victorian-era furnishings, and spacious bathrooms with air-jet tubs big enough for two. Our favorite rooms are upstairs and have partial water views: the Country French Room, with its cozy sloped ceilings, and the comfortable King Louis Room. On the main floor, the spacious Garden Room overlooks the backyard patio and rock garden waterfall. In the morning, the candlelight breakfast looks almost too good to be true—particularly since the food arrives on beautiful china from the owners' collection. You might find yourselves waking up to caramel-pecan French toast or a four-cheese omelet with orange-maple sausage and fresh fruit. Make sure to save room for the dessert course, which might include almond-filled crepes with raspberry sauce.
$$ *MC, V; checks OK; www.autumn-leaves.com.*

CAMANO ISLAND INN
🌀🌀🌀
1054 W Camano Dr, Camano Island / 360/387-0783 or 888/718-0783
This quiet, beautiful island, accessible by car (no ferry lines!) is a getaway that even some longtime Seattleites aren't aware of. And while technically not located in Skagit County (it's part of Island County, which also encompasses Whidbey Island), this island's serene charms are reminiscent of the Skagit Valley, and its nearby location makes it natural for inclusion here. At this luxurious waterfront inn with spectacular views, each of the six guest rooms has a private waterfront deck; from here, you're likely to catch sight of porpoises, bald eagles, whales, and sea otters—all with the Saratoga Passage and Olympic Mountains as the incredible backdrop. One of the most impressive accommodations is Room 1 (it's also the most expensive), which boasts a large jetted tub and king-size canopy bed; Rooms 2 and 4 offer jetted tubs on private decks. All the rooms feature goose-down feather beds, spacious bathrooms with heated floors, and plush robes, in addition to TV/VCRs and phones. In the afternoons, cozy up in the sitting room before the rustic river-rock fireplace and enjoy the Northwest art that fills this 1904 Arts and Crafts house. The fancy continental breakfast might include fruit parfait and moist coffee cake, along with delicious strong coffee, and you can choose between dining upstairs in your own room, or downstairs at a private table. After breakfast, the two of you can walk along the pebble beach to get even closer to the sea (and to each other), and kayaks are available to rent should you want to paddle the passage. But for the ultimate

relaxation, make arrangements for a hot-stone massage. In winter, check out the affordable specials.

$$–$$$ *AE, DIS, MC, V; checks OK for deposit; www.camanoislandinn. com.* ♿

THE HERON INN AND WATERGRASS DAY SPA
❂❂❂

117 Maple Ave, La Conner / 360/466-4626 or 877/883-8899
Relaxation and romance go hand in hand at The Heron, a stylish 12-room inn with pretty flower gardens and the on-site Watergrass Day Spa. Northwest art and a tasteful mix of antique and contemporary furnishings, subtle color schemes, sleek fixtures, and extremely comfortable beds make this among La Conner's most pleasing getaways. Several rooms have gas fireplaces and DVD players (with a selection of movies downstairs to choose from). The Romantic Suite has a Jacuzzi tub and does feel romantic, but it overlooks the parking lot. Lovebirds who prefer their romance with a view will enjoy Room 32, with its king-size bed and pretty garden. A Jacuzzi tub located in the inn's backyard doesn't offer the greatest privacy, but the views of farmland, Mount Baker, and the Cascades are spectacular around sunset; if you're lucky enough to find yourselves alone, hop in for a wonderful soak. In the morning, come downstairs to the pleasant dining room for breakfast, which might include beautifully arranged fresh fruit, homemade scones, and delicious eggs Benedict with citrus-tarragon hollandaise. For the ultimate relaxation, schedule a deluxe facial and massage. If you're ready to splurge, consider the inn's separate property, the splendid waterfront Heron's Nest guesthouse. Set on 2½ secluded acres west of the Inn, with views of Puget Sound, this two-level, 2,000-square-foot hideaway features two outdoor decks, a gourmet kitchen (you can have dinner catered), and a lovely grand stone fireplace. When you're not transfixed by the stunning view of Puget Sound through the floor-to-ceiling windows, adjourn for a heavenly soak in the private outdoor hot tub.

$–$$$** *(The Heron Inn);* **$$$$ *(The Heron's Nest) AE, MC, V; checks OK; www.theheron.com.*

LA CONNER CHANNEL LODGE
❂❂

205 N 1st St, La Conner / 360/466-1500 or 888/466-4113

LA CONNER COUNTRY INN
❂

107 S 2nd St, La Conner / 360/466-3101 or 888/466-4113
Of these two establishments owned by the same management company, we prefer the Channel Lodge, which is right on the water. Walk into this expansive, dark gray–shingled building set on the Swinomish Channel,

and you'll be immediately charmed by the glowing hardwood floors, huge stone fireplace, boldly colored area rugs, and pretty views. The lovely, antique-filled library and an outdoor patio overlooking the channel are our favorite places to relax and enjoy the quiet setting; La Conner's main street, eminently strollable, is just one block away. You'll find standard hotel-type features here, such as long, uninspired hallways and metal room doors; but all 40 units are beautifully decorated with Northwest flair, and most have water views and gas fireplaces (lit upon your arrival). The King Parlor rooms are the most desirable, with tall ceilings, Jacuzzi tubs, large tiled showers, and decks that overlook the water. The Queen Jacuzzi rooms are also very romantic, with Jacuzzi tubs, tiled showers, wooden shutters, and Northwest prints on the walls. Breakfast is a quick continental affair of fresh fruit, pastries, and granola. This romantic destination also has a not-quite-kissing cousin, the La Conner Country Inn, a nearby motel-style lodging with 28 rooms. The inn offers some pet-friendly and some smoker-friendly rooms, and has a casual country decor, but lacks the views and the coziness of the Channel Lodge. However, both accommodations are centrally located just a few steps away from the boutiques, restaurants, and antiques shops that inevitably draw lovers out for a starry-eyed, wandering stroll. $$–$$$$ *(La Conner Channel Lodge);* $–$$$ *(La Conner Country Inn) AE, DC, DIS, MC, V; checks OK; www.laconnerlodging.com.*

LA CONNER MAISON
◐◑◖

310 N 3rd St, La Conner / 360/391-0506 or 866/552-5526
Couples who dream of renting a charming French cottage but can't afford to cross the pond to Provence for the weekend will delight in this retreat. The owners of La Conner Maison offer two properties: the Garden Cottage, perfect for couples, and a new 2-bedroom property opening in 2005. The Garden Cottage is located in central La Conner, just a stone's throw from downtown restaurants and shopping—yet it feels very private. The building is located behind a pretty 19th-century Victorian that houses a gourmet food shop, so it feels shielded from street traffic even though it's adjacent to the main road into town. Cross the brick garden patio to your private entrance and step into a hideaway filled with cozy charm. Inside the studio-style space is an inviting lounging area with a vintage sofa and king-size bed dressed in natural-fiber linens; the separate bathroom has a two-person jetted tub. There's also a TV and stereo (bring your favorite romantic tunes). The cute kitchenette is stocked with a continental-style breakfast, including tasty baked goods, homemade jams, and fresh fruit (on the first morning only). The new two-bedroom guest house opening in 2005 will have more space and amenities but a similarly central La Conner location, and we're certain

it will offer the same signature style and attention to detail that makes the Garden Cottage such a wonderful retreat.
$$ *AE, MC, V; no checks; www.laconnermaison.com.*

SAMISH POINT BY THE BAY
✪✪✪✪

4465 Samish Point Rd, Bow / 360/766-6610 or 800/916-6161
It doesn't get any more private than this: your own spacious cottage on secluded Samish Point, a poetically beautiful piece of land surrounded by Samish Bay and Puget Sound. The charming Cape Cod–style house, located on 2 forested acres, is nestled among gorgeous old trees and a sweeping lawn. The house accommodates two to six (rates vary depending on the size of your party), but the most romantic choice is—naturally—to keep this sublime place to yourselves. This option won't be the cheapest, but the benefits are obvious: outside your door, 100 acres of beautiful wooded walking trails invite exploration and amorous adventure, and private sandy beaches are yours to discover. Inside, the cozy retreat features a bright living room with hardwood floors, a river-rock fireplace, gingham couches, and sliding doors that open onto a wooden deck where a completely private hot tub awaits you and your loved one. The white-tiled designer kitchen will be stocked with continental breakfast fixings when you arrive. Two guests normally stay on the main floor, where an immaculately clean, spacious bedroom features a king-size bed, pine furnishings, and master bath with pretty views of the lawn. Larger groups use the upstairs, where the two additional rooms have private baths, country linens, pine furnishings, and views of the pastoral landscape. Far away from any neighbors, with nary another building in sight, this is the ultimate in peaceful getaways. Bring your favorite food and drink and plan to settle in for a while—a hasty departure from this kind of romantic solitude seems downright silly.
$$$ *AE, MC, V; checks OK; www.samishpoint.com.*

SKAGIT BAY HIDEAWAY
✪✪✪✪

17430 Goldenview Ave, La Conner / 360/466-2262 or 888/466-2262
This luxurious waterfront hideaway, with two 600-square-foot suites, was designed by an architect specifically for those in search of a private romantic retreat. The spacious, shingle-style cottage housing both suites is nestled among Douglas firs and cedars just up the hill from the owners' home in a quiet residential neighborhood. The Bay Suite is done in soothing shades of dark blue and taupe, while the cozy Forest Suite features dark-green-and-plum decor; both suites have the same thoughtful layout, exquisite water views, and deluxe amenities. A fireplace awaits in the cozy living room downstairs in each suite; a tidy minikitchen adjoins. The impressive bathroom has an Italian-tiled, double-headed shower room with multiple

jets that emerge from the walls to massage you from all directions. The bedroom, upstairs, is designed to envelop you in a soothing cocoon, with a cozy feather bed, plush robes, and a skylight for moon watching. Just a step away is your own completely private deck (the suites are staggered, so you'll never see your neighbors) with two-person jetted spa tub. At night, sitting in your tub, you'll enjoy a sublime view of the moonlight on the bay. Subtle touches throughout, such as the glass blocks near the ceiling line, fresh flowers, and framed Northwest woodblock prints, complete the retreat. There are no phones or TVs to distract you from each other, but bring your own CDs for the in-suite stereo. Breakfast arrives at your door in the morning and includes fruit, coffee or tea, and delights such as crab-Havarti frittata and homemade muffins. This amount of privacy and comfort, seamlessly integrated into the natural beauty of the surroundings, is a rare gem indeed, and one that will surely inspire some kisses. It can be a little hard to find, so call ahead for detailed directions.

$$$ AE, MC, V; checks OK; www.skagitbay.com.

THE WHITE SWAN GUEST HOUSE
🖤🖤

15872 Moore Rd (Fir Island), La Conner / 360/445-6805
Commanding poplars bordering the long gravel driveway usher you to the door of this picturesque yellow Queen Anne farmhouse, set on a quiet country road 6 miles from La Conner. A warm greeting from friendly resident dogs, and the scent of freshly baked cookies in the kitchen, will make you feel immediately welcomed. In summer, the spectacular English garden invites the two of you to relax with a refreshing glass of iced tea; in colder weather, you can cozy up to the wood-burning stove in the parlor. Upstairs, three guest rooms, all named for their color schemes, offer tranquil views of the rural surroundings. Sunny buttercup walls and a king-size bed distinguish the spacious Yellow Room; the smaller Peach Room has a queen-size bed covered with a pretty patchwork quilt; and the Pink Room has rose-hued decor and a snug sitting area in a delightful window-lined turret. Unfortunately, all three rooms share just two baths down the hall; fortunately, both baths are quite spacious—one holds a large tiled shower, the other an elongated claw-foot tub that affords lovely views of the flower beds. For the most privacy, choose the modest, self-contained Garden Cottage, set beneath huge silver maples at the edge of the property. The open floor plan includes a living room and small kitchen with floor-to-ceiling windows overlooking the cedar deck. The simple bedroom upstairs has a cozy queen-size Shaker bed. The country continental breakfast is delivered to cottage guests; those staying in the main house are seated in the cheerful yellow breakfast room. You'll begin with fresh fruit smoothies, seasonal

strawberries, and homemade applesauce, followed by satisfying home-baked muffins.

$$ MC, V; checks OK; www.thewhiteswan.com.

THE WILD IRIS INN
✿✿✿

121 Maple Ave, La Conner / 360/466-1400 or 800/477-1400
Every detail at The Wild Iris exudes country refinement and promises amorous bliss. Although the two-story Victorian-style inn overlooks a parking lot, the parlor and the 20 individually decorated guest rooms more than compensate with their plentiful comfort and elegance. The deluxe Jacuzzi King and Queen suites are the most desirable, with contemporary furnishings, plush down comforters, extra-roomy spa tubs set near gas fireplaces, and views of the valley and the stunning Cascades. Some rooms have romantic white-veiled wrought-iron beds, while others feature white wicker or contemporary pine furnishings; all of the main-floor rooms include private patios that look out to pastoral scenes. The fanciful Cloud Room lives up to its name, with blue walls, wooden columns, playful murals of clouds, and billowy white gauze arranged over the king-size bed. Twelve suites have private tubs, but guests in rooms without one can use the beautiful community hot tub, set on a deck overlooking quiet farmland. In the evening, head downstairs to Le Jardin (call main number for more information), the inn's charming French-country restaurant, for a fine-dining experience that ranks among the most romantic in the valley. (Make reservations in advance, because dinner, served Tuesday through Saturday, is open to everyone, not just guests at the inn.) At your intimate table for two, you'll revel in the seasonally changing menu, which might include fresh salmon with peppercorn butter or grilled duckling breast with mushrooms, sun-dried cherries, and marsala sauce. A lavish complimentary breakfast is served in this same dining room; rose-scented fruit soup, poached eggs *en croûte* with roasted red pepper coulis, and homemade granola are just a few of the enticing dishes offered each morning.

$$–$$$ AE, MC, V; no checks; www.wildiris.com. &

Romantic Restaurants

KERSTIN'S
✿✿✿

505 S 1st St, La Conner / 360/466-9111
This cozy favorite, the former location of Andiamo and The Black Swan, has harbored many a romantic couple in its day. Views of the Swinomish Channel are superb, especially from the upstairs dining room or the tiny, charming deck; a busy parking lot across the street is the only thing you

won't want to gaze upon. On summer evenings, the soft blue twilight on the water reflects the calm inside the restaurant, where the warm walls are illuminated by sconces and the handful of intimate tables are covered with linens and flickering with candlelight. Gracious and efficient, the wait staff go out of their way to ensure that your dining experience is superb. The menu takes advantage of the valley's seasonal bounty, and you can count on every dish to be carefully prepared and presented. Try the moist, fall-off-the-bone-tender lamb shank served with cabernet sauce over roasted-garlic risotto; Samish Island oysters baked in the shell with garlic-cilantro butter; or a flavorful dish of pasta cooked to perfection. Desserts are equally tantalizing, so bring your sweet tooth along with your sweetheart. $$–$$$ *AE, MC, V; local checks only; lunch, dinner every day; full bar; reservations recommended.*

NELL THORN RESTAURANT & PUB
✪✪✪

205 E Washington St, La Conner / 360/466-4261
After one visit to Nell Thorn, you will find yourselves raving about the creative, delicious food and romantic charm—and plotting an imminent return. Soft lights illuminate the wood-beamed ceiling in the upstairs dining room, lilac walls and stained glass add color, tables feature white linen and candlelight, and well-chosen music sets a pleasing mood. Appetizers on the mostly organic, seasonal menu are delicious enough to make a meal of. Try the sweet onion gratin topped with crunchy homemade bread crumbs, or the warm scallop salad served on mashed potatoes with wilted greens. For your main dish, consider the flavorful Beach Bowl, the chef's choice of seafood simmered in lobster cream. Other tempting options include slowly braised lamb shank with cannellini bean–garlic stew; or a savory risotto or pasta. For dessert, we recommend the creamy *panna cotta* with fresh berries or a slab of the rich chocolate pâté. If you'd like to spend less money and enjoy a more casual ambience, eat in the main-floor pub instead. The environment isn't nearly as formally romantic, but the service is quick and efficient, and the excellent food speaks for itself. $$–$$$ *AE, DIS, MC, V; checks OK; lunch, dinner Tues–Sun (lunch Sat–Sun only in winter); full bar; reservations recommended; www.nellthorn. com.*

THE OYSTER BAR ON CHUCKANUT DRIVE
✪✪✪

2578 Chuckanut Dr, Bow / 360/766-6185
This elegant restaurant is a culinary milepost along famous Chuckanut Drive. Just 12 tables fill the tiny cedar dining room upstairs, which is lined with floor-to-ceiling windows that frame breathtaking views of Samish Bay and the San Juan Islands. The restaurant goes above and beyond to

make this a romantic retreat by supplying an award-winning wine list and discouraging children under 10. Service can be slow, but the presentation is always impeccable. The quintessentially Northwest menu features seafood and shellfish, along with unusual choices like grilled elk tenderloin and rack of Texas wild boar. The luscious wild salmon, perfectly grilled filet mignon, or local Samish Bay oysters fried to a golden crisp with a light parmesan-bread crumb crust are sure bets. Desserts include a light, creamy huckleberry and vanilla cheesecake and a decadent chocolate mousse. Recent renovations and a new fireplace have improved the interior, but this star in the Northwest restaurant firmament has never ceased to dazzle.
$$–$$$ AE, MC, V; local checks only; lunch, dinner every day; beer and wine; reservations recommended; www.chuckanutdrive.com.

THE RHODODENDRON CAFE
●●

5521 Chuckanut Dr, Bow / 360/766-6667
On the corner of a busy intersection along Chuckanut Drive, this tiny country cafe couldn't be more conveniently located—nor could the from-scratch cooking be more delicious. Decidedly casual, the cream-colored interior is sparsely furnished but cheery, with country fabrics and a handful of peach-colored tables. The cafe's excellent location helps fill tables, but so does its glowing (and ever-growing) reputation—and we'd have to agree, the food here is simply outstanding. Specials change daily but always include refreshing salads; delicious, lightly breaded and pan-fried Samish Bay oysters; savory pasta entrées; homemade soups and chowders; and tantalizing desserts. Pull in here for lunch after spending the day spellbound by the views from Chuckanut Drive's winding waterfront bluffs; you'll come very gently back to earth.
$$ AE, MC, V; checks OK; breakfast Sat–Sun, lunch, dinner every day Apr–Aug (lunch Wed–Sun, dinner every day Sept–Nov and Jan–Mar); closed late Nov–mid-Jan; beer and wine; reservations recommended.

BELLINGHAM

ROMANTIC HIGHLIGHTS

When you notice the number of lodgings in Bellingham that have received the coveted four-lip rating, you'll wonder if we've spent a little too much time being dazzled by the sparkling waters of Bellingham Bay. In fact, this small city deserves every last lip, and more. Its romantic, historic Fairhaven district is ideal for hand-in-hand strolling, and the advent of several luxurious new hotels and restaurants has only increased the city's appeal. The autumn leaves here are brilliant, but summer is perhaps the loveliest season, thanks in part to ample opportunities to enjoy it, including plentiful outdoor dining and bountiful parks. Although it hasn't managed to escape the suburban sprawl and shopping malls typical in cities of this size, Bellingham is nevertheless unique. Stay in town for waterfront meals and shopping, or set out for one of the other highly romantic destinations within easy reach. To the south is Chuckanut Drive, a famous stretch of road (Hwy 11) between Bow and Bellingham that was once part of the Pacific Highway; to the north is charming Lummi Island, accessible by a 10-minute ferry ride; to the east are the spellbinding slopes of Mount Baker (only an hour's drive away). With so many options on offer, Bellingham is truly a transcendent romantic destination.

The historic Fairhaven district is rich with diversions: Browse the shelves at **Village Books** (1200 11th St; 360/671-2626), then sit down with your new books in the next door **Colophon Cafe** or nearby **Tony's Coffees** (1101 Harris St; 360/738-4710) for an excellent espresso. During the summer, you can enjoy an alfresco lunch at nearly every cafe. For incredible views of the islands—not to mention the sunset—stroll **Boulevard Park**, located between downtown Bellingham and the Fairhaven district. If the two of you find good nightlife kiss-inspiring, Bellingham has some fun spots: **Calumet** (113 E Magnolia St; 360/733-3331; dinner Mon–Sat) is a hip eatery with an extensive wine and cocktail list, and the **Boundary Bay Brewery** (1107 Railroad St; 360/647-5593) downtown serves freshly brewed beers, along with a delicious lamb burger and other tasty pub food. Music lovers should consider timing their getaway with the summer **Bellingham Music Festival** (360/676-5997; www.bellinghamfestival.org; in August); you can spoil yourselves with more than two weeks of orchestral, chamber, and jazz performances.

For one of the prettiest drives in the state, take your loved one on a trip down **Chuckanut Drive** (Hwy 11; from Bellingham, follow 12th St south out of town; from Interstate 5 northbound, take exit 231). You'll be treated to forested cliffs plunging to the water's edge, and islands silhouetted on the horizon. Make a stop at beautiful **Larrabee State Park**, Washington's first state park (off Chuckanut Drive, 7 miles south of Bellingham; 360/902-8844; www.parks.wa.gov). Here, sandstone-sculpted beaches and cliffs provide an evocative backdrop for exploring abundant sea life—on weekends, however, the crowds might make your visit a little less than romantic. Avid hikers can get more privacy by following the trailhead directly across the road from the park with signs for Fragrance Lake. Climb about a mile straight uphill to the viewpoint, and you'll be amply rewarded for your hard work. With a spectacular view of the San Juan Islands almost to yourselves, this is definitely one of the region's best places to kiss. Mountain bikers will enjoy the **Interurban Trail**, formerly the electric rail route from Bellingham to Mount

Vernon and now a 5-mile trail connecting three parks along Chuckanut Drive: Larrabee State Park to Arroyo Park to Fairhaven Park (in Bellingham). Chuckanut will eventually lead you to the pastoral small town of **Bow**, which boasts some wonderfully romantic lodgings and restaurants (see the Skagit Valley section of this chapter).

Another romantic destination nearby is **Lummi Island**, one of the quietest islands of all the ferry-accessible San Juans. You'll be transported back to the days when these islands were still hidden treasures. Just 9 miles long and less than 2 miles wide, Lummi has no real town or parks to speak of, but because the ferries run so regularly, it makes an ideal day-trip. We suggest a long bike ride (there aren't any bike lanes, but neither is there much traffic) or an afternoon picnic, though the lovely accommodations may end up enticing you to spend the night. Not far from the ferry landing, the folks at the **Beach Store Cafe** (2200 N Nugent Rd; 360/758-2233) cook with fresh island produce; it's a local gathering place for pizza or clam chowder, but don't overlook the daily specials. **The Willows Inn** (see Romantic Lodgings) has a tiny, cute cafe offering great espresso, pastries, and sandwiches.

Those headed north to **Mount Baker** are most likely interested in either the stellar winter skiing or a spring or summer hike through breathtaking meadows filled with bright wildflowers. For a beautiful vista, make the drive to **Artist Point** (at the end of Mount Baker Hwy/Hwy 542; 58 miles east of Bellingham); if you can't get enough of the scenery, take one of the several hikes that depart from here. Be sure to stop along the way in Glacier for a picnic among sparkling views of the mountains and colorful wildflowers. Wine lovers can visit **Mount Baker Vineyards** on the way (12 miles east of Bellingham on Mount Baker Hwy/Hwy 542; 360/592-2300; call for seasonal hours); located in a cedar-sided, sky-lit facility, this winery's specialty is lesser-known varietals such as Müller–Thurgau and Madeleine Angevine.

Access & Information

Driving north from Seattle, Interstate 5 leads you right to Bellingham. Fly into **Seattle-Tacoma International Airport** (17801 Pacific Hwy S, SeaTac; 206/433-5388)—13 miles south of Seattle and 16 miles north of Tacoma—from where you'll have easy access to the interstate. To best explore the region, you'll need a car; most car-rental agencies have outlets at Sea-Tac. Train travel is romantic in its own right. **Amtrak** (303 S Jackson St, Seattle; 206/382-4125 or 800/USA-RAIL; www.amtrak.com) provides a link to Portland, Seattle, or Vancouver. You can arrange with several area lodgings to pick you up at the depot in Fairhaven. For more information on historic Fairhaven, contact the **Fairhaven Association** (360/738-1574; www.historicfairhaven.us).

Lummi Island is located off Gooseberry Point northwest of Bellingham.

Lummi is serviced by the tiny **Whatcom Chief ferry** (360/676-6759; www.
co.whatcom.wa.us/publicworks/), which leaves Gooseberry Point at 10
minutes past the hour from 7am until midnight (more frequently on weekdays). It's easy to find (follow signs to Lummi Island from I-5, north of
Bellingham); cheap ($5 round-trip for a car and two passengers); and quick
(6-minute crossing). The ferry returns from Lummi on the hour.

The **Mount Baker Highway** (Hwy 542) starts from Bellingham, parallels
the sparkling Nooksack River, and passes through little towns like Deming
and Glacier to reach two of the state's loveliest sights: 10,778-foot Mount
Baker and 8,268-foot Mount Shuksan. Skiers and snowboarders from all
over the world journey to the **Mount Baker Ski Area** (360/734-6771), 56
miles east of Bellingham. The mountain never lacks for snow—it's a glacier—but it's not always a skier's paradise and conditions vary. During the
1998–99 season, it set a world record for snowfall with 1,140 inches—on the
other hand, during the dry 2004–05 season, the resort was closed for much
of the winter. But when the snow falls, Baker is a famously popular destination, offering the kind of steep terrain that satisfies avid boarders. Call
ahead to get conditions if you're planning a ski getaway; in summer, you can
enjoy beautiful vistas and exhilarating day hikes.

Romantic Lodgings

CHRYSALIS INN & SPA
◐◐◐◐
804 10th St, Bellingham / 360/756-1005 or 888/808-0005
A spectacular waterfront setting and sleek luxury spa on the premises
make this new Northwest Craftsman–style hotel a smart, romantic retreat.
It's located within walking distance of historic Fairhaven, so you'll have
ample opportunity for pleasant strolls right outside your door. In the hotel's
foyer, a beautiful ironwood spiral staircase is a favored spot for romantic
photos to memorialize your getaway. All 43 guest rooms have oversize
soaking or jetted tubs, fireplaces, distinctive artwork, king-size beds with
down comforters, and cozy window seats overlooking the bay. The spacious
slate bathrooms feature plush robes, large glassed-in showers, and sliding
Japanese cherry-wood screens that can be opened for a vista from the
soaking tub. The desirable corner suites also have their own separate sitting rooms—they're more expensive, but you'll feel as though you could live
happily ever after here. The expanded continental breakfast, which includes
hot dishes, is served downstairs. But it's the spa that truly sets the Chrysalis
apart, and makes good on the inn's promise to provide a getaway for "body,
mind, and soul." Services offered include everything from expert massage—
choose from Swedish, deep tissue, reflexology, or hot stone—to high-tech
hydrotherapy tub or Vichy shower treatments. Inside the spa, soft music

and aromatherapy scents will immediately relax you; couples can schedule simultaneous treatments. After you've been pounded or doused into a state of relaxed bliss, slip into the inn's sophisticated dining spot, Fino Wine Bar, which has terrific water views. While the wood, metal, and glass interior can be noisy, the creatively prepared food is beautifully presented. Plans to refurbish the old dock in front of the hotel sound promising; strolling here under the moonlight could inspire more kisses—on top of those already encouraged by this soul-satisfying retreat.

$$$–$$$$ *AE, DC, DIS, MC, V; checks OK; www.thechrysalisinn.com.*

HOTEL BELLWETHER
✿✿✿✿

1 Bellwether Wy, Bellingham / 360/392-3100 or 877/411-1200
Exquisite views, luxurious rooms, and every amenity you could possibly desire—what more could you want for a backdrop to romance? Combining grand hotel luxuries with the decor of a cozy inn, this much-lauded Squalicum Harbor destination, which opened in 2001, offers the best of both worlds. Many of the 68 rooms overlook Bellingham Bay and boast terrific sunset views from private balconies or patios. Rooms come with gas fireplaces, and the spacious bathrooms have both glassed-in showers and soaking tubs with shutters, so you can either enjoy or close off the view. You won't exactly forget that you are in a hotel, but there are individual touches in the rooms, such as furniture imported from Italy and distinctive artwork. A turndown service provides fine chocolates on your Hungarian down pillow, and the dreamy beds are made up with Austrian linens. The dramatic Lighthouse Suite, a few steps from the hotel, offers three levels of seclusion; enjoy the surf, seagulls, seals, and boats passing right by your windows. One night here does come at cruise-ship costs, but for a special occasion, it might be worth the splurge. (Note: we can hardly imagine a more picture-perfect spot for a marriage proposal than the Lighthouse balcony at sunset.) If he or she accepts, the Bellwether is also a popular spot for weddings; on certain balmy Saturdays, they even host two in one day. Enjoy a libation and watch the sunset in the aptly named Sunset Lounge, or indulge in fine dining at the Harborside Bistro (see Romantic Restaurants). Breakfast and afternoon tea are served in the smaller, more intimate Compass Room. If you arrive by boat, you can "park" at the hotel's private dock.

$$–$$$$ *AE, DC, DIS, MC, V; local checks only; www.hotelbellwether.com.*
♿

SCHNAUZER CROSSING
✿✿✿✿

4421 Lakeway Dr, Bellingham / 360/734-2808 or 800/562-2808
Even after many years of operation, Schnauzer Crossing still sets the standard for bed-and-breakfasts in the Northwest. The contemporary wood-

and-glass home is nestled in a quiet residential neighborhood overlooking Lake Whatcom. Beautifully landscaped, the property features well-groomed gardens, a wisteria arbor, a charming koi pond with meditation garden—and, of course, the friendly but low-key schnauzers who inspired the inn's name. There are two accommodations in the main house and an elegant, self-contained guest cottage next door. The Garden Suite feels like a luxury apartment and features a private entrance, king-size bed and alcove sitting area, CD player, TV/VCR, wet bar, and wood-burning fireplace. The huge bathroom has a Jacuzzi tub for two, a roomy double-headed shower, and sumptuous robes waiting to envelop your relaxed selves. The smaller, adjacent Queen Room has a queen-size bed, views of colorful rhododendrons, and a private bath; two sets of doors shut this room off from the rest of the home, so your privacy is ensured. Set amid lofty cedar trees next to the main house, the picture-perfect guest cottage features tasteful Asian decor, hardwood floors, original Northwest artwork, a king-size bed, and a gas fireplace (plus an extensive movie and CD collection, and the appropriate gadgets for enjoying them). Other perks include the lovely, green-tiled bathroom with large Jacuzzi tub and a private wraparound deck with views of Lake Whatcom. The delicious gourmet breakfast might include Triple Sec French toast with blueberry sauce, baked oatmeal served with ice cream "snowballs," fresh-baked hazelnut scones, and fresh fruit; it will be served wherever you specify—including the privacy of your own suite, if that's your hearts' desire. No stay here is complete without a good, long, steamy soak in the outdoor hot tub, tucked next to the house beneath the towering trees. **$$–$$$** *AE, MC, V; checks OK; www.schnauzercrossing.com.*

SEMIAHMOO RESORT
◆◆◆◖

9565 Semiahmoo Pkwy, Blaine / 360/318-2000 or 800/770-7992
This sprawling resort set north of Bellingham on the sparkling bay waters of Washington's Canadian border used to be your grandmother's country club, with acres of award-winning golf and little else. Not anymore, thanks to a major renovation that upgraded the spa to a nearly 4,000-foot complex that includes ten treatment rooms, including one just for couples; a new adjoining health club complex offers a vast heated pool, Jacuzzi, and gleaming workout facility, as well. Add to this the nearby walking trails and three on-site restaurants, and it's clear that you can stay put for days—a romantic and relaxing concept in itself. The rooms are restful if a bit standard in decor, which includes white walls, blond-wood accents, seafoam green carpeting, and knotty-pine beds; spacious bathrooms are a plus. Best, even the lowest-level "classic" room is relatively spacious. If you choose an affordable "non-view" room, book one on the fourth floor for a pleasant view of the masts bobbing in the Semiahmoo marina. For a special weekend, try one of the "deluxe king" rooms; more than 40 of these have river-stone or

slate wood-burning fireplaces, others have small covered patios. The junior suites, offered with the romance package, provide even more lounging space. Our only caveat is that this resort caters to families with children: there's a kids' movie theater, organized kids' beach activities in summer, and, alas, kids frequently wreaking havoc in the otherwise-peaceful pool and Jacuzzi area. So, while an intimate getaway is certainly possible, the ambience is less than adults-only (especially in the high season). Summer brings as many as four weddings per weekend, as well. Still, despite the crowds, the resort is an appealing package; for absolute quiet, try the winter off season. The waterfront pub offers casual meals and a popular Sunday brunch. At the romantic dinner spot, Stars, a jazz pianist plays on weekend nights; the standard continental cuisine seems apt amid the traditional surroundings of striped wallpaper, seafoam green carpet, and linen-draped tables.
$$–$$$ *AE, DIS, MC, V; checks OK; www.semiahmoo.com.* &

SQUALICUM LAKE COTTAGE
◖◖◖◖

4367 Squalicum Lake Rd, Bellingham / 360/592-1102
You'll find few settings more serene than what greets you at this contemporary cottage, which overlooks a small lake and beautiful gardens that explode with flowers in summer. Once you've come down the rural, tree-lined gravel drive that leads to the property, you may feel as though you're arriving at your own private Walden Pond. The cottage has its own entrance and is separated from the owner's house by landscaping and ornamental grasses. With vaulted ceilings, six skylights, and plenty of windows, the 480-square-foot space is airy and bright. The comfortable main room has a sofa that takes in the view, TV with satellite reception, CD player, and compact but full kitchen. This will come in handy, since the country location means you'll have to drive to enjoy Bellingham's fine dining; it's so peaceful here that the most romantic option may well be to bring provisions and stay in for the evening. The tiny, cozy bedroom has a queen-size bed and basic full bath; you'll find bubble bath and a rubber ducky waiting for your enjoyment. To make the most of your getaway, arrange with the owner for the on-call masseuse to make a house call to the cottage. Other romantic touches include exquisite flower arrangements (the owner was formerly a professional florist), Swiss chocolates, and complimentary refreshments upon arrival. Breakfast, which is delivered to your door, includes goodies like homemade fruit breads, jams, yogurts, and fresh fruit compotes complete with edible flowers or mint from the owner's organic garden. In warm weather, you can breakfast at the teak table on your own front patio; a day that starts off this beautifully is almost guaranteed to be filled with romance.
$$–$$$ *MC, V; checks OK; www.sqlakecottage.com.*

THE WILLOWS INN
♥♥♥

2579 W Shore Dr, Lummi Island / 360/758-2620 or 888/294-2620
Embraced by rose arbors, vegetable patches, and scented herb gardens, this lovely retreat offers sparkling views of the Strait of Georgia and the forested hills of nearby Orcas Island. The owners, Judy Olsen and Riley Starks, also run nearby Nettles Farm, and they excel at creating a welcoming environment that will immediately put you at ease. You'll be impressed by the excellent food—even if all you have time for is a delicious scone and espresso in the small downstairs cafe. Weekend dinners and Sunday brunch are served in the upstairs main dining room, which features water views. The Willows also offers wine tastings, cooking classes, and Valentine's Day dinners complete with a special romantic menu. Of the four guest rooms (all with private baths) in the main house, two on the main floor have private entrances. There's also a very secluded small cottage for two, which has a tiny kitchen and a stunning view from its French doors and deck; a clawfoot tub, TV/VCR, and barbecue are included. A two-bedroom guest house with two suites is often rented to larger groups, but the suites are also occasionally rented separately. Both feature king-size beds; Thistle comes with an oversize Jacuzzi tub, and Heather has a double shower. But the best place to kiss here is definitely the cottage, which is adorable and serene. Breakfast is self-catered or, for a small extra charge, continental breakfast fixings can be stocked in the kitchen before you arrive. A complimentary basket of fruit and chilled juice is provided in both the guest house and the cottage.
$$–$$$ *AE, DIS, MC, V; checks OK; www.willows-inn.com.*

Romantic Restaurants

HARBORSIDE BISTRO
♥♥♥

1 Bellwether Way (Hotel Bellwether), Bellingham / 360/392-3200
An intimate refuge is on offer at this waterfront bistro located in the Hotel Bellwether (see Romantic Lodgings). Decorated in dark woods and crimson, the gracious dining room has white linens, romantic lighting, and elegant European antiques. You can time your meal to watch the sun sink slowly in the west, as most tables have views of Bellingham Bay; but the booths lifted slightly up from the main floor are the most romantic choices. Ensconced in the high-backed, cushioned banquettes, you'll enjoy more privacy, with the same view. Much of the menu has a Mediterranean flair, and risk-taking is usually rewarded; for example, the innovative coconut-lime seafood chowder is sublime. For your main dish, try one of the delicious fresh seafood specials or the horseradish-basted filet mignon. Excellent desserts, particularly the homemade sorbet and ice cream—one creamy version is

filled with chunks of divine homemade tiramisù—will encourage you to linger until the stars come out. Note that the adjoining Sunset Lounge has an outdoor patio perfect for enjoying summer-afternoon drinks.
$$$ *AE, DC, DIS, MC, V; local checks only; Canadian cash accepted; lunch, dinner every day, brunch Sun; full bar; reservations recommended; www. hotelbellwether.com.* &

MANNINO'S RESTAURANT
⬡⬡⬡

1007 Harris Ave, Bellingham / 360/671-7955
This well-loved, family-run Italian restaurant has played host to many a romantic tête-à-tête. After moving in 2003 from downtown to a splendid location in the historic Fairhaven district, this Bellingham favorite is better than ever. The most secluded tables in this two-level restaurant are on the upper floor; request one by the windows to overlook the quaint main street. A sophisticated color palette of taupe and white, tiled floors, framed prints of Italian architecture, and lofty ceilings create a soothing decor. Additional tables on the heated outdoor dining deck and on a tiny, secluded "proposal balcony" that fits just one table for two (it's designed specifically for that very special occasion) offer further romantic seating. The ground-level dining room is also elegant, but slightly noisier as it's close to the kitchen. The menu features well-prepared traditional Italian dishes, and every meal begins with a basket of warm, crusty bread served with garlic-infused oil and balsamic vinegar for dipping. Start with the *funghi al marsala*, crimini mushrooms sautéed with marsala wine on crispy toast points, or delicious mussels in a savory broth made with Prosecco, shallots, and tomatoes. Then continue your feast with one of the savory pasta dishes, such as linguine with chicken, spinach, and mushrooms in sherry-cream sauce, or a classic main-course preparation such as veal *piccata*. Service is friendly and efficient. Save room for dessert: the tiramisù here is the real deal.
$$$ *AE, DC, DIS, MC, V; local checks only; lunch, dinner every day; full bar; reservations recommended.* &

MILANO'S RESTAURANT AND DELI
⬡⬡

9990 Mt Baker Hwy, Glacier / 360/599-2863
Located in Glacier, between Bellingham and Mount Baker, this unassuming little Italian restaurant within a market and deli doesn't at first look deserving of a stop. But slam on those brakes! There's exceptionally tasty cuisine here in a surprisingly charming atmosphere. The star offering is the freshly made pasta with creative fillings and sauces; the clam-packed linguine *vongole* and the chicken Gorgonzola smothered in a rich, savory sauce are mouth-watering *speciale della casa*. They are rivaled by a slew of tasty raviolis, stuffed with spinach, porcini mushrooms, or smoked salmon. With

your dinner, enjoy a beer or a glass of wine from the well-priced selection; finish off with coffee and tiramisù. The deli also does a brisk business in take-out sandwiches for those headed to the mountains. Finding food this delicious in remote ski country should definitely inspire a kiss.

$$ *MC, V; local checks only; lunch, dinner every day; beer and wine; reservations recommended.* &

PACIFIC CAFE
◐◐◑

100 N Commercial St, Bellingham / 360/647-0800
Superb service, soothing ambience, and a well-established reputation for fine cuisine make this restaurant an excellent choice for a romantic evening out. Tucked into the Mount Baker Theatre building and overlooking busy Commercial Street, the Pacific Cafe will immediately envelop you in soft jazz, while low lighting and flickering candles create cozy intimacy at your table. The tasteful decor of watercolors and shoji screens in the small dining room won't distract you from each other—or from the delicious food. European, Hawaiian, Indian, and Malaysian cuisines, among others, influence the sophisticated menu choices; seafood dishes are specialties. Be sure to save room for one of the spectacular, freshly made desserts, which might include *lilikoi* (passion fruit) sorbet, butter-pecan ice cream, or hand-dipped Belgian chocolate truffles. The quality vintages will tempt you to splurge; if the two of you are oenophiles, call and inquire about the restaurant's special wine dinners. Reservations, in any case, are an absolute must.

$$–$$$ *AE, MC, V; local checks only; lunch Mon–Fri, dinner Mon–Sat; beer and wine; reservations recommended.*

SOUTH SOUND

ROMANTIC HIGHLIGHTS

Awe-inspiring mountain and water views, serene public gardens, an impressive arts scene, and quiet island retreats help make the South Sound good for a romantic getaway. Although a growing traffic problem, a surplus of uninspiring mini-malls, and chain stores galore aren't helping this region overcome its decidedly lackluster reputation, a short drive—or ferry ride—off the beaten path of Interstate 5 reveals that romantic surroundings are in plentiful supply. In the summer, visit one of the many gardens or pack a picnic lunch to enjoy at one of the spectacular viewpoints overlooking Puget Sound. In the winter, go antiquing in Gig Harbor or Tacoma, or take in the museums and theaters in Tacoma's revitalized downtown cultural district.

The area's two most breathtaking natural features are the mountains and Puget Sound; Mount Rainier appears in the east with the sunrise, while sunset brings a kaleidoscope of color over the snowcapped crags of the Olympic Mountains to the west. While the cultural activities on offer in the South Sound have year-round appeal, the region is most romantic in summer, when estate and garden tours offer chances for a romantic stroll, and the great outdoors opens for exploration.

Perhaps the most romantic destination in the region is lovely, peaceful **Vashon Island**. A short ferry ride from Seattle or Tacoma will whisk you here. In the summer or fall, leave the car at home and tour the island by bicycle; you can either bring your own bikes or rent them at **Vashon Island Bicycles** (9925 SW 178th St; 206/463-6225). Start with a coffee at the espresso counter adjacent to the **Stray Dog Café** (see Romantic Restaurants) and prepare for a leisurely day of sightseeing. For a view from the water, rent a kayak at **Vashon Island Kayak** (Jensen Point Boathouse; 206/463-9257) and choose from a day-trip around the island or the two-hour alternative. For delicious soups and freshly baked pastries, visit **Sound Food & Bakery** (20312 Vashon Hwy SW; 206/463-0888); weather permitting, sit at one of the outdoor tables in the backyard garden. Summer visitors can visit the u-pick lavender fields at **Lavenders on Vashon** (10425 SW 238th St; 206/463-5672; open July–Aug). When it's time for dinner, try the gourmet take-out fare from **Express Cuisine** (17629 Vashon Hwy SW; 206/463-6626). The menu at this eatery includes dishes such as prime rib, smoked salmon over linguine, and delicious soups—perfect for a romantic picnic dinner in your room—or claim a picnic table near the lighthouse and catch the sunset at **Point Robinson Park** (east end of SW Point Robinson Rd on next-door Maury Island).

Bordered by Commencement Bay, the once blue-collar mill town of **Tacoma** has long been in Seattle's shadow. However, thanks to recent preservation of historic homes and industrial buildings, and the opening of some excellent new museums, Tacoma's image is fast improving, and it now boasts the best of the South Sound's art, theater, and romantic dinner spots. The revitalized downtown cultural district is beginning to positively blossom. Opened in 2003, the sparkling new **Tacoma Art Museum** (1701 Pacific Ave; 253/272-4258; www.tacomaartmuseum.org) is a must for art lovers, and the much-heralded new **Museum of Glass** (on Thea Foss Waterway; 253/396-1768) houses some truly amazing glass sculptures. For great browsing at novelty shops and antiques stores, visit Tacoma's charming Proctor District; while you're here, enjoy a leisurely lunch at **The Old House Café** (2717 N Proctor St; 253/759-7336). Be sure and try one of their original desserts, such as luscious raspberry cake topped with whipped cream. For a romantic evening at the theater, the beautifully restored 1,100-seat **Pantages Theater** (901 Broadway Plaza) provides the perfect venue; ticket prices and production schedules are available from the **Broadway Center for the Performing**

Arts (253/591-5894; www.broadwaycenter.org). Cap off the night with a glass of wine and a delectable Brie plate at **Café Divino** (2112 N 30th St; 253/779-4226) in Tacoma's adorable Old Town section, near a quiet residential neighborhood overlooking the sound.

About 10 miles east of Tacoma sits the historic pioneer town of Puyallup, made famous by the annual September **Puyallup Fair** (253/841-5045; www.thefair.com). Spring and summer are the perfect times to explore the downtown sidewalk shops like **Candy's** (114 W Meeker Ave; 253/848-5640), where you can buy old-fashioned treats by the piece or pound. Read some sweet poetry in the new **Puyallup Public Library** (324 S Meridian; 253/841-5454) while enjoying the best view in town of Mount Rainier, or stroll just next door to the farmers market at the **Pioneer Park Pavilion** (253/841-5518; www.ci.puyallup.wa.us; 9am–2pm May–Oct). Grab a kiss and a bite at **From the Bayou** (see Romantic Restaurants). Then go on a historical tour of the **Meeker Mansion** (312 Spring St; 253/848-1770), built in the late 1800s by Puyallup's first mayor who earned, and then lost, his fortune growing hops. Tiptoe through the tulips at **VanLierop Bulb Farm** (13407 80th St E; 253/848-7272) where beautifully landscaped gardens come alive with more than 150 varieties of spring flowers.

If it's a hand-in-hand stroll you're in the mood for, visit some of the grand estates and public gardens in the area—you're certain to find some exceptional spots in which to steal a kiss. Start in **Olympia**, where you can stock up on picnic goodies at the **farmers market** (near Percival Landing; 360/352-9096; Thurs–Sun Apr–Oct, and weekends Nov–Christmas) and tour the **Yashiro Japanese Garden** (9th Ave and Plum St; 360/753-8447). North on Interstate 5 in the town of Lakewood, you can visit the **Lakewold Garden Estate** (12317 Gravelly Lake Dr; 253/584-4106), a 10-acre public garden with meandering paths, lush trees, and seasonal blooms. Before leaving Lakewood, visit the **Thornewood Castle Bed and Breakfast** (see Romantic Lodgings) and take the tour of the grounds, which include a sunken garden— just be sure to call ahead to reserve a spot. Last but not least, drive north to **Point Defiance State Park** (5400 N Pearl St; 253/591-5337) on the west end of Tacoma and stroll through the rows of dahlias, roses, and flowery arbors in the public gardens. Afterward, hop in the car and follow the signs down to the beach, just below the park area. This is a perfect spot to savor the last of your picnic fare as the sun goes down.

Access & Information

The two largest South Sound cities, Tacoma and Olympia, are most easily accessed via Interstate 5, the multilane highway that runs north/south through Western Washington. Several exits off Interstate 5 easily direct travelers to the main areas and attractions in both cities. Vashon Island is accessible only by ferry, from three docks: downtown Seattle (foot traffic only), West Seattle (Fauntleroy ferry), or Tacoma (Point Defiance ferry). Contact **Washington State Ferries** (206/464-6400 or 800/843-3779; www. wsdot.wa.gov/ferries/) for details. You can reach Gig Harbor via Highway 16 across the Tacoma Narrows Bridge (by 2007 a new bridge is scheduled to replace it, and the construction occasionally causes some rather unromantic driving delays). Boating remains an important part of Gig Harbor's identity; good anchorage and various moorage docks are here if you travel via watercraft. Be aware that traffic on both Interstate 5 and Highway 16 can be challenging and unpredictable during rush hour—and even on weekends.

Romantic Lodgings

ALOHA BEACHSIDE BED AND BREAKFAST
✿✿✿

8318 SR 302, Gig Harbor / 888/256-4222
Hawaii is more than a place—it's a state of mind. The Aloha Beachside Bed and Breakfast, perched just above the sound, certainly thinks so. And when guests espy the trickling waterfalls and lush gardens on the grounds and encounter the warm demeanor of innkeeper LaLaine Wong, they will be convinced, too. The Honeymoon Suite, located in the main house, is an obviously romantic choice, with gas fireplace, shower for two, bathtub overlooking the bay, and exquisite linens on a fluffy feather bed. Although a TV/VCR and romantic movies are available, the picture window gives a pretty amazing show of its own; turn out the lights and watch the moon rise over the water. The guest cottage, down the steps from the main house, offers two cozy rooms with queen-size beds dressed in soft cotton, water views, and a communal living space with kitchen where breakfast is served. Speaking of breakfast, count your calories somewhere else! LaLaine and her husband, Greg, whip up amazing breakfasts that can include sticky buns gooey with caramel sauce, fruit cocktail with whipped cream, delicious berry crepes, and Kona coffee. After savoring this hearty breakfast, work off a few of the calories you haven't counted by walking along the shore with the Wongs' dogs, Oreo and Charlie, or taking a dip in the pool. If you still need some relaxation, ask LaLaine to arrange a private massage for you and your sweetie.
$$–$$$ *MC, V; checks OK; www.alohabeachsidebb.com/photo-tour.htm.*

ARTISTS STUDIO LOFT BED AND BREAKFAST
✿✿◖

16529 91st Ave SW, Vashon Island / 206/463-2583
Stroll the 5 lovely acres surrounding the Artists Studio Loft B&B, and you will see where innkeeper Jacqueline Clayton gets her inspiration as

a painter. Guests might find themselves wanting to pick up a brush, too, once they see the lush gardens, goldfish pond, and personal artistic touches added to the grounds. The newest cottage, the River Birch, has a Jacuzzi tub, walk-in tiled shower, and fireplace. Two guest rooms (the Master Suite and the Ivy Room) in the main house feature warm, home-away-from-home ambience, while the two guest cottages promise the most privacy. The Arbor Cottage is decorated in a Northwest cabin style, complete with wood floors, green soapstone fireplace, and Jacuzzi tub for two. Those staying in the two guest rooms enjoy breakfast prepared by Jacqueline in the sun-filled kitchen of the main house. Guests in Arbor Cottage and the Aerial Cottage savor a more continental affair in the privacy of their own kitchens, where breakfast items include fresh juice, sweet pastries, and juicy Italian plums fresh from the garden. All accommodations are very reasonably priced, immaculately clean, and close to town.
$$–$$$ *AE, DIS, MC, V; checks OK; www.asl-bnb.com.*

BETTY MACDONALD FARM BED AND BREAKFAST
🌸🌸🕯

12000 99th Ave SW, Vashon Island / 206/567-4227 or 888/328-6753
Sweeping views of Puget Sound and Mount Rainier, access to a private beach, and spacious log cabin–like accommodations only begin to describe this storybook retreat just up the hill from the ferry dock. For 20 years, innkeeper Judith Lawrence has been providing a comforting, romantic get-away on the 17-acre property, which was once owned by the author Betty MacDonald. The Loft, which sits above the barn, provides the best view; on summer evenings, watch the moon rise from the porch while you savor a glass of wine and raspberries fresh from the garden (and a kiss or two). In the winter, couples can cozy up on the couch in front of a woodstove. The large Cottage has room for four, but couples who crave privacy can stay here and enjoy the same view as the Loft, in addition to the perfect romantic feature—a claw-foot tub overlooking a southwest view of the Sound. Light some candles and enjoy the tranquil silence. Breakfast goodies are provided in the fridge; take your pick from farm-fresh eggs, waffle mix, English muffins, homemade jams, and fresh fruits. In the afternoon, collect some juicy Asian pears as you stroll around the farm, and then walk down to enjoy them on the private beach.
$$ *AE, DIS, MC, V; checks OK; www.bettymacdonaldfarm.com.*

CHINABERRY HILL
🌸🌸🌸🕯

302 Tacoma Ave N, Tacoma / 253/272-1282
Built in 1889, this historic Victorian home perched above a quiet residential street in the Stadium District is beautifully maintained and oozing with romance. Charming antique furniture, wood floors, and an inviting fireplace

add to the ambience. We like the Pantages Suite in the main house for its amazing view of Commencement Bay and its vaulted ceilings, gold-accented Jacuzzi tub, and luxurious white linens. On cold nights, the Wild Rose Room is also inviting, as it includes appointments similar to those in the Pantages Suite—plus a gas fireplace. The best view in the house might just be the old servants' quarters, now the lush third-floor suite. It has two bedrooms, a kitchen, a dining area, and a claw-foot tub. For a little more privacy, try the Carriage Suite or the Hayloft; both are located in a converted carriage house at the back of the property. The most unique feature of the Carriage Suite is a Jacuzzi that receives water from an old hay chute. After a hearty breakfast—which can be served either in your room or in the dining room of the main house—take time to stroll through the beautiful landscaped garden in back and give the Buddha statue a lucky pat on the belly.
$$–$$$ *AE MC, V; checks OK; www.chinaberryhill.com.*

OLYMPIC VIEW BED AND BREAKFAST
◖◖◖◖

Three Tree Point, Seattle / 206/243-6900
This getaway lives up to its name, with a spectacular view encompassing sparkling Puget Sound, towering evergreens, and the snow-capped Olympic Mountains. The scenic Three Tree Point neighborhood is located much closer to Seattle than Tacoma (it's just 10 minutes west of Sea-Tac Airport), but nonetheless *feels* far enough out of the Emerald City to qualify as "south of Seattle" (thus its inclusion in this chapter). The two-story cottage itself is located adjacent to the beautifully landscaped main home (a minor drawback is that the parking is offered in the lower level's cluttered garage). The closest civilization is the old-fashioned, store-lined main street of downtown Burien, about five miles down the road, but you may not want to leave this private hideaway, complete with a Jacuzzi tub on the deck. You'll find all the comforts of home, including a fully equipped kitchen inside and a barbecue outside—perfect for preparing your own dinner of fresh Northwest seafood. Soothing decor is Northwest meets Pottery Barn, with hardwood floors, subtle color schemes, and historic seafaring photographs. A seating area is made for lounging, with leather chairs and sofa, a stereo with CD player, and cable TV along with a VCR and a wide array of movies. A partial wall separates the bedroom, with its king-size pillow-top bed, and the adjacent bath with walk-in shower, pedestal sink, lovely bath products, and plush robes. Come morning, the refrigerator is stocked with ready-to-prepare items such as buttermilk pancakes, cinnamon French toast, eggs and cheeses for omelets, as well as cereals and yogurts. Wake at your leisure and dine outside on a sunny deck surrounded by blossoming plants and shrubs, then start the day right with a relaxing soak in the Jacuzzi tub.
$$$ *MC, V; checks OK; www.olympicviewbb.com.*

THORNEWOOD CASTLE INN AND GARDENS
✿✿✿€

8601 N Thorne Ln, Lakewood / 253/584-4393
Nestled in a gated community on the banks of American Lake, this 19th-century estate is just minutes off Interstate 5 in quiet Lakewood, south of Tacoma. Be prepared: not one square foot of Thornewood Castle lacks romance. The "house that love built" has no trouble living up to its romantic history. Chester Thorne, a prominent banker in the late 1800s, bought a Gothic Tudor home in England that he then dismantled, shipping the pieces to Lakewood to be rebuilt for his bride, Anna Thorne. Now, more than 100 years later, not only has the home been placed on the National Register of Historic Places, but it also was the setting for the Stephen King movie *Rose Red*. Several restorations have returned it to its original grandeur. Enter through the heavy wooden front door to the grand living room, where soft music floats among fluffy couches and a crackling fire. Each guest room includes the most important romantic details, such as a gas fireplace, a bed piled with pillows and exquisite linens, thick terry-cloth robes, and a view of either the lake or the breathtaking estate grounds. For the ultimate romantic experience, stay in the Grandview Room, which features a luxurious king-size bed, an attached bath, a kitchenette, and a porch complete with Jacuzzi tub overlooking both American Lake and the beautiful sunken garden. Breakfast is served either in a large dining room or in the privacy of your own room. Since chances are very good you won't want to leave the estate once you've arrived, innkeepers Wayne and Deanna Robinson also offer boxed dinners on the weeknights and weekend dinners in the dining room.
$$$–$$$$ *AE, MC, V; checks OK in advance; www.thornewoodcastle.com.*

THE VILLA
✿✿✿€

705 N 5th St, Tacoma / 253/572-1157
If jetting off to the Old World for the weekend isn't in the cards, visit this authentic Italian villa in the charming Stadium District of Tacoma. The six romance-inspiring rooms are all named after Italian cities, but each offers completely different decor and romantic amenities. Innkeepers Greg and Becky Anglemyer have lovingly decorated their "ode to Italy" to reflect the charm and romance of the best inns around *la bella Italia*. The Sorrento Suite—which has been known to make new brides cry with happiness upon entering—is the primo room to reserve. Guests literally step into luxury, as the room boasts a fireplace, a king-size bed bedecked with tulle and twinkling white lights, and a sitting room complete with inviting couches where you and your special someone can sip complimentary wines. The Cimbrone Suite offers a private balcony overlooking the tranquil gardens, where peacocks sometimes wander by. Breakfast has several seatings and consists of

four delicious courses that might include cinnamon rolls, fruit with whipped cream, and an egg bake with potatoes and cheese. Attention to the smallest of details in every room, color schemes ranging from sour-apple greens to bright pinks, and a never-ending supply of romantic stories from the owners make the Villa a pocketbook-pleasing alternative to the real thing.
$$–$$$ *AE, MC, V; checks OK; www.villabb.com.* &

Romantic Restaurants

ANTHONY'S HOMEPORT
◐◐◖

8827 Harborview Dr N, Gig Harbor / 253/853-6353
This outpost of Anthony's, a popular seafood restaurant with several locations around Puget Sound, offers the best of Gig Harbor's natural beauty. While the interior decor is a bit predictable, with picture windows, dark woodwork, and white-linen tablecloths, the views of the harbor and Mount Rainier and an outdoor dining area help make this a great place to steal an across-the-table kiss. Premium Northwest seafood dishes such as alder-planked salmon with smoked sweet-pepper sauce and the refreshing seafood salad with Dungeness crab, bay shrimp, and avocado might momentarily take your attention away from each other; dessert will find you intimate again, gazing at each other while sharing a warm blackberry cobbler topped with vanilla ice cream. The downstairs Shoreline Room is a little more casual and features a lighter menu.
$$–$$$ *AE, MC, V; no checks; dinner every day; beer and wine; reservations recommended; www.anthonys.com.*

CLIFF HOUSE
◐◐◐

6300 Marine View Dr, Tacoma / 253/927-0400
The Cliff House has long been a romantic institution in Tacoma. With its formal decor and amazing views of Commencement Bay, Mount Rainier, and the Tacoma skyline, we can easily see why. Although the service can be unpredictable and the prices a little steep, this restaurant is still one of the area's top romantic destinations, where locals go for special occasions or for an utterly elegant dining experience. The restaurant prides itself on preparing local produce, seafood, and meats, and boasts tempting desserts such as cherries jubilee and crepes suzette flambéed tableside. White linens cover every table, and soft lighting definitely sets the mood for a kiss.
$$$ *AE, DC, DIS, MC, V; no checks; lunch, dinner every day; full bar; reservations recommended.*

EL GAUCHO

✿✿✿❲

2119 Pacific Ave, Tacoma / 253/272-1510

One of the newest dining establishments in Tacoma's rejuvenated downtown, Seattle's El Gaucho now has a southerly outpost, and it's a welcome addition to the scene. Descend the large staircase to the main dining floor where live music (at dinner only) welcomes you and tables glow with soft candlelight. Ask for a table on the landing overlooking the main floor, where you can sink into a comfy booth and enjoy your skillfully prepared dinner, which is served by a deft and attentive wait staff. If you've got carnivorous instincts, go ahead and try any of the steak dishes, which are deliciously satisfying and well worth the price. After dinner, every patron is given a complimentary platter of fruit, nuts, cheese, and crackers. But why stop there? Cap your romantic meal with a chocolate cake, rich cheesecake, or, for the most drama, bananas flambé or baked Alaska—flambéed tableside. This is truly an amazing dining experience.

$$$–$$$$ *AE, MC, V; no checks; dinner every day; full bar; reservations recommended; www.elgaucho.com.*

FROM THE BAYOU

✿✿

508 Garfield St, Parkland / 253/539-4269

Cajun- and Northwest-influenced cuisine is served with spicy flair at the Bayou, located just a stride or two from the Pacific Lutheran University campus. Sit outside on the French Quarter garden strewn with lush plantings, garden lights, playfully painted furniture, and murals. Inside, request the "love table," which is tucked away and decorated with romantic details. Known for food with soul, the Bayou serves up generous helpings of jambalaya, catfish, and red beans and rice. Try the steamboat artichokes stuffed with crab and roasted red pepper and topped with a creamy champagne sauce. For dinner, the pepper bacon–wrapped halibut topped with a tomato-and-caper cream sauce or the catfish platter smothered in a crawfish étoufée will have you thinking you are dining in New Orleans. Our favorite homemade desert is the cheesecake made with roasted coconut, almonds, and dark chocolate. If all this sounds fabulous, you might also try the owner's new establishment located in downtown Puyallup (328 S Meridian; 253/841-5640), which has similar down-on-the-bayou fare and ambience.

$–$$ *AE, DIS, MC, V; no checks; dinner Mon–Sat; beer and wine; reservations recommended; www.fromthebayou.com.*

THE GREEN TURTLE
❍❍❍
2905 Harborview Dr, Gig Harbor / 253/851-3167
The Green Turtle is a favorite with locals and visitors alike for its great food and festive, under-the-sea decor. Friendly owners Nolan and Sue Glenn, along with chef Roman Aguillion, keep the menu focused squarely on seafood, offering such delicious dishes as king salmon crusted with sesame seeds, spicy seafood sauté, and a to-die-for surf-and-turf featuring jumbo scampi in a creamy lemon sauce with filet mignon in cabernet demi-glace. Whatever you do, remember to save room for one of the Green Turtle's amazing desserts. We recommend either crepes suzette or chocolate mousse. If you've got a sunny day on your hands, make the most of it by dining on the deck overlooking the harbor.
$$ *AE, DIS, MC, V; checks OK; dinner Wed–Sun; beer and wine; reservations recommended; www.thegreenturtle.com.*

OVER THE MOON CAFÉ
❍❍◖
709 Court C, Tacoma / 253/284-3722
Tucked away on a slim city street near the Pantages Theater, Over the Moon Café has all the charm of a quaint Italian trattoria. Soft candlelight illuminates the split-level dining area, while from the open kitchen waft the enticing aromas of basil and garlic. The mood is relaxing, the wait staff is down-to-earth and unobtrusive, and the food is simply terrific. Try the pasta primavera with fresh tomatoes, shiitake mushrooms, broccoli, and basil, or the juicy Tuscan chicken topped with basil and mozzarella cheese. Both dishes are satisfying and refreshingly free of heavy sauces. For dessert, perhaps between bites of boysenberry-drenched cheesecake, read poetry to each other from the tiny books thoughtfully placed on every table.
$$ *AE, MC, V; checks OK; breakfast Sat–Sun, dinner Tues–Sat; beer and wine; reservations recommended.*

PORTOFINO
❍❍
101 Division St NW, Olympia / 360/352-2803
It's easy to overlook this small restaurant located next to an unattractive office building, but you'd be wise to seek it out, as Portofino, set in a charming 1890s farmhouse, offers a quiet, elegant alternative to the staggering number of chain restaurants in this area. The menu consists of inventive, skillfully prepared Pacific Northwest fare. For dinner, consider the savory prawn bisque or the crab cakes, the latter made from shrimp and crab shucked on the spot. If pasta sounds more appealing, try the ravioli, which changes daily. To up the romance quotient, choose a bottle from the extensive wine list. In the warmer months, a glass-enclosed porch lets you

enjoy the sunshine while you sup. Bustling traffic on nearby Division Street is distracting, but there's certainly enough charm here to inspire a kiss or two.

$$ *AE, MC, V; checks OK; dinner every day; beer and wine; reservations recommended.*

THE STRAY DOG CAFÉ
◐◐

17530 Vashon Island Hwy SW, Vashon Island / 206/463-7833

Don't let the name fool you—the Stray Dog Café has nothing of the ragamuffin about it. Instead, this small, intimate restaurant, smack-dab in the middle of town, has an urban flair that belies its island location—minus the big-city prices and cooler-than-thou attitude. Red walls, vaulted ceilings, tables covered with white linens, small votive candles, and fresh flowers set the tone for romance. The menu offers comfort food with a twist. Lunchtime offerings include a wonderful balsamic chicken salad and homemade soups; dinner options feature creamy risotto with saffron and juicy prawns, crispy chicken in a spicy cilantro sauce, or grilled strip steak in a mustard-cream sauce with roasted garlic mashed potatoes. Try one of the more inventive dishes—such as mango, cucumber, and shrimp salad—if you're in the mood for a little culinary adventure. The service can be inconsistent here, but it's a minor drawback, and this cozy eatery is worth the ferry ride. There's also a scrumptious Sunday brunch and a separate counter offering espresso drinks to go.

$–$$ *AE, DIS, MC, V; checks OK; lunch every day, dinner Wed–Sat, brunch Sun; beer and wine; reservations recommended.*

THE SAN JUAN ISLANDS

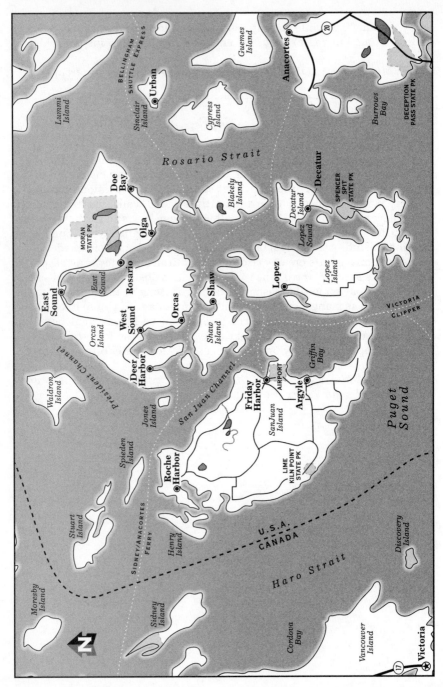

"Every kiss provokes another."
—MARCEL PROUST

♡ THE SAN JUAN ISLANDS

The San Juan Islands are, simply put, breathtakingly beautiful. There are 743 of these remote, varied islands at low tide and just 428 at high tide; 172 of them have names, 60 are populated, and 4 have major ferry service. Of the main islands, three—Lopez, Orcas, and San Juan—offer lodgings, eateries, and beautiful parks. But the best fact of all, and one not widely known, is that the islands are frequently sunny, since they lie in the rain shadow of the Olympic Mountains—most receive just half the rainfall of Seattle. Even with the pleasant weather, keep in mind that these islands are about as far north as you can go in the continental United States, and any flush on your cheeks will more likely be from the brisk air than from blazing heat. So much the better: there'll be lots of incentive to snuggle.

Deciding on one island won't be easy. You can opt for the convenience of one of the more populated islands, or, if you have access to a boat, you can enjoy a rustic holiday on one or more of the lesser-known islands. Deciding when to go is another tough one: the sparsely populated islands are positively overrun in summer, and getting your car on a ferry out of Anacortes can mean a three-hour-plus wait. While July and August are truly spectacular here, fall, spring, and winter are equally beautiful in their own ways. During the so-called quiet season, you'll find that rates are more reasonable, and you'll be better able to truly relax into the unhurried pace of island life. On the other hand, many restaurants and lodgings also have seasonal closures. To save time and frustration, check with the San Juan Islands Visitor's Bureau (360/378-9551 or 888/468-3701) for seasonal hours and rates whenever you choose a restaurant or island accommodation. The center can also provide good recommendations for campgrounds and outdoor activities.

The easiest way to reach the San Juans is via the Washington State Ferries (206/464-6400; www.wsdot.wa.gov/ferries/), which run year-round from Anacortes. Located a little more than an hour and a half north of Seattle, Anacortes is itself on an island: Fidalgo. Though most travelers rush through on their way to catch the boat, this small city is quietly becoming a destination in itself. (For more on Anacortes, see the Skagit Valley section of the Puget Sound chapter.) Companies such as Kenmore Air (425/486-1257 or 800/543-9595; www.kenmoreair.com) provide an exciting, if more expensive, way to reach the islands—via seaplane. No matter how you get here, these quiet islands will blow you away with their stunning beauty and romantic atmosphere.

SAN JUAN ISLAND

ROMANTIC HIGHLIGHTS

San Juan Island is nothing less than a northern vacation paradise. The largest and most developed of the San Juans, it is also the westernmost destination in the Strait of Juan de Fuca. It's so close to Vancouver Island that you can often see the interior mountains and the lights of Victoria twinkling in the distance. Packed with restaurants, bed-and-breakfasts, hotels, and enough shoreline to satisfy any nature lover, San Juan is an island escape par excellence. Driving through the island yields an ever-unfolding scenic masterpiece, and, on foot, you can joyfully explore the numerous parks. Be sure to spend some time browsing the shops and galleries in lively Friday Harbor, the island's main town.

If you like to do your kissing alfresco, say with a little picnic lunch and a soundtrack of birdsong, this island offers excellent options. Particularly noteworthy are the mid-19th-century sites of the **American and English Camps** (360/378-2240; www.nps.gov/sajh), established when ownership of the island was under dispute. (The Americans and British, in fact, shared joint occupation until 1872, when the dispute was settled in favor of the United States.) The American Camp, at the south end of the island, showcases open, windy prairie and beach; it ranks among the most glorious seaside spots in the San Juan Islands. Investigate the shoreline or meander through sand dunes and sea grass; plentiful opportunities for ducking out of sight into secluded and sheltered coves make this excellent terrain for lovers. You'll be mesmerized by views of both the Olympic and Cascade Mountains in this spectacular park. The English Camp, toward the island's northwest end, is wooded and secluded; if the two of you have the energy (and the hiking boots!), don't miss climbing the gorgeous uphill trail from English Camp to Young Hill. You'll hike through tree-canopied pathways and madrone forests to reach the majestic, windswept top. There are plenty of nice spots up here in which to catch your breath (and then lose it again to the view—or a kiss). Give yourselves at least an hour for this round-trip excursion, and bring along a picnic, because once you're atop Young Hill, you'll want to stay as long as possible. If this lovely hike leaves you hungry for more, explore beautiful **San Juan County Park** (50 San Juan Park Dr; 360/378-2992), on the island's west side. (With advance reservations, out-doorsy romantics can camp at one of 19 sites on a pretty cove.)

Another popular outdoor activity is whale-watching. If the thought of getting on a boat makes your sea legs feel wobbly, you can whale watch from terra firma at the nation's first official whale-watching park: **Lime Kiln Point State Park**, on the island's west side. Several pods of whales make regular trips through this area, and even if you don't catch a glimpse of them, you'll more than likely see a bald eagle or, if you time it right, a sensational sunset with the snowcapped Olympic Mountains in the distance. Folks flock here in summer, so bring your binoculars and patience; in qui-eter seasons, you and the seagulls might have the place to yourselves. After you've spotted a whale, learn about what you've just seen back in town at the excellent **Whale Museum** (62 1st St N; 360/378-4710 or 800/946-7227; www.whalemuseum.org), which features exhibits devoted to the beloved resident cetaceans.

But for a close-up look at the island's wildlife, nothing beats a boat. Take a nautical journey with **Western Prince Whale and Wildlife Tours** (1 block from ferry landing; 360/378-5315 or 800/757-ORCA; www.orcawhalewatch. com) or with **San Juan Boat Tours** (360/378-3499 or 800/232-6722; www. whaletour.com; prices start at $39 per person). This is the chance of a life-time to come face to face with harbor seals, bald eagles, or a pod of orcas, among other magnificent creatures. There are many whale-watching com-panies based on San Juan Island; look for the flyers posted all over the ferry landing. We suggest calling around to get the price and experience you're looking for (oh, and make sure to dress warmly). Kayaking couples should also follow this advice, as there are plenty of outfitters to choose from. Truly adventurous individuals who find a plunge into cold water the ultimate vacation experience may want to take advantage of the diving in the archi-pelago—some claim it's the best cold-water diving in the world. **Island Dive and Watersports** (2A Spring St; 360/378-2772; www.divesanjuan.com) offers rentals, charters, and classes.

If you leave your car at home—a great option in summer when the fer-ries are crowded—rent scooters at **Susie's Mopeds** (up the hill from the ferry dock; 360/378-5244 or 800/532-0087; www.susiesmopeds.com) or bikes at **Island Bicycles** (380 Argyle Ave; 360/378-4941; www.islandbicycles.com). Bicyclists be warned, however: roads can be steep and winding, without much in the way of a shoulder. There are plenty of wonderful bed-and-breakfasts, but if you'd like to stay for a week or more, look into **renting a house** on the island (360/378-3601 or 800/391-8190; www.windermere vacationrentals.com).

For a lovely picnic spot, visit the beautiful, fragrant grounds of **Pelindaba Lavender Farm** (off Wold Rd; 360/378-4248 or 866/819-1911; www.pelindaba. com; open every day May–Sept). The farm's new product gallery, cafe, and meeting place is one block from the ferry in Friday Harbor (150 1st St; 360/378-4248) and is open every day year-round. You can even cut your own lavender during the summer harvest. If wine tasting is on your agenda, visit **San Juan Vineyards** (3136 Roche Harbor Rd; 360/378-WINE (9463); www. sanjuanvineyards.com; open every day in summer); the tasting room is set in a renovated turn-of-the-20th-century schoolhouse. Oyster fans should visit **Westcott Bay Sea Farms** (904 Westcott Dr; 360/378-2489; www.westcottbay. com) off Roche Harbor Road, 2 miles south of Roche Harbor Resort—where you can help yourselves to fresh oysters at bargain prices.

Access & Information

The most popular way to reach San Juan Island is via the **Washington State Ferries** (206/464-6400 or 800/843-3779 in WA only; www.wsdot.wa.gov/ ferries/), which run year-round from Anacortes. From Seattle, Anacortes is approximately an hour and a half north by car. To avoid long ferry lines in summer, leave your car behind; many B&B owners will gladly pick up guests at the ferry dock with prior notification. Another option in summer for those willing to go without a car is the passenger-only **Victoria Clipper** (2701 Alaskan Wy, Seattle; 206/448-5000; www.victoriaclipper.com), which travels daily from downtown Seattle to San Juan Island.

   Kenmore Air (425/486-1257 or 800/543-9595; www.kenmoreair.com) schedules five floatplane flights per day during peak season; there are fewer flights in the off-season. Round-trip flights start at about $170 per person and leave from downtown Seattle at Lake Union and from north Lake Washington. A shuttle is available from Sea-Tac Airport to Lake Union. Luggage is limited by weight. **San Juan Airlines** (206/768-1945 or 800/874-4434; www.sanjuanairlines.com) flies into the airport on San Juan Island; the flight takes approximately 50 minutes. Either air service will be met by the rental-car operator on the island, M&W (360/378-AUTO (2886) or 800/323-6037).

Romantic Lodgings

FRIDAY HARBOR HOUSE
◖◖◖◖

130 West St, Friday Harbor / 360/378-8455
This sleek inn perched on a hillside offers posh, spare decor and views, views, views. The beautiful surroundings are decoration enough, and you'll delight in this professionally managed, subdued retreat where you'll find privacy, relaxation, and, yes, romance. Handsome slate floors and a stylish water fountain accent the small lobby, where guests receive their first taste

of the understated elegance that distinguishes Friday Harbor House. In most of the 20 rooms, floor-to-ceiling windows showcase unparalleled views of the water and the bustling marina below; on clear days, Orcas Island's Mount Constitution can be seen in the distance. (As with most places, the more you pay, the better the view; some of the less expensive rooms have parking-lot peekaboo views.) Taupe and sand colors, Craftsman-style furnishings, and Northwest touches—tasteful wooden carvings, beach rocks on the fireplace mantel, and paintings of San Juan scenes—characterize the rooms. Romance-friendly features in all rooms include gas fireplaces, dimmer switches, TVs, queen-size beds, and spacious bathrooms with Jacuzzi-style soaking tubs. Some of the rooms have tiny balconies, while others feature open tub areas so you can watch the glowing fireplace while you soak the night away. Located on the main floor, the polished dining room holds only a handful of tables, so intimacy is guaranteed. Floor-to-ceiling windows frame views of the picturesque marina. The delectable menu changes seasonally, tempting with dishes such as Westcott Bay Belon oysters on the half shell with blood-orange granita or duck confit with celery-root mashed potatoes and gremolata. In the morning, a complimentary, generous, continental buffet-style breakfast is served here; if the weather's nice, take your breakfast outside and watch the ferries come and go.
$$$–$$$$ *AE, DIS, MC, V; no checks; www.fridayharborhouse.com.* &

FRIDAY'S HISTORIC INN
◐◐◖

35 1st St, Friday Harbor / 360/378-5848 or 800/352-2632
Built in 1891, this three-story gray hotel was a youth hostel before it was reincarnated as a boutique hotel. Its location in the heart of Friday Harbor means that noise from the bustling streets below can pose a problem for guests seeking quiet refuge, but you may change your minds once you set foot in one of the luxurious suites (soft earplugs are included in bathroom baskets just in case). It would be hard not to feel pampered as you gaze at the beautiful harbor views from the San Juan Suite (on your soaring private deck) or bubble away in your jetted tub on the private courtyard of the Marrowstone Suite. Both suites feature king-size beds and luxurious robes. San Juan's bathroom features a jetted tub and a double-headed shower; the suite also has a large kitchenette and the best view in the house (well worth the climb up a couple flights of steps). Marrowstone boasts a separate entrance and gas fireplace, and is fully wheelchair accessible. The petite Orcas Suite is also pleasant, with a partial view of the harbor and a jetted tub in the room. The standard rooms are a good option for lower budgets. Try the third-floor Cypress, with its vaulted ceiling, queen-size bed, and large private bath with claw-foot tub. Most rooms have TV/VCRs and heated floors, some have wet bars and private balconies, some have Jacuzzi tubs, and four of the rooms share two common bathrooms. Romance seekers should note

that the accommodations in the daylight basement feel a little less inspiring. If you are looking for an amorous interlude, and if your budget can handle the slightly steeper tab, you will definitely prefer the extravagance of the suites. In the comfy main floor lounge, enjoy the antique pressed-tin ceiling and a substantial continental breakfast of rave-worthy fresh-baked scones, seasonal fruits, hot and cold cereal, yogurt, fresh juice, tea, and locally roasted coffee (fresh-baked cookies and coffee or tea greet you when you check in).
$$–$$$ MC, V; checks OK; www.friday-harbor.com. &

HIGHLAND INN
✿✿✿✿
West side of San Juan Island / 360/378-9450 or 888/400-9850
Linger on the long, covered veranda for spellbinding views of the water and snowcapped Olympic Mountains; submerge yourselves in the outdoor hydrotherapy hot tub and study the stars; or relax in a spacious suite as luxurious as it is cozy. Sound dreamy? We think so. When Helen King, the former owner of the renowned Babbling Brook Inn in Santa Cruz, California, moved north, she built the inn of her dreams in this spectacular, secluded hillside location. A romantic idyll is yours to be had in one of the two enormous suites, one at each end of the house. Though the suites have identical layouts and amenities, they differ in decor and ambience. The mocha-and-beige color scheme in the Haro Strait Suite is all elegance. The furry white throw rug laid before the fireplace invites you to lounge, and the king-size bed with intricately carved headboard, luxurious armchair, antique furnishings, and well-chosen artwork all add to the subtle opulence. The welcoming Whale Watch Suite is done in French country. Sink into the blue-denim sofa or gaze at the fire from the oversize blue and yellow armchair. Luxurious touches fill both suites, from the wood-burning fireplaces to the incredible marble bathrooms—each with a jetted tub for two and steam-cabinet shower. Both open onto the spectacular, 88-foot-long veranda. Amenities include satellite TV, VCR, CD player (plus a selection of videos and CDs to choose from), and a private telephone line. Staying here entails a winding drive from Friday Harbor, but the views are so good you won't mind the trip. Enjoy the delicious breakfast in the dining room or at a cozy table for two in your suite. Seasonally varied fare includes such tasty treats as freshly squeezed orange juice, fresh mango and blueberries served with raspberry compote, smoked salmon eggs Benedict, and apple bread with toasted pecans and coconut. In a word, divine.
$$$$ AE, DIS, MC, V; checks OK; www.highlandinn.com.

HILLSIDE HOUSE BED AND BREAKFAST
❍❍◖

365 Carter Ave, Friday Harbor / 360/378-4730 or 800/232-4730
Attractive landscaping and an inviting hammock welcome guests who wander up the path to this contemporary bed-and-breakfast, located in a residential neighborhood. There are six guest rooms on the upper main floor and in the daylight basement; a seventh option, the bright and spacious Eagle's Nest Suite, is perched on the top floor. All rooms have individualized country decor and Northwest flair, with arrangements of dried flowers, wide window seats with comfy pillows, private bathrooms (either in the room or across the hall—robes provided), and plush linens on raised beds with headboards. While most of the rooms are nearly identical in amenities, we recommend the upstairs rooms for their abundance of natural light; the downstairs rooms won't make you forget you're in a daylight basement, despite views of the front yard and Mount Baker, or the small back rock garden. (The nautically themed Captain's Quarters, with a private ground-floor entrance and a view of Mount Baker, is perfect for people troubled by stairs). But for a truly romantic getaway, the fairest room of all is the expansive Eagle's Nest Suite. Large windows toss lots of light into this third-floor loft, which has a private stairway from the comfortable common area, cathedral ceilings, a king-size bed, a sumptuous leather love seat, and a huge jetted tub with a skylight view of stars. A private deck for two over-looks the immediate neighborhood and frames views of water and Mount Baker. The warm and amiable hosts encourage guests to relax in their comfortable living room and on roomy outside decks with water views in the distance. When the birds start singing, sit down to a full breakfast that might include fresh fruit, a blue cheese–crab quiche or lavender-pecan pancakes, and homemade breads and muffins. Weather permitting, you can dine on the deck and watch the ferries come and go. There's also a bike barn if you bring or rent cycles. Call ahead about special events, which may include holiday parties, Victorian teas, and gourmet cooking classes.
$$–$$$ *AE, DIS, MC, V; checks OK; www.hillsidehouse.com.*

INN TO THE WOODS
❍❍❍

46 Elena Dr, Friday Harbor / 360/378-3367 or 888/522-9626
Follow the beach-stone path through towering fir trees to reach this spar-kling inn located between Friday and Roche Harbors. Once inside, you'll feel welcomed by the natural light, bright decor, and immaculate Berber carpeting. The wraparound porch has views to Sportsman's Lake, which harbors beautiful trumpeter swans. The new innkeepers have a passion for comfort and luxury: plush towels, silky-soft cotton linens and lofty pillows (two goose down and two hypoallergenic for each bed), and new Westin Heavenly Mattresses are standard in all four rooms; most have TVs with

satellite reception, and none have phones—perfect for your romantic retreat. For the most sumptuous option, we recommend the spacious Marilyn Suite, situated in a nice private spot at the end of the house and featuring views of the lake. It includes a four-poster mahogany bed with a taupe, claret, and burgundy coverlet over the down comforter, private hot tub on the deck, and spacious bathroom with single-person jetted tub. The St. John Room offers a king-size bed and a view of the woods; the cozy Lakeview Room, a queen-size brass bed and an antique writing desk. The Nautical Room, privately situated over the garage adjoining the main house, has blue and white decor, a king-size bed, and a private balcony overlooking the lake. Guests sit down to breakfast in the bright kitchen, sensibly soundproofed so morning noise never disturbs late sleepers. Indulge in a homemade full hot breakfast including such delectable treats as two-pepper crustless quiche or apple-topped baked French toast, as well as fresh fruit salads, coffee and tea, and freshly baked pastries. Tea and cookies or brownies in the comfortable common room are the perfect afternoon snack.
$$–$$$ *AE, DIS, MC, V; no checks; www.inntothewoods.com.*

LONESOME COVE RESORT
✿✿❦
416 Lonesome Cove Rd, Friday Harbor / 360/378-4477
Drive down the long, wooded gravel road and into the dreamy, sepia-colored past to secluded Lonesome Cove Resort, located on the northernmost part of the island. Six cabins with vintage Lincoln Log charm skirt a private pebbled beach, their decks and living rooms looking out across the channel to Spieden Island. Deer leisurely forage for fallen apples on the manicured lawn; beyond the beach, cormorants dive for their dinner; and several resident ducks waddle here and there, hoping for a handout. On a hill above the cabins you can sit (and kiss!) in solitude on a wooden bench beside a trout-stocked pond. Inside the cozy cabins, huge stone fireplaces (smelling romantically of wood smoke), exposed log walls, and full kitchens will help you relax in unfussy comfort. While linens are only average, everything is spotlessly clean and in good working condition. If you'd like to meet your fellow guests (some of whom have been coming back to Lonesome Cove's remote quiet since childhood), you can relax in the group lounge—situated on the other side of the drive from the cabins so you won't hear it if you don't want to—for impromptu evening happy hours. A small library can furnish you with a paperback, and—note to romantic boaters—a 100-foot private dock with power and water is available for guests from May through October; let your hosts know if you'll be arriving by sea. Be sure and stop in Friday Harbor or Roche Harbor to stock up on groceries, barbecue supplies,

and personal items, because once you settle in here with the right special someone, you won't want to leave.

$$ *MC, V; checks OK; 5-night minimum stay in summer; www.lonesome cove.com.*

ROCHE HARBOR RESORT
⬡⬡⬡

Roche Harbor / 360/378-2155 or 800/451-8910
This scenic, historic harbor and marina, protected by a tiny barrier island, is a yachting and tourist playground. As you wander the winding brick pathways through the resort's crisp white and dark green New England–style buildings, gazebos, rose gardens, sculpted hedges, and ivy-laden buildings, you may feel as if you have stepped back into a simpler time (albeit with a lot of other people). The four McMillin suites, renovated in 1999, are the most romantic accommodations. Overlooking the harbor with incredible water and sunset views, the sophisticated interiors boast high ceilings, polished wood floors, and leather wingback chairs facing gas fireplaces. Doors lead to a veranda stocked with wicker furniture. Bedrooms feature king-size four-poster beds; bathrooms have heated floors, double sinks, and claw-foot soaking tubs and separate showers. The suites are quite expensive, but Roche Harbor is a popular site for marriage ceremonies, and they offer the only acceptable on-site lodgings for the wedding night. Overnight accommodations are also available at the 20-room Hotel de Haro, but whatever you do, don't book one for a romantic getaway. While this historic hotel looks charming on the outside, the inside is literally scary, with sagging ceilings and floors, rickety stairways, dark Victorian decor, bathrooms with exposed plumbing, and doors that don't shut properly. Waterfront condominiums are also available, but we don't recommend them either. At the resort, booking guided kayak tours and whale-watching excursions is easy, and there are three restaurants on site: the formal McMillin's Dining Room with spectacular harbor views and an upscale Northwest-inspired menu; the casual lower-level Madrona Grill, which has waterfront patio dining in summer; and the Lime Kiln Café on the pier, with standard breakfast and lunch options. Guests should note that an immense new building project at the resort was scheduled to add almost 20 new residences in 2005—which means all the more people in the manicured gardens. Some of these romantic-looking Victorian-style townhomes will be available to rent, though.

$$$$ *AE, MC, V; checks OK; www.rocheharbor.com.* ♿

TRUMPETER INN BED & BREAKFAST
◉◉◉
318 Trumpeter Wy, Friday Harbor / 360/378-3884 or 800/826-7926
Set on an emerald-green lawn and surrounded by meadows, this bucolic spot 1½ miles from Friday Harbor allows for quiet romantic moments in a calming country atmosphere, nationally recognized for its exceptional birding. The cheerful exterior invites you inside to the six attractive guest rooms and two comfortable common areas (the innkeepers stay in a little cottage behind the inn and can be reached by intercom from the comfort of the common areas, if necessary). The rooms boast private baths, fluffy down comforters, pretty linens, views of the garden or meadow, and slippers and plush robes. Our favorite room for a luxurious getaway is the newly redone second-floor Bay Laurel, with its gas fireplace, private deck overlooking the pond, and king-size bed covered with a floral duvet. For a less pricey option, we love the Sage Room (also redone in 2004). It lacks a fireplace and balcony, but the corner location allows in plenty of clear San Juan Island light and views of lawn and pastures. An extra touch we love for romance and repose is the massage room, painted in deep, soothing plum and forest colors. Your hosts will happily arrange individual or couple's massages. When you're done, meander (in your robes) back to your room and collapse into utter relaxation. It's worth noting that this is one of only a few smaller accommodations that offer a wheelchair-accessible room. The friendly innkeepers prepare a delicious breakfast (and can accommodate any preferences); savor pear soufflé, smoked-salmon quiche, or the famous strawberry pancake basket at the dining table, elegantly set with lace, fine china, and silver. On balmy days, eat outside on the deck and enjoy views of the meadow with your meal. The grounds include cobblestone paths with rose-blooming trellis and arbor, and a cement-brick patio covered with flowering pots, along with plantings of lavender, napanthas, and ornamental grasses. Come evening, don't miss taking a dip in the outdoor hot tub, nestled among the lush plantings, surrounded by twinkling lights, and fenced on one side for privacy. Just be sure to turn off the jets for a moment, listen to the night sounds, and gaze at the stars. What a setting for a kiss.
$$$ DIS, MC, V; checks OK; www.trumpeterinn.com. ♿

TUCKER HOUSE BED AND BREAKFAST
◉◉◉
260 B St, Friday Harbor / 360/378-2783 or 800/965-0123
Friday Harbor is bursting with inns and hotels, but many are on the main drag or just off it—right in the thick of summer tourist craziness. Tucker House, built in 1898, is perched on a hill just two blocks south of the ferry landing—the perfect place from which to join all the craziness or to retreat from it when you're ready for some downtime and a leisurely kiss. The seven rooms and two suites in two houses and the three cottages that comprise

Tucker House's property are each named after a quilt-block design and painted in bold or neutral colors to coordinate with the namesake quilt on the bed. All rooms have private baths and TV/VCRs (with a video library in the common area). We have two favorite options for the ideal getaway. The Four Winds Suite, the loftiest room (with the loftiest price), features angled attic ceilings, a king-size bed with down comforter behind French doors, a sitting room with a comfortable couch, a spacious bath with a two-person Jacuzzi tub and separate shower, and a private balcony. Two tall captain's chairs allow you to sit (and kiss!) and see over your rail—if you're not afraid of heights. Among the cottages (where your pets can stay, too), the Goose in the Pond is our favorite and features a queen-size bed, a kitchenette, a woodstove, vaulted sky-lit ceilings, and a private entrance and patio. Breakfast here is simple yet tasty—and delivered to your room at the time you choose (fill out your preference sheet at check-in). A savory, individually baked hot breakfast casserole is accompanied by freshly baked muffins, bagels, granola, yogurt, and fresh fruit; coffee, tea, or hot chocolate and a selection of juices round out the offering. Be sure to take a moment in the parlor to listen to "Rhapsody in Blue" on the 1915 Steinway, retrofitted to be a player piano.
$$–$$$ *MC, V; no checks; www.tuckerhouse.com.*

Romantic Restaurants

DUCK SOUP INN
◖◖◖◖
50 Duck Soup Ln, Friday Harbor / 360/378-4878
Duck Soup Inn is the restaurant of choice for island-going lovebirds. Tucked into the woods, the arbor-fronted, shingled cottage overlooks a tranquil pond, and the wood-paneled dining room with stone fireplace, wooden booths, and high windows is completely charming. Chef-owner Gretchen Allison is committed to an ambitious kitchen using local seafood and seasonal ingredients, and she's succeeded admirably. If savory, fresh Northwest cuisine with a French touch excites your taste buds, you've come to the right place. Start with house-baked bread served with tangy anchovy paste and butter. A small bowl of perfectly seasoned soup, such as creamy tomato-saffron, and a large green salad accompany the ample portions. The menu is made up entirely of house specialties (and changes frequently)—try succulent sautéed prawns in wild blackberry sauce, apple wood–smoked Westcott Bay oysters, or grilled fresh fish. Herbs and edible flowers are grown in a kitchen garden on site. Desserts can be as light as mango sorbet or as indulgent as lemon-coconut cheesecake or pear-almond pie. Whatever

you decide to order, be assured that, from start to finish, every part of your meal will be delicious.

$$ *MC, V; no checks; dinner Wed–Sun (Apr–Oct); closed Nov–Mar; beer and wine; reservations recommended; www.ducksoupinn.com.*

FRONT STREET ALE HOUSE
◐◖

1 Front St, Friday Harbor / 360/378-BEER (2337)
Just about every town in the Northwest has its own brew pub, and Friday Harbor, thankfully, is no exception. While we wouldn't necessarily call this place romantic, the tall, comfortable bar stools, dark-wood tables and floors, long bar of polished wood, mullioned windows, and cheerful crowd of locals and visitors are certainly relaxing—and could definitely encourage at least one kiss. And, after a strenuous day of kayaking or bicycling, the tasty food and abundant beers will hit the spot. Try the Ale House Nachos, smothered with jack and cheddar cheeses, green onions, Roma tomatoes, sour cream, guacamole, salsa, jalapeños, kalamata olives (on request—definitely request them), and house-made Black Bean or Ass-Kicking Chili on top. Burgers are all excellent, and veggie patties can be substituted; traditional Old Country pub grub such as Bangers and Mash is also a solid choice. Beers from the San Juan Brewing Company (the official name of Front Street's brewery) are just what you'd expect from the Northwest—tasty, varied, and fresh. Try the Haro Strait Pale Ale or the Diablo Ale (brewed with chiles to spice things up a bit). If their small-batch Sin City Malt Liquor (named for "outer" islanders' nickname for Friday Harbor) is available, it's a must.

$ *AE, DIS, MC, V; no checks; lunch, dinner every day; full bar; reservations not accepted; www.sanjuanbrewing.com.*

THE PLACE BAR AND GRILL
◐◖

1 Spring St, Friday Harbor / 360/378-8707
You can cruise in here for a quick bite before you catch your ferry, but why not stay awhile? A far better plan is to enjoy a quiet dinner at this waterfront eatery while you watch everyone else rush for the boat. The three walls of windows at this restaurant perched on pilings—the oldest building still standing on the island—give diners excellent views of the ferry terminal and marina. White holiday lights frame each window to add cheer during the dark season, comfortable chairs complement tables set with fresh flowers and thick linen tablecloths and napkins, and light wood paneling softens the room. Locally made art, ranging from amateurish to professional, adds plenty of visual spice. And, best of all, the refined Northwest cuisine is well worth missing a boat or two for. Chef-owner Steven Anderson features a rotating menu of Northwest-eclectic cuisines, focusing on local and regional fish and shellfish, from British Columbia king salmon

to Westcott Bay oysters. Salmon might come with gingery citrus sauce; black bean ravioli could come topped with tiger prawns in a buttery glaze. In summer, crab cakes flavored with ginger and lemongrass are a sure bet. To finish, try the sumptuous crème brûlée or the warm chocolate pudding cake with toffee sauce, made with rich Belgian chocolate—a dream come true for chocolate lovers. A full-service bar, completed in 2002, blends in nicely with the decor and offers plentiful options for romantic libations.

$$ *MC, V; local checks only; dinner every day (Tues–Sat in winter); full bar; reservations recommended.*

ORCAS ISLAND

ROMANTIC HIGHLIGHTS

Horseshoe-shaped Orcas Island offers a breathtaking combination of gorgeous rural scenery, enchanting mountain wilderness, and several charming communities. Eastsound, in the central northern portion of the island, is the largest town and well worth exploring. Whether you're hoping for an intimate dinner, groceries and gas, or boutiques to browse, you'll find it here.

Artists of all types are drawn to these islands because of the natural inspiration to be found everywhere you look. For a pleasant afternoon excursion, explore the artists' studios scattered around the island. Housed in a classic log cabin, **Crow Valley Pottery and Gallery** (on Horseshoe Hwy to Eastsound from Orcas, just before golf course; 360/376-4260; www.crowvalley.com) carries work from more than 70 artists. The abundant variety of local pottery, paintings, jewelry, and sculpture make it easy to find a unique souvenir of your sojourn in this incredible part of the world. In summer, at the **Saturday Farmers Market** (10am–3pm May–Sept), you can meet artisans and browse their wares while stocking up on fresh provisions.

With Mount Constitution as the centerpiece of the incredible **Moran State Park** (800/233-0321), the topography of Orcas is the most dramatic of the islands—and provides many sublime opportunities for outdoor kisses. From the top of Mount Constitution—at 2,409 feet, the highest elevation on the San Juan Islands—the breathtaking view stretches to unbelievable distances. It's a pleasant hike (or an easy drive) to the summit, where a historic stone lookout tower looms well above the treetops. On a clear day, you can see Mount Baker, Mount Rainier, the Olympics, the Cascades, and the Gulf Islands, not to mention the entire San Juan archipelago and the coastal towns across the water. Even though this vantage point is typically swimming in tourists, the unrivaled view is simply not to be missed. On the way up the mountain, you will see a turnout on the right for Cascade Falls. A short, easy hike leads to a fern-lined stream and cascading waterfall. This scene provides a great photo opportunity—and a great setting for a kiss. Moran State Park is 13 miles northeast of the ferry landing. Once you enter the park, look for the 6-mile road to Mount Constitution, clearly marked on the left.

Stop in Eastsound along the way to the park for provisions at **Roses** (382 Prune Alley; store, 360/376-5805; restaurant, 360/376-4292), which recently moved into the old firehouse in town and added a cafe, and still sells gourmet cheeses, fresh breads, Northwest wines, and delicious bakery goods. Or do as the locals do and dine on fresh, organic, free-range delectable local foods in the old fire-truck bay.

A bit of history: The man responsible for Moran State Park was ship-building tycoon Robert Moran. His former mansion is now the focal point of **Rosario Resort & Spa** (see Romantic Lodgings), just west of the park. Even if you don't stay here, you may want to visit for a meal or to tour the **Moran Museum**, which takes up the second floor of the mansion. You can walk through rooms originally used by Moran family members, who built this mansion as their summer residence, and imagine what it must have been like to live here in simpler days. In the summer, a massive pipe organ that fills the music room is played during evening historical presentations, followed by a slide show. (Call the resort for more information.)

Orcas offers all kinds of opportunities for romance on the water. Propelling yourselves in a two-person kayak through the blue waters around the forested islands, for example, is nothing short of remarkable. Eagles and seabirds swoop across the water's surface, and otters and seals dart below. Truly, few outings can compare with watching the world from this vantage point. Happily, the strength of your arms (or lack thereof) has little bearing on the quality of the experience. All kinds of trips are possible, including custom tours, small classes, and—most romantic—guided evening and moonlight kayak tours. There are several kayaking outfitters, but we like **Shearwater Adventures** (360/376-4699; www.shearwaterkayaks.com). Prices start at $49 per person, reservations are required, and tours are available May to September and off-season by arrangement.

Another popular option is to cruise on an engine-propelled boat in search of the beautiful orca whales after which the island is named. Your best chances for spotting one of these magnificent creatures are May through September, with June and July being especially good whale-watching months. The tours on Orcas Island have a wonderful naturalist bent, so even if no whales make an appearance, you will get an expert tour of this region and probably spot porpoises, seals, or bald eagles. Just being out on the water is a wondrous experience, but spotting a pod of orcas gliding along with their massive dorsal fins cutting through the water will take your breath away. **Deer Harbor Charters** (360/376-5989 or 800/544-5758; www.DeerHarbor

Charters.com) leaves from Deer Harbor or Rosario Resort; **Orcas Island Eclipse Charters** (360/376-6566 or 800/376-6566; www.orcasislandwhales.com) departs from the Orcas Ferry Landing. Prices start at about $56 per person, and reservations are required; call for seasonal closures.

Access & Information

The most popular way to reach Orcas Island is via the **Washington State Ferries** (206/464-6400 or 800/843-3779; www.wsdot.wa.gov/ferries/), which run year-round from Anacortes. From Seattle, Anacortes is a little more than an hour and a half north by car. To avoid long ferry lines in summer, leave your car behind; many B&B owners will gladly pick up guests at the ferry dock with prior notification. Another option in summer for those willing to go without a car is the passenger-only **Victoria Clipper** (2701 Alaskan Wy, Seattle; 206/448-5000; www.victoriaclipper.com), which travels daily from downtown Seattle to San Juan Island (you have to catch another boat from there to reach Orcas).

Kenmore Air (425/486-1257 or 800/543-9595; www.kenmoreair.com) schedules five floatplane flights a day during peak season; there are fewer in the off-season. Round-trip flights start at about $170 per person and leave from downtown Seattle at Lake Union and from north Lake Washington. A shuttle is available from Sea-Tac Airport to Lake Union. Luggage is limited by weight. **San Juan Airlines** (206/768-1945 or 800/874-4434; www.sanjuanairlines.com) also flies into the airport on Orcas Island.

Romantic Lodgings

THE ANCHORAGE INN
✿✿✿
249 Bronson Wy, Eastsound / 360/376-8282
Situated on 16 acres of wooded beachfront land, the Anchorage Inn is far removed from civilization; the only human neighbors you'll have here are the other guests and the innkeepers (who built their dream home next door). A gravel road takes you to a two-story brown building that appears austere for a romantic getaway—until you realize that it blends in perfectly with the lightly forested surroundings so that, from the water, it doesn't seem to exist at all. The three suites, designed for maximum privacy (all entrances are from different directions), are simply but comfortably decorated, with hardwood floors and plants; each comes with a private entrance, queen-size bed, gas fireplace, standard bath, CD player, and kitchenette. Our favorite kissworthy treat: the carafe of ruby port. Enjoy your private cedar deck, which looks through the trees to the water and the distant lights of Eastsound. A

short walk from your suite is the two-person hot tub, available to all guests; a lighted path marks the way to its waterfront location (and alerts fellow guests that it's occupied, thus ensuring your privacy while you soak—and kiss), nestled beneath magnificent fir trees. Another nearby path leads down to a secluded pebbled beach—did someone say kiss worthy? Continental breakfast provisions and a selection of snacks are stocked in the kitchens; a tasty dish that's easy to heat (such as crab quiche or baked oatmeal) is delivered to your door in the evening so you can pop it in the microwave at your convenience in the morning. For romantics who prefer quiet, privacy, and plush simplicity, this inn will provide a wonderful refuge.
$$–$$$ *DIS, MC, V; checks OK; www.anchorageonorcas.com.*

BAYSIDE COTTAGES
❂❂❂
65 Willis Ln, Olga / 360/376-4330
Located on 12 acres near the tiny town of Olga, this waterfront hideaway offers several kinds of accommodation, the most romantic of which are two adorable cottages situated close to the owner's home on a hillside that slopes down to the water. The Lummi Cottage feels more like a getaway in the woods, with a classic Northwest frontal view of fir trees framing the water. Cypress is closer to the water, with a bigger deck and more expansive water views. Both have polished wood floors, queen-size beds nestled into alcoves, cozy sitting areas with real wood-burning stoves, and standard baths with pretty pedestal sinks. The tidy kitchens are well equipped with toasters, refrigerators, microwaves, and stoves. A three-minute drive from the main house brings you to the Bayside Cottage, isolated amid trees and right next to the water. Here, you'll have more space (for a slightly higher price), but the cabin's antiquated interior has tiny windows that don't take advantage of the view and make the interior seem a bit dark. Nonetheless, the antique curved-pine ceilings, pine wainscoting, and old-fashioned wood-stove lend charm. A full kitchen, satellite TV/VCR, simple room with queen-size bed, and full bath complete the amenities. The 700-square-foot Barn Loft, located behind the owner's house, is also a good choice. Inside, you'll find vaulted ceilings, wood floors, a large sitting area with two couches and a woodstove, and a full kitchen. The comfortable bedroom has a queen-size sleigh bed and adjacent standard bath. Best of all, the outdoor garden with wooden table is yours alone to enjoy. Other accommodations include the two-room Mount Baker Suite, located on the top floor above the garage of the main house, and several other houses in various locations, including the Wisteria Cottage in Eastsound. The newly renovated Peapod Cottage on 2 acres of waterfront (a larger three-bedroom, three-bath cottage shares the location) promises to add romance to the flock. Bring your own provisions, as breakfast is not included with your stay.
$$$ *MC, V; checks OK; www.orcas1.com.*

CABINS ON THE POINT
◑◑◑◖
Deer Harbor Rd, Eastsound / 360/376-4114
When you see the two Cape Cod cottages perched on the point, you won't be surprised to learn that couples frequently rent them for weeks at a time. Why not? After indulging in a lot of delightful lounging, you can kayak to Skull Island, pick flowers, picnic on the lawn, or take a quick dip in the chilly water. (We prefer a long soak in the waterfront hot tub, nestled beneath three trees: a madrone, a fir, and an old cedar.) For the ultimate in romance, book the Heather Cottage, a cozy, renovated 100-year-old cabin on the bluff. Inside, you'll find one of the nicest sleeping nooks we've ever seen: the queen-size bed is tucked into a windowed alcove overlooking the water, so the fiery sunsets linger right above the tips of your toes. Other features include hardwood floors, comfortable antiques, a slightly rustic full kitchen, and a wood-burning stove. The smaller Primrose is nestled among fir trees farther back from the water, but has charming cedar-planked walls, hardwood floors, a tiny woodstove, and a queen-size bed. The small, fully equipped kitchen has skylights; the separate bathroom has a shower. Located closer to the owner's house, Willow Cottage overlooks the flower garden (and driveway, making it slightly less private). It has two bedrooms, but the well-designed layout remains sufficiently cozy that one romantic couple wouldn't find it too large; the enclosed sun porch has great views of the water. Meals are not included in your stay, so bring your own groceries or journey 15 minutes to Eastsound. Romantic note: elopement and engagement packages are a specialty! Two other retreats operated by the same innkeeper are geared more toward multiple couples traveling together: Highlands House, a private home near Moran State Park with a 30-foot-wide cedar-and-glass living room; and Sunset House, the largest on offer, with beautiful views of the Cascades and neighboring islands.
$$$ *No credit cards; checks OK; www.cabinsonthepoint.com.*

INN ON ORCAS ISLAND
◑◑◑◑
114 Channel Rd, Deer Harbor / 360/376-5227 or 888/886-1661
This spectacular luxury inn is set on 6 acres overlooking an estuary at the top of Deer Harbor. The building is reminiscent of a weather-aged Cape Cod and fits in beautifully with the surroundings. The two antique bronze statues of Dobermans ("Harry" and "Wills") guarding the entrance provide the first hint of the elegance inside. Owners John Gibbs and Jeremy Trumble, who were formerly in the art business, have lined the walls with artwork; well-chosen colors and beautiful furnishings fill the eight rooms in the main house, the carriage house, and the stunning cottage (more on this especially romantic accommodation, below). Expect luxurious amenities such as 300-thread-count sheets and heated floors; rooms also have phones

and data ports (some have TVs). The two beautifully decorated king suites feature slate-tiled fireplaces and jetted tubs in the spacious bathrooms. Although it's the only room without a deck, our favorite is, nonetheless, the upstairs Harvest Suite. Shades of butter cream and sage green warm the room, and the grand wrought-iron bed and marble frieze of cupids on the wall add romance. Of the smaller, less expensive rooms, we like the aptly named Love Nest. For romantic ambience, however, nothing can compete with the superlative, completely private, and pricey Waterside Cottage, adjacent to the main house. It has vaulted ceilings, a slate fireplace with cozy sofa, a wet bar, a private porch, and a jetted tub and double-headed shower in the spacious bath. For guests staying here and in the Carriage House—located above the garage and equipped with full kitchen and cozy gingham couch—the three-course breakfast can be delivered. However, you might want to join other guests in the crimson-painted dining room for breakfast, which includes treats like coffee cake, fresh orange yogurt, and eggs Florentine. Bikes are available to guests, and kayaking and whale trips that leave from Deer Harbor are just a few steps away. For art lovers—and for other kinds of lovers—this is an idyllic spot.

$$$–$$$$ *AE, MC, V; checks OK; www.theinnonorcasisland.com.*

ORCAS HOTEL
❂❂

Orcas ferry landing / 360/376-4300 or 888/672-2792
The stately Orcas Hotel is probably the first thing you will see as the ferry pulls into the Orcas Island landing. "Hotel" is really a misnomer here, since nowadays that term conjures up generic lobbies and identical rooms. Nothing could be further from the truth of this striking Victorian inn trimmed by a white picket fence and enhanced by a flowering English garden. The view of the ferry dock and surroundings from the wraparound windows in the dining room and lounge—and from many of the rooms upstairs—is terrific. Many rooms in this 1904 landmark have been updated with private baths, but four of the twelve still share bathrooms; it was originally built as a boardinghouse. In terms of kiss-inspiring accommodations, we recommend only the two rather luxurious rooms, the Blue Heron and the Killebrew Lake, that have private balconies, whirlpool tubs in the bathrooms, and charming stained-glass windows. (Note that during high season, their high price tag is not exactly a bargain compared with other island accommodations that offer equal privacy and style for less cash.) As for breakfast, you have several options: our preference is to grab a delicious scone and strong coffee at the outstanding bakery downstairs—this is on the house if you're a guest. If it's omelets, pancakes, or other big beginnings that you crave, you pay for the meal and enjoy it in the formal dining room (Sundays only in winter). Since this hotel is located right at the ferry dock, it is affected by the exceptionally heavy tourist and car traffic during the summer. The

downstairs public rooms can get crowded with curious travelers when there is a delay in boarding the ferry.
$$$ *AE, MC, V; no checks; www.orcashotel.com.*

OTTER'S POND BED AND BREAKFAST OF ORCAS ISLAND
❶❶❶

100 Tomihi Rd, Eastsound / 360/376-8844 or 888/893-9680
This is one of the most bird-friendly places we've ever visited—both for lovebirds and for the feathered variety. The backdrop for this two-story country home is the pond, which looks like something out of a Monet painting and is home to hundreds of birds, including lots of red-winged blackbirds. Everything inside the house is contemporary, comfortable, cozy, and immaculately clean, if not wildly stylish—the owners have wisely chosen to let the serene views take center stage. Just off the huge deck overlooking the pond is the hot tub, housed in a pretty Japanese-style cottage complete with shoji screens for privacy. Of the five guest rooms, all of which have private baths and include plush robes, our favorites are the recently completed Goldfinch Room, the Swan Room, and the more moderately priced Chickadee Room. The Goldfinch, which is the newest addition, has a private entrance off the front porch, a king-size bed, a gas fireplace with brick mantel, generous skylights, a classic pedestal sink in the bathroom, and views to the garden out front. The light, airy Swan Room is located upstairs; it has a pretty pond view, a king-size bed, elegant country furnishings, and an extra-long clawfoot tub and double shower in the spacious bath. Due to its location on the main floor off the living room, the Chickadee Room feels less private, but it's as cute as its namesake, with a four-poster queen-size bed, a fluffy down comforter, a pond view, and an antique bathroom complete with authentic fixtures and claw-foot tub. Mornings are busy times here with all the bird life about, so come prepared with earplugs if you don't want to be up with the birds. A sumptuous five-course (!) breakfast will keep you singing all day.
$$–$$$ *DIS, MC, V; no checks; www.otterspond.com.*

THE RESORT AT DEER HARBOR
❶❶❶

31 Jack and Jill Ln, Deer Harbor / 360/376-4420 or 888/376-4480
At press time, Redmond, Washington–based Trendwest Resorts had just acquired The Resort at Deer Harbor to add to its WorldMark brand of condominium resorts. Renovations, including the addition of kitchenettes or full kitchens to each of the 26 units, were scheduled to finish up by the release date of this edition. Considering the abundance of gourmet food options on Orcas, either for take out or home preparation, we think private kitchen facilities will make this secluded spot all the more attractive for a romantic getaway. WorldMark also intends to maintain the charm and

diversity of the many accommodation choices here, including waterfront suites and historic cottages and hillside suites, as well as the delightful shingled deluxe cottages. These cottages, built recently with an eye toward Craftsman simplicity, offer partial to full water views and fresh, clean decor. Best of all, each features not one but two wonderful places to soak together: a hot tub on the deck, perfect for sunsets (but with no privacy), and a two-person jetted tub in the slate-covered bathroom. Romantic three-way fireplaces can be viewed from the king-size bed, tub, or sitting area. Top all this off with a CD player and TV/VCR, and you'll never want to leave. The only downside is that some cottages are close to the road (but in this tranquil hamlet, cars are rare). The historic clapboard cottages, used by apple pickers in the 1930s, are slightly rustic and small but cozy, with pot-bellied stoves and hot tubs on the decks. You'll feel almost as if you're living on your own private island in one of the waterfront suites, two of which feature two bedrooms (all have private hot tubs). Be sure to meander hand in hand around the docks of the Deer Harbor Marina and admire the boats in this beautiful cove. WorldMark condominiums are privately owned, and units are rented exclusively to club members. *$$–$$$$ AE, DIS, MC, V; checks OK; www.deerharbor.com.* &

ROSARIO RESORT & SPA
◖◖◖

1400 Rosario Rd, Rosario / 360/376-2222 or 800/562-8820
Rosario Resort, which has been plagued by management issues, seems to have worked out a lot of kinks in recent years. This gorgeous historic waterfront estate built by early Seattle industrialist Robert Moran is an Orcas Island landmark, but most of the rooms are not nearly as romantic as the setting. The most noteworthy part of the resort is the historic Moran mansion, a sparkling white home with groomed lawns and a luxurious interior. Inside the guest rooms, most of which are located on a hillside behind the mansion, the decor is upscale country. Pale blue, yellow, and cream colors in the striped curtains warm neutral-toned walls, and comfortable furniture and cotton calico-striped quilts combine to make the rooms much homier on the inside than the 1950s motel-style exteriors imply. All rooms have patios and wet bars, and some have deep, jetted tubs. Rooms in the 1100, 1200, and 1300 buildings are located near the water, the mansion, the three pools, and the luxurious spa. If you're willing to pay a lot for luxury, reserve one of the pricey (but lovely) cottages, either Cliff House, located on a short cliff directly over the bay and featuring a gas fireplace, king-size four-poster bed, long private deck, and posh marble bathroom with jetted tub and separate shower; or Round House, formerly the playhouse for the Moran children and now a quaint circular cottage on a little point, featuring a separate sitting room and a kitchenette (as well as sweeping views). Rosario is extremely popular in the summertime, and getting a reservation here can be diffi-

cult, so plan your getaway well in advance. Once you arrive—by seaplane if your budget can support it—check out the restaurants (see Romantic Restaurants), gift shops, kayaking concession, and dive shop. Don't forget to meander the grounds to find the perfect place to kiss—even with all the other guests milling about, Rosario has many private crannies. Above all, don't miss visiting the Moran mansion itself, which houses a museum and music room where you can catch a recital on the grand old organ.
$$$–$$$$ *AE, DC, DIS, MC, V; checks OK; www.rosarioresort.com.*

SPRING BAY INN
❀❀❀❀

464 Spring Bay Trail, Olga / 360/376-5531
Spring Bay Inn continues to live up to the stellar reputation for romance and relaxation it gained upon opening 14 years ago. In fact, we found it to be so spectacular we have a difficult time doing it justice with words. Start with a sea kayak built for two. Add to that a stretch of pristine coastline, early-morning stillness on the water, a friendly and informative guide, and plenty of wildlife. What do you end up with? A morning at Spring Bay Inn. Rain or shine, a kayaking adventure is offered every day at this unique and wonderful wilderness hideaway. (If the morning leaves you hungry for more and you can pass a basic skills test, you may be able to rent a double kayak for the afternoon.) On the off chance there's lightning or high winds (the only truly unsafe kayaking weather), a nature walk through the inn's 57 acres and the adjoining Obstruction Pass State Park is offered, instead. Don't be afraid of hunger during your morning exertions—Spring Bay offers *two* fresh-made breakfasts—outside your room at 7:30am is an extended continental complete with warm fresh-baked scones, cereal, juice, and coffee and tea; after the paddle, a full brunch with smoothies, fruit salad, vegetarian sausage, and a main dish (we had steel-cut oat waffles) is served in the common area. But that's not all: the lodge-style inn fits in perfectly with the towering cedars that surround it. The interior common area has a 14-foot-high exposed-beam ceiling, two river-rock fireplaces, and expansive windows overlooking a glorious scene of fir trees, the bay, a small marsh, and a trail leading to the pebbled beach—where a large hot tub awaits. (Guests can reserve private soaking times in this idyllic spot.) Upstairs, four generous guest rooms feature stylish Northwest simplicity and forest and water views; antique and contemporary furnishings, plush feather beds and down comforters, teeny wood-burning stoves, and tiled private baths with claw-foot tubs and separate showers round out the amenities. The two larger rooms at either end of the house have private decks—excellent for stargazing (and, need we say it, kissing). The main-floor Ranger Suite (the innkeepers are both former park rangers) is the grandest of all, with high ceilings, a pretty glass solarium, a wood-burning fireplace, a queen-size bed, a private entrance, and a small private courtyard with soaking tub with

low-speed jets. Check your e-mail (if you must) with the guest computer—or the inn's WiFi; better yet, serenade your squeeze on the piano or guitar in the common room—the innkeepers' only request: No "Heart and Soul" on the piano; no "Stairway to Heaven" on the guitar. You have to come up a long dirt road to get here, but rarely is a drive so amply rewarded. $$$–$$$$ *DIS, MC, V; checks OK; call for seasonal restrictions; www. springbayinn.com.*

TURTLEBACK FARM INN
✿✿✿

1981 Crow Valley Rd, Eastsound / 360/376-4914 or 800/376-4914
When the colors of the countryside come alive with the glow of daybreak, Turtleback Farm Inn is a delightful place to be. The inn overlooks 80 acres of hills, pastures, ponds, and orchards in the breathtaking Crow Valley. There are rooms in two locations: seven in the beautifully renovated, turn-of-the-20th-century farmhouse and four in the separate two-story Orchard House. The rooms in the farmhouse, all of which have private baths, range from charming to more charming. Less expensive options like the Nook are quite small; the Valley View Room is the most luxurious. Polished fir floors, fir wainscoting, and fluffy comforters full of Turtleback Farm's own cozy lamb's wool endow every room with elegant simplicity, and white muslin curtains and floral duvet covers lend a crisp country touch. Six of the seven baths are outfitted with porcelain and silver antique claw-foot tubs, separate showers, and pedestal sinks—tubs and sinks rescued, after years of romantic service, from the Savoy and Empress Hotels (the Orchard View room has a modern stall shower). The welcome omission of TVs and phones in the rooms guarantees your country getaway will be quiet. In the separate Orchard House, rooms have similar spacious, elegant bathrooms; taupe walls; polished floors; throw rugs; gas fireplaces; king-size beds; and private decks overlooking the orchard. Best of all, breakfast can be delivered in your room via a two-way pantry. Although newer, the house doesn't seem to have much soundproofing; we recommend the two top rooms for this reason. The innkeeper, who has published a cookbook, serves a dazzling breakfast. The view from the window-enclosed dining room is unfailingly lovely; choose your own table and enjoy. $$$ *DIS, MC, V; checks OK; www.turtlebackinn.com.*

Romantic Restaurants

BILBO'S FESTIVO

North Beach Rd, Eastsound / 360/376-4728
In the Northwest, it's a truism that most Mexican restaurants focus on good basic food, generous portions, and a festive atmosphere rather than the white-linen ambience of romance. Well, this popular spot is no exception, but happily, the setting—a small house with generous garden courtyards, mud walls, Mexican tiles, a fireplace, and Navajo and Chimayo weavings—has a good deal of charm. On the outdoor deck, carved wooden benches surround a blazing fire; a foliage-covered lattice conceals the patio from the road. Inside, the stone fireplace and soft lighting provide some romance—although the noisy bustle of the large groups and families who frequent this spot do not. The food is light and mildly spicy, with generous portions. If you order seafood, you'll find it to be remarkably fresh. Choose from among enchiladas, burritos, chiles rellenos, and mesquite-grilled specials. A word to the wise: this is a local favorite, so on busy weekends, call ahead or be prepared to wait. In summer, lunch is served taqueria style, grilled to order, outdoors.
$ *MC, V; local checks only; lunch every day (June–Sept), weekends only (Apr–May), dinner every day; full bar; reservations recommended.*

CAFE OLGA

Olga Junction (11 Point Lawrence Rd), Olga / 360/376-5098
Want to experience island dining the way islanders do? Travel a few miles south of Mount Constitution to this charming, remodeled 1936 strawberry-packing-plant-turned-rustic-cafe, art gallery, and gift boutique. The atmosphere is laid-back and casual, and the food is tasty and eclectic. New owners Beverly Simko and Robert Olmstead have changed the menu quite a bit, with the focus now on local, local, local. Expect halibut cakes and scallop cakes as well as other fresh local seafood, organic greens and veggies, and delectable desserts including lemon shaker pie and tiramisù. Everything is made from scratch—locals and visitors alike will be glad to know that the luscious fresh blackberry pie of old will still be available in late summer. Dining at this leisurely pace, you'll have plenty of time for each other. If you have to wait for a table (which is often the case), browsing in the art gallery is a nice way to pass the time.
$ *MC, V; local checks only; breakfast, lunch every day, dinner every day Jul–Labor Day; closed mid-Dec–Valentine's Day; beer and wine; reservations not necessary.*

CHRISTINA'S
◑◑◑

310 Main St, Eastsound / 360/376-4904
An island destination for 25 years, this heavenly little spot enjoys a terrific perch above Eastsound. Although the renowned Christina herself is no longer always in the kitchen, her unique touch has been carefully passed on to the chef now in charge, and the classic continental fare keeps patrons coming back. King salmon might come with scallops, sorrels, and Jack Daniels cream sauce; the fillet of beef could arrive with a horseradish potato gratin and an apple-shiitake demi-glace. Servings tend toward the generous; appetizers are sized to share or to enjoy as a light meal. The tasteful dining room has a Craftsman feel, with hardwood floors, copper-topped tables and—finally, after all these years—matching chairs, and wildflower arrangements; the effect is island elegant. Christina's is set directly on the waterfront, and views of the mountains surrounding Eastsound's inlet are fantastic, particularly from the sun porch. On pretty summer evenings, the open deck is an alluring alternative for dinner, and the views out here are even better. Local oysters are routinely on the menu.
$$$ *AE, DC, MC, V; checks OK; dinner every day (Thurs–Mon in winter); full bar; reservations recommended; www.christinas.net.*

ISLAND GOURMET
◑◑

188 A St, Eastsound / 360/376-7030
You may be surprised that we've recommended a place with no dining room, but chef-owner Sean Paul's cuisine deserves to be made an exception. Many Orcas Island lodgings have facilities to reheat food—and Island Gourmet offers everything to-go, so you can make your cozy room into a private five-star restaurant. Or, purchase "ready-to-eat" dishes, complete with napkins and flatware, and head out to a park or beach for a romantic picnic. French-trained Sean Paul (formerly of popular Sean Paul's Waterfront Restaurant) prepares new delectable dishes every day, including simple fare such as twice-baked potatoes and vegetarian lasagne, and more complex cuisine—try the beef medallions with raspberry and chipotle reduction or the applewood smoked salmon with sweet-hot pineapple sauce. Don't forget dessert, which can include tangy lemon meringue pie and Floating Islands (meringue islands in a custard sauce). In spring and summer you can build your own picnic basket in the wine-and-gourmet-accoutrements section of the shop, complete with blanket and wine glasses, napkins, flatware, and even fresh flowers—and, of course, a menu fit for a (courting) king.
$ *MC, V; local checks only; open 10am–7pm Mon–Sat (call for seasonal hours); wine.*

ROSARIO'S MANSION DINING ROOM
◖◖◖

1400 Rosario Rd (Rosario Resort & Spa), Rosario / 360/376-2222
A major renovation in 2002 turned the former two restaurants at popular Rosario Resort & Spa (see Romantic Lodgings)—the Compass Room and the Orcas Dining Room—into this current posh restaurant, which has become a romantic celebration destination for islanders and visitors alike. Quiet music, attentive service, and crisp white table linens are the perfect backdrop to gourmet Northwest-inspired food. Take a moment between courses to appreciate the view out large windows looking over Cascade Bay (where resident otters occasionally play) and the mouth of East Sound. Then return to your delectable dinner, which might start off with a baked Camembert with almonds and lingonberries or Caesar salad with house-made parmesan crisps. The main courses, such as sake-and-brown sugar–cured salmon with wild-mushroom butter sauce and horseradish potatoes or roasted Moulard duck breast with dried fruit compote have a Northwest flair and are full of local ingredients and fresh seafood. For dessert, don't miss the apple torte with caramel sauce. Be sure to arrive early enough before your reservation for an intimate cocktail in a polished-leather club chair in the Moran Lounge.
$$$$ *AE, DC, DIS, MC, V; checks OK; breakfast, dinner every day; full bar; reservations recommended; www.rosario.rockresorts.com.*

LOPEZ ISLAND

ROMANTIC HIGHLIGHTS

Lopez Island is among the better known of the San Juan Islands—it's one of the four stops on the ferry run—but when you come here, you still feel as though you've discovered a hidden gem. Miles of rolling farmland, gentle inclines, and pastoral quiet make it an idyllic spot to retreat from the rest of the world and focus on each other. The island is famous for friendly locals. It's also famous for having some of the best and easiest bicycling in all the islands: the mostly level 30-mile circuit is suitable for just about anyone who can balance on two wheels. If you don't bring a bike, rent one from Lopez Bicycle Works (2847 Fisherman Bay Rd; 360/468-2847; www.lopezbicycleworks.com); many bed-and-breakfasts are just a few miles' ride from the ferry terminal. Lopez Village, 4 miles south of the ferry dock on the west shore near Fisherman Bay, is the center of island activity. From mid-May through October, you can also rent kayaks (www.lopezkayaks.com).

For bird lovers, this island is a particularly wonderful spot. Visit the protected tide flats of Fisherman's Bay and narrow Fisherman Spit, accessible from **Bayshore Drive** (park at Otis Perkins Park), where you might spot horned grebes, double-crested cormorants, ducks, plovers, and yellowlegs, among many others. A paved road running down the middle of the spit makes walking and watching easy; keep your eyes open here for brants, snow buntings, and Lapland longspurs. There's beach access at Otis Perkins Park, and you can also dip your feet in the water and explore at Agate County Park. Be sure to bring along a picnic so you can spend all afternoon out. Pick up fixings in town at the **Lopez Village Market** (we recommend the hot chicken baked in Lopez Larry's Barbecue Sauce or San Juan Island Seafood's smoked salmon). Organic goods are available at **Blossom Organic Grocery** across the street, or, if you'd prefer a ready-made picnic, locals will point you in the direction of **Vita's** (360/468-4268), a Mediterranean-style takeout. If it's already lunchtime, eat at **Vortex Juice Bar and Café** (135A Lopez Rd, in the village; 360/468-4740). If you've been exploring all morning and are ready to sit down for lunch, try **The Love Dog** (1 Village Ctr; 360/468-2150), a casual spot for soups and sandwiches.

From Lopez, you can also take an easy day-trip to **Shaw Island**, the smallest, least populated, and least developed of the ferry-served San Juan Islands. The only business establishment on the whole island is a little general store at the ferry terminal. The Franciscan nuns who used to run the store—and the ferry dock—closed their convent in early 2004, turning over operations to a local couple. From the moment you step off the ferry, the utterly tranquil surroundings will make it impossible for you not to slow down and relax. The best way to enjoy Shaw is to pack up a picnic, hop on your bikes, and ride along the rural country roads to your own secluded stretch of shoreline or private meadow. The sunsets here are magnificent. With no distractions save an occasional sighting of a deer or a blue heron, and the continuous chirping of the birds, your day exploring Shaw Island will leave you deeply relaxed and contented (note: your only option for an overnight stay on Shaw are a few state campsites).

There are also plenty of simple romantic pleasures to be had by staying put on Lopez and exploring the village. Split a delicious hot fudge sundae, ice cream soda, or thick milk shake at Lopez Island Pharmacy's new old-fashioned **ice cream parlor** (Lopez Village; 360/468-2644). The ice cream is made on the island by the locally famous Lopez Island Creamery, and the unusual flavors can include cinnamon, mango, and Skor coffee. Stroll hand in hand at the **farmers market** in Lopez Village (10am–2pm Sat, summer only) and pick up handmade scented soaps or local berry jam for souvenirs. If this taste of local farm life leaves you eager for more, explore some of the 55 Lopez Island farms that help create this bounty. The map and brochure available from the **Lopez Community Land Trust** (360/468-3723) provides locations and a list of farms that sell their wares on site. Decorate your lodging with freshly picked bouquets at **Sticks and Stems Floral Gifts and**

Nursery (189 Hummel Lake Rd; 360/468-4377). At **Lopez Vineyard & Winery** (724-B Fisherman Bay Rd; 360/468-3644; www.lopezislandvineyards.com; call for hours), sip Madeleine Angevine or a cabernet-merlot blend in the tasting room, and then pick up a bottle to take home in the gift shop. It's a nice way to end a day of idyllic island exploring.

Access & Information

The most popular way to reach Lopez Island is via the **Washington State Ferries** (206/464-6400 or 800/843-3779; www.wsdot.wa.gov/ferries/), which run year-round from Anacortes. From Seattle, Anacortes is a little more than an hour and a half north by car. To avoid long ferry lines in summer, leave your car behind; with its flat farmland and mild hills, Lopez is the best place in the San Juan Islands for biking. **Kenmore Air** (425/486-1257 or 800/543-9595; www.kenmoreair.com) offers floatplane flights during peak season. Round-trip flights start at about $170 per person and leave from downtown Seattle at Lake Union and from north Lake Washington. A shuttle is available from Sea-Tac Airport to Lake Union.

More information is available from the **Lopez Island Chamber of Commerce** (PO Box 102, Lopez, WA 98261; 360/468-4664; www.lopezisland. com). Contact them in advance for a map of the island, or you can easily find one when you arrive at area lodgings.

Romantic Lodgings

BLUE FJORD CABINS
♥♥❮

Elliott Rd, Lopez Island / 360/468-2749 or 888/633-0401
These remote cabins offer a lovely forested setting near the water and a total escape from everything but each other. Sequestered beneath groves of cedar and fir trees, both chalet-style cabins are simply decorated, filled with light from overhead skylights, and feature open-beam ceilings and exposed cedar log interiors. The Norway cabin, hidden among the cedars, is best for couples who like sleeping in on long, leisurely mornings. The more exposed Sweden cabin catches the morning light—perfect for early risers who can't wait to get out and explore. The plain furnishings and distinctly 1970s color schemes are more than compensated for by the queen-size beds, full kitchens, large decks with forest views, and utter privacy. Near the innkeepers' house, seashells mark the beginning of a five-minute nature-trail walk to a "minifjord" in Jasper Bay. Savor the stillness as you relax (and kiss?) in the private gazebo on the beach, with the stunning view of Mount Baker in the distance. You might also catch a glimpse of your only other

neighbors here (besides the owners): bald eagles, blue herons, and a cluster of sea otters. Since this isn't a bed-and-breakfast, you're on your own for meals. Stock up in Lopez Village before arriving.
$$ *No credit cards; checks OK; www.interisland.net/bluefjord.*

EDENWILD INN
❀❀❀
132 Lopez Rd, Lopez Island / 360/468-3238 or 800/606-0662
This lovely inn is tailor-made for couples seeking a romantic island getaway. Thanks to meticulous attention to detail in the construction, this modern Victorian inn filled with lovely furnishings boasts the worn hardwood floors and antique-style light fixtures associated with the grand residences of earlier eras. However, unlike historic lodgings, which can sometimes offer inconvenience along with their period beauty, this manse offers eight utterly comfortable and spacious bedrooms, all with private baths. Continuing the best-of-both-worlds theme, the house is located in the center of Lopez Village, which means an easy walk to shops and restaurants—but the surrounding lawns, herb garden, wraparound clematis-draped porch, and arbor with antique white roses and wisteria will make you feel as though you're in the country. The rooms are simply but beautifully appointed with antiques, artwork, and beveled-glass windows. Some also include fireplaces and water views. Rooms 5 and 6 are particularly charming, with gorgeous sunset and water views, king-size Victorian sleigh beds, and comfortable sitting areas. While Room 5 is more streamlined, with taupe-colored walls, contemporary art, pounded copper-topped tables, and a bay-window sitting area, Room 6 (the official honeymoon suite) certainly tempted us with its cozy fireplace and claw-foot tub. The casual, self-serve breakfast of freshly brewed coffee, toaster choices, fresh fruits, yogurts, and cereals is available throughout the morning, so wake up whenever you please. Two-person tables in the simply decorated dining room overlooking the brick patio let you enjoy breakfast à deux. Ask the owners about information on the local cab service, which is available to whisk you to the inn from the ferry terminal or the airport if you arrive without wheels (a nice option in summer for avoiding ferry lines).
$$–$$$ *MC, V; checks OK; www.edenwildinn.com.* ᪥

INN AT SWIFTS BAY
❀❀❀❀
856 Port Stanley Rd, Lopez Island / 360/468-3636 or 800/903-9536
This beautiful Tudor home nestled above Swifts Bay is an ideal place to indulge in our three favorite Rs: relaxation, refreshment, and romance. Tucked among cedars, the inn is just minutes from a private beach and boasts a hot tub down a stone path at the edge of the forest. (Reserve a soaking time to ensure total privacy in this wonderful spot.) All five guest

rooms are tastefully appointed with comfortable furnishings. Only three of the five rooms have private baths, but the two rooms that share a bath are beautifully furnished with fine linens and lovely antiques. Romance seekers, however, should definitely head to one of the two attic suites, particularly desirable for their skylights, queen-size beds with goose-down comforters, gas fireplaces, private decks, and private entrances (one has a double-headed shower). If you can manage to leave all of this, sip tea next to the wood-burning fireplace in the richly decorated common room, or lounge in the courtyard for glimpses of wild birds. If the day is rainy, settle in with the portable headphones to watch a movie in the library (choose from more than 400 videos), or exercise in the small workout room, complete with sauna. Morning brings delicious breakfasts that include freshly baked muffins, homemade jams, a savory dish such as frittata, and the inn's secret-blend fresh juice and secret-blend coffee. If you are repeat guests, the owners promise you'll never have the same breakfast twice (unless, that is, you request it). A computerized guest-breakfast tracking system sees to it. How's that for detail-oriented service? You can drive, bike, hike, or get a ride (the innkeepers will arrange this) from your floatplane or ferry. $$–$$$ *MC, V; checks OK; www.swiftsbay.com.*

LOPEZ FARM COTTAGES AND TENT CAMPING
○○○◖
555 Fisherman Bay Rd, Lopez Island / 360/468-3555 or 800/440-3556
Each of the five cottages on this 20-acre farm offers a little oasis of privacy. A gravel road leads to the check-in hut, where you pick up your key, next to the 1907 Craftsman-style farmhouse. Key in hand, stroll the well-lit gravel path to your utterly private retreat nestled among the cedars. The Scandinavian-meets-Northwest cottages are designed strictly for couples—from the two Adirondack chairs placed in front of each unit to the double-headed showers in the bathrooms. All have hardwood floors, classic Craftsman-style furnishings and lighting, kitchenettes, queen-size beds, high ceilings with fans, and plenty of windows and French doors to let in light; yet each has an individual character, with decor in well-chosen colors, such as lavender or coral, and arrangements of fresh flowers. The newest and largest cottage, completed in 2002, features a king-size bed, large tiled bathroom, and private outdoor jetted tub. Guests in the other cottages have access to a jetted hot tub hidden in a cedar grove, surrounded by old barn panels for privacy. The lovely views take in green, tranquil fields punctuated by boulders. There are no telephones and only Cottage Five has a TV, so dim the lights, prop up the pillows, and enjoy the crackling fire. On warm evenings, you can sit outside and watch deer graze in the meadow. A breakfast basket of fruits and baked goods arrives in the early evening for the next morning, so there's no hurry to get up. (Note that if you prefer to camp, the 10 private

sites—with available showers—are among the most romantic we've seen.)
Sometimes, as with this island retreat, romance is pleasingly simple.
$$–$$$ *MC, V; no checks; www.lopezfarmcottages.com.*

MACKAYE HARBOR INN
◖◗

949 MacKaye Harbor Rd, Lopez Island / 360/468-2253 or 888/314-6140
Bikers, kayakers, beachcombers, and amorous travelers alike will find a
relaxing haven in this gracious sea captain's house overlooking MacKaye
Harbor. The tall white home, built in 1927, sits above a sandy, shell-strewn
beach, perfect for sunset strolls or for pushing off in a kayak. Each of the
five cozy guest rooms offers full or partial water views, although only
three rooms in the main house have private bathrooms (these, obviously,
are the best choices for romance). The Harbor Suite features a fireplace;
queen-size bed; and private, covered deck facing the beach in addition to
the private bath. The smaller, blue-and-white-accented Blue Room, with
simple furnishings, boasts almost the same view as the more expensive
Harbor Suite. The Captain's Room, done in a maritime motif, features
a queen-size bed and private bath with shower only; its location off the
main-floor parlor is not the most private, but it does boast a capacious new
private deck looking out over the water. The rooms are comfortable, though
the decor is more practical than beautiful. Adjacent to the main house, the
romantic Carriage House Studio is appointed with white wicker furnishings, Laura Ashley fabrics, a small but modern kitchenette, and a private
bathroom. The large Master Carriage House is geared for larger groups.
Mornings bring an expanded continental breakfast for those in the inn;
Carriage House guests should bring their own supplies. Couples can rent
a two-person kayak and paddle off to sea. Complimentary mountain bikes
are also available for guests' use, and after your hard work, enjoy fresh-
baked cookies in the afternoons.
$$–$$$ *MC, V; checks OK; www.mackayeharborinn.com.*

THREE SEASONS ON LOPEZ
◖◗◗

95 Weeks Rd, Lopez Village / 206/214-8551
Get away from the big city and become a part of island culture in this tiny,
newly constructed Cape Cod–style home just one block outside of Lopez
Village. This miniature, fully-furnished one-bedroom/one-bath home is
move-in ready (even if you do only get to live here for a few romantic nights).
White walls hung with tasteful art prints; cider-colored pine paneling; trim,
pale wood floors; pine pillars; and furniture of wood and neutral fabrics lend
a bright airiness to the cozy space, and a compact glass-windowed gas-log
stove will warm you on chilly island nights—as well as create the perfect
backdrop for a kiss or two. A queen-size bed with feather duvet, a soaking

tub, a TV/VCR, a stereo, and a washer and dryer round out the amenities in this ideal home-away-from-home. Although breakfast is not included, a five-minute hand-in-hand meander will bring you to the center of the quirky, artsy village where you can either shop for groceries to bring back to your barbecue (or your fully stocked kitchen) or simply dine leisurely at one of the multiple eateries—and not have to do the dishes! (Note that in winter, many local restaurants are closed.) Watch the evening wane over the bay from Adirondack chairs on your front porch.

$$ *No credit cards; checks OK; 1 week minimum stay Jul–Aug; www.three seasonsonlopez.com.*

Romantic Restaurants

THE BAY CAFE
◔◔◔
9 Old Post Rd, Lopez Village / 360/468-3700
Spending an evening at the twinkling Bay Cafe is part of any complete trip to this serene isle. Its close-to-the-beach location is spacious and full of windows, and still displays the same rack of Fiestaware plates and rowboat suspended from the ceiling that lent a whimsical feel to its long-ago original location. The spectacular, sweeping sunset view of Fisherman Bay and beyond could alone draw fans. It's a come-as-you-are kind of place—and people do just that. The oft-changing menu could include delicious seafood such as steamed mussels in a spicy Thai green chile–coconut broth, Oregon bay shrimp cakes, or grilled tofu with chickpea-potato cakes (vegetarians have plentiful options here). The daily seasonal fish special could be salmon, halibut, or fresh mahi mahi, and all the satisfying dinners include soup and locally grown green salad. Whatever you do, don't skip dessert. The chocolate gâteau and daily cheesecake—such as white chocolate–ginger—are dreamy.

$$ *AE, DIS, MC, V; checks OK; dinner every day (Thurs–Sat in winter; call for hours); full bar; reservations recommended; www.bay-cafe.com.*

OLYMPIC PENINSULA & LONG BEACH

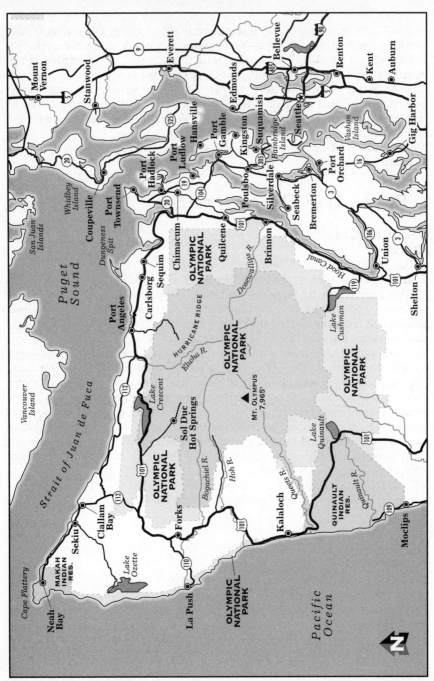

"You are always new. The last of your kisses was ever the sweetest . . ."

—JOHN KEATS

♡ OLYMPIC PENINSULA & LONG BEACH

If you and your sweetheart think one of the last of the western frontiers sounds ideal for your romantic getaway, you won't be disappointed by the vast, rugged, and immensely varied wonders of the Olympic Peninsula. To say this area will make you feel exalted is an understatement. It is a must-see for anyone venturing to the Northwest. Whether your idea of romance is a breathtaking mountaintop vista, the ethereal magic of a rain forest, a jazz concert and dinner at an elegant Italian trattoria, a sparkling lake surrounded by pristine forest, or a dip in the Pacific Ocean, you'll find it here. At the top of Hurricane Ridge at the northern edge of Olympic National Park, snowcapped peaks extend up to seemingly forever; in the forested territory below, old-growth evergreens reach heavenward to mesmerizing heights. Deeper into the woods to the west, the Hoh Rain Forest is a mystical Eden draped in moss and shadows. Farther out, the powerful Pacific Ocean explodes against the western shore of the peninsula. If you are in search of more tranquil scenery, visit Lake Crescent and Lake Quinault, sparkling blue jewels amid the mountains and trees. For small-town pleasures, Port Townsend offers an impressive array of cultural events, restaurants, and historic Victorian architecture.

The rugged geography and remote location of the peninsula mean it's far less crowded than other scenic destinations in the Northwest. If you're hoping to leave the world behind, you'll delight in the splendid isolation of the area, and it would be hard to find any place in Olympic National Park that does not inspire a truly romantic adventure.

Some of the wettest areas in the world are to be found here, just a few miles from the exceptionally sunny lavender fields of Sequim—the Olympic Mountains create a rain shadow. Romance in these parts will likely involve curling up beside a fireplace or under the covers with a cup of hot cocoa after

243

OLYMPIC PENINSULA & LONG BEACH

an invigorating hike or a visit to the windswept beaches of the Pacific. Just take our advice and be sure to bring a rain jacket—any time of year.

The southern coast of Washington is also a romantic draw. Of the many destinations here, the region, known as the Long Beach Peninsula, offers the most alluring escapes for travelers in search of romance. Forested hillsides, beautiful and isolated beaches, and wildlife refuges share space along this magnificent stretch of coastline. (While equally blessed with natural beauty, the northern sections of coast alternate between underdeveloped areas that lack top-notch accommodations and places where overdevelopment and hordes of tourists undercut the romantic mood.)

Crowds flock to the Long Beach Peninsula in July and August, but fortunately, numerous accommodations make it possible to find a private romantic spot even during the high tourist season—you just have to make your reservations well in advance. Those seeking total privacy or making a last-minute getaway, particularly on the coast, will have better luck visiting during the fall or winter, when romantic solitude is easy to come by.

PORT TOWNSEND

ROMANTIC HIGHLIGHTS

Port Townsend, a small town at the northeast corner of the Olympic Peninsula, is easily accessible compared with the rest of this expansive tract of land. Originally settled in the 1800s, the town's authentic and lovingly restored period architecture is its trademark. Beautifully cared-for gingerbread-trimmed Victorian homes are perched on a bluff overlooking the waterfront. Nearby parks—and a quaint main street lined with boutiques, antiques shops, and restaurants—project an aura of charm and tranquility. A favorite weekend getaway for Seattleites escaping hectic urban life, Port Townsend is sweet and slow paced all year long. A walk around the waterfront district and the bluffs above will give you outstanding views of the Olympic Mountains, Admiralty Inlet, and island-dotted Puget Sound.

Stroll along the main thoroughfare downtown, aptly named Water Street (and declared a National Historic District), and take in the beautifully restored buildings, the peekaboo views of the Sound and the islands, and the eclectic medley of antiques stores, art galleries, and gift and craft shops. Indulge in an ice cream or hot chocolate (depending on the weather) at one of the many cafes that dot the street, then visit the harbor, stopping at the edge to savor the sweeping views. If it's a gray day, take in a movie at the lovingly restored **Rose Theatre** (235 Taylor St; 360/385-1089).

Over the years, Port Townsend has earned a reputation as the hub of cultural activity on the Olympic Peninsula, with diverse events scheduled from spring through fall. Contact **Centrum** (360/385-3102 or 800/733-3608; www.centrum.org) for details about the many activities taking place both in Port Townsend and in the surrounding area. For jazz fans, an ideal romantic getaway would be to visit during **Jazz Port Townsend** (late July) or the **Port Townsend Blues and Heritage Festival** (early Aug). The **Wooden Boat Festival** (360/385-3628; www.woodenboat.org; early Sept) has gained international attention and offers both tours and the chance to see boat races. The nearby **Olympic Music Festival** (206/527-8839; www.olympicmusicfestival. org; late June–Labor Day) is another favorite summertime event. For general information about other local events, contact the **Port Townsend Visitor Information Center** (2437 E Sims Wy; 360/385-2722 or 888/ENJOYPT; www. ptchamber.org), or just drop by on your way into town. Whether you choose to enjoy an outdoor concert in a splendid setting, stroll around the picturesque harbor admiring the craftsmanship at the Wooden Boat Festival, or take advantage of the offerings that are here year-round, you're bound to find romance in Port Townsend.

There are parks and then there are parks, but there is only one **Chetzemoka Park**. This ocean-flanked patch of land at the corner of Jackson and Blaine Streets makes an ideal spot for a romantic picnic for two. Stock up at **Aldrich's Market** (940 Lawrence St; 360/385-0500), an authentic general store—but with a few gourmet goodies for modern pioneers. At the park, wander through scattered pines along a cliff with an eagle's-eye view of Admiralty Inlet and Whidbey Island. Thick grass, a children's swing set, a footbridge spanning a babbling brook, and a few well-spaced picnic tables make this picturesque park complete. Take the arbor walk to the gazebo overlooking the water or follow the paths past the gardens and waterfall.

Fort Worden State Park (200 Battery Wy; 360/385-4730) is another great destination. Miles of hiking trails are scattered throughout the 433-acre waterside park, and the turn-of-the-20th-century officers' quarters date back to a time when this area was part of the defense system protecting Puget Sound. Fly a kite in the vast field, go for a leisurely stroll along the beach, explore the deserted concrete bunkers on the hillside above, or head down to the lighthouse at the water's edge. If you time it right, you can also take in a concert, workshop, or festival in the old balloon hangar, now known as the **McCurdy Pavilion** (360/385-3102; www.centrum.org).

If spending so much time looking at the water makes you want to get out on it, consider a three-hour sailing trip aboard a **45-foot racing sloop** (Brisa Charters, 877/412-7472; www.olympus.net/brisa_charters). You can also take a **water taxi**, during the summer months, for either a one-hour tour of the waterfront or a three-hour tour to Indian and Marrowstone Islands (Boat Haven Fuel Dock or Point Hudson Long Dock; 360/379-3258).

Access & Information

You could drive around Puget Sound from Seattle to reach Port Townsend, but the more popular route is via a 35-minute ferry ride from Seattle to Bainbridge Island on **Washington State Ferries** (206/464-6400 or 800/843-3779; www.wsdot.wa.gov/ferries/), followed by a drive across the Agate Pass Bridge, north up the Kitsap Peninsula, and then over the Hood Canal Bridge. Beyond the bridge, head north to Port Townsend. As, of course, with any romantic getaway, it's best not to plan on rushing through here—you'll be on two-lane roads most of the way. Getting here is half the fun. Boats also dock in Port Townsend (from Keystone on Whidbey Island). The largest airline serving the peninsula is Horizon Air (800/547-9308; www.horizonair.com), which lands at Fairchild International Airport in Port Angeles. For general information about local events, contact the **Port Townsend Chamber of Commerce Visitor Information Center** (2437 E Sims Wy, Port Townsend, WA 98368; 360/385-2722 or 888/ENJOYPT; www.ptchamber.org).

Romantic Lodgings

ANN STARRETT BOUTIQUE AND HOTEL
♥♥♥

744 Clay St, Port Townsend / 360/385-3205 or 800/321-0644
Port Townsend's grand past has been beautifully and authentically revived in this ornate 1889 Victorian home set on a scenic bluff that's just a two-minute walk from downtown. A Gothic octagonal tower is the focal point of the mansion, and rich red-and-green-gabled detailing adorns the exterior. Inside, a free-hung, three-tiered circular staircase spirals up the tower. Be sure to stop and gaze at the eight-sided dome ceiling, where frescoes depict the four seasons and the four cardinal virtues. Every aspect of this inn's classic Victorian elegance will embrace you in stunning splendor. All nine guest rooms offer rich color schemes, original period furnishings, antique brass and canopied beds, and lace curtains. Honeymooners have been known to disappear for entire weekends in the grand and private Gable Suite, located at the top of the tower, which offers a king-size bed, skylights, water views, and a two-person soaking tub. All the bathrooms are private, albeit small. Downstairs, the pleasant and cozy first-floor rooms are a bargain, if you don't mind a detached bath in some and no water view in any; they feature exposed-brick walls, snuggly floral down comforters, and the soothing sounds of a burbling fountain in the garden outside. Next door, the Starrett Cottage holds a pair of two-room suites, which, although not quite as grand as those in the main house, are both private and spacious. The Honeymoon Suite, the top-floor cottage unit, is decorated in flamboyant, sumptuous Victorian style, with red walls, chandeliers, a gas fireplace, and

a Jacuzzi tub for two; the more subtly hued ground-floor Garden Suite has a river-rock gas fireplace and antique oak furnishings. It won't be easy to leave these gorgeous rooms, but trust us, the award-winning full gourmet breakfast, served in the elegant dining room of the main house, is worth getting out of bed for. The mansion is open for self-guided tours before guests check in, so be forewarned that the inn can feel like a museum for a few hours during the day.
$$–$$$ *AE, MC, V; checks OK; www.starrettmansion.com.* &

BAY COTTAGE
ⓞⓔ
4346 S Discovery Rd, Port Townsend / 360/385-2035
These two cabins, located about 6 miles from Port Townsend on a bluff at Discovery Bay, are casual, inviting, and full of charm. If you're looking for a homey escape with access to a private sandy beach, this is the place. The cabins, built in the 1930s, have low ceilings and are slightly weathered, but you'll be exceedingly comfortable here amid the handsome, country-style furniture and the sumptuous feather beds. Brass bed frames, claw-foot tubs, and private decks lined with clematis vines add to the charm. The surrounding rose gardens are fragrant, and the views of Discovery Bay and the Olympics are stunning. Both cabins feature full kitchens stocked with snacks and beverages. Meals are up to you, so bring along all the necessities for a light breakfast and perhaps a picnic lunch on the beach (picnic baskets provided) to take advantage of this premium location.
$$ *No credit cards; checks OK; www.baycottagegetaway.com.* &

BIG RED BARN
ⓞⓞⓔ
309 V St, Port Townsend / 360/385-4837
Owners Carol and Todd Eskelin have transformed this 110-year-old barn into a delightful and unusual romantic getaway located just a few houses down from Fort Worden State Park. The completely restored, cozy interior offers not only abundant privacy but also a gas fireplace, luxuriously comfortable bed, TV/VCR, stereo, microwave, toaster, and refrigerator, all in a rustic, uncluttered, fir-paneled setting. One of the romantic highlights here is the wonderful bathroom, which features a Jacuzzi tub for two overlooking a meadow, adjustable lighting, white tiles, fluffy white towels, scrub brushes, candles, bath salts, and fresh flowers. What more could you possibly need for a leisurely soak to put you in a relaxed and romantic mood? A breakfast basket of muffins, bagels or English muffins, fruit, coffee, and tea is set up prior to your arrival, allowing for maximum privacy and flexibility when you start your day. The barn overlooks the meadow behind the property in one direction, and the main house in the other. A porch with Adirondack chairs invites you to linger

outside and listen to the waterfall while you decide whether to stroll over to Fort Worden, down to the lighthouse, or along the beach into downtown Port Townsend—or not to go anywhere at all. Carol is more than happy to enhance special occasions or accommodate special requests. Pet owners will be pleased to know that pets are welcome.
$$ *MC, V; checks OK; www.bigredbarngetaway.com.*

THE CHANTICLEER INN BED AND BREAKFAST
✆✆✆
1208 Franklin St, Port Townsend / 360/385-6239 or 800/858-9421
The Chanticleer Inn changed ownership in 2002 and has a fresh new look as a result. Elegant yet homey, this 1876 Victorian cottage radiates luxury and comfort. Three of the main house's four guest rooms are located upstairs. The refreshingly unfussy Bay View Room boasts a private balcony with sweeping mountain and water views, a private bathroom with shower, and a queen-size sleigh bed. It's the charming Beach Haven Room, however, that stole our hearts. It features a crisp blue-and-yellow color scheme with white wicker cottage furnishings, and a sumptuous bathroom with a Jacuzzi tub—which, unfortunately, is located across the hall. All the rooms have feather beds and down comforters to ensure a luxurious night's rest, and a welcome basket with midnight snacks and bottled water is provided. Guests can choose from a light continental breakfast or a full breakfast served on fine china and crystal. Whether you seclude yourselves in the privacy of your room, enjoy the complimentary afternoon sherry and tea by the fireplace in the bright and elegantly appointed living room, or take advantage of the easy access to downtown attractions, you are sure to enjoy a gracious and relaxing stay.
$$-$$$ *AE, MC, V; checks OK; www.chanticleerinnbb.com.*

HOLLY HILL HOUSE BED AND BREAKFAST
✆✆✆
611 Polk St, Port Townsend / 360/385-5619 or 800/435-1454
This lovely Victorian bed-and-breakfast, located in the heart of Port Townsend's Historic District, has undergone extensive restoration and redecoration in recent years. The delightful result is a peaceful setting perfect for lovers. Surrounded by rose gardens and ancient holly trees, the home boasts a main-floor parlor filled with antiques and warmed by a glowing fireplace. Upstairs, three guest rooms are done up in handsome Victorian appointments. The spacious Colonel's Suite, with its striped navy-blue wallpaper, custom-built headboard, and deep soaking tub, overlooks Admiralty Inlet and the Cascades in the distance. Billie's Room also features a water and mountain view, and has a pretty blue floral duvet, brass lamps, and a shower in the private bath. A queen-size bed, an additional twin bed, and views of the garden are among the charms of Lizette's Room. Behind

the main house, the Carriage House holds two more guest rooms. Skyview's large skylight above the bed allows moonlight to beam in; Morning Glory is also a cozy option. Both Carriage House rooms open to the back patio, where flowerpots and wonderful gardens abound. Tea or lemonade and other treats are served here each afternoon. Be sure to take a look at the Camperdown elm off to one side of the yard; this unique tree actually grows upside down (you will have to see it for yourselves) and produces enough lush foliage to create a private little alcove that's perfect for shady summer kissing. In the morning, a bountiful full breakfast is served on fine china with crystal glassware, silver, and candles at one large table in the sun-filled formal dining room. Home-baked muffins, fresh fruit, and a hot dish such as a baked French toast are served, along with a detailed history of the 1872 home. **$$–$$$** *MC, V; checks OK; www.hollyhillhouse.com.*

HONEY MOON CABIN ON MARROWSTONE ISLAND
🌢🌢🌢

1460 E Marrowstone Rd, Nordland / 360/385-4644
Marrowstone Island, an idyllic spot full of summer homes, is connected to the mainland by a small bridge and is only a 20-minute drive from Port Townsend—but this is one place even most Northwesterners don't know about. Its seclusion and quiet beauty make the Honey Moon Cabin, set in 6 acres of woods, a spectacular romantic destination. The woods are filled with paths to explore, and a short walk reveals a rocky beach with remarkable views of the Olympics and Puget Sound. The cabin itself is essentially one large room, filled with lovely furnishings, attractive antiques, and plenty of cozy comfort. An oak-trimmed gas fireplace warms the sitting area, as does an entertainment center with a selection of movies. Two impressive murals, painted by a local artist, reside high on the cabin's walls beneath a cathedral ceiling, and the beautiful four-poster bed is covered in fluffy, soft, floral linens. Almost as big as the main room, the bathroom has a slate-colored tile floor, glass-block shower, and giant Jacuzzi tub. Outside, the wraparound deck is an excellent spot for barbecuing or simply for savoring the surrounding tranquility. If your idea of a getaway means staying put, you're in luck: the cabin features a full kitchen stocked with all the breakfast fixings you'll need, plus extra goodies like cold beer. There's also a washer/dryer—why not stay here all week? If you do venture out, pedal on a bicycle built for two to Nordland General Store (7180 Flagler Rd; 360-385-0777) to pick up a picnic lunch (we recommend the fresh oysters). You can also rent a kayak or canoe for exploring nearby Mystery Bay. For the mysteries of romance, you're on your own. **$$$** *No credit cards; checks OK; www.marrowstone.com/honeymooncabin.*

JAMES HOUSE BED AND BREAKFAST
◐◐◐◖

1238 Washington St, Port Townsend / 360/385-1238 or 800/385-1238
This striking Queen Anne home, lovingly decorated with re-covered and refinished period pieces and intricate, handcrafted wood moldings, is as Victorian as it gets in Port Townsend. And, since it's set right on the bluff overlooking town, the view is totally unobstructed. Most of the 12 guest rooms have impressive water views, and all have private baths. The elegant Bridal Suite, with its massive antique furnishings and crisp white linens, is the most grand. It features bay windows with unsurpassed water and mountain views, as well as soft lighting, a wood-burning fireplace, and complimentary champagne delivered upon request. Both the Bay and Chintz Rooms also have fabulous views of Admiralty Inlet and Whidbey Island. The Gardener's Cottage behind the main house is another good romantic option, with its private entrance and patio overlooking the gardens and water in the distance. Freshly baked cookies in the afternoon and complimentary sherry are nice extras, but the real treat is the full breakfast. Your morning repast may include fresh scones, baked pear with walnut-fruit filling, and a tasty egg dish. Next door, a modest brick house holds another romantic, albeit more expensive, lodging option called A Bungalow on the Bluff, which is managed by the James House. Because it is separate, guests of the bungalow have the option to take breakfast in the main house or have their meal brought out to them. The bungalow's style and decor is contemporary compared with the James House's Victorian-era setting. It includes a black-and-white color scheme and simple, more modern furniture. The room has a wood-burning fireplace and a picture window overlooking the port and town below; in the spacious slate-tiled bathroom, a corner Jacuzzi tub for two is set beneath a skylight. To be perfectly honest, kissing here is inevitable.
$$ AE, DIS, MC, V; checks OK; www.jameshouse.com.

MORGAN HILL VIEW LOFT
◐◐◖

606 Roosevelt St, Port Townsend / 360/385-2536 or 800/490-9070
The entire top floor of owner Ann Raab's home has been transformed into a romantic perch overlooking Puget Sound. Curl up on the feather bed in the turret's cozy nook and savor the panoramic view of the water. The sloped-ceiling sitting room has an inviting pillow-covered window seat/day bed, a TV/VCR, a sound system, and a kitchenette with a fully stocked breakfast that encourages you to start your day privately and at your leisure. Decorated in muted colors and an array of textures, the overall effect is contemporary, unfussy, and immensely soothing. You'll feel on top of the world here—and you're just a few minutes up the road from downtown and the lovely Chetzemoka Park. The Puget Passion package includes deluxe towels, books for romantic inspiration, and a massage mat with massage

videos and customized scented massage oil. With or without these extras, this is indeed an elegant getaway. When the windows are open, you can hear foghorns and seals; binoculars are provided for those who like to check out the passing ships or the seabirds. Ann is happy to suggest activities and outings, and will give directions to a romantic and little-known bluff perched on the edge of the sea. Rent her two available mopeds and follow Ann's "Kissing Tour" map for fun and adventure. A charming, though definitely less romantic, cottage next door accommodates families.
$$–$$$ *No credit cards; checks OK; www.morganhillgetaways.com.*

OLD CONSULATE INN/HASTINGS HOUSE
✿✿✿✿

313 Walker St, Port Townsend / 360/385-6753 or 800/300-6753
If pampering yourselves with modern creature comforts in the atmosphere of a bygone era is a combination that appeals, the Old Consulate Inn is exactly right for you. This venerable red Victorian inn boasts a fireplace-warmed parlor complete with antique organ and grand piano, a reading nook in the front parlor, and a billiards and game room in the basement. Tea (lemonade on sunny days) and cookies are served in the afternoon in the handsome, spacious floral dining room with water views, and liqueurs and desserts await in the evening. Elegant period antiques abound. Up the grand oak staircase you'll find eight private rooms, each with its own bath. Cozy alcoves, turret lookouts, canopied king-size beds, and expansive views of the waterfront are among the amenities offered here. Especially alluring (and more expensive) is the Master Anniversary Suite, with its antique wood-burning fireplace and four-poster canopied bed. The lacy Tower Honeymoon Suite is also one of our favorites, with water views from the bed and a claw-foot tub in the bedchamber. Enjoy a romantic soak in the glassed-in outdoor hot tub, which is set in a gazebo overlooking the bay. In the morning, the inn proudly presents its own blend of designer coffee along with a three-course, seven-dish breakfast served banquet-style, which includes fresh fruits, hot breads, gourmet egg dishes, and granolas. Savor the relaxed luxury of the Victorian era while you are here—you will have to return to the real world soon enough.
$$–$$$ *MC, V; checks OK; www.oldconsulateinn.com.*

RAVENSCROFT INN BED AND BREAKFAST
✿✿✿✿

533 Quincy St, Port Townsend / 360/385-2784 or 800/782-2691
The stately, Southern-style architecture of Ravenscroft sets it apart from the other—mostly Victorian—bed-and-breakfasts found in the Historic District of Port Townsend. This clapboard house with white trim and a long, gracious porch offers a welcome change. Inside, the entire inn is carpeted, creating a quieter environment than do the hardwood floors of many other

inns. Furnishings are a casual mix of wicker and antiques, and each room has individual character and style. All eight guest rooms, with immaculate, attractive baths, unlimited privacy, and room to spare, are delightful. Many have French doors that open onto a veranda with views of the bay and mountains; some have spacious sitting areas, four-poster beds, and decorative brick fireplaces. The least expensive accommodations, which instantly won our hearts, are the three secluded garden-level rooms, which feature exposed-brick walls and floral linens. Two rooms have nonfunctioning fireplaces; all three offer a cozy and affordable option for lovers on a budget. At the high end, the Admiralty Suite is a wonderful romantic splurge. Decorated in whimsical blue and yellow, this choice unit has a gas fireplace, a soaking tub, and a fabulous six-foot window seat overlooking the water and distant mountains. The Mount Rainier Suite offers a bay view, a gas fireplace, and a soaking tub for two, while the Fireside Room has a queen-size bed, a wood-burning fireplace, and French doors leading to the expansive veranda. Breakfast may include such delectable treats as frappés made from frozen berries, bananas, and yogurt; egg blossoms (a lavish creation featuring hollandaise sauce and phyllo dough); or pumpkin-apple waffles with pecan-caramel sauce. What a sumptuous way to start the day! Self-serve beverages are available all day long.

$$–$$$ *MC, V; checks OK; www.ravenscroftinn.com.*

Romantic Restaurants

FINS COASTAL CUISINE
◐⟨

1019 Water St, Port Townsend / 360/379-3474
This recent addition to the dining options of Port Townsend, on the second floor of a mall, has a spare and somewhat sterile interior, but boasts a charming terrace overlooking the water and islands beyond. With its intriguing menu, friendly staff, and second-to-none view, this is a delightful place for lunch on a sunny day. The lentil soup, with a sprinkling of fried leeks, is elegantly presented and utterly delicious. The well-prepared lamb burger on a ciabatta roll is a nice change from standard burger fare, and the crab cakes are abundantly flavorful. The specialty here is a clam chowder that's made to order with local clams and fresh seafood. There are several extravagant dessert options, along with a nice selection of microbrews. At dinner, the ambience remains fairly informal, but at a candlelit table overlooking the water, with fine food and wine—and the right companion, of course—you are sure to enjoy a casually romantic evening.

$$ *AE, DIS, MC, V; checks OK; lunch, dinner every day; full bar; reservations recommended; www.finscoastalcuisine.com.*

THE FOUNTAIN CAFÉ
ᴏ𝄢

920 Washington St, Port Townsend / 360/385-1364
If we awarded ratings of stars or chef's hats, the Fountain's consistently excellent food and pleasant service would easily earn the highest number of hats (or stars). To earn an equally high lip rating, however, other criteria must be met. Although we *oohed* and *aahed* with pleasure during our meal, the super-casual Fountain Cafe's tiny, dimly lit dining room is usually packed with people; and the green walls, along with closely arranged tables draped with funky tablecloths and topped with little bouquets and candles, make it feel more like a coffeehouse than a nice restaurant. But don't come here for the ambience—come for the creative, delectable food. You can't go wrong with seafood here—it is always fresh. You might want to start with Penn Cove mussels steamed with saffron, fresh herbs, and tomato, then move on to the locally smoked salmon, topped with a cream sauce and a hint of Scotch, garnished with caviar, and served with fettuccine. For dessert, try the warm homemade gingerbread cake on a bed of custard. For couples who like to romance their taste buds as well as each other, this spot is well worth a visit.
$$ *MC, V; checks OK; breakfast Sat–Sun, lunch, dinner every day; beer and wine; no reservations.*

LANZA'S RISTORANTE
ᴏᴏ𝄢

1020 Lawrence St, Port Townsend / 360/379-1900
Italian restaurants have a reputation for being a little noisy, but even on busy weekends Lanza's is always intimate and romantic. This could be due to the kitchen's location, hidden behind a thick oak door inset with stained glass, or to the subdued lighting and cozy booths. Painted gray and with one wall of exposed brick, Lanza's interior is reminiscent of a New Orleans jazz club. Live music Friday and Saturday nights reinforces this impression, but rest assured that the music is soothing rather than raucous, and the atmosphere is excellent for romance. As for the food, we recommend one of the fabulous pasta dishes, such as the *pollo bolognese* with chicken, prosciutto, and provolone in a marsala cream sauce. Seafood lovers can't go wrong with the Seafood Lorraine: scallops, clams, mussels, and shrimp tossed in a pesto wine sauce with tomatoes and green onions. If you feel like indulging in dessert (you are on vacation, after all), share a serving of Lanza's rich and decadent tiramisù.
$ *MC, V; checks OK; dinner Mon–Sat; beer and wine; reservations recommended; www.olympus.net/lanzas/.*

MANRESA CASTLE RESTAURANT AND LOUNGE
🌑🌑

7th and Sheridan Sts, Port Townsend / 360/385-5750 or 800/732-1281
Manresa Castle is one of Port Townsend's most recognizable landmarks. Proudly roosting on a hill overlooking town, this impressive building was built in 1892 to resemble a Prussian castle. From the 1920s until the 1960s, Jesuit priests used the castle as a training college, but since 1968 it has been operated as an inn and restaurant. Although the inn does not offer the most romantic accommodations in town, the restaurant and lounge are loaded with kiss-worthy ambience. The stately cocktail lounge is an irresistible setting for a romantic interlude, and next to it the inviting dining room has tall, lace-covered windows, soft lighting, and handsome wood furniture. The Swiss-German chef here has put together an inventive international menu, including a popular bacon-wrapped filet mignon and curry chicken Casimir. The excellent Sunday brunch makes for an exceptionally elegant start to the day.
$$–$$$ AE, DC, DIS, MC, V; checks OK; dinner every day (May–Oct), Wed–Mon (Oct–May), brunch Sun; full bar; reservations recommended; www. manresacastle.com.

SILVERWATER CAFÉ
🌑◖

237 Taylor St, Port Townsend / 360/385-6448
Although the casual ambience at this little cafe couldn't be called exceptionally romantic, the food and service here are so good that it merits a visit. Local artwork and brick walls lend character to the dining room, as do the high ceiling, numerous hanging plants, hardwood floors, and unadorned wood tables. Everything here is made from scratch, and the menu's range is surprisingly wide: The lemon baked brie with sautéed mushrooms and red onions is perfect for a light lunch, and the seafood is consistently fresh and fabulous. One especially inventive and wonderful dish is the Oysters Bleu: fresh oysters, bacon, and spinach in a light blue cheese sauce, presented on fresh black pepper linguine. It may be lacking in traditional romantic ambience, but after a beautiful day by the water, this is a distinctly warm and inviting spot to settle in for a tasty meal.
$$ MC, V; checks OK; lunch, dinner every day; full bar; reservations recommended.

T'S
🌑🌑🌑

2320 Washington St, Port Townsend / 360/385-0700
Formerly Lonny's, new owners Nancy and Gary Tocatlian have retained the relaxed elegance and Mediterranean ambience of this local favorite. The interior is warm and welcoming, and the food is outstanding. Tawny stucco

walls; soft lighting; a crackling fire; and tables and booths set with crisp white linens, olive oil, and flowers help set the mood for a memorable evening. Signature specials include applewood bacon–wrapped king salmon and rack of lamb served with horseradish and new potatoes. Fresh organic produce, free-range chicken, and local seafood enhance the menu, and the service matches the flawless presentations. The refined setting, distinctive and well-executed menu, and top-quality service make this a perfect choice for a special night out.

$$–$$$ *AE, MC, V; checks OK; lunch Mon–Sat, dinner Mon–Sun; beer and wine; reservations recommended; www.ts-restaurant.com.*

THE WILD COHO
♥♥

1044 Lawrence St, Port Townsend / 360/379-1030
Though not the fanciest spot in town, this bright little gem located a few blocks above Port Townsend's downtown manages to create a romantic atmosphere through careful attention to detail and a warm and intimate setting. The award-winning chef takes his food and ingredients very seriously, and it shows—whether you order the crab cakes, the polenta soufflé with mushrooms, or the salmon in sweet potato crust served with green onion butter and tomato relish. For dessert, the warm chocolate cake with handmade crème-fraîche ice cream and marionberry sauce is a sublime way to end the evening. Votive candles in miniature lanterns adorn the 12 tables, and the service is professional and friendly—all making this a special place for a romantic evening.

$$$ *MC, V; checks OK; dinner Wed–Sun; beer and wine; reservations recommended; www.thewildcoho.com.* &

OLYMPIC NATIONAL PARK, PORT ANGELES & LAKE CRESCENT

ROMANTIC HIGHLIGHTS

Whether you aim to be swept off your feet by the breathtaking mountain vistas at Hurricane Ridge or to savor the beautiful views from the shores of Lake Crescent; whether you want to set off on adventurous hikes or to visit boutique wineries, this area has it all—in abundance.

Although Port Angeles used to be more of a stopover point than a destination, a new crop of lodgings and restaurants is changing all that, and staying here is more worthwhile than ever before. The city can still be said to lack romantic atmosphere, but it's beginning to make the most of its prime location—including one of the most accessible entrances to Olympic National Park and a plum spot on the Strait of Juan de Fuca. Sequim, just east of Port Angeles and in the rain shadow of the Olympic Mountains, can boast of getting more sunshine than anywhere else in the region, making it the ideal destination when you need to count on an escape from the rain. Farther west, the sparkling blue jewel of Lake Crescent nestles among steep forested hills and offers all manner of water activities.

The spectacular **Olympic National Park** (for details, go to the visitor center at 600 E Park Ave, Port Angeles; 360/565-3130; www.olympic. national-park.com) is perhaps the biggest romantic draw on the peninsula, and doing justice to its incredible natural beauty in one paragraph is impossible. For romantic accommodations, unless you plan to camp, you're likely to stay in Port Angeles or Sequim, or on Lake Crescent.

The obvious place to begin is at the viewpoint on **Hurricane Ridge**, a drive up into the mountains to an elevation of 5,200 feet. On a clear day, the views of the park's trademark jagged peaks are simply breathtaking. If it's warm, hike out on one of the trails and enjoy a sunny picnic in a wildflower-filled meadow. Or, in winter, take a free guided snowshoe tour. Be sure to walk the short paved loop trail to savor the view of Vancouver Island and the Strait of Juan de Fuca. Although you won't be alone here, the views are worth the crowd, and you can lose much of the crowd, anyway, if you hike a little way out. Plan ahead and bring a picnic.

To avoid the crowds entirely, drive to **Deer Park**, southeast of Port Angeles in Olympic National Park (from Hwy 101, turn south at the sign for Deer Park; it's at the end of a 17-mile drive). However, this recommendation comes with a warning: the countless switchbacks and sharp turns on this mostly unpaved road can be downright hair-raising. Rest assured, however, that there's a payoff at the end: on a clear day, an enthralling view deep into the heart of the Olympics. And because of the road conditions, you are likely to find yourselves quite alone with the purple mountain majesty.

Twenty miles west of Port Angeles, enveloped by mountains and sky, **Lake Crescent** is Olympic National Park's deepest lake. This distinction makes it an enticing destination, and a sunny day here wreaks havoc with both your senses and your emotions. The drive around the lake is a monumental treat (unless you're inclined to car sickness—there are lots of curves). Access to the lake is limited to just a few areas: the small East Beach, which is usually crowded on summer days; some boat launches; and the shore fronting the **Lake Crescent Lodge** (see Romantic Lodgings). You can take an easy hike along the Spruce Railroad Trail, which hugs the northern side of the lake. If you don't mind a steep climb, hike up the Storm King Trail for a bird's-eye view of the lake in all its splendor; if you do mind, take the short, flat stroll through the forest to lovely Marymere Falls. Begin at the visitor center near Lake Crescent Lodge on the southern side of the lake.

While the park and Lake Crescent are the area's best-known destinations, consider opting for some less rugged activities around **Sequim**, where (remember?) the sun is likely to be shining. Walk along the **Dungeness Spit**, the longest natural sand spit in the United States and a refuge for birds, and enjoy the exceptional views. It's a 5½-mile walk along the narrow beach to the lighthouse at the end. Sequim, with all its sunlight, is the lavender capital of the region, so consider a drive into the hills above town to visit the **Cedarbrook Herb & Lavender Farm** (1345 S Sequim Ave; 360/683-7733; www.cedarbrookherbfarm.com), where lunch, dinner, and afternoon tea are served at the on-site cafe. Or indulge in some wine tasting at the scenic **Lost Mountain Winery** (3174 Lost Mountain Rd; 360/683-5229; www.lost mountain.com).

For a fun day-trip, hop the ferry (an hour and a half each way) across the strait and go for a stroll and high tea in **Victoria**, British Columbia.

Access & Information

Visitors coming from Seattle will find it easiest to reach this part of the peninsula by taking the 35-minute car ferry from Seattle to Bainbridge Island on **Washington State Ferries** (206/464-6400 or 800/843-3779; www.wsdot. wa.gov/ferries/). From there, cross the Agate Pass Bridge and drive north up the Kitsap Peninsula and over the Hood Canal Bridge. Beyond the bridge, two-lane Highway 101 makes a big loop around Olympic National Park and passes through Sequim, Port Angeles, and Lake Crescent. Another option is to arrive in Port Angeles by boat from Victoria, British Columbia, with the **MV Coho**, operated by Black Ball Transportation (360/457-4491; Feb–Dec twice daily, Jan one trip daily), or via the much-quicker **Victoria Clipper** (360/452-8088 or 800/633-1589; www.victoriaclipper.com), a foot-passenger ferry that runs two times daily in summer, and once daily in fall and winter. In summer, **Royal Victoria Tours** (888/381-1800; www.royaltours.ca) offers guided bus trips to Victoria and Butchart Gardens. Small planes land at airports in Bremerton, Jefferson County, Shelton, Sequim, and Port Angeles. The largest airline serving the peninsula is Horizon Air (800/547-9308; www.horizonair.com), which lands at Fairchild International Airport in Port Angeles. Average temperatures on the Olympic Peninsula range from 45 degrees F in January to 72 degrees F in August. Rainfall averages 2 to 3 inches per month, less in Sequim, and more—up to 121 inches annually—in Forks. For information on visiting the area, contact the **Port Townsend Chamber of Commerce Visitor Information Center** (2437 E Sims Wy; 360/385-2722 or 888/ENJOYPT; www.ptchamber.org) or the **North Olympic Peninsula Visitor & Convention Bureau** (360/452-8552 or 800/942-4042; www.northwest secretplaces.com/vcb/) in Port Angeles. The Olympic Peninsula's rainy winter weather may be nature's way of keeping visitors from overwhelming this exquisite area, so be a good sport—and bring some rain gear.

Romantic Lodgings

A HIDDEN HAVEN
◐◐

1428 Dan Kelly Rd, Port Angeles / 360/452-2719 or 877/418-0938
This bed-and-breakfast's big draw is its bucolic setting: the main house faces a lovely pond, with a footbridge leading out to a gazebo. The soothing rush of water from a waterfall can be heard nearby, and the light-filled grounds are tucked away among the tall trees outside Port Angeles. Although you'll feel as though you're a million miles away from it all, the convenience of easy access to Port Angeles, Lake Crescent, and Olympic National Park makes this a wonderful point of departure for exploring the area. Two room options cater specifically to romance. Our favorite room, in the main house, is the soft pink-and-green Garden Suite, which features a luminous sitting room with a vaulted ceiling and tall windows overlooking the pond, skylights, a big-screen television (DVDs available), and a Jacuzzi tub for two. If privacy is your greatest desire or if you plan a longer stay, ask about the two cottages, each of which offers a Jacuzzi for two (one is heart-shaped!), private deck, kitchen, living room, TV, fireplace, gas grill, and washer/dryer. The pond draws all kinds of wildlife and makes for excellent bird-watching. Brought to your room, a hearty country breakfast of eggs, hash browns, bacon, and fruit will get your day off to a delicious start.
$$$ MC, V; no checks; www.ahiddenhaven.com.

COLETTE'S BED AND BREAKFAST
◐◐◐◐

339 Finn Hall Rd, Port Angeles / 360/457-9197 or 877/457-9777
Colette's caters exclusively to readers of this book—that is, couples seeking a romantic getaway. Perched on a bluff overlooking the Strait of Juan de Fuca, with views of the passing ships and the twinkling lights of Victoria in the distance, the five deluxe rooms in this immaculate and well-groomed setting all offer water views. Specifically designed to afford maximum privacy, each room has a small private sitting area outside from which to enjoy the view. Owners Lynda and Peter Clark have gone out of their way to anticipate every need—and then some—of their guests. With remote-control fireplaces; thick robes; a vast collection of DVDs, videotapes, music, and upscale magazines to choose from; chocolates, fresh-baked cookies, and baskets of fruit awaiting guests upon arrival; Jacuzzi tubs for two; and birding books and binoculars, you'll lack for nothing here. In fact, the most compelling reason to leave the privacy of your room is to indulge in the multicourse breakfast, whose sumptuous options may include omelets with smoked salmon, Dungeness crab, bay shrimp, and dill; pumpkin waffles with apple cider syrup; strawberry champagne soup; a citrus medley with vanilla bean sauce; and lavender scones. You are also welcome to join other

guests for wine and cheese in the evening or to sit at the outdoor fireplace at sunset. Romantic packages for special occasions feature red roses, chocolate desserts, champagne, chocolate-covered strawberries by the bed, small gifts, and a card. And, if all this isn't enough for your very special someone, in-room fireside massages can also be arranged.

$$$ MC, V; checks OK; www.colettes.com.

DOMAINE MADELEINE
❤️❤️❤️

146 Wildflower Ln, Port Angeles / 360/457-4174 or 888/811-8376

Domaine Madeleine is recognized as one of the first bed-and-breakfasts in the area to cater specifically to lovebird couples. Longtime proprietor Jeri Weinhold upholds the B&B's romantic focus by going the distance to meet guests' requests of anniversary cakes, bedside chocolates, and fireside massages. She's a font of information—always ready to recommend romantic walks and hikes or local restaurants. With all this attention to romance, it's strange that the decor doesn't mesh with the overriding theme. The "East meets West" mélange of oriental scrolls and souvenirs, antique perfume bottles, and floral bedspreads clutter the spaces. It all seems outdated and too much. If you can put the excess aside, come to Domaine Madeleine for the views and the breakfast. The Ming Suite has a spectacular view of the Strait of Juan de Fuca and a vast private balcony; plus it has a fireplace and Jacuzzi tub for two. The Renoir Suite on the first floor shares the same view and boasts a large sitting room with a basalt fireplace, as well as a two-person shower. Separate from the house is the Rendezvous Room and The Cottage— both with kitchenettes. The Cottage's greenhouse-like sitting area looks out onto the private garden, offering a lovely serene and peaceful morning view. Domaine Madeleine's multicourse breakfast is an impressive and delectable experience. Enjoy the bread and cheese course and try one of the perfect chocolate-filled croissants, but save room for the main course. We delighted in tiger prawns with dill and puréed fennel over smoked marlin and a sweet potato purée side. And what is breakfast without dessert? Crepes suzette was the finale. Morning socializers will enjoy the experience of chatting with other guests, and hearing the owner's suggestions as she hovers nearby during the meal. Stretch your limbs following the dining extravaganza with a stroll through the several intimate garden areas, including one with a waterfall, pond, and bamboo bridge—or walk the groomed lawn hand in hand with your sweetheart while admiring the expansive horizon.

$$$ AE, MC, V; checks OK; www.domainemadeleine.com.

FIVE SEASUNS BED & BREAKFAST

1006 S Lincoln St, Port Angeles / 360/452-8248 or 800/708-0777
Surrounded by gardens, this Dutch Colonial home is a welcome addition to
the short list of romantic accommodations located in central Port Angeles.
The grand white house with its large porch and pillars will draw you into
the inviting living room, where antiques, built-in glass shelves, and a fireplace await. The five guest rooms (all with private baths) are named after
the Dutch words for the seasons—Indian summer is the fifth season—and
are decorated accordingly. The most romantic rooms are those with private
baths: Zoner (summer) features warm floral wallpaper and bedding, fine
antiques, a fireplace, and a jetted tub. Herfst (autumn) has a soaking tub,
hardwood floors, and a golden color scheme—and it sits above the rose
garden, from which fresh scents waft up to your room. By far the grandest
room, Winter (spelled the same in both languages) welcomes you with deep
red and green bedding, rugs, and curtains. A brass bed with white linen
creates a lovely contrast to the holiday colors. This room includes a small
dressing room and a separate sitting room with comfortable wicker furniture. Lente (spring) is furnished with white wicker and has a tub and shower
combination. Breakfast is a gourmet feast of Dutch babies with fresh fruit,
smoked salmon frittata, and custard and apples baked in a cinnamon pastry.
After you've eaten, stroll along the covered walkway or relax near the
property's soothing waterfall and goldfish pond.
$$–$$$ *AE, DIS, MC, V; checks OK; www.seasuns.com.*

LAKE CRESCENT LODGE

416 Lake Crescent Rd, Port Angeles / 360/928-3211
Lake Crescent Lodge rests on the bank of its enormous blue namesake, and
from your somewhat rustic cabin—heated by a woodstove or a stone fireplace—you can view this glassy stretch of water as it curves around forested
mountains that ascend magnificently in the distance. Breathe deeply in the
fragrant air that permeates this epic landscape. By far the most romantic
accommodations at the lodge are the Roosevelt Fireplace Cottages (no. 38, at
the far end, offers the most privacy). Ignore the lackluster decor, build a fire
in the wood-burning fireplace, and savor the splendid view from your plum
location at the water's edge. If a Roosevelt Cottage is not available, consider
a Singer Tavern Cottage. These cottages are lined up close to one another
near the main lodge, and foot traffic passes between them and the lake, but
the peach walls, hardwood floors, and plain interiors make for adequate
accommodations. Other options include budget-friendly motel-like units
and rooms on the second floor of the lodge—though these are less private
than the cottages and aren't exactly made for romance. The main lodge's
historic wood-paneled great room is cozy and has an inviting fireplace. The

old-fashioned glassed-in sun porch overlooking the water is a lovely place to sip a glass of wine and savor the darkening lake and mountain silhouettes at sunset (see Romantic Restaurants). The handsome historic property, reasonable rates, and proximity to the lake all make this one of the most romantic destinations in the area. Whether you use the lodge as a base camp for Olympic National Park, take a picnic lunch out on one of the available rowboats, or simply lounge by the lake in an Adirondack chair, the perfect location certainly makes this a good place to call home for a few nights. **$$–$$$** *AE, DC, DIS, MC, V; no checks; Nov–Apr only Roosevelt Cottages available (weekends only); www.lakecrescentlodge.com.*

LOST MOUNTAIN LODGE
🟋🟋🟋

303 Sunny View Dr, Sequim / 360/683-2431
Surrounded by 6 acres of sunny meadows and cottage gardens, this secluded bed-and-breakfast, opened in 2001, offers three spacious and refined suites. With amenities like vaulted ceilings, large floor plans, wood-burning fireplaces, king-size beds, down comforters, TV/VCRs, and comfortable sitting areas, this contemporary lodging makes for a very appealing getaway. The Creekside Suite features a luxurious bathroom with a double steam shower, soaking tub, fireplace, private deck overlooking the pond, high ceilings, and enough space to do yoga. Draw a bath, light a few candles (provided) and a fire in the fireplace, add some lavender crystals (also provided) to the water, and savor the view from the tub. The Moonbeam Suite's vaulted-ceiling skylights allow you to gaze at the moon from the comfort of your own bed. In the Sunnyview Suite, a window seat offers a lovely view over the mountains. The decor throughout is tasteful, soothing, and refreshingly unfussy. The owners, who are happy to help you plan your visit around the area, make you feel at home: sparkling cider, crackers, and crab dip are brought to your room shortly after your arrival, and hors d'oeuvres, wine, lattes, and dessert are served in the evenings. The plentiful and delicious breakfast of muffins, bagels, seasonal fruit, yogurt, juice, and coffee is assembled in a basket, and you choose whether you'd prefer to savor it in the privacy of your room, outside by the pond, or in one of the nearby meadows. This offers great flexibility for outdoor enthusiasts who want to head out early and for honeymooners who don't want to appear for breakfast at a set hour. A stargazing dip in the hydrotherapy spa is a romantic treat after you return from dinner in town. Check the Web site for special romance packages. **$$$** *MC, V; checks OK; www.lostmountainlodge.com.* ⅖

TUDOR INN
◕◕

1108 S Oak St, Port Angeles / 360/452-3138
The Tudor Inn is a good place to rest your weary bones after a day of hiking in Olympic National Park or exploring nearby Lake Crescent. Owner since 2001, Betsy Reed-Schultz has re-created a bit of the Old World in this historic Tudor home set in a residential neighborhood. Of the five accommodations here, the Country Room holds particular romantic interest, with its cathedral ceiling, pastoral mural, fireplace, and French doors that open to a private balcony with views of the Olympics in the distance. The Tudor Room, appointed with peach walls, dark woodwork, and a four-poster bed, features a down comforter and antique lace bedspread. The remaining three rooms are on the snug side, but each has a private bath, and their rates are quite affordable. The lovely main floor, filled with intricate European antiques, provides several comfortable places to relax; we especially like the living room, with its grand piano, white-stone fireplace, and plush red velvet couch. A bountiful three-course breakfast is served family-style in the formal dining room.
$$ *AE, DIS, MC, V; checks OK; www.tudorinn.com.*

Romantic Restaurants

BELLA ITALIA
◕◖

118 E 1st St, Port Angeles / 360/457-5442
Local institution Bella Italia is painted in sunny, warm colors, with an inviting bar, a pleasantly bustling dining room, and charismatic staff—this restaurant is an excellent romantic choice. A 2002 winner of the *Wine Spectator* "best wine list" award, the restaurant offers you a choice of more than 450 wines. With its renewed emphasis on using fresh, local ingredients, Bella Italia is well-positioned to attract foodies, as well. A combination of reasonably priced classics—chicken saltimbocca, pizzas, pastas, flank steak, duck, tiramisù—and a menu of daily specials featuring the catch of the day make this a tasty option after a day of hiking. Settle in to one of the candlelit booths, soak up the convivial atmosphere, and savor the fine flavors.
$$ *AE, DIS, MC, V; local checks only; dinner every day; beer and wine; reservations recommended; www.bellaitaliapa.com.*

C'EST SI BON
◕◕◕

23 Cedar Park Dr, Port Angeles / 360/452-8888
C'est Si Bon is at the tip of every local's tongue when they're asked to recommend a romantic spot for an evening meal. The bright turquoise, pink, and

purple exterior is slightly garish, but inside, the ambience is wonderfully elegant. A massive crystal chandelier hanging from the vaulted ceiling casts a warm glow upon rich fuchsia walls. Upholstered chairs provide comfortable seating, and silk flower arrangements are placed around the room and on every linen-covered table. The effect is grand, but the room becomes most lovely after the sun sets and the lights dim. A table by the window is best—you'll look out upon either rose gardens, fountains, or the flower-lined brick patio. Michéle Juhasz, chef and owner with her husband Norbert, prepares each entrée personally, so on busy weekend nights the wait can be lengthy; however, it's worth it. Try the tender and savory Cornish game hen with mushroom stuffing and rich brown sauce, or the delicious filet mignon with crabmeat in a rich cream sauce. If you are chocolate fans, do not miss the sumptuous chocolate mousse. Service fluctuates between eccentric and entertaining, and can be slightly intrusive, especially if you are enjoying a quiet tête-à-tête. Still, overall, the name says it all.
$$$ *AE, DIS, MC, V; checks OK; dinner Tues–Sun; full bar; reservations recommended; www.cestsibon-frenchcuisine.com.*

LAKE CRESCENT LODGE

416 Lake Crescent Rd, Port Angeles / 360/928-3211
Although this historic lodge's restaurant is rather spare, it's worth stopping here for a meal just for an excuse to linger over the incredible view. Breakfasts are abundant—French toast, pancakes, a flavorful medley of omelets—and lunches offer a good range of standard burgers, salads, and a wickedly creamy clam chowder. If you come for dinner, try to arrive before dark in order to enjoy the magnificent lakeside view. The dining room is casual and not especially romantic, but it does have character, and the food is a definite step up from standard hotel-restaurant fare. Seafood is the specialty, and you might enjoy halibut with risotto or delicate salmon encrusted in a potato pancake. Manager Bill Ahler knows his wines, and the wine list offers a carefully selected blend of local and regional specialties. The warm marionberry cobbler makes for a perfect finale.
$$–$$$ *AE, DC, DIS, MC, V; no checks; breakfast, lunch, dinner every day; closed Nov–Apr; full bar; reservations recommended; www.lakecrescent lodge.com.* ♿

TOGA'S

122 W Lauridsen Blvd, Port Angeles / 360/452-1952
With a name like Toga's, you might expect a sheet-clad staff or at least a Greek menu, but you won't find either at this excellent little eatery. Toga's (named after the young, entrepreneurial chef) is a modestly adorned, family-managed establishment boasting the most creative menu in town.

If only the overhead lights in the dining room were dimmed after dark, the small brass lamps and cream tablecloths would succeed in creating an intimate mood. European sauces and techniques are combined with fresh local ingredients to produce rich, inventive dishes, such as baked prawns stuffed with crab and topped by Jarlsberg and Gruyère cheeses, and broiled salmon and scallops served with a mustard-dill beurre blanc. A house specialty is "Jägerstein," in which the wait staff brings to your table an extremely hot stone on which you prepare your meat or seafood. The concept is similar to fondue, except that you use the stone to cook the food instead of a pot of hot liquid. Desserts are decadent, so bring a hearty appetite—you won't want to skip the famous Black Forest cake.

$$$ *AE, DIS, MC, V; checks OK; dinner Tues–Sat; call for seasonal closures; beer and wine; reservations recommended.*

HOH RAIN FOREST, WESTERN BEACHES & LAKE QUINAULT

ROMANTIC HIGHLIGHTS

If you really want to get away from it all, and we mean it all, there are few places as remote as the western and southern portions of the Olympic Peninsula. This is the place to come for an outstanding diversity of natural beauty—from majestic forests to ethereally beautiful beaches to sparkling glacier-carved lakes nestled among dense evergreens. Although the area gets plenty of visitors in the summer, many claim they love it best in fall and winter, when the crowds thin to a trickle and whoever's left can claim the glorious landscapes all for themselves. The weather can be fierce, but with the right person along, retreating to the coziness of your room after a day of braving the elements can be downright heavenly.

Just about everything you'll want to see is off Highway 101, which makes a loop around Olympic National Park. Allow extra time to get anywhere, as this is a two-lane road, not a major freeway. Once you leave 101, you'll find yourself on some narrow winding roads to the beaches or up into the forest.

For long, meandering strolls, visit the wide, windswept beaches between **Ruby Beach** and Kalaloch. Ruby Beach is accessible via a well-maintained trail. This pebbly stretch of coastline is graced with majestic sea stacks jutting up from the ocean. The beach is named for the rosy sand, which contains tiny garnets. Comb the beach for sand dollars, watch the gulls coasting above, listen to the pounding of the waves on the shore, and savor the robust landscape. What could be more romantic? Buy a kite at the **Kalaloch Lodge** gift shop (see Romantic Lodgings) and fly it on the beach, or build a bonfire, make s'mores, and watch a world-class sunset over the Pacific Ocean. Afterward, warm up with hot chocolate at Kalaloch Lodge.

To experience the raw power of the ocean, head to **Third Beach**, near La Push. Watching waves crash into the rocks here is a humbling experience. Two miles of coastline enclose the surf-pounded beach, where hidden caves and rock formations await exploration. To get here, follow the signs on Highway 101 to La Push. There is only one road that goes south of La Push along the coast; follow it 2 miles to the small sign that says "Third Beach" and an unmarked parking area at the trailhead. A three-quarter-mile walk on a forest path leads to the beach. Be very careful of the tides, as you could get trapped around a point or headland during an incoming tide. Know when the tides occur (buy a tide table or check the newspaper). Mere guesswork could get you in trouble.

The **Hoh Rain Forest** is a must-see, and the Visitor Center here will help you find the best romantic walk for your skill and energy levels (Hwy 101; 18 miles east of the highway, south of Forks; 360/374-6925). This majestic, ethereal forest demonstrates what Mother Nature can do with an abundance of moisture to thrive on (150 inches of rain annually). Every inch, including decaying trees, is covered with moss, lichens, mushrooms, ferns, and sorrel. You will also see some of the largest spruce, fir, and cedar trees in the world. Some are 300 feet tall and 23 feet around. Silence surrounds you as all traces of sky disappear under the canopy of moss-covered trees. On a rare sunny day, streams of light penetrate the thick foliage in a golden, misty haze. Don't miss the chance to share a kiss behind the curtains of moss. And since you simply can't avoid the moisture that oozes from the ground, be sure to wear waterproof shoes.

An entirely different landscape, with an abundance of its own romantic options, awaits you at **Lake Quinault** (off Hwy 101), a glacier-carved lake surrounded by cathedral-like firs. Rent a canoe, rowboat, or seacycle at **Lake Quinault Lodge** (see Romantic Lodgings). If you're staying there, ask the lodge to prepare a picnic basket for you, and head off in search of a secluded inlet. Or put together a picnic at the mercantile across the street from the lodge and hike in the majestic rain forest. As the southwest gateway to Olympic National Park, the Quinault Valley is the ideal point of departure for hikes up to scenic alpine meadows, small lakes, and ice-carved peaks; less-athletic types will be glad to know that there are several easy trails, including one to Campbell Grove with its enormous old-growth trees. The **ranger station** (on the lake's south shore; 360/288-2444) provides information on more strenuous hikes up the North Fork of the Quinault River, or to **Enchanted Valley**. The lodge also provides a list of hiking options, levels of difficulty, and things you're likely to see along each one. If a hike sounds too ambitious, drive around the lake, which takes about an hour and a half and offers magnificent bird's-eye views, as well as a glimpse of the biggest trees in the Northwest. Afterward, relax with a glass of wine in front of the fireplace at the lodge.

Access & Information

Lake Quinault is best accessed by car; the drive from Port Angeles takes a little over three hours. At the inland apex of the Quinault Indian Reservation, the lake is usually the first or the last stop on Highway 101's scenic loop around the peninsula's Olympic National Park and Forest.

Romantic Lodgings

EAGLE POINT INN
🌀🌀🌀

384 Stormin' Norman Ln, Beaver / 360/327-3236
Cradled on 5 acres in a bend of the Sol Duc River, this spacious log lodge is one of the most romantic places to stay in the area. Designed by Chris and Dan Christensen to perfectly combine comfort and style, the inn's three rooms also afford guests a great deal of privacy. The two elegantly rustic downstairs rooms have old-fashioned log-cabin walls and queen-size beds covered with thick down comforters. The exceptionally elegant wood-paneled baths feature elevated claw-foot tubs, from which you can admire the farmlands beyond as you soak, and stacks of thick white towels to wrap yourselves in when you climb out. The open, two-story common living quarters house Chris's collection of kerosene lamps and other interesting antiques, but leave plenty of room for guests to spread out in front of the fireplace, which is made of rocks from the Sol Duc River. The Christensens live nearby in what was the original lodge, and the generous breakfast is served family-style in the dining room.
$$ *No credit cards; checks OK; www.eaglepointinn.com.*

KALALOCH LODGE
🌀🌀

157151 Hwy 101, Kalaloch / 360/962-2271
The Pacific Ocean is in Kalaloch's front yard—and it's the primary reason to come here. During low tide, take a long, sandy hike along the shore, accompanied by seagulls drifting overhead. At high tide, you will hear the roar of the ocean surf. An overnight stay in one of the eclectic assortment of accommodations at this lodge will allow you to enjoy all the phases of the tides. The main lodge has 9 adequate rooms and a mediocre ocean-side restaurant (moderately priced breakfast, lunch, and dinner are served daily). Farther down is a motel unit with less than romantic rooms stacked tightly together.

On a bluff overlooking the ocean are the primo accommodations—20 cabins with views of the magnificent seascape. An additional 24 cabins are available, set back from the bluff and view. Several of the cabins have wood-burning fireplaces—having a roaring fire adds a bit of life to the merely hotel-standard decor and the sparsely equipped kitchens. Regardless of the Spartan quarters, the setting truly is magical. If you plan to spend most of your time outdoors, you probably won't mind the less-than-inspiring interiors. In the evening, after dinner, light a fire, turn the lights down low, and cuddle the night away. Note that due to its remote location, Kalaloch Lodge occasionally experiences power outages. Candlelight may be romantic, but the loss of your refrigerator, stove, and hot water is not.
$$–$$$ *AE, MC, V; checks OK; www.visitkalaloch.com.*

LAKE QUINAULT LODGE
🖤🖤

345 S Shore Rd, Lake Quinault / 360/288-2900 or 800/562-6672
Set in the heart of the Olympic Rain Forest, this grand cedar-shingled lodge overlooks serene Lake Quinault. A massive brick fireplace warms the lobby, and windows face the lake beyond a manicured front lawn edged by rhododendrons and hydrangeas. Add to this quiet setting a variety of intriguing hikes nearby and the opportunity for a lake cruise just before sunset, and the result is an incredible Northwest getaway. Originally built in 1924, then destroyed by fire in 1925 and rebuilt in 1926, Lake Quinault Lodge has seen many visitors in its day. Unfortunately, the lodge has also seen better days. Recent remodeling efforts included new carpeting, bedspreads, and curtains, but the overall effect is a confusion of rustic wood-paneled walls, wood and wicker furniture, odd lamps, and brass beds. The rooms that seem the most pulled together are the pastel-appointed Lakeside Units, but they are located in a separate, more motel-like building, so the lodge feeling is totally lost. Consider a rustic little room in the main lodge so you can at least appreciate the history and authenticity of the place. And if you're focused on the natural wonders of the area, and on your sweetheart, you should find it easy enough to forgive the decor. The range of amenities—heated indoor pool, saunas, massage service, boat rentals—combined with the gorgeous setting, make for a very comfortable stay. And then there is the restaurant—one of the best in the area—that offers a spectacular lake view and candlelight dinners (see Romantic Restaurants). Be sure to alert the staff if it's a special occasion; they can place wine and treats in your room ahead of time.
$$–$$$ *AE, DC, MC, V; checks OK; www.visitlakequinault.com.* ♿

LAKE QUINAULT RESORT
📍☕

314 N Shore Rd, Amanda Park / 360/288-2362 or 800/650-2362
New owners, Jonathan Hawkins and family, bought Lake Quinault Resort in 2003 and are in the process of making plenty of changes. While the 600 feet of waterfront along Lake Quinault remains a prize feature of this intimate establishment, changes include face-lifts to the original nine rooms' sterile, standard appearance and additions of two cottages, due to be finished in fall 2005. Five of the rooms offer full kitchens, while all share a wide deck overflowing with flower-filled planters, wisteria, and Adirondack chairs. On the grounds, there are many secluded outdoor spots—the gazebo just above the beach is especially inviting—from which to sit and savor the view. The Hawkinses carry on the original owners' tradition of inviting guests to campfires and stargazing on the beach in the evenings, including a bit of guitar playing. This is a pleasant option if you are seeking a quiet and secluded alternative to the massive and bustling lodge across the lake.
$$–$$$ *AE, DIS, MC, V; checks OK; www.lakequinault.com.* ♿

MILLER TREE INN
📍

654 E Division St, Forks / 360/374-6806
Romantic accommodations can be hard to come by in this area, but this pretty white house located on the edge of Forks offers a range of comfortably romance-inspiring rooms. While the older rooms feature nicely appointed, if simple, decor with floral wallpaper, lace curtains, and basic amenities, the two newer deluxe suites at the back of the house are the most romantic rooms by far. Very private and quiet, each of these crisp, contemporary suites offers views of the surrounding farmlands, an exceptionally comfortable king-size bed, a gas fireplace, a Jacuzzi tub for two, a TV/VCR, and a love seat. An abundant breakfast is served in the communal dining room in the morning, where guests can compare notes on their discoveries in the area. We hear the sumptuous gingerbread pancakes are truly magnificent, and, along with breakfast, the pleasant owners can provide detailed information about hikes. With the Hoh Rain Forest only 45 minutes away and the famous Olympic beaches a mere 20 minutes down the road, this is a snug retreat from which to explore this rugged portion of the Olympic Peninsula.
$$–$$$ *DIS, MC, V; checks OK; www.millertreeinn.com.*

Romantic Restaurants

LAKE QUINAULT LODGE
◐◐

345 S Shore Rd, Lake Quinault / 360/288-2900 or 800/562-6672
This restaurant is one of the best bets in the area and a great chance to visit the historic lodge if you are staying elsewhere. Enjoy a hearty breakfast and the gorgeous lake view as you savor your coffee and plan your day, or stop in for lunch. If you intend to come for dinner, ask about going on a predinner boat ride. At the very least, have a drink in front of the grand stone fireplace in the main lodge before moving into the dining room—very romantic. The dining room is vast, so ask for a table by the window to better savor the view, especially at dusk when the lights begin to sparkle around the edge of the lake. In a candlelit setting with crisp white linens, you are sure to enjoy a special evening in this unique setting. The menu offers a respectable selection of Northwest regional cuisine with an emphasis on seafood. The cedar-plank salmon is the specialty, and the halibut is very good. Share an order of berry cobbler for a very cozy way to end the evening.
$$–$$$ AE, MC, V; checks OK; breakfast, lunch, dinner every day; full bar; reservations recommended; www.visitlakequinault.com.

RIVER'S EDGE
◐◑

41 Main St, La Push / 360/374-5777
Location, location, location. This first business venture of the Quileute Native American tribe in La Push opened in 2002 and is off to an exciting start. Perched on the banks of the Hoh River right where it opens onto the majestic Pacific Ocean, River's Edge enjoys a gorgeous location in the old boat-launch building, complete with high ceilings and soaring windows facing the water, exposed beams, and sepia-toned photos of the Quileute tribe in earlier days. With its cheerful young staff, this restaurant is a surprisingly hip, cosmopolitan find on the edge of the peninsula. The kitchen offers a catch of the day that can't get much fresher, with a choice of baked potato, fries, or mashed potatoes. The rest of the dinner menu is simple, and the lunch menu offers a range of sandwiches and other standard fare. Note that no alcohol is served, though you are welcome to bring your own beer or wine. Though very informal and not especially romantic in the traditional sense of the word, River's Edge offers a world-class setting and hearty fare in an area with few dining options.
$$ MC, V; local checks only; breakfast, lunch, dinner every day; no alcohol; reservations not necessary. &

LONG BEACH PENINSULA

ROMANTIC HIGHLIGHTS

With 28 miles of accessible sand beaches, a number of beautiful parks and gardens, and some of the most intimate small-town restaurants in the Northwest, the Long Beach Peninsula is nothing short of a marvelous coastal destination—as long as you know when and where to visit. Although numerous developments and a long succession of shops, motels, and gas stations line the Pacific Highway, you can find parts of this area that are still surprisingly pristine. During the summer, however, crowds can be overwhelming—especially if it's a quiet retreat you're seeking. In July or August, the key to a successful intimate getaway is finding an idyllic spot and staying put. Fortunately, you'll find plenty of extremely romantic lodging options, some of which are even quickly becoming Washington's most sought-after sites for tying the knot. Another alternative is to visit during the quiet winter season and cozy up before a fire and a picture window to watch the fury of the storms along the coast. Above all, it's the natural beauty of the remote areas here that will inspire kisses.

A crown jewel among coastal Northwest parks, **Leadbetter Point State Park** is set at the northern end of the Long Beach Peninsula (3 miles north of Oysterville, on Stackpole Rd). The route to the park involves a peaceful drive through a canopy of leafy trees—a nice lead-up to the park itself, which is, simply, sublime. The two of you can wander hand in hand all day without running into another soul, so bring a picnic and a warm blanket and enjoy the vast expanse of sand flanked by stretches of dune grass, lupine, and wild strawberry. Your only neighbors will be the great blue herons, brown pelicans, bald eagles, and seals who call the place home. (In spring, aggressive black flies can create an unforeseen kissing obstacle.) This park is known as a great place to bird-watch in the spring and fall, but beach trails are flooded with deep water during the rainy season (Oct–May). On the drive back to your lodgings—there are none in the remote area around the park—stop in **Oysterville**, a picture-postcard of a tiny 19th-century sea town, listed as a Historic District on the National Register of Historic Places. **Oysterville Sea Farms** (1st and Clark; 360/665-6585 or 800/CRANBERRY) is the only industry here and sells the marvelous fresh oysters promised by the town's name—along with other goodies such as rich chocolate fudge.

On the southern end of the peninsula, explore the 3-mile scenic loop that begins at the town of **Ilwaco**. (In Ilwaco, you'll see signs for the loop.) From the parking lot for the North Head Lighthouse, a short walk along a pretty wooded trail ends in an astounding view of both the Pacific Ocean and the entire Long Beach Peninsula. Be it high noon or sunset, views from this vantage point—with the picturesque, century-old lighthouse in

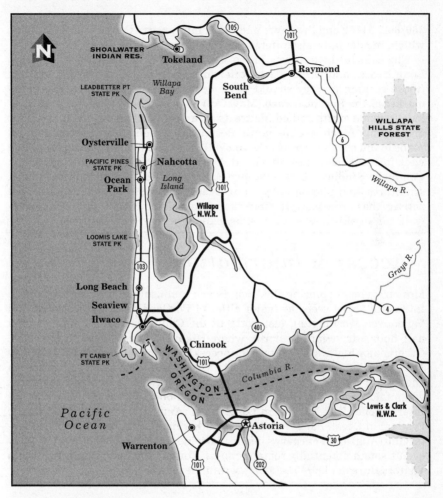

the background—are sure to inspire a kiss. For a small fee, you can climb to the top of the lighthouse and take a short tour. Continue driving south along the loop, pass through an entrance to the U.S. Coast Guard Station, and look for the path that leads to Cape Disappointment Lighthouse. The hike up is a bit steep, but you'll be glad you made the effort when you take in the view from this historic lighthouse, which has been guiding sailors into the Columbia River's entrance since 1856. Other highlights along the loop include **Cape Disappointment State Park** (formerly Fort Canby State Park), with its 16 miles of hiking trails (2½ miles south of Ilwaco off Hwy 101; 360/642-3078)—here you will also find Benson Beach, which affords a view of both lighthouses; the **Ilwaco Heritage Museum** (115 SE Lake St;

360/642-3446); and the **Lewis and Clark Interpretive Center** (360/642-3029), which, incidentally, also offers a wonderful view of the Columbia River.

The colorful little towns lining the Pacific Highway—Ilwaco, Seaview, Long Beach, and Ocean Park—offer lots of opportunities for exploration (those seeking privacy should steer clear during summer). The **Saturday market** at the Port of Ilwaco (May–Oct) is an excellent place to browse for locally made crafts and edible treats. **Seaview** offers some lovely spots for an intimate lunch (see Romantic Restaurants), and since it seems that all roads in town lead to the beach, you will undoubtedly find yourselves drawn west to stroll the dunes afterward. You can also check out the arts scene; **Campiche Studios** (101 Pacific Ave S; 360/642-2264) features watercolors, sculptures, and photography. Long Beach, the center of peninsula tourist activity, has crowded gift shops, amusement arcades, and a beach boardwalk for an old-time beach-holiday experience.

Access & Information

Most travelers exploring the Long Beach Peninsula by car approach from Interstate 5. Between the major cities of Portland and Seattle, you'll find Vancouver, Washington, just north of the Columbia River. Longview is a half-hour's drive farther north, where Highway 4 turns west to the coast. Other major highways that provide access to the region include US Highway 101 (to the south this runs to Astoria, Oregon; to the north, it connects via Highway 4 to Interstate 5). Unless you find festivals particularly romantic, you might want to work around the region's busiest weekends, such as the International Kite Festival in Long Beach (Aug), and the Northwest Garlic Festival in Ocean Park (June). On the other hand, Jazz and Oysters in Oysterville (Aug) and February's peninsula-wide Old Fashioned Valentine's Day events sound potentially romantic to us. Contact the **Long Beach Peninsula Visitors Bureau** (800/451-2542; www.funbeach.com) for details.

Romantic Lodgings

BLACKWOOD BEACH COTTAGES
🌼🌼🌼
20711 Pacific Wy, Ocean Park / 360/665-6356 or 888/376-6356
Romantic seclusion is a snap at these charming oceanfront cottages overlooking swaying beach grasses and sand dunes. After a warm welcome from the hosts—and a quick browse through the fine wines and hand-selected gifts at the on-site store—retire to your cottage for all the privacy you desire. The RV park right next door tends to be busy during the summer, but inside your pleasant retreat, you probably won't notice. Each spacious and taste-

fully appointed cottage has a comfortable living room with a gas fireplace, a fully equipped kitchen, and a bedroom and bath. For the most spectacular views of the glowing sunsets, choose from among the five oceanfront cottages: Spinnaker, with a cheerful pine interior; Beachcomber, tastefully decorated in floral prints and indigo; Mystic, with a color scheme of sunny yellow and blue; Klipsan Queen, which features vintage 1920s decor; and Sandbar, done in deep green with wicker furnishings. Three other recently built cottages offer woodland views only, but are still a stone's throw from the beach; Amanita, with soothing, rosy sand-colored walls and a luxurious bed with a dramatic carved headboard, is an excellent choice. In all the cottages, flowers, gourmet chocolates, and romantic music stashed next to CD players are thoughtful touches. The kitchens are stocked with coffee, hot cocoa, and tea, and guests are welcome to fresh herbs or vegetables from the owner's garden—but breakfast is not provided, so bring your own provisions. If your idea of vacation means never setting foot in a grocery store, you can order a specialty food basket from the owner. After so much privacy and tranquility, returning home will be harder than you think. $$–$$$ *MC, V; checks OK; www.blackwoodbeachcottages.com.*

BOREAS BED & BREAKFAST INN
🌑🌑🌑
607 N Ocean Beach Blvd, Long Beach / 360/642-8069 or 888/642-8069
Just as Boreas, the god of the north wind, brought clear weather to the Greeks, this bed-and-breakfast bearing his name will make clouds of stress disappear for amorous couples. The home is tightly tucked between other houses, but this will be forgiven once you see the spectacular coastal setting and the lovely interior—including a marble fireplace and baby grand piano in the living room. Choose from five gracious guest rooms, three of which have ocean views. The Dunes Suite is bright and airy, with a sage, rose, and cream color scheme and an Impressionist-style mural of the North Head Lighthouse, a regional landmark; the spacious, pretty bathroom features a luxurious jetted tub. One of our favorite picks for a weekend of relaxation and romance is the main-floor Garden Suite, which boasts French doors opening onto a private deck with views of the dunes—only a five-minute walk away. Upstairs, both the Pacifica and the Stargazer Suites have simply spectacular views of the ocean, while the smaller Hideaway Suite has a cozy, garret-style charm. All five rooms have private baths. The delicious breakfast served family-style at the dining room table might include omelets filled with wild mushrooms and smoked salmon, ginger pancakes with lime sauce, or French toast topped with Grand Marnier and almonds, along with organic coffee, hot chocolate, or one of dozens of teas. Don't forget to sign up for your time in the state-of-the art spa located in an enclosed cedar and glass gazebo in the dunes—it's reserved for one couple at a time, so you can

cherish your sunset soak in supreme privacy, with the gentle rustle of beach grass as a heavenly soundtrack.

$$$ *AE, DC, MC, V; checks OK; www.boreasinn.com.*

CASWELL'S ON THE BAY BED & BREAKFAST INN
◐◐◐◖

25204 Sandridge Rd, Ocean Park / 360/665-6535 or 888/553-2319
This stately Queen Anne Victorian–style house, recently built on 3 acres at the edge of Willapa Bay, has a top-notch reputation for romance—and deserves every bit of it. Surrounded by flower gardens and sweeping water views, the gleaming yellow house is close to attractions but well-removed from traffic and noise. You'll find it bright and airy inside, with high ceilings and excellent soundproofing. The five guest rooms, all with private baths and pleasant sitting areas, are located on the second floor. Two offer wonderful views of the bay, and the other three overlook the garden. Hand-carved antique bedroom sets and down comforters in the bedrooms, and soaps and lotions produced specially for Caswell's, along with deluxe sheets and towels in the baths, all add up to the feeling that you're making a luxurious getaway, indeed. Of particular romantic interest is the Terrace Suite, which has an expansive view of the bay and a lovely sitting room and balcony. The ornate French oak bedroom set from 1793 will make you feel like French aristocracy. You can have your breakfast delivered to your room if you choose the Terrace Suite; otherwise, guests feast on a full gourmet breakfast at one large table in the main-floor dining room. Children are not allowed at this romantic retreat, so breakfast is always a relaxing affair. Orange-pecan French toast; hash brown quiche; buckwheat pancakes; and a variety of frittatas, cobblers, and homemade pastries are some of the delicious ways in which you might begin your day. This is one of the most sought-after coastal wedding sites in the Northwest, so reserve early. The white gazebo by the water is an excellent little spot for kissing.

$$–$$$ *AE, DIS, MC, V; checks OK; www.caswellsinn.com.*

CHINA BEACH RETREAT
◐◐◐

222 Robert Gray Dr, Ilwaco / 360/642-5660 or 800/INN-1896
Nestled on a cove with serene views of Baker's Bay, this spacious, recently renovated wooden house–turned-romantic-getaway offers amorous couples a quiet escape from a busy world. Under the same ownership as the historic Shelburne Inn nearby, the house includes many luxurious, thoughtful touches, such as the addition of Victorian stained glass panels that cast romantic light in the rooms. Floor-to-ceiling windows in the living room invite contemplative and quiet time together; a dining room and pretty kitchen (available for coffee and tea only) round out the common areas. There are three guest rooms to choose from, all with private baths. Down-

stairs, the beautiful Kwan Yin Suite feels like a secret garden getaway, with a private entrance, views of flowering plum trees, and ornately carved furnishings. The two-person air-jet massage tub in the impressive bathroom has a marble relief panel of the Chinese goddess (the room's namesake) floating in the clouds. Upstairs, the bright and airy Sacajawea Room features yellow walls and crisp white linens, while green walls and patterned linens give the neighboring Lewis and Clark Room a cozier feel. Each queen-size bed has been raised on a wooden dais so you can enjoy a beautiful view of Baker's Bay while snuggling under the covers, and the baths, with massage tubs, are decorated by handcrafted tiles made by a local artist. Any stay here comes with a full breakfast at the Shelburne Inn, just five minutes up the road by car—although the quiet and seclusion at China Beach are such that you might find it hard to leave until you absolutely have to.
$$$ *AE, MC, V; checks OK; www.chinabeachretreat.com.*

THE SHELBURNE INN
◖◗◖◗

4415 Pacific Hwy S, Seaview / 360/642-2442 or 800/INN-1896
One of the Northwest's premier country inns, the Shelburne has a well-deserved reputation as a wonderfully romantic retreat. Inside the inn, filled with antiques and ornate tapestries, the ambience is so memorable that the setting—right on busy Highway 103—is the last thing you'll remember about your visit. (Traffic noise is hardly noticeable unless you sleep with the windows open at night—although those who are particularly sensitive might request a room away from the street.) The 15 small, comfortably elegant rooms and 2 luxurious suites all feature private baths, beautiful antiques, down comforters, lace pillows, and handmade patchwork quilts, and many have a balcony or deck. Some rooms have queen-size beds while others have doubles; some face the charming garden, while others offer less-inspiring street views. If you don't mind the climb, the third-floor rooms offer the best value. No matter which room you book, you can expect fresh flowers and freshly baked cookies awaiting you upon arrival. The highly romantic suites downstairs, furnished with remarkable antiques, are simply spectacular. Suite 17 boasts beautiful leaded-glass French doors opening to the inn's lush herb garden, while Suite 9 offers a graceful sitting room and bedroom partitioned by an exquisite wall of leaded glass. Guests who stay in the suites may choose the luxurious option of having breakfast delivered to their room in the morning. For everyone else, a gourmet breakfast is served family-style in the dining room, and the delectable treats might include a savory wild-mushroom omelet, potato and lamb hash with a coddled egg, or smoked oyster frittata. Homemade pastries, fruit, and colorful edible flowers and herbs are also offered. Lunch and dinner are available downstairs at the wonderful Shoalwater restaurant or the more casual Heron and Beaver Pub (see Romantic

Restaurants). For an extra-special occasion, consider splurging on a romance package: a bottle of champagne and a delicious appetizer waiting in your room will get the weekend off to an auspicious start.
$$–$$$ *AE, MC, V; checks OK; www.theshelburneinn.com.*

THE WHALEBONE HOUSE BED AND BREAKFAST
⬡⬡❰

2101 Bay Ave, Ocean Park / 360/665-5371 or 888/298-3330
This impeccably restored 1889 Victorian farmhouse draws its romantic appeal from pure, unadulterated historic charm. Set among colorful flower gardens bordered by the unusual white fence that inspired the inn's name— it's made from the vertebrae of a whale that washed up on shore in the early 1950s—the home is listed on the Washington Register of Historic Places. Due to its location on a main thoroughfare in Ocean Park, street noise is sometimes audible, and rooms are a bit small because of the home's authentic vintage character. Fortunately, the four guest rooms are filled with lovely antiques and heirlooms that recall local history, and each has a private bath. Upstairs, the Louise Rice Room offers the most romantic possibilities. Skylights allow for stargazing from a queen-size bed sheathed in cream-colored linens, and beautiful antique furniture adds ambience. Also upstairs, Artemisia's Parlor—so named because it was once the home's second-floor parlor—has distinctive charm. The S. A. Matthews Room downstairs adjoins the home's central area; it's less private, but the floral wallpaper and spacious bathroom with claw-foot tub make it a good choice, nonetheless. Mornings at the Whalebone bring a full country-style breakfast served at a long table in the dining area. Enjoy homemade muffins and scones, and a variety of delicious savory dishes such as the signature Whalebone Hash, which includes smoked salmon, capers, potatoes, and sour cream. After breakfast, relax on the beautiful enclosed sun porch.
$$ *MC, V; checks OK; www.whalebonehouse.com.*

Romantic Restaurants

THE ARK
⬡⬡❰

273rd and Sandridge Rd, Nahcotta / 360/665-4133
The true beauty of this acclaimed Northwest restaurant lies on the inside— so don't let the nearby oyster farm's industrial equipment, trucks, and buildings turn you away from this romantic spot. The inside rewards with cozy decor of wood and brick, large stone fireplace and dark-wood beams, and numerous window tables offering serene water views. While the interior changes little, big changes took place in 2004: After 25 years under the same ownership, this beloved restaurant—nationally known despite its

tucked-away location in this remote corner of Washington—has changed hands. Fortunately, the new owners have promised to leave the helpful, experienced staff in place and uphold the restaurant's longstanding policy of supporting local producers and creating seasonal menus. This is a very good thing, indeed, since The Ark is widely viewed as serving some of the finest food on the peninsula. The menu consistently features delicious fresh seafood, local blackberries, and other regional bounty. What's in season will determine what's on offer, but if it's available, start with Willapa Bay clams steamed in a savory broth of garlic and white wine, before moving on to excellent entrées such as the pan-fried salmon with citrus and crème fraîche or local lingcod served with chive potato pancakes and chipotle aioli. Save room for one of the seductive desserts; then sit back and watch the twinkling stars emerge over the water.

$$$ *AE, DIS, MC, V; local checks only; dinner Tues–Sun (summer), Fri–Sun (winter), brunch Sun; call for seasonal closures; full bar; reservations recommended; www.arkrestaurant.com.* &

THE DEPOT RESTAURANT
◐◐

1208 38th Pl, Seaview / 360/642-7880

This rather ramshackle former train depot might not impress you on first sight (although it looks good for its age, considering the building turns 100 years old in 2005)—but the delicious, creative fare and unique ambience inside will make a lasting impression. For the most romantic atmosphere, reserve a table on the outdoor patio, which is surrounded by ornamental beach grasses and equipped with heat lamps to keep things cozy—you can catch a sea breeze sitting here. Inside, the open kitchen entails unavoidable background noise, but the funky, down-home feel is still pleasant. The oft-changing menu is satisfyingly American and makes the most of local bounty. You'll find several ways to enjoy local oysters, including a crunchy fried rendition served with garlic aioli. For the main event, try the pan-seared giant prawns and scallops in a ginger-coconut broth with wasabi sticky rice, or one of the constantly changing specials, which are always delicious; steak is always on the menu. Wednesdays bring a fun, build-your-own burger night. Dessert is an absolute must, whether you choose the tiramisù; a seasonal fruit dessert such as a strawberry-rhubarb cobbler; or something decadent, like the chocolate ganache-filled upside-down bread pudding.

$$ *DIS, MC, V; checks OK; dinner Tues–Sun (summer), Wed–Sun (winter); beer and wine; reservations recommended; www.depot restaurantdining.com.*

THE 42ND STREET CAFE
◐◐◖

4201 Pacific Hwy, Seaview / 360/642-2323
This local-favorite restaurant may not look like much from the outside—in fact, it's housed in a building that was once a Coast Guard barracks moved from Fort Canby Station after World War II—but inside, tables adorned with flowers and colorful linens arranged around the country kitchen–style dining room make for a charming ambience. Lace half-curtains shield the view of the busy highway outside, and the service is cheerful and efficient. At lunch, try unusual offerings such as the chèvre fondue with apples, the smoked salmon Caesar salad, or the fried green tomatoes with cumin-orange mayonnaise. We also highly recommend the halibut and shrimp cake with parsley-caper mayonnaise. The dinner menu offers something for everyone, from well-prepared fresh seafood to roasted vegetable ravioli to steaks livened up with cranberry barbecue sauce or mesquite butter. For dessert, indulge in homemade lemon dainties, chocolate-and–ancho chile brownies, or cranberry bread pudding with walnut crème anglaise.
$$ *AE, MC, V; checks OK; breakfast, lunch, dinner every day; beer and wine; reservations recommended; www.42ndstreetcafe.com.* &

THE SANCTUARY
◐◐◐

794 Hwy 101, Chinook / 360/777-8380
Pardon the pun, but eating at The Sanctuary can be a simply heavenly experience. Located along Highway 101, this 92-year-old building was formerly the Methodist Episcopal Church of Chinook; today it retains the hushed, echoing atmosphere one might expect from such reverent beginnings. Original stained-glass windows, angel sconces, a pump organ, and leaded-glass door insets can be admired from the wooden pews, where diners sit at tables covered with white linens. Vaulted ceilings and polished wood floors add to the ambience. Pardon the pun once more, but the food here is divine, from the fresh local seafood to the Scandinavian specialties. For starters, try the *kottbullar* (Swedish meatballs) or the clam bisque. Move on to entrées such as the crisp panko-dusted jumbo prawns and crab cake or the chicken roulade with prosciutto, Jarlsberg cheese, and herbs. We also recommend the impeccable rack of lamb, well seasoned and smothered with an herb crust before being oven roasted. For the perfect ending to this—ahem—celestial meal, try the famous lemon cream sherbet or indulge in *krumkake*, waffle-like cones filled with whipped cream and topped with a light berry sauce.
$$–$$$ *AE, DIS, MC, V; checks OK; dinner Thur–Sun (hours change seasonally so call ahead); full bar; reservations recommended; www.sanctuary restaurant.com.* &

THE SHOALWATER
◒◒◒◒

THE HERON AND BEAVER PUB
◒◒◖

4415 Pacific Wy (The Shelburn Inn), Seaview / 360/642-4142
Can food be wildly romantic? At the Shoalwater, the warm, country-Victorian dining room at the Shelburn Inn (see Romantic Lodgings), we think you'll agree the answer is a resounding yes. Everything from the imaginative and wide-ranging menu is utterly fresh, delicious, and beautifully presented. Mouthwatering crab and shrimp cakes are kissed with sesame oil and ginger, and roasted herb-encrusted duck breast is served with a cranberry and truffle butter. The wine list here is so extensive that some bottles have to be stored off site, and the array of delicious desserts, including a delightful rose-geranium sorbet, will tempt you to indulgence. The decor charms, with leaded and stained-glass windows, high ceilings, soft candlelight, and crisp white linens on well-spaced antique tables. Reserve well in advance for the Shoalwater's popular wintertime winemakers' dinner series, featuring seven-course meals designed around wines from a visiting winemaker. The Heron and Beaver Pub is this destination's more casual sister, but shares the same kitchen: This tiny establishment re-creates that Old World magic of an English pub with a wide selection of excellent beers—and the welcome addition of excellent food. Some tasty items off the Shoalwater's menu are available, including delicious Cajun-style "blackened" Willapa Bay oysters; other fare includes classic comfort food with a twist, like the wild-mushroom–goat cheese lasagne. A deck overlooks the inn's beautiful Victorian gardens, so you can enjoy the pleasant outdoor seating on a balmy summer's day.
$$$** *(The Shoalwater);* **$$ *(The Heron and Beaver Pub) AE, DC, MC, V; checks OK; lunch, dinner every day, brunch Sun; full bar; reservations recommended; www.shoalwater.com (The Shoalwater) or www.shoalwater. com/pages/hubs/pub (The Heron and Beaver Pub).* ₤

NORTH CASCADES

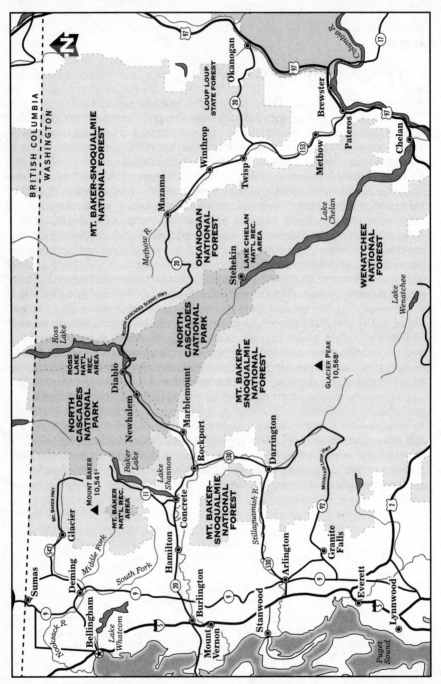

♡ NORTH CASCADES

Few regions in Washington have the romantic allure of the North Cascades. Set squarely in the northwest part of the state, this mountainous area is world-renowned for its ice-capped peaks, alpine meadows, and vast stands of old-growth forest. While the west side of the Cascades offers lush vistas, on the east side you'll find the authentic Old West—awash in hues of gold, bathed in hot summer sunshine, and blasted with cold, snowy winters. You'd be hard-pressed to find a square foot in this expanse that isn't magnificent—and highly romantic. Broadly speaking, the North Cascades includes a vast national park, encompassing Mount Baker (see the Bellingham section in the Puget Sound chapter); the North Cascades Scenic Highway (Hwy 20), which leads to the Methow Valley (pronounced "MET-how") east of the Cascades; and, farther south, pristine and popular Lake Chelan. In addition to the lake, the Chelan area is blessed with 300 days of sunshine a year; the springtime perfume of apple blossoms; and good skiing, hunting, fishing, hiking, and sailing. The top attraction is taking a cruise up Lake Chelan to the remote town of Stehekin.

The drive along Highway 20, the state's most northerly east-west route, is among the Northwest's most breathtaking journeys. After climbing mountain passes, it winds through the Methow Valley and the towns of Mazama, Winthrop, and Twisp. This exquisite region, relatively unscathed by development, boasts no cities, few resorts, and limited options for food and lodging. (The cute espresso stands lining the road are among the region's few nods to civilization.) The great outdoors is the romantic attraction here, and opportunities abound for hiking, camping, mountain biking, fishing, boating, and downhill and cross-country skiing. In winter, snow closes Highway 20 from approximately mid-November to mid-April, depending on the weather. Another popular way to get to this region is via the Cascade Loop, a series of connecting highways that passes through the northern section of the mountains. For more information on driving the Cascade Loop, see Access and Information.

Like the Alps, their European counterparts, the North Cascades possess extraordinary grandeur and majesty; their wild, elusive beauty makes them a worldwide draw. Part of what keeps this region so untamed and romantic is North Cascades National Park, a cluster of magnificent peaks that are part of the Cascade Range. This enormous, 505,000-acre national park, located just south of the United States/Canada border, contains jagged peaks draped in ice, 318 glaciers, and much-hidden wilderness. The park will not reveal its treasures easily, and they are best discovered on foot. Adventurous couples can explore 386 miles of maintained trails in the territory; less-athletic types can experience the splendor along the stunning roads that slice through the mountains. To request information about hiking in the area, contact North Cascades National Park headquarters (2105 Hwy 20, Sedro Woolley; 360/856-5700; www.nps.gov/noca/).

METHOW VALLEY

ROMANTIC HIGHLIGHTS

The journey to the Methow Valley is extraordinarily romantic. The route winds along the **North Cascades Scenic Highway** (Hwy 20), one of the Northwest's most famous routes. The two-lane road cuts through the mountains to provide stunning roadside mountain vistas and passes by brilliant jade-green and turquoise Diablo and Ross Lakes. Stop at the lookouts to stretch your legs and enjoy the spectacular views. By the time you descend into the Methow's wide-open valley and grassy meadowlands, a few hours' journey on the highway itself, you will have encountered peaceful farmland, dramatic ridges lush with evergreens, and the rugged mountains and immense glaciers of beautiful Rainy and Washington Passes. In summer, the Methow Valley offers a host of outdoor activities, including white-water rafting, fishing, horseback riding, mountain biking, and spectacular hiking in the North Cascades.

In the winter months, the Methow Valley becomes a sparkling, snowy paradise for **cross-country skiers**, with crisp, sunny days; views of soaring, ice-capped peaks; and opportunities for every ability level. The region boasts nearly 200 kilometers of well-groomed trails, the second-largest network in the country, all of which are maintained by the Methow Valley Sport Trails Association (MVSTA). A large section surrounds Winthrop's Sun Mountain Lodge (see Romantic Lodgings), where 44 miles of trail cut through rolling hills. Mazama's flat terrain and open meadows make it ideal for easy exploring. The system consists of four linked sections, many of which go directly past the valley's popular accommodations, so you can literally ski from your door. After an adventurous day outdoors, head back to your room and relax by the fireplace. (In summer, the trails are used by mountain bikers.) Ski season usually begins in early December and continues through March. For updates on snow and trail conditions, contact the MVSTA (509/996-3287 or 800/682-5787; www.mvsta.com). For the truly adventurous, there's the opportunity to try **heli-skiing** (see More Methow Valley Kisses).

Each town in the valley has its own unique romantic appeal. If you're heading east on Highway 20, tiny **Mazama** is the first stop on the map. We mean tiny—"town" consists of one store. Thankfully, the **Mazama Store** (50 Lost River Rd; 509/996-2855; www.methow.com/mazamastore) is a charming stop, with an espresso counter, tasty lunch options (get burgers hot off the grill in the outdoor picnic area in summer), and a fine selection of wines. Also, note that it offers the last gas pumps for more than 70 miles if you're traveling west across the mountains. If you're driving a reliable SUV or a sturdy four-wheel-drive car, devote your afternoon to a round-trip adventure up to Harts Pass via **Methow Valley Road** (County Rd 9140). The 19 harrowing miles up this steep, one-lane road, complete with hairpin curves, no guardrails, and 1,000-foot drop-offs, have a worthy reward: **Slate Peak**. At 7,440 feet, you've reached the state's highest drivable point. From this heavenly vantage point, snowcapped mountains rise in every direction, and the only sounds are birdsong and the gentle murmur of wind in the trees. A kiss here will take your breath away.

Open only in summer, Harts Pass offers campgrounds that will please outdoorsy couples, along with access to the famed Pacific Crest Trail. For more information on hikes or stays, contact the **Methow Valley Ranger District** (509/996-4003; www.fs.fed.us/r6/okanogan). If you prefer lower-altitude romantic pursuits, consider visiting in time for the **Methow Music Festival** (509/996-6000; www.methowmusicfestival.org), a summer classical-music series held in local barns and meadows.

For hand-in-hand strolls along quaint streets, the valley's best destination is the Western-motif town of **Winthrop**. The old-fashioned storefronts and boardwalks are popular with tourists; but not to worry, the town's incredible access to the pristine outdoors makes it easy as pie to find time alone. After the day's adventures, relax with a beer at the **Winthrop Brewing Company** (155 Riverside Ave; 509/996-3183; www.webspinnings.com/winthrop), in an old schoolhouse on the main street. **Winthrop Mountain Sports** (257 Riverside Ave; 509/996-2886 or 800/719-3826; www.winthropmountain sports.com) sells outdoor-activity equipment and supplies, and rents bikes, skis, snowshoes, and ice skates. On Saturday morning, travel the 8 miles from Winthrop to Twisp and explore the thriving **Methow Valley Farmers Market** (near the community center; mid-Apr–mid-Oct). You'll find local arts and crafts at the **Confluence Gallery** (104 Glover St; 509/997-ARTS; www. confluencegallery.com), summer theater performances at the **Merc Playhouse**

(101 Glover St; 509/997-PLAY; www.mercplayhouse.com), and wonderful pastries and fresh bread—hot from 9am to 11am—at cutely named **Cinnamon Twisp** (116 Glover St; 509/997-5030; www.cinnamontwisp.com). Also in Twisp, **Osprey River Adventures** (509/997-4116 or 800/997-4116; www.methow.com/~osprey) can introduce you to the joys of white-water rafting or help you organize a serene float trip on nearby rivers.

The tiny town of **Pateros**, located approximately 25 miles north of Chelan and 40 miles south of Winthrop, is among some of this region's best-known and -loved recreation destinations. It is **Amy's Manor** (435 Hwy 153; 509/923-2334; www.amysmanor.com), perched on a hilltop overlooking the Methow Valley, that puts Pateros on our romance map. The 170-acre property is a wonderful spot for outdoor weddings, and the hostess (a former chef) can cater the event from start to finish. Savory hors d'oeuvres feature herbs from her well-tended gardens, and her wedding cakes are made completely from scratch.

The months of December and January in the Cascades bring gray skies and short days, but also the chance to witness the stunning **bald eagle migration**. Along Highway 20, between the towns of Rockport and Marblemount, hundreds of bald eagles migrate to the Skagit River during salmon-spawning season. (Salmon die after spawning, which makes the river an eagle's easy feast.) All along the river banks, eagles soar overhead or perch in clear sight on exposed alpine branches; bring your binoculars for close-ups. The best view is from the river, via a two- to three-hour **float tour**. Call Chinook Expeditions (800/241-3451; www.chinookexpeditions.com), Wildwater River Tours (800/522-WILD; www.wildwater-river.com), or the Mount Baker Ranger District (2105 Hwy 20, Sedro Woolley; 360/856-5700; www.nps.gov/noca/challenger/ch6.htm) to find out about other float-trip operators.

Access & Information

Travelers tour the North Cascades via car (there are no airports or train service within this region) on the North Cascades Scenic Highway (Hwy 20), an east-west corridor that links Sedro Woolley near Interstate 5 (exit 230, 65 miles north of Seattle) to the town of Twisp. East of the Cascades, the Twisp–Chelan leg is connected by Highway 153 and US Highway 97.

Generally, the best weather for visiting the high country arrives mid-June to late September. Snow closes the North Cascades Highway—typically the stretch between Mazama on the east side and Diablo on the west—from approximately mid-November to mid-April, depending on the weather. In winter, visitors from Puget Sound reach the Methow Valley by crossing the Cascades via the longer, more southerly routes of US Highway 2 or Interstate 90. Highway 2 is part of one of the Northwest's most beautiful drives, the 400-mile Cascade Loop. This route takes in Leavenworth and Wenatchee (see the Central Cascades chapter), and heads north to Lake Chelan, Winthrop, and the North Cascades Scenic Highway (Hwy 20). The route can be accessed from Interstate 90 at Cle Elum by taking Highway 970 to US Highway 97 north, which joins US Highway 2 just east of Leavenworth. A brochure is available from the **Cascade Loop Association** (PO Box 3245, Wenatchee, WA 98807; 509/662-3888; www.cascadeloop.com).

For more information, contact the **Winthrop Chamber of Commerce Information Center** (220 Hwy 20; 509/996-2125 or 888/463-8469; www.winthropwashington.com). Methow Valley Central Reservations (14F Horizon Flat Rd, Winthrop; 509/996-2148 or 800/422-3048; www.methow reservations.com) books lodging for the entire valley and sells tickets for major events, such as mid-July's Rhythm and Blues Festival. Twisp has its own **Visitor Information Center** (509/997-2926; www.twispinfo.com). Another good source of information is the **North Cascades Visitor Center** (502 Newhalem St, Newhalem, WA 98283; 206/386-4495).

Romantic Lodgings

FREESTONE INN AND EARLY WINTERS CABINS
❂❂❂

17798 Hwy 20, Mazama / 509/996-3906 or 800/639-3809
A magnificent, three-story stone fireplace in the Great Room signals the grandeur of this beautiful, remote, two-story log inn. It's a quintessential romantic Northwest getaway, from the main lodge's rough-hewn exterior to the two luxurious hot tubs overlooking Freestone Lake. During summer, the trout-filled lake attracts fly-fishers; in winter it freezes over to become an ice-skating rink for guests. Hand-forged iron fixtures, warm wood-accented decor, and comfortable country furnishings make for a rustic yet elegant interior. The above-mentioned fireplace divides the sitting area from the restaurant, where a complimentary continental breakfast is served each morning. Evenings bring an elegant dinner (see Romantic Restaurants). The 21 guest rooms (4 are suites) feature lake views, subdued earth tones, wrought-iron and pine furnishings, and thick wool blankets piled on king-size beds. Other amenities include kitchenettes, TV/VCRs tucked in armoires, plush terry robes, cozy gas fireplaces, and private decks or patios. In the suites, you can open the shutters between the bedroom and bathroom for views of the lake and woods from your soaking tub. The 15 Early Winters Cabins, set next to the main lodge, offer total privacy and come in varying sizes ranging from studio to two bedrooms. Here, the simple country comforts include knotty-pine interiors, gas stoves, hardwood floors, casual furnishings, and private decks overlooking the tranquil creek. Three spacious Lakeside Lodges are designed for families or larger groups. The possibilities

for outdoor romance here are seemingly endless. Jack's Hut (509/996-2752), located across the parking lot, can help with arranging everything from horseback riding and fly-fishing to mountain biking, hiking, and white-water rafting. There is also an outdoor swimming pool, open during the summer. You can rent ice skates in winter or mountain bikes in summer, or sign up for fly-fishing lessons.
$$$ *AE, MC, V; checks OK; www.freestoneinn.com.*

MAZAMA COUNTRY INN
◗◗

42 Lost River Rd, Mazama / 509/996-2681 or 800/843-7951 (in WA)
For those seeking simple pleasures in a remote location, the Mazama Country Inn—and the town of Mazama, for that matter—will deliver exactly what your hearts desire. The lodge, set among evergreens at the foot of a mountain, offers 18 units, each with a private bath. Most rooms have been recently renovated and include king- or queen-size beds, gas stoves, patchwork quilts, new carpeting, jetted Jacuzzi tubs, and private decks. Best of all, you can enjoy romantic views of the North Cascades from nearly every window, with no televisions to distract you (telephones aren't in-room either, but we doubt you'll miss them). As for recreation, there is something for everyone here: horseback riding, heli-skiing, cross-country skiing, mountain biking, windsurfing, and sleigh riding. After a day of exercise, relax in the communal sauna and hot tub or try out the brand-new outdoor swimming pool (open May–Oct). There is also an on-site workout facility as well as squash and tennis courts. While three's a crowd when it comes to romance, people traveling in groups will appreciate the inn's 13 additional cabins, which can each sleep up to six people. Amenities vary from cabin to cabin (as do prices), but many include fully stocked kitchens, wood-burning stoves, TV/VCRs, stereos, and even washer/dryers. In summer, breakfast, lunch, and dinner are offered in the lodge restaurant; winter brings family-style breakfasts and dinners. In winter (mid-December through President's Day), when rates include meals, children under 10 aren't allowed, making this more of an adult-oriented haven. The coffee bar, which opens early, provides the perfect place to wake up while warming up by the fire and enjoying the view; mixed drinks, beer, and wine are served during the dinner hour.
$$ *MC, V; checks OK; www.mazamainn.com.*

RIVER'S EDGE RESORT
◗◗

115 Riverside Ave, Winthrop / 509/996-8000 or 800/937-6621
The Chewuch River serves as the picturesque backdrop for the simple cabins of this resort. Accommodations include three two-bedroom cabins (one is brand new); six three-bedroom cabins set next to the river; and five more modest, one-bedroom cabins farther back from the water. All offer ample

space and privacy, along with easy access to Winthrop's downtown shops, restaurants, and small brewery. For the romance-minded, we recommend the two-bedroom cabins, thanks to their scenic location and utterly private riverside hot tubs. The occupancy-based rates make them a good bargain. Four of the larger three-bedroom cabins have private hot tubs; the one-bedroom cabins share a single hot tub overlooking the river. In all the cabins, you'll find separate living areas; private baths; and bedrooms with comfortable queen-size, locally made, pine-log-frame beds covered with quilts. Polished hardwood floors and propane stoves warm up the living rooms, but the bare walls and lack of special touches don't exactly spell romantic luxury. Other amenities include comfortable couches, TV/VCRs, and CD players. The larger cabins have full kitchens for making your own romantic meals. Bring some provisions and an appetite for cooking. (Smaller cabins have kitchenettes.) Spend the evening out on the large deck, taking in views of the Chewuch River from the hot tub available to all guests. Once you witness the power and beauty of the rushing river, you won't want to leave this peaceful retreat.

$$–$$$ *AE, MC, V; checks OK; www.riversedgewinthrop.com.*

SUN MOUNTAIN LODGE
❂❂❂❂

Patterson Lake Rd, Winthrop / 509/996-2211 or 800/572-0493

Everything about the Sun Mountain Lodge is extraordinary, starting with the majestic drive up to this mountaintop resort. Built of massive timbers and stone, the beautifully renovated lodge interior is graced with immense wrought-iron chandeliers, stone floors, and rock-clad fireplaces. The 102 rooms range from rather standard to spectacular, although, fortunately, almost all offer views of the dramatic mountain panorama (a few rooms also overlook the roof, which isn't particularly romantic); some boast luxurious Jacuzzi tubs. Two newer buildings across from the lodge house 36 impeccable suites, where sliding glass doors open to stone patios with mesmerizing views. Each of these units has its own fireplace, elegant willow furnishings, and lush comforters; in winter, you can cross-country ski out your back door. The most luxurious accommodations are the Mount Robinson Rooms, which feature whirlpool tubs, beautiful sitting areas, fireplaces, and king-size beds with down comforters. One and a half miles below the main lodge, you'll find the Patterson Lake Cabins in a cottonwood grove overlooking a lake; for couples, the one-bedroom cabins are best, but be forewarned that the surrounding larger cottages do draw families. Sun Mountain Lodge offers every imaginable amenity: two heated pools, outdoor hot tubs, hiking trails, horseback riding, white-water rafting, a golf course, sailboats, sleigh rides, exercise equipment, mountain bikes . . . not to mention the totally outrageous, thoroughly intoxicating heli-skiing packages available for both downhill and cross-country skiers. Whether you

spend the day trying extreme sports or simply exploring the quiet woods nearby, an evening soak in one of two outdoor hot tubs will be in order. You can even splurge on a facial or massage in the newly expanded spa. The restaurant in the lodge offers unbeatable views and a menu that emphasizes regional cuisine (see Romantic Restaurants). Be sure and reserve early for summer or winter ski-season stays.
$$$–$$$$ *AE, DC, MC, V; checks OK; www.sunmountainlodge.com.*

WOLFRIDGE RESORT
♥♥
412-B Wolf Creek Rd, Winthrop / 509/996-2828 or 800/237-2388
Serenity reigns at this resort, which boasts a 60-acre riverside setting. Five log buildings contain sixteen units, which include two-bedroom town-houses, one-bedroom suites, hotel-style rooms, and three custom cabins. Although the accommodations are spacious and comfortable, it's the beautiful setting here that is extraordinary. The rooms feature oil paintings by a local artist, exposed-log walls, handcrafted wood furniture, and private standard baths. For truly private kissing, check out one of the three custom cabins, two of which were completed in 2004. The Wolf Hollow Cabin offers a living area with log-beam cathedral ceilings, a bedroom with both queen-size and single bed, a loft area, a kitchen, and a cozy pellet stove; it's not hidden from the main buildings but offers a sense of quiet seclusion. The Howling Wolf Cabin is set in the woods and includes a kitchen, dining area, and living room with gas stove with an upstairs bedroom, lounge area, and a bathroom with Jacuzzi tub. The largest and most decadent is the Whispering Wolf Cabin, which has a front porch overlooking the Methow River and includes a fully equipped kitchen, dining room, living area, and bedroom on the main floor as well as an upstairs bedroom, loft area, bathroom with Jacuzzi tub, and rear balcony. No matter where you stay, cathedral ceilings and private decks are the norm. Lovely ponderosas blow in the wind, mountain peaks dazzle behind a curtain of green forest, and a glorious meadow lets in the sun. Outdoor enthusiasts can cross-country ski or mountain bike on the trail system that runs right outside your door. When it's time to head back to the peaceful riverside setting of Wolfridge Resort, you'll discover the heated outdoor pool and a Jacuzzi in a river-rock setting—perfect for soothing sore muscles.
$$–$$$ *AE, MC, V; checks OK; www.wolfridgeresort.com.*

Romantic Restaurants

FIDDLEHEAD BISTRO
❂❂

201 Glover St, Twisp / 509/997-0343
This warm neighborhood bistro in downtown Twisp is an unexpected haven
for romance. With weekly menu changes, a lovely canopied deck in summer,
and live music three nights a week ranging from jazz to bluegrass to ragtime
piano, this is a wonderful place to dine. Locally grown organic vegetables and fruit are featured, and excellent bread from Anjou, an award-
winning bakery located outside nearby Cashmere, makes any meal here even
more delicious. Sample dishes include maple-roasted butternut squash and
chèvre cheese over fresh pappardelle pasta, cassoulet, and seafood risotto.
The owner greets all diners, and his staff is personable and knowledgeable.
The wine list is relatively short but offers exquisite choices, great prices, and
generously sized vessels (a glass of wine here is equivalent to two elsewhere).
Desserts are rich—don't pass up the Chocolate Ecstasy cake.
*$ MC, V; checks OK; breakfast, lunch, dinner Wed–Sun (dinner Wed–Sun,
brunch Sun in winter); full bar; reservations recommended.*

FREESTONE INN
❂❂❂

17798 Hwy 20, Mazama / 509/996-3906 or 800/639-3809
A stunning floor-to-ceiling river-rock fireplace in the center of the Freestone
Inn (see Romantic Lodgings), separates the lobby on one side of the room
from the restaurant on the other. In this intimate room, candlelit tables covered with white cloths provide the setting for dinners of Northwest specialties. Sit by the window in summer—the view overlooks Freestone Lake—or
cozy up by the fireplace come winter. The simple, elegant menu emphasizes
locally grown ingredients and offers a wine selection with plenty of Washington vintners. Start with an appetizer such as the poached leek, onion, and
goat cheese tart or try the roasted beet salad made with organic greens. New
chef Stuart Holm serves up entrées ranging from a tasty pan-fried pecan-
dusted rainbow trout to grilled Misty Isle Farms rib-eye steak served with
garlic roasted red potatoes, Gorgonzola butter, and black pepper jus. The
delicious desserts here include a d'Anjou pear tart with star anise cream or
a nightly chef's surprise that will drive chocolate lovers wild.
*$$$ AE, MC, V; checks OK; breakfast, dinner every day (reduced days in
winter); full bar; reservations recommended; www.freestoneinn.com.*

SUN MOUNTAIN LODGE
✿✿✿✿

Patterson Lake Rd, Winthrop / 509/996-4707 or 800/572-0493
Even if you've decided not to stay at the exquisite Sun Mountain Lodge (see Romantic Lodgings), consider indulging in a romantic meal at this flawless restaurant. Housed in a charming original section of the lodge, the dining room features wrought-iron chandeliers hung from log ceiling beams and cozy two-person tables and booths. All tables have beautiful views of the Methow Valley, and the effect is of dining in a tree house. Executive chef Patrick Miller offers Northwest-fresh cuisine made with high-quality ingredients and exquisite presentation. The pillowy, rich crab cakes are artfully surrounded by capers and swirls of infused olive oil. Many delights accompany the beef tenderloin—mashed Yukon Gold potatoes and a morel demi-glace, seared squash, and two elaborate horns of crispy turnip. The wild Chinook salmon cooked with orange-candied fennel might feature Dungeness-crab mashed potatoes and smoky bok choy. The staff offers good advice about the extensive wine list (focusing on many Northwest varietals) and provides seamless service. Though the food is delicious, the prices are a little steep for the amount that comes on your plate; fortunately, the incredibly romantic setting outweighs this minor drawback. Thoughtful touches like sorbet palate cleansers and chocolate truffles to conclude your meal only add to the overall experience. Lunch and breakfast are simpler, as is the menu in the adjoining Wolf Creek Bar and Grill (formerly Eagle's Nest Lounge; 509/996-4706).
$$$ AE, DC, MC, V; local checks only; breakfast, lunch, dinner every day; full bar; reservations recommended; www.sunmountainlodge.com.

More Methow Valley Kisses

If your idea of romance involves heart-stopping adventure, you can find it in the Okanogan National Forest, which encompasses nearly 2 million acres of northern Washington wilderness. While hikers and nature lovers marvel at the region's diverse surroundings—which rise from scenic grasslands to ponderosa pine forests to glades of Douglas fir as the elevation increases— extreme-sports types love it for the heli-skiing. The well-known North Cascade Heli-Skiing (Mazama; 509/996-3272 or 800/494-HELI; www.heli-ski.com), founded in 1988, is run out of the Freestone Inn in Mazama and can help you access a vast variety of runs, starting at altitudes of 7,500 to 9,000 feet and offering drops from 1,500 to 4,000 vertical feet. Skiing down these untouched powder runs is an unforgettably exhilarating experience.

LAKE CHELAN

ROMANTIC HIGHLIGHTS

Located south of the Methow Valley, 55-mile-long Lake Chelan is an exquisite blue jewel dropped amid the Cascades' ice-covered peaks. Boating on the fjordlike lake, which is never more than 2 miles wide and yet among the deepest in the nation, gives you the sense of floating right into the mountains. At Lake Chelan's northern tip, the tiny town of Stehekin offers one of the Northwest's most famously remote getaways.

Otherwise known as "the Enchanted Valley," the utterly unique **Stehekin** is accessible only by ferryboat or plane from the towns of Chelan and Manson, or via tough high-country trails that pass through the Cascade Mountains. Once you're here, it's easy to see why the Skagit Indians of long ago gave this river valley the name Stehekin (meaning "the way through") as they searched for a passage through the glacier-laden Cascades.

Today, this small community with a handful of residents and even fewer cars—every vehicle here had to be shipped in by barge—is celebrated for its glorious scenery and unparalleled quiet. Most establishments in Stehekin don't even have telephones; locals are often seen pedaling on bicycles to a centrally located pay phone. But what will astound you most are the jagged mountain vistas reflected in the glacier-fed waters of the clear blue lake.

The **ferry** departs from Chelan and takes between one and four hours, depending on which boat is running. Both the ferry and the little town of Stehekin can be a bit crowded with tourists on summer afternoons. Fortunately, most of these visitors are day-trippers only—which is why staying overnight here is so romantic. Once that passenger-laden boat departs for Chelan in the late afternoon, Stehekin's exquisite scenery and sublime seclusion are left to you. In summer, the minimum-stay requirements here are considerable, so don't plan on making this a quick stop. Restaurant options are limited, to say the least, and none are gourmet. Most central is the dining room at the **North Cascades Stehekin Lodge** (at head of Lake Chelan; 509/682-4494; www.stehekin.com), located above the ferry dock and open for breakfast, lunch, and dinner daily (restaurant closed Nov–Dec). **Stehekin Valley Ranch** (800/536-0745; www.courtneycountry.com), set at the farthest end of the valley, serves buffet-style dinners in rustic tent-cabins in summer (closed Nov–early June). For a sweet snack, bicycle to the nearby **Stehekin Pastry Company** (www.stehekinvalley.com/pastryco.htm; summer only), where the tantalizing, sugary smell of freshly baked cinnamon rolls fills the air. If you really want to pamper yourselves with fine wining and dining, cook for yourselves—and bring your own supplies, as there are no grocery stores out here, only what the locals call an "inconvenience store" selling overpriced beer and candy.

Your days here will be spent exploring the incredible natural setting—and keeping your eyes open for the abundant wildlife. Good day hikes include a pretty one along the lakeshore and another along a stream through the historic and lovely Buckner Orchard; or ride your bikes to take in the magnificent 312-foot Rainbow Falls. Note that only serious backpackers should embark on the rugged backcountry trails here. Winter brings fine opportunities for cross-country skiing or snowshoeing, though the town pretty much shuts down for the season, and lodgings and restaurants close or have limited operations. A National Park Service shuttle bus (509/682-2549) provides transportation from Stehekin to trailheads, campgrounds, fishing holes, and scenic areas mid-May through mid-October.

If your time is limited, or if you prefer to hover closer to civilization, stay in the resort town of **Chelan**, at the lake's southern tip. However, keep in mind that this is one of the state's most popular summer swimming, boating, and fishing destinations, and the hordes of visitors do detract from the romantic ambience. In warm weather, the lake's clear waters buzz with water-skiers, windsurfers, kayakers, and boaters. If you wish to join the fray, rent boats and water-ski gear at **Chelan Boat Rentals** (1210 W Woodin Ave; 509/682-4444). Otherwise, enjoy lakeside strolls or take a day-trip to Stehekin (see above). For the most romantic option, book a breathtaking aerial tour of the surrounding mountains with **Chelan Airways** (1328 W Woodin Ave; 509/682-5065 or 509/682-5555; www.chelanairways.com). At the **Deepwater Brewing & Public House** (225 Hwy 150; 509/682-2720; www.deepwaterbrewing.com), 2 miles outside of Chelan, enjoy microbrews and tasty pub fare at sunset on the outdoor terrace; there's even live music on summer weekends. For casual Mexican fare, visit **La Laguna** (114 N Emerson St; 509/682-5553), with its pleasant lighting; cozy booths; white stucco walls stenciled with flowers; and delicious, authentic tacos, burritos, and chiles rellenos. If nothing sounds better than an exotic drink, try the Chelan Sunset Margarita, a pretty and potent mix of tequila, melon liqueur, and cranberry juice.

If you're traveling to or from Chelan via the southern route past the town of Wenatchee, consider a stop at **Ohme Gardens** (just north of Wenatchee on US Hwy 97A, near its junction with Hwy 2; 509/662-5785; www.ohmegardens.com; closed mid-Oct–mid-Apr; small admission fee charged). This lush alpine retreat sits on a promontory 600 feet above the Columbia River, offering incredible views of the river, valley, city, and mountains. Amid this 9-acre display of mountain splendor are the gardens; take one of the footpaths that wander through colorful flower beds, splashing waterfalls, and lovely alpine meadows. Natural rock formations emerge from tranquil pools set among evergreens, and the Cascades provide a magnificent backdrop for it all. This garden would be Eden, and you and your sweetheart

Adam and Eve—if only it weren't for the thousands of other tourists who have also discovered it. Though the scenery is apt to inspire some kisses, the crowds will certainly inhibit your romantic inclinations; try to visit at an off-time, when other visitors are at a minimum.

Access & Information

Via Highway 20 and Highway 153, toward Pateros, link to Alternate Highway 97 south to reach the towns of Manson and Chelan. From the greater Seattle area, take Highway 2 to Wenatchee and head north on Alternate Highway 97. At Chelan, catch a boat or floatplane to Stehekin. For the latter, contact **Chelan Airways** (1328 W Woodin Ave; 509/682-5065 or 509/682-5555); they offer daily seaplane service to Stehekin ($120 round-trip), as well as scenic tours of the mountains.

Summer travel by water into Stehekin involves taking one of three boats: an old-fashioned tour boat, the **Lady of the Lake II**, or one of its two faster, more modern siblings. All boats offer day-trip options; those staying overnight simply disembark in Stehekin. The largest boat, *Lady II*, holds 350 people and takes four hours (it's a long, leisurely trip). Day-trippers have a 90-minute layover in Stehekin, so the real adventure here is the boat trip itself. *Lady II* departs Chelan daily at 8:30am and returns around 6pm ($22 per person round-trip; kids 6–11 travel for half price). The faster, smaller **Lady Express** shortens the trip to just over two hours one-way, with a one-hour stop in Stehekin before heading back (round-trip tickets $41). And finally there's the **Lady Cat**, a catamaran that whips across the lake at 50mph, makes the trip in 75 minutes, and costs $79 round-trip. Many people opt for the "combination trip," traveling uplake on the *Lady Express* and returning on the *Lady II*, which allows for a layover of 3 hours and 15 minutes in Stehekin and a return by 6pm. The faster boats in particular almost always book up early; advance purchase is necessary. During the off-season—November 1 through May 1—the boat schedule is cut back drastically, so always call ahead. For full details, contact the **Lake Chelan Boat Company** (1418 W Woodin Ave; 509/682-2224 or 509/682-4584; www.ladyofthelake.com).

For more information about Chelan, contact the **Lake Chelan Visitor Bureau** (PO Box 216, Chelan, WA 98816; 800/4-CHELAN; www.lakechelan.com). For more about the backpacking route to Stehekin, check with **North Cascades National Park** (360/856-5700) or the well-informed and helpful ranger station at Chelan (428 W Woodin Ave, Chelan; 509/682-2576; open year-round).

Romantic Lodgings

FLICK CREEK HOUSE
♥♥♥

Stehekin / 509/884-1730

If you thought the town of Stehekin was an isolated destination, just wait until you see this secluded retreat. Your definition of privacy will never be the same again. Hidden away along the shore of Lake Chelan, this post-and-beam cedar home is accessible only by boat, floatplane, or trail—a fact that pretty much guarantees you will have the property's 7 acres all to yourselves. Depending on the season, the daily passenger boat can drop you off and pick you up at your own private bay; just be sure to call ahead to find out if this is an option during your visit. Embraced by towering pines and fronted by a large deck, the two-story wood cabin is comfortably rustic, with modest furnishings and two bathrooms. Large picture windows and a very high ceiling showcase breathtaking views through the trees to McGregor's Peak. The view is no less phenomenal in the master bedroom upstairs, where a unique bed frame made from Stehekin lumber elevates the bed for advantageous viewing. Although the cabin sleeps up to 10 people, for the ultimate romantic getaway we recommend renting the entire place for yourselves. A second bedroom upstairs is oriented more to kids, but the third bedroom, on the main floor, features a four-poster bed and serene views of nearby Flick Creek. Also on the main level, a pretty blue-and-white kitchen offers modern appliances and a cozy love seat for two; all you need to bring is a week's worth of provisions and an appetite for romantic dinners for two. If you'd like to venture into town, follow the Lake Shore Trail 2½ miles into Stehekin, or make arrangements with the owners for boat transportation ($15 per trip). Also at your disposal are a private sandy beach, a barbecue and fire pit overlooking the water, and a complimentary 12-foot rowboat for quiet moments on the lake. As if all this weren't enough, breathtaking sunsets each evening come compliments of Mother Nature. After so much time in a gorgeous place with the one you love, you may never want to return to civilization.

$$$ *No credit cards; checks OK; closed Nov–Apr; www.stehekinvalley.com/ stehekinvacationrentals.htm.*

SILVER BAY INN
♥♥♥

10 Silver Bay Rd, Stehekin / 509/687-3142 or 254/377-3912 (May–Oct)

Sheltered on the tip of a tiny peninsula and surrounded by groomed lawns, Silver Bay Inn offers splendid isolation in a wondrous setting for those who can't wait to get away from it all. A waterside hammock sways lazily under a stand of trees, and a magnificent hot tub, new dock, and swimming area await at water's edge, lit at night only by the moon and shooting stars. Complimentary canoes, new rowboats, and beach cruiser bicycles are available, so guests can explore the surrounding country roads and waterways. There are several accommodation options, and it's a testament to the power of technology that all units feature wireless Internet service (free for guests). A passive-solar home (the innkeepers live next door) is rented as a single unit and sleeps up to five, but is definitely cozy enough for two. Antiques, local artwork, and country decor welcome you in the parlor and glass-enclosed sun porch; two bedrooms have beds covered with patchwork quilts and lots of rustic charm, particularly the upstairs room with its deep soaking tub and private lake-view deck. Stock up on groceries before you arrive to take advantage of the full kitchen (the nearest grocery store is in Chelan). The River View Room, a separate unit attached to the house, provides a much smaller and less expensive option; it includes a tiny bedroom, detached kitchenette, private entrance, and deck. For amorous couples, the two neighboring lakeside cabins with full kitchens and updated baths are best. They also feature cozy sleeping lofts, woodstoves, propane barbecues, and wraparound cedar decks with expansive water views. Breakfast is do-it-yourself, so come prepared with goodies. There's a five-night minimum-stay requirement for the cabins during the summer, and after your first heavenly night here, you'll understand why.

$$–$$$ *MC, V; checks OK; www.silverbayinn.com.*

Condos in Chelan

Some of the best accommodations in the town of Chelan are shore-side condos. Chelan Quality Vacation Properties (509/682-9782 or 888/977-1748; www.lakechelanvacationrentals.com), a rental clearinghouse, has listings for condos and private vacation homes in the area. Keep in mind that because each condo or house is privately owned, furnishings and styles vary greatly. Condos at Wapato Point (1 Wapato Point Wy, Manson; 509/687-9511 or 888/768-9511; www.wapatopoint.com), a full-fledged resort in neighboring Manson, are rented directly through its office.

CENTRAL CASCADES

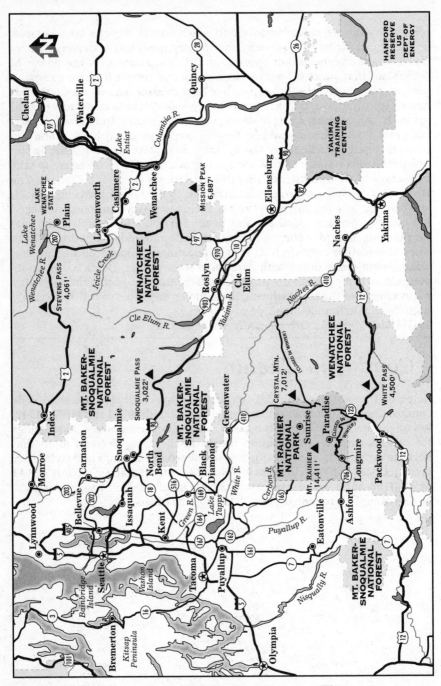

*"I have found men who didn't know how to kiss.
I've always found time to teach them."*

—MAE WEST

♡ CENTRAL CASCADES

If your vision of romance includes soaring snowcapped mountains, consider a visit to the Central Cascades, which are among the most spectacular and pristine peaks in the Pacific Northwest. The region offers plentiful opportunities to explore its natural treasures, including hiking, white-water rafting, horseback riding, golfing, bird-watching, and cross-country skiing. And all of it can be easily accessed via Interstate 90 or US Highways 2 and 12, which pass directly through the Central Cascades and serve as the main arteries between Western and Eastern Washington. Romantic destinations here include the Bavarian-style village of Leavenworth and the Stevens Pass and Lake Wenatchee recreation areas. Also near Leavenworth, you'll find two of the state's most magnificent outdoor destinations: the pristine Alpine Lakes Wilderness, with its mountain goats and sapphire-hued lakes, and the Wenatchee National Forest, with more than 2,600 miles of trails winding through some of the Cascades' most breathtaking scenery.

Each season of the year brings a new set of attractions in this area. In summer, enjoy beautiful mountain hikes in the clear, pine-perfumed air. Winter affords excellent downhill skiing at the resorts at Snoqualmie, Stevens, and White Passes, along with opportunities for romantic sleigh rides. In autumn, some of the state's most glorious foliage can be found along Highway 2, which is also the route to Leavenworth. This town's many festivals draw visitors year-round.

The Central Cascades are also home to one of the world's most beautiful mountains—Mount Rainier. On a sunny day, picnicking among wildflowers on one of the mountain's pristine meadows makes for one of the Northwest's most sublime outdoor experiences. The views at Paradise, one of the mountain's most popular summer destinations, simply must be seen to be believed. From Puget Sound, the mountain is an easy day-trip, but we highly recommend spending a romantic weekend at one of the nearby lodgings to truly take in the exhilarating alpine sights.

LEAVENWORTH & LAKE WENATCHEE

ROMANTIC HIGHLIGHTS

Tucked snugly in a valley on the eastern slopes of the towering Cascades, Leavenworth's mountain setting evokes that of a tiny village in the Swiss Alps. Faced with near extinction when its logging and railroad industry fell away, the town decided to make the most of this resemblance, and Leavenworth, the Bavarian Village, was born. This presents a contradiction for amorous couples. On the one hand, the pervasive, tourist-attracting Bavarian motif is more contrived than charming; on the other hand, the setting is truly spectacular. Fortunately, a number of luxurious getaways in the area tip the scales in Leavenworth's favor, and those willing to look beyond the faux-Bavarian decor will find some excellent retreats. And what about those chain outlets, like Dairy Queen, dressed up in German-themed facades? Well, you might be pleasantly surprised by how charming they look when snow completes the picture. Winter is indeed a pleasant time to visit, when cozy sleigh rides offer a romantic respite from the busy streets of town. Summer brings hot, sunny days and hordes of visitors. Amorous couples should plan ahead to avoid the busy festival weekends (see Access and Information), which occur throughout the year. For smaller crowds, crisp mountain air, and brilliant yellow-gold foliage on the alpine larches, we highly recommend a visit in autumn.

Icicle Road, off Highway 2, provides a link from Leavenworth to the incredible scenery within the Alpine Lakes Wilderness and Wenatchee National Forest. The views along the drive are spectacular, but we recommend stepping out of the car from time to time to get the full effect of the stunning natural beauty. On Icicle Creek you can watch the Chinook salmon run, late May through July, and spawn, in late August; or walk the mile-long nature trail at the **Leavenworth National Fish Hatchery** (12790 Fish Hatchery Rd, off Icicle Rd; 509/548-7641; leavenworth.fws.gov or www.salmonfest.org). Traverse the glorious terrain on foot with a trail map (see Access and Information), or just park along the road and follow one of the many marked paths that wind through the mountain landscape.

For pleasures of a more touristy sort, stroll hand in hand through the streets of Leavenworth itself. Intriguing shops include **Die Musik Box** (933 Front St; 800/288-5883; www.musicboxshop.com), with its dazzling—and sometimes noisy—array of music boxes; and **A Country Heart** (821 Front St; 509/548-5719), which offers country accents for the urban home. When a romantic respite is called for, visit **Cafe Mozart** (829 Front St; 509/548-0600; www.cafemozartrestaurant.com) for European charm, tasty German-style food, and afternoon coffee and pastries; if Italian suits your mood, try **Visconti's Ristorante Italiano** (see Romantic Restaurants).

On a crisp winter evening, a **horse-drawn sleigh or carriage ride** is an absolute must for a romantic thrill—many a marriage proposal has taken place here. Take in the splendid surroundings from your old-fashioned perch while the well-cared-for Percheron carries you through the snow; rides are available through **Mountain Springs Lodge** (19115 Chiwawa Loop Rd, Leavenworth; 509/763-2713 or 800/858-2276; www.mtsprings.com), or **Icicle Outfitters & Guides** (on the south shore of Lake Wenatchee; 509/669-1518 or 800/497-3912; www.icicleoutfitters.com).

Couples can also find a pleasant retreat at pretty **Lake Wenatchee**, although its popularity as a family destination in summer means you definitely won't have the place to yourselves. The lake is about a half-hour's drive from Leavenworth, and a state park at one end offers a large, sandy public swimming beach and campsites in the woods closer to the Wenatchee River and lake (888/226-7688; www.parks.wa.gov; overnight fee). Ask about day hikes on the north side of the lake (your best bet for privacy) at the **ranger station** (22976 Hwy 207, Leavenworth; 509/763-3103). Near the lake, resorts abound. Recreation seekers can play golf or tennis at **Kahler Glen Golf and Ski Resort** (20890 Kahler Dr, Leavenworth; 509/763-2121 or 800/440-2994; www.kahlerglen.com); there are also havens for couples at such retreats as **Natapoc Lodging** (see Romantic Lodgings).

Access & Information

Highway 2 heads east-west across Washington from Interstate 5 at Everett to Spokane. The highway winds its way up to Stevens Pass along the Skykomish River. Stevens Pass itself (exit 194 off Hwy 2; 206/812-4510; www.stevenspass.com) is a popular destination with Seattle-area skiers, offering downhill and cross-country (the Nordic center is located 5 miles east of the summit). Day lodges at the summit house half a dozen casual eateries. From the pass, Highway 2 descends to the turnoff for Lake Wenatchee (at Cole's Corner, about mile marker 85, turn onto Highway 207) and leads directly to Leavenworth.

Highway 2 is part of one of the Northwest's most beautiful drives, the 400-mile Cascade Loop. This route takes in Leavenworth and Wenatchee, and heads north to Lake Chelan, Winthrop, and the North Cascades Scenic Highway (see the North Cascades chapter). The route can be accessed from Interstate 90 at Cle Elum by taking Highway 970 to US Highway 97 north, which joins US Highway 2 just east of Leavenworth. A brochure is available from the **Cascade Loop Association** (PO Box 3245, Wenatchee, WA 98807; 509/662-3888; www.cascadeloop.com).

For more information on Leavenworth, along with helpful maps, check with the **Leavenworth Chamber of Commerce** (220 9th St; 509/548-5807; www.leavenworth.org). Excellent hiking information is available from the **Leavenworth Ranger Station**, just off Highway 2 (600 Sherbourne St, eastern edge of town; 509/548-6977).

Romantic Lodgings

ABENDBLUME PENSION
✿✿✿✿

12570 Ranger Rd, Leavenworth / 509/548-4059 or 800/669-7634
This elegant, sophisticated inn, which offers luxury in every detail, provides one of Leavenworth's most romantic retreats. Hand-carved, arched double doors open to reveal a gorgeous limestone foyer; a curved, wrought-iron staircase beneath a stained-glass skylight winds upward to six exquisite guest rooms (the seventh one is on the main floor). Every room, regardless of size, offers a romantic escape, and even the least expensive rooms include down comforters, TV/VCRs, tiled bathrooms, and fireplaces (one room, the Tannenbaum, even has two—both gas and wood burning). Soft lounging robes are provided for your comfort, and in-room therapeutic massages for two can be arranged upon request. The two most romantic rooms, the Dornröschen and Almrosen, have wood-burning fireplaces, Italian-marble bathrooms with whirlpool tubs discreetly opening into the rooms, and sun-drenched window seats with views. Relax in front of the fireplace, lounge on the snow-white canopy bed, take in the views of the valley and distant mountains, or unwind with a water massage in the double-headed shower—there is no shortage of good places to kiss at Abendblume. If you can muster the energy to leave your wonderful room, we suggest a visit to the outdoor Grecian spa, inlaid with Italian tiles, or the sumptuous common area, where you can snuggle up on an overstuffed couch in front of a crackling fire. But perhaps the ultimate place to share a kiss is over the dessert served every evening to guests by candlelight at intimate, two-person tables in the knotty-pine dining room. In the morning, a hearty German repast featuring sweet breakfast breads, a hot entrée, and an assortment of meats and cheeses is served in the same dining room, minus the candlelight. The gracious hosts are dedicated to fostering romance. Upon request, they will have champagne and chocolates or wine and cheese waiting for you in your room; they can even place a red rose on the pillow, dim the lights, and have your favorite soft music playing on the in-room CD player when you walk in. Ask and you shall receive. If you visit over the holidays, you'll be treated to their amazing Christmas decor, which always garners awards and acclaim.
$$–$$$ *AE, DIS, MC, V; checks OK; www.abendblume.com.*

ALL SEASONS RIVER INN
❍❍❍❡

8751 Icicle Rd, Leavenworth / 509/548-1425 or 800/254-0555
Perched on a bluff overlooking the Wenatchee River, this modern two-story cedar house's rather plain exterior belies the utter country-style comfort inside. The spacious living room boasts a river-rock fireplace and expansive views of the surging river, and teddy bears adorn both common-area couches and the beds in the lovely guest rooms. A deck overlooking the river adds another great way to enjoy this relaxing riverside location. Snow-capped Wedge Mountain peeks through the windows in the upstairs game room, and a separate TV room offers floral upholstered couches perfect for snuggling. All six enticing guest rooms have deliciously thick down comforters on queen-size beds (in keeping with the spirit of a romantic retreat, there are no TVs). Most of the rooms have private decks or patios, gas fireplaces, Jacuzzi tubs, tasteful wall stenciling, and sitting areas furnished with restored-antique love seats. Three recently completed two-room suites, complete with river views and cozy window seats, offer accommodations that are even more elegant. Our favorites are the spacious Evergreen and River View Suites, which feature double-headed showers and soothing color schemes. The third two-room suite, River Bend, offers serene views of the river from its Jacuzzi tub, nestled next to a large window in a cozy nook in the bathroom. Breakfast in the morning is a sumptuous spread of home-made granola, fresh zucchini bread, fruit parfait, Mexican tamale pancakes, savory sausage, and German potatoes. Ask about the innkeeper's recipe book if you'd like to try making this unforgettable morning meal at home. $$–$$$ MC, V; checks OK; www.allseasonsriverinn.com.

ENCHANTED RIVER INN
❍❍❍

9700 E Leavenworth Rd, Leavenworth / 509/548-9797
The Enchanted River Inn's secluded and lovely setting on the Wenatchee River has great romantic appeal. This recently renovated contemporary home, located just 30 feet above a serene stretch of the river, feels utterly removed from Leavenworth's busy streets, although town is within 5 minutes by car, or 15 minutes on foot. For the most romantic accommodations, check in to one of the two riverside suites, which boast glorious sunset views over Tumwater Mountain and Icicle Ridge. The sky-high rates seem a bit inflated given the rather standard, impersonal room decor, but fortunately, the stellar amenities help make up for such drawbacks. In the main-floor Starlight Suite, gaze at the stars through 12-foot-wide skylights from the king-size bed, or relax in the two-person Jacuzzi tub. There's a private entrance from the wraparound deck. The Sojourner Suite is by far our favorite, with its private lower-level location and direct access to the long shared deck. Features include a river-rock gas fireplace, 12-foot window

wall looking out to the river, private entrance, king-size bed, and TV hidden away in a large armoire. You might end up spending most of your time in the enormous, luxurious bathroom, where a softly lit alcove surrounded by blue pearl granite holds a gorgeous two-person Jacuzzi bathtub; heated tile floors; and the "J-Dream Shower," with two benchlike seats, an embedded stereo/CD player, and various body-spray, waterfall-shower, and steam-bath options. (Let the water heat up before you step in, or you might get a chilly surround-jet surprise.) Fresh flowers and plush robes are extra nice touches. The recently remodeled New Seasons Suite has an in-room two-person Jacuzzi and a freestanding fireplace, and the bathroom includes a shower/steam bath with a stereo and CD player, a bidet, and heated tile floors. In the morning, the delicious breakfast starts with homemade sorbet and a freshly baked cinnamon roll, followed by a Leavenworth breakfast burrito or other savory egg dish. All this is served in the bright, airy dining area or, in nice weather, river-side on the deck.
$$$ MC, V; checks OK; www.enchantedriverinn.com.

FEATHERWINDS LODGING
♦♦◖
17033 River Rd, Leavenworth / 509/763-0698 or 866/319-4637
This country getaway, comprising a B&B and a new luxury inn built in 2003, is a quintessential rural retreat located about 15 miles from the heart of busy Leavenworth. (There are also two large guest houses on the property, designed for groups.) The B&B is in a picturesque wood-shingled farmhouse surrounded by tall trees and wildflowers. Inside, the focus is on old-fashioned comfort, with three guest rooms offering cushioned window seats, private baths, TV/VCRs, and old-fashioned feather beds beneath pretty floral comforters. Our favorite is the main-floor room, which has a whirlpool tub set beneath corner windows in the sunny bathroom. The aroma of piping-hot coffee set just outside your door in the early morning will make it that much easier to get out of your warm bed and enjoy the generous breakfast served in the dining room. The Inn at Featherwinds, completed in May 2003, is a spacious and welcoming two-story structure with large fireplaces and lodge-inspired decor in the common areas. The rooms have country simplicity, with knotty-pine interiors, pale carpeting, in-room Jacuzzi tubs, private bathrooms, king-size beds, and balconies that look out into the trees. Furnishings are comfortable, if standard. There's one seating for the hearty multicourse breakfast, which you enjoy at individual tables. Year-round outdoor activities are available just outside your door. In winter, you can cross-country ski along a mile-long trail or roam the property's 9 wooded acres. In summer, guests can explore the area on complimentary bikes, relax in the large outdoor spa, or swim under the small waterfall that splashes into the outdoor pool. After you've worked up an appetite, an extra bonus

is the complimentary dessert served each evening to guests of both the inn and the B&B.
$$ *MC, V; checks OK; www.featherwinds.com.*

HOTEL PENSION ANNA
◒◒◖

926 Commercial St, Leavenworth / 509/548-6273 or 800/509-ANNA
The Austrian-style exterior of this bed-and-breakfast may suit only visitors with an affinity for the town's ersatz motif, but inside, anyone can love the comfortable rooms. Even the less expensive suites have thick down comforters, down pillows, stately armoires, and wood accents. (Plus, these rooms are a steal at less than $130 a night.) The pricier suites are really not all that pricey, considering their spa tubs, pretty half-canopies, sitting areas, and wood-burning fireplaces, in addition to the features listed above. Of the suites, try the second-floor Ottman Suite, with lavish red and gold decor, ornate tiled fireplace, and two-person Jacuzzi tub. All the rooms are named after valleys in Germany, and the common areas showcase colorful Bavarian mementos and antiques. For the most "heavenly" option, try the Chapel Suite or the Parish Nook, both of which reside in an old Catholic chapel adjacent to the main building. The innovative Chapel Suite, our favorite, boasts 15-foot cathedral ceilings, rich burgundy carpeting, and a two-person Jacuzzi tub set beneath leaded Gothic windows in the sitting room. While a few places in the room feel worn around the edges, the detailed tapestry above the ornate king-size bed, and the staircase leading up to what was once a choir loft, are nice touches. In the morning, all guests are welcome to enjoy a German-style continental breakfast in the bright, spacious breakfast room. The hearty fare of cheeses, sausages, fresh fruit, and breads can be enjoyed privately at tables for two, or you can have it delivered to your room if you stay in one of the suites.
$$–$$$ *AE, DIS, MC, V; checks OK; www.pensionanna.com.* &

MOUNTAIN HOME LODGE
◒◒◒◖

8201 Mountain Home Rd, Leavenworth / 509/548-7077 or 800/414-2378
This wonderful lodge is located a mile above Leavenworth in a breathtaking mountaintop setting. In summer, it can be reached by driving 3 miles of dirt road; in winter, a heated snow-cat picks you up from the parking lot at the bottom of Mountain Home Road. The slow, half-hour trip up the mountain is breathtaking, with its views of the snow-blanketed valley, and this thrilling ascent is part of the appeal of this unique bed-and-breakfast. Upon your arrival, the friendly innkeepers graciously welcome you to the cedar lodge, where a massive stone fireplace warms the Great Room, and wall-to-wall windows offer lovely views. The 10 charming guest rooms are decorated with quilts, log- or peeled-pine beds, restored antiques, and

outdoor-themed accessories. All rooms have private baths and views of the tranquil surroundings. Our favorite is the Cascade Suite, which features a river-rock gas fireplace, a handcrafted peeled-pine king-size bed, rustic bent-vine maple furniture, plush robes, and a lovely Jacuzzi tub. For a true romantic getaway, rent one of two custom-built pine cabins with amazing views, plenty of privacy, and amenities intended just for couples. Each cabin has a hand-carved king-size bed, private deck, reading loft, and river-rock spa tub, as well as fireplace. And just outside your door is a wondrous mountain playground. Borrow cross-country skis to enjoy miles of tracked cross-country ski trails outside the back door, snowshoe and sled, or try the 1,700-foot toboggan run. Summer activities include hiking, horseshoes, badminton, and tennis; the hot tub and swimming pool overlook a broad meadow and mountains. Evenings are cozy, with hors d'oeuvres and wine served next to the stone fireplace. An adjacent dining area with two-person tables is a good spot to enjoy gourmet meals served up by the lodge's talented chef (see Romantic Restaurants). Winter rates include transportation to and from the lodge, all meals, and unlimited use of recreational equipment (snowshoes, sleds, and cross-country skis).
$$–$$$$ DIS, MC, V; checks OK; www.mthome.com.

PINE RIVER RANCH
❀❀❀
19668 Hwy 207, Leavenworth / 509/763-3959 or 800/669-3877
If you're looking for some quiet country romancing, look no further than the Pine River Ranch. This charming 1940s ranch house is located about 14 miles west of the town center and feels worlds away from the tourist-filled streets of downtown Leavenworth. The ranch was once a dairy farm, and though it no longer operates as such, the old barn remains beautifully intact. Of the six suites, two are located in the original ranch house, with four more in adjacent white stucco buildings. All feature jetted tubs, fireplaces, small kitchenettes (complete with espresso machines), and sitting areas with satellite TVs, VCRs, and stereos. In the ranch house, choose from the two-room Evergreen Suite upstairs, with country decor and four-poster pine feather bed, or the main-floor Wildflower Suite, a bright, airy room with plenty of windows and a charming wrought-iron bed with canopy. The four detached suites offer even more privacy. Named after the lodgepole pine trees on view from its many windows, Lodgepole features a unique bed frame crafted from unfinished branches; Ponderosa showcases distant views of the mountains; and Natapoc and Nason both offer views of a pasture and tree-covered ridge. The interiors feature vaulted ceilings, richly colored linens made up on mammoth log beds, and river-rock hearths with gas fireplaces. Private entrances ensure your sense of self-sufficiency and seclusion. Those who like to sleep late will be happy to know there's no need to wake up early, as all the suites come with a full breakfast delivered to your doorstep. Treats

might include French toast with caramel-apple topping or smoked salmon quiche. After breakfast, explore the property's 32 acres, which include new landscaping and hiking and cross-country skiing trails with access to nearby Mason Creek.
$$$ *AE, DIS, MC, V; checks OK; www.prranch.com.*

RUN OF THE RIVER
◆◆◆◆

9308 E Leavenworth Rd, Leavenworth / 509/548-7171 or 800/288-6491
This elegant log inn on the bank of the Icicle River is an exceptional place to make your getaway with luxury and style. Vintage bicycles hung from the ceilings and vintage snowshoes on the walls add rustic charm to the interior, which is decorated with a whimsical outdoorsy theme. All six suites have plenty of luxury and space and come complete with river-rock fireplaces, hand-hewn four-poster burlwood log king-size beds, cozy quilts, jetted tubs for two surrounded by river rock, and work by local artists. The color and personality of the rooms immediately sets a fun mood. For its excellent views of the mountains and warm, inviting decor, the new Osprey suite is an excellent choice, though, in truth, all the suites boast plenty of solitude, comfort, and attention to detail. Book lovers should request one of the rooms with a reading loft. The romantic extras include soft robes, cozy cuddling nooks, private decks with wooden swings, and binoculars for watching wildlife in the nature refuge across the river. You'll also find satellite TVs and bubble kits, in case stargazing from the hot tub isn't entertainment enough. Amenities include the rather brilliant idea of vintage typewriters supplied with stationery; write each other romantic missives when inspiration strikes. Don't forget to place a candle in your "wish upon a star" candle holder and watch shadows and patterns dance on the walls and ceiling at night. Capressa self-grinding coffee makers are in all of the rooms, and gourmet breakfasts are served at the large dining room table in the main entry. The food is served in courses and may include fresh fruit, delicious fruit smoothies, personally monogrammed yogurt cups, savory frittata, organic chorizo sausage and eggs, pumpkin pancakes, and sweet fruit desserts. Although the rates may seem high, luxury comes with a price and the personal touches here make it worthwhile; however, value packages can often be found on their Web site between January and May. Take advantage of the in-room massage service, and don't hesitate to ask the innkeepers about what this area has to offer. They are very knowledgeable about good scenic drives, hikes, and mountain-bike trails. Maps and information are available to guests, as is complimentary use of mountain bikes and snowshoes in the winter. Borrow the Cannondale tandem bicycle for a romantic ride along Icicle Creek.
$$$–$$$$ *DIS, MC, V; checks OK; www.runoftheriver.com.*

Romantic Restaurants

THE ALLEY CAFÉ
◐◐◐

214 8th St (at the Alley), Leavenworth / 509/548-6109
Cuisine other than German *can* be found in Leavenworth, you just have to
find the right alleyway. At this charming Italian restaurant, two intimate
dining rooms offer a cozy hideaway for couples. The menu, featuring classic
pasta with house-made sauces and hearty dishes of halibut, salmon, and top
sirloin, provides a welcome respite from Bavarian specialties. Both dining
areas are filled with romantic detail, including chandeliers, wine-colored
carpets, rose-patterned wallpaper and attractive charcoal-gray walls, and
decorative curtain swags. On the linen-covered, candlelit tables, the paper
napkins are the only thing out of place. Try the penne pasta with Italian
sausage and peas in a rich mascarpone cream sauce, or the tasty black bean
ravioli stuffed with tomatoes and Serrano peppers. Select a special bottle
from the inviting wine list to go with your meal, and finish with a tiramisù
with freshly whipped cream or Chocolate Decadence, a rich flourless cake.
On Friday evenings, the soothing music of a local jazz trio adds to the ambience. When you step outside into the Bavarian-themed streets after dinner,
you will be delighted to have taken this unexpected romantic detour into
Italy.
*$$ AE, MC, V; checks OK; dinner every day; beer and wine; reservations
recommended; www.thealleycafe.com.*

MOUNTAIN HOME LODGE
◐◐◐◖

8201 Mountain Home Rd, Leavenworth / 509/548-7077 or 800/414-2378
The Mountain Home Lodge's motto is "1,000 feet closer to heaven," and
we couldn't agree more. Not only are you elevated to Leavenworth's supreme
mountain viewing spot, but also the food and accompanying ambience are
simply divine. Guests staying overnight at the lodge (see Romantic Lodg-
ings) receive priority seating, so be sure to make reservations in advance
if you plan on making the 2-mile journey from downtown. (In winter, the
lodge is accessible to nonguest diners only via the innkeepers' snowmo-
bile—exciting!) Before dinner, unwind in the Great Room, where appetizers
and complimentary wine is served in front of a crackling fire. The adjacent
dining room offers a handful of cozy tables for two. Soft lighting, white
tablecloths, and soothing music set the mood for romance, but nature itself
has provided the crowning touch: expansive panoramas of the snowcapped
Cascades showcased by large windows make you feel as though you're a
part of the scenery. A tasty prelude to your gourmet Northwest meal might
include apricot Brie wrapped in delicate phyllo, followed by homemade
bread and soup or salad. Just one entrée is prepared each evening, and it

might be applewood-smoked breast of duck with marionberry compote or delicious grilled yellow-fin tuna; a decadent chocolate tart might make a tempting finish. The wine list is graced by top Northwest offerings. With the menu decisions made for you, all that remains is to focus on the spectacular view and each other.

$$$ *DIS, MC, V; checks OK; dinner every day; beer and wine; reservations required; www.mthome.com/dining.html.*

VISCONTI'S RISTORANTE ITALIANO
●

636 Front St, Leavenworth / 509/548-1213
As romantic options are limited in Leavenworth, this restaurant does make the cut because the food is excellent and wine list outstanding, although the atmosphere does leave something to be desired (the crayons at the tables and kids' menu detract a bit from the adults-only mood you might be yearning for). Nonetheless, the attentive wait staff is well versed in their extensive Northwest-based wine list and is happy to recommend a favorite vintage. While Frank Sinatra croons on the stereo, enjoy an appetizer such as the fire-roasted mussels with aioli or freshly made bruschetta. The *spaghettini alla cozze* (spaghetti with mussels) and Veal saltimbocca are divine. Save room for a decadent dessert such as white chocolate–raspberry cheesecake or the infamous Visconti's Nightmare, a chocolate–peanut butter ice cream pie topped with chocolate sauce, caramel, and whipped cream, served in an Oreo cookie crust. To escape the din of the downstairs pub, request a table on the third floor, preferably a lovely window seat overlooking the village. If you venture to nearby Wenatchee, the restaurant has a location there, as well (1737 N Wenatchee Ave; 509/662-5013).

$$ *AE, DIS, MC, V; checks OK; lunch, dinner every day; beer and wine; reservations recommended; www.viscontis.com.*

More Leavenworth Kisses

Icicle Outfitters & Guides (on the south shore of Lake Wenatchee; 509/669-1518 or 800/497-3912; www.icicleoutfitters.com) offers everything from one-hour horseback rides to overnight trips; the overnight journeys come complete with meals, pack horses, saddle horses, a well-seasoned wrangler, a cook, tents, and the entire camp setup necessary for a two- to seven-day expedition. If you opt for this romantic adventure, you'll cross unspoiled wilderness and enjoy exhilarating views of glistening lakes, mountain streams, and snowcapped peaks. In the evenings after a hearty dinner, you can snuggle by the roaring campfire. **Eagle Creek Ranch** (509/548-7798 or 800/221-7433; www.eaglecreek.ws) is another full-service horse ranch that offers sleigh, buggy, hay, and trail rides as well as backcountry horseback-riding journeys. Make reservations well in advance, and confirm them again before your departure.

MOUNT RAINIER

ROMANTIC HIGHLIGHTS

Using poetic words to describe Mount Rainier is best left to the poets. For the kissing purposes of this book, suffice it to say that almost every inch of this mountain is romantic and utterly exquisite. An abiding symbol of natural grandeur in the Northwest, the peak soars 14,410 feet above sea level—several thousand feet higher than others in the Cascade Range—and makes an ideal place to get away from everything except each other. **Mount Rainier National Park** (360/569-2211; www.nps.gov/mora; $10 entry fee per vehicle, $5 entry fee per bicycle) is the center of all the action. Some of the mountain's main routes are closed in the winter, so find out about access ahead of time. The best romantic accommodations are located outside the park, in the town of Ashford, where you will find the Mount Rainier Visitor Association (see Access and Information), as well as a few stores and restaurants.

The single romantic highlight here is exploring the magnificent park. Three hundred miles of backcountry and self-guiding nature trails lead to ancient forests, dozens of massive glaciers, waterfalls, and alpine meadows lush with wildflowers during the mountain's short summer. The drives are almost as spectacular as the hikes. Getting to the popular destination of **Paradise**, located 19 miles inside the southwest entrance of the park, entails a wonderful journey. As the road climbs to 5,400 feet, views encompass lush old-growth evergreens, roaring **Narada Falls**, and glistening **Nisqually Glacier**. You might also spot foraging deer, brightly hued birds, mountain goats, soaring eagles, and brilliant wildflowers. Amid this natural splendor, Mount Rainier itself—draped in majestic snowy white—becomes larger and more magnificent as you ascend. At your destination, you'll find the Henry M. Jackson Memorial Visitor Center (just before Paradise; 360/569-2211, ext. 2328), housed in a flying saucer–like building, which offers snacks, a gift shop, and extensive nature exhibits. However, the best exhibit is the view itself. When you step out on the observation deck, you'll know why they call this Paradise.

If you've always wondered what it would be like to be on top of the world, **Sunrise** is a good place to find out. Open only during summer, this destination (6,400 feet) is the closest you can get to Rainier's peak without climbing. The old lodge has a visitor center (northeast corner of park, 31 miles north of Ohanapecosh; 360/663-2425; www.nps.gov/mora), a snack bar, and mountain exhibits. Once you arrive, you'll find that the inspiring trails offer everything from high-tech summit expeditions to relatively easy hikes; for one of the latter, make the short trek to a magnificent view of Emmons Glacier Canyon. No matter which trail you choose, you will enjoy the endlessly stunning landscapes—and each other.

On a fall afternoon, the mountain can be almost too glorious for words (even poets' words). You'll see what we mean when you drive over **Chinook Pass** (approach via Hwy 410; closed in winter). The scenery is so thrilling that you might even forget to kiss. Hills bathed in golden light, vivid red and amber trees, and crisp, clear air add up to one of the Northwest's most incredible autumnal experiences. The drive offers plenty of vista turnouts, hikes with dizzying switchbacks, and meadows you can explore hand in hand. Just be sure to come prepared. Comfortable hiking shoes, plenty of snacks and water, bug repellent, tissues, and a day pack will go a long way to ensure that Chinook Pass is the incredible experience it is meant to be. Also, be considerate of the wilderness and stay on the trails; behaving responsibly will keep this park's magnificent beauty intact for years to come. If you arrive from the north, you might stop for picnic goodies in Black Diamond. This relatively quiet, former coal-mining town is located on Highway 169, in Maple Valley, about 10 miles north of Enumclaw. **Black Diamond Bakery** (32805 Railroad Ave; 360/886-2741; www.blackdiamondbakery.com) boasts a wood-fired brick oven; the bread that comes out—26 different kinds, including cinnamon, sour rye, potato, and garlic French—is excellent and makes perfect fuel for a Rainier excursion.

Come winter, the two ski resorts in the Central Cascades offer the chance for snow-loving couples to hit the slopes. The state's best ski area, **Crystal Mountain Ski Resort** (off Hwy 410 just west of Chinook Pass, on northeast edge of Mount Rainier National Park; 360/663-2265; www.skicrystal.com) is located southeast of Enumclaw, with runs for beginners and experts plus fine backcountry skiing. **White Pass** (509/672-3101; www.skiwhitepass.com) is an off-the-beaten-path ski destination offering downhill (with a high-speed quad lift) and cross-country skiing; it's located 12 miles southeast of the park at the summit of Highway 12. At 4,500 feet, its base is the highest on the Cascade crest. A Nordic center near the day lodge serves cross-country skiers with about 18 miles of trails. Whether you decide to take to the slopes in winter, or explore the glories of spring, summer, or fall, Mount Rainier offers endless opportunities for romance and adventure.

Access & Information

Most people travel to Mount Rainier National Park by car. From Interstate 5 near Tacoma, Highways 7 and 706 connect the main Nisqually entrance, which is open year-round, to Paradise. Highway 706 goes right into the park. From Enumclaw to the north or Yakima to the east, you can take Highway 410 into the park; from both the southeast and southwest, Highway 12 intersects with Highway 123 to take you into the park.

Inside the park, Chinook and Cayuse Passes are closed in winter; you can take the loop trip or the road to Sunrise in late May through October. The road from Longmire to Paradise remains open during daylight hours in winter; carry tire chains and a shovel, and check current road and weather conditions by calling a 24-hour information service (360/569-2211; www.wsdot.wa.gov/traffic/passes). Of the five entrance stations (fee is $10 per automobile or $5 per person on foot, bicycle, or motorcycle), the three most popular are described here; the northwest entrances (Carbon River and Mowich Lake) offer few visitor facilities and have unpaved roads.

For more information, contact **Mount Rainier National Park** (360/569-2211; www.nps.gov/mora). You can also request a map and brochure with points of interest from the **Mount Rainier Visitor Association** (PO Box 214, Ashford, WA 98304; 360/569-0910 or 877/617-9950; www.mt-rainier.com).

Romantic Lodgings

ALEXANDER'S COUNTRY INN
🏚🍴

37515 SR 706E, Ashford / 360/569-2300 or 800/654-7615
Nestled at the edge of old-growth forest (and, unfortunately, next to a two-lane highway that leads to Mount Rainier), this quaint, blue-painted country inn is surrounded by a lush green lawn with winding walkways and wooden benches. Beyond the main house is a peaceful trout pond bordered by evergreens. Upstairs, the inn's spacious common room has a gas fireplace, but its sparse furnishings and dim lighting disappoint somewhat. Most of the 12 guest rooms are much the same—they are even slightly gloomy, although unique stained-glass windows do add some color and character. Moreover, when all the rooms are occupied in high season, you might hear your neighbors through the thin walls, although there are no TVs. For the most privacy and romance, book one of the two suites in the tower. The upstairs suite has two levels: there's a bright sitting room with antiques on the lower level, and a loft bedroom full of sunlight on the upper level. The downstairs suite features a cozy sitting room and an octagonal bedroom with redwood paneling and wraparound windows. Down the road, a spacious house and chalet offer accommodations for larger groups. Guests at the inn enjoy complimentary wine in the evening, and the dining room at Alexander's is a nice spot for an intimate meal (see Romantic Restaurants). Complete your evening with a soak in the new hot tub, sheltered in a half-enclosed gazebo that overlooks the pond. In the morning, the full country

breakfast offers fruit, home-baked muffins, bacon, and a main course like hearty pancakes or quiche. This generous repast will fuel you to explore the park, just a mile up the road; if you want to stay out all day, order a boxed lunch to bring along on your hike.

$$–$$$ *MC, V; checks OK; www.alexanderscountryinn.com.*

ALMOST PARADISE
❂❂❂

201 Osborn Rd, Ashford / 360/569-2540 or 888/569-2540

A long, wooded drive leads to a Northwest cedar mountain lodge–style home and guest cottages, where the private and luxurious accommodations provide an ideal setting for romance. Opened in 1998, Almost Paradise caters specifically to couples and is a welcome addition to romantic lodging options in the area. Choose from among the three guest cottages on the main property and a more remote cabin. The three comfortable cottages boast lots of romantic touches, such as wonderful outdoor Jacuzzi hot tubs, gas fireplaces, plush terry robes, and inviting queen-size beds. Other features include continental breakfast baskets in the well-equipped kitchens, private baths, TV/VCRs, and stereos (some romantic music is supplied, or bring your own). The decor and amenities in each accommodation differ slightly. Our favorite is the spacious Paradise Guest House, completed in 2000, with an open layout that includes sitting room and bedroom, light switches on dimmers, and an inviting hunter green sofa placed in front of the river-rock gas fireplace. Outside, relax in your private hot tub nestled among giant boulders enveloped in moss and ferns, and gaze out at towering evergreens. The Sunrise Guest House is cozier, with low ceilings and adjoining smaller rooms that include a bedroom with country linens, a sitting room with fireplace, and a small kitchen; an added bonus is the huge, beautiful dry sauna outside your sliding doors, which is entirely private. The newest accommodation on the property is the Rainier Cabin, with kitchenette and private outdoor hot tub, completed in 2003. But if you truly want to get away from it all, check into the Woodland Cabin, a five-minute drive from the main house. The appealing interior, with white and cedar-plank wainscoting, is absolutely charming, and old-fashioned wooden skis mounted on the wall add whimsy to the decor. A queen-size bed is fitted with an attractive wooden headboard. There's a standard bath, but for long soaks we recommend the outdoor hot tub. The breakfast basket is not included here, but there is a full kitchen, so come with supplies.

$$ *MC, V; checks OK; www.almostparadiselodging.com.*

JASMER'S AT MOUNT RAINIER
✿✿✿

30005 SR 706E, Ashford / 360/569-2682
If you think a sublime way to enjoy Mount Rainier National Park would be to have your own private retreat here, you're in luck, because Jasmer's provides just that. Choose between two cozy suites on the main property or a dozen cottages located throughout Ashford. Most are within a 5-mile drive of the park entrance, and quite a few provide enough privacy and refinement to satisfy your romantic needs. On the main property, the small, affordable suites offer cozy wood interiors, gas fireplaces, queen-size beds, and private baths with two-person showers; breakfast is not included, but the small refrigerator, coffee maker, microwave, and toaster, along with gourmet coffee and tea, mean you can prepare it yourselves. The hot tub tucked away in the woods is shared by both units; reserve private time for an evening soak. Of the individual cabins, our favorite is the Creekside, a two-bedroom cottage overlooking a creek with an expansive deck and completely private hot tub; it comes with a wood-burning stove clad in river rock, a full kitchen, pleasant Northwest-style country decor, and an entertainment center (there is no TV reception, so bring along a few romantic movies). Other less expensive options include the East Echo Chalet, a studio apartment with full kitchen, cozy woodstove, and queen-size bed; the private hot tub outside offers a wonderful way to view the stars. Cabins are individually decorated, and some have rather dated furnishings, so survey all the options before you make your choice. Stock up on favorite foods before you arrive; Ashford has only two small stores, which might not carry exactly what you're craving. Expect minimum-stay requirements in season. One more word to the wise: Be sure to make reservations well ahead of time. These places fill up fast.
$$–$$$ *MC, V; no checks; www.jasmers.com.*

MOUNTAIN MEADOWS INN AND B&B
✿✿◖

28912 SR 706E, Ashford / 360/569-2788
Located 6 miles from the entrance to Mount Rainier National Park, this inn offers a secluded retreat on 11 landscaped acres. A newly added half-mile nature trail leads guests on a lovely walk among the grounds—don't miss the thousand daffodils blooming in spring or the meadows filled with wild flowers in summer. You can soak in the luxurious, 23-jet hot tub nestled in a cedar grove; roast marshmallows over the bonfire; or explore the grounds—by foot or on skis—to revel in the great outdoors before you and your sweetheart even set foot in the park. Six guest rooms, all with private baths, are available; the guest house has three larger apartments, but they're designed more for families than romantic couples. We recommend staying in the main house, where you'll find spacious guest rooms filled with beautiful

antiques and romantic furnishings. Our favorites are the Sunnybrook Room, with its bright wicker furniture and 19th-century brass bed, and the spacious Chief Seattle Room, with an antique trunk and armoire, a king-size bed, and Native American artwork. This room also features large windows overlooking the garden. Don't oversleep or you'll miss the bountiful breakfast prepared by the chef-owner. Homemade muffins, berry scones, and fresh fruits whet your appetite for the fabulous main dishes that follow, such as quiche Huntington with artichoke hearts, fresh basil, and cheese; smoked salmon omelet; or Belgian waffles topped with fresh strawberries and cream.
$$–$$$ *MC, V; checks OK; www.mountainmeadowsinn.com.*

NATIONAL PARK INN AT LONGMIRE
◆◖
Mount Rainier National Park / 360/569-2275 or 360/569-2411
This inn, located 6 miles inside the southwest entrance of Mount Rainier National Park, operates as a bed-and-breakfast in winter and a standard hotel in summer. Although its view of the mountain is less commanding than that of the park's other lodge, Paradise Inn (see below), the National Park Inn offers nicer accommodations and a beautiful, woodsy setting. The 25 small guest rooms here are fairly standard, but special touches like log furniture, soft quilted bedspreads, and oak-framed mountain pictures make them snug and inviting. The majority have private baths. Of course, the best reason to stay here is to enjoy the national park and the majesty of Mount Rainier; you won't be spending much time in your room anyway. A complimentary breakfast, served in the casual dining room downstairs, is included in your stay during winter, and ski packages are also available. The dining room is open to the public year-round for breakfast, lunch, and dinner (inexpensive to moderate). While hardly gourmet fare, the restaurant's sandwiches, salads, and burgers are sure to satisfy hungry hikers and skiers. You'll also find a small museum with wildlife exhibits, a hiking information center (360/569-2211, ext. 3317), a general store and gift center, and snowshoe and cross-country ski rental (360/569-2411).
$$–$$$ *AE, DC, DIS, MC, V; no checks; www.guestservices.com/rainier.*

PARADISE INN
◆
Mount Rainier National Park / 360/569-2275
Renovations costing more than $1 million recently updated the guest rooms of this historic lodge with more due in 2006; unfortunately, a million dollars doesn't go as far these days as it once did. Our hopes for a newly romantic mountainside retreat were dashed as soon as we stepped inside the guest rooms. Even with new carpeting, draperies, and bedding, the rooms still leave a great deal to be desired. Don't be fooled by the inn's stately lobby,

which is an impressive, airy, open-beamed room built from massive logs. Large fireplaces and cozy tables and chairs are scattered throughout, providing many tempting places to snuggle up together with a hot drink. The rooms, however, are an entirely different story. Situated along dismal hallways, all 117 units are claustrophobic, with small windows and standard motel-style furniture. It's a shame that the management hasn't done more with this prime property, but the lack of competition for this awe-inspiring summer destination has let them get away with mediocre accommodations for years. Nevertheless, its unparalleled location on Mount Rainier makes Paradise Inn worth a visit. The views up here truly defy description—this is purple mountain majesty in all its glory. Romantically speaking, the main highlight of staying here is being this close to Paradise (see Romantic Highlights).

$$–$$$ *AE, DC, DIS, MC, V; no checks; closed Oct–mid-May; www.guest services.com/rainier.*

STORMKING SPA AT MT. RAINIER
🌢🌢🌢

37311 SR 706E, Ashford / 360/569-2964 or 360/569-2339

Just a mile from the entrance to Mount Rainier National Park, the Stormking Spa offers a wonderful option for those who don't really want to rough it. The two recently built cabins (which sparked the high lip rating) are luxurious retreats; take our advice and leave the rustic B&B and large three-bedroom cottage to the larger groups. In the Eagle cabin, vaulted ceilings, a gas woodstove, polished wood-slab tables, and a handcrafted wall hanging of snowcapped Mount Rainier create cozy ambience. The spacious bathroom boasts a two-person greenhouse shower and a beautiful slate-tiled floor; outside, your private hot tub awaits in a cedar gazebo strung with twinkling lights. The only possible drawback is traffic noise from the nearby highway, but in this country setting that's not really an issue. For total romantic seclusion, check into the smaller, more remote Raven, a round, yurt-style cedar cabin nestled against protected forest and a babbling creek. Inside, a queen-size bed is situated underneath a round overhead skylight, perfect for looking at the stars. The garden-inspired decor beautifully melds indoors and outdoors, with hand-painted ferns on the floor and walls, a charming white wrought-iron bench, and a river-rock gas fireplace. The creatively designed bathroom's oversize showerhead creates a waterfall effect. Your private, cedar-enclosed hot tub is just steps away. Outdoor lighting at both cabins is superb; small spotlights illuminate the beautiful old firs, giant ferns, birch trees, and well-designed plank and stone walkways. Both also have surround-sound stereo, and you can even channel music outside to your hot tub—soothing CDs are supplied in the room, or bring your own. Other amenities include robes and slippers; candles; fine chocolates; a microwave; a mini-fridge; a coffee maker; and a basket with coffee, tea, and muffins or croissants for the morning. Massages are also available. Call ahead for detailed directions if you plan to arrive at night.

$$–$$$ *MC, V; checks OK; www.stormkingspa.com.*

Romantic Restaurants

ALEXANDER'S RESTAURANT
⬡⬡

37515 SR 706E (Alexander's Country Inn), Ashford / 360/569-2300 or 800/654-7615

No one comes to Mount Rainier for the fine restaurants, but Alexander's does have a quaint charm and pleasant ambience, thanks to stained-glass windows and tables adorned with candles and flowers. Get cozy in a wooden booth lined with soft cushions; savor the warmth of the wood-burning fireplace; and peek out of the lace-curtained windows overlooking the old wooden waterwheel and surrounding yard. Ducks and deer are often seen cavorting outside, seemingly undisturbed by the highway traffic just beyond the white picket fence. During high season, arrive early to secure a seat in the front room, since the back "overflow" area has poor lighting and low ceilings. Try the fresh trout, typically caught the same day in the backyard pond, or the hearty stuffed green peppers. The excellent entrées are accompanied by fresh sourdough bread, and the service is attentive. At the end of your meal, satiate your sweet tooth with a chocolate torte with raspberry sauce or the famous blackberry pie.

$$–$$$ *MC, V; checks OK; breakfast, lunch, dinner every day (June–Oct), lunch, dinner Fri–Sun (Nov–May); beer and wine; reservations recommended; www.alexanderscountryinn.com.*

WASHINGTON WINE COUNTRY

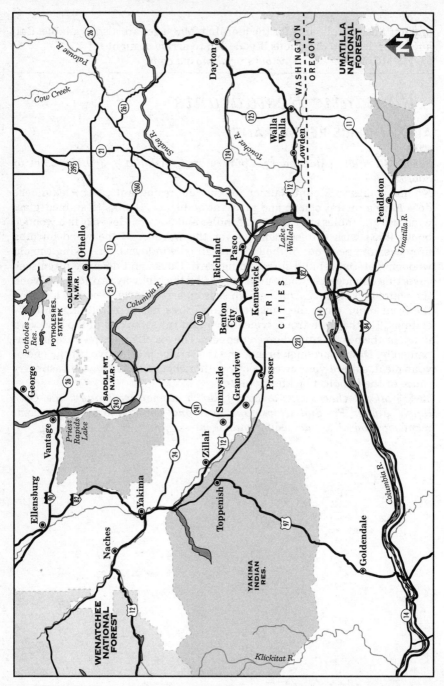

"Her lips on his could tell him better than all her stumbling words."

—MARGARET MITCHELL

♡ WASHINGTON WINE COUNTRY

Hundreds of days of sunshine each year and nearly 300 wineries—many of which are world-class producers, with tasting rooms open throughout the year—make this agricultural Eden southeast of Seattle a viable place for a romantic retreat. As its wine industry grows, Eastern Washington's reputation as a dry, monotonous landscape dotted with roadside fruit stands is giving way to the reality that it is, in fact, a worthy destination. Washington is the second-largest wine-producing state in the nation (behind California), and nearly 99 percent of the grapes for its wines are grown here, across a huge expanse of land that includes the Yakima, Columbia, and Walla Walla valleys. The state's vineyards enjoy hot, arid growing days and cool desert nights perfect for growing flavorful wine grapes. Washington wines offer something for every taste, from reds like merlot, cabernet sauvignon, and syrah to whites such as chardonnay, Riesling, sauvignon blanc, and semillon. The state is particularly known for its excellent red wines, with sweet cherry and berry flavors and complex, spicy aromas.

A weekend is too little time to visit—even briefly—all the wineries in the region, much less to relax and spend quality romantic time. A good idea is to book lodging in either Yakima or Walla Walla—each city has lots of romantic options—and explore the wineries within easy reach. Yakima is the preeminent city of central Washington as well as the seat of county government, and offers some pleasant hideaways despite its pronounced urban sprawl. Farther east, the quiet city of Walla Walla offers small-town ambience, tree-lined streets, a charming historic downtown, and a surprising number of excellent restaurants and inns. It's possible to experience both places in one trip, if you've got a little extra time and don't mind doing a lot of driving. The other cities of this golden, shrub-steppe landscape can't be described as truly romantic destinations, although each has its moments. Ellensburg boasts the Valley Café (see Romantic Restaurants), while the

Tri-Cities—Richland, Kennewick, and Pasco—feature some stellar wineries and private golf courses. During the scorching summers, the temperature often soars upward of 100 degrees F, and since most people explore this region by car, air-conditioning is a must. For the ideal romantic getaway, we recommend visiting in spring or fall, when the weather is balmier.

The idea of wine touring in this area is starting to catch on, and in Yakima and elsewhere, special-event weekends bring hordes of tourists to participating wineries. Normally, area winemakers are happy to have visitors and enjoy discussing their wines; but during these busy times the overall experience can be compromised. For the quietest and most idyllic retreat, plan in advance to avoid the crowds (see Access and Information).

YAKIMA VALLEY & WALLA WALLA

ROMANTIC HIGHLIGHTS

Yakima Valley winegrowers like to point out that their vineyards share the same latitude as the renowned wine regions of France. Unfortunately, the city of Yakima itself could never be confused with anywhere in the French countryside; however, beyond the strip malls and freeway exits of the city itself, you'll find some wonderful wineries in pretty settings. The stretch of countryside from Selah to Benton City reveals mile after scenic mile of lush orchards, cultivated fields, green-aisled hop yards, and vineyards, set off by rolling hills and a network of rivers and canals. Farther east, Walla Walla is filled with lush parks, shady boulevards, chic restaurants, and wine bars. Spring, when clouds of blossoms give the valley an ethereal beauty, is an especially lovely time to visit wineries; summer brings soaring temperatures and dry winds, and autumn ushers in the wine crush and cooler weather. Plan your trip right, and you'll return home with a few bottles (or cases) of wine and countless happy memories of your wine-country getaway.

Every winery, like every bottle of wine, has its own distinct personality. In our Romantic Wineries section, below, we highlight places that hold special interest for couples seeking romantic wine-country moments. (The list is not meant to indicate which wines in the region are best—a highly subjective matter, in any case.) For help in planning your trip, be sure to acquire the wine country brochure from the **Washington Wine Commission** (206/667-9463; www.washingtonwine.org). You can also pick up local touring maps at your lodging or at any winery. Some of the larger producers have vast tasting rooms and even vaster parking lots—but beyond this you'll find impressive grounds full of wonderful picnic spots. Other wineries are tiny, charming, and nestled along quiet back roads lined with vineyards. With **more than 100 wineries** in all to choose from, your days can be as busy, or as leisurely, as you please. A wine-country picnic is a must, and many local accommodations (see Romantic Lodgings) specialize in supplying provisions. A word to the wise: if you are planning a long day of wine tasting, choose a designated driver or book with a wine-tour company that provides transportation. **River City Tours** (888/486-9119; www.rivercitytours.com) in Richland offers regularly scheduled wine tours by bus or van, but by far the most romantic option is a luxurious day of exploring by limo. Try **Four Star Limousines** (509/521-7849; www.fourstarlimos.com) out of Kennewick or, in Yakima, **Moonlit Ride Limousine** (509/575-6846; www.moonlitride.com).

When you're ready to take a break from the wineries, explore Yakima's quaint **North Front Street Historical District**, which invites a hand-in-hand stroll and window shopping. If you stay into the evening, step into **Café Melange** (see Romantic Restaurants) for an Italian dinner. Or, if you're in the mood for something a bit more brisk, walk the **Greenway** (509/453-8280; www.yakimagreenway.org; enter at the east end of Valley Mall Blvd), a 10-mile-long path for walkers, runners, bicyclists, and inline skaters that follows the Yakima and Naches rivers. The paved path has nature-trail offshoots, where you might catch a glimpse of a bald eagle or blue heron overhead. If it's not walking at all but a long, leisurely lunch you have in mind, try the **Barrel House** (22 N 1st St; 509/453-3769), a cozy, inviting pub housed in a beautifully restored turn-of-the-20th-century building.

Traveling east takes you into true farm country, including the small towns of Prosser, Sunnyside, and Grandview. Aside from a handful of wineries, these towns offer little in the way of romance, although if it's time to stop for lunch, consider **Dykstra House Restaurant** (114 Birch Ave, Grandview; 509/882-2082). In this 1914 home, decorated with lace curtains and tchotchkes, you can enjoy wholesome sandwiches and great desserts. In Prosser, the Vintner's Inn at the venerable **Hinzerling Winery** (1524 Sheridan Ave, Prosser; 509/786-2163 or 800/727-6702) offers a prix-fixe dinner, available by reservation only, on Fridays and Saturdays; the bed-and-breakfast, housed in a 1907 Victorian-style house, is new and offers quaint rooms with private baths upstairs. A bit farther east around Benton City (which is decidedly pastoral, not urban) is the Red Mountain appellation, established in 2001. This is one of Washington's hottest wine regions, so be sure to stop at the wineries here, particularly **Terra Blanca** (see Romantic Wineries) and **Hedges Cellars** (53511 N Sunset Rd, Benton City; 509/588-3155; www.hedges cellars.com; call ahead for tasting-room hours).

One of the most appealing stops in the Tri-Cities is **Bookwalter Winery** (894 Tulip Ln, Richland; 509/627-5000 or 877/667-8300; www.bookwalter wines.com), which has a recently expanded wine lounge, live jazz, and an outdoor patio where you can order a plate of farmhouse cheese and a glass of wine while overlooking vineyards. Or enjoy views of the Columbia

River and fresh Northwest seafood at the new **Anthony's** in Richland (see Romantic Restaurants).

About 130 miles east of Yakima, **Walla Walla** is a wonderful example of just how romantic a small town in the wine country can be. Beautiful, original architecture lines the restored little downtown, where you can find wine-tasting rooms, charming restaurants, small shops, and galleries. The community is strong on the arts, and the **Walla Walla Symphony** (509/529-8020; www.wwsymphony.com) happens to be the oldest symphony orchestra west of the Mississippi. Performances are held in Cordiner Hall (345 Boyer Ave), on the grounds of the private **Whitman College** (509/527-5176), which anchors the town. The lovely campus is an idyllic spot for romantic strolls on warm summer evenings, when few students are about. The history of this valley, a stopping point for the Lewis and Clark Expedition in 1805, might intrigue you. An excellent interpretive center at the **Whitman Mission National Historic Site** (7 miles west of Walla Walla along Hwy 12; 509/529-2761) sketches the dramatic story of the original mission, which was settled by Marcus Whitman. It's easy to fill an entire weekend just tasting the vintages produced in this award-winning wine region. Downtown, there's the **Waterbrook** (31 E Main St; 509/522-1262) tasting room. Stroll through local produce at the farmers market in the summer or stop for a bite at the hot new **26 brix** (see Romantic Restaurants), an upscale restaurant with many local wines and French-style food with flair. Or, head to the outskirts of town, where you can try the award-winning wines at **Woodward Canyon Winery** (11920 W Hwy 12, Lowden; 509/525-4129; open daily) and **L'Ecole No 41** (see Romantic Wineries).

Access & Information

Most people visiting central and southeast Washington do so by car. Even if you fly here, you'll want to have a car for exploring. Numerous highways lead through often sparsely populated country to this dry, sunny corner of the state. Take advantage of rest areas and be sure your gas tank is full. In summer, bring sun block and a light sweater (for overactive air-conditioners and cool evenings); in winter, a turtleneck and a warm, wind-proof jacket should keep you toasty.

Interstate 90 is the most practical route to take from the Seattle area; it connects at Ellensburg with Interstate 82, which leads through the Yakima Valley to the Tri-Cities at the confluence of the Yakima, Snake, and Columbia Rivers. From there, Walla Walla is an easy trip via Interstate 82 and Highway 12. From Portland, Interstate 84—or the two-lane Highway 14 on the Washington side—leads to Eastern Washington. If you're heading to Ellensburg or Yakima, turn north on Highway 97. If your destination is the Tri-Cities, take Interstate 82/Highway 395. Note: the Tri-Cities includes Kennewick,

Richland, and Pasco, and freeway signs usually name one of those cities only instead of the region's nickname. Horizon Air (800/547-9308; www. horizonair.com) serves the small airports in Walla Walla and Yakima; many other airlines fly into the larger Tri-Cities Airport (3601 N 20th Ave, Pasco; 509/547-6352); most major car-rental companies also operate here.

A map highlighting Yakima wineries is available from the **Yakima Valley Winery Association** (800/258-7270; www.yakimavalleywine.com). For general information on planning a trip to Walla Walla, contact **Tourism Walla Walla** (29 E Sumac St; 877/998-4748; www.wwchamber.com); be sure to request the attractive winery brochure from the **Walla Walla Valley Wine Alliance** (509/526-3117; www.wallawallawine.com). Additionally, the **Washington Wine Commission** (206/667-9463; www.washingtonwine.org) offers a comprehensive booklet with an overview of wineries throughout the state. Before your trip, call to receive a copy of these publications or pick them up at hotels, B&Bs, restaurants, wineries, and other locations in the region.

Romantic Wineries

BONAIR WINERY
❍❍❶

500 S Bonair Rd, Zillah / 509/829-6027
This small Tudor-style winery offers a friendly and intimate tasting experience, and the owners' quirky personal influence is apparent from the moment you step into the tiny tasting room (which is just a few yards from their own home). After you sip a little chardonnay and merlot, wander the small, beautifully landscaped lawn, which has a waterfall rock garden, koi pond, and gazebo. Visitors are also welcome to stroll through the estate vineyards or picnic at the table placed in the shade (on busy weekends, bring a blanket just in case the table is taken). The serene setting has been known to inspire marriage proposals as well as kisses; if that's what you've got on your mind, and if you order two weeks in advance, the winery can create personalized labels for wine bottles that will help celebrate the special occasion. But any visit here is guaranteed to put you in high spirits. Bonair will accommodate weddings or parties of fewer than 75 people.
10am–5pm every day (Sat–Sun only Jan–Feb); www.bonairwine.com.

COLUMBIA CREST
❍❍❶

Hwy 221, Columbia Crest Dr, Patterson / 509/875-2061 or 888/309-9463
Twenty-six miles south of Prosser toward the mighty Columbia River awaits the largest winery in the state, set in complete seclusion and surrounded by 2,500 acres of estate vineyards. The tasting room is housed in a huge French-style chateau, complete with lake and fountains (and a chateau-

size parking lot). Visitors may choose four wines to taste from an impressive list of more than twenty that includes the winery's highly acclaimed chardonnay, merlot, and cabernet sauvignon; we think the delicious bubbly scores highest for romantic purposes. Self-guided tours of the wine-making facilities are available, and the gift shop offers gourmet cheeses, smoked salmon, and other goodies. Call ahead and arrange a day to linger and hold hands among the vines on a seasonal vineyard tour, $15 per person with a special tasting afterwards. Among the walkways and lush lawns outside are many pleasant spots for a picnic—with wine, of course.
10am–4:30pm every day; www.columbia-crest.com.

L'ECOLE NO 41
♥♥♥

41 Lowden School Rd, Lowden / 509/525-0940
At your first glimpse of the quaint brick exterior of this historic schoolhouse located outside Walla Walla, you might think you've found a small-town museum rather than a nationally acclaimed winery. Step inside, and you can experience the charm of both. With high ceilings, built-in bookshelves, and original windows and wood floors, the beautifully designed tasting room makes an excellent place to sample the spectacular L'Ecole No 41 wines. The tasting bar is made of slate, so you can take notes with chalk as you sip the famously rich merlot or delicate semillon; or skip the tasting notes, and write each other sweet nothings instead.
10am–5pm every day; www.lecole.com.

SAGELANDS VINEYARD
♥♥♥

71 Gangl Rd, Wapato / 509/877-2112
On sunny days you can gaze at Mount Adams from this winery, enclosed by stone gates and perched on a hill just 10 minutes south of Yakima. The stone building features massive carved wooden doors, a splendid tasting room, and a large sitting area. Outside, the scene is pure romance (if you subtract the crowds). The pretty grounds are brightened with flowers and shrubs, and concrete picnic tables and benches—arranged on a pleasant slope and shaded by canvas umbrellas—offer inspiring views of the surrounding hills and valleys. You probably won't find utter privacy at this popular spot, but the delicious, lush cabernets and merlots and the lovely surroundings make it more than worth a stop.
10am–5pm every day; www.sagelandswinery.com.

SILVER LAKE AT ROZA HILLS
❂❂❂

1500 Vintage Rd, Zillah / 509/829-6235
The lovely grounds—and the sweeping views of the valley—make this large tasting room a romantic, if not exactly intimate, stop. Perched atop a green hillside, the handsome Northwest-style building offers a spacious interior with a gift shop in addition to a tasting bar where you can sip a wide range of varietals, including a rich cabernet-merlot blend. Outside, picnic tables and a patio with additional seating provide plenty of space for relaxing with a glass of wine and soaking up the glorious vista of surrounding hills and vineyards. Kissing just seems like the right thing to do amid all this wine-country splendor.
10am–5pm every day (Apr–Nov), 11am–4pm every day (Dec–Mar); www.
silverlakewinery.com.

TERRA BLANCA VINTNERS
❂❂❂❂

34715 N DeMoss Rd, Benton City / 509/588-6082
The Red Mountain appellation is an exceptional place to grow grapes, thanks to the high calcium carbonate content that whitens the soil; Terra Blanca, located in this exclusive growing region, also happens to be an exceptional place to kiss. A beautiful, winding drive leads to the stone and iron gates that mark the entrance; the hilltop winery offers panoramic views of the sagebrush-dotted valley and high-quality syrah, merlot, cabernet sauvignon, and chardonnay vineyards. On special wine-event weekends, you can visit the man-made caves, sunk deep into the hill and lined with giant barrels where the wine can age at a consistent temperature and humidity. Stroll through 8 acres of landscaped grounds, kiss near one of the four waterfalls, gaze at your lover's reflection in the small lake, and explore the new 50,000-square-foot facility, designed around a Tuscan theme, slated to open in fall 2005.
11am–6pm every day; www.terrablanca.com.

THREE RIVERS WINERY
❂❂❂

5641 W Hwy 12, Walla Walla / 509/526-9463
Excellent wines and festive outdoor summer concerts draw couples to this expansive winery located 6 miles west of downtown Walla Walla. While the scale here is more gigantic than romantic, the sheer variety of wines on offer might put wine lovers in an amorous mood, whether live bands are playing or not. You can taste everything from merlot, syrah, and sangiovese to late-harvest Gewürztraminer. Or, swirl and sip on the award-winning Meritage red wine by the cozy fireplace or on the sunny deck. Established in 1999, Three Rivers is a noteworthy addition to the area, which has traditionally

been defined by smaller boutique wineries—this fact alone makes it an intriguing stop. You can tour the vineyards, barrel rooms, and cellar facilities; browse the gift shop; or play the winery's three short holes of golf. *10am–6pm every day; www.threeriverswinery.com.*

Romantic Lodgings

A TOUCH OF EUROPE B&B
✿ ✿ ✿

220 N 16th Ave, Yakima / 509/454-9775 or 888/438-7073
For a tranquil, pampered stay in charming Old World surroundings, book a room at this lovely Queen Anne Victorian home, which has an octagonal turret and exquisite period detail in every room. Built in 1889 by well-to-do Yakima pioneers, the home was once visited by Theodore Roosevelt; today, the friendly owners, Jim and Erika Cenci, offer an old-fashioned, elegant ambience that perfectly suits the house. All three guest rooms feature air-conditioning, private baths, beautiful antiques, down comforters, and freshly ironed sheets, and welcome you with fresh flowers and French chocolates. Wall-to-wall carpeting, while anachronistic, keeps noise to a minimum. The Prince Victorian Mahogany Room, the largest and most romantic of the three, is decorated with exquisite mahogany furniture, a beautiful handcrafted iron bed, and Italian wallpaper that perfectly matches the fine linens of green and gold. The similarly memorable Princess Victorian Mahogany Room has a detached bath in the hall, a gorgeous fainting couch, and an early 1800s queen-size bed. In keeping with the nature of an old-fashioned getaway, radios and TVs are absent. When you awake, descend to the elegant parlor, where tables adorned with lace tablecloths, silver candlesticks, lovely china, fine crystal, and fresh flowers await. Erika, a professionally trained chef, creates extraordinary breakfasts, as well as stunning multicourse dinners (see Romantic Restaurants). Breakfast might include warm chocolate scones, a delicious fruit dish with creamy mascarpone, apple-mango and raspberry-currant popovers, a chive-Brie omelet served with delicate blini, and a tempting platter of European cheeses, as well as a fruit smoothie and strong coffee. All is perfection. Request her gourmet lunch basket to make sure your romantic wine-country picnic food lives up to the fine wines.
$$ AE, MC, V; checks OK; www.winesnw.com/toucheuropeb&b.htm.

COZY ROSE INN BED AND BREAKFAST
✿ ✿ ✿ ✿

1220 Forsell Rd, Grandview / 800/575-8381
This cozy country retreat nestled into a landscape of orchards and vineyards offers a romantic reprieve for wine tasters and passersby. A new Italian-

inspired suite and dining room, completed in 2004, definitely give this locale a boost. Guests choose from five different suite options housed in separate structures that range in feel from grandma's cozy cottage, filled with florals and scented candles, to a plush Florentine retreat with top-notch linens and Old World furnishings. Each suite has a private entrance, a fireplace, a TV, a stereo system, and fresh flowers. The Irish House, set on the bottom floor of the farmhouse, offers a quiet, if unique, getaway. Ivy-stenciled walls, loud flower patterns, and small rooms make the surrounds slightly jarring, but the absolute quiet and privacy of its bedrooms, living rooms, and kitchen make up for its overdone decor. Bask under the starry glow in the shared outdoor Jacuzzi tub, filled with bubbles. By far the best room in the house is the new Sweet Surrender, which boasts a view of Mount Rainier and is lavishly decorated to emulate haughty Italian style. Pastoral fields just outside the window make those who squint a little think they are back in Northern Italy. A Jacuzzi tub, large vanity, and shower big enough for four is sure to start up some good clean fun. Breakfast before a wine tasting is a must, and huckleberry pancakes, homemade applesauce, ham, and fresh fruit will sharpen your palate for what's ahead. Guests can choose to have breakfast delivered or to dine in the Tuscan-style dining room with private tables for two. Dinner is available upon request (a nice option since there are no nearby restaurants). Couples can choose from five-course filet mignon dinners to pasta with an herbed cream sauce. Long, scenic country roads and nearby vineyards call for a romantic stroll for two.
$$–$$$ *MC, V; checks OK; www.cozyroseinn.com.*

GREEN GABLES INN
✪✪❧

922 Bonsella St, Walla Walla / 888/525-5501
This beautifully restored, historic 1909 house, set on a tree-lined residential street just across from the Whitman College campus, offers a quiet, relaxing retreat. The names of the five guest rooms are all inspired by the classic *Anne of Green Gables* children's books, but rest assured that the accommodations are not at all childish. For the most romantic experience, book the Idlewild, which features a romantic fireplace complete with a furry rug for lounging in front of the flames. Elegant 1940s mahogany furnishings; a king-size bed; a crystal chandelier; and pleasant, rose-patterned linens and decor complete the room. In the private bath, you'll find a single Jacuzzi tub (it could use an upgrade) and plush robes. The private deck is the perfect spot to enjoy a glass of the wine you bought during your winery tour—do bring your own, as the owners are not certified to supply it. If you don't mind the cozy quarters, the Mayflower (previously the maid's room) doesn't share walls with any other rooms and thus offers the most privacy; another pleasant option is Dryad's Bubble, with Maxfield Parrish prints on the walls and a small balcony. All rooms feature air-conditioning, soundproofing, and small

refrigerators neatly stowed away. Hot coffee arrives at your door in the morning, and a buffet-style breakfast is served downstairs in the pleasant dining room. The only thing that might interrupt your peace and quiet here is one of the high-volume Whitman College reunion or event weekends; the owners can help you schedule your visit to avoid these times. On warm summer evenings, the wraparound porch is a very romantic place to kiss. $$ *AE, DIS, MC, V; checks OK; www.greengablesinn.com.*

THE INN AT ABEJA
♥ ♥ ♥ ♥
2014 Mill Creek Rd, Walla Walla / 509/522-1234
This 100-year-old, 22-acre farmstead, which doubles as a working winery, is also among the most luxurious and romantic retreats in all of the wine country. The lovely setting, in view of the rolling Palouse and the Blue Mountains, and the exquisite taste that shows in every detail, put the Inn at Abeja at the top of its class. The three cottages and two suites have been taken from their practical uses—chicken house, carriage house, hay-lofts—and transformed into tastefully playful accommodations. Among the most romantic is the two-story Summer Kitchen Cottage, with a deck overlooking the vineyards, a sky-lit bath with a claw-foot tub, and a full kitchen and living room. Fresh flowers and lavender bath salts await your arrival—here, and in all the rooms—creating an utterly romantic ambience. Charm is also found in the Chicken House Cottage, with its vaulted ceilings, slate-tiled walk-in shower for two, airy full kitchen, and private deck over-looking the creek. (A claw-foot tub in the lovely, tiny adjacent bath house is at your disposal if you prefer to soak.) The Locust Suite boasts an impres-sive Northwest decor of Montana slate floors, overstuffed leather furniture, cozy gas-fired stove, and granite-tiled kitchen. The airy, two-story Carriage House Suite, completed in 2001, features a pretty four-poster bed and tiled sky-lit bath upstairs, and comfortable sitting, dining, and kitchen areas downstairs. The charming remodeled barn on the property, complete with fireplace and leather couches, is a common area, and the hearty gourmet breakfasts are served here.
$$–$$$ *MC, V; checks OK; closed Jan–Feb; www.abeja.net.*

INN AT BLACKBERRY CREEK
♥ ♥ ♥
1126 Pleasant St, Walla Walla / 509/522-5233
At the end of a winding, tree-lined driveway, this beautifully restored 1912 farmhouse, complete with wraparound porch, invites you in for a romantic retreat. At this inn, located around the corner from Pioneer Park and Whitman College, the residential quiet is interrupted only by the music of the nearby creek. The rooms are flawlessly decorated, the common areas are inviting, and an overall attention to detail makes Blackberry Creek a

delightful place to stay. The three guest rooms, Cezanne's Sanctuary, Monet's Retreat, and Renoir's Studio, all feature king-size beds, private baths with showers, and peaceful views. All are immaculately clean and feature lovely antiques, beaded lamps, wingback chairs, creamy peach-colored walls, and hardwood floors covered with plush Oriental carpets. In the bathrooms, adorned with fresh flowers, are slate-tiled floors, spacious showers, and thick robes. Tapestry draft stoppers can be placed in front of your door to muffle noise; sound tends to carry in a historic house like this. For this reason, we recommend Monet's Retreat, which shares no floor or ceiling with any another bedroom. Owner Barbara Knudson is an expert baker, and mornings bring freshly made croissants, coconut-yogurt coffee cake, or apple-nut muffins; these treats, along with fresh fruit and a main breakfast dish, are served in the pretty dining room. For a more leisurely option, order a breakfast tray and enjoy it in bed; or, in nice weather, adjourn to the beautiful garden for a morning picnic.
$–$$ *AE, DC, MC, V; checks OK; www.innatblackberrycreek.com.*

MARCUS WHITMAN HOTEL & CONFERENCE CENTER
✪✪✪
6 W Rose St, Walla Walla / 509/525-2200 or 866/826-9422
The Marcus Whitman joined the ranks of Washington's most elegant restored historic hotels when it reopened in 2001. Originally built in 1927, this is the only hotel of its kind in all of southeast Washington. The ideal location, within a block of downtown, makes it an easy stroll to restaurants and shops, and the rooms are remarkably affordable. Enjoy the magnificent lobby, complete with towering ceilings, original wood floors, and grand floral arrangements; dine on fine Northwest cuisine at The Marc restaurant; or sip champagne in the cozy Vineyard bar. Peek into the three enormous ballrooms or two banquet rooms, and you might see a wedding in progress. Rooms in the hotel are appealing, with burgundy and gold color schemes, Italian furnishings, and beautifully tiled bathrooms with pedestal sinks. Other amenities include phones, high-speed Internet access, and TVs. Book a comfortable King Deluxe Room—there are 24 of them—or consider one of the well-designed, two-room Junior Luxury Suites, with inviting parlor, separate bedroom, and plush robes. We suggest steering well clear of the rooms located in the "west wing," a restored 1970s motor inn adjacent to the original hotel. It's cheaper, but you get what you pay for; if you must stay here, rooms 23 or 24 on the third or fourth floor offer the most privacy. The place does fill up with conference guests on occasion, but fortunately, the grand and spacious surroundings mean you can find lots of intimate nooks and crannies.
$–$$ *AE, DC, DIS, MC, V; local checks only; www.marcuswhitmanhotel. com.* &

Romantic Restaurants

ANTHONY'S
♥♥♥

550 Columbia Point Dr, Richland / 509/946-3474
The brand new Anthony's overlooks Columbia Point Marina just off of the
Columbia River. Watch the sun melt away as you relax on the outdoor patio.
And when the desert night turns cool, snuggle closer next to the patio's fireplace or share a blanket provided by the restaurant. Inside, Anthony's boasts
hip Northwest architecture. The dining room is showy, with exposed wood
beams, several fireplaces, slate tile, brushed chrome, and nature-inspired
colors. All of the tables offer marina views, but ask for a window seat or sit
underneath the arches for a little more privacy. Start with the tempura ahi
roll with fresh ginger sauce, a few fresh oysters on the half shell, and a selection from of one of 130 Washington wines. Anthony's is well known for great
seafood, and their new Richland location holds close to that tradition. For
dinner, try Alaska wild Chinook salmon, fresh Dungeness crab, or applewood grilled steak. There is no better way to finish up a starry-eyed meal
than with the melting chocolate cake. It's served warm with a chocolate
syrup–filled center, vanilla ice cream, and raspberry sauce—a sure recipe for
some chocolate-flavored kisses! After dinner take a romantic stroll along the
Columbia River in nearby Howard Amon Park.
$$–$$$ *AE, MC, V; checks OK; lunch Mon–Sat, dinner every day, brunch
Sun; full bar; reservations recommended; www.anthonys.com.*

A TOUCH OF EUROPE B&B
♥♥♥♥

220 N 16th Ave, Yakima / 509/454-9775 or 888/438-7073
Without question, the most romantic meals in the valley are served at this
charming bed-and-breakfast (see Romantic Lodgings). The exquisite four-
to seven-course dinners here can be enjoyed by special arrangement only,
and calling early definitely pays off. (The first party to reserve an evening
gets to choose the courses and select the time; additional parties may reserve
places after that.) Dining here evokes the golden era of formal romance,
from the antique-filled front parlor to the magnificent Victorian dining
room, complete with a box-beamed embossed ceiling, exquisite stained-
glass cabinets, a cast-iron fireplace, and tables adorned with lovely crystal
and silver, fresh flowers, and candles. For the utmost privacy, reserve the
adjacent parlor, which can be shut off from the other dining room. Erika
Cenci—the versatile, talented chef—focuses on seasonal ingredients and
works with local growers. Starters—such as curried squash and pear soup
topped with delicate crème fraîche, citrus-dressed salad with ripe mango,
and fresh homemade bread—are delicious. Main dishes range from seafood
in a delicate saffron sauce over squid ink–saffron pasta to hearty roasted

lamb in red wine sauce. The refreshing desserts are unique confections. Guests bring their own wine to accompany dinner (no corkage fee); if you'd like to work around that very special bottle, the chef is happy to custom-design your meal to go with the wine, provided you call in advance.

$$-$$$ *AE, MC, V; checks OK; dinner every day; no alcohol; reservations by special arrangement only; www.winesnw.com/toucheuropeb&b.htm.*

CAFÉ MELANGE
◗◖

7 N Front St, Yakima / 509/453-0571
Formerly known as Deli de Pasta, this tiny, Italian-influenced cafe offers an inviting, homey ambience in the North Front Street Historic District. The delectable Italian cuisine is all made from scratch by the talented chef. The cafe has been in the same family for decades, and the delicious recipes and classic red-and-white decor haven't changed significantly since the early days. Start with the popular smoked salmon ravioli topped with basil-cream sauce, followed by lemon chicken or lasagne with five layers of robust flavor. Evening specials, such as baked aioli salmon, are simply outstanding. Sauces that might adorn your dish of homemade pasta include classic marinara, Alfredo, pesto, basil-cream, or lemon—you choose. Soups, salads, and crostini enhance the main dishes. The recently expanded wine list features more than 100 Washington state bottlings. Romantically speaking, the modest, plant-adorned interior does not really measure up to the high quality of the meals, although the small linen-draped tables are pleasantly decorated with candles and flowers. It's the superb food here that will arouse your passions.

$ *AE, MC, V; checks OK; lunch, dinner Mon–Sat; beer and wine; reservations recommended.*

GASPERETTI'S RESTAURANT
◗◗

1013 N 1st St, Yakima / 509/248-0628
Consistently voted the most romantic restaurant in town by local diners, Gasperetti's is an Italian hideaway complete with linen tablecloths, fresh flowers, intimate lighting, and delicious food. Don't be deterred by its less-than-promising location on a busy street lined with motels and tattoo parlors; as the parking lot filled with expensive vehicles indicates, this 39-year-old restaurant attracts a well-heeled crowd for special nights out. Inside, the two dining rooms display distinct personalities; one boasts comfortable banquettes and a lively ambience (we like this one best), while the quieter garden room features pretty frescoed walls. In both rooms, tables are set with silver and crystal, and service is friendly and professional. Brad Patterson, who helped owner John Gasperetti open the place, has returned as chef after working in Seattle's four-star Lampreia

restaurant. Local produce provides much of the inspiration here: cream of asparagus soup tastes as if the vegetables came straight from a nearby field earlier in the day; succulent halibut is served with a remarkably fresh and flavorful sauce of red and yellow peppers. A range of entrées, from pastas to Washington filet mignon in a sauce of marsala and Gorgonzola, are equally good. The award-winning wine list offers a good selection from Washington, California, and Italy.

$$ AE, DIS, MC, V; checks OK; lunch Tues–Fri, dinner Tues–Sat; full bar; reservations recommended. &

PATIT CREEK RESTAURANT
❂❂❂❂

725 E Dayton Ave, Dayton / 509/382-2625
Just 30 minutes east of Walla Walla in the town of Dayton lies one of the most highly rated restaurants this side of the mountains—and when it comes to romance, it just about soars off the charts. If you are looking for an intimate gem in a charming little town to enjoy after a day of winery hopping, stop your search here. By the way, when we say intimate, we mean *small* as well as romantic: the restaurant, housed in a transformed 1920s service station, has only 10 tables. The menu's focus is on classic French cuisine. Add to this the inviting wine list, strong on Walla Walla selections, and consistently stellar service, and Patit Creek makes an excellent place to celebrate a special occasion. Among the tempting choices on the menu, you might try the famous fillet steaks in green peppercorn sauce, or chèvre-stuffed dates wrapped in bacon. All ingredients are incredibly fresh, and the huckleberry pie for dessert is a must. It's recommended that you call to make reservations at least two weeks in advance.

$$ MC, V; local checks only; lunch Wed–Fri, dinner Wed–Sat; beer and wine; reservations recommended.

26 BRIX
❂❂❂❂

207 W Main St, Walla Walla / 509/526-4075
26 brix, newly opened in 2004, has a reputation for inspiring marriage proposals, including that of the restaurant's chef-owner Mike Davis. Everything about this restored 1899 hotel-turned-restaurant is elegant, and the nearly $650,000 renovation has updated the building's classic interior into cool urban style. The unpretentious restaurant received many accolades in Northwest and national publications, and the exquisite food, wine, and ambience promise to stir romantic appetites. Fresh flowers and watercolors adorn the restaurant's subtle ochre- and moss-colored walls. And, sparkling flights of wine glasses rest upon intimate, linen-clad tables. Jazz in the background, a candle at each table, and low lighting add to the romantic feeling, although mostly hard surfaces make the restaurant a bit noisy.

Order your favorite local Walla Walla vintage or ask the wine steward for a recommendation. Start off your evening of seasonal, French-influenced cuisine with the seared divers scallops served with grilled endive and capers, or the house favorite, a warm apple and watercress salad. Mains include the popular pan-roasted sturgeon, oxtail ravioli served on creamy polenta, or the braised Iowa lamb shank in a *braisage* reduction. The rich flavors and artful presentation will doubtless inspire some flirtatious taste trading, especially if you opt for the decadent three-course tasting menu ($50) or the chef's six-course tasting menu ($85). Finish with the sultry pear sorbet, the cheese plate, or the 26 brix hot chocolate. The main dining room offers many nooks and intimate corners. For a truly special evening, request the chef's table right in the hustle of the kitchen or hide away in the private wine room with its view of the cellar. As if all this isn't good enough, the restaurant's owners plan to renovate the old hotel's upstairs and expand the wine cellar. **$$$–$$$$** *AE, MC, V; local checks only; breakfast Sun, dinner Mon–Tues, Fri–Sat; full bar; reservations recommended; www.twentysixbrix.com.*

WHITEHOUSE-CRAWFORD
❂❂❂

55 W Cherry St, Walla Walla / 509/525-2222
Part of the romance of this airy, inviting restaurant is discovering such a sophisticated place in quaint Walla Walla. Although the numerous well-heeled diners, along with the framed letters from Chez Panisse's Alice Waters on the wall, prove that the restaurant is no secret, Whitehouse-Crawford still manages to feel like a hidden gem. Housed in a beautifully restored turn-of-the-20th-century planing mill, with high ceilings and a vast dining room of tables covered in white linen, the interior is reminiscent of a chic urban warehouse. It can get a little noisy, and the tables for two are rather close together, but the absolutely delicious food makes such drawbacks fade into the background. Chef Jamie Guerin, formerly of Seattle's acclaimed Campagne restaurant, creates excellent Northwest cuisine that is simple, fresh, and unpretentious, with an emphasis on seasonal ingredients. Tasty appetizers—try spicy calamari with ginger—pair well with many of the local wines on the extensive wine list. Entrées of salmon and pork tenderloin have unexpected twists: the Southwest-style salmon is served with black beans, corn, and squash in a piquant tomato sauce; pork is smoked and served with grilled fresh figs, shallots, and spaetzle. The luscious desserts include a classic crème brûlée and an award-winning twice-baked chocolate cake—a marriage of dense cake and chocolate soufflé. **$$–$$$** *AE, MC, V; checks OK; dinner Wed–Sun; full bar; reservations recommended; www.whitehousecrawford.com.*

VANCOUVER & ENVIRONS

*"There is nothing in kissing once; it's the second
time that counts."*

—MAURICE HEWLETT

♡ VANCOUVER & ENVIRONS

S et on the wild Pacific Ocean and embraced by British Columbia's Coast
Mountains, Vancouver, in our opinion, is one of the world's most romantic
cities. The area is Canada's fastest-growing metropolis, and the next several
years, climaxing with the 2010 Olympic Winter Games, is an opportune
time to visit. Surrounded on three sides by water and swaddled in a lush,
temperate rain forest, its magic derives as much from its dramatic natural
setting as from the distinctive cosmopolitan culture of the city. Vancouver
is an amalgam of 23 neighborhoods, each with its own unique character
and romantic appeal, including the bustling Granville Island and the sleek
shopping paradise of Robson Street. To the north, Vancouver's trademark
mountains—Cypress, Grouse, and Hollyburn—preside over the city. At their
base are the suburbs of West Vancouver and North Vancouver. In the neighborhoods and the beautiful parks, sublime kissing opportunities await
around seemingly every corner. For lovers who like their romance enhanced
by fine food, Vancouver offers an astounding diversity of restaurants, from
high-end to down-home, as well as public markets, ethnic-food outposts,
and award-winning wines from British Columbia's Okanagan Valley.

Vancouver's weather is the mildest in all of Canada, thanks to ocean currents and major weather patterns that bring warm, moist air in waves from
the Pacific year-round. Spring comes early, with flowers in full bloom by
early March. June, July, and August are the warmest months. Late-summer
and autumn days—through October—tend to be warm and sunny, with
occasional rain. Winter is the rainy season; it starts about November and
tapers off about March, but, as with its American neighbor to the south,
the rain is usually showers or drizzle rather than heavy precipitation. Perhaps the mild weather explains why this area is among the oldest human
habitations in North America. The area's First Nations peoples have been
telling their stories since time immemorial, and the myths of the Raven, the
Bear, and the Whale are woven into Vancouver's landscape in the form of
public art. Higher elevations experience the precipitation as snow, which
translates into excellent skiing on the area's three major ski hills during

the winter. We simply cannot recommend a romantic getaway to Vancouver strongly enough. Magic and romance abound here.

VANCOUVER

ROMANTIC HIGHLIGHTS

One romantic centerpiece of this very romantic city is **Stanley Park**. Walk, run, roller-blade, or cycle—on a tandem two-wheeler if you'd like—along the park's seawall; its 5½ miles (9 km) can be walked in 2½ hours at a brisk pace. A larger seawall system extends beyond the park: along the south shore of the city's harbor, and also along English Bay east to the end of False Creek. Take a day to stroll around the park itself, to discover hand in hand such spots as Lost Lagoon, Siwash Rock, and the **Vancouver Aquarium** (845 Avison Wy, Stanley Park; 604/659-3474). Just off the beaten paths, you will find secluded trails edged by towering fir, cedar, and hemlock trees. Deep in the park one feels as if moved to some primeval glade, though the city is minutes away. Stop for afternoon tea by the tennis courts at **The Fish House in Stanley Park** (8901 Stanley Park Dr; 604/681-7275)—views are as delicious as the thick cream on the scones. For the illusion of seclusion, try Third Beach for romantic park benches and great sunset views. Horse-drawn carriage tours are available March to October through **AAA Horse and Carriage** (604/681-5115). Another choice sunset spot for an after-stroll drink is a short walk from the park's English Bay entrance: the lounge of the ivy-shrouded **Sylvia Hotel** (1154 Gilford St; 604/681-9321).

For a different perspective on how nature frames Vancouver's beauty, go to **Spanish Banks**—a long, wide strip of gently inclined sandy beaches on the shore of Point Grey, toward the University of British Columbia campus. It's ideal for a lovers' stroll (or an iron-person run, for that matter). An hour before sunset, downtown's distant skyscrapers gleam a brilliant gold. At low tide, the beach stretches hundreds of yards out to sea. Vancouver's neighborhoods invite romantic wandering. **Yaletown**, home to the incredible four-lip-rated **Opus Hotel** (see Romantic Lodgings), feels like a whirling high-tech zone. For a taste of Vancouver's vibrant Asian-infused offerings, dine on the edge of Chinatown at **Wild Rice** (see Romantic Restaurants) and then catch a movie at the 12-screen **Tinseltown Cinema** (88 W Pender; 604/806-0799). If the excitement of crowds makes you feel romantic, amble with hands entwined through the lively **Granville Island Public Market**. Board one of the blue-and-white **False Creek Ferries** (604/684-7781; www. granvilleislandferries.bc.ca) from the dock behind the **Aquatic Centre** (Beach Ave near Thurlow St) to arrive by water. This fleet of 10 little passenger ferries provides service every five minutes, and you can also stay aboard for a mini-sightseeing cruise. Beyond the market, small artisan shops are fascinating to explore. Perhaps the quintessential Vancouver neighborhood is **Kitsilano**, affectionately known as Kits. Its main street, Fourth Avenue, put this enclave on North America's counterculture map in 1967 when it was considered Canada's Haight-Ashbury. Now it offers trendy clothing and home accessories stores (how times change), plus the organics-focused **Capers Market** (2285 W 4th Ave; 604/739-6676), where you can provision for a picnic on Kitsilano Beach. Just east of Capers, Yew Street takes a steep incline, plunging to the beach. Nearby, locals fill restaurant patios after they've finished a jog along the sand. If you visit during the three warm-weather months, take an ocean-side dip in the turquoise-blue salt water of **Kitsilano Pool** (2305 Cornwall Ave; 604/731-0011); it's one of the most beautiful pools in North America. More great neighborhoods lie across the harbor from downtown. A trip across the stunning **Lions Gate Bridge** presents picture-postcard views of the North Shore, Stanley Park, and Burrard Inlet. Loop westward from the end of the bridge along Marine Drive, and West Vancouver's prime shopping street eventually becomes a meandering swath that marries forest and sea. In less than 30 minutes, you can find unspoiled wilderness-for-two in **Lighthouse Park** (Marine Dr and Beacon Ln). On the way through quaint Ambleside, stop at the **Savary Island Pie Company** (1533 Marine Dr; 604/926-4021) for inspired picnic provisions. While on the **North Shore**, soar to the top of **Grouse Mountain** for superb vistas of the entire Lower Mainland. The 2,800-foot (850-m) ascent in the **Skyride gondola** (604/984-0661; www.grousemountain.com) to the alpine station (elevation 3,700 feet; 1,130 m) is utterly breathtaking. If you'd prefer, go straight up on pure body power: a less direct route is the 1.8-mile (2.9-kilometer) Grouse Grind hiking trail. At the top, reward yourselves with lunch at the casual **Altitudes Bistro** (604/984-0661). In winter, this is a popular ski resort during the day; night skiing (until 11pm) is even more romantic, with a swooshing descent toward the carpet of city lights spread out below. Finally, while it may not sound wildly romantic, it's fun to explore **Capilano Regional Park**, home to a fish hatchery, the huge **Cleveland Dam**, and the 450-foot (137-m) **Capilano Suspension Bridge** (3735 Capilano Rd; 604/985-7474), which crosses a uniquely picturesque canyon.

If cultural outings are your aphrodisiac, Vancouver's spectacular traditional venues and outdoor summer settings (such as an open-air First Nations longhouse that might feature chamber music) will inspire passion. The **Vancouver Opera** (604/683-0222; www.vanopera.bc.ca) and **Vancouver Symphony** (604/876-3434; www.vancouversymphony.ca) are the city's musical core, just as the **Playhouse Theatre Company** (604/873-3311; www.vancouverplayhouse.com) and **Arts Club Theatre** (604/687-1644; www.artsclub.com) are major stage players. Lovers of dance turn to **Ballet B.C.** (604/732-5003; www.balletbc.com). All summer, **Bard on the Beach**

(604/739-0559; www.bardonthebeach.org) fills two large tents with Shake-speare's wisdom on life and love—with British Columbia sunsets as a backdrop. The **Vancouver International Jazz Festival** (604/872-5200; www.coastaljazz.ca) is the highlight of a year-round calendar that showcases diverse performances, from all styles of jazz to blues and Latin music. The **Vancouver Recital Society** (604/602-0363; www.vanrecital.com) brings stellar international names to town as well as tomorrow's stars, and sponsors a summer chamber music series. For a midsummer fortnight, **Festival Vancouver** (604/688-1152; www.festivalvancouver.bc.ca) dominates the city morning, noon, and evening with scores of performances in many venues ranging from staged opera and organ recitals to world music and late-night jazz. (Comprehensive listings of what's going on appear in the free *Georgia Straight* weekly; the Queue section of Thursday's *Vancouver Sun*; and at the comprehensive Web site, www.ticketstonight.ca.) A strong anchor for the visual arts is the **Vancouver Art Gallery** (750 Hornby St; 604/662-4700; www.vanartgallery.bc.ca) in the heart of downtown. After taking in the striking architecture and impressive First Nations artifacts at the **Museum of Anthropology** (6393 NW Marine Dr; 604/822-3825), search out the secret garden located between the museum and the Point Grey Cliffs; once you find it, revel in views of 10 totem poles towering over grassy knolls while you share a secret kiss.

Vancouver is known as a shopping mecca. Millions of international tour-ists have made **Robson Street** a relentlessly trendy boulevard of prêt-à-porter boutiques and swank eateries. Art lovers will find jewelry and gifts made by local craftsmen in the **Vancouver Art Gallery** shop (604/662-4719); fashion lovers will delight at the string of flagship stores for international retailers (Zara, Armani Exchange, Gap) and local chains (Lululemon, Aritzia, Boys' Co.). Browsing, people watching, and latte sipping can easily fill an after-noon here. For higher-end shopping, visit **South Granville**, stretching from the south end of Granville Bridge to West 16th Avenue. Sometimes referred to as Gallery Row, this is also a haven for antiques stores filled with trea-sures imported from Japan, Indonesia, and India. With top eateries like **Vij's** and **West** (see Romantic Restaurants), this area is home to some of the best shopping and dining in the city, as well as the refurbished **Stanley Theatre** (2780 Granville St; 604/736-8423). Other cool neighborhoods for hand-in-hand exploring include **Yaletown**, where brick warehouses have been transformed into chic jewelry and clothing boutiques; and **South Main** or **SoMa** (as locals call the area around Main Street and Broadway), which has become Vancouver's hottest new shopping district with the "it" boutique **Eugene Choo** (3683 Main St; 604/873-8874) and rare collectibles mecca **Bak-er's Dozen** (3520 Main St; 604/879-3348). Vancouver's 60,000 East Indian immigrants have established their own shopping area called the **Punjabi Market** (in South Vancouver at 49th and Main Sts), where you can haggle for sexy, custom-fit Salwar Kameez clothing or Rajastani jewelry.

Access & Information

Vancouver International Airport (604/207-7077; www.yvr.ca) is a major international airport, with daily flights to all the continents. The modern, spacious, and well-designed airport is located 9 miles (15 km) south of downtown on Sea Island.

Two major highways connect greater Vancouver to the rest of British Columbia, other parts of Canada, and the United States. Highway 99, the main highway connecting Vancouver to Seattle and the rest of Washington State, leads south from the city across the fertile delta at the mouth of the Fraser River and connects with Interstate 5. It's about a three-hour drive between Vancouver and Seattle, crossing the international boundary at Blaine, Washington. The border crossing can add considerably to your travel time, particularly on weekends or during popular summer travel periods; your best bet is to travel at nonpeak times and to allow for possible traffic. Highway 99 also connects Vancouver to the ski resort town of Whistler, about a two-hour drive north of the city. Highway 1, the Trans-Canada Highway, winds through the Lower Mainland, up the Fraser River Valley, and east across Canada. If you drive, watch for rush-hour traffic between 7am and 9am on weekday mornings and 3:30pm and 6:30pm in the evenings. For regular updates on highway conditions in the Vancouver area and across the province, call 604/299-9000, ext. 7623; information is also available online through the **British Columbia Ministry of Transportation** (www.th.gov.bc.ca; click on "Road Reports").

For more information on activities, whether climbing Grouse Mountain or shopping downtown, contact the **Vancouver Tourist Info Centre** (200 Burrard St; 604/683-2000; tourismvancouver.com). Keep in mind that airfares, hotel rates, and admission fees are often lower from November through February, if you're undeterred by rain. In late January and early February, Tourism Vancouver promotes **Dine Out Vancouver**, with $15, $25, and $35 three-course dinners at the city's top restaurants.

Romantic Lodgings

ENGLISH BAY INN
◆◆◆

1968 Comox St, Vancouver / 604/683-8002
Chances are good that once you settle in, you won't want to leave this English Tudor hotel tucked away in Vancouver's West End. This is especially true if you land the fabulously romantic suite on the top floor (no. 5), a cozy two-level boudoir with a fireplace. It features a loft bedroom with a skylight, a sleigh bed with down comforter, and an extra-long Jacuzzi in the bathroom. There's also a garden-level suite with kitchen (no. 7) and four guest rooms to

choose from. The guest rooms are snug, but they make up for lack of space with turn-of-the-20th-century furnishings and four-poster beds. All rooms have private baths, terry robes, and private phones; two rooms have windows or French doors that open to the back garden. The antique-filled lobby has a garden view, and there's a bar where you can enjoy complimentary port or sherry. A fabulous breakfast is served in a formal dining room complete with gleaming Chippendale furniture, crackling fire, and ticking grandfather clock, but if you stay in the suites, you can have breakfast delivered. Stanley Park and English Bay are just minutes away by foot. $$$–$$$$ AE, DC, MC, V; checks OK; www.englishbayinn.com.

FAIRMONT WATERFRONT HOTEL
✪✪✪

900 Canada Place Wy, Vancouver / 604/691-1991 or 800/441-1414
Of the three Fairmont hotels in the area, we think the Waterfront is the most romantic. The large, tastefully appointed guest rooms are among the best in the city, and many have views of Burrard Inlet, where floatplanes, helicopters, and cruise ships come and go against a backdrop of fir-covered mountains. Ask for a corner room, or for one on the third floor with a private terrace overlooking herb gardens and the outdoor pool. All rooms feature marble bathrooms and original artwork. Two Fairmont Gold Club floors cater to guests' every whim, offering complimentary breakfast and late-afternoon hors d'oeuvres in a room with a view—and a large outdoor patio. Guests can pamper themselves in the health club's heated outdoor pool, large hot tub, and sauna. The other two Fairmont hotels are worth a mention here, too. The Fairmont Airport Vancouver (604/207-5200 or 800/441-1414), completed in 1999, is Canada's most technologically advanced and environmentally sound hotel; the waterfall in the lobby and floor-to-ceiling soundproof glass on all floors eliminate outside noise, making this an oasis of tranquility. To revel in the luxury of an earlier era, stay at the Fairmont Hotel Vancouver (604/684-3131 or 800/441-1414), where Old World elegance is apparent in every detail; there's also a lounge with brocade chairs and windows that reveal a slice of water and mountains between skyscrapers. $$$–$$$$ AE, DC, DIS, E, JCB, MC, V; no checks; www.fairmont.com. ₺

FOUR SEASONS HOTEL VANCOUVER
✪✪✪

791 W Georgia St, Vancouver / 604/689-9333 or 800/332-3442 (U.S.), 800/268-6285 (Canada)
You can imagine the turn-of-the-20th-century love affairs that must have been discreetly kindled here as you indulge in the luxury of this upscale hotel. Although it's located smack in the middle of the high-rise downtown core, many of the 376 guest rooms (including 79 suites) offer fabulous views of the city as well as peeks at the harbor. Snuggle into one of the

world-famous Four Seasons down-dressed king-size beds (also available for purchase, so you can re-create that Four Seasons feeling in your own home) in a bedroom with mirrored French doors; thick terrycloth bathrobes, luscious comforters, oversize towels, 24-hour valet and room service, and complimentary morning beverages in the lobby round out the amenities. For romantic vistas, try a Deluxe Corner Room with wraparound windows; for more space, including a separate parlor, try an Executive Suite. Facilities include a year-round indoor/outdoor pool, a health club (with iced towels!), and a rooftop garden. Order a couple of two-olive martinis and sit in the Terrace Bar, also known as the "leather bar" by the locals. Have breakfast or lunch in the soothing Garden Terrace amid what seems like a jungle, but is actually an award-winning garden of rare flora from Africa.
$$$$ *AE, DC, DIS, JCB, MC, V; no checks; www.fourseasons.com.* &

HOTEL LE SOLEIL
✿✿✿
567 Hornby St, Vancouver / 604/632-3000
Indulge in splendor at the boutique Hotel Le Soleil ("the sun"). Situated in the heart of Vancouver's downtown financial, shopping, and business districts, it's a sophisticated home base for a weekend of urban fun. The high-ceilinged lobby is a study in gilded opulence, featuring original oil paintings, a grand fireplace, and satin-covered sofas in the cozy sitting area. Like the lobby in this 119-room luxury boutique hotel, the guest suites are a little on the small side. But with their efficient layouts, the loss of space is not as noticeable as the value for the dollar is evident. Besides, the suites are beautifully decorated and furnished in tones of regal red and gold, focusing on Le Soleil's solar theme. Splendid beds draped with silk brocade coverlets, feather pillows, and down duvets are the perfect place to stay put in the morning, when complimentary in-room coffee and tea and the morning newspaper are delivered to your door. The snug, marble-tiled bathrooms are equipped with high-end bath products. Guests have access to the state-of-the-art YWCA fitness center next door for $11 per day, should you want to work out side by side before heading out to an indulgent dinner.
$$$ *AE, DC, MC, V; no checks; lesoleilhotel.com.* &

"O CANADA" HOUSE
✿✿◗
1114 Barclay St, Vancouver / 604/688-0555 or 877/688-1114
This sumptuous 1897 Victorian home in the West End is where the national anthem, "O Canada," was written in 1909. Filled with the comfort and grace one would expect in such a setting, the front parlor and dining room harken back to gentler times. Potted palms nestled in Oriental urns; the welcoming fireplace; large, comfy chairs; and soft lights, along with a glass of sherry in the evenings, complete the alluring picture of Old World comforts. A

Puppy Love

Some couples just don't consider a getaway romantic unless they can bring along their beloved golden retriever or adored calico kitty. Fortunately, the Northwest boasts an impressive number of romantic lodgings that will also accommodate your pet. In Portland, the **Hotel Vintage Plaza** (422 SW Broadway; 503/228-1212) welcomes pets with open arms. If you let them know you're bringing along that special four-legged friend, they'll stock a water bowl and pet treats in your room before your arrival; and if you need to go someplace your pet cannot go, there's a good chance that one of the notoriously pet-friendly staff members will be available for a brief dog sit.

Seattle's **Hotel Monaco** (1101 4th Ave; 206/621-1770) has a creative new amenity for those traveling with their dogs: Hotel Monaco dog coats, complete with the elaborate hotel logo embroidered on the coats, which are available on a complimentary basis for guests' use. At **W Seattle** (1112 4th Ave; 206/264-6000), the Pet Amenity Program provides plush pet beds and treats for your pooch.

But few cities can beat Vancouver, British Columbia, for welcoming four-legged critters. Visitors to Vancouver who think only the best will do for their furry friend will delight in the fact that the **Four Seasons Hotel** (791 W Georgia St; 604/689-9333) not only welcomes dogs and cats but also has a Pet Friendly Program, which includes a bowl handmade by a local ceramic artist, biscuits made in the hotel's bakery (with recipe card), and bottled Evian water. Dog beds are available on request, as are dog walks. Vancouver's **Sutton Place Hotel** (845 Burrard St; 604/682-5511) offers a VIP (Very Important Pet) program, which includes in-room dining for your pet with a menu that includes an Alberta T-bone steak for dogs and a fish entrée for cats. Finally, if you find yourselves in Vancouver without your dog, and you really wish you had some doggy company, the **Fairmont Waterfront Hotel** (900 Canada Place Way; 604/691-1991) has a black Labrador named Morgan and a golden Labrador named Holly on staff that will buddy up with you and accompany you on a walk around the seawall.

If you prefer to let your pet run wild and free, take him or her on your romantic excursion to the remote town of Tofino on Vancouver Island. At the pet-friendly **Wickaninnish Inn** (Osprey Lane at Chesterman Beach; 250/725-3100 or 800/333-4604), arrange in advance and water and food dishes, milk bones, and a comfy pet bed will await your arrival in the room. Best, you can hike from your front door down to the gorgeous beachfront, where tide pools and stretches of sand make for prime exploring for pets; a dog wash station at the beach access point stocks towels for easy cleanup. (For more information on pet-friendly romantic lodgings, see the index at the back of the book.)

—KATE CHYNOWETH

wraparound porch looks out onto the English-style garden. The late-Victorian decor that greets you at every turn continues into the six guest rooms, which have private baths and modern conveniences. The South Suite has an additional adjoining sitting room. The Penthouse Suite offers two gabled sitting areas, skylights, and a view of the downtown area. The separate, diminutive guest cottage, a new addition, also has a gas fireplace and a private patio. Parking is free, and the complimentary pantry is open 24 hours, should you need a late-night snack. Descend to the dining room in the morning for a memorable three-course gourmet breakfast that might entice with moist blueberry-lemon muffins, seasonal fresh fruit with mint, and hot Belgian waffles with homemade apple compote and cinnamon sugar. $$$ *MC, V; no checks; www.ocanadahouse.com.* &

OPUS HOTEL
●●●●
322 Davie St, Vancouver / 604/642-6787 or 866/642-6787
Fun-loving romantics will flip for this latest addition to the Vancouver hotel scene, a multimillion-dollar brick, granite, and glass cocoon in Yaletown. The bold design of each of the rooms in this boutique hotel takes as inspiration five fictitious personalities, from "Bob and Carol" of the hip 1960s couple-swapping farce to "Dede," an actress who loves animal prints and fake fur. All rooms and suites feature spa bathrooms with oversize vanities topped with unique stainless-steel sinks, luxurious European toiletries, and ultra-plush Frette robes. Courtyard rooms overlook a rooftop garden, and penthouse suites boast double-sided fireplaces, plasma-screen TVs, and deep soaking tubs. The rooms overlooking the street make up for the street-side location with floor-to-ceiling windows in the bathrooms, covered with two sets of blinds: one allows you to see out while nobody can see in; the other closes the room off entirely. Have an Ultra-Vox martini in the Opus Bar, the chic lounge in the lobby, and reserve a corner table in Elixir's (604/642-0557) plush velvet room for a French-bistro dinner. $$–$$$ *AE, DC, JCB, MC, V; no checks; www.opushotel.com.* &

PAN PACIFIC HOTEL
●●●◖
300–999 Canada Place Way, Vancouver / 604/662-8111 or 800/937-1515 (U.S.), 800/663-1515 (Canada)
Although this megahotel wouldn't seem to be a romantic destination at first glance, no hotel in Vancouver boasts a more stunning location or a more remarkable architectural presence. As part of the Canada Place conference facility, the Pan Pacific juts out into Vancouver's inner harbor with its five famous giant white sails—which are actually the roof of the convention center. Many of the 504 rooms showcase spectacular views of water, mountains, and sky. Soft color schemes, down comforters atop king-size

beds, and marble baths distinguish the rooms. For sheer indulgence, book a deluxe room, which features a luxurious sunken jetted tub, or a corner room, which comes with views from your tub. The more expensive rooms overlook the water and offer positively hypnotizing vistas of the floatplanes that come and go against the backdrop of Stanley Park, the Lions Gate Bridge, and the North Shore mountains. Share a libation with your loved one in the Cascades Lounge, just off the lobby, and watch ships sail off into the sunset. For an incredible dining experience, visit the Five Sails Restaurant (604/891-2892; reservations recommended) and request a window table overlooking the harbor and North Shore mountains. Try the luxurious lobster bisque, open ravioli filled with pan-seared prawns, or delicious seared duck, and finish with one of the desserts, which are nothing short of perfection.

$$$$ *AE, DC, E, JCB, MC, V; no checks; www.panpacific.com.* &

RIVER RUN COTTAGES
◐◐◐
4551 River Rd W, Ladner / 604/946-7778
This romantic B&B nestled among a community of houseboats in historic Ladner, 30 minutes from Vancouver, feels like such a getaway that Vancouverites themselves often escape here. In the exquisitely crafted Waterlily floating cottage, relax on a deck overlooking the North Shore mountains and Vancouver Island while watching the ducks, swans, leaping salmon, and bald eagles. Inside the cottage, you'll find a queen-size loft bed, a small kitchenette, a wood stove, pillowed window seats, and a CD player. (Note: if you are tall, you might have trouble negotiating the tiny claw-foot tub/ shower and sleeping loft.) Three onshore cottages built on pilings are just as alluring. Each has a private entrance, fireplace, CD player, and small refrigerator. The Northwest Room has a wood-burning fireplace and French doors that open onto the water; the Keeper's Quarters features a hand-built driftwood bed and a Jacuzzi tub; and the Netloft's spiral staircase leads up to a queen-size captain's bed and a Japanese-style soaking tub on the deck. A hot breakfast is delivered to guests along with the morning paper. If you're in the mood to go completely over the top, try the River Run's romance package: in addition to a three-course dinner at a local restaurant and a bottle of bubbly, the deal includes a tub of chocolate body paint (paintbrush optional). Be sure to make time to paddle the two-person kayak to nearby No Name Island for a romantic picnic (wash the chocolate off first).

$$ *MC, V; checks OK; www.riverruncottages.com.*

THISTLEDOWN HOUSE
✿✿✿✦

3910 Capilano Rd, North Vancouver / 604/986-7173
Set amid a half acre of lush lawns and gardens, yet only minutes from the city center, this sparkling white 1920s Craftsman-style home is a vision of peace and tranquility. All guest rooms offer private baths, soundproofed walls, thick terry robes, and either down or silk comforters, and two have gas fireplaces and separate sitting areas. But for your romantic getaway, you'll want to book the gorgeous Under the Apple Tree Suite, where you can take a bath by candlelight in the air-jet tub for two; sip complimentary vintage port in front of the fireplace in the sunken sitting room; and gaze through the bay windows at the spectacular tree that gives the suite its name. A delightful afternoon tea, including European pastries, fruit flans, and sherry is served on the porch overlooking the flower garden or in the living room by the fireplace, depending on the weather. Breakfast is a sumptuous four-course affair that might include homemade granola with mulled milk or stirred yogurt, a selection of breads and jams, sherried grapefruit, alder-smoked Pacific salmon in puff pastry, and fresh fruits.
$$$–$$$$ *MC, V; checks OK; www.thistle-down.com.* ♿

THE WEDGEWOOD HOTEL
✿✿✿✿

845 Hornby St, Vancouver / 604/689-7777 or 800/663-0666
Located in the heart of Vancouver's finest shopping district, across the street from the gardens and waterfalls of Robson Square and the glass courthouse, the Wedgewood offers Old World charm and scrupulous attention to detail. From the warm and personal service to the renowned Bacchus Restaurant (see Romantic Restaurants), this 83-room hotel is everything that a small urban luxury hotel should be—and then some. The large, finely appointed guest rooms, all with balconies, are grand yet homey. They feature genuine antiques, beautiful English chintz fabrics, half-canopied beds, and Italian-marble bathrooms with separate showers and soaking tubs. The penthouse suites include fireplaces, wet bars, and king-size beds; two have terraces with views, and several open into the bedroom from the bath through louvered windows. Nightly turndown service, an up-to-the-minute spa and fitness facility, and 24-hour room service are also offered. This is a very popular spot with honeymooners.
$$$ *AE, DC, DIS, E, JCB, MC, V; no checks; www.wedgewoodhotel.com.* ♿

Romantic Restaurants

BACCHUS RESTAURANT
◐ ◐ ◐ ◐

845 Hornby St (Wedgewood Hotel), Vancouver / 604/608-5319
This elegant retreat in one of the city's best hotels is consistently rated "most romantic restaurant in Vancouver" in local polls. Dark cherry–wood paneling and deep burgundy velvet couches create private niches, accented by extravagant bouquets of flowers. A pianist taps out everything from soft rock to lounge standards. The sensuous contemporary-French menu might include such delights as cappuccino of white bean soup with truffle oil, lobster rolls with mango and mint, roasted loin of venison with juniper jus, or a classic duck breast with savoy cabbage. For dessert, if you're in luck, the piquant lemon and lime tart will be on the menu; or, surrender to the malted milk chocolate terrine and house-made pistachio ice cream. Best of all, Bacchus offers fine French cheese, top-notch wines, and servers who cater to your every whim. The dimly lit Bacchus Lounge is furnished with leather chairs and plush velvet banquettes. On a rainy weekend afternoon, enjoy afternoon tea in front of the fireplace; in summer, indulge in cocktails next to the windows opening onto the street. Every Wednesday in the lounge, the chef offers a soul satisfying bistro dish paired with wine from the same region of France for $20 ($28 with wine).
$$$ *AE, DC, MC, V; no checks; breakfast, lunch, dinner every day, brunch Sat–Sun; full bar; reservations recommended; www.wedgewoodhotel.com.*
&

BIN 941 TAPAS PARLOUR
◐ ◐ ◐

941 Davie St, Vancouver / 604/683-1246

BIN 942 TAPAS PARLOUR
◐ ◐ ◐

1521 W Broadway, Vancouver / 604/734-9421
Leave busy Davie Street behind and squeeze into the small, high-energy Bin 941, located in the West End. Glowing lighting and upbeat club music create a warm ambience that will make you feel naturally inclined to get intimate with your date—while rubbing shoulders, unavoidably, with the next table. At Bin 942, located at Broadway and Granville, the mood is more subdued somehow, although the music is just as pumping and there's just as much of a crowd. At both spots, you can stay long into the night, nibbling on a progression of enticing cross-culture "tapatizers" with sensual flavors from Italian to Indonesian. Consider a pound of mussels done (superbly) any of four ways; fat crab cakes with burnt orange–chipotle sauce; or charred bok choy and shoestring *frites*—a haystack of hand-cut, seasoned Yukon golds—it's

the city's best-tasting potato bargain. A savvy wine list at the Bins makes it a pleasure to pick out a special bottle to celebrate the occasion.
$$ *MC, V; no checks; dinner every day; beer and wine; no reservations; www.bin941.com.*

BISHOP'S
✿✿✿✿

2183 W 4th Ave, Vancouver / 604/738-2025
You know things are getting serious if your date reserves a table upstairs at this highly acclaimed, intimate 40-seat restaurant located in the trendy Kitsilano district. Everything bears the Bishop trademark of light, understated elegance and bright, graphic color—from the exquisite contemporary art on the walls to the lavish floral arrangements and fine linens on the table. John Bishop warmly greets his guests and is assisted by a staff whose service is as polished as the silver. You may even spot some celebrities here enjoying a romantic tête-à-tête of their own. Simplicity is the key to chef Dennis Green's zealous use of seasonal and organic ingredients. Dungeness crab is perfectly matched with pear-cranberry chutney, and wild sockeye or spring salmon is grilled to perfection—while in season, of course. Other standouts include the rack of lamb with truffle-and–goat cheese mashed potatoes; the sablefish, smoked then steamed, with truffle brandade cake and herb-horseradish sabayon; and the pan-seared scallops in a sweet red pepper–and-chive bisque, topped with a crisp potato pancake. For dessert, share a serving of the moist ginger cake pooled in toffee sauce or the legendary Death by Chocolate. Manager Abel Jacinto oversees an eclectic list of fine wines, and couples who enjoy clinking glasses but find they can rarely finish a bottle will be delighted with the stunning selection of more than 50 half-bottles.
$$$–$$$$ *AE, DC, MC, V; no checks; dinner every day; closed for 2 weeks in Jan; full bar; reservations required; www.bishopsonline.com.*

BLUE WATER CAFE
✿✿✿

1095 Hamilton St, Vancouver / 604/688-8078
We can't think of many ways to spend an evening more romantically than barhopping in this posh seafood restaurant in Yaletown. Your first stop in this 100-year-old converted warehouse: the main bar, to slurp Fanny Bay oysters and sip champagne. Next: the sushi bar, for wild salmon sashimi with chilled sake. Finally, settle into a plush banquette in the dining room for the towering three-tiered signature seafood platter piled high with spot prawns, Dungeness crab, Pacific tuna, sea urchins, mussels, and geoduck clams. For dessert, you might want to go light with one of the homemade fruit sorbets. At some point in the evening, try a concoction of chilled vodka and freshly squeezed juices from the menu of hand-shaken cocktails at the

Ice Bar. The wine list is extensive, with a good selection of British Columbia's best wines. There's a heated terrace outside for alfresco dining.
$$$–$$$$ AE, DC, E, MC, V; no checks; lunch Mon–Fri, dinner every day, brunch Sat–Sun; full bar; reservations recommended; www.bluewatercafe. net. &

C
●●●
1600 Howe St, Vancouver / 604/681-1164
C offers exotic seafood in Zen-like surroundings with an unbeatable view across False Creek to Granville Island. Chef Rob Clark creates cutting-edge dishes with dramatic flavors and stunning presentations, and his appetizers are not to be missed. Share C's signature starter—caviar in a gold-leaf pouch—to start things off right. Move on to the Skeena River wild salmon prepared any way (C has a direct line to the local catch) or the octopus-wrapped scallops. Or, try the "taster box" with green tea–cured gravlax, ahi tuna tartare, and five-spice roasted duck breast. Don't think twice if the special sounds delicious—order it up, they're consistently fabulous. In summer, the patio is the place to spend an entire afternoon lingering over lunch. Expect a broad range of international wine labels on C's eclectic wine list; wine service is informative without being pretentious or intrusive.
$$$$ AE, DC, E, MC, V; no checks; lunch, dinner every day; full bar; reservations recommended; www.crestaurant.com.

CRU
●●●
1459 W Broadway, Vancouver / 604/677-4111
Coffee and butterscotch tones from the tall-backed banquette running along one wall sets the tone for this warm and intimate room. The focus at Cru (the name refers to the French term for "growth of grapes") is "fun and easy," and the menu definitely gets this point across: each item is color coded with eight components of the wine list (with descriptions such as crisp, luscious, juicy, smooth, and big), and all wines are sold by the glass. Simply choose the food or wine you would like to order and then use the color-coded menus to match them up to each other. This allows you to explore how different foods interact with various wine grapes and styles. Try a three-course prix fixe, offered with "mix and match" choices, or go for casual small plates that are all large appetizer sizes. Chef/co-owner Dana Reinhardt has elevated Caesar salad to an art form—a slight grill imparts a hint of smoke, and the croutons are made to order. They may just have the best duck confit in town—crackling skin outside and a hint of vinegar perfectly balances the rich meaty flavor. Save room for the lemon curd fool with seasonal berries, the poached stone fruits in Japanese plum–wine sabayon,

or the bitter chocolate torte with port-stewed rhubarb served with a big dollop of crème fraîche.

$$ *AE, MC, V; no checks; dinner every day; full bar; reservations recommended; www.cru.ca.* &

IL GIARDINO DI UMBERTO
◗◗◗

1382 Hornby St, Vancouver / 604/669-2422
Romance-seekers love Umberto Menghi's charming Tuscan restaurant, with its high ceilings, tiled floors, flickering candlelight—and its wonderful vine-draped terrace for dining alfresco in summer. One of Canada's best-known restaurateurs, Menghi has a syndicated TV show; has written five cookbooks; and owns Villa Delia, one of Italy's best cooking schools. Ask for one of the two most romantic tables, which are table 20 (in one of the side alcoves overlooking the restaurant) and table B20 (a hideaway on the patio). Menghi's emphasis is on reinventing traditional pasta and game dishes in a lighter, more contemporary style: try *tagliolini* in a lobster sauce; tender veal with a mélange of lightly grilled wild mushrooms in a Bambolo (Umberto's label) wine sauce; and osso buco with saffron risotto. For dessert, go for the prize-winning tiramisù—the best version of this classic in town. Expect swift, polished service and a solid wine list.

$$$–$$$$ *AE, DC, MC, V; no checks; lunch Mon–Fri, dinner Mon–Sat; full bar; reservations recommended; www.umberto.com.*

LA TERRAZZA
◗◗◗

1088 Cambie St, Vancouver / 604/899-4449
This Yaletown dining room—with its romantic lighting, dark-painted interior, and lush drapes—could well serve as the set for a postmodern performance of *Romeo and Juliet*. La Terrazza lives up to its name: in warm weather, a row of French doors open onto a large terrace, which adds an alfresco atmosphere to the inside tables. The cuisine is inventive, modern Northern Italian. Start with the seared Quebec foie gras on poached pear, toasted brioche, and late-harvest wine reduction, or the extraordinary, juicy boneless short ribs. Simple yet inspired pasta dishes include the made-in-house tortelloni or the chewy little *strozzapreti* ("priest stranglers") Bolognese. However, the kitchen's creativity shines even brighter when it comes to the main courses. Try grilled bison in a huckleberry-port sauce served with a pasta *galette*, or pan-seared duck breast in Calvados. Heavenly. The service is discreet yet attentive, and the wine list is complete yet not overbearing.

$$$ *AE, DC, E, MC, V; no checks; lunch in Dec only, dinner every day; full bar; reservations recommended; www.laterrazza.ca.* &

LUMIÈRE
❂❂❂❂
2551 W Broadway, Vancouver / 604/739-8185

FEENIE'S
❂❂❂
2563 W Broadway, Vancouver / 604/739-7115
These two restaurants are the culinary stars of Vancouver's West Side. Lumière is more formal, with soft gray-green tones, fine Frette linens, crystal stemware, and clever lighting. Here, couples can choose from one of three seasonally driven, seven-course tasting menus ($100), including a sublime vegetarian selection; there's also the chef's twelve-course signature menu ($130). For an additional $50 to $65, the expert staff will serve carefully selected wines to accompany each menu. Outstanding dishes to consider (if they're offered) include acorn squash velouté with spaghetti squash and poached quail's egg from a fall vegetarian menu; foie gras terrine with truffles and poached figs from the chef's tasting menu; squab breast poached in olive oil with matsutake-mushroom risotto from the Lumière signature menu; and pan-seared spring salmon with *lentilles du Puy*, pancetta, and crispy shallot salad from the seafood tasting menu. Desserts come in flights: luscious caramel apple sits beside gala apple sorbet and a spiced biscuit; the white chocolate–filled gingerbread cannoli rubs shoulders with pumpkin mousse. The Tasting Bar, set within the restaurant, offers a dozen scaled-down, lower-priced versions of Lumière classics. In 2003, the energetic chef also opened a bistro next to Lumière, Feenie's, and these days it's a terrifically popular spot. The main room features slick, high design, and to one side, there's a sexy all-red room with bar and tables, modular and curvy like a spaceship. The menu is fun—everything from the $8 Feenie's Weenie to a superb Peking duck clubhouse sandwich; there's excellent Alsatian pizza, too, as well as a justly renowned calamari sandwich. Dine à la carte or try the $35 prix-fixe menu. The cocktail and beer lists are serious, too.
$$$$ *(Lumière);* $$ *(Feenie's and The Tasting Bar) AE, DC, MC, V; no checks; dinner Tues–Sun; full bar; reservations recommended; www. relaischateaux.com.* &

PARKSIDE
❂❂❂❂
1906 Haro St, Vancouver / 604/683-6912
It doesn't get any more romantic than holding hands under table No. 10 at Parkside, and that's because the food is even more fabulous than the ambience—after all, this is where local chefs impress their dates. The menu's 20 small plates are each priced under $20, and the clever wine list comprises 60 bottles, each under $60 (there is also a reserve wine list and a tasting menu for $40). The only problem is making a decision: all of chef Andrey

Durbach's dishes are as delicious as they are tempting. Begin with the warm salad of red mullet, *lentilles du Puy*, and sauce *vierge*; the mullet, with its crispy crackling exterior and delicate flaky interior, will linger as a delightful memory, as will the silkiest foie gras parfait with pear chutney. If it's a wintry night, go for ever-so-slowly braised veal cheeks with polenta and the thickest, richest sauce. To go with a summer breeze on the patio, try heirloom tomato salad with Dungeness crab bisque. Elegant finales include a smooth *dulce de leche* caramel flan, or a chocolate tart with warm sour cherries. **$$–$$$** *MC, V; no checks; lunch in Dec only, dinner every day; full bar; reservations recommended; www.parksiderestaurant.ca.*

QUATTRO ON FOURTH
🔹🔹🔹

2611 W 4th Ave, Vancouver / 604/734-4444
Patrick Corsi and the accommodating staff at this comfortable Italian restaurant in the heart of Kitsilano make sure dining here is a treat in any season. In winter, the restaurant emanates mystery and romance with candlelight, crimson-washed walls, and the glow from rustic, wrought-iron chandeliers. In summer, couples love to dine alfresco under the lights twinkling on the lush garden patio. Start with the impressive and generous antipasto platter, which includes such items as grilled tiger prawns, crab and salmon cakes, and salmon gravlax. The raw swordfish, sliced razor thin, is superb, as are the grilled radicchio *bocconcini* (fresh mozzarella balls wrapped with radicchio and prosciutto with cherry vinaigrette) and portobello mushrooms. Entrées to consider include grilled beef tenderloin cloaked in aged balsamic syrup; pistachio-crusted sea bass; and spicy deboned Cornish game hen. For pasta lovers, Spaghetti Quattro (playfully marked "for Italians only") rewards with a well-spiced sauce of chicken, chiles, black beans, and plenty of garlic. The mostly Italian wine list is stellar, and Quattro has the largest selection of grappa in Vancouver. It's also worth checking out the restaurant's sibling, Gusto di Quattro (1 Lonsdale Ave, North Vancouver; 604/924-4444), across from the Lonsdale Quay Market on the North Shore. **$$$** *AE, DC, MC, V; no checks; dinner every day; full bar; reservations recommended; www.quattrorestaurants.com.* &

TOJO'S
🔹🔹🔹🔹

202–777 W Broadway, Vancouver / 604/872-8050
Sushi lovers will delight in this renowned restaurant, whose acclaim draws visiting celebrities and local sushi fanatics alike. Sit at the 10-seat sushi bar and hold hands while chef-owner Hidekazu Tojo, respectfully known as Tojo-san, dazzles your palate. One of the best-known sushi maestros in Vancouver, this beaming, mustachioed chef is endlessly innovative, surgically

precise, and committed to fresh ingredients. Among the most outstanding selections are the Tojo's tuna or "special beef" (very thin beef wrapped around asparagus and shrimp) and the suntan tuna, a lightly fried red tuna wrapped with seaweed and served with Japanese plum sauce. Tojo-san also created the "BC roll" (barbecued salmon skin, green onions, cucumber, and daikon), now found in almost every Japanese restaurant in Vancouver. Japanese standards such as tempura and teriyaki are always reliable, and daily specials are usually superb: try pine-mushroom soup in the fall, steamed monkfish liver from October to May, and cherry blossoms with scallops and sautéed halibut cheeks with shiitake mushrooms in the spring. One more thing: the cold Masukagami sake is hot at Tojo's.
$$$$ *AE, DC, JCB, MC, V; no checks; dinner Mon–Sat; full bar; reservations recommended; www.tojos.com.* &

VIJ'S
♥♥♥♦
1480 W 11th Ave, Vancouver / 604/736-6664
Bombay native Vikram Vij's imaginative, home-cooked Indian fare is a sensual delight. Courtesy and simplicity rule, as Vij himself waits carefully on all who arrive, greeting you with a glass of chai before discussing his seasonal menu, which changes every three months. The decor is minimalist and casual; coal-black walls and East Indian ornaments allow the food to take center stage. Start with a glass of Vij's fresh-ginger-and-lemon drink, and don't pass on the standout appetizer—small samosas filled with ricotta and served with a five-spice Bengali sauce. For entrées, you can almost always count on an aromatic curry (lamb "popsicles" in a fenugreek-and-cream curry) or a delicious *saag*, creamy, lightly spiced spinach. A short but excellent wine list and an eager-to-please staff help make this an unforgettable evening out. Or, you can slip next door into Vij's new venture, Rangoli (604/736-5711), for lunch or tea, dinner until 8pm, or a feast from the take-out fridges (prices are very reasonable). You can pick up curries, cumin rice, chutney, chapati, and naan. There's even a special dessert to go: Chocolate Sparkle cookies—truffles you bake at home, developed by Canada's leading chocolatier, Thomas Haas, and flavored with Vikram's own *garam masala*, a blend of ground spices.
$$–$$$ *AE, DC, MC, V; no checks; dinner every day (Vij's), lunch, dinner until 8 pm every day (Rangoli); beer and wine; no reservations; www.vijs. ca.* &

WEST
♥♥♥♥
2881 Granville St, Vancouver / 604/738-8938
David Hawksworth, who returned to his Vancouver roots after working alongside many of London's leading chefs, is the city's best European-

trained chef, which means foodies-in-love will want to make this place a certain stop. The sophisticated, contemporary menu offers three seasonal multicourse tasting menus. The "West" menu begins with wild bluefin tuna tartare, segues into nori-wrapped Dungeness crab, and concludes with a tasting of chocolate. Other signature dishes not to be missed include the foie gras and chicken-liver parfait on apple *gelée*; halibut with Salt Spring Island mussels; and braised lamb shank sided with thyme-nutmeg gnocchi. The beautifully designed dining room features a separate cherry-wood and marble bar (it seats 10) against a ceiling-high "wall of wine." The "wall" includes a custom-built refrigeration system that keeps the wines within two degrees of optimum temperature. You'll love pastry chef Rhonda Viana's desserts and chocolates and the fine cheese selection from Les Amis du Fromage, a highly esteemed Vancouver cheese shop. The early (before 6pm) prix-fixe menu is a steal at $29 and perfect if you are heading across the street to the Stanley Theatre. The wine list offers a well-chosen selection and has garnered many awards. The service is seamless. **$$$$** *AE, DC, E, MC, V; no checks; dinner every day; full bar; reservations recommended; www.westrestaurant.com.* &

WILD RICE
◗◗
117 W Pender St, Vancouver / 604/642-2882
This thoroughly modern Chinese restaurant boasts industrial resin–topped tables under 21-foot ceilings, and offers an intriguing spot for a romantic evening. The hip crowd here is great for people watching—if, of course, you can take your eyes off each other. The traditional elements of Chinese cooking—ginger, soy sauce, wild mushrooms, chile oil, and rice—are revamped here into ingenious-tasting platters perfect for sharing. Crispy, bite-size duck and rabbit wontons arrive stacked like an *inukshuk*. (This term, pronounced ee-nook-shook, refers to a balanced stone cairn in the shape of a person, which is used by the Inuit (Eskimo) and First Nations peoples to mark high points of land and good hunting and fishing spots. You can see them in Canada along lakes and rivers.) Signatures, called Favorite Sons, include Chinatown Sweep—spicy barbecued pork atop a stir-fry and deep-fried chow mein noodles, and a stack of shiitake-dusted beef over cloud ear mushrooms and crispy rice triangles. Duck, beef, and wild boar feature heavily, but there are delicious options for seafood lovers, too: a tower of honey-roasted British Columbia sablefish atop a golden-fried rice paddy is so impressive it elicits admiring gasps from other diners. Choose your sipping pleasures from the tea menu or the small but admirable wine list. **$$–$$$** *AE, MC, V; no checks; lunch Mon–Fri; dinner every day; full bar; no reservations.* &

LOWER MAINLAND BRITISH COLUMBIA

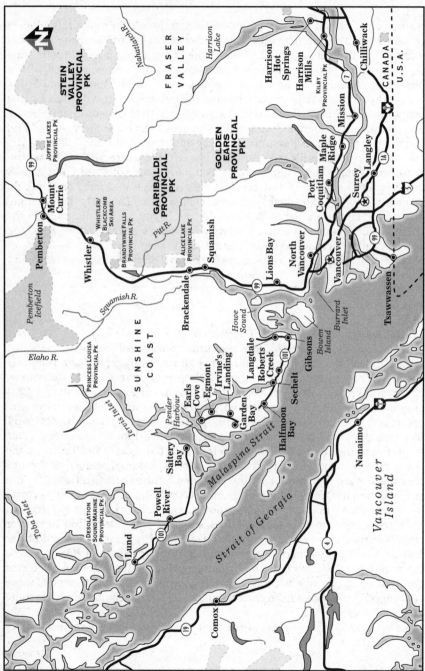

"Kisses are a better fate than wisdom."
—E. E. CUMMINGS

♡ LOWER MAINLAND BRITISH COLUMBIA

The lower mainland is truly a jewel in British Columbia's crown. Not only does it incorporate Whistler, one of the world's most glorious ski resorts, but it also harbors the Fraser River Valley, the Sea to Sky Highway, and the magnificent shoreline stretch known as the Sunshine Coast.

A world-renowned alpine mecca, Whistler offers romance-seeking recreationalists every activity imaginable, year-round. And all this adventure, in its achingly beautiful mountain setting, is serviced by an abundance of world-class dining and lodging options. The village snakes along the valley and is presided over by the twin peaks of Blackcomb and Whistler, both of which soar to heights over 7,000 feet (2,000 m). The skiable terrain on offer comes to over 7,000 acres and caters to all ability levels. In its evolution to an all-season resort, Whistler now also offers award-winning golf courses for sun-kissed days during the summer. Advance reservations for lodging and dining are recommended, and minimum-stay requirements are usual in the high season (May through September, and all holidays). For pocketbook-friendly romantic weekend getaway packages, consider visiting in the shoulder seasons (October through April, not including holidays). Ninety minutes north of Vancouver, Whistler is accessible by the beautiful Sea to Sky Highway (Hwy 99). Floatplanes are a quick way to travel in summer. Visitors from the United States generally fly into Vancouver's airport and rent a car for the drive up to Whistler (see Access and Information).

The other major romantic draw in this region is the beautiful Sunshine Coast, which lives gloriously up to its name. With a total of between 1,400 and 2,400 hours of sunshine annually, bright days outnumber gloomy ones by a wide margin. The area benefits from a rain shadow cast by the Vancouver Island mountains, which catch most of the moisture coming off the

Pacific (though clouds regroup in the Coast Mountains to the east, providing sufficient winter snow to coat trails for cross-country skiing). This region also marks the end of the world's longest highway, the Pan-American—known as Highway 1 or 101 in parts of the United States and Canada—which stretches 9,312 miles (15,020 km) from Chile in South America to the tiny town of Lund on the Sunshine Coast. Before you reach the highway's end, however, there's an 87-mile (140-km) stretch between Langdale and Lund offering everything the Sunshine Coast promises, including unspoiled beaches, biking, hiking, and ski trails; canoe and kayak routes; and spectacular coastal viewpoints.

WHISTLER

ROMANTIC HIGHLIGHTS

Getting from Vancouver to Whistler is a romantic adventure in itself. The **Sea to Sky Highway** (Hwy 99) connecting the two is rated as one of the "Most Romantic Drives in North America" by Robb Report magazine and one of the "Ten Best Drives" by National Geographic Traveler. The views of fir-covered mountains that tumble sharply into island-filled Howe Sound, North America's southernmost fjord, are breathtaking, and there are dozens of romantic spots where you can stop and drink it all in. At Shannon Falls, about an hour north of Vancouver, hold hands and walk down the winding footpath for a view of the falls. At six times the vertical drop of Niagara Falls, this is the fifth-largest waterfall in the world, plummeting 1,100 feet (335 m). Near the town of Squamish, the highway climbs beyond Howe Sound into spectacular Garibaldi Provincial Park, which is surrounded by 10,000-foot peaks and crowned by the exploded volcanic remnant known as the Black Tusk.

Whistler actually comprises four cheek-by-jowl communities: Whistler Village (the main hub), Upper Village (at the base of Blackcomb Mountain), Creekside (the southernmost community, at the original gondola base of Whistler Mountain), and Village North (the northernmost development, which consists of the Marketplace and Town Plaza). Although all four areas have grown exponentially with the completion of a number of multimillion-dollar condominiums, retail stores, and restaurants, walking in any of the pedestrian-only villages still evokes the intimate feel of a small European resort. Sociable plazas are accessed via broad pedestrian-only boulevards, unexpected byways, and pathways that connect the various communities. Both Whistler and Blackcomb mountains can be accessed from any of the four villages, thanks to a well-organized series of interconnecting high-speed lifts and gondolas.

Once you arrive at Whistler, unpack and hit the slopes—the season even stretches into the summer, with skiing and snowboarding available on the Horstman Glacier. The best place to steal a kiss is the slow-moving old triple chair, the Crystal, which serves one of the quieter spots on Blackcomb and tops out at the rustic **Crystal Hut**—where you can feast on the best waffles in town, loaded with berries, whipped cream, and syrup.

The Valley Trail network (maps available at a variety of Whistler/Blackcomb outlets or at www.findwhistler.com) winds through the region, stringing together lakes like precious baubles and offering lovers many paths to stroll hand in hand. **Pane e Formagio** (102–4369 Main St; 604/935-0470) is a good spot to gather tasty picnic supplies. In winter, rent cross-country skis and try the quieter, lower tech, and (we think) more spiritual skiing on winter trails around Lost Lake. Be sure to take along a thermos of soup or a hip flask of something belly-warming to share. Hiking and mountain-biking trails follow old logging roads and veer away into the hills in all directions. For an absolutely incredible hike, visit **Ancient Cedar Forest** (head north along Hwy 99, past Emerald Estates to the trailhead marked by the Cougar Mountain sign; the hike takes about three hours). Here, you'll be seduced by a grove of wizardlike trees, a mysterious cairn garden, and mountain lakes complete with waterfalls. For a winter alternative, snowmobile the access road, then approach reverently in snowshoes with **Cougar Mountain Wilderness Adventures** (36–4314 Main St; 604/932-4086; www.cougarmountain atwhistler.com).

For an escape from the bustle of the village, follow an age-old American romantic tradition and hit the road—northbound. Take scenic Highway 99 to Pemberton—stopping along the way at **Nairn Falls Provincial Park**. Walk out along the boardwalk here to view the hypnotic, surging water of the Green River as it flows through the park, carving its way through a mass of granite. Having picked up volume from the Soo River and Rutherford Creek on its way from Green Lake in the Whistler area, the Green River swirls and crashes its way along until it reaches a fracture in the granite. Suddenly, its broad shape is transformed into a thundering column of white water as it drops 197 feet (60 m) at Nairn Falls. One of the best spots in the world to catch thermal wind-currents, Pemberton in summer offers up the sight of the brightly colored sails of parasailers circling in the sky.

For some sit-down adventures, explore the wide variety of romantic restaurants in and around the resort. A slow-paced and luxurious morning can be had over coffee and brunch at **Crepe Montaigne** (116–4368 Main St; 604/905-4444) or **La Brasserie des Artistes** (4232 Village Stroll; 604/932-3569). The Fairmont Chateau Whistler hosts Sunday afternoon tea in its elegant, Old World **Mallard Lounge** (see Romantic Lodgings). **The Den at Nicklaus North** (604/932-7631; www.whistlerweb.net/resort/sleighrides), in conjunction with Blackcomb Sleighrides, offers lovers a quintessential winter experience, combining an open sleigh ride with fondue. The hottest place to cozy up to one another in the evening is **Bearfoot Bistro's Champagne Bar** (see Romantic Restaurants). A new dining arrival, **Après** (103–4338 Main St; 604/935-0200) beckons you for tapas and wine pairings with intimate booths and a hip, sophisticated ambience. Film buffs will love the **Havana Lounge Classic Theatre Café** (4–4433 Sundial Pl; 604/905-6440) for its desserts, exotic teas and coffees, and twice-nightly showings of black-and-white classics.

Access & Information

From Vancouver, it's a 90-minute drive up the scenic Sea to Sky Highway (Hwy 99) from West Vancouver through Squamish to Whistler. (Follow Hwy 1 west until just before Horseshoe Bay, then take the Squamish–Whistler exit to Hwy 99 north.) If you're coming from the BC Ferry terminal at Tsawwassen, Highway 17 provides the link to Highway 99. A word to the wise: on the drive, please don't allow yourself to get distracted by your partner or the breathtaking views—the curves of the road demand constant attention. If you decide you don't want to miss a single second of spectacular scenery, take the three-hour bus journey with Perimeter Transportation (604/905-0041) or Greyhound Canada (800/661-8747) and snuggle up to enjoy the view. Whistler Air (604/932-6615 or 888/806-2299; www.whistlerair.ca) offers a 30-minute floatplane service between Vancouver and Whistler twice daily from June 1 to September 30.

Border crossings (and customs) link Washington State and the lower mainland at four locations. The busiest crossings are at Blaine, Washington, where Interstate 5 links with Highway 99 at the Peace Arch, and at Douglas, where British Columbia's Highway 15 begins. The others are located just south of Aldergrove, British Columbia, and at Huntingdon-Sumas just south of Abbotsford, British Columbia. After September 11, 2001, security at the borders was significantly tightened: allow two to five hours to make the crossing at peak hours and be sure to carry a passport as proof of citizenship. The nearest major airport is **Vancouver International Airport** (9 miles/15 km south of downtown on Sea Island, Richmond; 604/207-7077; www.yvr.ca).

The **Whistler Chamber of Commerce** (604/932-5528) and **Tourism Whistler** (604/932-4222; www.mywhistler.com) can provide up-to-date information about activities, accommodations, and the array of annual festivals that spill onto the mountains and the villages' cobbled streets.

Romantic Lodgings

DURLACHER HOF ALPINE COUNTRY INN
◐◐◐

7055 Nesters Rd, Whistler / 604/932-1924 or 877/932-1924

Can't make it all the way to the European Alps for your romantic getaway? At Durlacher Hof, your bilingual hosts, Erika and Peter Durlacher, have created an authentic Austrian experience right here in the Coast Mountains. From the imported European slippers proffered when you walk in the door to the tiled *Kachelofen* (old-fashioned farmhouse fireplace) that radiates heat throughout the cozy lounge area, their country inn feels like the real thing. Eight guest rooms evoke the original 1970s spirit of Whistler, with hand-carved pine furniture and comfortable beds with goose-down comforters. Two suites on the third floor are particularly romantic, with Romeo-and-Juliet balconies, jetted tubs, cushioned reading alcoves, and skylights. Erika's lavish breakfasts afford a new reason to smile when the sun comes up: a sideboard groans under a feast of special dishes, perhaps *Kaiserschmarren* (pancakes with stewed plums), freshly baked breads, and lean Schinkenspeck ham. A warm fire and afternoon tea with fresh-from-the-oven cakes welcome guests back from the slopes in the winter; it's served on the patio in summer. A hot tub and sauna are available to warm weary bodies in addition to the soaking tubs found in some of the guest rooms. Escaping the rat race is your only option here—the inn has no televisions, one computer jack, and only one telephone. From the moment you arrive to the last cup of *gluhwein* late at night, the innkeepers' exacting standards will make you feel welcomed and pampered. You can also enlist their assistance in arranging dog sledding, horse-drawn sleigh rides, canoeing, or bicycling expeditions.

$$$–$$$$ MC, V; checks OK; www.durlacherhof.com. &

EDGEWATER LODGE
◐◐◖

8841 Hwy 99, Whistler / 604/932-0688 or 888/870-9065

If you didn't think it was possible to find anything off the beaten path in well-trodden Whistler, the Edgewater Lodge will come as a nice surprise. In a resort where space is at a premium, the Edgewater, nestled on 45 environmentally sensitive acres on Green Lake, is a gem. The ambience is unpretentious, the air is unbelievably fresh, and the lodge's 12 rooms guarantee privacy and attentive service. The lodge's restaurant—one of Whistler's best-kept secrets—doubles as a lobby and sitting room with facilities for making tea and coffee. But what really sets this lodge apart is the immediate access to the outdoors that you'll enjoy. Whistler's recreational Valley Trail connects the property with the rest of Whistler; Meadow Park Sports Centre—complete with indoor skating rink, fitness center, and swimming pool—is adjacent, as is the Nicklaus North golf course. Though the rooms themselves are unspectacular—and ready for a face-lift—the expansive bay windows provide an ideal nook where you can curl up together and enjoy the untainted views of the spectacular mountains—Armchair and Wedge to the northeast, Blackcomb to the east, and Whistler to the south. Toast each other as you watch the sun set from the lakeside hot tub.

$$–$$$ *AE, DC, MC, V; local checks only; www.edgewater-lodge.com.* &

FAIRMONT CHATEAU WHISTLER RESORT
◐◐◐◖

4599 Chateau Blvd, Whistler / 604/938-8000 or 800/441-1414

If you're really looking to splurge, the Chateau Whistler is the ultimate honeymoon getaway—or, if you haven't gotten that far yet, an ideal place to pop the question. It's the grande dame of Whistler—a venerable matriarch presiding over the base of Blackcomb Mountain, enjoying the most privileged location in town. The valet parks not only your car but also your ski gear, so you can grab your beloved a hot buttered rum or piping hot chocolate from the urn bubbling in the corner. The Great Hall lives up to its name. Gaze at the floor of giant slate slabs covered with oversize hooked rugs, the two mammoth limestone fireplaces, and the 40-foot-high beamed ceiling. Folk-art birdhouses and weathered antique furnishings warm up the lodge-style grandeur. The hotel's Fairmont Rooms are 400 square feet and feature king-size beds (a more spacious choice than the petite 300-square-foot Moderate Rooms with queen-size beds). Suites are elegantly appointed, offering comfortable sitting rooms (some have fireplaces) and bedrooms as well as spacious European-style bathrooms. The duplex suites on the top floor are grand in both size and comfort. For an unforgettable (your wallet won't soon forget, either) experience, upgrade to the Fairmont Gold Floors. Dubbed "a hotel within a hotel," these luxurious rooms give guests private check-in, concierge services, and their own wood-paneled lounge with fireplace—where a fully stocked bar (on the honor system) and hors d'oeuvres are available in the evening, and a continental breakfast is offered in the morning. Of the amenities all guests can enjoy, the spa is especially swank, offering facials, body wraps, and herbal and aesthetic treatments, as well as massage and shiatsu. The health club has a heated pool flowing both indoors and out, allowing swimmers to splash away under the chair lifts or soak in the Jacuzzi under the stars. Outside, there's a 58-foot (18-m) lap pool that plays underwater music. The resort also has three tennis courts—and even its own 18-hole golf course, designed by Robert Trent Jones Jr. The on-site restaurants—The Wildflower; the Mallard Lounge, with cigar room and outdoor fire pits (Robin Leach proclaimed this "the premier address at Whistler"); and Portobello—complete this impressive overall picture.

$$$$ *AE, DC, DIS, MC, V; no checks; www.fairmont.com/whistler/.* &

FOUR SEASONS RESORT WHISTLER
✪✪✪✪

4591 Blackcomb Wy, Whistler / 604/935-3400 or 888/935-2460
Just minutes away from the ski lifts for Blackcomb and Whistler mountains, yet secluded enough for total privacy, this new resort, opened in 2004, exudes warmth from the moment you enter the welcoming lobby with its wood-burning stone fireplace. A variety of stones, wood, and granite materials blend seamlessly with the outdoors, and exotic furnishings add sophistication to interior designs. A theme of woven textures, from chair-backs to stunning wall divisions, unify and highlight some eye-popping British Columbia art, including a spectacular forest painting by renowned artist Gordon Smith. The hotel's 242 rooms carry on the luxurious rustic feel with a fireplace in each spacious room, all decorated in warm, earthy hues. Each room has a stellar view of surrounding mountains, and some balconies are totally secluded. Personalized service takes all the "grunt work" out of skiing: As soon as you arrive, your equipment is sent to the ski concierge at the bottom of Blackcomb Mountain, and at the end of the day, a Four Seasons staff member is stationed at the hill to help with your skis and boots. And there's a lot more perks: a private yoga or Pilates workout can be arranged, followed by a visit to the spa and the couple's treatment room, where the microfiber blankets feel like cashmere and each massage table has an adjustable heating pad. Pamper yourselves with any one of eight massages, or a body wrap with clay harvested from British Columbia's glacial lakes, fresh wild seaweed, and wildflowers. Bask in the outdoor pool or the three Jacuzzi tubs; plus, just to make sure you're warm enough, hot chocolate shots are delivered every half hour. And, be assured that someone has already laid out fluffy towels for both of you.
$$$$ *AE, DC, DIS, MC, V; no checks; www.fourseasons.com/whistler.* ♿

PINNACLE INTERNATIONAL RESORT
✪✪✪◖

4319 Main St, Whistler / 604/938-3218 or 888/999-8986
This 84-room lodging might well be Whistler's most romantic small hotel, thanks to the many couple-oriented amenities in each room: seated shower for two, double Jacuzzi tub in a mirrored nook with a view of the fireplace (and just a leap from the king-size bed), TV/VCR, voice mail, full kitchen, Judith Jackson aromatherapy bath products, bathrobes, and wineglasses filled with Hershey's kisses. All rooms also have air-conditioning, a big plus on hot summer nights. The Pinnacle was refurbished in 2001 with a warm Renaissance theme, which goes well with the excellent Italian restaurant downstairs, Quattro (which also does the in-room catering; see Romantic Restaurants). The long-time staff offers genuinely great service, and the boutique feel is a welcome change from the impersonal quality of larger hotels. There's also something satisfying in knowing that all rooms offer

Whistler Reservation Companies

One romantic alternative to hotels and B&Bs is to rent a privately owned condominium or home. Such properties are very popular and widely available in Whistler, and run the gamut from basic one-bedroom condominium units to elaborate log homes. This style of accommodation will appeal to do-it-yourself types, those who are likely to enjoy preparing romantic dinners at home and lazy sleep-ins, and who won't miss the services of the concierge or maid. Staying in a condo or private home can also offer better value, especially if you are planning on sharing with friends. Often, the private amenities—including more space, fully equipped kitchens, entertainment units, or in-house laundry facilities—can also clinch the deal. The variety of properties available is extraordinary, as is the variety of decor—remember, you're relying on the individual owner's taste, as opposed to a professional interior decorator's overall design aesthetic. Couples choosing this route should clarify variables, such as check-out times, maid service, and personal taste, with the property manager in advance. It's also advisable to have the property manager's contact information in Whistler, in case issues come up upon your arrival.

Several management companies in the area handle the marketing, rental, and maintenance of these residences, and most represent different units in the same complexes: try **Whistler Resort Homes** (604/932-7466 or 888/932-7966; www.whistlerresorthomes.com); **Tourism Whistler Central Reservations** (604/932-4222 or 800/944-7853; www.mywhistler.com); and **Powder Resort Properties** (604/932-2882 or 800/565-1444; www.powderproperties.com). High-end luxury homes are also available through **Whistler Chalets and Accommodations, Ltd.** (604/932-6699 or 800/663-7711; www.whistlerchalets.com).

Alternatively, you can bypass the "middleman" entirely and deal directly with homeowners through full-service online booking agencies such as **AlluraDirect.com** (604/707-6700 or 888/425-5872; www.alluradirect.com).

the same use of space and facilities—there are no second-class guests; there are no upgrades. Note that, ironically, "roadside" rooms get a better view of Sprout Mountain than "mountain view" rooms, which look out over the resort. Be sure to take a romantic stroll in the park and follow the meandering art walk up toward the base of Blackcomb.
$$$ *AE, MC, V; no checks; www.pinnacle-hotels.com.* &

SUNDIAL BOUTIQUE HOTEL
🔷🔷

4340 Sundial Crescent, Whistler / 604/932-2321 or 800/661-2321
For the complete Sundial Boutique experience, reserve a room with private hot tub and fireplace; phone the concierge a few days ahead and order groceries, candles, and champagne; arrive at the hotel; and snuggle in the comforts of your room. Renovations have transformed the space (it was formerly The Westbrook). Details in slate, granite, and fir shout Whistler, from floor to ceiling and all the way up to the roof, which offers a hot tub and stupendous views. You could almost reach the Blackcomb gondola from your balcony; in fact, the hotel's just a stone's throw away from the village. Each spacious room has a large kitchen area (the granite countertop doubles as a desk), heated slate bathroom floor, warm earth tones, and luxurious furnishings, all making this boutique destination a perfect getaway. Only 49 rooms make this hotel (the only owner-operated one in Whistler) feel like an intimate, "homey" inn. The 24-hour concierge can arrange everything, from doggie day care to personal chef service.
$$$$ *AE, MC, V; no checks; www.sundialhotel.com.* ♿

THE WESTIN RESORT AND SPA
🔷🔷🔷

4090 Whistler Wy, Whistler / 604/905-5000 or 888/634-5577
The Westin's luxury all-suite hotel aims to sweep lovers off their feet—and straight into bed. All of the suites feature custom-designed "heavenly beds," made up with luscious 280-thread-count Egyptian cotton sheets and down comforters. While the suites themselves feel more like high-tech apartments than quiet, cozy getaways, modern romantics will find much to be happy with here, including the upscale kitchen appliances (even ice machines), high-speed Internet access, and video games. A choice location perfectly positioned just steps from the Whistler gondola provides a little distance from the nightclubs that tend to plague the sleep of visitors in the heart of the village. An indoor/outdoor pool and a health and fitness facility are available to guests for a daily resort fee; there are also soaking tubs in each of the rooms. The Aubergine Grille (604/935-4338), a soaring room with a mountain-view terrace, offers excellent food, while après-ski drinks can be enjoyed in the quiet, swanky FireRock Lounge.
$$$$ *AE, DC, MC, V; no checks; www.westinwhistler.com.* ♿

Romantic Restaurants

ARAXI RESTAURANT & BAR
⬡⬡⬡⬡

4222 Whistler Village Sq, Whistler / 604/932-4540
Whatever you do, save an evening for a romantic dinner at Araxi, one of Whistler's culinary cornerstones. It's located in the middle of action central—Whistler Village Square—with sought-after patio dining during the summer. (It can be jam-packed some nights, but worth the wait, or grab a seat at the bar.) The seafood and oyster bar has Whistler's best selection of oysters with no less than six varieties to choose from (the listing reads like a minicourse in Oysters 101, describing where each oyster comes from and its unique flavor). Tailor-made for lovers is the two-tiered seafood tower appetizer, piled high with oysters, marinated shellfish, smoked fish, and albacore tuna sashimi paired with sparkling Okanagan Blue Mountain Brut. The new-style *hamachi* sashimi embellished with flying fish roe, silky tuna, and a drizzle of yuzu dressing bursts with textures and flavor. Renowned and award-winning chef James Walt's main courses come in dizzying array, and many use local ingredients. Also, Araxi gives vegetarians a special menu offering a satisfying selection (which is somewhat hard to find in Whistler). The expansive and impressive wine cellar is yours to explore every night. For dessert, share the pineapple Tarte tatin, served with fresh Tahitian vanilla and coconut sorbet.
$$$ *AE, DC, MC, V; no checks; lunch May–Oct, dinner every day; full bar; reservations recommended; www.araxi.com.* ♿

BEARFOOT BISTRO CHAMPAGNE BAR
⬡⬡⬡

4121 Village Green (Listel Whistler Hotel), Whistler / 604/932-3433
André St. Jacques, the irrepressible manager of the Bearfoot Bistro, goes to great lengths to provide deluxe wining and dining, and culinary aficionados book as much as a year in advance to secure a table for their next visit (apparently undeterred by the rather exorbitant prices). With the opening of the sexy Champagne Bar, fans and newcomers have the chance to discover the Bearfoot's charms—and at more affordable prices. The bar itself—cast in solid pewter and lined with high-backed leather stools—is a showpiece. But the visual highlight is the frozen ice river incorporated into the bar, drilled with champagne (or martini) glass–sized holes. Hidden fiber optics provide a magical light fantastic that floods your bubbly with an electric rainbow. The Champagne Bar offers a tapas-style dining experience made up of West Coast ingredients with a French-bistro influence—be sure to try the tamari-marinated sablefish with Pemberton plum vinaigrette, or warm smoked salmon with champagne and caviar sauce. An unusually wide range of wines and champagnes are available by the glass, or you can order a

bottle from the 36-page wine "bible." It's practically a small museum for oenophiles, with treasures like Château Mouton-Rothschild going back to 1945, and Moët & Chandon to 1914. The bar opens at 2pm and serves light snacks until the kitchen opens for dinner; for a romantic après-ski experience, lounge here in the late afternoon and indulge in champagne. **$$–$$$** *AE, DIS, MC, V; no checks; dinner every day; full bar; reservations recommended; www.bearfootbistro.com.* &

CARAMBA!
⬡⬡

12–4314 Main St, Whistler / 604/938-1879
The fun, boisterous, Mediterranean-influenced Caramba! offers a refreshing alternative to lovers looking for good food, quick service, and an informal atmosphere. The high-energy staff deals out big, soul-satisfying portions of down-home pasta (try the spaghetti and meatballs), pizza, and roasts. Start with the savory baked goat cheese served with a tomato coulis and garlic toast points. Munch on a melanzane pizza heaped with roasted eggplant, Roma tomatoes, and goat cheese. Then tuck into the spit-roasted free-range chicken or the locals' choice: pot roast braised in red wine. The open kitchen, earthy hues, and alderwood-burning pizza ovens lend a warm feel to the room. Drinks are reasonably priced. Prefer a night in? They'll whip up a take-out meal in 15 minutes.
$ *AE, MC, V; no checks; lunch Fri–Sun in winter, every day in summer, dinner every day; full bar; reservations recommended; www.caramba-restaurante.com.* &

CIAO-THYME BISTRO
⬡⬡

1–4573 Chateau Boulevard, Whistler / 604/932-7051
Formerly known as Chef Bernard's and still run by Bernard Casavant, Ciao-Thyme Bistro maintains the same warm ambience and friendly service that the casual eatery has always been known for, but now offers an intimate addition: the pub next door, which has a cozy bistro feel, hardwood floors, a small lounge area, and just a handful of seats. Here you'll find a well-thought-out selection of local wine and beer, and that rare Whistler spot that feels like a hideaway; time it right and you might have a waiter all to yourself. The restaurant consistently has a bustling breakfast crowd (the all-day eggs Benny made with free-range eggs is popular with locals), but it slows down as the day progresses, and the pub next door transforms into a romantic little hideaway for a late lunch or dinner. Whenever possible, the restaurant relies on local and organic ingredients. Campbell River salmon is wildly popular in a star anise–infused sandwich at lunch and seared with delicious salmon ravioli at dinner. The slow-cooked lamb shank with wine essence, two potatoes, celeriac terrine, and Pemberton root vegetables is

a labor of love. If you visit in summer, linger over a romantic meal on the serene outdoor patio surrounded by a garden of herbs, flowers, and vegetables.

$–$$$ *AE, DC, MC, V; no checks; breakfast, lunch, dinner every day, brunch Sat–Sun; full bar; reservations recommended; www.findwhistler. com.* &

THE EDGEWATER LODGE'S LAKESIDE DINING ROOM
⬡⬡⬡

8841 Hwy 99 (Edgewater Lodge), Whistler / 604/932-0688 or 888/870-9065
The Lakeside Dining Room in the Edgewater Lodge (see Romantic Lodgings) is Whistler's best-kept secret. Revelling in the solitude of its own undeveloped 45-acre Green Lake estate, this intimate restaurant (only 12 tables, plus seasonal lakeside garden seating) features memorable cuisine and outstanding service. This is the perfect spot for a romantic tête-à-tête during the sunset hour. The very traditional menu is remarkably appealing. Start with chef Thomas Piekarski's escargot with basil pesto and parmesan baked in garlic butter; then progress to the Heidelberg schnitzel of tenderest pork loin topped with a hunter's mushroom sauce and accompanied by rich mashed potatoes; or order the sweet and tender local venison, raised on the lodge's own ranch in northern British Columbia, deliciously prepared in a peppercorn and cognac sauce. Finish the evening with a slice of the luscious signature dessert: Black Tusk chocolate cake.

$$$ *AE, MC, V; no checks; dinner every day; full bar; reservations recommended; www.edgewater-lodge.com.*

FIFTY TWO 80 BISTRO AND BAR AT FOUR SEASONS RESORT
⬡⬡⬡

4591 Blackcomb Wy, Whistler / 604/935-3400 or 888/935-2460
The bistro and bar (named after the number of vertical feet from the top of Blackcomb Mountain to the village below) in the Four Seasons Resort (see Romantic Lodgings) are warm and welcoming, designed with romance and relaxation in mind, with high-back chairs in the bistro and dark leather club chairs in the bar. On warmer days, dine on the heated outdoor terrace with wood-burning fireplace, and year-round enjoy views of the beautifully landscaped courtyard and stream with mountain views beyond. Executive chef Jason McLeod has geared the lunch menu to hungry skiers, with practical and efficient items such as the mouthwatering Reuben sandwich and a juicy burger with back bacon. Everything satisfies; the house-smoked salmon with crisp roasted potato and citrus crème fraîche listed as a first course could be a meal unto itself. Attention to detail is noteworthy (asparagus is peeled, the soup is served in individual terrines). Seafood shots are a steal

at four dollars, and chef McLeod creates perfection on a plate with lamb two ways: a New York strip of lamb and a braised lamb cheek, slow roasted and served with prosciutto and Pemberton salsify. If you visit in the fall, try the pine mushrooms, handpicked by the restaurant's own staff. Leave room for the hot chocolate dessert: a molten *manjari* cake made with Valrhona chocolate, a hot chocolate shooter, and chocolate ice cream will transport you. The extensive wine list features many British Columbia wineries and has a separate list of B.C. boutique bottles, featuring several by the glass. **$$–$$$$** *AE, DC, MC, V; no checks; breakfast, lunch, dinner every day; full bar; reservations recommended; www.fourseasons.com/whistler.* &

LA RÚA RESTAURANTE
❍❍❍

4557 Blackcomb Wy (Le Chamois), Whistler / 604/932-5011
La Rúa is sure to win your hearts with its deep-red dining room filled with bold works of art. This is fine dining at its best: You can expect a commitment to the highest-quality ingredients, excellent service, and a great wine list from owner and former bullfighter Mario Enero (who also owns the vibrant and midrange Caramba! restaurant, reviewed in this chapter). Start with the ahi tuna with *togarachi* spice, sesame spinach, and shiitake mushrooms. If you have a hearty appetite, split one of the toothsome pastas, then move on to any of the outstanding lamb dishes: try the rack served with caramelized garlic sauce and mint dumplings, or the shank set atop roasted root vegetables and lentils. Save room for the homemade biscotti and chocolate truffles. The outdoor patio is the place to be on a balmy night, but quiet romantics beware—when this high-energy spot gets crowded inside, it also gets noisy. **$$$** *AE, DC, MC, V; no checks; dinner every day; full bar; reservations recommended; www.larua-restaurante.com.* &

QUATTRO AT WHISTLER
❍❍❍❍

4319 Main St (Pinnacle International Resort), Whistler / 604/905-4844
Enjoying good food in good company, with a steady flow of wine and conversation and a commitment to living with *abbondanza* (Italian for "the passion and poetry of life")—what better way to enjoy a romantic evening in Whistler? The moment you pass through the doors at Antonio and Patrick Corsi's restaurant at the Pinnacle International Resort (see Romantic Lodgings), you're embraced by the delicious aromas of *la cucina leggera*, that is to say, "the healthy kitchen." The ambience is warm and intimate, and the unusual wall art of tiles embossed with crowns, hearts, and allusions to infinity (by Vancouver artist Sid Dickens) conveys an appreciation for the art of love. A 2002 reconnaissance mission to Italy for key staff at the three sibling Quattro restaurants resulted in the innovative Postcards from Italy series,

which injected some 70 new dishes into the kitchen's repertoire. The signature experience at Quattro, and a must for romance seekers, is the impressive antipasto platter, featuring no fewer than a dozen items (including lamb sausage, grilled radicchio bocconcini, and salmon gravlax). The pasta dishes are equally inspired. Try the fusilli with white truffle–infused wild mushrooms, sage, and shaved grana in a light cream sauce. The pistachio-crusted sea bass and mesquite-grilled Alberta beef tenderloin with a rosemary and peppercorn rub are also irresistible. Finish with Italy's "holy wine"—*vin santo*—with biscotti for dipping.

$$$ *AE, DC, MC, V; no checks; dinner every day; full bar; reservations recommended; www.quattrorestaurants.com.* &

RIM ROCK CAFE AND OYSTER BAR
◐◐◐

2117 Whistler Rd (Highland Lodge), Whistler / 604/932-5565 or 877/932-5589

In winter, call ahead and book a table for two by the stone fireplace at this cozy retreat in the unprepossessing Highland Lodge near Creekside. Filled with a hip local crowd, the romantic Rim Rock is proof that fresh seafood and wondrous cuisine can be found in this mountainous setting. Start with any of the hot or cold oyster selections—classic Rockefeller is a favorite, also try Fanny Bay oysters topped with vodka, crème fraîche, and caviar. Main courses range from herb- or chèvre-infused salmon to pan-fried halibut in a potato crust to a mouthwatering caribou with porcini-mushroom cream sauce and wild-mushroom gnocchi and cranberry relish. In summer, book a table on the back patio and dine amid the fresh herbs in the chef's garden.

$$$ *AE, MC, V; no checks; dinner every day; closed mid-Oct–mid-Nov; full bar; reservations recommended; www.rimrockwhistler.com.*

SPLITZ GRILL
◐

4369 Main St (Alpenglow), Whistler / 604/938-9300

Sometimes there's nothing more satisfying than a big, juicy burger after a day on the slopes, and Splitz Grill is the best place in Whistler to get that satisfaction. It's been a long time since a hamburger (or any of its '90s-style chicken, salmon, or lentil cousins) has been this thick and tantalizing. Splitz strikes the right chord in the hearts of locals by offering a not-so-humble grilled sandwich on a crusty bun with a choice of umpteen toppings, ranging from sauerkraut and tahini to sprouts and salsa. Regulars go for the garlicky Italian sausage burger. And there's something very romantic about splitting an ice cream float, chocolate shake, or banana sundae with your sweetheart. A satisfying meal here, including thick, house-cut fries, comes to what you might pay for a single glass of wine at some of Whistler's more upscale locales.

$ *V; no checks; lunch, dinner every day; beer and wine; no reservations.*

TRATTORIA DI UMBERTO
❍❍❍
4417 Sundial Pl (Mountainside Lodge), Whistler / 604/932-5858
Two large, romantically lit dining rooms separated by a massive open kitchen welcome you to this lively establishment, which feels imported directly from Northern Italy. Animated conversation is as much a part of the atmosphere here as the rustic Italian decor, the potted plants and the sculptures, and the poolside view. Classic Tuscan starters include beef carpaccio topped with shaved Parmesan, and the hearty minestrone is guaranteed to take the chill off. But it's the entrées, like the half roasted chicken, Tuscan style, and the cioppino (a saffron- and fennel-laced stew combining crab, prawns, mussels, and a variety of fish in a rich tomato broth) that will have you singing the kitchen's praises. Pasta and risotto dishes include the signature *lasagne al forno* and smoked-duck-and-portobello risotto. A respectable wine list, desserts large enough to share, and rich cappuccino complete the experience.
$$$–$$$$ *AE, DC, MC, V; no checks; lunch, dinner every day; full bar; reservations recommended; www.umberto.com.* ♿

VAL D'ISÈRE
❍❍❍
4314 Main St (Bear Lodge), Whistler / 604/932-4666
Val d'Isère offers a grand combination: excellent people watching in a comfy, romantic setting. Nearly every seat in the house has a street-level view of the plaza. The interior is brasserie style, from the tiled floor to the white porcelain fireplace with fleur-de-lis motif. Superchef-owner Roland Pfaff presides over this French kitchen with overtones from Alsace, which offers a range of palate-pleasing delicacies. Regulars become dreamy eyed at the mere mention of his house onion-and-bacon tart and the signature crab ravioli. One glance at the menu and you're in for the long haul: Start with the delicate rabbit and blueberry pâté to share, then move on to any one of the "slow cooking" mains, all superb and created with classic French technique, such as pot-au-feu (beef flank simmered in a heady beef broth with root vegetables and horseradish) or fall-off-the-bone duck confit with braised pork and chorizo sausage. Don't forget the must-have side of *pommes frites*. Chocolate crème brûlée is definitely created for lovers; just don't fight over the last bite. Wines from France, the United States, and

Canada grace the impressive cellar list, providing selections to complement each dish.

$$$$ *AE, DC, MC, V; no checks; dinner every day; closed after Canadian Thanksgiving and open again before American Thanksgiving; full bar; reservations recommended; www.valdisere-restaurant.com.* &

SUNSHINE COAST

ROMANTIC HIGHLIGHTS

Ocean, wilderness scenery, and sleepy step-back-to-yesteryear villages make the Sunshine Coast one of the most romantic destinations in British Columbia; it has the added charm of being surprisingly affordable. The region is accessible by ferry from Horseshoe Bay in West Vancouver, then via Highway 101 until Earls Cove, where travelers take another scenic ferry ride across Jervis Inlet, a body of water that divides the Lower and Upper Sunshine Coast regions. Roughly speaking, the Lower Sunshine Coast stretches from the ferry at Langdale and Earls Cove, occupying the Sechelt Peninsula, while the Upper Sunshine Coast is between the ferry terminal at Saltery Bay to Lund, on the Malaspina Peninsula. The Pacific deeply indents the coastline at Howe Sound, Jervis Inlet, and Desolation Sound; Jervis and Desolation attract a steady stream of marine traffic in summer. Much of the Sunshine Coast is naturally hidden, which means it's a terrific spot for couples who love to explore. Intriguing side roads with colorful names like Redrooffs and Porpoise Bay lead to romantic places that don't announce themselves until you all but stumble upon them.

Strung along the highway running south to north between the two ferry terminals are Gibsons and Sechelt, two of the larger towns, and a series of delightful villages: Roberts Creek, Smugglers Cove, Secret Cove, Pender Harbour, Garden Bay, Irvines Landing, and Egmont. Amazingly, the entire Sunshine Coast can be traversed by car in a few hours if you rush, but this is not a rushing type of place. You can easily spend a week here exploring. Fans of the TV show *The Beachcombers* (which holds the record for being the longest running television series in Canadian history—19 years) will want to drive into Lower Gibsons to visit the town where it was once shot, have lunch at **Molly's Reach** (647 School Rd; 604/886-9710), and flash back to the past. If you take the upper road (North Rd) off the ferry, you will bypass Lower Gibsons and meet up later with Highway 101. Northbound, the Roberts Creek Road, just past the public Sunshine Coast Golf and Country Club, leads to the tiny, funky village of the same name. Order a couple of ice creams at the **Roberts Creek General Store** (1147 Flume Rd, Roberts Creek;

604/885-3400) on Flume Road, stroll the long pebble beach, or indulge in a sumptuous European-style dinner at the **Creekhouse** (see Romantic Restaurants). Couples won't want to leave "the Creek" without picking up a box of exquisitely molded "kama sutra" chocolates from **Geneviève Lemarchand** (3733 Sunshine Coast Hwy, Roberts Creek; 604/885-4617). Call ahead before stopping by for these naughty novelties. Afterward, hike the forested trails of **Cliff Gilker Park** (3110 Sunshine Coast Hwy/Hwy 101, Roberts Creek; 604/885-6802; www.scrd.bc.ca) or, if golf is an interest, get out your clubs at the **Sunshine Coast Golf and Country Club (**3206 Sunshine Coast Hwy/Hwy 101, Roberts Creek; 604/885-9212; www.sunshinecoastgolf.com). The **Chaudire**, an old ship that was sunk to form British Columbia's first artificial reef and thus draw recreational divers, will lure couples who like to explore underwater. **Porpoise Bay Charters** (604/885-5950 or 800/665-DIVE) will take you to the wreck and other dive sites, as will **Suncoast Diving** (604/740-8006 or 866/740-8006), which has a well-equipped shop in Sechelt. When visiting the bustling town of Sechelt, pop into **The Old Boot Eatery** (5530 Wharf 108a; 604/885-2727), a favorite Italian neighborhood cafe. Try the seafood linguini or homemade meatballs, and enjoy the local scene. There is always a buzz at the Boot. Proceeding up the coast to Halfmoon Bay, divert to get ice cream at the **Halfmoon Bay General Store** (5642 Mintie Rd; 604/885-8555) or tasty European sandwiches at the **Upper Crust Gourmet Market** (5642 Mintie Rd; 604/885-3600). If you are into wild scenery, there are many great hiking options. An easy and wonderful way to experience the coastal wilderness is the 1-mile (1.6-km) round-trip hike around **Smuggler Cove Provincial Marine Park** (1.2 miles/2 km west of Halfmoon Bay; 604/898-4678; wlapwww.gov.bc.ca/bcparks/infocentre.htm). Next is **Secret Cove** (a sheltered harbor located approximately 10 miles/16 km north of Sechelt), a favorite with yachties. In summer, enjoy the eclectic boat traffic from the floating **Upper Deck Café** (Secret Cove Marina; 604/885-3533) where fresh seafood reigns. A suggestion: have the mouthwatering crab and prawn cakes. Contact the **Secret Cove Marina** (604/885-3533 or 866-885-3533) for restaurant reservations and information on fishing or sightseeing charters. Farther north, watch the sign for **Lord Jim's Resort Hotel** (5356 Ole's Cove Rd, Halfmoon Bay; 604/885-7038 or 877/296-4593; www.lord jims.com), a great spot for a lingering drink, great meal, and a bird's-eye view of Thormanby Island in the distance.

It's hard to tell where the freshwater lakes end and the saltwater coves begin at the north end of the Sechelt Peninsula. Narrow fingers of land separate the waters around Agamemnon Channel from a marvelous patchwork of small and medium-sized lakes. Three ocean-side communities are grouped around the indented waterway known as Pender Harbour: Madeira Park, Garden Bay, and Irvines Landing. At Madeira Park, head to **The Hamburger Stand** (12901 Madeira Park Rd; 604/883-9655), where burgers, milk shakes, and fries are miraculously produced out of a rustic trailer.

Enjoy your burgers in peace and quiet at the picnic area in front of the **Harbour Gallery Artists Co-op** (Madeira Park near the Government Wharf; no phone), where there's a beautiful view of Pender Harbour. A romantic—and ecologically minded—hiking destination is the new **Francis Point Marine Park** (turn at Francis Peninsula Rd and follow to end of Merrill Rd; www.naturalists.bc.ca/clubs/associate/ag2_fp.htm), an important 180-acre piece of pristine waterfront on the Francis Peninsula west of Madeira Park. Its towering old-growth Douglas fir, windswept pines, mossy headlands, and intricate coves have made the area world famous.

North of Pender Harbour, Highway 101 winds around Ruby Lake and climbs above it, allowing a good view of the lake, its setting, and beyond. Each May, Ruby Lake Resort hosts the **Ruby Lake Wood Duck Wilderness Festival** (604/883-2269 or 800/717-6611; www.rubylakeresort.com) in honor of the beautiful bird's reappearance; considering that these are entirely monogamous birds, we think them quite romantic indeed.

An impressive natural show occurs twice daily in **Skookumchuck Narrows Provincial Park** (on Hwy 101, just before the road ends at Egmont; 604/898-3678), about 7 miles (12 km) north of Ruby Lake. Watch in amazement while one of the largest saltwater rapids on Canada's West Coast boils as tons of water forces its way through Skookumchuck Narrows at the north end of Sechelt Inlet. A 2.5-mile (4-km) walking/cycling trail leads from the outskirts of Egmont to viewing sites at North Point and nearby Roland Point. At low tide, the bays around both points display astonishingly colorful and varied forms of marine life: giant barnacles, colonies of sea stars, sea urchins, and sea anemones.

Egmont is the access point to one of the Sunshine Coast's treasures—Princess Louisa Inlet and Chatterbox Falls. This swatch of phenomenal wilderness can be seen on a full-day cruise aboard the large **Malibu Princess** (604/883-2003), on a smaller vessel with **Sunshine Coast Tours** (604/883-2280 or 800/870-9055), or with **High Tide Tours Water Taxi** (604/883-9220 or 866/500-9220) for a romantic trip for two.

Egmont is also the end of the Lower Sunshine Coast. From here, take the picturesque, 50-minute ferry ride from Earls Cove through the fjords of Jervis Inlet to Saltery Bay. As you drive to Powell River, consider a stop at romantic Palm Beach Park, a well-kept secret in an area known as Lang Bay.

If you're hungry in Powell River, pop in to the cute **La Casita Mexican Restaurant** (4578 Marine Ave; 604/485-7720) for a Dos Equis and a bowl of *sopa de lima* (tortilla and lime soup)—you'll feel like you're in Puerto Escondido. The tiny fishing village of Lund, some 33 miles (54 km) from Saltery Bay, is the end of Highway 101, which started 9,312 miles (24,000 km) away in the South American country of Chile. It is also the gateway to Desolation Sound, renowned as one of British Columbia's most spectacular marine parks. If staying overnight at the edge of civilization sounds romantic, check out the lovingly restored, historic **Lund Hotel** (1436 Hwy 101; 604/414-0474; www.lundhotel.com). But first, fortify yourselves with a blackberry-cinnamon roll from nearby **Nancy's Bakery** (on the wharf; 604/483-4180). A jaunty red water taxi called the **Raggedy Anne** (604/483-9749) ferries pedestrians from Lund to nearby Savary Island. Here you'll find a land of enchantment, with tropical white sand and warm aqua-hued water, no electricity, only a few cars, and no campsites. Fortunately, kiss-worthy accommodation and a warm welcome await at **Savary Lodge B&B** (3114 Malaspina Promenade; 604/483-9481).

Access & Information

The Sunshine Coast is accessible from the rest of the lower mainland via a combination of car and ferry, or by floatplane. Travelers aboard **BC Ferries** (604/444-2890 or 888/724-5223 in BC; www.bcferries.bc.ca) leave Horseshoe Bay in West Vancouver aboard one of eight daily sailings for a 45-minute ride to Langdale on the Sechelt Peninsula.

Border crossings (and customs) link Washington State and the lower mainland at four locations. The busiest crossings are at Blaine, Washington, where Interstate 5 links with Highway 99 at the Peace Arch, and at Douglas, British Columbia, where BC's Highway 15 begins. The other crossings are located just south of Aldergrove, British Columbia, and at Huntingdon-Sumas just south of Abbotsford, British Columbia. The nearest major airport is **Vancouver International Airport** (9 miles/15 km south of downtown on Sea Island, Richmond; 604/207-7077; www.yvr.ca). Highway 1 (the Trans-Canada Highway) runs east-west and links the south Fraser Valley with Vancouver.

Highway 101 links Langdale with Earls Cove, 50 miles (80 km) to the north. A 650-minute ferry ride from Earls Cove crosses Jervis Inlet to Saltery Bay. Highway 101 makes the second leg of this journey 37 miles (60 km) north to Lund. BC Ferries also connects Powell River on the Malaspina Peninsula with Comox on the east side of central Vancouver Island. Those traveling up the entire coast or returning via Vancouver Island should ask at the Horseshoe Bay terminal about special fares, as there may be discounts (up to 30 percent) if you complete the circle tour (of all four ferry rides).

Romantic Lodgings

BEACHCOMBER MARINE SPA AND COTTAGE
❤❤❤

6398 Gale Avenue N, Sechelt / 604/885-0900 or 877/399-2929
Driving from the Sunshine Coast's largest town, Sechelt, through a sub-urban-style neighborhood to the Beachcomber, you may begin to wonder: is this really the road to romance? Keep driving—it is. Owners Chris and Ann McNaughton's new custom-built home on beautiful Sechelt Inlet has been planned with the three keys to a romantic getaway—comfort, privacy, and tranquility—firmly in mind. And despite other homes nearby, the surrounding grounds provide a peaceful sense of seclusion. Choose from two rooms in the main house or a separate cottage. There are views from every room of the airy, spacious two-level stucco home with strikingly carved cedar entry posts. Soothing contemporary decor in neutral tones invites you in. The two large rooms (Arbutus and the Driftwood, each with a private entrance) on the house's lower level both have access to a comfy sitting room with a TV and selection of videos. There's also a private room for massage or body treatments that can be scheduled in advance with a local masseuse. The third accommodation, and the most romantic, is the separate Beachcomber Cottage, located a dozen steps closer to the water. Luxurious touches in all three accommodations include dreamy queen-size beds, heated floor tiles in the bathrooms, and two-person jetted tubs situated so that you can watch soaring eagles or the moon and stars over the mountains and inland sea. You can have breakfast upstairs in the main house, or your hosts will deliver a breakfast basket to your door.
$$ *AE, MC, V; no checks; www.beachcomberbb.com.* ♿

BONNIEBROOK LODGE
❤❤❤

1532 Ocean Beach Esplanade, Gibsons / 604/886-2887 or 877/290-9916
If you're fantasizing about a romantic getaway that's close to the ocean and offers fabulous food and a private beach, this is an ideal destination. Located at Gower Point, this 1922 yellow clapboard lodge was remodeled by owners Karen and Philippe Lacoste. For the most romance, reserve an ocean-view room or suite in the main lodge or one of the "romance suites" nestled in an old farmhouse beside the lodge along Chaster Creek. The two penthouse guest rooms on the lodge's third floor have vaulted ceilings, private balconies, and captivating views of the water. The two one-bedroom suites on the second floor have king-size beds and private balconies with ocean views. And the three romance suites are at ground level and look out toward the forest. All of the accommodations feature gas fireplaces, overstuffed sofas, pine armoires, TV/VCRs, oversize showers, two-person Jacuzzi tubs, and cozy terry-cloth robes. The lodge's intimate, French-inspired restaurant,

Chez Philippe, is well designed for an intimate dinner for two. Call ahead to reserve table 63 at sunset (trust us) and choose between à la carte selections and the reasonably priced four-course *table d'hôte* menu; start with a slice of duck galantine—a boneless duck stuffed with goose liver and pistachios—before diving into the outstanding seafood ragout or a savory rack of lamb. In winter, a crackling fire lights up the dining room with the Old Country ambience of a French *relais*. Come morning, a hearty breakfast is served here, which might include a pesto omelet, fresh baked goods, and homemade strawberry jam; if you're staying in a suite, you can have it delivered. After breakfast, explore the lodge's deliciously private stretch of beach, which leads to nearby Chaster Park.
$$–$$$ *AE, MC, V; no checks; www.bonniebrook.com.* &

COUNTRY COTTAGE BED & BREAKFAST
❀❀❀
1183 Roberts Creek Rd, Roberts Creek / 604/885-7448
Philip and Loragene Gaulin's 2-acre farm offers two very romantic accommodations: the vintage one-room Rose Cottage, tucked inside the front gate, and the large Cedar Lodge, next to the sheep pasture. The sweet Rose Cottage comes complete with fireplace, small kitchen, and tartan blanket-covered queen-size bed. Farther back on the property is the Cedar Lodge, a tree house for grown-ups with its wood and stonework interior, giving a Northwest country-lodge ambience. Snuggle under a Hudson Bay blanket on the loft queen-size bed. Skylights brighten the room on even the most determinedly gloomy days, and a wood-burning river-rock fireplace glows in one corner. There's also a full kitchen, so bring supplies (if you forget something, there is a grocery store nearby). On Sundays in winter, guests are welcome to accompany Philip on his weekly backcountry ski outing in nearby Tetrahedron Park. Get ready for a day of exploring: breakfast, delivered to your door, may include farm-fresh eggs scrambled with smoked salmon or Belgian waffles that Loragene cooks up on her wood-burning stove. Couples with beloved dogs will be pleased to know that their furry friends are welcome.
$$–$$$ *No credit cards; checks OK; www.countrycottagebb.ca.*

DESOLATION RESORT
❀❀❀
2694 Dawson Rd, Okeover Inlet / 604/483-3592
You'll find unforgettable West Coast adventure—including kayaking, boating, and hiking—as well as romance at Desolation Resort. The quiet of the resort's 7 wooded acres is broken only by the lapping of waves on the shore, the cry of the loons on the water, and the squawks of ravens as they swoop among fir trees. The lodgings consist of 10 uniquely designed oceanfront chalets perched on pilings overlooking the pristine waterfront of

Okeover (pronounced "oak-over") Arm. Fir floors flow into patterned pine walls and ceilings below steep-pitched cedar-shake roofs. The rustic cabins are simply furnished, and beds are inviting, with warm comforters spread atop flannel sheets. Wide verandas offer sweeping views, and stairs lead to a floating dock. Cabins 1, 2, 6, and 7 have outdoor hot tubs. Carved figures of herons, gulls, and an ancient mariner sit on the pilings, and canoes and kayaks are for rent at the resort. The chalets also feature full kitchens, but no food is supplied, and no meals are served at the resort, so be sure to bring every gourmet item your hearts might desire. Managers are on site to help you check in—otherwise, you are entirely self-sufficient, which is an ideal level of privacy for any intimate getaway.
$$ *AE, MC, V; no checks; www.desolationresort.com.* &

HALFMOON BAY CABIN
✿✿✿✿

8617 Redrooffs Rd, Halfmoon Bay / 604/885-0764 or 866/333-2468
Seeking serenity? Privacy, luxury, and every convenience await you at this romantic gem—all you need to bring are the groceries and the love. Surrounded by an English-country garden and set on a hill overlooking its own beach, this rustic yet luxurious 1,292-square-foot (120-square-m) waterfront log cabin features a massive stone fireplace, skylights throughout, and thoughtful touches from fine linens to the latest glossy magazines. The cabin's two bedrooms feature queen-size feather beds and pine furnishings. While there is enough room here for two couples, the cozy decor makes it equally suitable for two people. The master bedroom's huge bath boasts a Jacuzzi tub and French doors leading to a sun deck with a private outdoor shower and gas barbecue. A cabana on the beach is furnished with everything you could possibly need: lounge chairs, a wet bar, a full fridge, a barbecue, and a wonderful cedar-walled shower. Best of all, the owners are off the premises, providing you with the ultimate privacy. With its breathtaking views, Halfmoon Bay Cabin is a gem for romantics any month of the year.
$$$–$$$$ *AE, DC, MC, V; no checks; www.halfmoonbaycabin.com.* &

ROSEWOOD COUNTRY HOUSE BED AND BREAKFAST
✿✿✿(

575 Pine St, Gibsons / 604/886-4714
In 1990, owner Frank Tonne felled and milled the timber growing on his steep slope overlooking the Strait of Georgia and built this 1910-inspired Craftsman-style mansion, fitted with classic doors and windows rescued from old Vancouver houses. Both inside and out, the home hearkens back to the spacious elegance of an earlier era. White walls and blond wood give the house a warm, honeyed glow, perfectly complemented by Oriental rugs and period furniture. There are two ground-floor suites complete with private bathrooms, fireplaces, stained-glass windows, and French doors that open

onto the lush flower gardens. Elegant furnishings highlighted with lace, chintz, and fresh flowers complement the astounding ocean and garden views from spacious, private decks; the Garden Suite also has a beautiful soaking tub. Wake up to a serene world where sparkling wine, orange juice, and a delicious breakfast are served in the airy sun-room; guests can also request breakfast in bed, rolled in on a silver tea-service trolley. Co-owner Susan Tonne Berryman handles all the details. Romantic multicourse seafood dinners (available to guests only; reservations required in advance) are also offered, served in a private dining room or on the patio. This is a justifiably popular spot, so we recommend booking several months in advance for weekends between May and October.
$$–$$$ *V; checks OK; www.rosewoodcountryhouse.com.* ⅗

RUBY LAKE RESORT
❤❤❤❤
Ruby Lake, Madeira Park / 604/883-2269 or 800/717-6611
Explore an enchanted wilderness complete with a bird sanctuary, a floating bridge, and waterfall gardens at this romantic retreat. Developed by the engaging and hospitable Cogrossi family, who hail from Milan, Ruby Lake Resort has a lot going for it. Above a lazy lagoon are 10 motel-like cedar cottages with rustic pine furnishings and TVs; some cottages have full kitchens. Across the road are two lakeside "Dreamcatcher" B&B suites, which were added in 2002. All 12 of the units have their own entrances, soaking tubs, and fireplaces, but the most romantic ones are the latter two with no TVs and the sunlit lake just outside the patio. Also incredibly romantic in an outdoorsy fashion are the 2004 additions—lakeside tents with a touch of luxury. On a cedar platforms, they have the allure of a safari abode with handcrafted four-poster beds and lovely fabrics. (When it's a mite chilly for your love to keep you warm, there are in-flame, eco-friendly stoves available.) The family's restaurant (see Romantic Restaurants) draws accolades for its fine Northern Italian cuisine and fresh seafood. But, the real treat here is the wildlife—waterfowl flock by the hundreds to the resort's private lagoon, eagles drop by for a daily feeding around 6pm, and occasionally a black bear is spotted in the nearby forest. In his spare time, chef Aldo Cogrossi builds birdhouses; more than 40 adorn the sides of cabins, telephone poles, rooftops, and the neighboring Suncoaster Trail, perfect for mountain biking and hiking. Aldo's wife, Brigit, is the resort's in-house registered massage therapist, and a spa opened in summer 2005. How romantic to luxuriate in a spa treatment surrounded by the sights, sounds, and fragrances of the forest.
$$–$$$ *AE, MC, V; no checks; closed Dec–Mar; www.rubylakeresort.com.*

SUNSHINE COAST RESORT
✿✿✿

12695 Sunshine Coast Hwy, Madeira Park / 604/883-9177
Pop the question, spend your honeymoon, or just put your regular lives on hold at this spectacular oceanfront resort with sweeping views of Pender Harbour and the surrounding mountains. A new lodge, opened in 2002, offers 10 units, ranging from deluxe rooms and one-bedroom suites to a magnificent two-bedroom penthouse. Amenities here include decks, fully equipped kitchens, TV/VCRs, soaking tubs, and stone fireplaces in the suites. Outside, there's a giant outdoor Jacuzzi tub set right above the water. Other accommodations include cottages and one- and two-bedroom apartments. There's also a full-facility 38-slip marina and full-hookup RV sites in a beautifully landscaped park. Guests can get a lift on the resort's motor boat to visit restaurants across the bay. Canoeing, sea kayaking, scuba diving, art walks, golfing, sailing tours and lessons, floatplane sightseeing, and other activities can be arranged with the knowledgeable staff.
$–$$$ *AE, MC, V; no checks; www.sunshinecoast-resort.com.* &

WEST COAST WILDERNESS LODGE
✿✿✿

Egmont (call for address) / 604/883-3667 or 877/988-3838
To commune with nature and with each other, it is worth the drive to the end of the lower Sunshine Coast to find this tucked-away treasure. The large post-and-beam lodge overlooks inlets spangled with verdant islands. Nestled into the woods are 5 minilodges with 20 rooms. Choose an ocean (read "spectacular") or forest view and enjoy the peaceful ambience of a simple but charming room. Fluffy quilts (14 rooms have king-size beds), rustic antique furnishing, and floor-to-ceiling windows welcome. Adventuresome romantics will be in their element as kayaking, canoeing, rock climbing, mountain biking, hiking, and heli-hiking, as well as boat tours are all options. You can kiss in a helicopter as you take a sightseeing tour above towering mountains and plunging waterfalls. *The* place to kiss here is the main lodge's spacious wraparound deck that boasts one of British Columbia's best sunset views, with the last rays painting the mountain-backed ocean in warm apricot hues. Other kissing options are in the well-placed hot tub, on the beach, and along wooded paths. The lodge's restaurant, Inlets, has garnered praise since opening in 2003—the menu lives up to the views, which says a lot. For the ultimate treat, arrive by floatplane from Vancouver.
$$–$$$ *AE, MC, V; no checks, www.wcwl.com.*

WILDFLOWERS BED & BREAKFAST
⬢⬢⬢⬢

5813 Brooks Rd, Halfmoon Bay / 604/885-7346 or 877/399-2929
A long, winding driveway leads to this forested haven where sun-dappled lawns boast luxuriant gardens and waterfowl bask in a man-made lagoon. The accommodations—two spacious, elegant cottages tucked into evergreens and gardens—stand separately from the owners' hilltop home. Both cottages have fireplaces, king-size canopy beds, comfy seating areas, soaking tubs, and small kitchens. (Note that the Iris has a particularly sexy bathroom.) Art, weavings, and fabulous fabrics add up to eye-pleasing decor; well-traveled owners, Doug and Darcy Long, have impeccable taste and know just what to bring home from their worldly jaunts, such as the Fijian *tapa* cloth above the bed in the Iris suite. A feeling of total privacy pervades the place, whether you're relaxing in a wicker lounge and listening to birdsong, soaking in the hot tub beside the lagoon, or indulging in a spa treatment in your room. Breakfast can be served in your suite when you wish—mornings are memorable with dishes such as blueberry and cream cheese–stuffed French toast; in summer, strawberries marinated in Grand Marnier; and, in winter, a soothing, seafood bisque. While you may wonder about choosing this forested, tucked-away haven in an area famous for its ocean views, the choice is more than justified. With pampering touches—designer robes, wine, and chocolates—this getaway defines a romantic retreat.
$$ *MC, V; no checks; www.wildflowers-bb.com.*

Romantic Restaurants

BLUE HERON INN
⬢⬢⬢

5521 Delta Rd, Sechelt / 604/885-3847 or 800/818-8977
Almost every table in the Blue Heron shares the magnificent waterfront view of the Sechelt Inlet (complete with blue herons, if you're lucky). Lamps at every table and a fieldstone hearth warm the wood-beam interior. Co-owner Gail Madeiros makes sure you're comfortable, while her husband, chef Manuel, makes sure you're well fed. Stand-out dishes here include the fresh clams, a carpaccio-style roast loin of veal, grilled wild salmon with fennel, smoked sablefish with hollandaise, and halibut fillet topped with a red onion–and-strawberry salsa. A creamy Caesar salad and a bouillabaisse for the soul are also excellent. The presentations are stunning, the arrival of each dish is perfectly timed, and the service is top notch.
$$ *AE, MC, V; no checks; dinner Wed–Sun; full bar; reservations recommended.* ♿

CAFÉ NEW ORLEANS
◐◐◖

450 Marine Dr, Lower Gibsons / 604/886-6722
There is a touch of Bourbon Street in the seaside village of Gibsons. For romance enhanced with the tinkle of piano ivories and mouth-watering Creole dishes, head to Café New Orleans. In summer, the patio seating is sublime with ocean views and soft breezes. In winter, hold hands by an expansive window seat and, warmed by candle glow, watch the lights of Cypress Mountain twinkle on the water. The whole setting smacks of warm, fuzzy feelings and the menu items by ex–New Orleans chef Stephen Hassingerare is dazzling. Start with Dungeness crab cakes with sweet corn *mâche choux* and red pepper rouille or New Orleans popcorn shrimp with spicy Creole mustard sauce. Dinner choices include blackened catfish with cornbread sausage dressing; steak lovers will savor the spice-rubbed sirloin with rosemary potatoes, vegetables, and blue cheese–compound butter. On weekends there is live entertainment—soft jazz, of course.
$$ MC, V; local checks only; dinner Tues–Sun, brunch Sat–Sun; full bar; reservations not necessary.

THE CREEKHOUSE
◐◐◐

1041 Roberts Creek Rd, Roberts Creek / 604/885-9321
Diners often follow a meal at Yvan Citerneschi's quiet restaurant with a romantic walk down to the beach to see the twinkle of distant lights on the mainland and Vancouver Island. Located in an unassuming neighborhood, this pleasant dining room with a view of a tree-filled garden is decorated simply, with white walls, light wood floors, flowers on the tables, and original contemporary art. On any given night you may choose from 10 seasonal entrées, including wild boar, rack of lamb Provençal, sautéed prawns, or locally caught rabbit. A mango mousse lights up the evening. Service is knowledgeable and friendly.
$$$ MC, V; no checks; dinner Wed–Sun; full bar; reservations recommended. ♿

LAUGHING OYSTER RESTAURANT
◐◐◐

10052 Malaspina Rd, Powell River / 604/483-9775
Romantic couples will be charmed by both the food and the spectacular views at the waterfront Laughing Oyster, whose split-level design means everyone has a good view of Oeuvre Arm, particularly from the large patio. On dark and stormy evenings, you might prefer a corner table beside the fireplace. Start with a microbrew and a spinach Caesar salad or British Columbia mussels, cooked to perfection. First timers should consider the Seafood Harvest for two or David's Cajun Bouillabaisse, seafood delicacies

in a spicy prawn and beer sauce. The casual ambience and generous portions make this spot a favorite with locals. Even those who aren't big oyster fans rave about the flavor of these oysters, which are brought fresh off the restaurant's dock and right to your table. The staff is unwaveringly friendly, with the right degree of attentiveness. The reasonably priced wine list isn't long, but is thoughtfully chosen.
$$$ *AE, MC, V; no checks; lunch, dinner every day, brunch Sun; closed Mon–Tues Oct–Mar; full bar; reservations recommended; www.laughing oyster.bc.ca.* &

RUBY LAKE TRATTORIA
❍❍❶
Ruby Lake (Ruby Lake Resort), Madeira Park / 604/883-2269 or 800/717-6611
"To eat good food is to be close to God," says the character Primo in the film *Big Night*. Brothers Giorgio and Aldo Cogrossi could have been the models for the restaurateurs in that film. Chef Aldo cooks up generous portions of Milanese home-style dishes, while his eager-to-please brother, Giorgio, greets guests with open arms. Aldo's Northern Italian specialties, using organic vegetables and herbs from the family garden, will please you from the first to the last bite. The dish of house-smoked salmon tossed with farfalle is a creamy and smoky delight, and the veal, a good test of any Italian restaurant, is fork tender, marinated, grilled, and topped with a sauce of chanterelle-mushroom reduction. Another favorite is the pan-fried snapper with sautéed baby squash. There's also spaghetti con Gamberi, a classic Italian seafood dish topped with local swimming scallops and fresh Garden Bay mussels steamed with tomato, white wine, and garlic. The wine list is mostly Italian, with some local Okanagan highlights, and offers plenty of appealing and affordable options. Save room for the tiramisù—and do not pass on the homemade nectarine crisp, when in season.
$$ *AE, MC, V; no checks; lunch, dinner every day (summer only), call for hours in spring and fall; closed Dec–Mar; full bar; reservations recommended; www.rubylakeresort.com.*

VICTORIA & VANCOUVER ISLAND

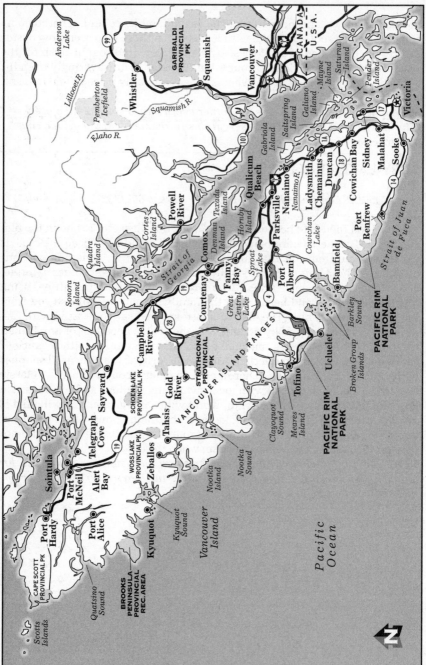

"A kiss has often proved a more potent arouser than any storm."

—E. M. MOORE

♡ VICTORIA & VANCOUVER ISLAND

Visiting Vancouver Island is an unconditional romantic must—it simply has everything that two people in love could want. Covered by deep forests and boasting pristine wilderness, this enormous island is perhaps best known for the charming city of Victoria, although its rugged beaches and the mountain range that spans its nearly 300-mile length are equally compelling. The beautiful and unspoiled central west coast is mostly undeveloped, except for the remote towns of Tofino and Ucluelet, where romance abounds. The north-central section is a vast, rugged, mostly uninhabited terrain. The highly civilized Victoria, on the southern tip of the island, presents a stark contrast to the rest of the island's untamed nature. Lavish gardens, elegant tearooms, and Old World architecture, along with a multitude of tourist traps and scores of international visitors, define the capital of British Columbia. (The self-conscious and whimsical "more English than the English" character is part of what draws the crowds.) Not far from Victoria, there are other attractions, such as exquisite scenery along the southwestern coast near the small town of Sooke, and the wineries of the Cowichan Valley and the Saanich Peninsula, each less than an hour's drive from Victoria.

Sublime romantic getaways can be had here year-round. The Pacific Ocean moderates the climate to make this region's weather the mildest in all of Canada. Expect lovely summers and cool winters with comparatively less rain than much of the rest of the Pacific Northwest. The dramatic tempests that lash the western coast in winter inspired the concept of storm-watching getaways. In peak season (May to August), crowds are thickest, prices are highest, and tourist services are best. Gardens and greenery are freshest in May and June; days are sunniest in July and August. The shoulder months of April and September are ideal for quieter, reduced-rate travel (note that some hotel rates do not drop until mid-October). Rates are often quite low

December through February, especially for U.S. travelers, who have enjoyed a favorable exchange rate in recent years.

If this island's diverse attractions strike you as a lot of ground to cover, you're right. Vancouver Island is approximately the same size as England; would you expect to get acquainted with the entire country in one visit? Suffice it to say, any sojourn here should last at least the weekend, preferably longer, and one trip won't be enough. Those staying in downtown Victoria can leave the car at home, while those exploring more remote areas might bring a vehicle, or rent one upon arrival. If you drive, reserve ferry times in advance (the boats get incredibly busy in the summer months) and come prepared with maps, as roads are not always clearly marked. Package vacations abound; **Clipper Vacations** (206/448-5000 or 800/888-2535; www.clipper vacations.com) offers a romantic Vancouver Island Spa Trail getaway, which includes transportation from Seattle and appointments at one of the island's top spas.

For more information, contact **Tourism Vancouver Island** (250/754-3500; www.islands.bc.ca) or **Tourism Victoria** (250/953-2033 or 800/663-3883; www.tourismvictoria.com). American travelers should keep in mind that the cost ratings in this section are figured in Canadian funds and correspond with the chart at the front of the book. This means, for example, that an establishment ranked as moderately priced ($$$) might have rates that appear expensive until you convert them to U.S. dollars. And, innkeepers are well accustomed to converting funds for travelers from the States.

VICTORIA

ROMANTIC HIGHLIGHTS

There's no way around it: Victoria attracts visitors by the thousands. But even in summer, when the crowds swell beyond romantic tolerance, the charms here are undeniable. The famous Fairmont Empress Hotel, stately Parliament buildings, gorgeous Butchart Gardens, lovely parks and museums, cozy restaurants, and Edwardian-style shops—all nestled on a thriving harbor with the snowcapped Olympic Mountains in the distance—make this little city a romantic haven. Choosing where to stay can be a challenge; hundreds of lodgings in Victoria describe themselves as romantic. (Our advice: If you decide to stay at a place not recommended here, do your research. We have found that second-rate rooms can sometimes lurk even in hotels with the most storied reputations.)

Victoria is a wonderful walking city, and if you stay within a 10-block radius of Government Street, everything you'll want to see and do is easily accessible. Parking is difficult, and really, the only reason to bring a car is to explore the out-of-town parks, gardens, wineries, or rugged coast-line. You can always rent a car when you arrive. **Victoria Harbour Ferries** (250/708-0201; www.harbourferry.com) offers tours of local waterways in adorable 12-passenger ferries. Lovers of the great outdoors can take whale-watching tours with the **Prince of Whales** (812 Wharf St; 250/383-4884 or 888/383-4884; www.princeofwhales.com); chances of orca sightings are best May through September. You can also try an outing with Victoria's **Oak Bay Beach Hotel and Marine Resort** (250/598-4556 or 888/668-7758; www. oakbaybeachhotel.bc.ca). Their Crescent Moon trip includes sunset kaya-king, a tasting of Dungeness crab and wine on a secluded beach, and tele-scope viewing of the glorious night sky. Then there's the timeless appeal of traveling by horse-drawn carriage: catch **Victoria Carriage Tours** (250/383-2207 or 877/663-2207; www.victoriacarriage.com) at the corner of Belleville and Menzies Streets.

While in Victoria, if wooing your beloved is on your agenda, we recom-mend an age-old tactic: chocolate. At **Roger's Chocolates** (913 Government St; 250/384-7021; open every day), the handmade chocolates are made fresh daily according to original recipes dating back to the late 1800s. Beyond edible delights, the shopping in Victoria is divine. Look for English and Irish goods along Government Street, where you will also find the stately **Munro's Books** (1108 Government St; 250/382-2464) and the exotic **Silk Road Aromatherapy & Tea Company & Spa** (1624 Government St; 250/704-2688). Explore the charming shops along Trounce Alley, and then duck into the romantic **Tapa Bar** (620 Trounce Alley; 250/383-0013) for lunch or late-afternoon sangría. **Re-Bar Modern Food** (50 Bastion Square; 250/361-9223), with its wholesome meals and fresh juices, is a local favorite. Another good lunch choice is **Herald Street Caffe** (546 Herald St; 250/381-1441), a short stroll north in Victoria's old town. It's been serving fine, innovative West Coast cuisine for more than 20 years in its stylish, high-ceilinged dining room; the seasonally changing menu relies on locally raised fare (it's good for dinner, too). If it's a relaxed ambience, great pub food, and a tall cold glass of beer you're hankering for, visit **Spinnakers** (308 Catherine St; 250/386-2739), one of Canada's first brew pubs, or the atmospheric water-front **Canoe Brewpub** (450 Swift St; 250/361-1940) near Chinatown.

The lush parks of Victoria make for wonderful romantic strolls. On the southern edge of downtown, the city's beloved **Beacon Hill Park** boasts 184 acres of manicured gardens interspersed with natural forest and meadows. At the rightfully renowned **Butchart Gardens** (800 Benvenuto Ave; 250/652-5256 or 866/652-4422; www.butchartgardens.com), 13 miles (21 km) north, chances are good it'll be a little too crowded to kiss—but these astonishing, elysian, 55-acre gardens will leave you breathless. High-lights include the Rose, Japanese, and Italian gardens, afternoon tea (see Afternoon Tea Kissing), Saturday night fireworks in July and August, and festive Christmas light displays. To discover a lesser known gem, visit **Abkhazi Garden** (10-minute drive or bus ride from downtown; 250/598-8096; www.conservancy.bc.ca/abkhazi; open 1–5pm Wed–Sun and holidays, by appointment Oct–Apr), known as "the garden that love built." **Victorian Garden Tours** (250/380-2797; www.victoriangardentours.com; tours start at $35 per person; reservations required) offers relaxed, small-group guided walks through some of Victoria's most beautiful public and private gardens. All transportation is provided, and a traditional English tea can be arranged. You can also find peace and quiet at **Mount Douglas Park** (5 miles/8 km north of town off Hwy 17; exit to Cordova Bay Rd and follow it south to the park). Far from tourists and the hubbub of the city, this 500-acre rainforest on the ocean's edge is miraculously quiet and serene; take a picnic down the beach trails to the winding shoreline or climb the 700 foot (213-m) summit for a 360-degree view of Victoria, the ocean, and the mountains of Washington State. If a wildly scenic afternoon drive sounds romantic, take the **Malahat** (Trans-Canada Hwy/Hwy 1, from Victoria to Mill Bay), which is one of the prettiest routes on the island. Lush Douglas fir forests hug the narrow-lane highway, which takes you past **Goldstream Provincial Park** (3400 Trans-Canada Hwy/Hwy 1; 250/478-9414; www.goldstreampark.com), where hundreds of bald eagles gather to feed on salmon between mid-December and February. At the summit, northbound pullouts offer breathtaking views over Saanich Inlet and the surrounding undeveloped hills. You can enjoy the view while lunching on the deck of the **Malahat Mountain Inn** (265 Trans-Canada Hwy/Hwy 1; 250/478-1944) or splurge and spend the night at the luxurious **Aerie** resort (see Romantic Lodgings).

The Malahat is also the gateway to Vancouver Island's wine country, centered in the **Cowichan Valley** and on the **Saanich Peninsula**; both regions are less than an hour north of Victoria. A short hop on the **Mill Bay Ferry** (250/386-3431; www.bcferries.com) links the valley and peninsula and creates a romantic circle tour from Victoria. En-route highlights include the **Zanatta Winery** (5039 Marshall Rd, Duncan; 250/748-2338; www.zanatta.ca), with its charming on-site restaurant, Vinoteca on the Vineyard, and **Victoria Estate Winery** (1445 Benvenuto Ave, Brentwood Bay; 250/652-2671; www.victoriaestatewinery.com), where you can dine on the wraparound veranda overlooking the vineyards or have a romantic picnic on the lawn. **Abigail's Hotel** (see Romantic Lodgings) can arrange chauffeured-limousine tours of Saanich Peninsula wineries, or you can stay in the heart of wine country at the **Brentwood Bay Lodge & Spa** (see Romantic Lodgings).

Above all in Victoria, be sure to embrace the charm of a long, leisurely afternoon tea; some assume it's a fussy thing to do, but we see lots of romantic potential in long afternoons of conversation and decadent treats. While afternoon tea at the Fairmont Empress Hotel is the most famous—and it certainly is wonderful—Victoria offers many other delightful opportunities to enjoy tea. Presentations differ widely, as do prices. No other town in

North America offers this delightful ritual with as much style, dedication, and abundance as Victoria, and it's worth taking advantage of while you're here (see Afternoon Tea Kissing).

Access & Information

From Seattle, the **Victoria Clipper** (206/448-5000 in Seattle, 250/382-8100 in Victoria, or 800/888-2535 elsewhere; www.victoriaclipper.com) zips to downtown Victoria via a high-speed, passenger-only catamaran (the journey generally takes between two and three hours). You can also get to the island via **Washington State Ferries** (206/464-6400 in Seattle or 888/808-7977 elsewhere; www.wsdot.wa.gov/ferries/). A two- to three-hour trip runs mid-March to late December, once or twice daily, from Anacortes, Washington—via the scenic San Juan Islands—to Sidney, British Columbia, 17 miles (27 km) north of Victoria by Highway 17. Reserve at least one day prior to departure. At Anacortes, cars should arrive at least one hour early; check-in times at Sidney can be longer, so call ahead for details. **Black Ball Transport** (360/457-4491 in Port Angeles, or 250/386-2202 in Victoria; www. ferrytovictoria.com) operates the MV *Coho* car-and-passenger ferry from Port Angeles on the Olympic Peninsula to downtown Victoria, a 95-minute trip across the Strait of Juan de Fuca. There are two to four sailings daily; reservations are not accepted, so call a day ahead for wait times. **Victoria San Juan Cruises** (360/738-8099 or 800/443-4552; www.whales.com) offers a three-hour, passenger-only cruise—which includes whale watching and a salmon dinner—between Bellingham and Victoria's Inner Harbour. The service runs between mid-May and early October.

BC Ferries (for information: 250/386-3431 or 888/223-3779 in BC; for car reservations: 604/444-2890 or 888/724-5223 in BC; www.bcferries.com) runs car ferries from the British Columbia mainland (Tsawwassen terminal) into Swartz Bay, 20 miles (32 km) north of Victoria. The sailing is approximately an hour and a half. Car reservations cost $15 in addition to the fare each way. On some sailings, staterooms are also available for an extra $25.

The fastest way to travel, of course, is by air, straight to Victoria's Inner Harbour. Kenmore Air (425/486-1257 or 800/543-9595; www.kenmoreair. com) makes regular daily floatplane flights from downtown Seattle. From Sea-Tac International Airport, Horizon Air (800/547-9308; www.horizonair. com) flies into **Victoria International Airport** (1640 Electra Blvd; 250/953-7500), 15 miles (25 km) north of the city. From downtown Vancouver and Vancouver International Airport, Helijet International (800/665-4354; www. helijet.com) can get you to Victoria by helicopter. Harbour Air Seaplanes (604/274-1277 or 800/665-0212; www.harbour-air.com) carries passengers from Vancouver Harbour to Victoria Harbour; from Vancouver International Airport, fly Air Canada (888/247-2262; www.aircanada.ca).

Once you arrive, stop by the centrally located **Tourism Victoria Visitor Info Centre** (812 Wharf St; 250/953-2033; www.tourismvictoria.com) for maps and information. They can also provide details about the lush wine country in the Cowichan Valley, a 45-minute drive from downtown, and on the Saanich Peninsula, 30 minutes north of Victoria. For accommodations reservations, contact **Tourism Victoria** (800/663-3883; www.tourismvictoria.com) or **Hello BC** (888/435-5622; www.hellobc.com). Victoria's bus system, operated by BC Transit (250/382-6161; www.bctransit.com), can take you anywhere in the city; call for information about bus routes. If you are not a resident of Canada, you might qualify for reimbursement of the goods and services tax (GST) charged on some purchases. Most lodgings provide the required forms and information explaining how you can submit your receipts for reimbursement.

Romantic Lodgings

ABBEYMOORE MANOR BED & BREAKFAST INN
◐◐

1470 Rockland Ave, Victoria / 250/370-1470 or 888/801-1811
This stately 1912 mansion is home to one of Victoria's most relaxed and friendly bed-and-breakfasts. A 20-minute stroll from the Inner Harbour in the stately Rockland district, the Abbeymoore has the wide verandas, dark wainscoting, and high ceilings of its era, but the ambience is strictly informal, from the helpful, easy-going hosts to the free snacks, soft drinks, and coffee on tap all day. Three levels of accommodations rise in romance quotient as you climb. Two one-bedroom, ground-level suites have kitchens, jetted tubs, phones, TVs, and private entrances. They're attractive enough, with hardwood floors and modern decor, but lack views and do allow children and pets. Of the two, the Honeymoon Suite, with its bed tucked into a cozy curtained nook, has the most romantic potential. On the first floor, above the main floor public rooms, are five phone- and TV-free, adults-only rooms. Our favorite is the spacious, carpeted Master Bedroom, with its king-size four-poster bed, rose-colored chaise longue and settee, deep bathtub, and access to a broad, upper floor veranda. The veranda is shared with the Iris Room, but a row of planters and plenty of space create privacy. The equally large Rose Room at the back of the house has no view or bathtub (just a shower), but has all the other makings of a couple's getaway, with its antique tiled fireplace, four-poster queen-size bed, hardwood floors, Oriental rug, and big leather sofa. Three smaller rooms charm with such individual touches as claw-foot tubs or sleigh beds. The most private option is the Penthouse Suite, an adults-only hideaway under the eaves with its own entrance and staircase. Occupying the whole top floor, the suite is modern and airy, though not lavish, with a kitchen, skylights, and light wood floors.

The best feature is the bed: tucked under a gable behind French doors, it's set before a little dormer window with views of treetops and glimpses of the ocean. Whichever room you choose, count on luxurious touches, such as 600-thread-count cotton sheets; down comforters; thick, fluffy towels; CD players; and wine glasses. In-room spa services are also available, and the hosts can book just about any tour or activity available in Victoria. Public areas include a wide veranda and a parlor, more cozy than elegant, with a fireplace and a mix of antique and not-quite-antique furniture. A multicourse breakfast featuring daily baked goods and fresh, local seafood is served in the pretty sun-room or, on fine days, on the terrace. There's a big group table, but privacy-minded couples can opt for a table for two. *$$$ MC, V; no checks; www.abbeymoore.com.*

ABIGAIL'S HOTEL
❂❂❂
906 McClure St, Victoria / 250/388-5363 or 800/561-6565
Abigail's is all 1930s Tudor-style gables, gardens, and crystal chandeliers. There are 17 oddly shaped rooms in the original four-story building; the more recently constructed adjacent building contains an additional 6 spacious rooms and, from the exterior, replicates the look and feel of its older neighbor. Down comforters, fresh flowers, and crystal goblets feature in all five room categories; some of the midpriced rooms boast a two-sided wood-burning fire, which lets you enjoy the glow from the bedroom or the tub. In the original building, the top-floor Honeymoon Suites are the grandest. These boast marble bathrooms, vaulted ceilings, wood-burning fireplaces, and Jacuzzi tubs for two. (This European-style inn has no elevator, however, so if climbing up three flights of stairs sounds unromantic, don't book one of these.) Our favorites are the stately, spacious Coach House rooms in the new building, where dark-wood wainscoting beautifully flatters the William Morris–print wallpaper and fabrics; Arts and Crafts stained-glass lamps, a king-size four-poster bed, a writing table, a wet bar, an armoire, and a leather love seat make up the furnishings. Each Coach House room has a wood-burning fireplace and oversize jetted tub; Room C1 has a balcony. Much of the traffic noise from busy Quadra Street is muffled by wooden shutters, tapestry drapes, and good soundproofing, but light sleepers may want to request a room as far from the street as possible. A three-course breakfast is served at a communal table in the small, airy dining room that looks onto the patio garden; guests can have the meal delivered to their rooms for a fee. In the main building, a wood-burning granite fireplace warms the library on the main floor, where drinks and hors d'oeuvres are served each afternoon. Abigail's also offers a wine-tasting getaway package, complete with a chauffeured limousine to transport you through scenic countryside to some of the island's best wineries. *$$$–$$$$ AE, MC, V; no checks; www.abigailshotel.com.*

Afternoon Tea Kissing

Visitors from far and wide come to the **Tea Lobby** at the Fairmont Empress Hotel (721 Government St; 250/389-2727 or 800/441-1414; www.fairmont.com/empress) for its famous afternoon tea, served daily. It's undoubtedly the most formal tea in Victoria, and the setting is posh beyond words. Locals are bemused by the exorbitant prices ($30 to $55 Canadian per person depending on the season), but to visitors, traditional afternoon refreshments at this landmark are a sheer delight. In the main tea room, stately columns, soaring rosy ceilings, marble fireplaces, and portraits of Queen Mary and King George V create a splendid Old World ambience. Nestle into an overstuffed floral chair and savor tea sandwiches of smoked salmon, cucumber, or carrot and ginger, and sip the Empress's own blend of tea while a pianist plays softly in the background.

For a more casual setting, a delicious Scottish tea, and more laughs than you thought were possible during the tea ritual, visit the popular **White Heather Tea Room** (1885 Oak Bay Ave; 250/595-8020). At this unassuming little shop in Oak Bay, the warm, gregarious hostess—Scottish, of course—does much of the baking herself. Our favorite treats include the savory goat cheese bites, rich Scottish shortbread, lemon-curd tarts, and apricot-hazelnut-ginger scones. Among the tempting teas, the tasty Mad Hatter's Blend seems a good fit for the friendly, bustling atmosphere. Best of all, the grand tea for two, called, in proper Scots tradition, the Big Muckle Giant Tea, costs less than tea for one person at the Empress in high season. Fresh flowers adorn the tables, each china cup has a different pattern, and the tea cozies are handmade. Located about 10 minutes by car from the Inner Harbour, it's a favorite with locals. You can also call ahead for a picnic lunch.

Some of the best tea in town can also be found, well, out of town. A 10-minute jaunt on Victoria Harbour Ferries (250/708-0201) transports you from the Inner Harbour back in time, to the peaceful oasis known as the **Point Ellice House** (2616 Pleasant St; 250/380-6506). Afternoon tea is served at this historic Italianate villa on the croquet lawn, where views of the water and gardens inspire a feeling of serenity, and clusters of white wicker chairs are arranged on the lush grass. Tea servers wear the traditional dresses of servants in the late Victorian era, and the surrounding gardens are fragrant with poppies, honeysuckle, jasmine, and lavender.

For the most magnificent views of flowers, visit the Dining Room restaurant at **Butchart Gardens** (800 Benvenuto Ave; 250/652-8222 or 866/652-4422). Although tea is a bit pricey, the views of brilliant flowers from every window make this a delightful place for an afternoon respite.

—KATE CHYNOWETH

THE AERIE
❂❂❂❂
600 Ebedora Ln, Malahat / 250/743-7115 or 800/518-1933

A beautiful half-hour drive from Victoria leads to this grandiose creamy-white Mediterranean-style villa complex (although some guests arrive via helicopter at the landing pad). Views of the distant Olympic Mountains, tree-covered hills, and a peaceful fjord below are utterly spectacular. While the famously opulent interior—full of overstuffed sofas, ornately carved mirrors, and fabric-draped four-poster beds—may overwhelm those with simpler tastes, you can choose among the 35 rooms and suites to find one that fits your style. There are a variety of room styles in three buildings, and most offer tubs for two, private decks with glorious views, and sensuous appointments. Among the most lavish are the multilevel Aerie Suites in the main building. Each boasts a large hydro-massage tub framed by columns in the center of the room, a gas fireplace, a king-size four-poster canopied bed, and an extra-large deck. Unfortunately, some decks offer little privacy, while others have the tennis courts or parking lot in the foreground of their vistas. We prefer the less ornate (but equally expensive) Residence Suites, which share a nearby building with the resort's six-room spa. The decor here is simpler, yet equally luxurious, with grand leather sleigh beds, large soaking tubs, gas fireplaces, and steam showers. The standard rooms, located one floor below the main building's reception area, are not nearly as grand—but are still quite expensive. Some have small balconies with incredible views, although they don't feel very private due to the neighboring balconies all around. Romantics seeking the ultimate in privacy (and scenery) may opt for one of the six suites in the new two-story Villa Cielo, opened in 2004, 300 feet up and away from the main building. Terraced gardens, complete with a reproduction of Michelangelo's *David* at center stage, are the serene foreground to a 200-degree view of Finlayson Arm and the distant mountains of Washington State. The studio, one-, and two-bedroom suites range in size from 800 to 1,400 square feet, and all have French doors leading to private decks or balconies, gas fireplaces, and enormous bathrooms with both tubs and showers for two. The decor varies, but all the suites have a masculine aesthetic, with rich fabrics, dark woods, creamy walls, leather-inlaid furniture, and Asian rugs on glowing cherry-wood floors. Guests here have their own lounge area, but also have access to the resort's facilities, which include two kiss-worthy spots for an evening dip: an outdoor hot tub with a view and a beautiful glass-enclosed pool. A generous full breakfast, included with your stay, is served in the elegant dining room overlooking the inspiring mountain scenery. Dinner at the Aerie Dining Room, which is open to non-guests, is also a four-lip experience, with food that is as spectacular as the view. Food-loving couples may enjoy one of the culinary foraging or cooking seminar packages, or join the chef for his daily menu discussion.

$$$$ *AE, DC, MC, V; no checks; www.aerie.bc.ca.*

ANDERSEN HOUSE BED & BREAKFAST
❤❤❤

301 Kingston St, Victoria / 250/388-4565 or 877/264-9988
While many historic homes are filled with antique furnishings from the eras in which they were built, this 1891 Queen Anne Victorian is decorated with free artistic style. From the moment you enter the bright and open parlor, with its high ceiling, hardwood floor, African masks, and Picasso- and Cubist-influenced artwork, you know that the Andersen House is run by an artist. Each of the four rooms has a distinctive personality and is decorated with a mixture of antiques, hand-knotted Persian tribal rugs, stained-glass windows, and contemporary art; all have private entrances and offer romantic touches such as robes, champagne goblets, and CD players. Our romantic favorite is the sunny Casablanca Room. Here, you can soak in the air-jet tub for two set by the windows, relax on the inviting queen-size bed, open the French doors to your private deck for magnificent views of the Olympics, or descend the curved staircase to the lush garden. Also on the top floor, the spacious Captain's Apartment has a separate sitting room, views of the Parliament Building, and a colorful Art Deco–inspired stained-glass window beside the air-jet tub. The ground-level Garden Studio has a two-person Jacuzzi tub and, just outside, a kiss-worthy, ivy-draped patio with an outdoor fireplace. The dining room's 12-foot ceilings and dramatic chandelier are rendered homey by the breakfast table, where mornings bring a gourmet feast. The backyard is the best place to kiss on the whole property; during the day, dappled sunlight streams through the branches of 100-year-old weeping willow, pear, and apple trees onto a graceful brick patio and garden statues. For an even more secluded experience, ask the proprietors about their other venture, Bay Breeze Manor (contact the same toll-free number as above), a scenic 10-minute drive from downtown. This exquisitely restored 1885 Victorian farmhouse boasts two spacious rooms that provide the utmost in privacy and romance, with wood-burning fireplaces, original art, sea views, and beautiful gardens. The farmhouse also has access to a beach.

$$$–$$$$ *MC, V; no checks; www.andersenhouse.com.*

BEACONSFIELD INN
❤❤❤

998 Humboldt St, Victoria / 250/384-4044 or 888/884-4044
Owners Bob and Dawna Bailey uphold the tradition of Old World elegance that has long been the hallmark of this beautifully restored Edwardian manor, located just a few blocks from the downtown core. As you pass

through a plant-filled sun-room with fountain to the main entrance, with its rich mahogany walls and roaring fireplace, you'll feel immediately at home. A full afternoon tea, with pastries, crumpets, and scones, or evening sherry is served in the impressive library, where walls of bookcases and a fireplace provide a cozy ambience. Fresh flowers from the garden await in each of the nine guest rooms. Choosing from among so many delightful options can be difficult, but rest assured, all the rooms have gorgeous antiques, fine linens, down comforters, and lovely color schemes. On the main floor, the rosy-toned Parlor Room has three walls of original leaded stained-glass windows, making it the brightest of all. Upstairs, the especially handsome Emily Carr Suite offers high ceilings, hardwood floors, navy-blue print wallpaper, a massive polished bedstead, and a two-person Jacuzzi tub with views of the wood-burning fireplace; the bathroom boasts a crystal chandelier and a two-person shower. The Veranda Room next door is considerably smaller and has no fireplace, but you'll hardly notice once you discover the jetted tub for two surrounded on two sides by picture windows. The friendly hosts and staff are professional, unobtrusive, and readily available, and a complimentary full breakfast is served at intimate dining room tables or by the fountain in the adjacent conservatory.
$$$–$$$$ *AE, MC, V; no checks; www.beaconsfieldinn.com.*

BRASS BELL FLOATING BED AND BREAKFAST
◑◑◖

475 Head St, Hidden Harbour Marina, Victoria / 250/748-1033
Docked at a quiet, private marina on Victoria's beautiful outer harbor, the *Thalia Bee*, a vintage 1931 wooden motor yacht, and the *Dreamboat*, a 42-foot 1947 cruiser, each offers a unique floating romantic retreat. It's about a 10-minute drive to downtown Victoria from this secluded marina, but guests can leave the car parked and sail to the dock on the Harbour Ferries, a fleet of 13 adorable boats that provide pedestrian transport around Victoria Harbour. Whichever boat you choose is yours alone, and ranks among the most charming on-board accommodations we've seen. Lovingly restored, the interior of the *Thalia Bee* features glowing woodwork, polished brass, fringed lampshades, floral upholstery, and a cozy ambience. Step into the Wheelhouse and note the uninterrupted views of the harbor; down two steps is the cozy aft cabin, appointed with brass lamps with floral shades, comfortable carpets, a cozy rose-patterned double settee, framed needlepoint work, and lace curtains. The cozy stateroom has a double berth and is best suited to couples who are willing to share a very small space. Glossy white paint and yellow linens deliver some charm, and opening the forward hatch allows a sea breeze on warm summer evenings. The head/bathroom has an electric toilet and a handheld shower; while this doesn't offer much luxury, showering at the Brass Bell is guaranteed to be memorable (and you'll probably laugh about it together later). Across the dock

is the *Dreamboat*. Newly renovated with custom-built settees and teak and holly flooring, it's roomier, if less cozily romantic, than the *Thalia Bee*. The *Dreamboat's* covered cockpit offers fabulous views out to the harbor; you might even catch sight of the family of otters that live nearby. Both vessels have down duvets, CD players and stereos, tiny TV/VCRs, and galleys with fridges, microwaves, coffee makers, and kettles. Included in your stay is breakfast at the Dockside Café, a three-minute walk away (you'll receive vouchers). Since breakfast is at your leisure, make your coffee on board and enjoy the morning on the boat while soaking up one of the most unusual waterfront views in Victoria.

$$$ *AE, MC, V; no checks; Dreamboat closed Oct–May; www.brassbell.net.*

BRENTWOOD BAY LODGE & SPA
◔◔◔◔

849 Verdier Ave, Brentwood Bay / 250/544-2079 or 888/544-2079
This modern cedar-sided resort opened in 2004 on the Saanich Peninsula, a quiet area of wineries, organic farms, and sheltered coves 20 minutes north of downtown Victoria. Private decks or balconies in each of the 33 rooms overlook the sails of Maple Bay Marina and the untouched forested hills beyond. The decor is hip, up-market West Coast, from the serene sage-green walls and carpets to the big gas fireplaces (standard in every room), and the hand-crafted king-size beds with leather inset headboards and chic black bedspreads. The bathrooms are impressive: shutters above the tub open so you can take in sunset views while you soak, and the river rock–based shower has both head and body jets. And, each room offers free long-distance calls to anywhere in North America. The resort's spa scores top romance points with its couple's room, where, in side-by-side treatment beds, you can hold hands during your mud wrap, followed by a private rainforest shower for two. Just past the spa's lounge, an outdoor pool, hot tub, and plenty of tempting loungers overlook the bay. The serene vibe here belies the sheer volume of things to do. From the lodge you can take a sunset cruise aboard a glass-domed eco-cruiser or board a water taxi for a five-minute jaunt to the famous Butchart Gardens (you can even paddle to the gardens in a kayak). Cycle the country roads, tour a winery or two, learn how to make an underwater movie at the on-site PADI (Professional Association of Diving Instructors) dive center, or catch an art opening—the whole resort is a gallery displaying the works of top British Columbian artists. Upon arrival you are greeted with sparkling wine from a local vineyard and therein, it just gets better. Keep things cozy in the morning by opting for breakfast in bed, delivered in a big wicker basket that includes freshly baked pastries warm from the oven. The Arbutus Grille and Wine Bar (see Romantic Restaurants) also beckons couples with its stellar views and stand-out food.

$$$$ *AE, MC, V; no checks; www.brentwoodbaylodge.com.* ♿

FAIRHOLME MANOR
◆◆◆◆
638 Rockland Pl, Victoria / 250/598-3240 or 877/511-3322
Few accommodations are as grandly romantic as those at Fairholme Manor, an exquisitely restored 1885 Italianate mansion set alone on an acre of parklike lawn in historic Rockland, just a 15-minute walk from the ocean or downtown. Thanks to excellent planning by proprietors Sylvia and Ross Main, every tasteful, spacious room in this adults-only inn has its own appeal, although we have our kiss-worthy favorites. One of these is the Olympic Grand Suite, which features Viennese antiques, lovely original artwork, a luxurious king-size sleigh bed, a sparkling chandelier and robin's egg–blue ceilings, and an immaculate white sofa in front of a wood-burning fireplace; the full bath boasts a double soaking tub. Step out to your deck for sweeping views of snowcapped peaks, the dazzling water, and the lush gardens of the adjacent lieutenant-governor's house. Another sublimely romantic spot is the Fairholme Grand Suite on the main level, which tastefully combines an indulgent, Las Vegas–style glamour with European elegance. Here, you'll find a spa room with 14-foot-high ceilings and a large double air-jet Jacuzzi surrounded by potted palms. After your leisurely soak, wake up under the double-headed shower for two. There's a king-size bed and a fireplace; bay windows look out upon the gardens. Other romantic options include the lovely Rose Room, an upstairs apartment-style unit with a kitchen, two bedrooms, and a wonderfully private deck. A separate wing offers slightly smaller rooms that are nonetheless highly romantic; we particularly like the Penthouse, with its picture windows, full kitchen, king-size bed, and double air-jet tub. The Tuscan is a cozy room with a country-cottage feel and a garden view. All rooms offer Internet connections, views, telephones, TV/VCRs, CD players, fireplaces, mini-fridges, coffee makers, robes, fresh flowers, imported chocolates, and floating candles. For an additional charge, breakfast can be served in your room, although the charming dining room, with vast windows, soaring ceilings, dramatic artwork, and pretty tiled fireplace, may lure you down in the morning; several delicious courses, featuring free-range eggs and produce from the inn's own garden, are served on china atop tables set with linen and silver. For the ultimate indulgence, you can book in-room spa services, including a massage for two.
$$$–$$$$ *AE, MC, V; no checks; www.fairholmemanor.com.*

FAIRMONT EMPRESS HOTEL
◆◆◆◆
721 Government St, Victoria / 250/384-8111 or 800/441-1414
Palatial and utterly elegant, the Empress Hotel is to Victoria what Big Ben is to London, the Eiffel Tower is to Paris, and so forth. The $45 million renovation of the 1908 building is old news, but the results still look new—and unequivocally spectacular. Among the Empress' dominions are the opulent

Palm Court, with its magnificent stained-glass ceiling; the grandly formal Empress Dining Room; and the unique Bengal Lounge, a British Colonial–inspired room that's perhaps the best place in Victoria to sip a martini. Alas, in high season, these public areas can feel like a museum, crowded with tourists. Still, you would be remiss if you didn't visit the handsome, eminently comfortable Tea Lobby (see Afternoon Tea Kissing). Outside, in the perfectly tended rose garden, potential kissing spots await discovery among the magnolia trees and flower-covered trellises. An overnight stay here is definitely worthwhile, although rates can be steep (the off-season is much more reasonable). There are more than 90 room configurations, but all 477 rooms have private baths, polished furniture, ceiling fans, and down comforters. If you can afford to splurge, request one of the 40 Fairmont Gold rooms or suites: "first-class" doesn't begin to describe the experience. Guests and nonguests are welcome to visit the hotel's Willow Stream Spa, which offers a range of conventional and alternative treatments. With this much romance under one roof, it's hardly surprising that the Empress is a favorite spot for elopements, anniversary celebrations, and second honeymoons.
$$$–$$$$ *AE, DC, DIS, MC, V; no checks; www.fairmont.com/empress.* &

HUMBOLDT HOUSE
❀❀❀
867 Humboldt St, Victoria / 250/383-0152 or 888/383-0327
This tall and skinny "shotgun"-style Victorian home, located next to the well-groomed grounds of St. Ann's Academy, specializes in romance—from champagne with the in-room breakfasts to jetted tubs in every room. For the most privacy, we recommend rooms on the top floor so you won't hear your neighbors walking above you. Those who enjoy dramatic color schemes of red and black might like the Mikado and Oriental Rooms, both of which are spacious. We like Edward's Room, with its British Colonial theme and carved elephants guarding the fireplace, but the street-side location makes it susceptible to noise. Our favorite is the bright Gazebo Room, with its pretty lawn and orchard views, Italian-tiled Jacuzzi area, and hand-painted vines on the vaulted ceiling. The Celebration Room is extremely frilly, with an immaculate white queen-size bed crowned by a lace canopy and lighted archway, sculptures of angels, and a glittering chandelier hanging overhead. All the rooms have wood-burning fireplaces, CD players, and Jacuzzi tubs tucked into elevated corners. When you arrive, pop open the waiting split of champagne or nibble on the homemade chocolate truffles. Champagne reappears at breakfast, when your morning meal is delivered through the two-way butler's pantry in each room. There's no contact with the outside world, so the two of you can enjoy your morning in your own romantic universe. One caveat: those who like to maintain some mystique may find the washing arrangements tricky. Instead of a traditional

bathroom, each room has a hand-held shower in the in-room Jacuzzi and a pedestal sink, also in the bedroom; only the toilet is behind closed doors. The same owners also operate the more traditional White Heather Cottage, a 1925 English country–style cottage near Beacon Hill Park. Each of the two rooms has pretty country floral decor and a private bathroom; they share a living room, dining room, sun deck, and kitchen. There is no staff on site, and breakfast is delivered to your door.
$$$$ *AE, MC, V; no checks; www.humboldthouse.com.*

VILLA MARCO POLO INN
✿✿✿

1524 Shasta Pl, Victoria / 250/370-1524 or 877/601-1524
Villa Marco Polo is a feast for the senses, from its magnificent rooms and stunning villa-style grounds to romantic boons like fine linens, fresh flowers, hardwood floors, lovely antiques, and fireplaces in every room. Originally built in 1923 as a wedding gift for the daughter of an influential family, the Italian Renaissance–style mansion has been lovingly restored with superb taste and attention to detail. Secluded on a quiet street in Rockland, an exquisite old neighborhood about five minutes by car from the Inner Harbour, this adults-only retreat offers both formal beauty and a relaxed atmosphere. All five rooms here offer sublime ambience, but we have three romantic favorites. On the second floor, the luxurious and completely soundproofed Zanzibar Suite has a lovely fireplace and a king-size bed. French doors and a balcony take in views of the mountains and water. The bathroom, beautifully done in gold and white, has a double soaking pedestal tub, glassed-in shower for two, and romantic lighting. Equally grand is the Persia Suite, at the opposite end of the house; it offers an additional bonus for lovers: a jetted tub for two set next to the windows in the magnificent bathroom. It also boasts garden, ocean, and mountain views; a Persian rug and tapestries; and a king-size canopy bed. The Silk Road Room on the main floor is smaller, but highly original, with an arched barrel vault ceiling and a hand-painted mural of flying angels. For additional romance, ask about specials with roses and champagne, or spa services. Mornings bring four-course gourmet breakfasts in the elegant dining room, which is graced with an Italian crystal chandelier; steps lead to a lower garden room with two tables for two. Privacy-craving couples can request to be seated here or at a table on the terrace.
$$$–$$$$ *MC, V; no checks; www.villamarcopolo.com.*

Romantic Restaurants

THE ARBUTUS GRILLE AND WINE BAR
◐◐◐◐

849 Verdier Ave (Brentwood Bay Lodge & Spa), Brentwood Bay / 250/544-2079 or 888/544-2079
The Arbutus Grille and Wine Bar—the Brentwood Bay (see Romantic Lodgings) resort's showcase restaurant—has a cool, almost urban, edge with two-story-high sea-view windows, art-covered walls, and an open kitchen with a wood-fired grill. The locally sourced menu showcases the best of Vancouver Island's bounty, such as Salt Spring Island goat cheese tart with Venturi-Schulze balsamic vinegar, and aromatic Cowichan Bay roasted duck breast with smoked pork-hock cassoulet and port-duck essence. And the seared local sablefish with smoked black cod brandade, celery, and chervil jus is outstanding. Pastry chef Bruno Feldeisen (with a chocolatier background that includes two Michelin three-star hotels) creates his signature banana cream pie, chocolate ice cream, banana wafer, and mango-caramel sauce that is so addicting you may need an order to go. For casual meals, try the resort's marine pub (where you can order high-end pizzas with the skinniest crusts, sandwiches, and hearty chowders) or the bakery/deli/coffee bar, where you can fill your picnic basket with wood oven–baked bread, locally made cheeses, and decadent pastries. An on-site wine shop, carrying hard-to-find local vintages, reminds us that, yes, these folks have thought of everything.
$$$$ AE, MC, V; checks OK; breakfast, lunch every day, dinner Wed–Sun; full bar; reservations recommended; www.brentwoodbaylodge.com. &

BRASSERIE L'ECOLE
◐◐◐

1715 Government St, Victoria / 250/475-6260
Those of the bread, wine, and thou school of romance will delight in this cozy French restaurant tucked between two Chinatown grocery stores. Chef-owner Sean Brennan, together with sommelier-owner Marc Morrison, have taken this heritage building—once a schoolhouse for Victoria's Chinese community—and turned it into a classic, nostalgic brasserie, complete with sensuous pomegranate walls, 100-year-old fir floors, lofty ceilings, and candlelight. Thirteen white linen–draped tables line the narrow room; a slate-topped bar, with room to dine, runs parallel. In summer, two tables in a tiny greenery-filled courtyard make a romantic alfresco dining spot. Brennan, one of Victoria's better-known chefs, uses meat and produce from local organic farms in his hearty and unpretentious French-country cooking. The menu changes daily but always includes the classics: oysters on the half shell, duck confit, onion soup, and steak *frites* along with such fresh-from-the-market specials as wild Sooke trout with lentils, squash,

and brown butter. Blackboards list the day's specials, desserts, oysters, and impressive selection of European cheeses. The wine list is extensive, predominately French, and user friendly—everything on it is available by the glass. Beer drinkers are spoiled for choice, too, with more than 50 mostly European varieties to choose from.

$$$ *MC, V; no checks; dinner Tues–Sat; full bar; reservations recommended; www.lecole.ca.* &

CAFE BRIO
❂❂❂

944 Fort St, Victoria / 250/383-0009 or 866/270-5461

Looking as if it belongs somewhere in Tuscany rather than on Victoria's Antique Row, this restaurant offers a dining opportunity with distinctly Italian charm. The patio, edged by ornate wrought-iron gates, frames the sun-kissed yellow entrance. The interior is warmly welcoming, with earthy colors as the backdrop for a neo-Renaissance decor that includes Italian wall statues, gilt-framed mirrors, lighting fixtures salvaged from an old mansion, and modern artwork. Unfortunately, the narrow dining room can have a decidedly unromantic decibel level. The noise can't be helped, but you can find some measure of seclusion in one of the pine booths, just right for two. The lighting is so romantically subdued that some diners have trouble reading the menu. Fortunately, you can't go wrong here: the food, though pricey, is consistently, blissfully delicious. The menu changes daily based, in part, on what's in season at local organic farms. Appetizers might include braised sablefish or handmade ricotta gnocchi with wild forest mushrooms and creamed sweet corn. Entrées range from red wine–braised beef short ribs to olive oil–poached albacore tuna or a delightful linguine with chanterelles, pancetta, cream, and fresh herbs. The wine list is well chosen, with a good selection of West Coast wines and minimal markups. Desserts are decadent and everything, including the ice cream, is made in house: try the pear tarte Tatin, or the rich dark chocolate timbale.

$$$$ *AE, MC, V; no checks; dinner every day; full bar; reservations recommended; www.cafe-brio.com.* &

CAMILLE'S
❂❂❂❂

45 Bastion Square, Victoria / 250/381-3433

Camille's is Victoria's most seductive restaurant, and from the moment you enter this irresistible lower-level restaurant, you'll see why. The bustle of downtown immediately fades to a memory as you settle in for quiet conversation and hand-holding over your table. Two dining rooms are tucked in here, but for romantic purposes you should request a seat in the second one, hidden away in the back. Hundred-year-old brick walls adorned with contemporary art mix well with linen tablecloths, stained-glass lamps, and a charming assortment of decorative books and wine bottles. A few individual tables are separated from the rest of the room by wooden partitions that create extremely private booths. The affable staff works to make your experience as warm and wonderful as you can imagine. Be sure to read the wine list, which is not only witty and entertaining, but also offers suggestions for special-occasion wines. The internationally inspired, seasonally changing menu emphasizes fresh fish, local meat, and seasonal produce; locally raised game is a specialty. Start with appetizers such as phyllo triangles stuffed with goat cheese and caramelized shallots, or a five-peppercorn-crusted ahi tuna carpaccio. Good entrée choices include a pan-seared duck breast with fig, orange, and sherry compote; the rack of lamb; or, in season, the divine baked halibut. For dessert, indulge in the tiramisù spiced with a citrus liqueur, or share the maple-orange crème caramel. It's almost as sweet as a kiss.

$$$ *MC, V; no checks; dinner Tues–Sun; call for seasonal closures; full bar; reservations recommended; www.camillesrestaurant.com.*

IL TERRAZZO RISTORANTE
❍❍❍
555 Johnson St, Victoria / 250/361-0028

You'll find a true taste of Italy in this beautiful restaurant tucked away on Waddington Alley. Inside, the tables are a bit too close together and the room is always bustling, but the romantic charm of the restaurant makes up for these slight drawbacks. Exposed-brick walls and archways are adorned with colorful artwork, while wrought-iron candelabras hang overhead. Hardwood floors and candles create an intimate yet casual ambience. Six outdoor fireplaces and heaters mean alfresco dining on the covered terrace is possible nearly year-round, and it's a charming spot embellished with flower baskets, multi-colored tiled tables, candles, and wrought-iron chairs. Of the excellent Northern Italian cuisine served by the knowledgeable wait staff, we recommend the *funghi arrosto* (a portobello mushroom baked in a focaccia-crumb and herb crust, sliced and tossed with baby spinach), risotto with clams and Italian sausage, and veal tenderloin medallions with Cambozola cheese, grapes, and herbs. Classics, like osso buco and scaloppini, frequently appear on the specials list and are always a good bet, as are the salmon and halibut, as only fresh, local fish is served here. For more casual evenings, try the wood-oven pizzas. An extensive wine list showcases a range of fine Italian and New World wines.

$$$ *AE, DC, MC, V; no checks; lunch Mon–Sat (Mon–Fri in winter), dinner every day; full bar; reservations recommended; www.ilterrazzo.com.*

PAPRIKA BISTRO
◐◐◖

2524 Estevan Ave, Victoria / 250/592-7424
The sophisticated decor and clean, modern aesthetic of this excellent little restaurant offers a change of pace from the more ornate and formal downtown scene. The restaurant draws a fun-loving crowd of well-heeled locals, and on busy weekend nights, it can get noisy. However, the delicious food makes it well worth living with the less-than-ideal acoustics. In the four tiny dining rooms, including an intimate six-seat wine room, walls of butter yellow and pepper red feature lovely artwork, and every polished wooden table is adorned with candles. Among the appetizers, the goat cheese and spinach salad with caramelized shallots is a standout. Main courses tempt with an array of seafood and meat; the chef is Hungarian, and one or two of the dishes betray his heritage. The main theme, however, is classic French cooking using such fresh local products as venison, rabbit, and duck. And do pay attention to the specials. On our visit, they included a juicy rib-eye steak with caramelized onion mashed potatoes and halibut in a coconut-lemongrass broth with delicious local mussels. A charcuterie menu features each day's house-made galantines, terrines, sausages, and pâtés. Desserts, including creamy crème brûlée and the refreshing sorbet, are also made in house. The worldly wine list offers plenty of choices by the glass and half bottle, and every vintage has been tasted by the owners. As if this spot needed more to recommend it, we'll add that the martinis are excellent.
$$$ *AE, MC, V; no checks; dinner Mon–Sat; full bar; reservations recommended; www.paprika-bistro.com.*

SOOKE

ROMANTIC HIGHLIGHTS

Located a half-hour west of bustling Victoria, Sooke is a friendly, if unremarkable, little town, but the surrounding area is renowned for its natural splendor. Along with pristine coastline and serene views, it offers romantic solitude and some sublime accommodations for couples. The entire coast between Sooke and Port Renfrew, farther west, is filled with excellent parks with trails leading down to ocean beaches. Quiet time together and outdoor exploration will be highlights of any stay in this region. If you drive here from Victoria, stop to see the magnificent former **Dunsmuir family castle**, done in the medieval style, at Royal Roads University (2005 Sooke Rd, Victoria; 250/391-2511 or 250/391-2600, ext. 4456; www.hatley castle.com). The exquisite grounds are open daily, dawn to dusk.

Sooke takes its name from the T'Sou-ke people, the first inhabitants of the area. Once identified with its logging and fishing industries, Sooke's economy now relies far more on tourism, with visitors from all over the world exploring the area's kiss-worthy beaches and incredible hiking trails. Summer is a popular time to visit, but the shoulder seasons are ideal for enjoying the slow, small-town pace and moderate climate without the crowds. There are few restaurants, but romantic lodgings abound. Sooke is also home to a thriving art community and one of the largest juried fine-arts shows in British Columbia, which draws approximately 10,000 people each year in August. You can look at art year-round at the **Blue Raven Gallery** (1971 Kaltasin Rd; 250/881-0528; www.blueravengallery.com) or the **Sooke Fine Art Gallery** (6703A W Coast Rd; 250/642-6411; www.sketching.com). For local crafts and organic vegetables, on Saturdays stop by the **Sooke Country Market** (at Otter Point Rd and Sooke Rd; 250/642-7528; May–Sept). It might not be highly romantic, but hearty diner fare and an authentic local experience can be found in the booths of the '50s-era **Mom's Cafe** (2036 Shields Rd; 250/642-3314). Or try the traditional pub fare at the historic **17 Mile House** (5126 Sooke Rd; 250/642-5942).

Enjoy a walk made for nature lovers, bird lovers, and lovers in general along **Whiffen Spit**, a narrow point that stretches far out into the water. From here, the sublime dining room at **Sooke Harbour House** (see Romantic Restaurants) is only moments away. For a longer hike, an ideal destination is the 3,512 acres of wilderness in **East Sooke Regional Park** (from Sooke, follow Hwy 14 toward Victoria, go right on Gillespie Rd, then right on E Sooke Rd to reach the park entrances at Anderson Cove Rd and Pike Rd; go left to reach the Aylard Farm entrance; www.sookeoutdoors.com/eastsookepark).Here, trails winding through pristine forest and beautiful beaches offer phenomenal views. Aylard Farm is an easy excursion and an excellent place to have a romantic picnic. At Anderson Cove, on the Sooke Basin, embark on a vigorous hike for sweeping views of the Olympic Peninsula. At Pike Road, you'll find an old logging road that winds through forest and meadow to the beach, where purple sea stars can be spotted in the tide pools. For a cool dip on a hot day, check out the natural swimming holes at **Sooke Potholes Provincial Park** (3 miles/5 km north of Sooke at the end of Sooke River Rd).

For an afternoon excursion, visit the beautiful shoreline stretches known as **French Beach** (13 miles/21 km west of Sooke on Hwy 14) and **China Beach** (23 miles/37 km west of Sooke on Hwy 14, past the small town of Jordan River). Both are rugged, romantic spots where you can ramble through secluded groves of trees and explore spacious beaches dotted with tide pools. French Beach is easily accessible, and the area offers beautiful trails through second-growth forest, as well as a nicely maintained 69-unit campground that is one of the most picturesque sites on the entire island to set up a tent for two (800/689-9025; www.discovercamping.ca for reservations). Whales migrating north to feeding grounds in spring and returning south in the fall often delight visitors by stopping to feed in this area. Getting to China Beach, via a 15-minute walk through a mature **West Coast rain forest**, does require some surefootedness, but your reward is a truly magnificent sandy beach. At either location, you can bask on the shore in solitary glory—and yes, these are both wonderful places to kiss. If you are in the mood for more vigorous exploration, a 45-minute forested hike leads from the China Beach parking lot to **Mystic Beach**, where shallow caves, a waterfall, and dramatic sandstone cliffs await. If it's too wet to picnic, you can cozy up over burgers and cheesecake at the homey **Country Cupboard Café** (402 Sheringham Point Rd; 250/646-2323) near French Beach.

Sooke is famous for whale watching, and orcas are visible in local waters between May and October. The grace and agility of these giant mammals is amazing. Boat excursions are highly recommended; **Sooke Coastal Explorations** (6971 W Coast Rd/Hwy 14; 250/642-2343; www.sookewhalewatching. com; closed Nov–Apr) has an impressive 95-percent sighting record. No matter how many times you encounter these creatures, a sighting makes for a singularly romantic experience.

Access & Information

Sooke is located approximately 30 to 40 minutes by car (depending on traffic) west of Victoria on Highway 14. If you are coming from the Swartz Bay Ferry Terminal, follow the Patricia Bay Highway toward Victoria and turn at the McKenzie exit. This will take you to Highway 1. Proceed on Highway 1 to the Sooke-Colwood exit, take the exit, and follow Highway 14. For more information, check out the Sooke community Web site (www. sookenet.com) or contact the **Sooke Visitor Info Centre** (2070 Phillips Rd; 250/642-6351 or 866/888-4748; www.sooke.museum.bc.ca), located in the same building as the Sooke Region Museum.

Romantic Lodgings

COOPER'S COVE GUESTHOUSE
♥♥♥

5301 Sooke Rd, Sooke / 250/642-5727 or 877/642-5727
For couples with a passion for fine food, finding an accommodation with a gourmet cooking school attached might be the answer to a fond dream. This adults-only, waterfront bed-and-breakfast, nestled along the coastline in Sooke, is home to the cooking school of chef Angelo Prosperi-Porta and makes for a culinary retreat extraordinaire. On offer are unique packages such as The Chef's Table, where a lively, interactive dinner allows you to

learn some of the tricks of the trade (and enjoy absolutely delicious Italian-influenced cuisine). The romance here extends well beyond the kitchen to the comfortable, sunny rooms with waterfront views. All four secluded, soundproofed rooms are delightful, with private decks or balconies, fireplaces, fridges, water views, luxurious down comforters, plush robes, and slippers. Fresh flowers, chocolate truffles, and decanters of sherry greet you upon arrival. Our romantic favorite is the Blue Heron Room, complete with a private entrance, hardwood floors, a king-size sleigh bed, and a private hot tub on a secluded ocean-view deck. Below the house, a hot tub perches on a lovely glass-screened deck adorned with potted palms. Colorful flower, herb, and vegetable beds spill over the terraced gardens to the harbor below. In the morning, delicious breakfast feasts are prepared by Angelo himself. Enjoy smoked salmon and Swiss chard omelets, strawberry crepes touched with peach liqueur, or waffles topped with an orange-walnut sauce at a window-side table for two. Certainly, with all these good ingredients, you can whip up your own recipe for romance.
$$$ MC, V; no checks; closed Jan; www.cooperscove.com.

HARTMANN HOUSE
✿✿✿✿

5262 Sooke Rd, Sooke / 250/642-3761
From the glorious, flower-filled gardens to the bay-windowed exterior draped with pink flowers in season, this handcrafted, cedar-sided bed-and-breakfast sets the stage for romance. Inside are two large, self-contained suites, each with a whirlpool tub for two, a handcrafted wooden shower stall, a two-sided fireplace, a kitchenette, a TV and stereo, wide-plank fir floors, and fluffy robes. Each has a private entrance from the garden, and, because they are set on opposite sides of the house with no adjoining walls, quiet and seclusion are assured. The Honeymoon Suite, the slightly larger of the two, was built around a four-poster "barley twist" king-size canopied bed, hand-carved from western red cedar. It's one of the most romantic beds we've ever seen, and from here you can look through the two-way fireplace to an oversize whirlpool tub encircled by emerald-green tile. Chinese wool carpet, black-and-white photographs, chintz fabric, and gorgeous woodwork lend elegance to this open, light-filled room. The Hydrangea Suite is similarly luxurious, with a handcrafted sleigh bed and French doors leading to a secluded garden-side patio. In the morning, breakfast is delivered to your room; in nice weather, adjourn with your goodies to the garden, just outside. Expect such decadent fare as spiced rhubarb parfait, fluffy omelets, and heart-shaped blueberry bran muffins.
$$$ MC, V; no checks; www.hartmannhouse.bc.ca.

MARKHAM HOUSE
✿✿✿

1853 Connie Rd, Sooke / 250/642-7542 or 888/256-6888
This pale-yellow Tudor home, tucked away on a gorgeous 10-acre estate, offers an intimate getaway on the outskirts of Sooke. The immaculately groomed grounds include a hot tub in a gazebo, a small river, a trout pond, a putting green, and iris gardens with more than 100 species of this regal flower. Relax by the parlor fireplace amid the innkeepers' eclectic combination of Scottish and Asian antiques, or open the French doors and lounge on the patio overlooking the pond. The full breakfast is served either here or in the nearby breakfast room. Three guest rooms occupy the second floor of the main house. The Garden Suite feels like a spacious apartment, with blossoming cherry trees outside the windows, an inviting double Jacuzzi tub, a fireplace with sitting area, and a king-size bed. The elegant design scheme includes matching chandelier and wall sconces and antiques ranging from an 18th-century Chinese chest to a mirrored Scottish armoire. The two smaller rooms feature feather beds, views of the gardens, electric fires, and private baths (one is detached); chocolates and turndown service in all the rooms, and tea and pastries in the parlor each afternoon are much-appreciated touches. A trail from the house leads to the honeymoon favorite, Honeysuckle Cottage. Here, comforts include Oriental throw rugs on the hardwood floors, a queen-size feather bed, a kitchenette neatly stowed in a pine armoire, and a cozy living room with old-fashioned woodstove, CD player, and TV/VCR (though just for videos). The decor is rather mismatched, but the glorious privacy more than makes up for it. Revel in your own private hot tub on the wooden deck. In the morning, Honeysuckle Cottage guests can join the others for breakfast in the main house or opt to have a basket of goodies delivered to their door.
$$–$$$ *AE, DC, DIS, E, JCB, MC, V; checks OK; www.markhamhouse.com.*

POINT NO POINT RESORT
✿✿✿

1505 W Coast Rd, Sooke / 250/646-2020
The pure, rugged beauty of Point No Point offers a sublime retreat from civilization. Set on a mile of waterfront and 40 acres of untamed wilderness, this resort has been welcoming travelers since the early 1950s (the original cabins are still standing). Today, there are 25 units available, and while some cabins have slightly outdated furnishings, all include such romantic essentials as full kitchens, private bathrooms, wood-burning fireplaces, and water views, and cater to those who eschew TV and phones in favor of remote beauty. The most recently built cabins (which earned our high lip rating) include the Blue Jay and Otter, two sides of a luxury duplex with 18-foot-high windows and spacious living rooms. In each bathroom you'll find a marble soaking tub and two-person shower. Yet another bonus is the

private hot tub on the deck—a truly memorable place to kiss. Other romantic choices are the Eagle and Orca, two relatively new stand-alone log cabins with private outdoor hot tubs. (Several of the older private cabins have hot tubs, as well.) Trails with tunnels of foliage lead down to a nearby inlet and three gorgeous sandy beaches—yet more fantastic kissing spots. Meals are not included in your stay, so bring your own breakfast provisions. The dining room serves a highly rated lunch, afternoon tea, and dinner (dinner Wed–Sun only). The water and mountain views from the sunny dining room are simply breathtaking. Binoculars are placed at every table in case an eagle soars overhead or a whale happens to swim by in the distant surf. **$$$** *MC, V; checks OK; www.pointnopointresort.com.*

RICHVIEW HOUSE
◔◔◔◔

7031 Richview Dr, Sooke / 250/642-5520 or 866/276-2480
Hand-woven wall hangings and earthy kilim-style carpets on the hardwood floors reflect the low-tech, naturalist simplicity of this waterfront getaway. Located at the end of a quiet dead-end road just steps from Sooke Harbour House and Whiffen Spit, the home overlooks a broad lawn and offers unobstructed views of the Olympics and the water. (The grounds lack secluded nooks, so come prepared to kiss out in the open.) All three rooms have private entrances, deep soaking tubs on secluded decks, and panoramic views of the Strait of Juan de Fuca. Each room also has a fireplace or woodstove, a queen-size futon-style bed, and simple wooden furniture. In the downstairs Garden Spa Room's bathroom, a green-marbled, double-headed shower doubles as a steam bath. Place a drop of lemongrass essential oil in the steam spout, sit on the wooden stools, and inhale. It's downright therapeutic. This room, located just off the living room, is protected from some noise by double doors (but, unfortunately, not from noise coming from above). The two upper-floor guest rooms feature skylights, radiant-heat floors, and wood-burning fireplaces made of beach stone and slate. A small TV/VCR is available on request, but there are no phones; we highly recommend that you arrive here ready to leave the world behind. Coffee or tea is delivered to your room before breakfast; couples desirous of privacy can have breakfast in their room as well, although the bright dining area is an excellent setting. As the morning fog subsides to make way for the sun, enjoy such treats as cantaloupe in a ginger-honey sauce, rhubarb-pecan muffins with peach-mango jam, caramelized sweet rolls, and a breakfast soufflé with sautéed pears.
$$$ *MC, V; checks OK; www.bnbsooke.com.*

THE SNUGGERY BY THE SEA B&B
🌢🌢🌢

5921 Sooke Rd, Sooke / 250/642-6423 or 877/642-6464

The star attraction at this bed-and-breakfast, and the reason for the high lip rating, is the lovely Sisiulth Cottage, a luxury cabin nestled above the serene waters of Sooke Harbour and surrounded by towering firs. Designed by a local architect and completed in 1999, the structure imitates a West Coast First Nations plank house, from the authentic cedar planking to the exterior carved with the two-headed spirit (called a Sisiulth) that protects entrances to First Nations peoples' homes. A wall of windows and an outside deck showcase the view. The open floor plan is split into two areas by a grand double-sided gas fireplace set in copper and designed to evoke a First Nations fire pit; overhead skylights call to mind the traditional smoke hole. Add to this romantic interior an air-jet thermal massage tub set in a glass-enclosed nook overlooking the water, and you have a unique retreat. On the bedroom side of the fireplace, the queen-size bed's carved red-cedar headboard depicts two ravens reaching to the moon; on the opposite side, the comfortable sofa and sitting area share space with a well-equipped small kitchen. The separate bathroom has a pedestal sink and glassed-in shower. The cliff-top cottage was built as close to the water as the bylaws allow; the main house is closer to the road, and this is where breakfast is served. Upstairs in the house are two additional rooms, but these are not highly recommended; the decor lacks warmth and style, although polished wood floors and private baths do offer some comforts. Morning fare of Belgian waffles, eggs Benedict, or seafood omelets is served in the dining room of the main home. Cottage guests can either come here to enjoy the full breakfast or have simpler continental goodies such as fresh fruit and muffins delivered to their front door.

$$–$$$ MC, V; no checks; www.snuggerybnb.com.

SOOKE HARBOUR HOUSE
🌢🌢🌢🌢

1528 Whiffen Spit Rd, Sooke / 250/642-3421 or 800/889-9688

It's no wonder that Sooke Harbour House has gained nationwide acclaim and earned an excellent reputation for both its inn and its restaurant (see Romantic Restaurants). Located at the end of a quiet road, the fantastic water's-edge setting, abundant elegance, and Northwest charm make Sooke Harbour House a sublime, albeit quite expensive, getaway. No detail has been overlooked in the 28 rooms, which feature captivating views of Sooke Bay, the Strait of Juan de Fuca, and the Olympic Mountains. Thoughtful luxuries include wood-burning fireplaces, inspired local artwork, fine linens, comfortable sitting areas, vaulted ceilings, beautiful furnishings, wet bars, balconies or patios, and a variety of soaking or jetted-tub options. The Thunderbird Room, a split-level, top-floor suite with a king-size bed, steam shower with a view, claw-foot tub, *and* a soaking tub on the deck, is outstanding. The ground-level Harbour Seal Room also ranks high, with a huge double-headed steam-bath/shower, private jetted tub on the terrace, and expansive king-size bed. The Blue Heron Room, one of the most popular rooms, has the best view in the house and a large whirlpool tub placed beside a river-rock fireplace. Leaving these sumptuous accommodations isn't easy, but thankfully, the lavish complimentary breakfast—hazelnut–maple syrup waffles with loganberry purée, or fresh garden vegetable quiche with scones and preserves, for example—is delivered to your door in the morning. Between May and October, and on off-season weekends, a picnic lunch is also included with your stay. As an added indulgence, you can also book an in-room spa service. From the luxurious in-room extras—such as fresh-cut flowers, plush robes, and decanters of fine port—to the spectacular waterfront setting, the amenities make this spot one of British Columbia's best kissing destinations, indeed.

$$$$ *AE, DC, MC, V; checks OK; call for weekday closures Dec–Feb; www. sookeharbourhouse.com.* &

WINTER CREEK HOUSE
❂❂❂❂

3070 Phillips Rd, Sooke / 250/642-4768 or 866-642-4768
Imagine a beautiful, handcrafted luxury cottage on a remote country road with its own naturally occurring 100-foot-high waterfall cascading just outside the windows. Believe it or not, this incredibly romantic haven exists, a mere 10-minute drive from town into the Sooke Hills. Specifically designed for intimate getaways, the house is billed as "a cottage with a conscience," although we think adjectives like *private, unique*, and *sublime* also fit. But then, modesty is typical of this sensitively designed retreat, which focuses on what nature brings to us, rather than what we bring to it. Gently placed on 40 acres ultimately destined for the Land Conservancy, the cottage was built by the owners from hand-milled cedar. It boasts a warm, inviting interior with vaulted spruce ceilings, exposed beams of old-growth cedar, and Afghan tribal rugs on glowing fir floors. The open floor plan includes a cozy love seat, where you can warm your feet by the gas fireplace while gazing through the picture windows out to the forest and waterfall. The queen-size featherbed has a luxurious down comforter made from natural fabrics and tiny handmade "sleep pillows" (scented sachets of lavender and chamomile); the bathroom is appointed with rich woods and handmade soap. Bring your favorite romantic music for the CD player (there's also a small selection on hand), or simply enjoy the serene sounds of the woods and water. Robes, slippers, fresh flowers, wine glasses, and candles complete the picture. The kitchenette, stocked with graceful Asian-style teapots and dishware, provides a cozy spot to indulge in your breakfast, which is delivered at the time you arrange. Options might include stuffed, baked French toast; fresh fruit;

and delicious homemade granola. In the evening, climb into the outdoor Japanese-style soaking tub of yellow cedar with gentle, circulating jets, and turn on landscape lights to illuminate the magnificent surrounding trees and waterfall. We simply can't imagine a more spectacular setting for romance. (About that waterfall: water flow is greatly reduced in the summer months, so to fully enjoy it, visit between late September and May.)
$$$ *MC, V; no checks; www.wintercreekhouse.com.*

Romantic Restaurants

MARKUS' WHARFSIDE RESTAURANT
◗◗◗

1831 Maple Ave S, Sooke / 250/642-3596
This little fisherman's cottage overlooking Sooke Harbour has been transformed into a simple, art-filled Mediterranean restaurant. With just nine tables in two little rooms, the feel is intimate, but not crowded. Every table, both inside and out on the sunny patio, has a water and—on a clear day—a mountain view, but should the clouds roll into the bay, you can also enjoy the moveable feast of local art on the gallerylike walls. Both rooms have a casual charm, with slate floors, warm colors, Latin music, white linen, and low lights, but our favorite is the fireplace room, with a cozy hearth on one side and a picture window on the other. Chef Markus Wieland, who trained in Europe before running Vancouver's successful Alabaster restaurant, applies his considerable talents to the great bounty of wild seafood and organic produce available locally. Everything on the menu is made from scratch, with the exception of the delicious bread, which is sourced from a local bakery. Starters include Tuscan seafood soup and baked goat cheese with roasted garlic. For a main course, try the sautéed prawns with white wine–and–garlic-butter sauce, the veal with sage and prosciutto, or the tempting daily risotto special.
$$$ *MC, V; no checks; lunch Tues–Fri, dinner Tues–Sat (call for winter closures); full bar; reservations recommended; www.markuswharfside restaurant.com.* ♿

SOOKE HARBOUR HOUSE
◗◗◗◗

1528 Whiffen Spit Rd, Sooke / 250/642-3421 or 800/889-9688
Prepare yourselves for a memorable experience—Sooke Harbour House (see Romantic Lodgings) lives up to its stellar reputation for romance. The menu reads like an exotic novel, and every dish comes out looking glamorous, many adorned with colorful, edible blossoms. Owners Frédérique and Sinclair Philip and their team of chefs have garnered international attention for their dedication to the freshest local ingredients combined with a good

deal of energy and flashes of innovation. Organically grown herbs from the inn's own gardens complement what dedicated island farmers, fishermen, and the wilderness provide. Offerings change daily, but sample entrées range from silver gray rockfish with caramelized apple juice, lemongrass, ginger, and tamari sauce, to seared squab and foie gras medallion with a preserved berry, sage, and squab stock reduction. Thrill seekers can book ahead for the Gastronomic Adventure and enjoy a flight of seven to nine chef-selected courses. Sooke Harbour House's award-winning wine list features excellent French vintages and an impressive array from British Columbia itself. You'll pay dearly for all this attention to detail, but this is a meal you won't soon forget. The dining room, located on the main floor, boasts a lovely fireplace that casts a warm glow over the room, delightful Northwest art, and tables adorned with white linen, fresh flowers, and a single tapered candle. Try requesting a window seat so you can also partake of the wonderful views of the strait and the surrounding gardens while you dine. The blooming passionflowers climbing the exterior walls of the dining room are a delightfully fitting detail.

$$$$ *AE, DC, MC, V; checks OK; dinner every day (call for seasonal closures); full bar; reservations required; www.sookeharbourhouse.com.* &

TOFINO

ROMANTIC HIGHLIGHTS

Getting to this remote, rugged stretch of coast is half the fun, and once you arrive, the wild, unruly, romantic appeal of the region will capture your hearts. During the high season—July and August—the best accommodations are usually booked many months in advance. However, if you plan ahead, warm and sunny days will be your reward. With gorgeous weather and fewer crowds, September is an ideal time to visit. In winter, the two of you can curl up and watch the legendary storms lash the coast. Traveling to Tofino by car makes for a beautiful journey along Highway 4, which crosses Vancouver Island and winds by rivers, lakes, and soaring snow-covered peaks (from Victoria, the trip takes about five hours). Be sure to plan for a stop at **MacMillan Provincial Park** (20 miles/32 km west of Parksville on Hwy 4), with its sky-high old-growth forest of Douglas firs and 800-year-old cedars. Nature trails lined with magnificent trees draped in moss invite you to commune with nature (and each other). Highway 4 is passable year-round, but try to avoid making the drive at night, as the scenery is not to be missed—and neither are the road's many winding curves. The road splits at the highway's end, with one fork heading north to Tofino, the other south to Ucluelet. Both towns, which began as fishing villages, pride themselves on their natural beauty and wilderness and are known as whale-watching destinations; in March and April, 20,000 gray whales make their annual migration past these shores. The more-frequented of the two destinations is Tofino, mainly because of its impressive number of wonderfully romantic accommodations. Ucluelet offers fewer amenities, but you'll nonetheless find a growing cluster of craft shops and galleries, excellent beach access, and stunning coastal rainforest walks along the recently built Wild Pacific Trail. And even if you're staying in Tofino, it's worth the 30-minute drive to the chic **Boat Basin Restaurant** in Ucluelet, set within the upscale **Tauca Lea Resort & Spa** (see Romantic Lodgings). For more casual, hearty posthike meals, try the **Matterson House** (1682 Peninsula Rd, Ucluelet; 250/726-2200; breakfast, lunch, dinner daily).

Most of Tofino's incredible getaways are within a stone's throw of the beach's infinite romantic possibilities: cuddle up and enjoy the pounding surf, hike through the trees along the shore, or head into the chilly water for a salty frolic. In **Pacific Rim National Park Reserve** (250/726-4212), you'll quickly discover why the aptly named Long Beach—all 11 sandy miles (19 km) of it—epitomizes many people's idea of the remote, rugged northern Pacific. The best way to explore it is by hiking the beach, headlands, and woodland trails; stop by the visitor center just inside the park entrance for a free hiker's guide. You can also ask for tips on whale watching and on where to see the permanent colonies of basking sea lions. Before you set off, pick up a boxed lunch in town at **Breakers Delicatessen** (4–131 1st St, Tofino; 250/725-2558), a hearty sandwich from **Caffé Vincenté** (441 Campbell St; 250/725-2599), or some organic global takeout from **So-Bo** (1084 Pacific Rim Hwy; 250/725-2341), a catering trailer at the Tofino Botanical Gardens. The fresh fish tacos with tropical salsa are sublime.

Excellent beach walks can also be had on **Chesterman Beach**, the longest beach outside the park, located 3 miles (5 km) south. Watch the many surfers trying to catch waves, or take the plunge yourselves with lessons at the popular **Inner Rhythm Surf Camp** (250/726-2211 or 877/393-SURF; www.innerrhythm.net). This reliable outfitter also supplies wetsuits, booties, gloves, and boards, so you can get out there and share salty kisses in the rolling breakers.

For a quieter excursion, spend an afternoon exploring Tofino's small shops and cafes. The mood in this town, tucked between the surf-pounded oceanfront and calm inner inlet, is unpretentious and amiable. You might stroll through galleries like the longhouse of the **Eagle Aerie Gallery** (350 Campbell St; 250/725-3235 or 800/663-0669) or **House of Himwitsa** (300 Main St; 250/725-2017 or 800/899-1947) to see First Nations masks, jewelry, and gifts. For refreshment, join locals for organic coffee and baked treats at the **Common Loaf Bake Shop** (180 1st St; 250/725-3915), enjoy sashimi with a view at **Tough City Sushi** (350 Main St; 250/725-2021), or try lunch or dinner at **Schooner on Second** (331 Campbell St; 250/725-3444). This historic central Tofino restaurant—part red clapboard building, part old schooner—offers great fresh seafood (try the Dungeness crab fresh off the boat). Tofino's newest hot spot is **Shelter** (601 Campbell St; 250/725-3353), a hip seafood restaurant at the edge of the village. South of town, stroll through the indigenous plants at the 12-acre **Tofino Botanical Gardens** (1084 Pacific Rim Hwy; 250/725-1220); afterward, enjoy a late-afternoon glass of wine or a tasty bistro supper on the patio of **Cafe Pamplona** (see Romantic Restaurants), located in the gardens.

When it comes to romance, Clayoquot Sound's famous **Hot Springs Cove** should be on your agenda. Here, a short walk through an ancient cedar rain forest brings you to a succession of five calming geothermal pools fed by a trickling waterfall. A number of boat and floatplane companies supply transportation; try the Hot Springs Explorer day-trip with **Remote Passages Marine Excursions** (250/725-3330 or 800/666-9833; www.remote passages.com; Mar–Oct), with marine stops that may include a sea cave and a seabird nesting island, and plenty of chances to spot whales and other wildlife en route. This outfitter also offers sea-kayaking and bear-watching excursions, as well as whale watching, one of Tofino's main attractions. (There are numerous charter companies, so it's easy to arrange trips once you arrive.) Maybe seeing a spout of water explode from the ocean surface, followed by a giant, arching black profile, provides the excitement; or maybe it's simply getting out on the open water; whatever the reason, a sighting of these miraculous creatures is best shared with someone special. Although the peak of the gray whale northern migration season is March and April, these magnificent mammals are present near the coastline from March to October. Humpbacks can be seen between June and September, and transient orcas, as well as sea otters, sea lions, and other marine life, may be spotted anytime.

If you'd rather be on the water yourselves, paddle with **Remote Passages Sea Kayaking** (250/725-3330 or 800/666-9833; www.remotepassages. com) or the **Tofino Sea Kayaking Company** (320 Main St; 250/725-4222 or 800/863-4664; www.tofino-kayaking.com), which offers kayak rentals and guided tours with experienced naturalists. For the ultimate bird's-eye view, explore the region's remote corners on the floatplanes of **Tofino Air Lines** (250/725-4454; 866/486-3247; www.tofinoair.ca). Day-trips include Hot Springs Cove, remote beaches, and Cougar Annie's Garden, where miles of unique moss trails wind through the ruins of a turn-of-the-20th-century wilderness homestead. Whether your getaway here includes unforgettable outdoor adventure or simply curling up at your oceanfront lodging and listening to the waves roll in, Tofino is sure to inspire kisses.

Access & Information

Travelers arrive at Tofino primarily by car, via the winding mountainous route of Highway 4 (five hours from Victoria). From Vancouver, take the ferry from Horseshoe Bay to Nanaimo. Drive north on the Island Highway (Hwy 19) to the Parksville bypass. Turn west, onto Highway 4, to cross the island (from this point, it takes approximately two and a half hours). Continue on Highway 4, past the Ucluelet junction, north to Tofino. Regency Express (604/278-1608 or 800/228-6608; www.regencyexpress.com) flies to Tofino from Vancouver Airport's South Terminal. It's a good idea to rent a car here (try Budget; 250/725-2060). The Pacific Rim Whale Festival (mid-Mar–early Apr) hosts events in Tofino and in Ucluelet; contact the **Tofino Visitors Info Centre** (250/725-3414; www.tofinobc.org).

Romantic Lodgings

A SNUG HARBOUR INN
🌢🌢🌢🌢

460 Marine Dr, Ucluelet / 250/726-2686 or 888/936-5222
Perched on a cliff above the Pacific, this luxurious bed-and-breakfast enjoys stunning views of the rocky shoreline and outlying islets where harbor seals, whales, and eagles play. Terraced decks, incredible views, plenty of windows, large rooms, and gorgeous bathrooms are all assets of this luxurious retreat. A pathway called the "stairway from the stars" leads to a private pebbly beach below, and a helicopter pad is available for guests who arrive by air. On the main deck, a big hot tub under the stars makes a grand place to kiss. Of the six phone- and TV-free guest accommodations, four are exquisite waterfront rooms appointed with fireplaces, unique furnishings, private decks with spectacular ocean views, and lavish private bathrooms with jetted tubs. For romance, try the Sawadee or the Lighthouse rooms. The Sawadee Room has captivating ocean views, a two-tiered deck, a king-size bed, and a soothing blue-and-green color scheme. Soak in the double jetted tub set next to the two-sided beach-stone fireplace. The dramatic Lighthouse Room winds up three levels; the bedroom has views from all sides through portholes and picture windows. Two forest view rooms (one unit allows pets; the other is wheelchair accessible) are located in a separate building. These feature private entrances and private covered decks, two-person jetted tubs, corner fireplaces, heated ceramic floors, comfortable pine furnishings, and king-size beds. Mornings bring the scent of delicious three-course breakfasts, which you can enjoy at a big harvest table or an intimate table for two in the great room with spectacular view, or in the privacy of your room.
$$$–$$$$ *MC, V; no checks; www.awesomeview.com.* ♿

BRIMAR BED & BREAKFAST
○○❮

1375 Thornberg Crescent, Tofino / 250/725-3410 or 800/714-9373

Pull into the tree-lined gravel drive of this elegant New England–style home, located just steps from spectacular Chesterman Beach, and the kiss-worthy aspects become immediately apparent. The light-filled interior boasts a large common space and an elegant dining room, where delicious breakfasts are served in the morning. Three tastefully decorated rooms have ocean views and private baths. The bright and airy honeymoon suite, known as The Loft, is the only room on the top floor, and thus extremely private. Charming features include a wrought-iron queen-size bed, lovely pale green walls, a wood-burning stove, a glassed-in shower, and a spacious claw-foot tub set beneath a skylight so you can watch the stars while you soak (a tasteful screen separates it from the main room). The Sunset, on the floor below, features a spacious bathroom, king-size bed, and a TV in an armoire. The smallest room, the Moonrise, has lovely views but less charm: the TV sitting on the dresser draws too much attention to itself, and the private bath across the hall features a shower but no bathtub. However, for romance on a budget, it's not a bad option. The elaborate breakfast is served family-style downstairs, and everything, from the homemade breads and granola to the asparagus-cheese torte and crispy waffles with mixed berries, is excellent. After this indulgence, you can stroll right onto the beach without even putting on your shoes.

$$$ MC, V; checks OK; www.brimarbb.com.

CABLE COVE INN
○○❮

201 Main St, Tofino / 250/725-4236 or 800/663-6449

Tucked at the edge of Tofino's town center, this cozy retreat is an excellent bet when you have romance on your minds. Don't be fooled by the unpretentious exterior of this building: the guest suites are luxurious, and the private decks have magnificent views past the wharves to Meares Island and out to the open sea. Steps lead to the sheltered cove below the inn where a fire pit, crab cooker, and gazebo await. Marble Jacuzzi tubs and glass showers for two are distinctly romantic attractions in most rooms; two have standard bathrooms but private hot tubs on their decks. Beautiful, softly colored linens cover the handsome mahogany-toned four-poster beds, and fireplaces add a warm glow to every room. Sliding wooden doors open to private decks equipped with cedar chairs, perfect for soaking up the beautiful scenery; one corner room has a wraparound deck. Sunlight pours in through skylights in the second-floor rooms. Add colorful Northwest art, a cozy wood-burning stove in the upstairs lounge surrounded by cushy leather couches, and an adults-only policy, and you have a recipe for relaxation and romance. Although this inn has the privacy and professionalism

of a hotel, the innkeepers live right next door and see to personal touches, making it feel more like a bed-and-breakfast. Hot beverages are brought directly to the rooms every morning, and a variety of refreshments are on hand in the common sitting room for all to enjoy. A continental breakfast is served in the morning.
$$$ *AE, MC, V; no checks; www.cablecoveinn.com.* &

CLAYOQUOT WILDERNESS RESORTS & SPA
❂❂❂❂
Quait Bay / 250/726-8235 or 888/333-5405
This luxurious wilderness resort in remote Clayoquot Sound is accessible only by boat or floatplane. The most romantic (and the most rugged) option here is to make your way to the inn's Wilderness Outpost on the banks of the Bedwell River, but you can also stay in the main lodge, housed in a floating barge on Quait Bay. Two all-inclusive packages, Eco-Adventure or Spa, have specific check-in and check-out days. Book for three, four, or seven nights, and hike pristine coastline, ride horses in the outback, relax in the state-of-the-art spa, or do all of the above. The main lodge, 30 minutes by water taxi from Tofino, is moored next to a huge wilderness area, home to thousand-year-old cedars, two private lakes, and a waterfall-fed swimming hole. We spotted a magnificent black bear here during our visit; it's partly due to such sightings that all outdoor activities are done with guides or in groups. While this detracts from your privacy, it does provide more safety. The rooms at the main lodge are cozy and carpeted, with warm yellow walls, country-style pine king-size or twin-size beds, private decks, and efficient bathrooms appropriate to ship's quarters. The jetted tub on the deck is for all guests to enjoy. Come evening, guests dine on truly outstanding Pacific Northwest cuisine at a long table by the fire or at intimate tables for two. The state-of-the-art Healing Grounds Spa adds to the pampering with a rainforest-themed sauna, a massage room for two, a yoga room, and natural outdoor cedar hot tubs. The spa is open to day visitors, so you can make the trip from Tofino if the overnight package rates are too much of a splurge. If you choose the Wilderness Outpost, you'll sleep in roomy safari-style tents—outfitted with Oriental rugs, remote-controlled woodstoves, hand-made furniture, and private decks—and enjoy fresh seafood and fine wine on china and crystal. By day, explore by horse, mountain bike, canoe, or kayak; by night, relax in one of the three wood-fired hot tubs or saunas, have a massage in one of the spa tents, and enjoy the deep silence. Cost includes airfare from Vancouver, meals, alcoholic beverages, and all activities and/or spa treatments.
$$$$ *AE, MC, V; no checks; packages for 3, 4, or 7 nights only; closed Nov–Apr; www.wildretreat.com.*

EAGLE NOOK WILDERNESS RESORT & SPA
◐◐◐◖

Barkley Sound / 250/723-1000 or 800/760-2777

No roads lead to the wilderness oasis of Eagle Nook, and that's what makes it special. Set on a private 70-acre peninsula on the edge of a marine reserve, this remote, adults-only, phone- and TV-free getaway caters to outdoor-loving couples who revel in luxury after a day of kayaking, fishing, beachcombing, or exploring the coast by helicopter. By day, you can hike out to a private beach on the property or kayak the pristine blue waters of the Broken Group Islands, part of Pacific Rim National Park Reserve. Every package includes a cruise to see harbor seals, cormorants, bald eagles, and possibly whales in the surrounding watery wilderness; if the weather's nice the guide will drop each couple off at their own deserted beach for a romantic picnic lunch. (The romance package includes a cruise for just the two of you.) Back at the resort, guests dine on beautifully prepared West Coast or Continental meals at tables for two set before floor-to-ceiling ocean-view windows. After dinner, you can soothe kayaking-weary muscles in the lodge's oceanside hot tub or cedar-hut sauna, stroll to the kiss-worthy gazebo to watch for phosphorescence in the bay, or head to the two-room spa for a luxurious massage. The 23 lodge rooms are all large and comfortable with private bathrooms, ocean views, fluffy duvets, and feather pillows, though the decor is more reminiscent of a high-end business hotel than a wilderness retreat. Our choice for a romantic getaway is one of the two secluded one-bedroom cabins next to the main lodge, where water-view decks, king-size beds, wood stoves, and kitchenettes assure comfort and privacy. Breakfast, or even dinner, can be delivered to your room or cabin, though you won't want to miss dining at the lodge. Most guests book packages that include meals and air fare from Seattle or Vancouver, although you can drive to Ucluelet and meet the resort's water taxi for an exciting cruise through the wildlife-rich sound to the resort.

$$$$ *AE, MC, V; no checks; closed Oct–May; www.eaglenook.com.*

LONG BEACH LODGE RESORT
◐◐◐◖

1441 Pacific Rim Hwy, Tofino / 250/725-2442 or 877/844-7873

Although it's been open only since spring 2002, this beautiful cedar-shingled resort on the beach at Cox Bay has already stolen many hearts. Nestled among towering trees with spectacular views of the ocean and just steps from a seemingly endless stretch of sand, this 41-room haven offers an immediate sense of a retreat from the world at large. You get all the five-star amenities in a completely informal, relaxed setting—minus the stiffness of fancy resorts. The great room typifies the lodge's naturalist decor, with its dramatic granite fireplace, floor-to-ceiling windows, and a "woven wall" of fir. Plush armchairs, unique furniture, and cozy lamps warm up the space.

The guest rooms feature luxurious beds made up with fine linens and slate-tiled bathrooms with soaking tubs and walk-in showers. Nine rooms have forest views, but most of the rooms look out on the beach and have either jetted single tubs or a two-person soaking tubs. The simply decorated rooms come in a variety of sizes, but even the regular beachfront rooms offer kiss-worthy views and comforts. Twenty two-bedroom cabins—featuring full kitchens, two full bathrooms, fireplaces, living rooms, and private patio hot tubs—offer another option for those who like more space or wish to travel with another couple. One of these cabins is fully wheelchair accessible, though the main lodge is not. We strongly recommend a visit to the dining room; not only is the room itself truly inviting, but also the kitchen uses many fresh, local ingredients, with delicious results.
$$$$ *AE, MC, V; no checks; www.longbeachlodgeresort.com.*

MIDDLE BEACH LODGE
◑◑◑
400 MacKenzie Beach Rd, Tofino / 250/725-2900 or 866/725-2900
A long road veers off the highway and into the forest, where the private, romantic Middle Beach Lodge and its more recently constructed counterpart perch above a pristine beach and the roaring Pacific. Each of the two main lodges has a large lobby graced with a massive stone fireplace and weathered antiques, all backed by panoramic views of the pounding surf. The simple, rustic guest rooms have sophisticated touches, including natural-fiber curtains, hand-carved chairs, and tastefully unique artwork—such as the antique wooden oars that adorn some walls. The spare decor makes the lavish beds, piled high with fluffy comforters, even more inviting. The Lodge at the Beach is kept romantic and quiet with an adults-only policy; rates here are surprisingly reasonable; and many of the 26 cozy, phone- and TV-free rooms feature full oceanfront views and private balconies (with the beach this close, even the rooms without such advantages deserve romantic consideration). The newer, pricier Lodge at the Headlands welcomes kids over age 12 but still supplies plenty of ambience, especially in the ocean-facing Headland Suites, which offer—in addition to the lodge's finest water views—gas fireplaces, soaking tubs, TV/VCRs, king-size beds, and private decks where you can feel the salt spray on your lips. For additional space, or for larger groups, there are also duplex, triplex, and free-standing cabins, some with additional bedrooms or hot tubs on private decks. The lodge serves a continental breakfast of home-baked goods and jams. Weekends and high season bring fresh fish barbecues served in the dining room. With all the long, leisurely beach walks you're going to be taking, you're sure to work up an appetite.
$$–$$$$ *AE, MC, V; no checks; www.middlebeach.com.* ♿

TAUCA LEA RESORT & SPA
🌢🌢🌢

1971 Harbour Dr, Ucluelet / 250/726-4625 or 800/979-9303
Tucked away on a private island in Ucluelet Inlet, this cluster of blue-stained cedar condos, complete with a spa and restaurant, has all the makings of a secluded getaway. Although this ecologically managed resort attracts families and active outdoor types, it's also a perfect place for couples to curl up together in front of the fire and watch the coast's famous storms lash at the windows. There's little need to leave your suite: each of the one- and two-bedroom apartment-sized units is serenely decorated in an airy, West Coast style, with leather armchairs or sofas and furniture hand-crafted from cedar milled on the property. Each has a fully equipped kitchen, private balcony (some are more private than others), gas fireplace, dimmer lights, and views of the harbor or the sheltered inlet. Bathrooms have deep soaking tubs, and about half of the units have outdoor two-person air-jetted tubs on their balconies. A continental buffet breakfast is served in the resort's Boat Basin restaurant; it can be delivered to your suite for an extra fee. You will, of course, want to head out at some point—to walk hand in hand through the rainforest along Ucluelet's Wild Pacific Trail, kayak through the clear waters of the Broken Group Islands, or indulge in a pampering treatment at the serene rainforest-themed spa. Try the aromatherapy massage for two or a couple's Rainforest Bath in a private grotto of slate and cedar. Both are part of the aptly named Couple's Bliss-Out Weekend package. The resort's stellar Boat Basin Restaurant (250/726-4644) is a chic, airy space with plenty of cedar, striking First Nations art, and romantic candlelight; the seasonally changing menu tempts with options such as duck breast with salal berry jus and wild cedar-plank salmon. In winter, reserve ahead for a window seat with a view; in summer, a table on the deck is sublime. *$$$–$$$$ AE, DC, MC, V; no checks; www.taucalearesort.com.*

WICKANINNISH INN
🌢🌢🌢🌢

Osprey Ln at Chesterman Beach, Tofino / 250/725-3100 or 800/333-4604
This exquisite property is set on a rocky cape that juts out from the western tip of Chesterman Beach. Dramatic white surf crashes against the jagged rocks that front the inn, while a forest of fir and cedar provides seclusion on the land side. Known for pioneering the concept of winter storm watching, this inn is one of the few places on Vancouver Island booked year-round, not least because it flawlessly melds luxury and elegance with natural West Coast surroundings. From the moment you pass beneath the grand cedar-beamed entrance and step into the inviting lobby, where floor-to-ceiling windows offer breathtaking views of the ocean, you will know you've come to the right place. The artful environment includes architectural details by master carver Henry Nolla, handmade driftwood chairs, and furniture

custom-crafted from recycled old-growth fir. This theme extends to the 75 guest rooms and suites, all of which feature ocean and beach views, fireplaces, and thoughtfully placed private balconies that provide the utmost privacy; many have double soaking tubs set before ocean-view windows. A major new addition, Wickaninnish-on-the-Beach, located just steps away from the original lodge, opened in 2003 with 30 new rooms and suites. All feature luxurious amenities similar to the rooms in the original building, but with more space; the smallest rooms are more than 600 square feet, while lofts soar up to 1,100 square feet. The top-floor Canopy Suite, with its four picture windows and shower and tub for two, is among the most romantic, and most expensive, places to stay in the province. Where else can you lie on a fabric-draped four-poster bed and gaze at the summer night sky, even during a storm? Fiber-optic panels in the ceiling accurately re-create the constellations as you'd see them over Tofino in mid-June. However, you might want to redirect your splurge when you hear what comes next: The Cedar Sanctuary is a completely private couple's spa cabin built on the tip of a rocky promontory, where you can both enjoy a massage treatment available from the soothing, full-service Ancient Cedars Spa. For sublime relaxation, try the hot-stone massage, done with smooth stones that are coated with essential oils. The crowning glory is The Pointe Restaurant (see Romantic Restaurants).
$$$$ *AE, DC, MC, V; no checks; www.wickinn.com.* &

Romantic Restaurants

CAFÉ PAMPLONA
❤❤
1084 Pacific Rim Hwy, Tofino / 250/725-1237
Tucked away in the Tofino Botanical Gardens, a short drive from town, this unique, simple, and charming spot is a terrific bet for a delicious meal. You'll like the local-haunt feel, which is manifested in everything from the ever-changing displays of art by island artists to occasional performances by local musicians. Inside the intimate dining room, a wall of French doors opens onto a patio where all sorts of plants flourish; an antique stove adds to the cozy ambience. During the day, overhead skylights fill the dining room with light, and in the evening, candles add flickering warmth to the simple wooden tables. The menu relies on local produce and organic fare fresh from the garden. Choose between a frequently changing à la carte menu, which includes tempting starters such as fresh oysters and organic local greens, or the three-course menu, which can also be paired with wine. Service is friendly, and you are as welcome to enjoy the artwork over a cup of coffee or herb tea as you are to swing by around dusk to enjoy

a glass of wine on the patio. While you're here, be sure to stroll around the lovely gardens.

$$$ AE, MC, V; no checks; lunch, dinner every day (mid-Mar–mid Oct), dinner Wed–Sun, brunch Sun (mid-Oct–mid-Mar); call for seasonal closures; beer and wine; reservations recommended; www.cafepamplona.com. &

THE POINTE RESTAURANT
◔◔◔◔

Osprey Ln at Chesterman Beach (Wickaninnish Inn), Tofino / 250/725-3106 or 800/333-4604

Memories of your romantic dinner at The Pointe in the Wickaninnish Inn (see Romantic Lodgings) simply will not fade. Everything here is memorable, from the magnificent decor to the massive wood-burning stove with hammered-copper hood and chimney to the intensely original cuisine. Step inside the dining room and marvel at the natural cedar posts and beams in the soaring 20-foot ceiling. The restaurant is perched over a rocky headland, and waves crash just outside the 240-degree panoramic windows; during winter storms, the dramatic surf can even splash up against the glass. Any time of year, the glorious sunsets are breathtaking. Even with the bar near the entrance, the dining area remains quiet throughout the evening, and your table feels like your personal island, with its beach-rock candle, fine china, and crystal. To top it all off, service is attentive without being pretentious. Chef Andrew Springett's distinctly West Coast Canadian menu focuses on fresh local seafood—including delicious oysters—and produce, much of it organic; everything, including the breads and desserts, is made in house from scratch. An à la carte menu features Long Beach Dungeness crab, grilled wild salmon, and excellent vegetarian selections, although, if you can stand the splurge, we think the most romantic option is the daily multicourse tasting menu. Just one such culinary adventure might include hickory-smoked tiger prawns, a caramelized shallot and Boursin cheese–stuffed veal loin, and a spiced white chocolate parfait with a merlot-poached pear. Add the wine-pairing option to savor a different delicious British Columbia vintage with every course. What we're really saying is, when you go to The Pointe, go big and expect to pay for it. You will be amply rewarded.

$$$$ AE, DC, MC, V; no checks; breakfast, lunch, dinner every day; full bar; reservations recommended; www.wickinn.com.

RAINCOAST CAFÉ
◔◔◔

120 4th St, Tofino / 250/725-2215

Simply put, this is one of the best restaurants in Tofino. The decor of this 12-table dining room is sleek and modern—as is the menu, which focuses

on local, sustainable seafood, organic meats, and creative vegetarian dishes, often with Asian or other global twists. Fortunately, this isn't the sort of chrome-and-metal place where an abundance of noise and glare discourages intimate evenings; here, soft jazz flows from the speakers, wooden tables are adorned with candles, and a relaxed ambience sets the stage for romance. This might be because the owners, Lisa Henderson and Larry Nicolay, are a husband-and-wife team, or simply because the food puts a magic spell over all who arrive. Try the popular seafood soba, a dish of buckwheat noodles with local shrimp, clams, and wild salmon in a savory lime-miso sauce. Or, sample one of the tempting specials, which change nightly; on our visit, a delicious Concord grape–and-sake-ginger salmon was served with local vegetables and tender couscous. Vegetarians will delight in the gamashio-breaded tofu, shallow fried and served with a sweet chile, mirin, and soy glaze, or the rich chick pea curry with mango raita. For dessert, try chocolate peanut butter pie. With its laid-back charm and Pacific Rim sophistication, the RainCoast Café is the perfect place for a prelude to a kiss.
$$$ *AE, MC, V; no checks; dinner every day; beer and wine; reservations recommended; raincafe@island.net.* &

SOUTHERN GULF ISLANDS

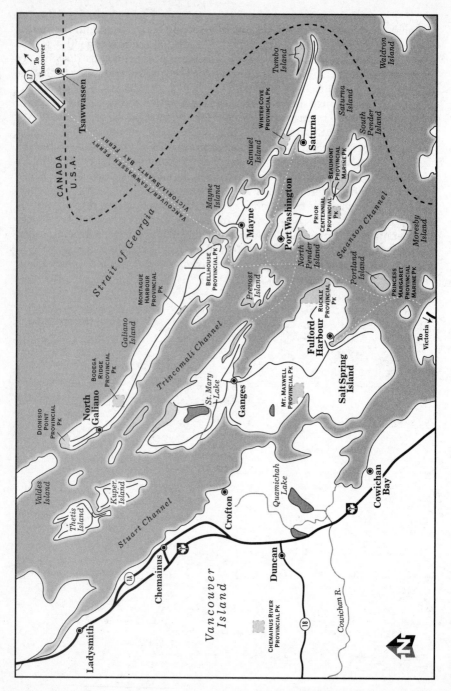

"A kiss though sometimes seen is never heard."
—ANON.

♡ SOUTHERN GULF ISLANDS

Scattered like a heavenly constellation in the blue ocean, the Southern Gulf Islands lie between Vancouver Island and mainland British Columbia. Hundreds of forested isles, whose populations vary from zero to several thousand, make up this group, and all of them are havens of transcendent splendor and solitude. So many islands can make it difficult to know which one to visit, but thanks to kiss-intensive research, we discovered which islands rate highest on the romance scale. For intimate getaways, we most highly recommend the islands of Salt Spring, Mayne, Galiano, Pender, and Saturna. All are accessible via the ferry terminal at Swartz Bay outside Victoria, or from Tsawwassen outside Vancouver. If you're visiting in summer, book your ferry passage and accommodations ahead of time. Depending on your island destination, you can arrange to arrive by floatplane.

From the air or by boat, these islands look like paradise. Once you land, you'll find that natural beauty and recreational opportunities do indeed abound. Located in the rain shadow of Vancouver Island's mountains, the Gulf Islands are considerably less rainy than Vancouver (to be safe, though, bring rain gear in winter). The islands, which are mostly inhabited by artisans, retirees, and small-scale organic farmers, can feel quite remote, and some lack even a bank machine or a well-stocked store, so plan accordingly. The widest selection of inns, eateries, shopping, and services are to be found on Salt Spring and Galiano Islands.

If you are planning to visit more than one island during your trip, we can't emphasize enough the importance of contacting BC Ferries (250/386-3431 or 888/223-3779; www.bcferries.com) for schedules and reservations. Island-hopping is not as easy as you would think, with some ferries offering only limited transportation at odd hours designed to cater to local inter-island commuting. It's possible to get stranded on one of the smaller islands overnight if you don't pay close attention to return sailing times (there aren't any at all on some days). We recommend bringing along a healthy sense of adventure and a store of patience when relying on ferry transportation between the islands. If you plan to bring a car from the mainland, we also recommend making a reservation, especially in the peak summer months; there is (so far) no extra charge for reservations on Gulf Island routes. Island hoppers may also want to check out BC Ferries' SailPass, which offers multiple crossings for a set fare. On summer weekends, it can be less stressful and less expensive to leave the car at home; most inns and B&Bs offer ferry pickup. Bring your own bike or rent one; the islands (with the exception of busy Salt Spring) are wonderful (if hilly) for cycling. It's also easier to island hop without a car: during July and August, Gulf Islands Water Taxi (250/537-2510; www.saltspring.com/watertaxi) runs foot passengers from Mayne and Galiano to Salt Spring.

Romantic travelers visiting these islands might find themselves stopping over at some point at Sidney, British Columbia, the nearest town to BC Ferries' Swartz Bay terminal and the destination of the ferry from Anacortes, Washington. Most people don't stay here for long—but we highly recommend that you stop for an unforgettable meal at **Dock 503** (from the Hwy 17 Beacon Ave exit, drive Harbour Rd to Van Isle Marina; 250/656-0828; dock503.vanislemarina.com; lunch Mon–Sat, dinner every day, brunch Sun; call for seasonal closures; reservations recommended). The delicious fare consistently wins awards from gourmet-food magazines, and the menu changes seasonally to make the most of fresh local produce. You might start with grilled Vancouver Island oysters or a caramelized purple onion tart, then tuck into local free-run ostrich tenderloin or halibut cheeks with baby bok choi. Save room for dessert; we recommend the dark chocolate and caramel tart or the steamed ginger molasses cake. The heated patio, open on sunny days, overlooks the hundreds of sparkling sailboats in the marina. Eating here is an excellent way to get your island getaway off to a delicious start.

SALT SPRING ISLAND

ROMANTIC HIGHLIGHTS

Salt Spring Island, the largest and most vibrant of the Southern Gulf Islands, dotted with pastoral farms and artisan studios, is packed with sublime places to stay. Due to the veritable explosion of B&Bs here (approximately 100 at last count), choosing accommodations can be tricky, but we have uncovered the best this island oasis has to offer. Due to Salt Spring Island's considerable size and popularity, we recommend calling the properties you hope to visit well ahead of time for both reservations and specific directions. The beautiful summer weather draws crowds, but quieter retreats can be found in the shoulder seasons of spring and fall; clear, crisp weather and the island's delightful Fall Fair make September an ideal month to visit.

If you do nothing else on this island, don't miss the breathtaking panorama from the top of **Mount Maxwell** (7 miles/11 km southwest of Ganges via the Fulford-Ganges Rd and Cranberry Rd). Endless views are just the beginning of what you'll experience at the end of the (very) bumpy gravel road that takes you to the top. Scenery this magnificent and inspiring is hard to describe—suffice to say, we think your kisses will be very eloquent. To the north are the snow-covered mountains of the Canadian Rockies; to the south stands the glacial peak of Mount Baker; all around are the forested islands and the sparkling, crystalline waters of the Strait of Georgia. For a romantic seaside walk, nothing beats **Ruckle Provincial Park** (10 minutes from the Fulford Harbour ferry dock, turn right on to Beaver Point Rd). If strolling through a beautiful garden sounds appealing, visit **Everlasting Summer** (194 McLennan Dr; 3¾ miles/6 km from Fulford Harbour toward Ruckle Park; 250/653-9418; open 10am–5pm daily; closed Dec–Feb), a popular wedding site that features a gorgeous display garden filled with a profusion of scented herbs, old-fashioned roses, and edible flowers, along with an excellent gift shop.

The seaside village of Ganges merits an afternoon of strolling; it offers plenty of cozy waterfront restaurants, charming cafes, and boutiques that carry the work of local artists and artisans. For a casual lunch, you can cozy up under the spreading plum tree at the funky, outdoor **Treehouse Café** (106 Purvis Ln, Ganges; 250/537-5379), where live music fills the air every summer evening, or enjoy a ciabatta sandwich and French-pressed coffee on the marina-side deck at **Auntie Pesto's Café & Delicatessen** (Grace Point Square, Ganges; 250/537-4181). Two slightly pricier downtown spots offer seafood, casual fare, and waterfront patios: the serene **Calvin's Bistro** (133 Lower Ganges Rd, Ganges; 250/538-5551; www.calvinsbistro.com), where both Swiss and Thai classics appear on the evening menu, and the busy, sometimes over-busy, **Oystercatcher** (Harbor Bldg, Ganges; 250/537-5041; www.oystercatcher.ca)—downstairs, visit the traditional English pub complete with fireplace. For a quintessential local experience, along with water views and great food (and no children), check out **Moby's Marine Pub** (124 Upper Ganges Rd, Ganges; 250/537-5559), an island mainstay for the past 20 years. It's across the harbor, about a half mile by road northeast of Ganges; a foot passenger ferry, delightfully dubbed the *Queen of DeNile*, can whisk you there in the summertime. If you're touring the island, plan a lunch stop at the **Raven Street Market Café** (321 Fernwood Rd, Ganges; 250/537-2273). Some of the island's best, and best-value, meals appear from the wood-fired oven at this little grocery-store-cum-cafe, hidden away at the island's northern tip.

If you're a couple who loves the arts, plan to be here on the weekend so you can visit the **Salt Spring Island Saturday Market** (Centennial Park, Ganges; 250/537-4448; www.saltspringmarket.com; Apr–Oct). Go early to avoid the crowds, and explore the delights that await in every stall: hand-crafted jewelry, unique pottery, hand-smoothed wooden bowls, delicious gourmet treats, and more. We're certain you'll find a special memento here that you will treasure for years to come. Another way to discover artisans on the island is to take the **Studio Tour** (free map available at Ganges Info Centre; 250/537-5252; www.saltspring.com/studiotour). It's entirely self-guided, so you choose which of the 30-plus studios you'd like to visit; at the studios, you can either simply look and enjoy or buy something to take home. A bona fide cultural adventure, touring the studios often takes you along some of the island's most lovely and remote back roads, where the views and island tranquility may even inspire you to create art yourselves—or at least an artful kiss.

Winemaking is a relatively new art form on Salt Spring, with two wineries starting production in recent years. At **Garry Oaks Winery** (1880 Fulford-Ganges Rd; 250/653-4687; www.garryoakswine.com; open for tastings noon–5pm daily May–Oct), be sure to check out the meditative labyrinth on site. You can also stay overnight in a loft room for two overlooking the vineyards. At the charming **Salt Spring Vineyards** (151 Lee Rd, off 1700 block Fulford-Ganges Rd; 250/653-9463; www.saltspringvineyards.com; open noon–5pm daily June–Sept) you can taste wines or stay in the romantic on-site B&B (see Romantic Lodgings).

More wine, plus cheese, chocolate, and other sensual delights are the quarry on an **Island Gourmet Safari** (250/537-4118; www.islandgourmet safaris.com). Guide Wendy Hartnett takes small groups, or private pairs, to visit some of the island's most intriguing farms, wineries, breweries, studios, and more.

Access & Information

BC Ferries (250/386-3431 or 888/223-3779; www.bcferries.com) offers service to Salt Spring Island from the Tsawwassen ferry terminal, on the mainland, 22 miles (35 km) south of Vancouver. Tsawwassen is located near the Canada/U.S. border, and is only about a two-hour drive from Seattle when there is no traffic at the border crossing; with traffic, the trip can take considerably longer. From Vancouver Island, two BC Ferries routes serve Salt Spring Island. From Victoria, ferries leave Swartz Bay and land 35 minutes later at Salt Spring's Fulford Harbour. North of Victoria, the mill town of Crofton offers a short ferry trip to Salt Spring's Vesuvius Bay, on the island's northwest side.

An alternative route to Salt Spring Island for travelers coming from the United States is to take **Washington State Ferries** (206/464-6400 or 888/808-7977; www.wsdot.wa.gov/ferries/) from Anacortes to Sidney, British Columbia; then make the short drive to the ferry terminal at Swartz

Bay, and then transfer to BC Ferries for the 35-minute ride to Salt Spring's Fulford Harbour. Although this route involves two ferry lineups and can end up taking an entire day, it does make for a memorable and scenic trip.

You can also arrange to arrive by floatplane. **Harbour Air Seaplanes** (604/274-1277 or 800/665-0212; www.harbour-air.com) offers regular service from Coal Harbour in downtown Vancouver to Salt Spring and South Pender Islands, and from Vancouver Airport's south terminal to Salt Spring, South Pender, Mayne, Galiano, and Saturna Islands (a two-passenger minimum applies on some flights). **Kenmore Air** (425/486-1257 or 800/543-9595; www.kenmoreair.com) makes scheduled flights from Seattle to Salt Spring between March and October; charters are available the rest of the year.

There's no public transportation on Salt Spring (or any of the Gulf Islands) but determined romantics can visit car-free with a judicious use of taxis, bike rentals, pick-up services offered by most B&Bs, and the Ganges Faerie Mini Shuttle (250/537-6758 or 250/538-9007; www.gangesfaerie. com), which runs foot passengers between the ferry terminals and the town of Ganges. Be sure to confirm these services are still available before flying in or walking on to the ferry, though, as taxi and shuttle companies tend to come and go with the seasons. Cyclists take note: the roads are beautiful, but winding, narrow, and hilly.

For more information, contact the **Salt Spring Island Visitor Info Centre** (121 Lower Ganges Rd, Ganges; 250/537-5252 or 866/216-2936; www.salt springtoday.com). Also, **Tourism Vancouver Island** (335 Wesley St, Ste 203, Nanaimo; 250/754-3500; www.islands.bc.ca) can give you information on touring the Gulf Islands.

Romantic Lodgings

ASTON HOUSE BED & BREAKFAST
⬡⬡⬡⬡

205 Quarry Dr, Salt Spring Island / 250/538-1868 or 866/538-1868
Tasteful and serene, this waterfront bed-and-breakfast has the refined comforts of, say, the island getaway of an established European artist—which is precisely what it is. Hosts Eric and Mariette Klemm—he's a well-known painter and photographer in his native Germany, she's a hotel professional—perfected their innkeeping skills operating the luxurious Cocoa Island Relais & Chateaux resort in the Maldives. The gleaming white two-story home, designed by the artist himself and built in 2003, sits on a bluff facing south over Vesuvius Bay. The foyer, indeed the whole house, is a gallery for Eric Klemm's abstract oils and dramatic landscape photography, as well as works by other island artists. A guest living room, where afternoon tea is served, is inviting with deep leather armchairs and a changing feast of art. French doors lead to an outdoor table for two; beyond that is a hilltop

gazebo. Both spots have views through the forest to the sea. Upstairs are two sumptuous guest rooms, each lush with oil paintings, sculptures, French-country fabrics, a duvet-topped plantation-style four-poster bed, and such creature comforts as a gas fireplace, phone, TV/VCR, and fridge stocked with soft drinks and local wine. Each bathroom has a big jetted tub with a separate shower, heated tile floors, and cozy terry robes; French doors lead to a wide water-view deck, equipped with loungers and a table, and invisible from the neighboring balcony. Of the two rooms, we prefer Room One, which has a king-size bed and an armoire to hide the TV; Room Two has a queen bed and its TV sits on an antique side table. Breakfast is a multicourse affair, served when you choose, at tables for two in the sunny breakfast room, garden, or gazebo; if you prefer, you can relax over a Continental breakfast on your balcony. Add modern soundproofing, a no-kids-under-12 policy, in-room spa services, and a path winding down to a private beach, and you've got a great spot for a grown-up weekend away.

$$$$ *AE, MC, V; no checks; call for seasonal closures; www.astonhouse.ca.*

CLOUD 9 OCEANVIEW BED AND BREAKFAST
ôôôĉ

238 Sun Eagle Dr, Salt Spring Island / 250/537-2776 or 877/722-8233
This romantic retreat couldn't be more aptly named. By the time you travel the long and winding road that leads to this tastefully modern, spacious, and elegant home—set high above the water with views of Galiano Island, Mount Baker, and towering Black Tusk to the north—you'll feel as though you've arrived on cloud nine, indeed. All three rooms are luxuriously appointed with private entrances, hand-knotted Persian rugs on heated acid-wash floors, Craftsman or sleigh queen-size beds topped with cotton sheets and down duvets, and electric fireplaces on slate hearths. Expansive picture windows take in the scenery (but you won't see any neighbors) and French doors lead to private patios where unobstructed views of water and islands will take your breath away; binoculars are on hand for deer and eagle spotting. Stereos, satellite TVs, VCRs, robes, slippers, coffee and tea makers, and mini-fridges stocked with wine and water round out the impressive amenities. Fresh flowers grace each room, and chocolate and champagne await your arrival. The most romantic choices are the Celeste and Orion suites, located in the stylish Coach House, completed in 2003 and set beside a tranquil pond about 100 feet from the main house. Sunshine pours through skylights in the bedrooms and bathrooms, which feature luxurious Jacuzzi tubs and separate showers. Each spacious room is a private haven with state-of-the-art soundproofing and a completely secluded patio. The third room, called the Morningstar Suite, is on the lower floor on the main house, next to a lounge available to all guests. Its private bathroom is across the hall, though no one else has access to the hallway. Breakfast can be served in the main house, in your room, or on your private patio, and

might include delicious orange-cream scones, fresh fruit, and a satisfying hot dish. In the evening, gaze at the stars from the hot tub perched practically on the cliff's edge.

$$$ *MC, V; no checks; www.cloud9oceanview.com.*

CRANBERRY RIDGE BED AND BREAKFAST
◗◗◖

269 Don Ore Dr, Salt Spring Island / 250/537-4854 or 888/537-4854
This bed-and-breakfast is set on a bluff offering magnificent 180-degree views of the surrounding islands and inlets, and the imperial snowcapped mountains of the mainland. Two broad decks, one off the upper level lounge and another shared by the guest rooms, take in the magnificent scenery. The three charming and immaculate guest rooms are located on the lower level. In every room, cozy sitting areas appointed with wicker and willow furniture look out to the stunning scenery through picture windows and floor-to-ceiling sliding glass doors. Our recommendation for romance, the Twig Haven, is tucked around the corner and offers the most privacy, plus a wood-burning fireplace, a Jacuzzi tub in the bathroom, and a delightful heart-shaped bent-willow love seat. From the hand-bent willow bed you can watch the sunlight filtering through the trees to your private covered deck: the effect is like staying in a well-appointed tree house. The slightly larger, but less secluded, Country Rose has a king-size bed; a Jacuzzi tub; an electric fireplace; and wicker, rather than willow, furniture. The smaller White Wicker room has an en-suite powder room with a toilet and sink, and a private bath and shower across the hall. All rooms have added comforts, like luxurious feather beds, duvets, handmade patchwork quilts, slippers, and terry-cloth robes, and all have private entrances opening onto the expansive deck with large hot tub (although particularly from the White Wicker, views from your windows may include other guests enjoying the tub). In all of the rooms, sherry, bottled water, fresh flowers, locally made soap, and chocolates on the pillows are wonderful touches. You can also enjoy the scenery from the upper-level deck or relax in the upstairs guest lounge, with its wood-burning fireplace, modern pine furniture, and local artwork. For ultimate relaxation, book a massage in the inn's spa room. And we haven't even mentioned the delicious gourmet breakfast, which might include quiche or crepes, fruit parfaits, and freshly baked goods: this feast is delivered in baskets to your room so you can take it out to the deck, if you so desire.

$$$ *MC, V; no checks; www.cranberryridge.com.*

SALT SPRING VINEYARDS BED AND BREAKFAST
◐◐◐◖

151 Lee Rd, Salt Spring Island / 250/653-9463
Vineyards are inherently romantic, but a secluded winery on a beautiful island tops the charts—particularly when the proprietors have years of experience in designing intimate, romantic retreats and keep their rates refreshingly low. Salt Spring Vineyards, created by Jan and Bill Harkley, the former owners of River Run Cottages in Ladner, British Columbia (awarded the highest lip rating in our previous editions), combines the luxuries of romance with the seductive setting of a working winery. You can meander through lush rows of grapevines (punctuated by roses) and visit the tasting room—although your first delightful sip may come when you indulge in the carafe of wine that waits in your room upon arrival. Most of the wines, including the pinot gris and pinot noir, are made from grapes picked right here. The two lovely rooms offer tasteful, country-style decor, private baths and entrances, CD players with romantic music, neatly stowed microwaves and fridges, and cozy sitting areas where your breakfast is delivered in the morning; you can enjoy it here or out on your private deck or balcony. In the spacious Winery Room, located above the tasting room adjacent to the main house (note that the tasting room opens to visitors at noon), you'll enjoy spectacular views of the terraced vineyard and fir-covered valley from the room and its Juliet balcony. In the colorful bathroom, there's a slipper-shaped soaking tub and a showerhead set directly in the ceiling (no curtains here; the whole room becomes your shower). In the main house, the smaller Vineyard Room has a jetted two-person tub and French doors leading to a large, private outdoor deck. Guests also have access to the outdoor jetted tub nestled below a flower-covered trellis, which overlooks the vineyard. The morning meal features produce and fruit grown on site (there are 50 different fruit trees on the property), locally roasted coffee, and organic eggs from a neighboring farm—and it's all the more delightful because you can enjoy it in blissful privacy. Trust us—we have your best interests at heart when we urge you to book here at once.
$$ MC, V; checks OK; www.saltspringvineyards.com.

SKY VALLEY INN BED & BREAKFAST
◐◐◐

421 Sky Valley Rd, Salt Spring Island / 250/537-9800
Imagine you and your beloved have been invited to stay at a friend's villa in the South of France, where you can spend your days lounging by the pool; lingering over coffee and home-baked goods at the breakfast table; or poking around in the garden, admiring the dahlias and sunflowers. This central Salt Spring B&B replicates just that kind of Mediterranean ease, with trails through 11 acres of forest, two friendly dogs, and a nearby lake thrown in. Three rooms, done in a pretty French country–style, all have private baths,

duvets, feather beds, and such luxurious details as fresh flowers, robes, and handmade soaps. Each also has a private entrance opening onto an ivy-draped courtyard, home to the inn's 20-by-40-foot heated outdoor pool. The roomy Ivy Master Suite is our romantic choice, with its gas fireplace, vaulted ceiling, and mahogany four-poster king-size bed. Best of all, it has views from both sides, with access to the courtyard and to an exterior deck. The deck, with its jaw-dropping views across the Gulf Islands to the mountains of the mainland, is accessible to all guests, but chances are you'll have it to yourselves. Two smaller, though still spacious, rooms are also charming. The Wisteria Room is cozy with French toile wallpaper, reclaimed fir floors, and a queen-size bed. The Garden Room is light and airy, with a king-size bed and white oak floors; it's also the most private as it's in a separate structure from the main house, connected by a breezeway. The view-blessed dining and living rooms are warm with recycled fir floors and a big river-rock fireplace. Guests gather here at a big pine table for lavish breakfasts featuring homemade jams, and organic herbs and fruit from the garden. Wine and hors d'oeuvres are served in the courtyard each evening.
$$$ *MC, V; checks OK; www.skyvalleyinn.com.*

Romantic Restaurants

HASTINGS HOUSE
✿✿✿✿

160 Upper Ganges Rd, Ganges / 250/537-2362 or 800/661-9255
For a romantic—and very formal—evening out, the atmospheric dining room at this exclusive English country–style retreat is simply a sublime choice. An enormous Inglenook fireplace warms the living room where cocktails are served prior to dinner. In the dining area, a large stone fireplace, upholstered chairs, candlelight, and white linens provide understated luxury. In warm weather, tables on the enclosed veranda are ideal for a summer supper. Though prices are lofty, the food is nothing short of magnificent. The multicourse prix-fixe menu (you can opt for three or five courses, with four entrée choices) changes daily, relying on fresh local ingredients (many from the inn's gardens) and offering such appetizers as celeriac and prosciutto bisque with chive cream and seared spring salmon with pattypan squash and nasturtium jus. Entrées range from peppered pheasant breast with orchard pears to saffron-steamed halibut with rosemary ratatouille. Salt Spring Island lamb is almost always available, but sells out quickly each evening. The well-rounded wine list features a good selection of local and island varietals.
$$$$ *AE, MC, V; no checks; dinner every day, closed mid-Nov–mid-Mar; full bar; reservations required; www.hastingshouse.com.* &

RESTAURANT HOUSE PICCOLO
◆◆◆◆

108 Hereford Ave, Ganges / 250/537-1844
Once you've sampled House Piccolo's delicious food and charming ambience, you'll see why this intimate restaurant is reputed to be one of the region's finest. We also happen to think it's among the most romantic. Chef-owner Piccolo Lyytikainen, a member of the prestigious Chaîne des Rôtisseurs, specializes in upscale European cuisine. Set in a tiny heritage house, House Piccolo's candlelit ambience achieves romance without formality. Just nine tables, covered in ivory and blue linens, are scattered throughout two tiny connecting dining rooms, each appointed with copper kettles, antique dishes, and pretty watercolors. In summer, another six tables appear on the patio. Starters include herb-crusted beef carpaccio and a delicious prawn-and-scallop brochette. Main dishes range from charbroiled filet of beef with Gorgonzola sauce to roasted Muscovy duck breast, as well as Salt Spring Island lamb. Chocolate lovers should not miss the decadent, baked-to-order, warm chocolate timbale. All portions are beautifully presented, and the excellent wine list, with its extensive selection of both European and Vancouver Island varietals, has been judged among the best in the world by *Wine Spectator* magazine.
$$$$ MC, V; local checks only; dinner every day; full bar; reservations recommended; www.housepiccolo.com.

MAYNE, GALIANO, PENDER & SATURNA ISLANDS

ROMANTIC HIGHLIGHTS

Among the beautiful Southern Gulf Islands, Mayne, Galiano, Pender, and Saturna Islands each have their own unique romantic appeal. Mayne Island, the smallest of the group, offers serenity, the highly romantic Oceanwood Country Inn, and quiet seclusion. Galiano, which boasts many protected parks and spectacular hikes, is an excellent choice for outdoorsy couples. Pender is actually two islands—North Pender and South Pender—linked by a short bridge. On green and rural South Pender, you can explore Mount Norman, part of the new Gulf Islands National Park Reserve, and treat your honey to a night at Poets Cove Resort and Spa, the archipelago's only full-service luxury resort. The most remote island, Saturna, is blessed with plenty of parkland and is home to the well-loved Saturna Island Vineyards. Whether you visit just one or all four, traveling through these exquisite islands could be defined as romance itself.

On Mayne Island, the tiny village of Miners Bay offers a small museum, a Saturday farmers market, and a handful of shops. You can browse the stacks at quiet **Miners Bay Books** (478 Village Bay Rd; 250/539-3112), stock up on supplies at the small grocery stores, or visit the **Sunny Mayne Bakery Café** (472 Village Bay Rd; 250/539-2323); in summer, call ahead and they'll pack your lunch. With picnic in hand, you're ready to explore the island's beautiful trails. For vigorous exercise, hike up Mount Parke to reach Mayne's highest point; the trail winds uphill for about an hour beneath leafy foliage before reaching a bluff with views of ferries crossing Active Pass. This lovely spot makes an excellent place to reward yourselves with your picnic. Afterwards, you can stop for a snack at the **Morningstar Café** (574 Fernhill Rd; 250/539-5987) near the park entrance; be sure to check out the two arts and crafts galleries next to the cafe. For a more leisurely stroll, visit **Marine Heritage Park** (off Bennett Bay Rd). A wide quarter-mile trail leads to Campbell Point, where you might spot purple starfish and exotic jellyfish in the tide pools and watch otters and seals at play. If all you want to do is roll out of bed and then roll out the picnic blanket, drive to Georgina Point Heritage Park (open every day, 9am–dusk). Lush grass surrounds the spectacular 1885 landmark lighthouse, and the wooden gazebo is a popular spot for weddings. Another romantic spot is the Japanese Garden at Dinner Bay Park, slightly more than half a mile (1 km) south of the Village Bay ferry terminal. Built by local volunteers to commemorate the island's early Japanese settlers, this pretty acre has a peaceful, contemplative air. For a romantic half- or full-day trip on a crewed 33-foot sailboat (lunch included), contact **Island Charters** (250/539-5040). Or if you prefer, do the paddling yourself with **Mayne Island Kayak, Canoe and Bicycle Rentals** (Miners Bay; 250/539-5599; www.maynekayak.com), or **Blue Vista Kayaking and Cycling** (250/539-2463 or 877/535-2424; www.bluevista resort.com). Both outfits offer kayaking instruction and tours; they also rent mountain bikes. A cycling tour of the island takes about five hours; there are some steep hills, but the small size and minimal traffic make Mayne a good bet for cyclists.

After your outdoor fun, relax on the deck of the historic **Springwater Lodge** (400 Fernhill Rd; 250/539-5521) in Miners Bay, which has been in continuous operation since 1892. The interior is well worn and the pub fare is standard, but the views from the deck at sunset are spellbinding.

Considering it's the closest of the Southern Gulf Islands to Vancouver (1 hour via the Tsawwassen ferry), Galiano Island feels surprisingly wild. Renowned for its protected land and well-maintained parks, this is an excellent place to enjoy pristine island beauty in natural surroundings. The jewel in this island crown is the eminently kiss-worthy **Montague Harbour** (5 miles/8 km west of ferry dock at Sturdies Bay), on the island's west side, a lovely, sheltered bay with glorious sunset views, beaches, camping areas, and picnic tables. For an artful afternoon, take a self-guided tour of island art studios, using the locally available map and watching for the numbered signs along the road. Or, for a seafaring adventure, book an afternoon cruise on a 43-foot sailboat sloop, the **Odyssey II** (250/539-5667 or 800/970-7464; departs Montague Marina; $45 per person), operated by the friendly hosts of the Bellhouse Inn (see Romantic Lodgings). No matter what other activities may tempt you, however, our highest recommendation is the island's romantic, secluded walks.

All the hikes we recommend on Galiano are easy to find with the help of a local map, readily available when you arrive on the island. For the most spectacular views, hike up **Mount Galiano** (trailhead off Phillimore Point Rd). The hour-long climb gets steep in some places, but trust us, it's worth it. Kisses will be in order as you stand beneath the rare Garry oak trees at the summit and enjoy spectacular views of Navy Channel. Hike the trail along Bodega Ridge and you'll find Lovers Leap View Point—aptly named, we think, since the views over Trincomali Channel to Salt Spring Island are enough to make anyone jump into the arms of their love. If a long walk sounds like too much, you can still enjoy exquisite views by visiting **Bluffs Park** with a beach blanket and delicious lunch in tow. For picnic provisions, shop for specialty foods and organic goods at **Daystar Market** (Georgeson Bay Rd; 250/539-2505); you'll find pastries, espresso, and a full lunch menu at the adjacent, vegetarian-friendly cafe. Otherwise, you can find both hearty pub food and local color at the **Hummingbird Pub** (Sturdies Bay and Georgeson Bay Rds; 250/539-5472), fresh baked breads and pastries at the **Trincomali, Bakery, Deli & Bistro** (2540 Sturdies Bay Rd; 250/539-2004), or a funky diner atmosphere and live entertainment at the **Grand Central Emporium** (2470 Sturdies Bay Rd; 250/539-9885).

North and South Pender Islands are rich in beaches. **Mortimer Spit** (at the western tip of South Pender) and **Gowlland Point Beach** (at end of Gowlland Point Rd on South Pender) are among 30 public ocean-access points on the two islands.

To take advantage of the fabled Gulf Island view scape, the trails on **Mount Norman** (accessible from Ainslie Rd or Canal Rd on South Pender), part of the Gulf Islands National Park Reserve, are steep but rewarding. The gentle terrain of South Pender is particularly appealing for cyclists; rent bikes at **Otter Bay Marina** (2311 MacKinnon Rd; 250/629-3579) on North Pender. Your best bets for kiss-worthy dining are both at South Pender's **Poets Cove Resort and Spa** (see Romantic Restaurants). Choose from elegant West Coast cuisine at Aurora Restaurant, or high-end casual fare at Syrens Lounge.

Remote and hard to get to, Saturna Island offers the ultimate get-away-from-it-all experience. One of the largest of the Southern Gulf Islands, Saturna is also the least populated. Crowds are simply not part of the picture here—nor are banks, cash machines, or drug stores, so come prepared. Most of the island is now part of the Gulf Islands National Park Reserve, so outdoor options abound. Embark on a floating adventure with **Saturna Sea Kayaking** (250/539-5553; www.gulfislands.com/saturnaseakayaking), or bring a bike and explore; although roads are steep and many are unpaved, bikers rarely run into traffic. For beach walking, you couldn't ask for more than the pristine shoreline of **Winter Cove Park** (near the junction of Winter Cove Rd and East Point Rd). Civilization has made it to the island in the form of the delightful **Saturna Island Vineyards** (8 Quarry Trail; 250/539-3521 or 877/918-3388; www.saturnavineyards.com; open daily May–Oct, by appointment the rest of the year), on the island's southern shore, with its charming tasting room, wine shop, and bistro. The bistro terrace (open for lunch daily May–Oct), with its Mediterranean-influenced fare and ocean and vineyard views, is a prime spot for a romantic lunch. For dinner, the most kiss-worthy option is the restaurant at the **Saturna Lodge** (see Romantic Restaurants). Otherwise, dining options are limited.

While the **Lighthouse Pub** (102 East Point Rd; 250/539-5725; lunch, dinner every day) will do in a pinch, it's not exactly romantic. Another option is the wholesome fare served at **Saturna's Café** (101 Narvaez Bay Rd; 250/539-2936; breakfast, lunch Wed–Sun May–Oct and Wed, Fri–Sun Nov–Apr; dinner Wed–Sat May–Oct and Wed, Fri–Sat Nov–Apr) tucked inside the general store.

Access & Information

BC Ferries (250/386-3431 or 888/223-3779; www.bcferries.com) offers daily trips to the islands. Mayne (ferry terminal at Village Bay), Galiano (ferry terminal at Sturdies Bay), and Pender (ferry terminal at Otter Bay) can be accessed from the Tsawwassen ferry terminal on the mainland, 22 miles (35 km) south of Vancouver. Tsawwassen is located near the Canada/U.S. border and is only about a two-hour drive from Seattle when there is no traffic at the border crossing; with traffic, the trip can take considerably longer. Advance reservations are recommended (and can be made at no additional charge) when traveling between the British Columbia mainland and the Southern Gulf Islands. From Tsawwassen, access to remote Saturna (ferry terminal at Lyall Harbour) is via a transfer at Mayne Island. From Vancouver Island, BC Ferries serves all four islands from the Swartz Bay ferry terminal, located north of Victoria.

Tourism Vancouver Island (335 Wesley St, Ste 203, Nanaimo; 250/754-3500; www.islands.bc.ca) offers information on touring the Gulf Islands. For more information on Galiano, you can also contact the **Galiano Chamber of Commerce Travel Info Centre** (250/539-2233 or 866/539-2233; www.galianoisland.com). You can view maps of Mayne Island and find other helpful information at the **Mayne Island Chamber of Commerce** Web site (www.mayneislandchamber.ca). The **Pender Island Visitor Info Centre**

(250/629-6541; www.penderisland.info) has information about Pender. Island hopping is possible, but ferry schedules are complex and sailing times do not always match up well. One alternative for passenger-only interisland travel is the **Gulf Islands Water Taxi** (250/537-2510; www.saltspring.com/watertaxi). On summer weekends, it can be less stressful and less expensive to leave the car at home; most inns and B&Bs offer ferry pickup. Bring your own bike or rent one; the islands (with the exception of busy Salt Spring) are wonderful (if hilly) for cycling.

Romantic Lodgings

THE BELLHOUSE INN
♦♦◖

29 Farmhouse Rd, Galiano Island / 250/539-5667 or 800/970-7464
The drive to get here winds past beautiful meadows dotted with grazing sheep, but once you arrive at this turn-of-the-20th-century farmhouse, it's the waterfront view that will take your breath away. With all the elements of the quintessential B&B retreat—a historic home with a fascinating history, excellent hosts who make you feel welcome at once, and absolutely delicious breakfasts—the Bellhouse Inn offers a peaceful setting perfect for focusing on each other. Located on the southern tip of Galiano Island, about a 10-minute drive from the ferry dock, the house is surrounded by beautiful fruit trees, manicured lawns, and 5 wooded acres for you to explore. Inside, the decor feels comfortably worn in and authentic; the common-area fireplace burns real wood (one of the two resident dogs may be curled up in front of it), bookshelves are filled with intriguing titles, and you can spot passing whales through the big picture window. Of the three phone- and TV-free guest rooms on the second floor, our romantic favorite is the Kingfisher. It's the most peaceful and private as it doesn't share walls with the other rooms and also has the best view: French doors open to a private balcony, where a weeping willow and a flowering crab apple tree frame the view of sparkling water. The bathroom features a Jacuzzi tub (although the well-worn tub needs replacing). There are two other smaller rooms on the second floor. These include the Orca—done in shades of taupe and green, with a private bathroom across the hall—and the adorable Eagle, with pretty yellow walls and peekaboo ocean views from the deck. A four-course breakfast is served each morning at an antique table in the dining room, or outside on the deck, weather permitting. The feast includes local fruit and creamy yogurt, delicious scones served with homemade jam, and a hot dish such as a breakfast wrap filled with scrambled eggs and topped with hollandaise. Bellhouse Park, just next door, is a lovely place to stroll hand in hand.
$$–$$$ *MC, V; Canadian checks only; www.bellhouseinn.com.*

GALIANO INN AND SPA
✪✪✪✪

134 Madrona Dr, Galiano Island / 250/539-3388 or 877/530-3939
We don't think it's an overstatement to say that while Galiano Island has
always been a beautiful spot, this boutique hotel and spa, opened in 2001,
has transformed it into a sublime romantic destination. Housed in two
Northwest-shingled buildings surrounded by flower gardens and perched
at the edge of the water, the inn is filled with warm decor that evokes the
Mediterranean—from hand-troweled yellow walls and imported floor tiles
to grand wrought-iron chandeliers. The spacious reception area—which
doubles as an inviting lounge—welcomes you with high ceilings, a blazing
fire in the impressive stone fireplace, and soft leather couches. Through
the French doors, you can glimpse the lush lawn stretching to the water's
edge. Wood-burning fireplaces, sitting areas, and private balconies or patios
with exquisite waterfront views grace every spacious room, and all feature
luxurious down comforters and Italian-tiled bathrooms with Jacuzzi or
soaking tubs. Amenities throughout include minibars, CD players, robes,
and coffee and tea makers, but, in keeping with the peaceful ambience, no
TVs. Choosing the most romantic accommodation might be difficult; Oceanfront King rooms offer the most space, with king-size beds and inviting
sofas; the Oceanfront Queens have queen-size wrought-iron canopy-style
beds or wooden sleigh beds and wingback armchairs in front of the fireplaces. No matter which you choose, you'll enjoy the lovely views of Active
Pass and Mount Baker from your room, as well as from the dining room,
where the complimentary breakfast is served. Supreme relaxation awaits
at the on-site Madrona del Mar spa, where you can enjoy a massage for two
in an ocean-side cabana or soak your cares away in a sea mineral flotation
bath. Other delights here include a seaside hot tub, a meditation garden,
the Oceanfront Patio Grill (open summer only) for alfresco lunches on the
water; and the elegant restaurant Atrevida (see Romantic Restaurants).
$$$ *MC, V; checks OK for deposit; closed Nov–Mar; www.galianoinn.com.*

OCEANWOOD COUNTRY INN
✪✪✪✪

630 Dinner Bay Rd, Mayne Island / 250/539-5074
Enveloped by lush gardens, towering trees, and a sweeping view of Navy
Channel, this large Tudor home holds 12 magnificent guest rooms, extremely
cozy and inviting common areas, and an elegant restaurant with superlative
views. All rooms except the Daffodil have water views; eight have private
decks and fireplaces as well as whirlpool or deep soaking tubs. We don't
have space to list all our favorites, but the Lavender Room is certainly one; it
boasts two plushly carpeted levels, a queen-size canopy bed with handsome
blue-striped fabric, a deep soaking tub facing a wood-burning fireplace and
window, and a private deck overlooking the water. The light, airy Fern Room

is equally attractive, with a pretty yellow-and-green color scheme and similarly deluxe features. The largest room is the top-floor Wisteria Room: it has all the amenities, including a Japanese soaking tub on its private deck, but lacks some coziness due to the massive square footage. Of the smaller rooms, our favorites are the Ivy Room, with its jetted tub in a lovely tiled bathroom and a pale green, white, and pink color scheme; and the Rose Room, which has its own rustic wooden balcony, striped pink-and-white satin love seat, and white wicker bed. Relax in the garden room, with its terra-cotta–tiled floor and floral tapestry chairs—afternoon tea is served here or in the library. A double-sided fireplace warms both rooms. If weather permits, soak in the outdoor hot tub or wander through the herb and flower gardens. The elegant downstairs dining room (see Romantic Restaurants) serves breakfast to guests only and dinner by reservation. The morning meal is luxurious and might include freshly squeezed juice, perfectly flaky croissants, seasonal fruit, and oat pancakes with berry compote and syrup. Our earnest recommendation is that you pack your bags this minute and take advantage of what this first-class inn has to offer.

$$$–$$$$ *MC, V; Canadian checks only; closed Nov–mid-Mar; www.ocean wood.com.*

POETS COVE RESORT & SPA
❀❀❀❀

9801 Spalding Rd, South Pender Island / 250/629-2100 or 888/512-7638
This pretty, wooded cove near the Gulf Islands National Park Reserve has long been the locals' favorite spot to propose. Poets Cove Resort & Spa, opened here in 2004 as one of the biggest developments yet on the Gulf Islands, has what it takes to inspire, if not a proposal, at least a highly romantic getaway. The nautical-themed main lodge is home to Aurora Restaurant (see Romantic Restaurants), the chic Syrens Lounge, and the serene Susurrus Spa, where a lit waterfall tumbles over a steam grotto. We recommend the spa's Romantic Interlude treatment, which starts with time alone together in the grotto, followed by a fireside massage for two. The lodge's 22 guest rooms all have ocean and sunset views, gas fireplaces, king-size or twin-size beds, lush duvets, and large private balconies. Bathrooms are a treat, with heated tile floors and shutters next to the soaker tub so you can take in the sea view while you bathe. Even the sensuously soft robes are a cut above. The two- and three-bedroom Arts and Crafts–style cottages, on the hillside above the lodge, are beautifully finished with vaulted ceilings, wood-burning fireplaces, and sweeping water views from large heated decks; some have private hot tubs. A well-equipped galley kitchen means you may never have to leave the cottage, especially if you order the Raw Menu Service: chef-prepped fixings for a romantic meal are delivered to your door, so you can woo your beloved with your culinary talents without the prep or the cleanup. (Other groceries can be delivered, too, but conventional room

service isn't available.) Slightly older, two- and three-bedroom villas at the top of the property have kitchens and more space, but lack the full-on views and architectural charm of the cottages. Also on site, a marine center for resort guests and visiting yachtees has an outdoor pool, a hot tub, and a market for high-end provisions; another pool, a tennis court, and a fitness center for resort guests opened in 2005. An activity center offers kayaking, sailing, fishing charters, whale watching, mountain biking, guided hiking, vineyard trips, scuba lessons and more; staff here can also direct you to the best local kissing spots. Getting to Poets Cove can be an adventure in itself, whether you seaplane directly to the pier, hop a water taxi from Sidney on Vancouver Island, or bring your car on BC Ferries. If you do drive, call for directions. This hideaway is, quite genuinely, hidden away.
$$$$ *AE, MC, V; checks OK; www.poetscove.com.* ♿

SATURNA LODGE
⬡⬡

130 Payne Rd, Saturna Island / 250/539-2254 or 888/539-8800
This French-style country inn overlooking Boot Cove offers easy access to the ferry dock, and houses Saturna's only spot for a kiss-worthy evening meal. Seven guest rooms with wine-inspired names are equipped with simple pleasures; most offer queen-size beds, down quilts, pine furnishings, private bathrooms, and views of either the cove or surrounding farmland. Sauterne, named for the sweet white wine, is considered the honeymoon suite; its private balcony affords views of the water, and the private bath holds a soaking tub. Sunny Aligot, reminiscent of vintages from the golden coast of Burgundy, features a four-poster queen-size bed and an old-fashioned claw-foot tub with commode sink in its private bath. Tokay's dormer ceilings, country wallpaper, and lovely view of Boot Cove make it a cozy option, as well. Avoid Ambrosia (which has two twin-size beds) and Napa; they are usually rented together to groups or families and share detached bathrooms down the hall. After a full day spent exploring the island (the lodge has bikes on hand if you're in an energetic mood), relax in the hot tub overlooking the gardens. Mornings begin with a complimentary full breakfast for two, served in the restaurant, on the patio, or, if you're staying in Sauterne or Riesling, on your own private patio. Evenings here are a treat: diners often boat in from other islands to take advantage of the daily three-course prix-fixe menu that might include a starter of Salt Spring Island mussels, main of roast pork tenderloin, and Frangelico tiramisù for dessert. Windows wrap around the simple, comforting dining room; a crackling fire makes it even more inviting on a cool evening. On warm evenings, dine outside on the deck overlooking the bay.
$$–$$$ *MC, V; Canadian checks only; closed Jan–mid-March; www. saturna.ca.*

Romantic Restaurants

ATREVIDA
◐◐◐◖

134 Madrona Dr (Galiano Inn and Spa), Galiano Island / 250/539-3388 or 877/530-3939

Every seat in this glass-enclosed restaurant offers spectacular water views and memorable romantic ambience. Sit at one of the tables covered with white linen and set with silver, and listen to the jazz piano or classical guitar that is played on weekends. A seasonally changing menu features locally raised, often organic, fish, meat, and produce. You can start with Mayne Island organic greens, Salt Spring Island goat cheese on a warm cedar plank, or Galiano Island steamed scallops. Mains might be beef tenderloin with rosemary, panko-crusted halibut, or sandalwood-smoked spring salmon. Vegetarians are well served with such creative entrées as quinoa, shiitake, and pine nut–stuffed tomatoes or sun-dried tomato and lemon-pesto shrimp penne. With so few fine dining options on the island, this combination is a considerable draw. The wine list offers a tempting array of mostly New World choices, including a good selection of British Columbia wines. In the summer months, an outdoor patio doubles as the inn's casual lunch spot, so when the sun shines you can enjoy an alfresco lunch on the water.

$$$$ MC, V; no checks; lunch every day (in summer); dinner every day; closed Nov–Mar; full bar; reservations recommended; www.galianoinn. com.

AURORA RESTAURANT AT POETS COVE RESORT & SPA
◐◐◐◐

9801 Spalding Rd, South Pender Island / 250/629-2100 or 888/512-7638

Book a window seat or a table on the terrace for a front row view of the cove's glorious sunset. The evening seascape, over yachts at harbor and the wooded hills across the inlet, is enough to set a romantic mood, but it doesn't stop there. Inside, there's plenty of elbow room between the solid, undraped wooden tables; the lighting is soft, service is friendly and efficient, and the big room feels calm, despite the open kitchen. In winter, when the sun sets long before dinner time, you might forgo the window seat for one of the intimate curved banquettes by the fireplace. Chef Martin DeBoard's locally sourced fare is quite luscious. A Gulf Islands–style bouillabaisse is rich with scallops, mussels, and salmon in a fennel and saffron broth; the seafood cakes are small but flavorful. Many of the mains come as "duos," offering two different treatments of one entrée. A duo of Gulf Island lamb, for example, arrives with cheese and garlic–stuffed sirloin and a balsamic vinegar–marinated tenderloin; the Cowichan Valley duck duo includes both breast and confit. The wine list is short but interesting, ranging from local and affordable to outrageously splashy. Desserts, including ice cream, are all

made in house. The chocolate caramel frozen mousse or apple and almond tart nicely round out a sensuous meal. For lunch, or a more casual dinner, the resort's Syrens Lounge offers burgers, pasta, fish-and-chips, and sea views in a chic, postmodern pub.
$$$–$$$$ *AE, MC, V; checks OK; breakfast, dinner every day (Aurora Restaurant), lunch, dinner every day, some closures in winter (Syrens Lounge); full bar; reservations recommended; www.poetscove.com.* &

OCEANWOOD COUNTRY INN
◆◆◆◆

630 Dinner Bay Rd, Mayne Island / 250/539-5074
With its welcoming atmosphere, incredibly fresh ingredients, beautiful food presentation, and stunning views of the terraced gardens and the glittering Navy Channel, this restaurant captures the finest aspects of the island experience. Housed on the ground level of the impeccable Oceanwood Country Inn (see Romantic Lodgings), the warm, intimate dining room features pale yellow walls and decor in a cozy fern-pattern fabric. Tastefully chosen background music sets the mood, and an attractive bar gleams in the corner. Jonathan Chilvers, the proprietor, is a knowledgeable and witty host—be sure to ask for his wine recommendations. Service is exemplary, and the food is extraordinary from start to finish. The daily four-course menus are good examples of regional fare, making the most of such fresh, local products as wild salmon and island-raised lamb. Start with some delicious homemade bread, which might include rosemary-almond and garden herb whole wheat (made with herbs snipped from the garden outside). The prix-fixe menu might include such delicacies as roasted beet soup with horseradish cream, cornmeal-crusted oysters with red pepper couscous, a refreshing course of blackberry-ginger sorbet, and a tender herb-crusted halibut or Mayne Island leg of lamb. A creative, delicious dessert, such as white chocolate mousse tartlets with house-made blackberry ice cream, completes the experience. The restaurant's wine list features excellent vintages from British Columbia.
$$$$ *MC, V; Canadian checks only; dinner every day; closed Nov–Mar; full bar; reservations required; www.oceanwood.com.*

OKANAGAN VALLEY

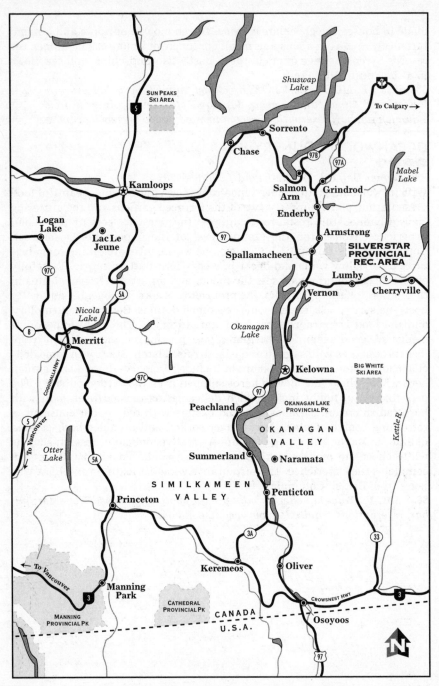

♡ OKANAGAN VALLEY

First-time visitors to this sun-drenched, semi-arid valley in British Columbia's southern interior, four hours east of Vancouver by car, may be surprised by the array of landscapes here, which range from the verdant green pastures near Vernon at the north end to prickly pear cacti and rattlesnakes in the southern desert near the U.S. border. Just as surprising is the variety of cultural landscapes on offer—everything from fruit stands and tiny, rustic wineries on rural back roads to the urbane buzz of chic eateries and gallery vernissages in Kelowna's burgeoning arts district. Kelowna (population approximately 150,000 including outlying areas) is the largest city in the Okanagan, and its location, midway between Penticton in the south and Vernon in the north, makes it a convenient base for exploring the valley.

Okanagan Lake, the crown jewel in a necklace of lakes extending in a north-south axis from Vernon to Osoyoos, is a narrow fjord approximately 79 miles (128 km) long, carved by Pleistocene-era glaciers. Its depth prevents it from freezing in most winters, and its moderating influence and expanse has made the valley a mecca for agriculture, tourism, and residential development, all of which manage to cohabit in relative harmony in a narrow valley corridor bounded by rugged, sparsely populated landscape to the east and west. Most valley towns are on the lake, making a visit to the beach and a cool dip a mandatory (and refreshing) part of the Okanagan summer experience.

When you combine the languor of summer heat with views of lush orchards and vineyards, sparkling lake waters, and a bounty of regional food and wine, romance is never far away. July brings 85 degree F (35 degree C) temperatures. Annual wine festivals in January, May, August, and October are good times to visit for romantic food and wine. Quieter times are in June or September, when the weather—and the tourist traffic—is more moderate. If you like to combine sports with romance, you'll be happy to know that golf courses abound, and three major ski resorts—Apex near Penticton, Big White close to Kelowna, and Silver Star outside of Vernon—offer winter days of skiing, boarding, or snowshoeing, followed by cozy nights curled up in front of a chalet's roaring fire. (For more on ski resorts, see Access and Information.) You can also spend some time searching for the Okanagan's most famous resident, the lake monster Ogopogo—although we personally don't believe the rumor that wine tasters have a habit of seeing the mysterious creature more frequently than other folk.

KELOWNA & REGION

ROMANTIC HIGHLIGHTS

Kelowna's pristine landscapes and agricultural roots are still very much in evidence, and a 10-minute drive in any direction can take you either to immaculately cultivated orchards and vineyards, or to a relatively untouched natural area populated by ancient bunchgrasses, ponderosa pines, and California quail. Despite the ubiquitous strip malls and big-box outlets lurking unattractively on the outskirts of Kelowna, the downtown area along the lakeshore remains vibrant and diverse, with a pleasing mix of accommodations, restaurants, historic buildings, galleries, and independent retail shops.

With Kelowna serving as the hub, the entire Okanagan and Similkameen Valleys have become a formidable wine destination—nearly 60 wineries dot the map between Vernon and the U.S. border. (Refer to our Romantic Wineries section for a selective list of the most kiss-worthy destinations.) With so much to see, a romantic wine tour can easily disintegrate into a frazzled marathon. Our advice: start early and pick just a few wineries to visit each day.

A leisurely pace will get you from one end of the valley to the other— Vernon to Osoyoos—in less than three hours, not including time spent touring and tasting. Count on at least a one-hour drive between Penticton and Kelowna or between Penticton and Osoyoos.

Major roads like Highway 97 are well marked with signs for individual wineries, but finding your way on some of the back roads can be tricky. Be sure to pick up the latest **BC Wine Institute touring guide**, which includes maps and information, at any tourism office; copies of the guide can also be ordered by contacting the **Thompson Okanagan Tourism Association** (800/567-2275; www.totabc.com) or the **British Columbia Wine Institute** (800/661-2294; www.winebc.com). The guide also lists winery hours; most larger wineries are open year-round, but hours for smaller wineries will vary with the seasons, so call ahead.

A good place to start your tour is the **Wine Museum** (1304 Ellis St,

Kelowna; 250/868-0441), located within the historic Laurel Packinghouse in Kelowna. The museum's helpful staff also manage a well-stocked wine boutique, often the site of special events.

Kelowna alone has six wineries, but a true wine tour will take you to towns south of Kelowna along Highway 97. Driving 25 minutes south will get you to wineries in the towns of Westbank (home of scenic favorites Quails' Gate and Mission Hill), Peachland, and Summerland. Farther south on Highway 97, you'll encounter the towns of Penticton, Naramata, Okanagan Falls, Oliver, and Osoyoos—all of which boast romantic wineries. Approaching Oliver, you'll see a long, sloping benchland the locals refer to as the "Golden Mile." It is home to so many vineyards and wineries that the town of Oliver has declared itself "the Wine Capital of Canada."

For the ultimate in pampered wine touring, turn over all of the driving and details to the professionals. **Okanagan Wine Country Tours** (1310 Water St, Kelowna; 250/868-9463 or 866/689-9463; www.okwinetours.com) offers half-day, full-day, and overnight tours with optional vineyard lunches or dinners. Rates start at $40 per person for a three-hour afternoon tour. **Wildflower Trails and Wine Tours** (1116–1765 Leckie Rd, Kelowna; 250/979-1211 or 866/979-1211; www.wildflowersandwine.com) specializes in half- and full-day tours, which combine winery visits with easy to moderate hikes in the area's unique landscape. Other customized touring options include visits to artisan cheesemakers, orchards, boutiques, and art galleries. Rates start at $39 per person for a two-hour excursion.

A more casual approach might be to explore **Kelowna's cultural district** (www.kelownasculturaldistrict.com), where you can spend the better part of a day strolling, window shopping, and taking in performances and exhibitions. One good romantic bet is strolling the lakeside pathways from the floating bridge north to the edge of **Knox Mountain Park** (north end of Ellis St; about 1¼ miles/2 km from downtown)—it makes for a perfect after-dinner walk. In warm weather, bring a picnic lunch to the park itself and explore to your hearts' content. The artsy **Bohemian Bagel Cafe** (363 Bernard Ave; 250/862-3517), which has some of Kelowna's best sandwiches, is a great place to gather a picnic. Trails and a picnic area at the top of the park's access road offer spectacular views. Another local favorite is the 4¼-mile (7-km) **Mission Creek Greenway** (www.greenway.kelowna.bc.ca), a tree-lined path on the banks of Mission Creek. In fall, the creek's waters come alive with the bright red hues of spawning kokanee salmon. An additional 6 miles (9 km) of trail through dramatic canyon landscapes was completed in 2005—ideal for a leisurely bicycle ride and picnic.

There are also plenty of romantic gardens in Kelowna. **Elysium Gardens** (2834 Belgo Rd; 250/491-1368; www.elysiumgardens.com) is a 3-acre perennial garden containing more than 1,000 plant varieties. It's open to the public from April to October ($5 admission), but it's also a popular spot for weddings, and if a ceremony is in progress, that section of the garden is closed to the public. Don't miss the **Kasugai Garden**, a traditional Japanese garden built in tribute to Kelowna's sister city, Kasugai, Japan. The tiny, enclosed garden is tucked in behind city hall, with entrances off both Water Street and Queensway Avenue. It's a peaceful, lovely spot for a romantic meander at any time of year. The 2.4 acre **Guisachan Heritage Park** (1060 Cameron Ave) is a gracious tribute to its former owners, the Earl and Countess of Aberdeen, and the luxuriant gardens and restored manor house provide scenic surroundings for picnics, weddings, and special events such as an Annual Garden Show in early July.

The Okanagan Valley's romance is also wonderfully captured in the work of the many talented artisans and artists who reside here. **The Okanagan Cultural Corridor guide** (available at www.okanaganculturalcorridor.com or various local outlets) directs you to dozens of studios, galleries, performances, and cultural attractions where you can partake of authentic regional culture.

Access & Information

Kelowna is located on Highway 97; most visitors travel to the region by car. From the Trans-Canada Highway (Hwy 1), you can enter the Okanagan Valley from the east via Highway 97 at Sicamous, or from the west via Highway 3 (the "Hope Princeton Highway"), or via Highway 5 (the Coquihalla) and Highway 97C (the Coquihalla "Connector"). The region is also well served by Air Canada Jazz (888/247-2262; www.aircanada.ca), Central Mountain Air (888/865-8585; www.flycma.com), Horizon Air (800/547-9308; www.horizonair.com), Regional 1 (888/802-1010; www.regional1.ca), and WestJet (800/538-5696; www.westjet.com) at the **Kelowna International Airport** (250/765-5125).

If you're traveling by car in the Kelowna area, you'll encounter the Okanagan Lake Bridge, the longest (⅞ mile) floating bridge in North America. It is the sole link from downtown Kelowna to the west side of Okanagan Lake and was built in 1958 to replace a ferry service. Given the traffic that now clogs the three-lane crossing, some might think that the ferries weren't so bad after all. However, if you avoid peak summer hours (and Friday afternoons on holiday weekends), you should be fine.

For information on wineries and other activities in Kelowna, contact the **British Columbia Wine Institute** (1737 Pandosy St, Kelowna; 800/661-2294; www.winebc.com), **Thompson Okanagan Tourism** (1332 Water St, Kelowna; 800/567-2275; www.totabc.com), or **Tourism Kelowna** (544 Harvey Ave, Kelowna; 800/663-4345; www.tourismkelowna.com).

If skiing is on your agenda, you can contact the ski resorts directly. Less than an hour's drive southeast of Kelowna, **Big White Ski Resort** (Big White Rd, 14 miles/23 km east of Hwy 33; 800/663-2772; www.bigwhite.com)

boasts the highest elevation of any winter resort in British Columbia (5,760 feet/1,755 m), offering 2,700 feet (810 m) of vertical drop, 2,565 acres of patrolled terrain, and a multi-million dollar expansion in 2004 that added two chair lifts, six runs, a state-of-the-art ski and snowboard terrain park, an on-mountain day lodge, and more accommodations. Near Vernon, **Silver Star Mountain Resort** (Silver Star Rd, east of Hwy 97; 250/542-0224 or 800/663-4431; www.skisilverstar.com) is the main draw for winter recreation in the north Okanagan Valley, offering 2,500 (762 m) feet of vertical drop, 2,725 acres of skiable terrain, 10 lifts, and 50 miles (80 km) of forested trails for cross-country skiers and snowshoers. **Apex Mountain Resort** is 21 miles (33 km) west of Penticton (on Green Mountain Rd; 250/292-8222 or 877/777-2739; www.apexresort.com). With 67 named runs, including a series of black-diamond powder chutes on the slopes below Beaconsfield Mountain (elevation 7,187 feet/2,178 m), Apex more than holds its own. It has 2,000 feet (600 m) of vertical drop, 1,112 acres of skiable terrain, and five lifts.

Romantic Wineries

CEDARCREEK ESTATE WINERY
◑◑◑

5445 Lakeshore Rd, Kelowna / 250/764-8866 or 800/730-9463
CedarCreek Estate Winery, like the vines that surround it, clings perilously to the steep slopes of the historic Okanagan Mission District some 7½ miles (12 km) south of downtown Kelowna. Stunning vineyard views and immaculately kept gardens make a scenic setting for the Mediterranean-style boutique and tasting room; after your tasting, you can enjoy a tapas lunch at the Vineyard Terrace. The Platinum Reserve and Estate Select chardonnays and pinot noirs have won many awards. Look also for some excellent dessert wines, including ice wine. A tasting room and deli at the winery's Greata Ranch vineyard, between Summerland and Peachland, offers a second location for the CedarCreek experience. Gourmet lunch baskets are available, and an inviting terrace with a lake view creates the perfect setting for a casual, sun-kissed lunch.
10am–6pm every day (May–Oct), 11am–5pm (Nov–Apr); www.cedarcreek. bc.ca.

GRAY MONK ESTATE WINERY
◑◑◔

1055 Camp Rd, Okanagan Centre / 250/766-3168 or 800/663-4205
The Gray Monk winery clings to the hillside in the center of its spectacular, steep-sloped vineyards, and this prime location high above Okanagan Lake is proudly designated as an official Ogopogo spotting site. While the name

Ogopogo actually comes from a cheap burlesque ditty, the mythology of the "lake demon" was widely accepted among the Okanagan First Nations. Gray Monk is perhaps best known for its Alsatian-style Gewürztraminer, but other good bets include a fine pinot gris and an excellent un-wooded chardonnay. The winery also makes a blended white it calls Latitude 50, which celebrates its location 25 minutes north of downtown Kelowna. The Heiss family's famous hospitality extends throughout the year for events and special tastings; between April and October, the Grapevine Patio Grill, with its incredible vista of lake and vineyards, is a perfect setting for a romantic sunset dinner.
10am–5pm every day (Apr–Oct) with extended hours in July–Aug, 11am–5pm Mon–Sat (Nov–Mar), noon–4pm Sun (Nov–Dec only); www.graymonk.com.

HAWTHORNE MOUNTAIN VINEYARDS
⬢⬢⬢

Green Lake Rd, Okanagan Falls / 250/497-8267
A picture-perfect patio setting and panoramic views are your first rewards at the end of the winding road leading to this winery from the main highway. The secluded setting and Old West charm of the buildings will make you feel as if you have traveled back in time. Inside the tasting room, more rewards await in the form of bottles of fruit-juicy Gewürztraminer, merlot, cabernet sauvignon, and a first-rate sparkler, the SYL Brut (SYL is the acronym for "See Ya Later," a local moniker for the ranch that once occupied the site). Assemble your lunch from the deli case in the wine shop, buy a bottle of your favorite wine, and then head out to the patio or one of the many walking trails on site for a truly romantic wine-country picnic.
9am–5pm every day; www.hmvineyard.com.

MISSION HILL FAMILY ESTATE
⬢⬢⬢⬢

1730 Mission Hill Rd, Westbank / 250/768-6448
The sheer architectural scale of Mission Hill, with its homage to European grandeur, will take your breath away. The winery dates back to 1981, but the real story began in 1992 with the arrival of winemaker John Simes, who came from New Zealand with the goal of putting Mission Hill wines on the world wine map. Countless awards later, he has done just that. Furthermore, Mission Hill has just completed a $32 million expansion, complete with a terrace restaurant and a 12-story bell tower that looks out over the entire valley. After your tour (the hushed and intimately lit barrel cellar is a good spot to get close), be sure to visit the elegantly appointed tasting room. Best bets include the chardonnay, merlot/cabernet, pinot noir, and pinot gris; specialties such as viognier and shiraz are also worth trying. To celebrate a special occasion, linger over lunch on the outdoor dining terrace or take

a private tour followed by a culinary workshop led by winery chef Michael Allemeier and come away with a new appreciation for food, wine, and each other.

10am–5pm every day; www.missionhillwinery.com.

NK'MIP CELLARS WINERY
❍❍❍
1400 Rancher Creek Rd, Osoyoos / 250/495-2985 or 800/665-2667
At the eastern edge of Osoyoos, Highway 3 begins its dramatic sweep up Anarchist Mountain, and here, situated on a spectacular bench overlooking the shores of Osoyoos Lake, you'll find Nk'mip (pronounced in-ka-meep) Cellars Winery and the Nk'Mip Desert & Heritage Centre, both owned and operated by the Osoyoos Indian Band. This is a true desert setting for western-style romance; on a hot summer day, follow the Heritage Centre's landscape trails with the fragrance of antelope brush and sage in the air. You might round a corner and encounter an authentic dwelling or one of the interpretive guides explaining the traditional uses of wild plants. Across the road, cool off in the winery's stunningly designed tasting room as you admire the Turtle Island floor mosaic and sample the chardonnay, pinot blanc, pinot noir, and merlot, all produced from grapes grown in the band's own vineyards.

9am–5pm every day (in summer), 9am–7pm (July–Aug only), 10am–4pm every day (Nov–May); www.nkmipcellars.com.

QUAILS' GATE ESTATE WINERY
❍❍❍
3303 Boucherie Rd, Kelowna / 250/769-4451 or 800/420-9463
Quails' Gate can trace its roots all the way back to the early 1900s, when the Stewart family was in the tree fruit business. The delightful setting boasts an early–20th century log-house tasting room and an exquisite vineyard that tumbles down the property to Okanagan Lake. The Old Vines Patio, open May to October, is a magical spot for a late dinner on a summer night; it offers fresh, seasonal cuisine and a panoramic view that has encouraged more than one prairie couple to consider a move and career change. Burgundy-style pinot noir and chardonnay are the focus at Quails' Gate, but don't miss an opportunity to taste their chenin blanc, chasselas, or dry Riesling. The winery has also developed a cult following for its Old Vines Foch, a shiraz-style blockbuster red that is rarely seen outside the winery.

10am–5pm every day (extended hours in summer); www.quailsgate.com.

RED ROOSTER WINERY
◐◐◖

891 Naramata Rd, Penticton / 250/492-2424
This dynamic winery reflects the charm and energy of its owners, Beat and Prudence Mahrer, Swiss-born lovers of life, food, wine—and, yes, poultry. The setting for the winery's new visitor center, on the famously sunny Naramata Bench, allows for sweeping views of orchards, vineyards, and Okanagan Lake. A visit here should include a sampling of their excellent White Meritage, as well as a tasting of a noteworthy pinot gris and a robust Bordeaux-style red blend called The Golden Egg. Light snacks are available on the scenic patio, and you are welcome to bring your own picnic. Before you depart, toss a coin into the wishing fountain—you never know! *10am–6pm every day (Apr–Oct), by appointment in winter; www.red roosterwinery.com.*

SUMAC RIDGE ESTATE WINERY
◐◐

17403 Hwy 97, Summerland / 250/494-0451
Sumac Ridge is a lovely spot surrounded by vineyards and has the distinction of being one of British Columbia's first estate wineries. Its diverse selection of varietal wines includes a very tasty Gewürztraminer, a fine pinot blanc, and one of the country's best *méthode-champenoise* sparklers: Stellar's Jay Brut, named after the brash, metallic-blue tricksters of the bird world. Red wine lovers can test out the best chocolate match with an excellent Meritage blend or single-varietal labels of cabernet sauvignon, cabernet franc, merlot, and pinot noir. The Cellar Door Bistro adjoining the tasting room is one of the valley's best winery restaurants. *9am–9pm every day; www.sumacridge.com.*

TINHORN CREEK VINEYARDS
◐◐◖

32830 Tinhorn Creek Rd (Rd No. 7), Oliver / 250/498-3743 or 888/484-6467
High atop Oliver's famous Golden Mile of vineyards and wineries, the architecturally splendid tasting room at Tinhorn's custom-built facility is not to be missed. Take the self-guided tour or experience the desert landscape firsthand by embarking (with a newly purchased bottle) on one of the local hiking trails. Tinhorn Creek specializes in an informal but informative approach to wine, and events throughout the year—including dinners with celebrity chefs and top-notch performers in the on-site amphitheater—make it a favorite with locals and visitors alike. Best bets include the merlot, cabernet franc, pinot gris, and Gewürztraminer. The affiliated Wine Lovers' Club provides devoted fans with a three- to four-night stay in luxurious self-catering vineyard guest suites, as well as personalized tours,

tutored tastings, a wine-and-food-pairing workshop, and special discounts and ticket offers.
10am–5pm every day; www.tinhorn.com.

Romantic Lodgings

THE CEDARS INN
◆◆◆◆

278 Beach Ave, Kelowna / 250/763-1208
This lovingly restored, circa-1908 heritage home contains two beautiful guest rooms, and the gracious hospitality of proprietors David Anderson and Jane Matéjka is reflected in every detail. European linens, pillowy down comforters, well-appointed private bathrooms, and added luxuries like in-room music, robes, candles, and amenity trays all add to the ambience. The Garden Room, with its dramatic four-poster bed, chaise longue, and claw-foot tub big enough for two, is a couple's haven; but after you partake of the morning coffee and newspaper delivered to your door, you might be tempted out by a signature breakfast of mascarpone French toast with triple-berry compote, served poolside or on the terrace in the lush, mature gardens. Among the many other perks that make this inn truly special are picnic baskets on request (for an additional charge), courtesy bicycles to explore the mansion- and tree-lined Abbott Street corridor, in-room massage and beauty services, and complimentary late-afternoon wine and hors d'oeuvres from the inn kitchen, including specialties such as crostini with blue cheese, pear, walnut, and brandy.
$$$ MC, V; no checks; closed Dec; www.cedarsinnokanagan.com.

GRAND OKANAGAN LAKEFRONT RESORT AND CONFERENCE CENTRE
◆◆

1310 Water St, Kelowna / 250/763-4500 or 800/465-4651
Despite some drawbacks, "the Grand" remains the grande dame of hotels in Kelowna's downtown. Its sprawling lakefront architectural presence and wide range of services, including several restaurants and a fitness center, offer everything you expect from a large hotel. Shops, lakeshore parks and pathways, and the cultural district are just minutes away, a real benefit for those who like to explore on foot. Standard rooms are, indeed, pretty standard, but Jacuzzi suites are a step up, with big tubs right in the rooms. The pastel decor in the South Tower is quite dated, but newer lakeside rooms in the North Tower, particularly the "romance" and other themed suites, are far more inviting (and expensive). For ultimate privacy with the comforts of home, you might consider one of the two-bedroom Deluxe Condos. But it's the accommodation packages, with their range of perks, that make a stay

at the Grand worth considering. These packages are themed around wine touring, spa treatments, gambling at the adjoining casino, golfing, and, of course, romance. Who says that the resort's honeymoon package (one night's accommodation in a suite with Jacuzzi, champagne, flowers, chocolates, and an in-room breakfast for two) is only for newlyweds?
$$$ *AE, DC, DIS, MC, V; no checks; www.grandokanagan.com.* &

HOTEL ELDORADO
●●●◖
500 Cook Rd, Kelowna / 250/763-7500
Hotel Eldorado's recent three-story expansion featuring 30 new rooms and 6 luxury suites sets a new standard for premium accommodation in the Okanagan, with plenty of opportunities for romance. The property provides a unique combination of history, setting, and boutique-style attention to detail; you'll feel at home and pampered at the same time. The original hotel has 19 rooms, which, although rich in heritage and charm, are a little too close to the action of the busy lounge, restaurant, and waterfront to offer a quiet, romantic setting. With the expansion, you have new, quieter room options. You'll find luxury appointments throughout, from the warm cork flooring to fine linens and colorful canvasses by Kelowna artist Wendy Porter. Romance packages—including one-night stay, rose-petal turndown service, welcoming goodies, and breakfast for two—are good values, and options such as dinner in the well-loved waterfront dining room, wine tastings, wine tours, and bubbly are easily arranged. The spacious luxury suites are worth every penny, with jetted platform tubs, fully stocked kitchenettes, showers big enough for two, and lovely views of Okanagan Lake. In each suite over the fireplace there is also a 42-inch plasma TV with built-in DVD player, but somehow we imagine you might be too busy romancing to use it.
$$$ *AE, DC, MC, V; no checks; www.eldoradokelowna.com.* &

MANTEO RESORT WATERFRONT HOTEL AND VILLAS
●●●
3762 Lakeshore Rd, Kelowna / 250/860-1031 or 800/445-5255
Manteo makes a striking architectural statement with its cluster of buildings in rich Mediterranean hues of red and ochre. The motto here is "Always exceed expectations," and this waterfront boutique facility has indeed set a new standard for hospitality in the region. Full wedding services are offered, as are a host of special getaway and romance packages. In the main hotel, a contemporary and comfortable one-bedroom lake-view suite is your best bet, with separate kitchen and living area and luxurious bedroom with full bath. Each suite has a private balcony where you can end the day with a glass of wine and a rosy-hued sunset. For complete and luxurious privacy, consider one of the much larger two-story villas adjacent to the hotel. These villas are in high demand and, with only 14 available, are often booked a

year or more in advance. Located within steps of the lake, the villas feature fantastic views and every imaginable convenience. The first floor holds a garage, outdoor patio with barbecue, fully equipped kitchen, and comfortable living area with fireplace; on the second floor you'll find a king master suite and queen second suite, both with en-suite bathrooms and balconies. Appointments are top-notch throughout, including the bed linens and comforters. The Wild Apple Grill (250/860-4488) offers casual lakeside dining, and those deserving of a little extra pampering can take advantage of a full range of spa services at Beyond Wrapture (250/860-0033; 888/860-WRAP). Try Vinotherapy, with a grape-pip scrub, wine body wrap, and a grapeseed oil massage that will soothe mind and body. Aquarians of all sorts can choose from indoor and outdoor pools, four hot tubs, a private beach, and any number of water sports.
$$$$ *AE, DC, MC, V; no checks; www.manteo.com.* &

NARAMATA HERITAGE INN & SPA
✿✿❢

3625 1st St, Naramata / 250/496-6808 or 866/617-1188
This perfectly restored 1908 hotel reflects a grand past, when hardy entrepreneurs understood the importance of frontier elegance and hospitality. Proprietors Norm and Janette Davies say that "a million miles away is closer than you think," and by the time you travel the winding road from Penticton to the lakefront village of Naramata and enter the inn's welcoming foyer, the two of you will feel as though you've made a clever escape into a quieter, more genteel time and place. Twelve rooms with wine-country themes all feature private balconies, high ceilings, antique furnishings, claw-foot tubs, large fluffy towels, and beautiful comforters. The historically appropriate decor is executed with admirable restraint. Subtle colors and an absence of flowered chintz help set a refreshingly uncluttered tone to this heritage setting, although dedication to historical accuracy means that modern soundproofing techniques are not at hand; you may occasionally hear what your neighbors are up to, and vice versa. An Aveda spa is located within the hotel, and for the ultimate in pampering, services can be easily packaged with a stay. Add in the lake view, landscaped grounds, and the intimate Rock Oven Dining Room (open seasonally), and you'll see why the hotel is also a choice spot for weddings. The Cobblestone Wine Bar and Restaurant offers more casual indoor and patio dining, an admirable list of local wines, and menu specialties cooked in "The Rock," the hotel's wood-fired stone oven. The oven-crisped thin-crust pizzas are particularly good, especially when accompanied by artisan beer from Penticton's Cannery Brewing Company. Local musicians make regular appearances on Friday nights, adding to the "best kept secret" ambience.
$$$ *MC, V; no checks; www.naramatainn.com.* &

Romantic Restaurants

BOUCHONS BISTRO
○○○(

105–1180 Sunset Dr, Kelowna / 250/763-6595
Bouchons Bistro is all about Gallic charm, authentic bistro cuisine, and a truly hedonistic wine cellar, all combining to form the very essence of romance. Its magic is personified by the talent of chef-owner André Bernier, the gracious hospitality of maitre d's Richard Toussaint and Martine Lefèbvre, and a staff that pampers you without intruding. The restaurant's location within Kelowna's cultural district means seating and parking are in high demand, and occasionally boisterous weekend evenings may find you drawn into the good-natured fun at the next table. Weekday nights are better suited for quiet conversation. The kitchen admirably responds to seasonal cravings (a winter game menu, for example), but the specialties at the heart of the menu read like a Francophile's dream: wild boar rillettes, cassoulet, bouillabaisse, braised rabbit in Dijon mustard and tarragon, and duck confit glazed with honey and spices. We are particularly taken with the cones of *pommes frites*, served with every entrée. The *table d'hôte* menu, offering an appetizer, main course, and dessert for a fixed price, changes frequently and is consistently excellent. After dinner, you'll be tempted by fine cheeses, desserts, port, ice wines and a wonderful flight of three aged Grand Marnier tasters.
$$$ AE, MC, V; no checks; dinner every day; closed mid-Feb–mid-March; full bar; reservations recommended. &

FRESCO
○○○○

1560 Water St, Kelowna / 250/868-8805
Opened in 2001, Fresco has already become the region's most highly recommended and awarded destination for those seeking an exceptional dining experience. We think the reputation is justified. Co-owners Rodney Butters and Audrey Surrao have created an elegantly restrained space featuring ambient lighting; soft music; and an unobtrusive, professional staff. The warm tones of this historic building's original brick wall, uncovered during restoration work, provide a backdrop for unique works of art (including a spectacular oil painting reputed to lend a romantic glow to those who are seated beside it), flickering candlelight, crisp white table linens, and the sparkle of fancy stemware. Add to this chef Butters' sublime food and an impressive wine list, and what you have is a recipe for romance. The menu reflects a contemporary West Coast bounty of seasonal and organic ingredients. Classic techniques, sophisticated presentation, seafood, and the occasional Asian accent are hallmarks. A four-course prix-fixe Signature Collection showcases favorites such as oat-crusted Arctic char, double-

smoked bacon and spinach flan, grilled Pontiac potatoes with browned maple butter, and the famous double chocolate–mashed potato brioche dessert served with sorbet of Second Wind Farm raspberries and warm bitter chocolate sauce. Tantalizing seasonal specials could prove difficult to resist; we're certain the endlessly creative *amuse-bouche* that precedes every meal will. The wine list is an impressive array of both domestic and imported wines, including some rare finds—the staff here are passionate and knowledgeable about wine, so be sure to seek out their recommendations. A chic little lounge area now occupies the restaurant's prime window frontage, offering ideal people watching for martini-sipping patrons.
$$$ *AE, DC, MC, V; no checks; dinner Tues–Sun; full bar; reservations rec-ommended.* &

THE HARVEST DINING ROOM
✿✿✿

2725 KLO Rd (Harvest Golf Club), Kelowna / 250/862-3177
Good news for golfers: one of the country's best golf courses takes its dining room seriously (and good news for nongolfers: you'll love it here, too). The large room can be quite noisy when full, but the huge windows provide a panoramic view of the beautiful grounds sweeping down toward Okanagan Lake. Executive chef Paul Cecconi has a passion for local seasonal cuisine, and the menu reflects his commitment to the best ingredients. A late-autumn menu might include a brown sugar–cured duck breast and sausage, accom-panied by leek whipped potatoes, roasted root vegetables, and a Calvados reduction. Service is attentive and friendly, and a knowledgeable sommelier will guide you through the extensive selection of local and imported wines, which includes rare finds from wineries such as Calliope, Poplar Grove, Burrowing Owl, and Leonetti. Kelowna's best burger is available in the adjoining Harvest Grill: the freshly ground beef patties are grilled to order, smothered in aged cheddar and onions on house-made cheese kaiser buns, and served with steak-cut fries.
$$$ *AE, DC, MC, V; no checks; lunch, dinner every day; full bar; reserva-tions recommended; www.harvestgolf.com.* &

THEO'S
✿✿✿

687 Main St, Penticton / 250/492-4019
The warm hospitality of the Theodosakis family has made this restaurant a local institution for more than 25 years. On cold winter nights, the seats around the capacious fireplace are in big demand, but in any season you'll enjoy an intimate courtyard ambience filled with beautiful art and antique tapestries, colorful table linens, and charming family photographs. You can choose to sit in either a small outdoor courtyard or a large indoor "court-yard" on the ground floor, filled with spectacular bougainvillea, where a

glass ceiling allows light to fill the atrium by the stairwell and the upper mezzanine dining area. The large menu features consistently good Greek specialties, such as *dolmathes avgolemono*; tender grape leaves filled with herb-laced rice and ground beef and baked with a traditional Greek lemon sauce; and lamb shoulder, baked in the oven on a tray of Greek oregano branches and flavored with garlic, lemon, and an Okanagan white wine–and-mustard sauce. For dessert, seek out the sinfully good *bougatsa*, a creamy custard wrapped in phyllo pastry and topped with whipped cream, crushed nuts, and cinnamon. The impressive list of local wines reflects the owners' passionate support of the booming local wine scene. Cushion-smothered benches in the lounge area and by the fireplace are irresistible for lingering by candlelight with an after-dinner ouzo. The chef himself may wander by and toast you with *"stin egia mas"* (to your health!).

$–$$ *AE, MC, V; no checks; lunch, dinner every day; full bar; reservations recommended; www.eatsquid.com.* &

WATERFRONT WINES
◐◐◐

103–1180 Sunset Dr, Kelowna / 250/979-1222
The chic little jewel box of a lounge at Waterfront Wines is a fitting companion to the adjacent specialty wine store. It's the kind of place you may visit to start or end a romantic evening on the town; the location in the city's cultural district is close to hotels, theaters, galleries, museums, and the local casino, as well as a lovely waterfront park, ideal for an evening stroll. For privacy, booth seating is available, but you'll need to arrive early (or really late) for the choice spot near the front window. Fresco alumnus Mark Filatow has a deft hand in the tiny open kitchen; smaller portions are ideal for sharing—you'll want to order several items. Favorites include a goat cheese fritter (the cheese comes from Carmelis, the newest star in Okanagan artisan cheesemaking) served with a smoky eggplant relish, and the lip-smackingly good chile salt–dusted calamari in a lime, coriander, and palm sugar glaze. The wine list offers "blondes" (white wines), "red heads" (red wines), and "air heads" (bubblies) by the glass or by the bottle, and the cocktail list features everything from retro to contemporary. Toast each other with a glass of Blue Mountain Brut as you watch Kelowna's beautiful people at play.

$$–$$$ *AE, MC, V; no checks; dinner Tues–Sat; full bar; reservations recommended; www.waterfrontwines.com.* &

Wedding Index

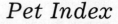

Pet Index

PUGET SOUND

Whidbey Island
Country Cottage of Langley
Island Tyme

Skagit Valley
La Conner Country Inn

SAN JUAN ISLANDS

San Juan Island
Tucker House Bed and Breakfast

Orcas Island
The Resort at Deer Harbor

OLYMPIC PENINSULA & LONG BEACH PENINSULA

Port Townsend
Big Red Barn

Olympic National Park, Port Angeles & Lake Crescent
Lake Crescent Lodge

Hoh Rain Forest, Western Beaches, Lake Quinault
Kalaloch Lodge

NORTH CASCADES

Methow Valley
Freestone Inn and Early Winters Cabins
Mazama Country Inn

CENTRAL CASCADES

Mount Rainier
Mountain Meadows Inn and B&B
Stormking Spa at Mt. Rainier

WASHINGTON WINE COUNTRY

Yakima Valley & Walla Walla
The Inn at Abeja

BRITISH COLUMBIA

VANCOUVER & ENVIRONS

Vancouver
Fairmont Waterfront Hotel
Four Seasons Hotel Vancouver

LOWER MAINLAND BRITISH COLUMBIA

Whistler
Edgewater Lodge
Fairmont Chateau Whistler Resort
Four Seasons Resort Whistler
Sundial Boutique Hotel
The Westin Resort and Spa

Sunshine Coast
Country Cottage Bed & Breakfast
Desolation Resort

VICTORIA & VANCOUVER ISLAND

Victoria
Abbeymoore Manor Bed & Breakfast Inn
Abigail's Hotel
Fairmont Empress Hotel

Sooke
Markham House
Point No Point Resort
Sooke Harbour House

Tofino
A Snug Harbour Inn
Eagle Nook Wilderness Resort & Spa (cabins only)
Long Beach Lodge Resort
Middle Beach Lodge
Tauca Lea Resort & Spa
Wickaninnish Inn

SOUTHERN GULF ISLANDS

Salt Spring Island
Cloud 9 Oceanview Bed and Breakfast
Salt Spring Vineyards Bed and Breakfast

Mayne, Galiano, Pender & Saturna Islands
Poets Cove Resort & Spa (cottages and villas only)
Saturna Lodge

Index